From Socrates to Plato

Plato's

Charmides, Laches, Euthyphro,

Euthydemus, Apology, Crito,

Protagoras, Meno and Phaedo

Newly translated with extensive notes

By Don Adams

CONTENTS

ABOUT THE TRANSLATOR

Don Adams received his Bachelor of Arts degree from Reed College where he studied philosophy and classical Greek. From there he went to Cornell University and studied with Terence Irwin, Gail Fine and Norman Kretzmann. His Ph.D. dissertation was a comparative study Of love and friendship in the moral theories of Socrates, Plato, Aristotle and Aquinas. He has taught logic and the history of European philosophy, especially ancient Greek philosophy, at about half a dozen colleges and universities across the USA. He is now Professor of Philosophy at Central Connecticut State University.

INTRODUCTION

Why did Plato become a Platonist? I've selected these nine dialogues because I think that they provide a good answer that question.

In the *Charmides*, *Laches*, *Euthyphro* and *Euthydemus* I think that we see the Socrates who originally inspired Plato's inherent genius. Socrates did not rest content with conventional wisdom regarding the most valuable possessions for a mortal: the virtues. Socrates boldly rejected the facile and servile notion of Pindar's that "custom is king of all" (Herodotus, *The Histories* 3.38.4). Perhaps we can rest content with purely relative mythological "truths" such as: it is true-among-Athenians that Orithyia was abducted by the god Boreas (*Phaedrus* 229b4-a7); perhaps we can also resign ourselves to some of our purely subjective "truths" such as: it is true-for-Ctesippus that Clinias is the most beautiful young man (*Euthydemus* 274b5). But is there no escape from the domination of custom? Are we forever doomed to be dragged through life by our purely subjective feelings? Is true freedom of thought utterly beyond our capacity?

Probably Plato was asking himself these kinds of questions when he noticed a most remarkable and absurd man: in Socrates Plato saw a genuinely free thinker. While Socrates accepted the relativity of belief in some areas, he relentlessly sought an absolute basis for our convictions regarding what is most important in life (*Euthyphro* 5c8-d5, 6d9-e6). And while he was no less susceptible than any of us to the subjectivity of perception (*Charmides* 155d3-4), he never lost his capacity for comprehending his own inclinations within a broader self-critical perspective (*Charmides* 155d4-e3).

But how are we mere commoners to depose, or even question, our King Custom? Actually, it's easier than you think. With just a bit of Socratic probing, King Custom questions himself (*Charmides* 159b1-160d4, *Laches* 190e4-191b7, *Euthyphro* 7c10-d5). It is at this point that cultural conservatives who are out to protect and preserve the existing power structure begin to get concerned or even hostile (*Apology* 22e6-23e3, *Meno* 94e3-95a1). Socrates, however, was intellectually fearless and indefatigable. Besides, we already have reason to think that some of our beliefs have an absolute basis and have some objective validity: we can settle disputes about who is swifter than whom by measuring who accomplishes more in the same amount of time, e.g. finishes a race before any other contestant (*Laches* 192b1, and see note on *Euthyphro* 5d1). Perhaps we can settle disputes about right and wrong in a similar way, with some sort of objective "science of measurement" operating on some absolute facts (*Protagoras* 356d4).

While this is an interesting line of inquiry, it is also troubling. While it makes sense that disputes about who is faster than whom can be settled by objective temporal measurements of absolute accomplishments, it is not clear that normative truths about right and wrong are reducible to any non-normative truths. Perhaps it is true for the most part that crime doesn't pay (*Apology* 25c5-e4), but can the full value of living your life virtuously and honorably be cashed out in an objective count of absolute material rewards accrued or punishments avoided? Doesn't the true value of virtue transcend all temporal benefits and detriments, thereby justifying the noble sentiment that when we consider what we ought to do, we must not weigh the prospects of life or death or anything other than this one thing: whether we will do what is right or what is wrong (*Apology* 28b5-9)?

But if virtue truly does have just such a transcendent value that cannot be reduced to any purely temporal benefits or detriments, then is there any way that we mundane creatures of crude clay could possibly come to know about it? If human knowledge is limited by the chains of mortal perception are we are forever denied any transcendent knowledge? Homer's Muses represent one possible solution to this problem: perhaps the gods will grace us with their blessed inspiration. That's a prospect worth taking seriously, but when Socrates talked with prophets, seers, poets, rhapsodes and others who sometimes claim to have special access to divine minds (e.g. *Euthyphro* 3e3, *Ion* 536c2), he found that (a) they don't actually understand the allegedly divine words they convey, (b) non-inspired bystanders can usually explain their allegedly inspired expressions better than they can, and (c) all too often their special talent leads them to over-estimate the extent of their expertise (*Apology* 22a8-c8). No. If there was a time when the gods dispensed wisdom to mortals, tending to us as shepherds tend their flocks, that time is long past (*Statesman* 271d3-e2, 274b5-6). Now we must take responsibility for the course of our lives (*Statesman* 274a3-b1, d3-6).

If our understanding of the transcendent value of virtue does not come to us by the grace of the gods, then perhaps there is something inherently transcendent about our understanding. If this is correct, then the question becomes whether there is within us some immortal spark of the divine. If there is more to us than meets the mortal eye, then perhaps what we call discovery is really a form of recollecting the divine truths imprinted on that immortal spark (*Meno* 81a5-d5, *Phaedo* 72e3-77a5). Death, in that case, need not be the catastrophic loss we fear it to be (*Apology* 40c4-41d7). We should, therefore, face our own inevitable demise with equanimity and hope (*Crito* 43b3-11, 43d7-44b4, *Phaedo* 63b4-c7).

My approach to translation. Most translators try to remain faithful to the vocabulary and sentence structure of the text they are translating. I think that's wrong-headed: if you want to be faithful to what Plato actually wrote, then learn Greek and read Plato yourself. The whole point of a translation is to make the original text accessible to people who cannot read the original language. In my view, a translator's primary job is to help readers avoid misunderstanding the text. Plato wrote these dialogues about two and a half millennia ago, he was a pre-Christian, polytheistic pagan. There are opportunities for misunderstanding all over the place. Obviously the notes are there to help with specific problems, but there are two general problems I should mention at the outset.

First, there is a real problem with Plato's vocabulary—especially his vocabulary having to do with learning, intelligence, knowledge and wisdom. I could give you four Greek words that correspond to those four English words, but think about it and you'll easily start to see the problems. All of those English words could be lumped together as simply referring to being "smart;" but we could also probably double or triple the number by distinguishing, e.g., different ways of learning, different kinds of intelligence, knowledge and wisdom. To make matters worse, the same is true for the four Greek words: each one has a range of meanings and associations. How do you accurately express a potentially fuzzy mixture of Greek words into a fuzzy mixture of English words?

There are two ways I solve this vocabulary problem. First, on particularly difficult passages I write a note. Second, I make every effort to stick just as closely to English common sense as Plato sticks to Greek common sense. Socrates' philosophy in these dialogues is *protreptic*. A protreptic philosopher meets you where you are, and helps you to see for yourself where you need to be a little more sophisticated in your thinking. Socrates uses language with ordinary looseness, and only tightens things up on an as-needed basis. So I think it is wrong to try to maintain a one-to-one correspondence between the Greek and the English—the Greek is natural and loose, and the English should be too.

Aside from vocabulary problems, there are many problems with syntax in Plato's Greek—especially for a translator. The Greeks often use longer sentences than we are now used to in English. This was easier in Greek than it is in English because Greek is a highly inflected language so it is usually easy to tell which verbs belong with which subjects, and which adjectives belong with which nouns. My solution is simply to break the long sentences down into shorter sentences. Unfortunately, this gives a very different flavor to the text, but I think it makes the English just as clear and easy to follow as the original text would have been.

The text. This is a translation of the Oxford Classical Texts edition of Plato's dialogues, which was edited by the Scottish classicist John Burnet (1863-1928), and was originally published in 1903. Burnet consulted the work of editors before him, but he also consulted all of the Greek manuscripts he could get his hands on. The oldest of these manuscripts is sometimes referred to as the "Codex Bodleianus." It is a "codex" because it is in book form, it is not a scroll; and it is "Bodleianus" because it is in the Bodleian Library in Oxford, England. But more often this old manuscript is called "Codex Clarkianus" because it was sold to the Bodleian in 1803 by the intrepid English mineralogist and traveller Edward Daniel Clarke (1769-1822). Clarke obtained the codex on the island of Patmos (where John had his famous "Revelation" in the Christian scriptures), and it may have been on the island for many centuries. It was created in 895 CE at a cost of 21 gold pieces, paid for by Arethas, Archbishop of Caesarea. The Codex Clarkianus was created more than a thousand years after the death of Plato, but that does not necessarily mean that it differs greatly from Plato's original. During the 3rd and 2nd centuries BCE, the librarians at Alexandria, Egypt, developed a tradition of careful scholarship that aimed at preserving manuscripts, so what we have today may be very close to what Plato wrote.

I apologize for those pesky numbers and letters strewn through the translation, e.g. [43a]. Those numbers are actually page numbers from the edition of Plato's works published by the classical scholar Henri Estienne (a.k.a. Henricus Stephanus) in 1578. In the Stephanus edition of Plato's works, the *Crito* begins on page 43. The letters "a" through "e" divide a page into fifths, so 43a refers to the top fifth of page 43, and 43c refers to the middle of page 43. These numbers and letters are standard, so they will be the same in any translation. John Burnet preserves the Stephanus page numbers, and he adds line numbers, so the *Crito* begins on 43a1 and ends on 54e2. I use these line numbers in the notes.

How to read these dialogues. There are plenty of notes on each dialogue at the back, but I urge you to ignore them the first time you read each dialogue. Wrestle with the ideas and argments on your own first, and start to develop your own opinion on the subject Socrates discusses. When you've finished reading the dialogue, then start to look through the notes to see if I have answered the questions you had. I think that Plato's dialogues will pique your curiosity, and I hope that my notes help you to develop your own philosophical thinking.

CHARMIDES

Setting: Athens, south of the Acropolis, in the wrestling-school of Taureas. Probably the year is 430 BCE. Socrates tells about a conversation he had the day after he returned from the battle at Potidaea.

Characters (in order of appearance):
SOCRATES (469-399; about 40 years old, from a middle class family, not handsome at all; his name is traditionally pronounced "SOCK-ra-teez," though "so-KROT-ays" is closer to the original)
CHAEREPHON (devoted friend of Socrates, probably about the same age as Socrates; his name is traditionally pronounced "KAI-re-fon," though "khai-re-FONE" is closer to the original)
CRITIAS (c.460-403; about 30 years old, from an aristocratic family; well educated, sophisticated and accomplished; cousin of Plato; in 404 he was one of the Thirty Tyrants to lead Athens after losing the Peloponnesian War, he was killed when the democratic faction took control of the city; his name is traditionally pronounced "KRIT-ee-us," though "kree-TEE-oss" is closer to the original)
CHARMIDES (d.403; probably a teenager, from an aristocratic family; well educated, extremely good looking and charming; his name is traditionally pronounced "KAR-mid-eez," though "khar-MEE-days" is closer to the original)

Dramatic Structure:
Prologue: Socrates describes the setting (153a1-b2)
Parodos: Socrates meets Charmides (153b2-158e5)
Episode #1: Socrates examines Charmides (158e6-162b11)
Episode #2: Socrates examines Critias (162c1-175a8)
Exodos: Charmides is eager to continue (175a9-176d5)

SOCRATES. [153a] We returned yesterday evening from the army's camp at Potidaea,* and because I had been away so long I was glad to head for the places I used to frequent. I was especially eager to visit the wrestling-school of Taureas, across from the shrine of the Queen.* When I went in, I saw that the place was packed. I knew most everybody, but there were some people I didn't know. When they saw me [b] show up unexpectedly, they gathered around me and gave me a very warm welcome.

Of course you know how enthusiastic Chaerephon is: once he saw me, he jumped up, ran over to me, and grabbing my hand he said, "Socrates! How did you make it through that battle?"* You see, shortly before we left, there had been a battle at Potidaea and in Athens people were just learning about it.

"As you see me now," I answered.

"It was reported here that the fighting was extremely fierce [c] and that many people you and I know were killed."

"That report is true, I'm sorry to say."

"And you were in the battle?" he asked.

"I was."

"Well come over here and sit down; tell us all about it. We have not yet received a clear account of the whole battle." With this, he brought me over to sit next to Critias, the son of Callaeschrus. So I sat down, greeted Critias and the others kindly, and told them all about the battle, answering every single one of their questions.

[d] When we'd had our fill of such matters, I began asking them about how things were in Athens, about the present state of philosophy, and about the young men, if any among them had distinguished

himself in wisdom or beauty or both. Critias then looked at the door [154a] because a group of young men were coming in, trading insults with one another, and a large crowd was following behind them.

"Well, I don't think you'll have to wait very long to find out* who is beautiful.* These young men coming in now are the advance guard for, and admirers* of, the one who is, for the moment at least, thought to be the most beautiful. So he's probably almost here.

"Who is he, and who is his father?"

"Actually, I think you already know him, though he was very young when you left for Potidaea. [b] He is Charmides, the son of my cousin Glaucon, which makes him my nephew."

"By god, you're right, I do know him," I said, "and even as a child he was impressive. I won't be surprised if he has grown into quite a fine young man."

"Well, here's your chance to see for yourself what kind of a young man he's grown into." Just as he said this, Charmides entered the room.

Trust me, my friend, when I say that I am as useless as a white line in white marble* when it comes to measuring beauty because pretty much everyone at that age seems beautiful to me. [c] But the moment Charmides entered I was struck by his stature and beauty, and there was such a commotion and uproar that I thought absolutely everybody in the room admired him—not to mention the many admirers that came in following after him. It is not surprising that older men like us would be struck by his beauty, but I paid close attention to the boys, and everyone from oldest to youngest had his eyes on Charmides: everyone gazed at him as if he were a statue.*

[d] Over the noise Chaerephon called out to me, "How does he look to you, Socrates? Isn't his face handsome?"

"Extremely handsome."

"Yes, but if he is going to strip down for a wrestling match you won't even notice his face because his form is so superbly beautiful."

The others immediately agreed with Chaerephon on this point. "By Herakles,"* I replied, "if your description is accurate, the boy must be utterly irresistible—if, that is, he also possesses one additional feature, a small thing,* really."

"What is that?" asked Critias.

[e] "If his soul* also happens to be well formed, which is likely since he is a member of your family, Critias."

"Oh, he certainly is beautiful and good in this respect also," Critias replied.

"Well, then, let's have him strip down for an intellectual wrestling match and view the form of his soul. At his age I'm sure that he's eager for an intelligent discussion.*

"Absolutely, since he's already a philosopher and a poet, [155a] as far as he and others are concerned."

"This fine trait, my friend Critias, has belonged to your family for a long time because you are descended from Solon.* So why not call him over here and give us a demonstration? Even if he were younger there would be nothing shameful* in our having a discussion with him in your presence, after all, you are his cousin and guardian."

"Quite right, well said," answered Critias, "we'll call him over here." [b] And speaking to his attendant he said, "Boy,* call Charmides over here and tell him that I want to introduce him to a healer* because of the weakness he's been complaining about in the morning." Then he turned to me and said, "Just recently he's been complaining of a headache when he wakes up in the morning. Is there any reason you can't pretend that you know a remedy* for his headaches?"

"None at all," I said, "just let him come over."

"Oh, don't worry, he'll come."

And he did. It was actually pretty funny [c] because everyone already seated started pushing and shoving to make room so that Charmides would sit next to him. The lad on one end of the bench was pushed so far that he had to get up, while the boy on the other end was actually knocked off and rolled over on the floor. Anyway, Charmides came and sat down between Critias and myself, and suddenly I felt quite at a loss* for words. I felt almost as if the wind had been knocked out of me, and I lost confidence in my ability to converse easily with him. Well, Critias told him that I was the one who knew the remedy, so he turned his [d] irresistible eyes to me and was about to plunge right in and ask me about it when everyone in the gymnasium surged* around us on all sides. Then—my noble friend*—I saw inside Charmides' cloak,* felt inflamed and like I wasn't in control of myself, and I thought how wise* Cydias* was in the ways of erotic desire to warn someone, "do not put the fawn before the lion to be devoured by him." [e] Actually, I almost felt as if I were the fawn about to be devoured by the beast of desire. Despite all this, when he asked me whether I knew of a remedy for his headache, I answered—though with some difficulty—that I did.*

"What is it?" he asked.

I told him that it was a leaf, but there is a charm* to go with the remedy, so that if you utter the charm when you use the leaf, the remedy will make you completely healthy, but that without the charm, the leaf is of no benefit.*

[156a] "Then I'll write it down as you tell it to me."

"If you persuade me,* or even if you don't?" I asked.

He laughed and agreed, "If I persuade you, Socrates."

Surprised that he remembered my name, since he was so young when I left for Potidaea, I asked "Are you so sure of my name?"

"If I am not mistaken. In fact, a lot of people my age have talked about you while you were gone, and I do remember you spending time with Critias when I was little."

"Excellent! That makes me feel more at home with you, and that I can [b] speak freely in explaining what sort of thing the charm happens to be. Just now, I was at a loss to point out its power* to you. That's because its distinctive power can do so much more than just cure a headache. I suppose you have heard the following sort of thing about good doctors: if somebody comes to them with eye problems, they say it is impossible for them to attempt to heal the eyes alone; instead, at the same time they must also apply some therapy to the whole head if they are going [c] to cure the eyes. But then they go on to say that it would be stupid to think that you can treat the head without treating the whole body. It is this kind of thinking that leads them to apply their therapies to the body as a whole, trying to heal the part and the whole together at the same time. Or haven't you ever heard doctors explain their approach that way?"

"Oh yes, I certainly have," he said.

"And do you think it makes sense; do you accept their principle?"

"Yes, absolutely."

[d] When I heard him approve of that principle I regained my confidence, and gradually I was able to compose myself. So I said, "That is exactly the sort of thing my charm* is. I learned it from a Zalmoxian doctor* when I was in the army in Thrace—these doctors are said to be able to make someone immortal. Anyway, this Thracian affirmed that the view of Greek doctors I went through just now is all well and good as far as it goes,

'But Zalmoxis,' he said, 'our King—who also happens to be a god—goes further. [e] He adds that just as you shouldn't try to heal the eyes without the head, or the head without the body, so also you shouldn't try to heal the body without the soul. This is the reason why the proper treatments of many illnesses have escaped the Greek doctors: they neglect the whole, which really should be their main focus because if the whole is not in good condition, then it is impossible for any part to be in good condition. Everything in the body and in the person as a whole, both the good and the bad, originates in the soul* and flows from there, as from the head [157a] to the eyes. So we must treat the soul first and foremost if we want the head and the rest of the body to be in good condition, and we must treat the soul with certain charms—the charms of fine words that bring temperance* into the soul. And once temperance has been established in the soul, it will be easy to bring health to the head and [b] to every other part of the body.'

So when he taught me the remedy and the charm he said to me,

'Never let anyone persuade you to use this remedy to treat his head without first using the charm to treat his soul. This is the great error* doctors today make: they separate temperance from health.'

He gave me very strict instructions never to let anyone persuade me to use the remedy without the charm, no matter how wealthy, well born, or handsome he happens to be. [c] I swore an oath to him that I would obey his instructions, and I must keep my oath. So, my dear Charmides, if you agree to my teacher's terms, and allow me first to treat your soul with the Thracian charm, then afterwards I will apply the remedy to your head. If you do not agree to these terms, then I'm sorry, my friend, but there's nothing I can do for you."

When he heard this, Critias exclaimed, "What a godsend Charmides' headaches will turn out to be if he is forced to improve his mind in order to improve his head! [d] And I can tell you, Socrates, that not only does Charmides surpass every young man his age in the beauty of his form, but also in that quality you say the charm is for—temperance, right? Didn't you say that the charm is supposed to bring temperance into the soul?"

"Yes, exactly right," I answered.

"Well, you should know that he is considered to be the epitome of temperance, and in every other respect second to no one his age."

"It certainly would be right for you to excel like this, Charmides: [e] I don't think that anybody here could easily point out two Athenian families,* other than your own father's and mother's, that would be more likely to produce finer or nobler offspring by being united through marriage. Your father is descended from Critias, the son of Dropides, and his house has been celebrated in the poems of Anacreon, Solon and many others for its beauty, [158a] its virtue* and for everything else that is considered to be part of happiness. Your mother's family is no less remarkable. It is said that her brother, Pyrilampes, never found an equal with respect to beauty or stature, no matter where he went as ambassador to the great Persian King, or throughout Asia. Coming from two families like that it would be no wonder if you are preeminent in every way. [b] I can see perfectly well, Charmides, son of Glaucon, that you live up to these expectations with respect to your physical form. Truly blessed is the son your mother bore if in addition to this physical beauty you are naturally inclined to temperance and all the other qualities that Critias here has claimed for you."

I summed things up by saying, "Well, then, here is where we stand. If temperance is already in you and you are sufficiently temperate,* then you actually do not need any charms at all, whether from Zalmoxis the Thracian, Abaris the Hyperborean,* or anybody else. I can just give you the remedy for your headaches right now. [c] But if you are still in need of temperance, then the charm must be recited before I give you the remedy. So I'd like to hear from you whether you agree with Critias that you are sufficiently temperate or are still in need of it."

Charmides blushed, which made him even more beautiful—a proper sense of shame* is very becoming in a young man. Then he gave the very considerate* answer that it wasn't easy to affirm or deny what Critias had said about him. [d] "If I deny that I am temperate," he said, "then first of all, that would be a strange thing to say about myself, but also, I would be saying that Critias and many other people, according to him, are wrong about me. But on the other hand, I can't go around boasting that I am temperate. So I don't really have an answer for you."

"That is a very smart thing to say, Charmides," I told him. "So perhaps you and I should investigate together whether or not you are temperate [e] so that you won't be forced to say something you don't want to say, and I won't resort to medicine against my better judgment. If that is acceptable to you, then I am eager to begin the investigation. But if you'd rather not, then we can let it go."

"Oh, it is not just acceptable to me, I am really eager to begin the investigation with you. Let's proceed however it seems best to you."

"Here is the best way, I think, for us to proceed with our inquiry. Obviously if temperance is present in you, [159a] then you have some opinion about it, because necessarily by being within you—if it is within you—it gives you some perception of it, from which you would be able to form an opinion about what temperance is and what qualities it has. Does that seem reasonable?"*

"Yes it does," he agreed.

"And since you know how to speak Greek, you can express your opinion in words, can't you?"

"Maybe," he tentatively agreed.

"So in order for us to discern whether temperance is in you or not, please tell us, in your own opinion, what do you say temperance to be?"

[b] At first he hesitated* and wasn't exactly eager to give an answer, but then he said that temperance seemed to him to be doing everything in an orderly and calm manner, like walking down the road, or participating in a discussion, and everything else like that. "So all in all," he said, "what you are asking about seems to me to be a kind of calmness."*

"Well done, Charmides. Certainly people do say that calm people are temperate, so let's look into this. [c] Tell me, is temperance among the fine things?"*

"Yes, it certainly is."

"And when you are in your writing class, which is finer: to get your lesson correctly* written down quickly or calmly?"

"Quickly."

"And when it comes to reading? Is it finer to be able to read a passage quickly, or if it takes you a long time to read it?"

"Reading is like writing: it is finer to be able to do both quickly."

"And how about in your cithara lessons? Is it finer to play a piece of music straight through without having to stop to find the notes? Or how about wrestling? Is it finer to execute wrestling moves quickly, or slowly?"

"Oh no, in both cases it is finer to act quickly."

"Is it the same in boxing and martial arts?"*

"Yes, certainly."

"What about running sprints and hurdles? Isn't it the same in those cases also? In fact, can't we sum things up when it comes to physical tasks? [d] Isn't it true that accomplishing things promptly and quickly is fine, and that it is quite the opposite when you can do these things only slowly and with difficulty? Aren't those actions embarrassing?"*

"So it seems."

"And it seems to us," I said, "that with respect to the body, it isn't the calmer actions, but rather the quicker and more efficient actions that are the finer ones. Is that true?"

"Yes, it certainly is."

"But temperance is a fine thing?"

"Yes."

"Therefore, with respect to the body, it is not calmness but quickness that would be more temperate, since temperance is fine."

"So it seems."

[e] "What's next?" I continued. "Is it finer to learn well or to learn poorly?"

"To learn well, of course."

"But to learn well is to learn quickly, isn't it? And to learn poorly is to learn slowly?"

"Yes."

"How about when it comes to teaching? Isn't it finer if your students learn the material quickly as opposed to taking a long time and having a great deal of difficulty?"

"Yes."

"What's next? What about memory? Isn't a quick and agile memory finer than a memory that works only with difficulty and only at a very leisurely pace?"

"An agile and quick memory is finer," he said.

[160a] "And I bet that you've had more than one teacher tell you that you are an 'astute' pupil. But doesn't being 'astute' mean that you have a sharp or keen intellect,* not a calm or leisurely one?"

"Yes, that's true."

"Therefore, when it comes to understanding what you are taught, whether in your writing lessons, your cithara lessons, or anything else, the finest student is not the one who learns things most calmly, but rather the one who learns things most quickly?"

"Yes."

"And what about intellectual inquiry and deliberation? I don't think that it is anything to be proud of if you have great difficulty in figuring out what to do, or in discovering the answer to a question, or if you can go about these only if you are not in a hurry. I think that person is worthy of praise [b] who can succeed quickly and easily. What do you think?"

"Yes, that's right."

"So in all tasks, both physical and intellectual, to be agile and quick in succeeding is finer than to be slow and calm?"

"I suppose it is."

"Therefore, from this argument it follows that temperance would not be a kind of calmness. It also follows that the temperate life would not be the same as the calm life because if it is temperate, then it must be fine. From this argument it seems that there are only two alternatives. [c] First, from all that we've gone through, it looks as if none of the calm actions in life are finer than the quick and vigorous actions. The only alternative is that if we keep looking we'll be able to find some cases where the calm actions are finer than the quick and vigorous ones. But no matter which of those two alternatives is true, in either case it will not turn out that temperance is calmness any more than that temperance is acting quickly and vigorously, whether in walking, talking or in any other activity. [d] The calm life would be no more temperate than the life that is not calm since in this argument temperance was placed among the fine things, and quick actions appear to be no less fine than calm actions."

"I think you've summed things up correctly, Socrates," he concluded.

"Well, then, try again, Charmides. Think carefully about cause and effect. If temperance is in you, then it must have a specific sort of effect on you. Try to figure out what temperance must be like in order to produce that kind of effect. Put this all together* and [e] bravely tell me what temperance seems to you to be.

He took his time and very bravely looked within himself. Finally he said, "I think that the effect temperance has on someone is that it gives them a sense of shame and sometimes makes them feel ashamed* of themselves. What causes those effects is modesty, and so I think that temperance is modesty."

"Ah, very good, Charmides," I said. "Now, didn't we just agree that temperance is a fine thing?"

"Certainly."

"And surely temperate men are good* men, aren't they?"

"Yes."

"But something cannot be good if its result is not good,* can it?"

"Certainly not."

"Alright, and you do agree, don't you, that temperance is not only fine but also good?"

[161a] "I think so, yes."

"But don't you believe Homer* when he says that modesty is not good for a needy man."

"I do."

"Well, then, it seems we have said both that modesty is good, and also that it is not good."

"So it seems."

"But temperance is just good if it makes men good and not bad when it is present."

"Yes, I think you put that correctly."

"And so, since modesty is no more good than bad, temperance would not be modesty [b] if temperance is good only."

"I think you are right about that, Socrates. Oh, but wait! Tell me what you think about this view of temperance that I just remembered hearing from someone. If I remember correctly, he said that temperance is minding your own business.* Please examine this and tell me if you think that the one who said it is right."

"Rascal! You heard this from Critias here, [c] or from some other wise man."

"What does it matter who I heard it from, Socrates?"

"No, you are quite right, it doesn't matter. Whoever said it, we should certainly consider whether it is actually true."

"You are definitely right about that."

"We're agreed, then. But my concern, Charmides, is that it seems to be some sort of riddle; I'd be very surprised if we were able to determine whether or not it is true.

"What do you mean?"

[d] "Well, I don't think that whoever said temperance is 'minding your own business' really meant it literally. Let me tell you what I have in mind. First of all, can we agree that your writing teacher is in the business of writing and reading?"

"Sure."

"And, of course, he taught you how to read and write his own name, and he taught each of you how to read and write your own names. But didn't he also teach you how to write the names of your friends? And surely you are just as adept at reading and writing the names of your enemies as well, aren't you?"

"Oh, yes, of course we can both read and write names other than our own."

"And when you write down your neighbor's name, are you being a busybody and intemperate?"

[e] "No, of course not."

"But if reading and writing someone's name is a form of minding someone's business, then aren't you minding someone else's business if you are writing someone else's name?"

"I hadn't thought of it that way, but I guess so."

"Can't we extend this to other ways of minding someone's business? For example, what about medicine, building, weaving, or any other craft whose business it is to produce some definite result?*"

"Certainly."

"Well, think about it: would a city be well organized if it had a law commanding each person to weave and wash his own cloak, to cut leather for his own shoes, to produce his own oil jars, his own strigils, and everything else? [162a] And what if the law absolutely forbade anyone to mind anyone else's business? For example, it didn't allow anyone to produce shoes or oil jars for anybody else?"

"No, that city wouldn't be well organized at all."

"But if the city is temperately governed, then it would be organized well, wouldn't it?"

"How could it not be?"

"Well," I said, "then temperance wouldn't be minding your own business, at least not if I'm interpreting this riddle correctly."

"I don't see how it could be."

"So now you see why I think that the one who said temperance is minding your own business was giving you a riddle. Surely whoever said it [b] wasn't so simple-minded as to mean it in the way I just interpreted it, was he? The person who told you this wasn't being silly, was he?"

"No, not at all! Really, I thought he was very wise."

"That settles it, then: he must have been deliberately giving you a riddle to puzzle out, given how difficult it is to know* what he meant* precisely by the phrase 'minding your own business'."

"Possibly."

"So what is 'minding your own business'?"

"By god, I don't know," he said. Then looking over at Critias he smiled a little and said, "I suppose it's possible that even the one who said it didn't know."

[c] At that point Critias couldn't restrain himself any longer. For a while he had clearly been uncomfortable because he was eager to protect his reputation with Charmides and the others, and it was only with great difficulty that he kept himself from jumping into the conversation. Obviously what I had suspected earlier was true: Charmides had indeed heard that account of temperance from Critias. It turns out that Charmides didn't want to answer questions about it himself, [d] rather he wanted Critias to give the answers. That's why Charmides added the somewhat dramatic "By god" when he admitted that he had been refuted again. This pushed Critias over the edge, and like a playwright who is angry with an actor about how he is delivering the lines, he looked right at Charmides and said, "So, Charmides, you think just because you don't know what was meant by the one who said that temperance is 'minding your own business,' that he himself doesn't know?"

"But Critias," I said, [e] "it's no surprise that someone as young as he is wouldn't know what it means. You, on the other hand, because of your age and your studies are likely to understand it. So if you agree that temperance is what that person said it is, and you are willing to take up the argument, nothing would please me more than to consider with you whether that claim is true."

"I do agree with that analysis of temperance," he said, "and I am willing to take up the argument."

"Wonderful! So tell me, do you agree with my point that all craftspeople make something?"*

"Yes."

[163a] "Then do they seem to you to be making their own things only? Don't they also make things for others?"

"Oh yes, they do make things for others."

"Well, then, are they temperate if they don't only make their own things?"

"Is there anything that prevents them from being temperate?"

"Nothing as far as I am concerned," I said. "But look, isn't there a problem for someone who says that temperance is 'minding your own business,' but then says that people who mind other people's business are temperate?"

"Ah! But I only agreed that someone who *makes* things for others can still be temperate. I never agreed that it is possible to be temperate if you mind other people's business."

[b] "Tell me, then, are you denying that making things for others is a form of minding their business?"

"I certainly am, just as I would also deny that *making* and *working* are the same thing. I have learned this from Hesiod* who said, 'work is no disgrace.' Surely he could never say that if by 'work' or 'minding one's own business' he meant the sort of things you were talking about just now—cutting leather for shoes, selling salt-fish, or working in a brothel.* We can't think that Hesiod was including that kind of work, Socrates. He must have been distinguishing between, on the one hand, working at one's proper business, or minding one's proper business, and, [c] on the other hand, just any kind of making or business-dealings, because obviously making something can be a disgrace if there is nothing fine about it.* 'Work' can never be a disgrace because he only calls something a 'work' if there is something fine and beneficial about it. Clearly he thinks the same way about 'minding' one's own proper business: only fine and beneficial things can possibly be one's own proper business, what is harmful is somebody else's business. That is how we must understand Hesiod and any intelligent person who says that 'minding one's own business' is temperance."

[d] "Ah, Critias, right when you mentioned 'making and working' I had a pretty good idea of where you were going. It doesn't surprise me at all that you restrict 'one's own *proper* business' to doing good things, and that you won't count making something as 'minding one's own proper business' unless you are making good things. I've heard Prodicus* draw many distinctions between words like that. I have no problem with you giving a word whatever meaning you want, as long as you make it clear what meaning you are giving

it.* So let's be clear about this. [e] '*Making*' good things or '*doing*' good things,* or whatever word you want to use here, that is what you say temperance is. Am I right about that?"

"Yes," he agreed.

"So the person who does bad things is not temperate; only the person who does good things is temperate?"

"Doesn't it seem that way to you, Socrates?"

"Whether it seems that way to me or not isn't the issue. Right now we are not inquiring into what I think, but rather into what you said just now."

"Oh, then, in that case, yes. I deny that the person who makes bad things and not good things is temperate, and I affirm that the person who makes good things and not bad things is temperate. However, to be perfectly clear, I would rather put my point by saying that temperance is the doing of good things."

[164a] "And that may well be true," I said, "however, it surprises me that you think temperate people can be ignorant of their own temperance."

"But I don't think that at all, Socrates."

"Weren't you just a moment ago talking about craftspeople who make things for others, and didn't you say that nothing prevents them from being temperate?"

"Yes, I did say that. What of it?"

"Well, nothing, except don't you think that when a doctor makes someone healthy, [b] he is producing a result that is beneficial both for himself* and also for the person he heals?"

"Certainly I do."

"And whoever does this is doing what he ought to do?"

"Yes."

"And the one who is doing what he ought to do is temperate?"

"He is temperate, yes."

"Well, does a doctor necessarily know when he is beneficially healing someone and when he is not?* In general, does a craftsperson know when he is and when he is not going to benefit from what he is doing?"

"Perhaps not."

"Well, then, perhaps a doctor can act beneficially or harmfully [c] without knowing himself which he is doing? Although, when he acts beneficially he is acting temperately, according to your account. Isn't that what you said?"

"Yes, I did say that."

"So, then, sometimes someone can act beneficially, and in doing so he acts temperately and he is temperate, but he lacks the self-knowledge to realize that he is in fact temperate?"

"But that, Socrates, could never be. In fact, if you think in any way that it is necessary to draw this conclusion from my former admissions, then I for my part would rather retract them. [d] I would not be ashamed to admit that I spoke incorrectly, but I would be ashamed to agree that someone can be temperate who does not know himself."

"In fact," Critias continued, "I would almost say that temperance is this very thing: to know oneself. I am in complete harmony with whoever dedicated that inscription at Delphi.* You see, I think that it was dedicated in order to serve as the god's direct address to anyone entering the temple. It is as if the usual, "Welcome!" is not the correct greeting, [e] but instead we should urge one another to be temperate. That is how the god addresses those who enter his temple, not using the usual greeting that mortals use—or at least that is what I believe the person who dedicated the inscription was thinking when he dedicated it. Whenever anyone enters the temple, the god always says to him nothing other than "Be temperate!", but like a prophet, he speaks enigmatically, since "Know thyself!" and "Be temperate!" [165a] mean the same thing—as I maintain, and as the words themselves declare. Although, it is understandable how someone might think that they mean different things, like the later people who dedicated the inscriptions "Nothing in excess" and "Oaths bring ruin."* Clearly whoever dedicated those inscriptions thought that "Know thyself!" was just a piece of advice, and didn't realize that it was actually intended as the god's direct address to the one who enters his temple. So they thought they would dedicate equally useful advice by dedicating their sayings. Here is my point, Socrates, in saying all this. [b] I want to leave that previous argument to you: perhaps you were more right, perhaps I was, but whichever was the case, we didn't really make anything very clear. Now I want to recommend this account of temperance to you, unless you already agree that temperance is to know oneself.

"Oh, but Critias," I said, "you are talking to me as if I professed to know the answer to my question, and that I could simply agree with you if I so desired. That is not how it is. In fact I am always inquiring into the truth of whatever is put forward precisely because I do not know* what the truth is. [c] If you let me consider the matter for a moment I am certainly willing to say whether I agree or not; just give me some time to think it over."

"By all means, think it over."

"Alright, I'm thinking it through, and I think that if temperance is a kind of knowledge,* then it would have to be a knowledge of something. Wouldn't you agree?"

"Yes, certainly. It is a knowledge of oneself."*

"Well, take medicine for an example. Medicine is knowledge of health, isn't it?"

"Certainly."

"Now, suppose you asked me, 'Since medicine is the knowledge of health, what use is it to us, and what does it produce?' [d] In that case, I should say that it is of no small use to us, it produces health, and that is a fine result for us. Would you accept that answer?"

"Yes, I would accept it."

"Then suppose you went on to ask me about building, which is the knowledge of how to build. If you were to ask me, 'What results does building produce?' I would answer 'Buildings.' And it would go this way with the other crafts. Therefore, you should answer this same question about temperance, since you say that it is the knowledge of oneself. Suppose I ask you, 'Critias, [e] since temperance is the knowledge of oneself, what fine result does it produce for us that makes it worthy of the name?' What would your answer be?"

"But Socrates, you are not conducting the inquiry properly. It's nature isn't like the others, and in fact the other crafts aren't even all like one another, but you are conducting the inquiry as if they are all similar. For example, take the crafts of calculation or geometry, what results do they produce? Do they produce things the way that building produces buildings and weaving produces cloaks, and the other crafts produce all their various results? [166a] Can you point to any result of calculation or geometry that is like these results of other crafts? No, you can't."

"What you say is true,* Critias. However, what I can point out to you is the subject matter of each of these forms of knowledge, and I can show you that in every case the subject matter of the knowledge is distinct from the knowledge itself. For example, calculation is the knowledge of both even and odd numbers, and their numerical relations to one another. Isn't that true?"

"Oh, yes, that is certainly true."

"And the craft of calculation is distinct from the even and odd numbers that one uses when one performs a calculation?"

"Of course."

[b] "And the craft of weighing deals with things that are heavy or light, but the craft is not itself a heavy thing or a light thing, the craft of weighing is distinct from the heavy and the light. Do you agree?"

"I do."

"So tell me, then, if temperance is a form of knowledge, what is its subject matter that is distinct from temperance itself?"

"There you go again, Socrates. You pursue the investigation by looking into how temperance differs from the other forms of knowledge, but then at the end you ask for how it is just the same* as the others.

Temperance is not like the others. All the other forms of knowledge are the knowledge of something else, not of themselves; [c] temperance is the only form of knowledge that is of other forms of knowledge* and also of itself."

"In fact, Socrates," Critias continued, "I think that you are deliberately doing what you just now denied* that you are doing: you are trying to refute me rather than investigating the issue at hand."

"Oh, no, Critias, you misunderstand me. If I try to refute something you say it is for exactly the same purpose that I would have [d] in examining something that I say, namely, in order to discover whether I was guilty of thinking that I knew something I did not in fact know. That is what I am doing now; I am investigating the issue at hand primarily for my own sake, but also for the sake of you, my companions. Or don't you think that it is a good common to pretty much everybody to reveal how things really are?"

"Well, yes, I do agree with that."

"Excellent! Then please boldly answer the question in whatever way seems right to you, and pay no attention to whether it is Critias [e] or Socrates who is refuted. Just focus on the issue at hand, and consider what comes out* of the refutation."

"That's just what I'll do, Socrates; your point is a fair one."

"Alright, then, let's start afresh," I continued, "how do you want to characterize temperance?"

"Here's what I say," he answered. "Temperance is the only form of knowledge that is a knowledge of itself and of the other forms of knowledge."

"And does it follow that if it is a knowledge of other forms of knowledge, then it is also a knowledge of ignorance? For example,* if I know who has medical knowledge, then would I also know who lacks medical knowledge; that is, can I tell a real doctor from an impostor?"

"Yes, certainly."

[167a] "So only the temperate man* will know himself, and he will be able to discern what he knows and what he does not know, and likewise with other people: he will be able to determine when someone thinks they know something and they actually do know it, and when they think they know something but in fact they do not know it. And only the temperate person will be able to do all this. In sum, temperance, being temperate, and knowing oneself are all one and the same thing: to know what one knows and what one does not know. Is that what you are saying?"

"That is what I am saying," he agreed.

"Ok, well, as the saying goes, 'third time's a charm.'* [b] Let's take a fresh look at this, and divide our inquiry into two parts. First, let's consider whether or not it is even possible to know that you know the things that you know, and to know that you do not know the things that you do not know. Second, if we find that this kind of self-knowledge is possible, then we should consider what benefit this self-knowledge would be to us."

"Yes, that is how we ought to consider the matter," Critias agreed.

"Alright, then tell me, Critias, whether you are more resourceful than I, because I am quite at a loss. May I explain to you why I can't see a way forward?"

"Certainly."

"Well, if we stick with the account of temperance you just gave, then doesn't it all come down to this: there is one special form of knowledge that is not a knowledge of anything other than itself, [c] the other forms of knowledge, and all the forms of ignorance?"

"Certainly."

"But, then, look at what a paradoxical thing we are trying to say, my friend. If we tried to say this same thing in other cases, I think that you would immediately see that it is impossible."

"How would it be impossible? What cases are you talking about?"

"Consider this kind of case. Can you imagine a kind of vision that is unlike every other kind of vision because it is not a vision of anything other than itself, the other forms of vision, and all the forms of non-vision? [d] It doesn't see color, but rather itself and the other forms of vision. Do you think there is such a thing?"

"By god, no I do not."

"What about a form of hearing that doesn't actually hear any sounds, but hears only itself, the other forms of hearing, and all the forms of non-hearing?"

"No, I don't think there is such a thing as that either."

"Well instead of taking all the senses one by one, what if we put them all together and asked about perception? Is there a form of perception that is only a perception of itself, the other forms of perception, and all the forms of non-perception?"

"No, I certainly don't think so."

[e] "Well, how about desire?* Do you think there could be a form of desire that is not a desire for pleasure,* but only for itself and for other forms of desire?"

"No."

"How about a wish that doesn't wish for some good, but wishes only itself and other wishes?"

"Absolutely not."

"Or a love that doesn't love anything beautiful, but loves only itself and other forms of love?"

"No."

"Have you ever observed a fear that wasn't afraid of anything terrible, [168a] but feared only itself and other forms of fear?"

"I have never observed any such thing."

"How about an opinion that wasn't an opinion on any particular issue but was merely an opinion of itself and other opinions?"

"No."

"But we appear to be saying that there is a form of knowledge that isn't knowledge of anything that you learn, it is merely knowledge of itself and other forms of knowledge."

"That is what we are saying."

"Wouldn't it be paradoxical if there were such a thing? Nevertheless, just because it is difficult to believe that there can be such a thing we should not conclude definitively that it is impossible. Let's consider this further, shall we?"

[b] "Yes, you are quite right about that, Socrates."

"Alright, this knowledge we are discussing is a knowledge of something, and it has the function of being of something. Isn't that right?"

"Yes, it is the knowledge of itself, so it is the knowledge of something," Critias said.

"Notice that other things have this same function of being of something. For example, the greater is necessarily greater than something, isn't it?"

"Yes, I suppose it is."

"It is greater than something that is lesser."

"Necessarily."

"Well, then, can you imagine finding something that is greater, but it isn't greater than any of the things that others are greater than. It is only greater than itself, and greater than the other things that are greater. [c] And notice further that if the greater is always greater than what is lesser, if it is greater than itself, it is simultaneously lesser than itself. Wouldn't that have to be true?"

"It would be entirely necessary, Socrates."

"And isn't the greater-lesser pair like the double-half pair? If something is the double of the other doubles, and also it is the double of itself, then wouldn't it simultaneously be half of itself?

"That is true," Critias agreed.

"And if it is true for greater-lesser, and double-half, then the same thing would be true for more-less, wouldn't it? If you said that something is more than itself, you'd have to agree that it is simultaneously less than itself. Isn't it the same with everything whose function it is to be relative to something, for example: heavier-lighter, older-younger, and so on? [d] Hearing is another example of what I'm talking about. Don't we say that the function of hearing is to hear sound?

"Yes."

"So if there is a form of hearing that hears itself, then it would simultaneously have to have a sound that it was hearing, because if it had no sound, it couldn't be heard, could it?"

"Necessarily."

"Then we could say the same thing about sight, couldn't we? If there is a form of seeing that sees itself, then it would have to have a color that it was seeing, because if it had no color, [e] it couldn't be seen, could it?"

"Certainly not."

"Notice, Critias, that all the examples we've gone through of applying a thing's proper function to itself can be divided into two groups. First, some of them seem to us to be absolutely impossible; for example, doesn't it seem impossible for one thing to be simultaneously greater and lesser than itself, or simultaneously double and half of itself?"

"It certainly does."

"Members of the second group don't seem totally impossible, but they do seem highly implausible, for example, the hearing that hears itself and the seeing that sees itself. We might add the motion that moves itself or the fire that burns itself. [169a] Some people will deny that these are real, but I suppose that others won't. What we need, my friend, is for some great man who is competent in such matters to determine once and for all that there is nothing whose nature includes the function of being in relation to itself, as opposed to being in relation to something other than itself, or who can tell us that actually there are some cases where something has the function of being in relation to itself, although in other cases this is not so. And finally, if it actually is possible that some things have the function of being in relation to themselves, is knowledge among them—the kind of knowledge that you say temperance is? I certainly do not believe that I myself am qualified to determine these matters, [b] and so I cannot conclude definitively whether it is even possible for there to be such a thing as the knowledge of knowledge. And even if it is possible for there to be such a thing, I cannot accept that it is temperance before considering whether it is beneficial or not. For I divine* that temperance is a beneficial and good thing. So, then, son of Callaeschrus, since you have put forward the view that temperance is the knowledge of knowledge and of ignorance, please demonstrate that such a knowledge is even possible, and after demonstrating that it is possible, [c] go on to demonstrate that it is beneficial. If you do both of those things, then I will be satisfied that what you say about temperance is correct."

When Critias heard this, and saw that I really was quite confounded,* he too became confounded. It was like when you see someone yawn, and then suddenly you feel like you have to yawn. But because he had a reputation to maintain among those who were present, he was too embarrassed to admit that he was unable to demonstrate either of the things I had asked him to demonstrate. [d] So he said something that wasn't very clear, concealing* the fact that he was just as confounded as I.

But I wanted the conversation to continue and so I said, "How about this, Critias? If it is ok with you, why don't we concede that this knowledge of knowledge is possible? At a later date we can examine whether or not it is actually possible. Instead, let's go back to a point that we touched on earlier.* Supposing that a knowledge of knowledge is possible, how does such knowledge make it possible for us to know what we know and what we do not know? That is what we say it is to "know oneself" and to be temperate, isn't it?"

"Yes, indeed, Socrates. And what you say adds up, [e] because a man is such as what he has, a man with self-knowledge will be self-knowledgeable and will know himself. It's like when a man has swiftness he is called swift, and when he has beauty he is called beautiful. So also a man who has knowledge is knowledgeable, and a man who has self-knowledge will be self-knowledgeable."

"I do not dispute your point, Critias, that the person who has self-knowledge is self-knowledgeable. But what I want to focus on is how the person with self-knowledge is bound to know what he knows and what he does not know."

[170a] "But the two are the same, Socrates. To possess self-knowledge just is to know what you know and what you do not know."

"Maybe," I said, "but I'm afraid that I'm being my same old ignorant self, because I still don't understand how self-knowledge is the same thing as knowing what you know and what you do not know."

"What's the problem?"

"Look at it this way. Is the knowledge of knowledge going to be able to do anything more than draw the simple distinction that this is a case of knowledge, but that is not a case of knowledge?"

"No, that's as much as it can do," Critias agreed.

"Then is this knowledge of knowledge the same thing as knowledge and ignorance of health, [b] or knowledge and ignorance of justice?"

"Certainly not."

"Because the knowledge and ignorance of health is for the doctor to determine, and the knowledge and ignorance of justice is to be determined by the person with political knowledge. Neither one of these is the kind of 'knowledge of knowledge' that you and I are discussing."

"Of course."

"Obviously, because we are saying that temperance is self-knowledge, but we wouldn't say that to be temperate is to be a doctor. So if someone lacks both medical and political knowledge, and possesses only the sort of self-knowledge that you and I are discussing, then it seems he won't know about health or justice, the only thing he will know is that he knows something, and that he has a particular bit of knowledge. And he'll know this both about himself and about others, won't he?"

"Yes."

"Then how will he know that he knows* by means of this knowledge? [c] It is the doctor's medical knowledge that allows him to know that he knows about health. It is the musician's knowledge of music that allows him to know that he knows about harmony. It is the builder's knowledge of building that allows him to know that he knows about building. It is not temperance, self-knowledge, or to "know thyself," that allows any of these people to know that they know these things, is it?"

"It seems not," Critias admitted.

"If temperance is restricted to only the knowledge of knowledge, and does not also include the knowledge of health or the knowledge of building, then is there any way that it can allow someone to know that he knows about health, or to know that he knows about building?"

"There is no way it could."

"So the person who lacks medical knowledge, or who lacks the builder's knowledge, won't know what the doctor knows or what the builder knows. If all he has is self-knowledge, then he will know only that he has knowledge. In general, knowledge of knowledge only allows you to know *that* you know, not *what* you know."*

"I suppose so."

[d] "Therefore, temperance and being temperate would not be the same as knowing *what* you know and *what* you do not know; it seems that it would only amount to knowing *that* you know one thing, and *that* you do not know another thing."

"That seems reasonable."

"So the person with the restricted 'knowledge of knowledge' that you and I are discussing will not be able to discern* whether someone who claims to know something actually knows it. The only thing it will allow him to know is *that* someone has some knowledge, temperance won't tell him *what* the other person knows."

"So it seems."

[e] "And doesn't it also follow that the temperate person will be unable to distinguish between the person who is truly a doctor, and the person who falsely claims to be a doctor, and likewise with the other forms of knowledge? Think of it this way. If the temperate person—or anybody else for that matter—intends to distinguish the true doctor from the impostor, how will he go about it? Obviously he cannot ask medical questions because the temperate person does not profess to have any knowledge of medical matters. And on the other hand, the only knowledge the doctor has is about medical issues regarding health and sickness. Isn't that so?"

"Yes it is."

"So because the doctor only has the knowledge of health and sickness, he won't have the 'knowledge of knowledge' you and I have been discussing, which is the knowledge that only the temperate person* has."

"Yes."

"And furthermore, because the doctor does not have the 'knowledge of knowledge,' he won't even have knowledge of medical knowledge, [171a] since medical knowledge happens to be a form of knowledge."

"Quite true."

"The temperate person will know *that* the doctor has knowledge, but if he is ever going to put someone to the test in order to distinguish the true doctor from the impostor, won't he have to ask questions about the actual subject matter of medical knowledge? The different forms of knowledge are not distinguished by knowledge, are they, but by subject matter, by what they are knowledge of?"

"Yes, that is how they are distinguished."

"And we've already said that the doctor's knowledge is distinguished from the other forms of knowledge because it's subject matter is health and sickness."

"Yes."

"And if anybody wanted to inquire into medical knowledge, [b] he would necessarily have to inquire into what is within the subject matter of medical knowledge, and not what is outside of its distinctive subject matter."

"Of course."

"So if this inquiry is to be conducted properly, it must focus on that in virtue of which medical knowledge is actually *medical*; it would have to focus on health and sickness, wouldn't it?"

"So it seems."

"Now, in order to put a self-proclaimed doctor to the test, we would have to consider both his words and his deeds: we would have to consider if what he says about health and sickness is actually true, and if what he does to promote health and ward off sickness is actually correct."

"Necessarily."

"But could anyone do either of these things if he himself did not have medical knowledge of health and sickness?"

"Not at all."

[c] "Then only a true doctor is able to put other doctors to the test. The temperate person cannot do this unless he happens also to be a true doctor."*

"That is so," Critias agreed.

"Don't we then have to conclude that if temperance is nothing more than the restricted 'knowledge of knowledge' that we've been considering, then the temperate person will be unable to distinguish the true doctor who actually knows the medical craft from the person who does not know it but only pretends that he is a real doctor, or who falsely thinks that he knows the medical craft? And the temperate person won't be able to determine any genuine practitioner of any other craft except his own, like any other craftsperson?"

"So it seems."

[d] "Then what benefit is there for us in temperance if it is like this? I think that things haven't turned out quite as we expected them to. At the start, when we first laid down the proposition that the temperate person knows what he knows and what he does not know, and he knows that he knows the former, and that

he does not know the latter, and that he would be able to recognize the very same knowledge in others—at that point it seemed as if temperance would have very far-reaching benefits for us, because those of us with temperance would go through life without ever making a mistake,* and we would be unerring guides of whomever we governed. [e] For we would never even attempt any task we did not know; instead, we would seek out those who did know it and hand it over to them. And we'd apply the same standard to those we governed: we would never entrust to them anything they wouldn't do correctly, and so we would never entrust anything to them that they did not know. The result would be that any household that was governed by temperance would be well governed, and any city that was ruled by temperance would be well ruled. The same would be true everywhere that temperance was in charge. For with every error* [172a] eliminated, and with correctness guiding all of our actions, in those conditions every action would necessarily be well and finely done, and those who do everything well would be happy.* Tell me, Critias, when we originally said that temperance is to know what one knows and what one does not know, isn't this the tremendous good we thought it would be for us?

"Certainly, yes, that is exactly it," he said.

"But now do you see that we have been unable to find any such knowledge no matter where we look?"

"I do see that."

[b] "Well, how about this? Since the knowledge of knowledge and ignorance did not turn out, upon our examination of it, to provide the benefit we expected, could the good that it provides be the following? Perhaps the one who possess it is able to learn more easily,* and when he learns things, he sees them all the more clearly because he doesn't just learn each particular thing, in addition he also learns the knowledge of the things he learns. That means he would be able to make an excellent examination of other people who are learning the same things. In contrast, people who lack this knowledge of knowledge will only be able to carry out a much weaker and less efficient* examination. Could it be, my friend, that these [c] are the only advantages there are to temperance, and that we have been looking for and seeking out a much greater benefit than it is really capable of?"

"Perhaps you are right, Socrates."

"Maybe so, but maybe not. Actually, I am now wondering if we are going to come up empty handed* after all this searching. I think I've just noticed a paradoxical result* of thinking about temperance in this way. Let's take a fresh look at it if you don't mind. Let's grant the proposal you made at the beginning, that temperance is to know what you know and what you don't know, and let's grant that such a knowledge of knowledge is possible. [d] Given all this, let's ask again what benefit temperance would be. Because, Critias, I am now doubting that we were right to agree that temperance—if it is what we are saying it is— would be such a great good when it comes to governing our households and cities."

"How so?"

"Because I think we agreed too easily that it would be a great good for us if we did only the things we know, and gave it to those who know to do the things that we do not know."

[e] "Weren't we right to agree to that?"

"Now I don't think so," I said.

"That truly does sound paradoxical, Socrates!"

"By the dog,"* I said, "it certainly does seem paradoxical, doesn't it? This is why I'm afraid that we are not conducting the investigation correctly. The truth of the matter is, Critias, that if temperance is what we are saying it is, [173a] then it now seems clear to me that it does us no good whatsoever."

"What are you saying, Socrates? Please explain this so that we both understand your meaning."

"I think I'm speaking nonsense here, but nevertheless, anyone with an ounce of self-respect must investigate what appears to them to be the case, and they must not casually ignore it."

"Well said."

"Then hear my dream. I don't know whether it has come through the gate of horn* or the gate of ivory. If temperance is what we are now defining it to be, and if it ruled our lives, [b] then everything would be done according to knowledge. For example, no impostor would ever deceive us into thinking that he was a pilot if he wasn't really a pilot. We would be able to detect any fraud who claimed to be a doctor or a general but lacked genuine medical or military knowledge. If that is how things were, then wouldn't we be healthier than we are now, and wouldn't we be far safer from the hazards of sailing and the dangers of war than we are now? And even when it comes to our shoes, our clothing, our tools and so on, [c] wouldn't all of our equipment be superior because it was all provided by people who actually knew what they were doing—by true craftsmen? If you want, we could even add divination* here as the knowledge of future events, and say that if temperance ruled us, we would never be deceived by charlatans, but we would employ only true diviners who would give us accurate information about the future. So equipped, the human race [d] would act and live knowledgeably—this much I accept—because temperance would guard against ignorance sneaking in and having a hand in anything we did. However, what we have not yet been able to establish, my dear Critias, is that if we did everything knowledgeably, then we would actually be doing well, and we would actually be happy."

"Ah, but Socrates, can't we establish it this way: you'd be very hard pressed to find any other route to the goal of doing well if you reject knowledgeable action?"

"Perhaps, Critias, if you will instruct me on one small point: *which* knowledgeable action are you referring to? Knowledgeable shoemaking?"

[e] "By god, no!"

"Knowledgeable bronze-working?"

"Not at all."

"Knowledgeable weaving or carpentry, then?"

"Certainly not."

"But then aren't we giving up the claim that the one who lives knowledgeably lives happily, because all these people live knowledgeably, but you do not agree that they live happily. Or perhaps I have not yet mentioned the particular kind of knowledgeable living that will make us happy: perhaps it is the person I mentioned just a moment ago, [174a] the diviner who knows what will happen in the future. Is that it?"

"Yes," said Critias, "and one more person."

"Who? Do you mean the person who doesn't simply know the future, but who also knows the present and the past, the person who is ignorant of nothing? Let's grant that there is such a person. I think you will accept that no one lives more knowledgeably than he does."

"Certainly not."

"Then there is just one thing further I want you to tell me: exactly which knowledge of his makes him live a happy life? Or do they all equally make him live happily?"

"Oh no, they do not all equally contribute to his living a happy life."

[b] "Then which one contributes most to his doing well? If he's a gambler, then is it his knowledge of which horse will win the race, or what number will come up on the dice?"

"Of course not, don't be ridiculous."

"His knowledge of calculation?"

"Not at all."

"His knowledge of health?"

"That knowledge certainly contributes more than the others," Critias answered.

"And the knowledge that contributes the most is what?"

"The knowledge of good and bad."

"What?! Do you mean to tell me that all this time you've been leading me around in a circle,* hiding from me the fact that it isn't living knowledgeably that makes us do well [c] and be happy, not even if we combined all the other forms of knowledge besides the one form that really matters: the knowledge of good and bad? Look at it this way, Critias. Suppose you take away the knowledge of good and bad from all the other forms of knowledge. Won't medical knowledge still produce health? Shoemaking will still give us shoes, won't it? Weaving will still provide us with clothing, knowledge of piloting will keep us safe at sea and the general's knowledge will save us in battle. Isn't that correct?"

"Yes, they will."

"But then, my dear Critias, if you take away the knowledge of good and bad from each of these, [d] then you are also taking away from them the function of benefitting us and making us do well in our lives."

"True."

"And this knowledge of good and bad is not temperance—not if temperance is the knowledge of knowledge and ignorance. And the knowledge of good and bad turns out to be the form of knowledge that is beneficial for us, so that if temperance is not the knowledge of good and bad, then temperance will not be beneficial for us."

"Why won't temperance still be beneficial? Because if it is the knowledge of the other forms of knowledge, [e] then it will include* knowledge of the knowledge of good and bad; and if temperance governs the knowledge of good and bad, then it will be beneficial for us."

"Then will temperance make us healthy? Isn't that the function of the doctor's knowledge? Will temperance perform the functions of the other crafts, or will each craft still perform its own distinctive function? Didn't we agree a while ago* that temperance is only the knowledge of knowledge and ignorance, and not of anything else? Isn't that so?"

"It appears so."

"Then temperance will not be the craft that produces health?"

"No."

[175a] "We attribute the production of health to a distinct craft, don't we?"

"Yes."

"Then temperance will not produce the benefit of health, because we just attributed that benefit to a distinct craft."

"Correct."

"Then how is temperance beneficial if it produces no benefit?"

"Apparently it will not be beneficial."

"So now you see, Critias, that I was right* to blame myself, and it was reasonable to fear that my search for temperance would come up empty handed. That which everybody agrees is the finest thing of all [b] would not have appeared useless to us if I had been of any use in the investigation. As things stand, we have been completely defeated, and have been unable to discover to which of the real things* the lawgiver gave the name of temperance."

"Furthermore," I continued, "we conceded many things that we were unable to prove. For example, we granted* that a knowledge of knowledge is possible despite the fact that our reasoning did not allow it—in fact, our reasoning actually denied such a thing. Then we conceded* that this form of knowledge included other forms of knowledge, [c] despite the fact that our reasoning did not allow it, so that the temperate person would turn out to know that he knows what he knows, and to know that he does not know what he does not know. This really was too generous of us, because our reasoning did not support the claim that the knowledge of knowledge included the other forms of knowledge, like medical knowledge or the general's knowledge. In effect, we were accepting that someone knows something that in fact he does not know, and I can think of nothing more unreasonable* than that."

"Well, be that as it may," I went on, "although we helped ourselves to these additional assumptions to which we were not entitled, [d] our inquiry was still unable to discover the truth of the matter. In fact, our inquiry positively mocks the truth: after accepting various assumptions and things we just made up on the spot, our inquiry had the audacity to make temperance appear to be of no benefit to us whatsoever."

Finally, bringing the conversation back to where it began, I turned to Charmides and said, "This failure doesn't really bother me for my own sake; but for your sake, Charmides, I am deeply concerned if, despite having such a fine form in your body and [e] being most temperate* in your soul, you gain no advantage from this temperance, and it doesn't benefit you in this present life. And I'm really annoyed if that Thracian charm I took so much trouble to learn has turned out* to be worthless. But I really don't think that this is possible; rather, I must be a very poor investigator because temperance is a great good, and if you do have it, Charmides, [176a] then you are truly blessed. So look and see whether or not you are indeed temperate and have no need of the charm, because if you possess temperance, then I would advise you to believe that I am useless and unable to discover anything through inquiry, and to believe that the more temperate you are, the more happy your life will be."

Charmides responded by saying, "By god, Socrates, I certainly do not know if I have or do not have temperance. How would I know either way when you admit that you and Critias have been unable to discover what it is. [b] But I'm not quite persuaded by you, Socrates, about the charm; I think that I do need it, and I would willingly be charmed by you every day until you say that I have been sufficiently treated."

"Very well!" said Critias. "If you do this, Charmides, I will take it as full proof that you are indeed temperate—if you allow Socrates to charm you, and you don't abandon him for anything."

"I shall follow him and not abandon him. It would be terrible [c] if I did not obey you, my guardian, and did not do what you urge me to do."

"I do urge you to do this," Critias said.

"Then I shall do it," replied Charmides, "and I shall begin this very day."

That's when I spoke up, "Here now, what are you two planning?"

"Nothing," said Charmides, "the planning is already complete."

"Am I to have no choice in the matter," I asked?

"None whatsoever," Charmides continued, "since I am now under orders.* So now you should plan what you will do."

[d] "There's nothing left to plan, since no one could oppose you once you have set out to do something and will overcome all opposition."

"Then don't even try to oppose me," he said.

And I replied, "I will not oppose you."

LACHES

Setting: Athens, probably in a wrestling-school. The dialogue takes place after the battle of Delium (424 BCE) and prior to Laches' death in the battle of Mantinaea (418). There is no indication of whether the dialogue is set before or after the Peace of Nicias (421).

Characters (in order of appearance):
LYSIMACHUS (over 50 years old, undistinguished member of an important aristocratic family; his name is traditionally pronounced "lye-SIM-uh-cuss," though "loo-SIM-ah-khoss" is closer to the original)
NICIAS (c.470-413; around 50 years old, a wealthy aristocrat; experienced politician and general; his name is traditionally pronounced "NICK-ee-us," though "nee-KEE-oss" is closer to the original)
LACHES (c.475-418; around 50 years old, from an aristocratic family; his name is traditionally pronounced "LAKE-eez," though "LAH-khays" is closer to the original)
ARISTIDES (probably a teenager, probably a bit spoiled, son of Lysimachus; his name is traditionally pronounced "air-RISS-ti-deez," though "are-is-TAY-days" is closer to the original)
THUCYDIDES (probably a teenager, probably a bit spoiled, son of Melesias; his name is traditionally pronounced "thoo-SID-i-deez," though "thou-kou-DEE-days" is closer to the original)
SOCRATES (469-399; around 50 years old, from a middle class family, not handsome at all; his name is traditionally pronounced "SOCK-ra-teez," though "so-KROT-ays" is closer to the original)
MELESIAS (over 50 years old, undistinguished member of an important aristocratic family; his name is traditionally pronounced "mel-EE-see-us," though "mel-ay-SEE-oss" is closer to the original)

Dramatic Structure:
Prologue: Lysimachus asks for advice (178a1-179a1)
Episode #1: Speeches on the value of *hoplomachia* (179a1-190e2)
Episode #2: Socrates asks Laches what courage is (190e3-194c1)
Episode #3: Socrates asks Nicias what courage is (194c2-199e12)
Conclusion: All agree to continue their education (199e13-201c5)

LYSIMACHUS. [178a] You have seen* the men fighting in armor, Nicias and Laches, but Melesias and I did not tell you why we asked you to come and see the demonstration with us. We'll tell you now because we think we ought to speak freely* with you: we asked you here to advise us.

Some people refuse to take such requests seriously, and if [b] someone asks for their advice they don't say what they really think. Instead, they guess what the other person wants to hear and tells them that, even if they don't really believe it. But we think that you are both quite knowledgeable* and that once you have formed a judgment, you will say what you think plainly and honestly. That is the spirit in which we asked you here today; we'd like your honest advice about the matter we'd like to discuss. [179a] The following is the issue about which I have made such a long prologue.

This is Melesias' son right here; he's named after his grandfather, Thucydides.* And this is my son; he's named after his grandfather—and my father—Aristides. Melesias and I are resolved to raise them as well as we possibly can and not to do what most fathers do, which is simply to let their children do whatever they want once they become teenagers.* Starting immediately, we want to do our best to raise them as well as possible.

Knowing that [b] you both have sons* of your own, we thought that if anybody is likely to have given serious thought to what kind of training is going to turn their sons into the best men they can be, it is you two. But if by chance we are wrong about you, and in fact you have not often paid serious attention to this matter, then we remind you that you should not neglect it. In any case, we urge you, please help us work out the best way to care for our sons. And I should tell you, Nicias and Laches, how we reached this decision, even though it will take a little while to explain.

As I said earlier, we shall speak freely with you, so I should tell you that Melesias and I are messmates,* and our boys are now old enough to join us. [c] Well, we both have many stories to tell our sons about the admirable* deeds of their grandfathers in both war and peace, successfully governing the affairs of the city and her allies. However, we have no deeds of our own to tell them about. Consequently, we are quite ashamed of ourselves in front of our own sons, and we blame our fathers [d] because while they were off tending to the affairs of others,* they left us to do as we pleased. We point all this out to our sons and tell them that if they don't think carefully about themselves, and if they don't take our advice, then they will grow up to be like us, without any glory or honor. However, if they do take great care, then perhaps someday they will be worthy of the names they bear. They have agreed to follow our advice, and so we are investigating what course of study, or what line of business, would make them the very best.*

[e] Someone advised us that this line of study we have just seen—learning how to fight in armor*—is an admirable one for our sons to take up. He praised this man in particular who just put on the demonstration for us and told us that we really ought to come see him. That seemed like a good idea to us, so we decided to come here and to bring you along to see the demonstration, and to give us your advice, and perhaps also to become partners with you in making sure that we raise our sons well. [180a] So that is the partnership* we would like to share with you.

And now, for your part, would you please give us your advice about this line of study: do you, or do you not, think that our sons ought to learn how to fight in armor? But also, please tell us if you think that any other study or business is good for a young man. And finally, tell us whether you would like to join us as partners in this enterprise.

NICIAS. Well I commend both of you Lysimachus and Melesias on your plan, and I am ready to join your partnership. I think that Laches here will also join us.

LACHES. [b] Quite true, Nicias. And I very much agree with what Lysimachus just said about his own father and Melesias' father. In fact, it applies not only to them but also to us and to everyone who is actively involved in the affairs of the community. It seems to be a general rule that people who occupy themselves with public matters are a bit careless about their own children and their private affairs generally, and don't pay enough attention to managing them. Well said, Lysimachus.

But I am surprised that you would ask for our advice about educating your children [c] without also asking Socrates for his advice. First, he's actually from the same town* as you. But second, he spends all his time in exactly the sorts of places you are looking into for your sons, places that are devoted to the fine education and training of young men.*

LYSIMACHUS. What? Has Socrates studied the proper training of young men?

LACHES. He certainly has.

NICIAS. And I am in as good a position as Laches to prove it, because just recently he recommended to me [d] a music* teacher for my son, a student of Agathocles named Damon.* No only is Damon a most accomplished musician, but in every other way he is quite a worthy mentor for young men of that age.

LYSIMACHUS. Well, in that case, I'll address myself to all three of you, Laches, Nicias and Socrates. You see, men of my age don't get out and about as much as you younger men, and so we are often quite out of touch with what is going on. And so, son of Sophroniscus,* if you have any good advice for your neighbor [e] you should share it. In fact, you owe it to me* to give me any advice you can because you are my friend through your father. You see, he and I were close friends for a very long time, and up until the day he died we never had a falling out. And hearing your name has just reminded me of something: I have often heard my son and his friends talking about someone named "Socrates," and praising him in the highest terms, but I never asked [181a] whether they were talking about the son of my old friend Sophroniscus. Tell me, boys, is this the Socrates whose name you keep mentioning?

ARISTIDES. Yes, father, this is he.

LYSIMACHUS. Well, then, by Hera,* I'm certainly glad to know that you are a credit to your father, Socrates, and that our families will renew their ties with each other.

LACHES. Quite right, Lysimachus, don't let him get away. I am witness to the fact that he is not only a credit to his own father, [b] but also to our entire country.* He stayed with me during the retreat at Delium* and I can assure you that if more of our soldiers had chosen to be like him, our country's honor would have been preserved and would not have fallen on that day.

LYSIMACHUS. Socrates, this is high praise indeed that you are receiving, especially because it is given by people who deserve to be believed when it comes to the conduct they are praising you for. I hope you understand how happy I am to hear such things about you, and how much I'd like us to be friends. [c] Really you should have visited us much sooner and considered us to be like family. Starting today, that's how it should be. Please come visit us and get to know us and our sons so that we can preserve the bonds of friendship between our families. Do remember to visit, and I'll be sure to remind you.

But now tell me what you think about the issue I've raised? What seems right to you? Do you or do you not think that it is worthwhile for us to have our sons to learn fight in armor?

SOCRATES. [d] I certainly will try to advise you on this to the best of my ability, and to do everything you just said about preserving the bonds of friendship between our families. However, since I am younger and less experienced than Laches and Nicias, I ought to listen to them and learn from them. If I have anything to add to what they say, then I'll explain it and make my case to all of you. So Nicias, why doesn't one of you two* begin?

NICIAS. Certainly, Socrates. In my opinion, [e] this study is beneficial in many ways for young men to know.

First, it strengthens and improves the body, which is absolutely necessary for young men, and is far better than what they tend to waste their time doing when they have free time. No form of physical exercise [182a] gives them a better workout.

Second, no exercise is more suitable for a free man than fighting in armor and horsemanship.* No one is being better trained for this great contest* in which we are engaged, and for the accomplishments it demands of us, than those who being trained in these military arts.

Third, this study will be of some use in battle when a man must fight in formation with many other soldiers. But its greatest usefulness will be when the army has broken formation* and he has to fight one-on-one, either because he is pursuing someone who is defending himself, [b] or because he is defending himself against someone who is attacking him. The one who knows this skill will suffer no harm from a lone attacker, and probably more than one attacker will do him no harm either because he'll always have the advantage over them.

Fourth, this study induces the one who learns it to pursue other noble studies. For everyone who learns how to fight in armor wants to learn what comes next, which is tactics. And once he's mastered tactics and is proud of his achievement, [c] he'll be eager to pursue the entire art of generalship. Of course, I'm sure you'll acknowledge that studying tactics and developing the leadership skills involved in generalship are very noble pursuits—well, learning to fight in armor leads the way to these further studies.

There's one additional point—and not a small one—to add here: this knowledge will make every man who learns it more daring and more courageous* in battle than he would be without it. Nor should we neglect to mention a point that some may think unimportant. Learning this skill gives a man an impressive bearing and poise when such an appearance is most important, [d] when it will strike fear into his enemy.

Therefore, Lysimachus, as I said, I think that we ought to teach young men these things, and I've explained why I think this. But if Laches has anything different to say, I'd be glad to hear it.

LACHES. Well, Nicias, it is difficult to say of any branch of learning that it ought not be studied, since all knowledge seems to be good. And so if fighting in armor [e] is indeed a genuine branch of learning, as its teachers claim, and as Nicias says, then we ought to study it. However, if it is not a genuine branch of learning, and if those who promise to teach it are deceiving us—or even if it is a legitimate branch of learning, but not a very important one, then what is the use in studying it?

I say this because of the following observation: I think that if there were anything to it, then the Spartans wouldn't have overlooked it. They care about nothing in life except to discover and to practice [183a] the arts that give them an advantage over others in war. And even if the Spartans have overlooked it, surely the men who teach fighting in armor would not overlook the fact that the Spartans are more interested than any other Greeks in these arts, and that if they earned the respect of the Spartans they would make a fortune everywhere else charging fees for lessons. It would be just like tragedians who earn the respect of us Athenians: if anyone thinks that he can write a good tragedy he doesn't bother producing it outside Attica, [b] he comes straight here to Athens. On the contrary, I've noticed that these self-proclaimed teachers of fighting in armor treat Sparta as a sort of sacred ground they cannot touch—they won't put a single toe inside Spartan territory. Instead, they go to all the cities around it and make their demonstrations there, especially in the cities that would agree their military skills are inferior.

[c] Second, Lysimachus, I have come across quite a few of these characters in action, and I've seen what they're like. So we can consider their deeds, not just their words. I can tell you that not one of them has ever distinguished himself in battle. In fact, it almost looks as if they deliberately avoid real action. In every other art, the one who practices and studies diligently ends up making a name for himself, but these experts are just extremely unlucky,* I guess.

Take this Stesilaus here for example. [d] We just watched his demonstration in front of a large crowd, and we heard the grand claims he made for himself. Well, I have witnessed a far better demonstration of his true abilities and the true worth of his art, though it was entirely unintentional on his part. He was a soldier on a ship that happened to ram a cargo vessel, and he was fighting with something that is as distinctive among weapons as he is among soldiers—a spear-sword.* There's really nothing to say about him on that voyage except for how events fell out* with that clever weapon, [e] because during the battle it got stuck in the other ship's tackle.* He kept pulling at it, but he couldn't get it unstuck, and the two ships were passing by each other. He had to keep moving along the deck to keep a grip on his weapon until the other ship started pulling away. Finally, he was at the stern of the trireme still clutching the spike on the butt end of his spear [184a] when the crew of the other ship broke out in laughter and applause at the show he'd put on. Somebody threw a big rock at him and missed, and he had to let go of his clever weapon. At that point, even the crew of his own ship couldn't contain themselves anymore and they broke out in laughter at the sight of the spear-sword sticking out of the transport.

Perhaps there is something worthwhile in what Stesilaus teaches, as Nicias has said; I can only tell you what I've seen. [b] In my view, whether it is a legitimate branch of learning that is almost useless, or it is something that people like Stesilaus falsely claim to be a legitimate branch of learning, in either case it isn't worth studying. In fact, it seems to me that it is actually detrimental. Look, if a coward thinks he knows this art, it will only make him reckless* and his true character will be even more obvious to all; if a courageous person knows it, then he won't be able to make the smallest mistake without being vilified.* [c] You see, as a general rule, people get really annoyed if you claim that you know more than they do about something, and so unless you really are much better than everyone, you'll be a constant target for mockery if go around claiming to know this skill.

Well, anyway, that's my opinion of the matter, Lysimachus. But like I said from the beginning, don't let Socrates go until he tells you his opinion of studying this skill.

LYSIMACHUS. Oh yes, by all means, Socrates, I certainly do ask this favor of you, [d] especially because it seems that our council is split and we need someone to break the tie. If Nicias and Laches had agreed with one another there would be less need for a third opinion, but as you see, they are on opposite sides of the issue, so I would really like to hear with whom you cast your vote.

SOCRATES. What, Lysimachus? Do you really intend to go along with the majority?*

LYSIMACHUS. Is there any other way to decide the issue?

SOCRATES. And what about you, Melesias? [e] Would you do the same? Consider a different case. Suppose we were trying to decide how your son ought to train for an upcoming athletic competition. Should we follow the opinion of the majority, or of someone who had actually been educated and trained by an athletics master?

MELESIAS. In all likelihood* the latter, Socrates.

SOCRATES. And therefore you would rather listen to him than to the four of us?

MELESIAS. Probably.

SOCRATES. Knowledge, I think, is necessary for judgment, not numbers, if you intend to judge well.

MELESIAS. Of course.

SOCRATES. Therefore, shouldn't our first order of business be [185a] to find out if any of us is an expert in the matter we are investigating? Because if one of us is an expert, then we ought to listen to him and not to the rest of us; and if none of us is an expert, then we ought to go find one. Surely the matter that you and Lysimachus are investigating is not a trivial one. Aren't our children the greatest of our possessions? They may turn out well or badly, and the fortunes of the entire family lineage depends upon which.

MELESIAS. That's quite true, Socrates.

SOCRATES. So we really should put a lot of thought into this.

MELESIAS. Certainly.

SOCRATES. [b] Well, then, how should we go about this? How about the way I was just suggesting? If we were considering which of us was an expert in a particular athletic competition, wouldn't we look for three things: whether he had actually learned about, practiced, and had good teachers in, that sport?

MELESIAS. That seems right to me.

SOCRATES. And before we do that, shouldn't we be clear on what it really is that we are looking for teachers in?

MELESIAS. What do you mean?

SOCRATES. Perhaps my point will be clearer this way. I don't think that we actually agreed on exactly what we are asking about when we ask which of us is or is not an expert, [c] and which of us has or has not been educated.

NICIAS. But Socrates, isn't it obvious that we are asking about fighting in armor, and whether or not young men ought to learn how to do it?

SOCRATES. Yes, Nicias, but when someone asks whether or not to apply a certain ointment* to the eyes, are they concerned about the ointment or the eyes?

NICIAS. The eyes.

SOCRATES. [d] It's like when someone is considering whether or not to put a bridle on a horse, and when do to so. The whole point of his inquiry is the horse, not the bridle.

NICIAS. True.

SOCRATES. If we were to put this in the form of a single principle or rule, we might say that whenever someone considers one thing for the sake of another, the real point of his inquiry is that for the sake of which* he is inquiring, and not that which is for the sake of another.

NICIAS. Necessarily.

SOCRATES. So when we look for an advisor, we have to find someone who is an expert in that for the sake of which we are inquiring.

NICIAS. Certainly.

SOCRATES. [e] And right now we are inquiring into a branch of study for the sake of the souls* of young men?

NICIAS. Yes.

SOCRATES. So what we actually ought to be considering is this—whether any one of us is an expert in training* the soul, and whether he is able to train souls well, and whether any of us has had good teachers in how to train souls well.

LACHES. Ah, but Socrates, haven't you ever noticed that some people who have had no teachers are actually more expert than those who have had teachers?

SOCRATES. I have, Laches. However, you would not simply take their word for it if they claimed to be experts unless they actually demonstrated their expertise with some work that they had done well, [186a] in fact you might ask for several demonstrations.

LACHES. Yes, that's certainly true.

SOCRATES. Therefore, Laches and Nicias, since Lysimachus and Melesias have asked for our advice about their sons, and they are so concerned that their souls become the best they possibly can, we should start by pointing out to them, if we can, teachers who satisfy the following three conditions: first, they have good souls themselves;* second, they have actually trained the souls of many young men; and third, they have taught us how train the souls of young men well. [b] But in deference to Laches' point, if one of us denies that he has ever had a teacher of this kind, then he should point to some work that he has actually accomplished—some souls that are acknowledged to have been made better by him, whether Athenian or foreigner, free or slave. And if we can do neither—if we can show neither teachers nor works of our own— then we ought to tell Lysimachus and Melesias to look elsewhere for advisors. We dare not risk corrupting our friends' sons; that would make us guilty of one of the most serious accusations* friends can make against each another.

Let me be the first to say that [c] I have never had a teacher in this subject, although I've wanted one ever since I was young. The only ones who claim to be able to make someone fine and good* are the Sophists,* but I don't have the money to pay their fees, and I have been unable to discover the craft on my own.

I wouldn't be surprised if Nicias or Laches has learned or discovered it: they have more money than I do, so they could have paid someone to teach it to them; and they are older than I am, so they could have discovered it on their own. On top of that, [d] they seem to be able to teach others—surely they wouldn't have lectured us so confidently on the activities that are worthwhile or worthless for the young if they weren't sufficiently confident in their knowledge.

Now, on the one hand, I do believe this about them. But on the other hand, they disagree with one another. So I'm puzzled. I therefore urge you, Lysimachus, just as Laches urged you not to let me go until I answered your question, don't let Laches or Nicias go. Question them like this,

"Socrates [e] denies that he is sufficiently knowledgeable about this subject to tell which of you two is correct because he's never learned the subject from a teacher, and he's never discovered it on his own. So each of you, Laches and Nicias, should tell us who is the most intelligent person you've ever come across on the subject of the nurture of the young. Have you learned this subject on your own or did you learn it from someone who knows it? And if you learned it from someone else, [187a] who were your respective teachers, and who were their colleagues? If you are too busy with the affairs of the city and don't have enough free time* to teach us yourselves, then we can go to your teachers or their colleagues and by gifts or favors or both, persuade them to train our children and yours so that they won't turn out to be disgraces to their ancestors. And on the other hand, if you discovered it on your own, then give us an example of someone that started out worthless but was turned, by your training, into someone fine and good. Because if this will be your very first attempt at training young men, [b] then you won't simply be risking the proverbial Carian*—no, you'll be risking your own sons, and the sons of your friends, and you'll be guilty of, as the saying goes, 'beginning pottery with a pithos.'* Tell us which of these alternatives applies to you and which does not."

That's what you should find out from them, Lysismachus. Don't let them off the hook.

LYSIMACHUS. In my opinion, gentlemen, Socrates has made a good point. [c] But it is up to you, Nicias and Laches, to decide whether you want to be questioned about these things, and to explain yourselves. Obviously* Melesias and I would be very pleased to hear you answer Socrates point by point since, as I said from the very beginning, we asked for your advice, thinking that, as seems quite likely, you have given careful thought to this issue, especially given the fact that your sons, like ours, [d] are about the age to be educated.* So if you have no objection, join with Socrates and investigate the issue, asking and answering each others questions honestly. He was right to say that we are considering one of the most important issues of all, so I hope that you will agree to help.

NICIAS. Oh, Lysimachus, I can see that you aren't familiar with Socrates, only his father, or that if you have met him before [e] it was when he was very young, probably when he accompanied his father to the temple or some town meeting. Clearly you are unfamiliar with the adult Socrates.

LYSIMACHUS. Why do you say that, Nicias?

NICIAS. I don't think you understand that anyone who gets near enough to Socrates to be drawn into a conversation with him is inevitably forced to give an account of himself—no matter what the original topic of conversation was—and there's no escape for him until [188a] he's given Socrates a full account of how he's been living his life. Once he's reached that point, Socrates won't let him go until he's been well and thoroughly put to the test.* I am well aware of what it's like to be put to the test by Socrates, and I know there's no escaping it if we engage him the way you suggested, Lysimachus, and I am perfectly willing to go through the ordeal. You see, I really enjoy these encounters with him, and I don't think it's a bad thing to be reminded that you have failed to live up to your principles in the past, [b] or that you are failing to do so now. In fact, I think that if you don't try to escape being called to account like this, it tends to make you more thoughtful and responsible in the future. What is it that Solon* says?

"I desire to learn as long as I live"
and

"Think not that you'll become a sage
Simply by reaching a very old age."

So I don't see anything horrible or horrific* in being put to the test by Socrates. And anyway, from the beginning I was all but certain that with Socrates here, the focus of the discussion would end up being ourselves and not our sons. [c] So, I repeat, I have no objection to spending time with Socrates anyway he wants; but see how Laches feels about it.

LACHES. My view of discussion, Nicias, is quite simple—or if you wish, you might say that I have not one but two* views of discussion.

To one person I might seem to be a discussion-lover, but then to another person I might seem to be a discussion-hater. For whenever I hear a man discussing virtue,* or any kind of wisdom, if he is a true man and worthy of his speech, [d] then I am absolutely delighted to behold how fitting and harmonious are the things said, and the one saying them. In fact, "harmonious" seems just the right word to use—such a man is a musician, having tuned himself to a far more beautiful harmony than you'll ever hear from a lyre or some other entertaining instrument. He has made his life a symphony of word and deed, attuned not to the Ionian,* Phrygian or Lydian scale but to the one true Greek scale: the Dorian. I am delighted to listen to such a man, [e] and when I do I am thought to be a discussion-lover because I am so eager to hear every word he has to say.

It is exactly the opposite with a man whose deeds do not fit his words. I find it positively painful to listen to such a man, and the better he speaks, the worse I feel about it.

Now, as for Socrates, I have no experience engaging him in discussion, but with respect to his actions [189a] I can honestly say that I have found them to be worthy of the finest words. So if his advice is in harmony with his deeds, then I am willing to heed it; I'm certainly not averse to learning something from the man. I agree with Solon, though I would add one thing: I am willing to learn many things as I grow old, but only from a worthy man. I don't take well to being lectured at, and I probably look like a dimwit unless Solon concedes to me that my teacher should be a good man. It doesn't even matter if my teacher is younger than I am or hasn't made a name for himself.

[b] So, Socrates, I put myself in your hands: teach me or refute me as you will, and maybe you, in turn, will learn something from me. You earned my undying respect that day we faced danger together and you

gave proof of your virtue in the only way that a man's virtue can be well and truly proven. Speak as you please; completely disregard the difference in our ages.

SOCRATES. [c] Well, it seems that no one* could accuse you two of being unwilling to consider the issue and to render whatever counsel seems best.

LYSIMACHUS. No, indeed, Socrates, they could not. So now the task is ours—since I now count you as one of us. Please take my place and for the sake of our sons find out what we need to know from Laches and Nicias, and please also give us your own advice in the course of the discussion. You see, because of my age I sometimes forget what questions I intended to ask—and sometimes even the answers I get—and if there's a digression I find my mind wandering and I completely lose the thread of the discussion. [d] So you all carry on the conversation amongst yourselves. I will listen as closely as I can; Melesias and I will accept whatever conclusion you reach.

SOCRATES. Alright, then, Laches and Nicias, it looks like we have our work cut out for us. I can see two different ways that we might proceed. The first is what we started with just a moment ago—we could ask each other what teachers we have had in this subject, or whom we have actually improved.

[e] But I think we could also achieve our goal if we proceed more from first principles. Suppose that we happen to know* about something—let's just call it x—and we also know that there is something we could improve by adding x to it. Now, if we understand how to add x to it, then clearly we understand x—the very thing about which we are supposed to be giving advice as to the best and easiest way to acquire it.

Maybe it's not easy to figure out what I mean; let me try it this way. [190a] Suppose we happen to know about sight, and we also know that we could improve someone's eyes by adding sight to them. Now, if we understand how to make this person's eyes see again, then clearly we understand sight—the very thing about which we are supposed to be giving advice as to the best and easiest way to acquire it. If we don't actually understand what sight is, or what hearing is, then we can scarcely be considered doctors for the eyes or the ears, and our advice about [b] the best way to add sight to someone's eyes, or hearing to their ears, isn't worth consulting.

LACHES. True, Socrates.

SOCRATES. And aren't we being asked to give advice about the best way to add virtue to souls in order to improve them?

LACHES. Certainly.

SOCRATES. So first and foremost don't we have to know what virtue is?* Because if we don't know at all what virtue is, [c] then how could we possibly advise someone on the best way to acquire it?

LACHES. There's no way we could, Socrates.

SOCRATES. Therefore,* we claim to know what virtue is.

LACHES. We do.

SOCRATES. And if we know what it is, it follows that we can say what it is.

LACHES. Obviously.

SOCRATES. But let's not start with the whole of virtue—that might be biting off more than we can chew. Let's begin with just part of it and see whether we have a sufficient grasp of it [d] to make our inquiry easier.

LACHES. Let's do as you wish, Socrates.

SOCRATES. Well, then, which part of virtue should we choose? Perhaps we should begin with the part of virtue that is most obviously relevant to fighting in armor. Most people would say that's courage, wouldn't they?

LACHES. Yes, they would.

SOCRATES. Well, then, Laches, our first task is to say what courage is. Second, after that, just as we were talking about adding sight to eyes and hearing to ears, we will consider [e] how courage may be added to our young men, and by what studies and activities we can accomplish this goal. So tell me, Laches, what is courage?

LACHES. By god, Socrates, that's not hard to answer. If a soldier is willing to remain in formation* to fight the enemy and not flee, you can be sure that he is courageous.

SOCRATES. Well said, Laches. But maybe I am to blame* for not formulating my question clearly, because you did not answer the question I had in mind, you answered a different one.

Laches. What do you mean, Socrates?

SOCRATES. [191a] I'll tell you, if I'm up to the task. That man is courageous who, as you put it, fights against the enemy while remaining in formation.

LACHES. That's what I say.

SOCRATES. And so do I. But what about another soldier who fights against the enemy while fleeing, not remaining?

LACHES. Fleeing? How?

SOCRATES. The way the Scythians are said to fight fleeing as well as pursuing.* And also the horses of Aeneas, whom Homer praises, describing them as "swiftly running this way and that," [b] and he says that they know how to pursue and how to flee. He also praises Aeneas himself for his knowledge of fear, describing him as "author of rout."*

LACHES. Ah, yes, quite, Socrates. Homer was talking about chariots, and you were referring to the Scythian cavalry. Quite right, horses do fight as you say, but hoplite soldiers fight as I described.

SOCRATES. Except perhaps for Spartan hoplites, Laches. [c] They say that at the battle of Plataea* the Spartans were not willing to stand and fight against the Persian troops that use wicker shields. Instead, they turned and fled, and when the Persians broke formation the Spartans wheeled about—just like the cavalry tactic—and they won the battle.

LACHES. That's true, Socrates.

SOCRATES. Well, you see, then, that's what I meant just now when I said that I was to blame for the fact that you did not answer my question well: I didn't ask the question well. [d] I meant to ask you not only about courageous hoplite soldiers, but also about courageous soldiers in the cavalry and in general about courage for any kind of soldier. And not only about those who are courageous in war, but also about those who are courageous when facing dangers at sea, or when facing illness or poverty or who are courageous in politics. And not only about those who are courageous when facing pains or fears, but also those who courageously fight [e] against desires or pleasures*—regardless of whether they are standing their ground or turning their backs. There are courageous people in all these circumstances aren't there, Laches?

LACHES. Yes, indeed there are, Socrates.

SOCRATES. So all of these are courageous, but some of them are courageous when facing pleasures, others when facing pains, others desires, or fears and so on. And I suppose there are also cowards in all of these circumstances as well.

LACHES. Certainly.

SOCRATES. What, then, is each of these: courage and cowardice? But let's begin with courage. What is the same in all of these cases?* Or, are you still not clear on what I mean?

LACHES. Not entirely.

SOCRATES: [192a] Here's what I mean. It's like if I were to ask you what quickness is, whether it be quickness in running, playing the kithara,* talking, learning or in many other activities, and which we have in just about any action worth mentioning whether it be when using our arms, legs, mouth, voice or mind. Don't you too refer to quickness in all these kinds of actions?

LACHES. Certainly I do.

SOCRATES. Then if someone should ask me, "Socrates, what do you call that which is named 'quickness' in all these actions?" I would answer, [b] "Speed is the capacity* to accomplish much in little time, whether in speaking, running or in any other activity."

LACHES. And you would be correct.

SOCRATES. Then you try, Laches, to give the same kind of answer about courage: say what capacity is one and the same in pleasure and pain and in all the activities we were going through just now, and is named "courage."

LACHES. It seems to me to be an endurance of the soul, [c] if I must say what it's nature is in all circumstances.

SOCRATES. Yes, that is exactly what you must do if we are going to find an answer to our question. Well, then, here's what I think. I believe that not every instance of endurance seems to you to be an instance of courage, and I think I can give you a clear sign of this. I am almost certain, Laches, that you think courage is one of the very fine capacities.

LACHES. Oh, the finest, to be sure.

SOCRATES. And intelligent* endurance is both fine and good?

LACHES. Certainly.

SOCRATES. [d] What about unintelligent endurance? Isn't that completely the opposite? Isn't it harmful and bad?*

LACHES. Yes.

SOCRATES. And do you call anything like that fine, if it is bad and harmful?

LACHES. That wouldn't be right, Socrates.

SOCRATES. So therefore, because* this sort of endurance is not fine, but courage is fine, you would not agree that this sort of endurance is courage.

LACHES. That is true.

SOCRATES. Then intelligent endurance would be courage, according to your account.

LACHES. So it seems.

SOCRATES. [e] Well, then, let's see what exactly we need to be intelligent about.* Is intelligent endurance intelligent about absolutely everything, both important and unimportant things? For example, suppose someone endures intelligently when it comes to spending money, knowing that by spending his money this way he will make a substantial profit. Would you call him courageous?

LACHES. By god, no I would not.

SOCRATES. Well how about a case where a doctor is treating a case of pneumonia in his son or someone else, [193a] and he intelligently endures in applying the correct therapy despite the complaints of his patient?

LACHES. Oh no, that's not a case of courage at all.

SOCRATES. Then what about a case where a man endures in war and is willing to continue fighting? Suppose he has intelligently calculated that allies will help him, and that his enemies will have fewer and inferior allies to help them, and that he occupies a strategically superior position* on the battlefield. Which of the two would you say is more courageous: the one who intelligently endures, having calculated that he has all the advantages, or the one who is in the opposite situation, but still endures and fights on?

LACHES. [b] I suppose the second man is, Socrates.

SOCRATES. But that is unintelligent endurance* compared with the first man.

LACHES. That's true.

SOCRATES. And do you say that the one who endures in a cavalry battle with knowledge of horsemanship is less courageous than the one who endures it without knowledge of horsemanship?*

LACHES. It seems so to me.

SOCRATES. And you'd say the same thing about someone who endures in attacking with a sling or a bow or in using some other such craft?* The one who endures with knowledge is less courageous than the one endures without knowledge?

LACHES. [c] Certainly.

SOCRATES. And what about someone who is willing to climb down into a well to dive for something lost in it, and he endures in this task although he has no idea of how to do it safely? Do you say that he is more courageous than the person who does the same thing, and is actually skilled at it?

LACHES. Yes. What else could someone say, Socrates?

SOCRATES. Nothing, if that is what he thinks.*

LACHES. But that is what I think.

SOCRATES. But you acknowledge, Laches, that people who endure these kinds of risks are less intelligent than those who are skillful at them.

LACHES. So it seems.

SOCRATES. [d] But didn't this sort of unintelligent recklessness and endurance seem to us a moment ago to be shameful and harmful?*

LACHES. It certainly did.

SOCRATES. And we agreed that courage is a fine thing.

LACHES. We did agree on that.

SOCRATES. But now, on the contrary, we are saying that this shameful thing—unintelligent endurance—is courage.

LACHES. Apparently.

SOCRATES. And do you think that we are correct to say this?

LACHES. No, by god, Socrates, I do not.*

SOCRATES. Well, then, by your account, Laches, you and I are not tuned to the Dorian mode* [e] because our deeds do not harmonize with our words. People would likely call us courageous if they had witnessed some of our deeds on the battlefield, but I think they would deny it if they heard us talking just now.

LACHES. That's the truest thing either one of us has said so far!

SOCRATES. Do you think we are in fine shape as things stand?

LACHES. Not at all.

SOCRATES. Then why don't we try to apply our own principle?

LACHES. Which principle do you mean?

SOCRATES. [194a] The principle of endurance. If you are willing, let us persevere and endure in the inquiry so that courage itself will not laugh at our craven retreat in the face of adversity. After all is said and done, we may still find that courage is endurance.*

LACHES. I am certainly ready and willing to continue the investigation and not surrender, but I am not accustomed to discussions like this. I'm really feeling motivated to emerge victorious, and that makes me really annoyed [b] at being unable to express what I have in mind. I'm sure that I understand what courage is, but somehow it has run away and I'm unable to capture it in words.

SOCRATES. But, my friend, a good hunter must continue the chase and not give up.

LACHES. Oh, yes, absolutely.

SOCRATES. Would you like Nicias to join in the hunt? Perhaps he's more resourceful than we are.

LACHES. [c] Yes, by all means, I would like Nicias to join us.

SOCRATES. Nicias, if you have any additional resources, please come to the aid of your friends, men who have been caught in a tempest of argument and are lost at sea.* You see that Laches and I have become puzzled, so perhaps by saying what you think courage is you will solve our puzzle, and confirm our beliefs about it.

NICIAS. Actually, for a while now I've been thinking that you and Laches have not been defining* courage properly, because you are not using something that I heard from you,* Socrates, something that I thought was quite well said.

SOCRATES. What was that, Nicias?

NICIAS. [d] I have often heard you say that each of us is good in respect to the things in which he is wise, and bad in respect to the things in which he is ignorant.*

SOCRATES. By god, Nicias, what you are saying is true.

NICIAS. Therefore, if in fact the courageous man is good, then it is clear that he is wise.

SOCRATES. Did you hear that, Laches?

LACHES. Yes, I did, but I'm not sure what he means.

SOCRATES. I think I understand him; he seems to be saying that courage is a kind of wisdom.

LACHES. What kind of wisdom, Socrates?

SOCRATES. [e] Are you asking Nicias this question?

LACHES. I am.

SOCRATES. Then tell him, Nicias, in your own words, what kind of wisdom courage is. Obviously it is not flute playing.*

NICIAS. Of course not.

SOCRATES. Nor is it kithara playing.

NICIAS. Certainly not.

SOCRATES. Then what kind of knowledge* is it? Or can you at least say what it is knowledge *of?*

LACHES. Well put, Socrates, that's an excellent question. Nicias should tell us what kind of knowledge he claims courage is.

NICIAS. If you insist, Laches, I claim that [195a] courage is the knowledge of what is to be feared and dared in war or in anything.

LACHES. What a strange thing to say, Socrates!

SOCRATES. Why do you say that, Laches?

LACHES. Why do I say that? Well, obviously wisdom and courage are two separate things.

SOCRATES. That is just what Nicias denies.

LACHES. Yes, by god, he does, but that's just silly.

SOCRATES. Then let's instruct him without insulting him.*

NICIAS. It looks to me, Socrates, that Laches wants to show that there's nothing in what I say because it was just shown that there was nothing in what he said.

LACHES. [b] Actually, Nicias, it is quite easy to show that there's nothing in what you say. When someone is sick, who knows what is to be feared, doctors or courageous men? Or do you call doctors courageous?

NICIAS. Not at all.

LACHES. It's the same with farmers, isn't it? What is to be feared in farming is known by the farmer, and it's the same with all the other crafts: what is to be feared and what is to be dared in any craft is known by the expert in the craft, [c] and that doesn't automatically make them courageous.

SOCRATES. What do you think, Nicias? Laches seems to have a point.

NICIAS. He has a point, but it's not true.

SOCRATES. Why not?

NICIAS. Because he thinks that the doctor knows something more about medical treatment than just sickness and health. But he knows only so much. Laches, do you think that a doctor knows in each particular case whether health or sickness is more to be feared by his patient? Don't you think that in many cases it is better* for a sick person not to recover? Tell me this: [d] do you say that it is always better to live, and do you deny that there are many cases where death is the more excellent* alternative?

LACHES. Oh, yes, I certainly do agree that in some cases it can be nobler to die.

NICIAS. Then compare a man for whom death is more advantageous than life, and another man for whom life is more advantageous than death. Are the very same things to be feared equally by both men?

LACHES. I wouldn't agree to that at all.

NICIAS. And would you attribute this knowledge to the doctor, or to any craftsman other than the one who knows what is and is not to be feared, whom I call courageous?

SOCRATES. Do you understand where he's going with this, Laches?

LACHES. [e] I certainly do: he's calling seers* courageous. Who else would know when it is better for someone to live or to die? But, Nicias, would you claim to be a seer yourself, or would you say that you are neither a seer nor courageous?

NICIAS. What? Are you saying that it is part of the seer's craft to know what is to be feared and what is to be dared?

LACHES. Of course I am. Who else would know that?

NICIAS. The man I am referring to, my friend. The seer knows only the signs of what will be—whether it be death, disease, financial ruin, [196a] victory or defeat in war or in any other contest. Why do you think the seer will know more than anybody else who is better off suffering or not suffering these things?

LACHES. I just don't get it, Socrates. What's his point? He denies that the seer is courageous; he denies that the doctor is courageous; he denies that everybody is courageous—except maybe god. If you ask me, Nicias simply doesn't want to admit that [b] he's got no idea of what courage is, and he's just coming up with answers that conceal the fact that he's just as lost as we are. You and I could have done the same thing if we had wanted to conceal the fact that we were contradicting ourselves. I can see why lawyers* would talk like this in a courtroom, but why would someone dress himself up in words like this in what is supposed to be a conversation among friends?

SOCRATES. [c] I completely agree with you, Laches, that unscrupulous verbal tricks are quite out of place among us. But let's see if he has a real point to make and isn't just talking for the sake of talking. Let's ask him to explain more clearly what he has in mind. If there's something in what he says we'll agree with him, and if not, we'll explain to him why not.

LACHES. You go ahead and ask him whatever you want, Socrates. I've asked all I care to.

SOCRATES. Ok, then, I'll ask questions on behalf of both of us.

LACHES. That's fine with me.

SOCRATES. Then tell me, Nicias—or, rather, tell us, [d] since Laches and I are partners in the argument—do you say that courage is the knowledge of what is to be feared and what is to be dared?

NICIAS. I do.

SOCRATES. And this is not something that every man would know—neither the doctor nor the seer know it, and they will not be courageous until they do. Isn't that what you are saying?

NICIAS. That's it exactly.

SOCRATES. Well, then, the old saying, "any dog or pig knows that" won't apply to courage, will it?

NICIAS. Certainly not.

SOCRATES. [e] Then obviously you don't even believe that the mythical Crommyon sow* was courageous. I'm not saying this to be funny, but because I think it is necessary for anyone who affirms your theory to deny courage to any wild animal, or else to accept that a wild animal—a lion, leopard or boar—is so wise as to know what very few human beings ever know since they are so difficult to learn. Necessarily, anyone who agrees with you must say that a lion, stag, bull and monkey* all have the same natural disposition with respect to courage.

LACHES. [197a] Aha! That's it, Socrates, by god you've put that well. Be honest, Nicias: are you seriously going to claim that these wild animals—whom everybody agrees are courageous—are wiser than we are? Or will you be so bold as to declare that everybody is wrong and that these animals are not courageous?

NICIAS. Laches, I do not call animals courageous if they don't know enough to be afraid of what is to be feared; I call them fearless or mindless. Do you think I would call children courageous [b] who are unafraid simply because they don't know they are in danger? I think that being unafraid is not the same thing as being courageous. In my opinion, only very few have genuine courage with forethought, but many men, women, children and animals are reckless, bold and fearless without any forethought whatsoever. So you see that what many people, yourself included, call an act of courage, [c] I call reckless; it is only shrewd acts that I will call courageous.

LACHES. Look, Socrates, how well he thinks he's dressing himself up in words. Those whom all agree are courageous he is trying to deprive of the honor.

NICIAS. Not you, Laches. Rest assured that I call you wise—along with Lamachus* and many other Athenians—if you are in fact courageous.

LACHES. I could answer you in kind, but then you'd just call me a "true Aexonian."*

SOCRATES. [d] No, don't answer him, Laches. I think you've overlooked the fact that he received this wisdom from our friend Damon, who is a student of Prodicus,* and Prodicus, you know, has a reputation for being the finest of Sophists at drawing distinctions between words like this.

LACHES. Well, that kind of quibbling about words is more appropriate for a Sophist than for a man whom the city has honored with a position of leadership.

SOCRATES. [e] And yet, my friend, it is also appropriate for the greatest leaders to have the greatest intelligence. I think that what Nicias says is worthy of consideration; let's see what he's got in mind by using the word "courage" in this way.

LACHES. You go ahead.

SOCRATES. Ok, but don't think for a moment that I'm letting you out of our partnership in the investigation. I expect you to pay attention and to examine what we say critically.

LACHES. Fine. I'll do that if you think I ought to.

SOCRATES. Yes, I do think you ought to. So now, back to you Nicias. Please start over. [198a] You know that right from the beginning we considered courage to be a part of virtue.

NICIAS. Certainly.

SOCRATES. And you agreed that it is part, and that there are other parts, and that taken all together it is called virtue?

NICIAS. Of course.

SOCRATES. And do you agree with me about the other parts? I call temperance, justice and others like them parts of virtue with courage. Do you also?

NICIAS. [b] I certainly do.

SOCRATES. Let's not proceed too quickly. We are all agreed on this first point, so let's next consider the second point. We need to be sure that we all have the same idea of what is to be feared and what is to be dared. I'll tell you what we think, and if you don't agree with us, show us where we are wrong.

We think that what is to be feared is that which causes fear,* and what is to be dared is that which does not cause fear. What causes fear are bad things in the future, not ones in the present or past, because fear is the expectation of something bad. Isn't that what we think, Laches?

LACHES. [c] Yes, exactly, Socrates.

SOCRATES. You've heard our view, Nicias; we say that future bad things* are to be feared, and future good things—or at least things that are not bad—are to be dared. Do you say the same thing or something different?

NICIAS. Oh, yes, that's just what I say.

SOCRATES. And the knowledge of these things you call courage?

NICIAS. Precisely.

SOCRATES. So now let's see whether you agree with Laches and myself on a third point.

NICIAS. What is that?

SOCRATES. [d] I'll tell you. Laches and I have the following view about how many forms of knowledge there are. We reject the view that there is one form of knowledge about how things happened in the past, another form of knowledge about how things are happening in the present, and still a different form of knowledge about how things might turn out best in the future. We think that this is all just one form of knowledge. For example, we think that there is just one form of medical knowledge about health, past, present and future. [e] It's the same with farming, which is the knowledge of how crops grew in the past, how they grow now, and how they will grow in the future. And you two are my witnesses about military knowledge: the general makes the finest projections about how things will turn out, so that he is the master and not the servant of the seer because he has a finer knowledge of war, [199a] both regarding what is happening and what will happen. We even have a law* that the general outranks the seer, the seer does not outrank the general. Isn't that what we say. Laches?

LACHES. It is.

SOCRATES. What about you, Nicias? Do you concur with us that each form of knowledge covers the same things regardless of whether they are in the past, the present or the future?

NICIAS. I do. I concur with you, Socrates.

SOCRATES. And courage is the knowledge of what is to be feared and what is to be dared. [b] That is what you say, isn't it?*

NICIAS. Yes.

SOCRATES. And we've agreed that what is to be feared are future bad things, while what is to be dared are future good things.*

NICIAS. Certainly.

SOCRATES. And the same form of knowledge covers the same things in the future and at any time?

NICIAS. It does.

SOCRATES. Then courage is not only the knowledge of what is to be feared and what is to be dared because those cover only how things will turn out in the future, for better or worse. Since courage is a form of knowledge, it must also cover the present and the past, [c] like all the other forms of knowledge.

NICIAS. So it seems.

SOCRATES. Then your answer, Nicias, has only given us a third* of courage, although we asked about the whole of courage. But now, as it seems, in your view courage is not only the knowledge of what is to be feared and what is to be dared, but actually covers pretty much anything good or bad regardless of past, present or future. [d] I think that would be your view now. Would you accept that alteration to your account of courage?

NICIAS. Yes, that seems right to me.

SOCRATES. But isn't this a really unexpected result? Is any part of virtue left out if a man knows all goods, past, present and future, and likewise with respect to bad things? Would such a man lack temperance, justice or piety when it belongs to him alone to take* all due precautions for what is and is not to be feared in dealings with both gods and mortals, [e] and to provide what is good? After all, because of his knowledge he is correctly and well informed both about what is good and about what is bad.*

NICIAS. There does seem to be something in what you say.

SOCRATES. In that case, Nicias, courage would not simply be part of virtue, it would be all of virtue.

NICIAS. So it seems.

SOCRATES. But we said that courage is only one part of virtue.

NICIAS. We did say that.

SOCRATES. And that is not what we are now saying.

NICIAS. No, it isn't.

SOCRATES. Then we have not discovered what courage is.

NICIAS. It seems not.

LACHES. I would have thought that you would make the great discovery of what courage is, my fine friend, [200a] since you looked down your nose at the answers I gave to Socrates. I had such great hope* that you would have found it because of Damon's wisdom.

NICIAS. It's all well and good for you to laugh at me now, Laches. Apparently you think nothing of the fact that earlier you were shown to know nothing of courage. It seems all you care about is that I'm in the same boat, and that neither one of us knows something that any self-respecting man ought to know. [b] It's an all too typical human failing to look at your neighbor's faults and not your own. I actually think that what I've said in our discussion so far has been quite reasonable, and even though my view does need to be corrected in some way, I should be able to revise it with the help of Damon—whom you ridicule, although you've never even met the gentleman—and with the help of others. Once I've sorted things out, I'll gladly share it with you. [c] It seems to me that you could do with a bit more learning.

LACHES. Ah, you are a wise one,* Nicias. In any case, I would advise Lysimachus and Melesias to pay no attention to you or to me when it comes to the education of their sons, but instead to stick with Socrates here, like I said at the beginning, and not let him go. If my own sons were the same age, that's what I would do.

NICIAS. I certainly agree with you on that. If Socrates is willing to take these young men under his wing, I would look no further. In fact, [d] if he is willing, I would gladly entrust my son Niceratus to his care. But I find that whenever I ask him to do this, he always turns me away and recommends someone else. But, look, Lysimachus, see whether Socrates will listen to you.

LYSIMACHUS. It would be right for him to do this for me, Nicias, since I would be willing to things for him that I wouldn't do for very many others. So, what do you say, Socrates? Will you help us out and do what is best for our sons?

SOCRATES. [e] Lysimachus, it would be terrible for me to refuse to help in doing what is best for anybody. And if in this conversation I had shown that I know what Laches and Nicias do not know, then it would indeed be right for me to do ask you ask. But in fact, we are all at a loss here. Why should any one of us be preferred to the others? Under the current circumstances I don't think that any one of us [201a] should be preferred.

Since this is how things stand, perhaps there is some advice that I can give you. I should tell you, my friends—and we don't have to go spreading this around*—that all of us together should look for the best teacher we can find for ourselves first, and then for our sons, regardless of expense or anything. I certainly cannot advise us to remain in our current condition. And if anyone laughs at us [b] for going back to school at our age, I will quote them that line from Homer,* "modesty is not good for a needy man." Let's disregard what others might say about us, and together do what is best for our own education, and for the education of our children.

LYSIMACHUS. I like what you say, Socrates, and since I am the oldest among us, I am the most eager to learn with our young men. But I ask you this favor: [c] come to my house tomorrow morning without fail, so that we can consult about this. But for now, let's end our meeting.

SOCRATES. I will do just as you say, Lysimachus. I'll come to you tomorrow morning, god willing.*

EUTHYPHRO

Setting: Athens, outside of the court of the Archon Basileus. The year is 399 BCE. While waiting for his trial to begin, Socrates talks with Euthyphro, who has come to court to prosecute his own father for homicide.

Characters (in order of appearance):
EUTHYPHRO (an acquaintance of Socrates', probably younger than Socrates; his name is traditionally pronounced "YOU-thi-froh," though "eh-oo-THOO-frone" is closer to the original)
SOCRATES (469-399; 70 years old, from a middle class family, not handsome at all; his name is traditionally pronounced "SOCK-ra-teez," though "so-KROT-ays" is closer to the original)

Dramatic Structure:
Parodos: Euthyphro meets Socrates at court (2a1-4)
Episode #1: Socrates explains his case (2a5-3e6)
Episode #2: Euthyphro explains his case (3e7-5a2)
Episode #3: Socrates asks Euthyphro about piety (5a3-15e2)
Exodos: Euthyphro leaves (15e3-16a4)

EUTHYPHRO. [2a] Something strange must have happened, Socrates, for you to leave the Lyceum* and spend your time here at the King's Porch.* Surely you are not involved in a lawsuit like I am.*
SOCRATES. No, Euthyphro, I'm not involved in a lawsuit; I'm involved in what is called an indictment.*
EUTHYPHRO. [b] What? Someone has indicted you? I can't believe that you would indict anyone.
SOCRATES. Oh, no, I haven't indicted anyone.
EUTHYPHRO. So someone else has indicted you?
SOCRATES. Yes.
EUTHYPHRO. Who?
SOCRATES. I don't really know* him, Euthyphro, but he seems to be a young man that hasn't made a name for himself yet. I think his name is Meletus* and that he is from Pittheus. Do you know him? He has straight hair, not much of a beard, and a hooked nose.
EUTHYPHRO. No, I don't know him, Socrates, [c] but what is his indictment against you?
SOCRATES. What sort of indictment is it? Not a trivial one, to be sure. For someone so young he has understood* something of great importance since, as he claims, he knows how young people are corrupted* and who corrupts them. Perhaps he is a wise man who, seeing that I am ignorantly* corrupting young men of his generation, brings an accusation against me to the King's Court, like a boy telling his mother* about the misdeeds of another.
He seems to me to be the only one [d] to begin his political career correctly, since the correct way to begin is to care* first about the young, and about how to ensure that they become as good as possible—as a reasonable farmer cares first and foremost about the good of the young plants* and then tends to the rest afterwards. Perhaps Meletus is first [3a] clearing us away who—as he says—corrupt the current crop of young men. Next, obviously, he will care about the older generation, and so will be responsible for the greatest and most widespread good in the city, which will be the likely result of a political career with such a beginning.
EUTHYPHRO. I would certainly like him to do us some good, but I fear that the result will be quite the opposite. It seems to me that he's making his start in politics by ineptly damaging the very heart of the city* by trying to wrong you. Tell me, what exactly does he say you are doing to corrupt the youth?

SOCRATES. [b] I know it sounds strange, my friend, but he says that I make gods, and he says that because I make new gods and do not acknowledge* the old ones, he lodged his indictment against me on behalf of the old gods.

EUTHYPHRO. I see, Socrates, this is about the divine sign* that you say comes to you on occasion. He's lodged this indictment against you because of your innovation with respect to the gods, and he puts it in a slanderous way so that he can haul you into court, knowing full well how easy it is to misrepresent such things to a jury. The same thing happens to me [c] when I speak about divine matters in the legislative assembly: when I foretell an event that will happen in the future they deride me as if I'm out of my mind despite the fact that I have never said a single thing that didn't turn out to be true. Really, Socrates, they are just jealous of us and of everybody like us. We shouldn't be anxious about people like that, we should confront them with confidence.

SOCRATES. Yes, my friend, you are probably right that their derision is unimportant. It seems to me that Athenians don't really care if they think a man is clever, as long as that clever man doesn't try to teach others his own peculiar wisdom. It's only when they think that [d] he's going to make others like himself that they get angry—either out of jealousy,* as you say, or for some other reason.

EUTHYPHRO. Well, I certainly have no desire to test their patience with me.

SOCRATES. And I think you are safe because you generally keep your wisdom to yourself and don't try to teach it to others. Unfortunately, I fear that I appear to them to be too generous, talking at great length with anyone who will listen—and I do this without charging a fee;* in fact, I would gladly pay people if they were willing to listen to me. So if they are just going to deride me, [e] as you say they deride you, then we might have an enjoyable time in court laughing and joking around. But if they take me seriously, it is unclear to all but you seers* how things will turn out.

EUTHYPHRO. Perhaps nothing will come of it, Socrates, and you will win your trial as I shall win mine.

SOCRATES. Yes, you mentioned that you are involved in a lawsuit, Euthyphro. What is it about? Are you prosecuting or defending?

EUTHYPHRO. Prosecuting.

SOCRATES. Whom?

EUTHYPHRO. [4a] Someone whom I am thought to be insane for prosecuting.

SOCRATES. Who could that be? Are you prosecuting someone who can fly away?

EUTHYPHRO. Oh, no, Socrates, he's much to old to fly.

SOCRATES. Who is it?

EUTHYPHRO. My father.

SOCRATES. Your father!

EUTHYPHRO. Certainly.

SOCRATES. What is your accusation? What is the lawsuit about?

EUTHYPHRO. Homicide.

SOCRATES. Herakles! You must have a highly sophisticated understanding of the legal situation to bring such a lawsuit—there's no way that the average man on the street could rightly* prosecute [b] his own father.

EUTHYPHRO. Yes, by god, Socrates, I do have a very highly sophisticated understanding of the legal situation.

SOCRATES. And the one your father killed was a member of your family? I suppose that's obvious because you wouldn't bring a case of homicide against your own father unless he killed a member of your own family.

EUTHYPHRO. Oh, Socrates, surely you cannot seriously think that it matters whether the one killed was a member of my family or not. The only thing we must look for is whether the killer was right to kill* or not: if he was right, then we must leave him alone; but if he was not right to kill, then we must prosecute him, even if he shares [c] our hearth and meals. This is because there is equal pollution* in both cases—

what matters is not whether you are related to the killer, but whether you associate with him knowing full well that he is guilty but you do not purify yourself and him by prosecuting him.

In this case, the one who died was an employee of mine that we hired to do some work on our farm on the island of Naxos.* One day he got drunk, flew into a rage at one of our domestic slaves, and killed him. My father tied his hands and feet and put him in a ditch to hold him while he consulted with the Interpreters* about what to do. [d] While he waited for an answer, he neglected the man he had bound and didn't take care of him on the grounds that he was a murderer and it didn't really matter what happened to him, even if he died—which is exactly what happened. Hunger, cold and his restraints killed him* before the messenger could come back from the Interpreters.

That is why my father and the rest of my family is angry at me. They say that in prosecuting my father* for murder I am taking the side of a murderer. On top of that, they say my father didn't actually kill the man, but even if he did, the man was a murderer and so could be killed with impunity* so I shouldn't give him a second thought; [e] but for a son to prosecute his own father for murder is impious.

Oh, Socrates, how badly they misunderstand the divine as it relates to what is holy* and what is unholy.

SOCRATES. But you, by god, Euthyphro, do you have such an accurate knowledge of divine matters, and of what is holy and unholy, that in the case you describe you are not afraid that by prosecuting your own father you will be doing something impious?*

EUTHYPHRO. I'd be good for nothing, Socrates, [5a] and Euthyphro would be no different from most people if I did not have accurate knowledge of all such things.

SOCRATES. Well, that's wonderful* Euthyphro! With you in my corner as my teacher, Meletus would be no match for me. I could call him out before the trial and tell him that I have always thought it very important to understand divine matters, and since he is accusing me of wrongdoing by making things up and innovating in that regard, I can tell him that I've become your student.

"Come now, Meletus," I could say to him, "if you agree that Euthyphro [b] is wise in divine matters, then you must think that my beliefs too are orthodox and you must not prosecute me. But if you do not agree, then you shouldn't indict me for corrupting the younger generation, you should indict my teacher for corrupting the older generation—both myself and his own father: he's corrupting me by his teachings, and he's corrupting his father by correcting and punishing him."

If he's not persuaded by that argument, and he refuses to drop his case against me, or he indicts you instead, I can simply make the same argument in court to the jury.

EUTHYPHRO. Yes, by god, Socrates, if he tried to indict me [c] I think I'd have no trouble revealing the weakness of his position and turning the tables on him: in the end, the inquiry would be about him rather than about me.

SOCRATES. I can see that, my friend, and that's exactly why I want to become your student. I know that this Meletus, and everybody else, turns a blind eye to you, but focuses on me so sharply that he indicts me for impiety.* So now, by god, tell me what you just said you clearly understand: what sorts of things are the pious* and the impious, [d] both in homicide and in other cases? Or isn't piety itself in itself one and the same* in every action? And isn't impiety, on the one hand, the opposite of piety in every case, and, on the other hand, isn't it like itself,* having one sort of character* with respect to impiety in everything that is impious?

EUTHYPHRO. Entirely so,* Socrates.

SOCRATES. Then tell me, what do you say piety is, and what do you say impiety is?

EUTHYPHRO. Well then, I say that piety is what I am now doing: to prosecute the wrongdoer,* whether he kills someone or steals from a temple or commits any such violation—whether that person be your father [e] or mother or anyone else—and not to prosecute is impious.

In fact, Socrates, I'll give you clear proof that the law requires us to prosecute any wrongdoer, no matter who he may be, and it is a proof that I have given to others. People believe that Zeus is the best and most just of all the gods, [6a] but they also believe that he put his own father in chains for swallowing his sons* without any right to do so—and his father had castrated his own father for other reasons—and yet they are angry with me for prosecuting my father for actually doing something wrong! They say about me exactly the opposite of what they say about the gods.

SOCRATES. Well, there you have it, Euthyphro. Isn't this exactly why I am being prosecuted, because when anyone says these things about the gods I find it difficult to believe them?* Maybe this is why Meletus has indicted me. I suppose that [b] if you know as much about these things as you claim, then I should concede this point* to you—what else can I say when I freely admit that I do not actually know about such things. So in the name of Zeus, the god of friendship, tell me: do you believe that these stories about Cronus and Ouranos are true?

EUTHYPHRO. Oh, yes, Socrates, I do. In fact, I know of things that are even more amazing—things of which most people are ignorant.

SOCRATES. And do you think that the gods wage war against each other, and that they carry on terrible feuds and battles and do all the sorts of things that the poets sing about, [c] and which are depicted in our great works of art and on our temples—especially on the embroidered sacred mantle of Athena which we carry to the Acropolis during the Great Panathenaea?* Do we say* that these stories are actually true, Euthyphro?

EUTHYPHRO. Not only are they all true, Socrates, but as I said just now, if you'd like I can tell you many other stories about the gods that will truly amaze you.

SOCRATES. It wouldn't surprise me if you are right about that. But tell me those stories some other time—what I'd really like to hear from you is [d] a clearer answer to the question I asked you. Because, my friend, you did not give me a sufficient answer when I asked you what piety is. You said* that what you are doing now is pious—prosecuting your father for homicide.

EUTHYPHRO. And what I said is true, Socrates.

SOCRATES. Perhaps. But you also say that many other actions are pious, don't you Euthyphro?

EUTHYPHRO. Yes, I do.

SOCRATES. Remember that I did not ask you to teach one or two of the many pious things, but rather to teach me what the form* of piety itself is, by which all pious things are pious. You do say, don't you, that it is by one character [e] that impious things are impious and it is by one character that pious things are pious? You remember that, don't you?

EUTHYPHRO. I do.

SOCRATES. Then teach me this character itself. Teach me what it is so that by looking at it and using it as a paradigm I could say that anything done by you or anyone else that is such* is pious, and what is not such, I could deny is pious.

EUTHYPHRO. If that is what you want, Socrates, I'll tell you.

SOCRATES. But that is what I want.

EUTHYPHRO. Then here it is: what is dear to the gods* is pious, [7a] what is not dear to the gods is impious.

SOCRATES. Superb, Euthyphro! That is just the sort of answer I was looking for. Whether it is true or not I don't yet know, but obviously you will teach me that what you say is true.

EUTHYPHRO. Of course.

SOCRATES. Well, then, let's investigate what you say. A person or thing that is dear to the gods* is pious, but a person or thing that is hated by the gods* is impious; piety is not the same thing as impiety, but in fact is completely the opposite. Is that so?

EUTHYPHRO. It is.

SOCRATES. And this account of piety and impiety seems well formulated?

EUTHYPHRO. [b] I think so, Socrates.

SOCRATES. But, Euthyphro, didn't you also say that the gods disagree and quarrel with one another, and even that some of them become enemies to one another?

EUTHYPHRO. Yes, I did say that.

SOCRATES. And what are the disagreements about that cause the gods to hate each other and become enemies to one other? Let's consider it this way. Suppose you and I disagreed about a quantity, for example how many teeth* someone has. Surely a disagreement like that wouldn't cause us to hate each other and to become enemies, would it? Wouldn't we quickly settle it by counting their teeth?

EUTHYPHRO. [c] Of course.

SOCRATES. And it would be the same with an issue of longer and shorter: we'd simply measure the two things in question and settle the issue quickly, wouldn't we?

EUTHYPHRO. Certainly.

SOCRATES. And if we disagreed about which of two things is heavier, we'd simply put them both in the scales, weigh them, and decide the issue.

EUTHYPHRO. Obviously.

SOCRATES. Then what kinds of disagreements cause us to become angry with one another, or even to become enemies, when we are unable to settle it? Perhaps you don't have an answer* on the spur of the moment like this, so consider what I think about it. [d] I think that the disputes that can turn people into enemies are disagreements about what is just and what is unjust, admirable and shameful, good and bad.* Isn't this true about you and me and all people, that when we are unable to reach some decision about these things, we become enemies to each other?

EUTHYPHRO. Yes, exactly, Socrates, it is disagreement about those sorts of things that causes the trouble.

SOCRATES. Then what about the gods, Euthyphro? If they disagree with one another, won't they disagree about these same things?

EUTHYPHRO. Necessarily.

SOCRATES. [e] Therefore, according to your account, some gods will think that a particular action is right, good and admirable, but other gods will disagree and think that it is wrong, bad and shameful? They wouldn't form factions against each another if they didn't disagree about these kinds of things would they?

EUTHYPHRO. That is correct.

SOCRATES. And whatever the gods think is right, good and admirable they love; but whatever they think is wrong, bad and shameful they hate?

EUTHYPHRO. Certainly.

SOCRATES. But don't you say that the very same things* some gods think are just, [8a] other gods think are unjust? Isn't it exactly this kind of dispute that makes them form factions and start wars against each other?

EUTHYPHRO. It is.

SOCRATES. So it seems that one and the same thing will be both hated and loved by the gods;* the very same thing will be god-hated and god-loved.

EUTHYPHRO. So it seems.

SOCRATES. And therefore, on your account, Euthyphro, one and the same thing will be both pious and impious.*

EUTHYPHRO. I'm afraid you are right.

SOCRATES. Then you did not answer the question I asked, because I did not ask you what is both pious and impious, but it appears that what some gods love, other gods hate. [b] So Euthyphro, think about what you are now doing to your father, bringing him to court to punish him: I wouldn't be surprised if this is dear or acceptable to Zeus, but not to Kronos or Ouranos, or acceptable to Hephaestus but not to Hera,* and there might be other gods who find it acceptable and others who find it unacceptable.

EUTHYPHRO. Oh, but Socrates, I think that there is no disagreement among the gods on this because they all hold that anyone who kills wrongly must be brought to justice.

SOCRATES. Well, as far as that goes, Euthyphro, isn't it the same among humans? Have you ever heard [c] anyone argue that someone who kills wrongly, or has done something else wrongly, does not need to be brought to justice?

EUTHYPHRO. There's no end of disputes about this in the courts. People commit all kinds of crimes and they'll say or do anything at all to escape punishment.

SOCRATES. But they don't actually admit that they acted wrongly and then go on to argue* that they should not be brought to justice, do they?

EUTHYPHRO. No, not at all.

SOCRATES. Then people will not literally say or do anything at all to escape punishment—they won't dare argue that [d] they should not be brought to justice if they've done wrong. Don't they simply argue that they did no wrong?

EUTHYPHRO. That's true.

SOCRATES. So no one disputes that the wrongdoer must be brought to justice. What they disagree about is who the wrongdoer is, what he did, and when* he did it.

EUTHYPHRO. That's true.

SOCRATES. Then* isn't that exactly what the gods will disagree about, if they do indeed fight about right and wrong, as you claim they do? Since nobody—neither god nor [e] man—would dare to deny that the wrongdoer must be brought to justice.

EUTHYPHRO. Yes, Socrates, I suppose that's generally true.

SOCRATES. I think that when there is a dispute—whether among men or gods, if gods engage in disputes—it is about particular actions: some say that the action was done rightly, and others say that it was done wrongly. Isn't that so?

EUTHYPHRO. Certainly.

SOCRATES. [9a] Come then, my friend Euthyphro, and teach me so that I may become wiser. What proof do you have that all the gods think your employee suffered a wrongful death: he had killed one of your slaves and he died after the master of the household bound him and was waiting to hear from the Interpreters what he ought to do? And what proof do you have that all the gods think it is right for a son to prosecute his father for killing someone in those circumstances? Please, try [b] to show me clearly that all the gods think that this particular action of yours is right; if you can show me this, I will forever praise your wisdom.

EUTHYPHRO. Ah, yes, Socrates, I certainly can demonstrate this to you quite clearly, though it is no small task.

SOCRATES. Oh, I understand. You think I am not as smart as the jurors who will try your case because you'll demonstrate to them but not to me that what your father did was wrong and that all of the gods disapprove of it.

EUTHYPHRO. I'll prove it quite clearly, Socrates, if they will actually listen to what I have to say.

SOCRATES. [c] They will listen to you if you appear to be a good speaker.*

But hold on, Euthyphro. Something just occurred to me while you were speaking, and I asked myself,

"Suppose Euthyphro does teach me that all the gods think what his father did was wrong. What would I have learned about piety and impiety? This particular act, as it appears, would be god-hated, but we just saw that piety and impiety cannot be defined* this way since an action that is god-hated will also seem to be god-loved."

So I'll let you off the hook, Euthyphro. Have it your way: all the gods [d] think that your father acted wrongly and what he did was hated by all of them.

But what about this? Is this a way to correct our last account of piety: what is hated by all the gods is impious, and what is loved by all of them is pious? If it is loved by some and hated by others, then it is both pious and impious, or it is neither pious nor impious. Do you want to define piety and impiety this way?

EUTHYPHRO. Is there anything to prevent us from doing so?

SOCRATES. I certainly wouldn't prevent it, Euthyphro. The question is whether you can teach me what you promised to teach me by adopting it.*

EUTHYPHRO. [e] Well, I do say that this is what piety is: what all the gods love. And the opposite, what all the gods hate, is impiety.

SOCRATES. Should we examine this account to determine whether it is correct, Euthyphro? Or should we give it a pass and just accept it without consideration simply because someone has said it?

EUTHYPHRO. We must examine it. But I do think that we've got it right now.

SOCRATES. [10a] Soon we'll have a better understanding of whether it is the right account or not, my good friend. Consider this: is piety loved by the gods because it is pious,* or is it pious because it is loved by the gods?

EUTHYPHRO. I don't know what you mean, Socrates.

SOCRATES. I'll try to say it more clearly, then. There are situations where we will say that something is being carried, and that someone is doing the carrying; or we'll say that one person is being led while another person is doing the leading; or that one thing is seen while another is seeing. You understand, don't you, that in all these kinds of situations the two are different from each other?

EUTHYPHRO. Oh yes, I understand that.

SOCRATES. So you understand that being loved is one thing, and loving is another thing.

EUTHYPHRO. Of course.

SOCRATES. [b] Then tell me, when something is being carried, is it being carried because someone is carrying it* or for some other reason?

EUTHYPHRO. Oh, no, that's the reason.

SOCRATES. And when someone is being led, we say that they are being led because someone is leading them, don't we? And when something is seen, the reason we say it is seen is that someone sees it?

EUTHYPHRO. Certainly.

SOCRATES. So it is not because something is being seen that someone sees it.* Quite to the contrary, it is the fact that someone is seeing it that explains the fact that it is being seen. When one person is being led, they don't have a leader because they are being led, rather they are being led because someone is leading them. And it's the same with being carried. Something isn't first being carried, and then because it is being carried someone has to then carry it—what is primary is the fact that someone is carrying something, and it is because someone is carrying it that it is in the state of being carried.

Is what I'm trying to say [c] clear to you, Euthyphro? Here's my point. In general, it is not because something is becoming that something makes it become, rather it is because something is making it become that it is becoming. And it is not because something is being acted upon that something is acting upon it, rather it is because someone is acting upon it that it is being acted upon. Do you agree?

EUTHYPHRO. I do.

SOCRATES. Well, isn't being loved like becoming something or being acted upon by something?

EUTHYPHRO. Certainly.

SOCRATES. Then the same thing is true in this case that is true in those cases we were just talking about. It is not because something is loved that it is loved by those who love it, but rather it is because someone loves it that it is being loved.

EUTHYPHRO. Necessarily.

SOCRATES. [d] Then what do we say about piety? According to your account, it is loved by all the gods, isn't it?

EUTHYPHRO. Yes.

SOCRATES. Because it is pious, or do they love it for some other reason?

EUTHYPHRO. No, it is because of this.

SOCRATES. So the gods love it because it is pious,* and not the other way around: it is not pious simply because the gods love it?

EUTHYPHRO. So it seems.

SOCRATES. But on the other hand, Euthyphro, something is loved by the gods, or god-loved, simply because they love it.

EUTHYPHRO. Of course.

SOCRATES. So, Euthyphro, the god-loved is not piety, nor is piety the god-loved, as you claimed. These are two distinct things.

EUTHYPHRO. [e] How so, Socrates?

SOCRATES. We agree that piety is loved because it is pious, and we deny that it is pious simply because it is loved, don't we?

EUTHYPHRO. Yes.

SOCRATES. But it's exactly the opposite for the god-loved. The god-loved is god-loved simply because* it is loved by the gods, and not the other way around: it is not loved by the gods because it is god-loved.

EUTHYPHRO. I see. That's true.

SOCRATES. But if the god-loved and piety were one and the same thing, then the exact same thing would be true of both:* if piety were loved [11a] because it is pious, then it would be equally true that the god-loved is loved because it is god-loved; and on the other hand, if the god-loved is god-loved simply because the gods love it, then piety would be pious simply because the gods love it. But you see now that the two cases are quite the opposite of one another: piety is loved because it is pious, but the god-loved is god-loved simply because the gods love it.

So, Euthyphro, it seems that when I asked you what piety is you did not want to tell me its essence* but only some non-essential property: it happens to be loved by all the gods. [b] What it is you have not said. Please don't hide this from me. Go back to the beginning and say what piety is—regardless of whether it is loved by the gods or has any other non-essential property, since we are not disagreeing about any of that. Please do me the favor of telling me what piety and impiety are.

EUTHYPHRO. But Socrates, I am at a loss as to how to tell you what I have in mind. Somehow every time we make a definite statement, it won't stay put, instead it leads us around in circles.

SOCRATES. Then your statements are like the works of my ancestor [c] Daedalus.* If I had been the one to make those claims you'd joke that my words are like the works of Daedalus that wander off and won't stay where you put them. Unfortunately, you'll have to find some other joke because the words are yours, not mine, and they don't want to stay with you.

EUTHYPHRO. That joke seems about right to me, Socrates. You are the Daedalus here. I'm not the one who keeps making the statements wander away—[d] if it were up to me they would stay put.

SOCRATES. Well, in that case, my friend, I suppose that somehow I've managed to become cleverer at the craft than he, because he made only his own works wander away, but apparently I can do it not only with my own words but also with the words of others. But the most ingenious aspect of my craft is that I am wise unwillingly: I would much rather have accounts that stay put and don't wander away [e] than to have all the wisdom of Daedalus and all the gold of Tantalus.*

But enough of this joking around. Since you seem reticent to venture another account of piety, I'll jump right in here to help you teach me about it. But don't you give up; pay close attention* and critically examine every step.

Look, don't you think that everything pious is necessarily just?

EUTHYPHRO. I do.

SOCRATES. And do you also think that everything just is necessarily pious? Or would you say that although [12a] all pious things are just,* not all just things are pious because some just things are pious while other just things are not pious?

EUTHYPHRO. I don't quite follow you, Socrates.

SOCRATES. But Euthyphro, you are younger and wiser than I am. I guess you are just being reticent because of your great wealth of wisdom.* Concentrate, my friend; what I'm saying isn't too difficult to understand because my point is the opposite of the poet who wrote the lines*

Zeus has done this and brought it all to pass,

[b] But you refuse to speak this truth,

For where there is fear, there too is reverence.

I disagree with the poet. Shall I tell you why?

EUTHYPHRO. Oh, yes, please do.

SOCRATES. I don't think that "where there is fear, there too is reverence." I think that lots of people fear sickness, poverty and many other things, but they don't revere or respect what they fear. Don't you agree?

EUTHYPHRO. Of course.

SOCRATES. On the other hand, however, where there is reverence, there too is fear. Whenever someone approaches some matter with reverence and a sense of shame, don't you think that he fears and recoils* [c] from earning a disgraceful reputation?

EUTHYPHRO. Yes, he does recoil.

SOCRATES. That's why I don't think it is correct to say that "where there is fear, there too is reverence." I think that in cases where you have reverence, you also have fear; but I don't think that every case of fear also involves reverence. Fear includes more than reverence, because reverence is one kind* of fear just as odd numbers are one kind of number. So we wouldn't say that "where there is a number, there too is an odd number" since the number could be even; but we would say, "where there is an odd number, there too is a number" since an odd number is necessarily a number. Do you follow that reasoning?

EUTHYPHRO. Certainly.

SOCRATES. That's the sort of question I was asking you a moment ago [d] about piety and justice. Would it be true to say that where there is justice, there too is piety? Or would it rather be true to say that where there is piety, there too is justice, because there are cases of justice that are not also cases of piety? Is piety one kind of justice? Shall we say that or something else?

EUTHYPHRO. Oh, yes, that is correct.

SOCRATES. Then consider what follows as a consequence. If piety is one part of justice, then it seems we must discover what sort of part it is. So for example, if you were to ask me which kind of numbers are the even numbers, and what it is to be an even number, I would say that it is to be evenly divisible by two.* Don't you think that is a good answer?

EUTHYPHRO. I do.

SOCRATES. [e] Then try to teach me which kind of justice piety is so that we can convince Meletus to stop the injustice he is doing by prosecuting me for impiety. We can tell him that I have been sufficiently educated by you on what is pious and holy, and also on what is impious and unholy.

EUTHYPHRO. Well, then, Socrates, I think the part of justice that is pious and holy is attending* to the gods. The rest of justice is attending to our fellow human beings.

SOCRATES. That sounds fine to me, Euthypyro. However, [13a] there is just one small point I'm not getting, because I don't quite understand what you mean by "attending." Surely you are not saying that we "attend" to the gods the way we do in other cases. For example, we say that it is not everybody who "attends" to horses, but only the knowledgeable horse trainer. Isn't that true?

EUTHYPHRO. Certainly.

SOCRATES. Horse training is taking care of, or "attending to," horses. Isn't that the phrase people use for taking care of horses?

EUTHYPHRO. Yes.

SOCRATES. And it's the same with dog trainers, isn't it? They are the ones who take care of, or "attend to," dogs. No one other than dog trainers do that for dogs, do they?

EUTHYPHRO. No.

SOCRATES. Because dog training is taking care of dogs?

EUTHYPHRO. Yes.

SOCRATES. And we could say the same thing about the herdsman and cattle, couldn't we?

EUTHYPHRO. [b] Certainly.

SOCRATES. And holiness and piety towards the gods is like that, Euthyphro? Is that what you are saying?

EUTHYPHRO. I am.

SOCRATES. And whenever someone attends to something it is always for the very same end, that is, for the benefit and the good of whatever is being tended? Do you see that horse trainers attend to horses in order to benefit them and make them better? Do you agree?

EUTHYPHRO. I do.

SOCRATES. And isn't it the same with dog trainers and the dogs they tend, [c] as well as herdsmen and the herds they tend, and so on? Or do you think that attending in these cases is directed to harming those who are served?

EUTHYPHRO. By god, no I do not think that.

SOCRATES. So you think the point of attending is to benefit?

EUTHYPHRO. Of course.

SOCRATES. Then since piety is attending to the gods, its point is to benefit the gods and to make them better? Would you say that when you do something pious you are making some god better?

EUTHYPHRO. By god, Socrates, I would say no such thing.

SOCRATES. I didn't think so, Euthyphro, not at all. In fact, it was in order to clarify* exactly this point that I asked you [d] what you meant when you said that piety is attending to the gods. I didn't think that you meant this sort of thing.

EUTHYPHRO. You are quite right about that, Socrates.

SOCRATES. Then what kind of attending to the gods is piety?

EUTHYPHRO. The kind that slaves give to their masters.

SOCRATES. I understand. Piety is a kind of service to the gods.

EUTHYPHRO. Exactly.

SOCRATES. Then tell me whether you agree about this. Any craft the doctor employs serves to accomplish the doctor's function,* which is to make someone healthy.

EUTHYPHRO. Yes, I agree.

SOCRATES. [e] And what about the crafts employed by the shipbuilder? What function do they serve?

EUTHYPHRO. Making a ship, obviously.

SOCRATES. And the crafts employed by the house-builder are of service in building a house.

EUTHYPHRO. Yes.

SOCRATES. Then tell me, my friend, what function is served by our service to the gods? Surely you know this since you claim to have the finest understanding of divine matters of all people.

EUTHYPHRO. And I speak the truth when I say that, Socrates.

SOCRATES. Then tell me, by god, what is that marvelous result that the gods accomplish by means of our service to them?

EUTHYPHRO. The gods do many fine things, Socrates.

SOCRATES. [14a] As do generals, my friend, but you could easily sum up the result they accomplish by saying that they achieve victory in war, isn't that correct?

EUTHYPHRO. Of course.

SOCRATES. Farmers also do many fine things, but you could sum them up by saying that they produce food from the land.

EUTHYPHRO. Certainly.

SOCRATES. Then what about the many fine things that the gods do? How would you sum them up?*

EUTHYPHRO. As I said a moment ago,* Socrates, [b] it is a tremendous undertaking to learn all these things accurately. But roughly, piety is the knowledge of how to say and do what is gratifying to the gods, whether through prayers or sacrifices. Whoever does this, saves families and the common goods of cities. Whoever does the opposite is impious; he ruins and destroys everything.

SOCRATES. Surely you could have given a much briefer summary in answer to my question if you had wanted to, Euthyphro. Obviously [c] you are not very eager to instruct me. Just now you were so close,* but you turned away; if you had answered my question then I would have learned* sufficiently about piety from you. But as the old saying goes, "the lover must follow wherever the beloved leads," so again I have to ask you what piety is: aren't you saying that it is the knowledge of sacrifice and prayer?

EUTHYPHRO. I am.

SOCRATES. And to sacrifice is to give to the gods, but to make a prayer is to ask for something* from the gods?

EUTHYPHRO. Yes, that's exactly right, Socrates.

SOCRATES. [d] So on this line of reasoning it would follow that piety is the knowledge of asking from and giving to the gods.

EUTHYPHRO. Yes, you've understood my meaning quite well.

SOCRATES. Well, I am quite eager for your wisdom and so I am paying close attention so that I don't miss anything.* Tell me, what is this service to the gods? You say that it is to ask from and give to them?

EUTHYPHRO. I do.

SOCRATES. And to ask correctly is to ask only for those things that we actually need from them?

EUTHYPHRO. Sure.

SOCRATES. [e] So then to give correctly is to give only those things that they actually need from us? Surely there is no skill* in giving someone something that they don't need.

EUTHYPHRO. That's true, Socrates.

SOCRATES. Well in that case, Euthyphro, then piety is the art of commerce* between gods and human beings.

EUTHYPHRO. Commerce! Well, I suppose you can call it that if you like.

SOCRATES. I'd like to call it that only if it's true. But tell me, what benefit can come to the gods because of the gifts that we give them? [15a] Everyone can plainly see what they give us: there isn't a single good we possess that isn't a gift from the gods. But what benefit do they receive from us? Or are we totally taking advantage of them in this exchange so that we get all good things from them, but they get nothing from us?

EUTHYPHRO. Oh, Socrates, do you think that the gods could possibly benefit from anything we give them?

SOCRATES. Well, then, what is the point of giving them gifts?

EUTHYPHRO. Worship, veneration and, as I just said,* they are gratified.

SOCRATES. [b] So, are you saying that piety is the part of justice* that gratifies the gods but does not benefit them and is not dear to them?

EUTHYPHRO. Oh, but Socrates, I do think that of all things, piety is the most dear to the gods.

SOCRATES. So it appears that piety is what is dear to the gods.

EUTHYPHRO. Yes indeed.

SOCRATES. Then will you be surprised if your statements appear to wander away* and won't stay put? And will you accuse me of being the Daedalus who makes your statements wander off when in fact you are the one who is far more skilled than Daedalus? You make your own statements come full circle. Don't you see that your latest account of piety has come back to the exact same account you gave earlier?* [c] Don't you remember we already showed that piety and what is dear to the gods are not the same thing, they are quite distinct from one another?

EUTHYPHRO. I do remember.

SOCRATES. And are you aware that just now you said that piety is what is dear to the gods, which is nothing other than what is god-loved, isn't it?

EUTHYPHRO. Certainly.

SOCRATES. So either we were wrong to reject this account earlier; or if we were right to reject it then, we are wrong to accept it now.

EUTHYPHRO. So it seems.

SOCRATES. Then we need to start all over from the beginning and ask what piety is. I will never willingly give up the quest* until I have learned what it is. [d] Don't abandon me, but concentrate and focus all your attention now and tell me the truth. If anybody knows the truth about piety, you do, and I must hold onto you like Proteus* until you tell me. Obviously if you didn't know exactly what piety and impiety are you would never have dared* to prosecute your own father for killing a hired hand—you would have been afraid to incur the wrath of the gods and the condemnation of mortals. I'm certain that you think you know exactly what is pious and what is not. So tell me Euthyphro, and don't hide your thoughts from me.

EUTHYPHRO. Some other time, then, Socrates. Right now I'm in a hurry and it is time for me to leave.*

SOCRATES. What are you doing, my friend? Are you really going to take away all the hope I had of learning from you what is pious and what is not, thereby escaping Meletus' indictment? I planned to show him that I had become wise in divine matters because of Euthyphro, and that I would no longer be making up new gods out of ignorance but would live a much better life from now on.

EUTHYDEMUS

Setting: Athens. Socrates tells Crito about a conversation he had yesterday in the Lyceum.

Characters (in order of appearance):

CRITO (a contemporary of, and devoted friend to, Socrates; author of seventeen philosophical dialogues; he was wealthy and managed Socrates' money quite well; his name is traditionally pronounced "CRY-toe," though "KREE-tone" is closer to the original)

SOCRATES (469-399 BCE; from a middle class family, not handsome at all; mentor to Plato; his name is traditionally pronounced "SOCK-ra-teez," though "so-KROT-ays" is closer to the original)

EUTHYDEMUS (an older contemporary of Socrates, sophist from the wealthy island of Chios; his name is traditionally pronounced "you-thi-DEE-mus," though "eh-oo-THOO-day-moss" is closer to the original)

DIONYSODORUS (brother of Euthydemus, his name is traditionally pronounced "DY-oh-NISS-oh-DOOR-us," though "dee-on-oo-SAW-door-us" is closer to the original)

CLINIAS (very handsome Athenian, probably a teenager; his name is traditionally pronounced "KLIN-ee-us," though "clay-NEE-oss" is closer to the original)

CTESIPPUS (clever young man from Paeania in the countryside east of Athens; perhaps a little older than Clinias; he was present at Socrates' death, *Phaedo* 59b9; his name is traditionally pronounced "ktee-SIP-us," though "KTAY-sip-oss" is closer to the original)

Dramatic Structure:

Prologue: Crito asks Socrates about the sophists (271a1-272e1)
Parodos: Socrates describes the setting (272e1-275d3)
Episode #1: the Sophists defeat Clinias (275d3-277c7)
Socrates' Protreptic A: love wisdom and virtue (277d1-282e6)
Episode #2: the Sophists defeat Ctesippus (283a1-288b2)
Socrates' Protreptic B: seek knowledge (288b3-290d8)
Interruption: Crito is astonished at Clinias (290e1-293a9)
Episode #3: the Sophists defeat Socrates (293b1-304b5)
Exodos: Socrates asks Crito to study with him (304b6-307c4)

CRITO. [271a] Who were you talking to* in the Lyceum yesterday, Socrates? There were so many people gathered around that I couldn't hear anything clearly, so I popped my head up to get a peek—it looked like you were talking with a stranger. Who was it?

SOCRATES. Which do you mean, Crito? There were two.

CRITO. The one second on your right, [b] sitting next to Axiochus' son—and by the way, Axiochus' son seems to have grown quite a lot; he's almost as big as my son Critobulus, who is a bit small for his age, but this boy looks quite well grown—a fine and good lad.

SOCRATES. Euthydemus is the one you are asking about, Crito. And the man sitting on my left was Dionysodorus, his brother; he was part of the conversation too.

CRITO. I don't know either of them, Socrates. It seems they're new here. [c] I suppose they are sophists. Where are they from? What wisdom do they profess?

SOCRATES. By birth I think they are from the island of Chios to the east, but they joined the colony at Thurii* in Italy. They were exiled from Thurii and since then they've spent a few years travelling around.

You asked about the wisdom they profess—it's amazing, Crito. You know the Olympic sport called the Pankration, right? We call it "*Pan*-kration" because they use *all* fighting styles: boxing, wrestling, kicking and so on. Well, these two brothers are not just sophists, they are *Pan*-sophists!* They surpass those Acarnanian brothers [d] who fight just with their bodies; these Pansophists do so much more than that. First of all, they are very skilled in physical combat and they will fight all comers—they are experts at armed combat and [272a] can make anyone else an expert too, if you pay their fee. But second, they are fierce competitors in legal battles and they can teach someone how to speak in court or to deliver a written speech. Up to now their expertise only extended this far, but now they have completed their skill set by adding the one form of combat they hadn't mastered, so that no one will be able to withstand them. They have become skilled at fighting with words and can refute [b] any claim whatsoever—whether it be true or false. So I have it in mind, Crito, to hand myself over to them: they say that in a short time they can make anyone as skilled as they are in these forms of combat.

CRITO. What? Socrates, aren't you afraid that you are too old for that?

SOCRATES. Not at all, Crito. In fact I can give you a clear proof that I'm not too old to learn from them. They actually admitted that they were already quite old when they made their start on this wisdom I desire: eristic. Just a year or two ago they weren't wise. [c] In fact, my only fear is that I'll be an embarrassment to them the way I've embarrassed Connus my kithara teacher. The boys who attend kithara class with me laugh at him and call him the "Elder Educator."* I'm afraid that someone might call them something like that, and so they won't want to take me on as a student. I've persuaded some other old guys like myself to come along with me to my kithara lessons, [d] and I'm going to try the same thing with these men. Why don't you join us, Crito? We'll take your sons as bait; I'm sure that in order to get them as students they'll be willing to teach us too.

CRITO. I have no objection, Socrates, if that seems like a good plan to you. But first explain to me what the wisdom of these men is so that I'll know what we'll learn from them.

SOCRATES. Certainly. I can't say that I didn't pay close attention to them because I did and I remember it well and I'll try to tell you everything from the beginning.

[e] By the will of some god I happened to be sitting alone in the undressing room outside the bath where you saw me later, and I had it in my mind to leave. But when I got up, my usual divine sign* came to me and so I sat back down and waited. [273a] It wasn't long before Euthydemus and Dionysodorus came in followed by a bunch of their students. They had made a couple of turns on the covered walkway when Clinias came in—that's Axiochus' son, the one that you quite rightly said has grown so much. He had a whole host of admirers following behind him, including Ctesippus of Paeania, who has a fine and good nature although he is a bit full of himself like many young men are. [b] Anyway, right from the entrance Clinias saw me sitting alone and instead of taking the walkway he just cut straight across and sat down beside me on my right—as you said. Well, when they saw him, Dionysodorus and Euthydemus stopped and talked to each other, occasionally glancing over at us—I was paying close attention to them—and then they came over; Euthydemus sat next to Clinias and Dionysodorus sat on my left. Everybody else sat where they could.

[c] I said hello to the two brothers since I hadn't seen them for a while and then said to Clinias, These two men, Euthydemus and Dionysodorus, are wise, and not in trivial things but in important things. They know everything about war, all the things you need to know if you are going to be a good general: tactics, command, and fighting in armor. On top of that, they know how to make someone capable of defending himself in court if anyone ever wrongs him.

[d] Looking at one another they laughed a little and dismissed my comments. Euthydemus said, We don't bother with those things anymore, Socrates, they aren't really worth our time.

I was amazed and said, Then your real business must be fine indeed if matters as important as these aren't worth your time. By the gods, please tell us what this fine business is.

Virtue, he said. We think that we are the finest teachers of virtue, and the quickest.

[e] Oh, Zeus! I said. That *is* a fine business. Where did you find such a gift of Hermes?* The last time you visited Athens I remember you two claiming to be clever at fighting in armor and so that's what I was thinking about just now when I introduced you. But if you now truly have this knowledge, then please be gracious to us. I am clumsily addressing you two as divine* [274a] in the hope that you will forgive me for my earlier comments. But see if what you say is true; the magnitude of what you are claiming is such that it wouldn't at all be surprising for me to doubt it.

Know well, Socrates, that this is so.

Then in my view, this one possession of yours makes you more blessed than the Great King of Persia and all his vast wealth. But tell me if you intend to demonstrate this wisdom.

That is exactly why we are here, Socrates, to demonstrate our wisdom [b] and to teach it, if anyone wants to learn it.

I promise you that everyone who doesn't have it wants it: first, myself, then Clinias here, then Ctesippus and these others, I said, pointing to the admirers of Clinias who had gathered around.

You see, Crito, I mentioned Ctesippus because he had been sitting far from Clinias, and when Euthydemus leaned in to talk with me [c] he blocked Ctesippus' view of Clinias, so Ctesippus got up and sat down right in front of us. He wanted to watch his beloved Clinias,* but he was also genuinely interested in the discussion. Anyway, after he moved in, all of Clinias' other admirers moved in too, and then all the followers of Euthydemus and Dionysodorus did the same. So I pointed to them all and told Euthydemus that they all wanted to learn. [d] Ctesippus agreed wholeheartedly and so did the others, so I asked them to demonstrate to everybody the power of their wisdom.

So I said, Euthydemus and Dionysodorus, do your very best in every way to oblige these young men, and me as well: demonstrate your wisdom. Obviously it would be no small task to demonstrate all wisdom, so just tell me this one thing. Are you able to make someone good only if he is already convinced that he ought to learn from you? [e] What about someone who believes that virtue cannot be taught? Or what about someone who does believe that virtue can be taught, but does not believe that you two can actually teach it? Is it the same craft or a different one to persuade someone that virtue can be taught and also that you can teach it?

It's one and the same, said Dionysodorus.

Then would you say that you two are more highly qualified than anybody else [275a] to turn someone to philosophy and get them to care about virtue?

That is what we think, Socrates.

Then hold off on everything else and just make this one demonstration: persuade this young man here to love wisdom* and to care about virtue. If you do that, we'll all be satisfied. He happens to be in exactly the condition I just described, and everybody here, myself included, greatly desire that he become the best person he can be. He is the son of Axiochus, the grandson of Alcibiades the Elder [b] and cousin of the famous Alcibiades the Younger: his name is Clinias. He is young, and so we are afraid that someone might turn his thoughts to the wrong sort of business and corrupt him.* So you two have arrived at the best time possible. If you don't mind, then, please talk with him right here in front of us all.

That's almost word-for-word what I said to them, Crito.

Then boldly and courageously Euthydemus answered, Oh, we don't mind at all [c] as long as the boy is willing to answer our questions.

He's quite used to answering questions, I told them. He's so popular that people are always coming up to him, asking him questions and engaging him in conversation, so he'll answer your questions boldly.

How can I adequately recount what happened next, Crito? It's not a small job to relate such stunning wisdom. [d] So I should begin like the poets do, I'll invoke the Muses, especially Mnemosune.

I think Euthydemus began like this. Clinias, who are the ones who learn, the wise or the ignorant?

The poor lad blushed when he heard what a grand question he had been asked. Being at a loss for words, he looked to me for help. I saw that he was flustered, so I said, Be bold, Clinias [e] and answer bravely, just say what appears to you to be true.* This might be a very good experience for you.

Dionysodorus then leaned over to me with a big smile on his face and whispered in my ear, Even before he answers I can tell you, Socrates, that he's going to be refuted whichever way he answers.

While he was saying this, Clinias gave his answer and so I didn't have a chance to warn him. [276a] He said that the wise are the ones who learn.*

So then Euthydemus asked, Are there people that you call teachers?

Clinias agreed that some people are teachers.

And the teachers are teachers of learners? For example, you and the other boys have a kithara teacher and a writing teacher, and so you boys are the kithara learners and the writing learners, isn't that so?

Clinias said that it was so.

And isn't it also true that while you are learning, you do not know the things you are learning?

No, we don't know the things we are learning.

[b] Then are you wise when you don't know these things?

No, not at all.

So if you are not wise, then you are ignorant?

Very much so.

So if you are learning what you do not know, then you are learning while being ignorant?

The boy nodded agreement.

Then the ignorant are the ones who learn, Clinias, and not the wise, as you thought.

Right when he said this, laughter and applause broke out from the followers of Euthydemus and Dionysodorus, [c] almost as if they were a chorus coming in on cue from their conductor. Before Clinias could even take a breath Dionysodorus jumped in like a substitution in a ball game and immediately asked him, But what about when your writing teacher dictates a passage* and expects you to write it down accurately from memory? Which of the students get it right, the wise or the ignorant?

The wise, Clinias said.

Then the wise are the ones who learn, Clinas, and not the ignorant, as you just said to Euthydemus.

[d] Cheers and laughter broke from their followers in admiration of their wisdom, but those of us who were devoted to Clinias just sat there in stunned silence. Euthydemus noticed this and in order to amaze us all the more he didn't let Clinias off the hook, but kept the questions coming. Like a ballet dancer in a pirouette, he spun the argument around on the lad and asked, Do learners learn what they know or what they do not know?*

Dionysodorus leaned in to me again and whispered, [e] This is just like the last one; no matter which answer he picks he'll be refuted.

Oh, Zeus! I said. That first question seemed fine* on its own.

All of our questions are like this, Socrates: inescapable.

I suppose this is why your students hold you in such high regard.

At this point Clinias answered Euthydemus and said that learners learn what they do not know,* so Euthydemus asked [277a] the same sort of questions he had just asked. Well, then, Clinias, tell me, don't you know the letters of the alphabet?

Yes, I do.

All of them?

Yes.

And when someone dictates a passage for you to write down, that passage will be spelled using a bunch of letters?

Yes.

So you know what he dictates, since you know all the letters of the alphabet.

I suppose so, Clinas replied.

And what follows from this? You aren't the one who learns from dictation; it's only the one who hasn't learned all the letters of the alphabet who learns from dictation, isn't that so?

But no, that can't be right, Clinias said, because I do learn from dictation.

[b] Aha! So you admit that you learn what you already know, since you admitted that you already know all the letters?

Clinias agreed to that.

So you didn't answer correctly, Euthydemus concluded.

No sooner had Euthydemus said this than Dionysodorus picked up the argument like a ball and aimed it right at the lad, Euthydemus is deceiving you, Clinias. Wouldn't you say that to learn is to acquire knowledge* of what you are learning?

Yes.

And to know is to have knowledge that you've already acquired?

Yes.

[c] And so *not* to know is *not* to have acquired knowledge yet?

That's right.

Ok, and what about people who acquire something?* Do they already have what they acquire?

No, they don't.

And you've already agreed that those who do not know, do not have?

Clinias nodded.

And the learners are among those who acquire, not those who already have?

Therefore, Clinias, the learners are not those who know, but those who do not know.

[d] At that point Euthydemus was ready to take Clinias down for a third time,* just like in a wrestling match, but I noticed that the lad was sinking fast and I wanted to give him some breathing room so that he wouldn't surrender. So I gave him some encouragement and said, Clinias, don't be surprised if these arguments are unfamiliar to you. Perhaps you don't see what these visitors are doing with you: they are treating you the way the initiates into the Corybantic mysteries* are treated: the initiate sits on a throne and the Corybantes dance and play around him. [e] That's what these two are doing with you now: they are dancing circles around you and playing games with you to prepare you for initiation. So now think of these arguments you've just heard as the first Sophistic mysteries.

The first mystery you must learn is that—as Prodicus says—*language is a precision instrument.** These two visitors are proving that you didn't know people use the verb "to learn" in two different senses: first, people use it in a case where someone starts out with absolutely zero knowledge of something, [278a] and then later acquires some knowledge of it; but second, people also use this same verb in cases where someone starts out with some knowledge of something, and then uses this knowledge to inquire further and gain additional knowledge, either about some action or some claim. Normally people use the verb "to understand" in the second case, but sometimes they do use the verb "to learn" in that case also. This has escaped your notice, as they have just proven: one and the same word can refer to people in the opposite states, both to the one who knows and also to the one who does not know. There was something similar in the second question they asked about [b] whether people "learn" what they know or what they don't know.

These questions are games for students, which is why I said that these two are playing games with you. I call them games because simply learning them, even if you learned all of them, doesn't bring you one step closer to knowing the real truth. But you would be able to play these games* on other people, tripping them up because one word can be used in more than one sense. It's like offering someone a chair and then pulling it out from under them when they go to sit in it, [c] laughing at them when you see them sprawled out on their backside. So don't take these questions too seriously; it's just a game they've been playing with you.

Obviously when they are done joking around they will get to more serious matters, and I will personally see to it that they keep the promise* they made to me. They said that they would give a demonstration of their protreptic wisdom,* but now it seems to me that they thought they should begin by playing games with you. So Euthydemus and Dionysodorus, [d] I think we've had enough of the joking around; you can stop now. Please give the demonstration of your protreptic skill that you promised: convince the lad that he ought to care about wisdom and virtue.

But before you do that, I'll show you the sort of thing I mean, and what I'd like to hear from you. And please don't laugh at me if my approach seems amateurish and unprofessional. It is only because I'm eager to hear your wisdom that I'm going to risk looking foolish in front of you, doing this my own way. [e] So please listen, and restrain yourselves and your students from laughing. But you, son of Axiochus, please answer me.

Everybody wishes* to do well, don't they? I asked. This is one of those questions I just said I was afraid you would laugh at: it's stupid even to ask such a question. Who doesn't wish to do well?

Nobody, answered Clinias.

[279a] Very well, I said, the next question is obvious: since everyone wishes to do well, how would we do well? By having many good things? Maybe this question is even more ridiculous; how else would we do well than by having good things?

I agree.

Ok, then, so of all the things there are, which are good for us? This too doesn't seem hard to answer; we don't need to seek out some prestigious dignitary to find out. Everybody would say that wealth is good. Do you agree?

Yes, I do.

So health, [b] beauty, and all the other bodily blessings are also good?

Yes.

How about being born into an aristocratic family with power and honor in your own country? Those are all clearly good, aren't they?

I agree.

What good things are left? How about temperance, justice and courage? By god, Clinias, would we be correct in placing these among the good things or not? It's possible that someone will dispute that claim, but how does it seem to you?"

Oh, those are definitely good things, Clinias said.

[c] Well, then, should we add wisdom to our chorus of good things? What do you say?

Wisdom does belong among the good things.

Think carefully so that we don't leave out any good things worth mentioning.

I can't think of anything else to add.

Then, remembering something else, I said, By God, we've left out the greatest of goods!

What's that? He asked.

Success! Everybody, no matter how simpleminded they are, says that success is the greatest good.

That's true, Socrates.

But then I thought about it again and said, [d] We almost made ourselves look ridiculous just now.

How so? Clinias asked.

Because by adding success in with the other goods we mentioned before, we are mentioning the same thing again.

What do you mean?

Once you have already put something on your list, it is silly to add it again and say the same thing twice.

How are we doing that?

Wisdom is success.* Any child knows that. Clinias was surprised to hear me say that; he is so young and ingenuous. I saw his surprise and so I asked him, [e] Don't you know that when it comes to performing flute music well, flute players are the most successful?

He agreed.

So, I said, in reading and writing, your reading and writing teachers are the most successful?

Certainly.

And when it comes to the dangers of a sea voyage, do you think that anyone is more successful, as a general rule, than wise pilots?

Oh not at all.

And what if you were on a military campaign? With whom would you rather risk victory and defeat: [280a] a wise general or an ignorant one?

A wise general.

And if you were sick would you take your chances with a wise doctor or an ignorant one?

A wise doctor.

And that's because you think the results would be better with a wise doctor than with an ignorant one?

He agreed.

So everywhere wisdom makes people succeed. Wisdom doesn't make mistakes, it acts correctly and succeeds or else it would no longer be wisdom.

[b] I don't know exactly how, but in the end we agreed that to sum it all up, the person who has wisdom had no additional need of success. When this was settled, I asked whether this point affected anything we had agreed upon earlier. Re-capping what we had said I asked, Didn't we agree that we would do well and be happy if we had many good things?

He agreed.

And would the good things we had make us happy if they didn't benefit us, or if they did?

If they benefitted us, he said.

[c] And would they benefit us if we only had them but didn't actually use them? For example, if we had a lot of food but didn't actually eat it, or we had water but we didn't drink it, would either benefit us?

No, not at all.

Then, if every craftsman had all the materials needed for his craft, but he didn't actually use them, would he do well simply by possessing all that he needs in order to do his job? Take a carpenter for example. Suppose he has all the tools and wood he needs but he never actually builds anything. Would he actually benefit [d] from what he has?

No.

Then, if a man had money and all the other things that we just said are good, but he never used them, would he be happy simply because he possessed good things?

No, not at all, Socrates?

So if you intend to be happy, then it's not enough to possess good things like these; you have to actually use them or there will be no benefit in possessing them.

That's true.

[e] Well then Clinias, are these two things together sufficient to make someone happy: having good things and using them?

I think so.

If he uses them correctly or incorrectly?*

Correctly.

That's a good answer, I said, because if someone uses something incorrectly things can turn out worse than if he'd just left it alone and not used it at all. Do you agree that in between good and bad there is the possibility of [281a] neither good nor bad?

Yes, I agree with that.

So in the case of carpentry, like I was saying just before, it is the carpenter's knowledge that successfully completes a carpentry project?

Yes.

And how about when it comes to making clothes? Isn't it the tailor's knowledge that does the job correctly?

Yes, that's right.

Isn't it going to be the same with all the things that we said at first are good? When it comes to money, health and beauty, [b] isn't it knowledge that leads us to the correct and successful* use of all these kinds of things?

Knowledge does that, yes.

So it seems that with every possession and in every action, knowledge provides for people success and the achievement of their goals.*

Clinias agreed.

Then, by god, I said, what benefit is there in other possessions without wisdom and intelligence? Which of the following two men would benefit more: a stupid man who has many possessions and does many things, or a smart man* who has few possessions and does little? Think of it this way. The one who does fewer things [c] will make fewer mistakes, won't he? And if he makes fewer mistakes, then he'll do less badly, and if he does less badly, he'll be less wretched.

Very much so.

Now, which of the two would do less: a poor man or a rich man?

A poor man.

And which of these two: a weak man and a strong man?

A weak man.

How about a man of low rank and a man of high rank?

The man of low rank.

And a coward as compared with a man with courage and temperance?

A coward.

A lazy man and a hard worker?

A lazy man.

I gave a few more comparisons, like between a slow man and a fast man, [d] a man who is hard of hearing and a man who has very acute hearing and so on. We agreed with one another on every point. So in sum, Clinias, I said, it seems likely that with all the things that we at first said were good, the issue about them is not to figure out how they are in themselves good by nature,* but rather the issue seems to be this: if they are led by ignorance, then they are worse than their opposites—and how bad they are is determined by how well they serve such a bad master; but if they are led by intelligence and wisdom, then they are greater goods. But in themselves, [e] neither one of them is worth anything.

Yes, he said, it seems to be just as you say.

Then what is the result of all that we've said? Haven't we reached two conclusions: first, none of the other things is either good or bad; and second, wisdom is good and ignorance is bad?

He agreed.

[282a] Then what is left for us to consider? I asked. Since everybody wishes to be happy, and it's been revealed that we become happy by using things, and using them correctly, and correctness and success are provided by knowledge; it seems to follow necessarily that every man should in every way do his utmost to become as wise as possible. Isn't that true?

Yes.

So then, what do we say about someone who believes that his father's first priority should be to give him wisdom, and not just money? [b] And what if he thinks the same way about his guardians, his friends and those who claim to love him—regardless of whether these self-proclaimed lovers are fellow citizens or visitors from another city? Is there anything shameful in begging and pleading with them to give him some wisdom? Can you blame someone who is willing to do anything honorable* in the service of a friend or lover, or really anyone, for the sake of wisdom? Or don't you think that's the way it is?

I think you are completely right about that, Socrates.

[c] But is wisdom something that can be taught, or does it come to a person on its own? We have yet to consider this issue; you and I haven't agreed on this yet.

Oh, but it does seem teachable to me, Socrates.

I'm very pleased to hear you say that, Clinias; you've spared me a very long inquiry on whether wisdom is teachable or not. So now then, since you do think that it can be taught, and you agree that it is the only thing that can make a person happy and successful, [d] wouldn't you say that it is absolutely necessary to love wisdom, and have you set your mind to do exactly that?

Yes, Socrates, to the best of my ability.

I was glad to hear it, and I turned to Euthydemus and Dionysodorus and said, That is my example of the sort of protreptic discussion I want from you two. It was probably amateurish and plodding, so perhaps one of you will give us a demonstration of a protreptic discussion that is more professionally crafted. Or, if you don't particularly want to do that, [e] perhaps you will pick up where I left off and take the next step: show the young man whether he must acquire every kind of knowledge in order to be happy and to be a good man, or if there is just one kind of knowledge that he must learn, show him what it is. As I said at the beginning, it really does matter to us a lot that he becomes wise and good.

SOCRATES. [283a] That's what I said, Crito, and I paid especially close attention to what would happen next. I was looking especially to see how they would begin, and how they would handle the discussion, encouraging the young man to pursue his training in wisdom and virtue. Dionysodorus, the older brother, began the discussion, and we all watched him closely, expecting that we were about to hear some amazing arguments, [b] which is what we got. In a way it was amazing, Crito—the argument he began with—and it is worth your time to hear how it was an encouragement to virtue.*

Tell me, Socrates, Dionysodorus said, when you say that you and these other people desire that this young man become wise, are you joking or is this what you truly desire? Are you really serious about this?

This question made me wonder if they thought we were joking from the start when we first asked them to talk with the young man. Perhaps that's why they treated the discussion the way they did, joking around and not taking it seriously.* [c] When I considered this possibility I went to great lengths to assure him that we were truly very serious about this.

To this Dionysodorus replied, Careful, Socrates. You might end up denying what you just said.

I am being careful, and I'm sure that I won't deny what I've said.

Very well then, he said, you claim that you want him to become wise?

I certainly do.

And what about right now? Is he wise right now or not?

He says he is not wise yet. He's no braggart.

[d] But you say that you want him to become wise and not to be ignorant?

We all agreed.

Then you want him to become who he is not,* and who he is now you no longer wish him to be.

It disturbed me to hear this, and he immediately took advantage of my state to say, So since you wish him no longer to be who he is now, it seems you wish that he were dead. What a wonderful bunch of friends and lovers you all turn out to be since you all wish for the destruction of your favorite!

[e] Ctesippus was really upset when he heard this and he said, Thurian visitor,* if it weren't so rude I'd wish destruction upon you for uttering such a lie—something that shouldn't even be said out loud—that I wish him destroyed.

Euthydemus stepped in here and asked, What's this, Ctesippus? Do you really believe that it is possible for someone to lie?

By god, yes of course it is; I'd be crazy not to think so.

And when someone lies, is he saying something* about the matter at hand or is he not saying anything?

[284a] Obviously he is saying something, Ctesippus answered.

And if he is saying something, then he isn't saying something about what he isn't saying anything about?

Of course.

And he is saying something real,* something that is separate from all the other things that he's not saying anything about?

Certainly.

Then by saying that, he is saying something that really is?

Yes.

Well, then, Euthydemus continued, the one saying something that really is, is saying something that really is true,* so that if Dionysodorus is saying something that really is, he is speaking the truth and he isn't lying as you claimed earlier.

[b] Yes, said Ctesippus, but someone who says what Dionysodorus said earlier isn't saying something that really is.

But, said Euthydemus, things that are not real are not?

Correct, they are not.

Then there is nowhere that the things that are not are?

Nowhere.

Then is there any way for anyone to act on these things that are not so as to bring them over from nowhere to somewhere?

It doesn't seem so to me, said Ctesippus.

Then when orators speak before an audience, are they doing nothing?

No, they are doing something.

[c] And would you agree that doing something is accomplishing something?*

Yes.

So speaking is both doing and accomplishing?

Yes.

Therefore, no one speaks what is not, because if he were speaking, then he would be accomplishing something, and you just agreed that it isn't possible to accomplish anything: you agreed that it is impossible to bring something over from nowhere to somewhere. So according to your own account, no one tells a lie; if Dionysodorus is speaking, then he is speaking the truth.

Yes, by god, Euthydemus, however, although he is saying things that are in a certain way, he's not saying them as they really are.

Dionysodorus jumped in at the point and answered, What do you mean in saying this, Ctesippus? [d] Are there some who say things as they are?

Yes, there are, and those who speak the truth are fine and good people.

Ok, then. Would you say that good things go well and bad things badly?

Yes, I would.

And so what about these fine and good people—as you call them—who speak the truth? Do they say things as they are?

Yes, they do.

So these good people speak badly of things that are bad, if they say things as they are?

Yes, by god, said Ctesippus, they most certainly do; especially when they are speaking about bad people. And if you take my advice, you'll be careful not to be included among them, [e] or else good people will say very bad things about you, because you should know this for a fact: good people speak badly of the bad.

And do they speak loudly of the loud and warmly of the warm? Euthydemus asked.

Indeed they do; and they also speak lamely of the lame, like your arguments so far.

An insult! Dionysodorus objected. Now you are just insulting us.

By god no, Dionysodorus, I'm not trying to insult you, I'm trying to warn you as a friend, and to persuade you never to make such a wild accusation as you did earlier when you said that I wish this young man here, about whom I care a great deal, [285a] no longer to be.

At this point it seemed to me that the conversation could get out of hand, and so I tried to lighten the mood by talking with Ctesippus cheerfully, Since we asked our two visitors to give us a demonstration, and they are generously obliging us, I think that we can accept what they are saying and not quibble about the word.* Suppose they do know how to "destroy" someone, so as to turn a person who lacks both virtue and wisdom into a virtuous and wise person. Perhaps they have learned this on their own, [b] or perhaps they've learned from someone else a form of "destruction" or "death" that allows them to kill a bad man and then resurrect him as a good man. If they do know this—well, clearly they know it, at least they claim that the craft they recently discovered is to make good people out of bad ones—then let's go along with them. Let them "destroy" Clinias and make him wise; and then let them do the same to the rest of us. [c] If you young people are afraid, then I'll be the guinea pig*—let them run the experiment on me first since I'm an old man, I'll take my chances with Dionysodorus as I might with Medea the sorceress. Let him destroy me, and if he wishes, boil my butchered carcass in his cauldron; he may do as he wishes as long as he makes me a good person.

Me too, Socrates, Ctesippus chimed in. I'm ready to hand myself over to our visitors. If they wish, they may flay me more than they are already doing as long as my hide isn't turned into a wineskin—as Apollo did when he flayed Marsyas—they must turn my hide into virtue. [d] Dionysodorus thinks that I am angry with him but I am not, I am simply contradicting the things that, in my opinion, are not well said. Please, Dionysodorus, don't call contradiction an insult; an insult is something quite different.

Well, then, Dionysodorus said to Ctesippus, do you make an argument on the assumption that there is such a thing as contradiction?

[e] Yes, indeed, I certainly do! Don't you think there is such a thing as contradiction, Dionysodorus?

But surely you cannot actually prove that one person has contradicted another.

No? Listen and you'll hear Ctesippus contradicting Dionysodorus right now.

I suppose you can support your claim?

Certainly.

All right, then. Tell me, are there words for each of the things that are?

Certainly.

And do those words express or define* each thing as it is or as it is not?

[286a] As it is.

And do you recall, Ctesippus, we just proved* that no one says things as they are not, because no one speaks what is not?

What of it? Asked Ctesippus. Aren't you and I still contradicting one another?

But are we contradicting one another if we are both speaking the definition of the same thing? In that case, aren't we both saying exactly the same thing?

Yes, in that case we are, agreed Ctesippus.

And what about a case where neither one of us expresses the definition of the thing? [b] Would we be contradicting each other in that sort of case? Wouldn't that case be completely different? Neither one of us is calling the thing to mind, isn't that so?

Ctesippus agreed to this also.

So then what about the case where I express the definition of the thing, and you express a different definition of a different thing,* are we contradicting each other then? Or is this final possibility a case where I am expressing one thing and you aren't talking about it at all? How can you say that the person who isn't talking at all is contradicting the person who is talking?

At this Ctesippus was silent. I was amazed at the argument, and asked, What are you saying, Dionysodorus? [c] I have actually heard this argument many times from many people and it never ceases to amaze me. The followers of Protagoras* used it quite a lot, and so did people even before Protagoras.* It is always amazing to me how it refutes every other argument, and how it even refutes itself!* But I think I will finally learn the truth about this argument from you. Aren't you saying, basically, that it is impossible to say anything false? Isn't that really the point of your argument? Someone is either speaking the truth or he isn't speaking at all?

Yes, that's it, Dionysodorus agreed.

[d] Well, would you say that although it isn't possible to *say* what isn't true, it is possible to *believe* what isn't true?

No, it's not even possible to *believe* what isn't true.

So it's impossible for anyone to have a false belief?

Utterly impossible.

Then there is no such thing as ignorance, and no one is ignorant? Because this is exactly what ignorance is—or would be, if it exists—to have a false belief about something?

Correct.

So it's not possible to have a false belief?

No, it isn't.

Really? Tell me, Dionysodorus, do you truly believe that no human being is ignorant, or are you just presenting this argument in order to raise a paradox?

[e] Just go ahead and refute me.

But if nobody has a false belief, is it possible to refute* someone according to your account?

No, it is not possible, said Euthydemus.

Then Dionysodorus did not bid me to refute him just now?

How can someone bid what is impossible? Do you ever tell someone to do something impossible?

The reason I ask, Euthydemus, is because I don't quite understand these clever and sophisticated things. I'm afraid that I am, in a way, a bit thick* when it comes to them. So please excuse me if I sound naive, [287a] but look at it this way. If it isn't possible to say something false, or to have a false belief, or to be ignorant, then isn't it equally impossible to go wrong or make a mistake* when you do something? Aren't you saying that it is impossible for someone who does something to make a mistake?

Yes, that is exactly what we are saying.

Ok, well, then, here's my naive question. If it isn't possible to make a mistake in saying, thinking or acting—if things really are so—then, by god, what have you come here to teach?* Didn't you say just a little while ago* that [b] if anyone wanted to learn virtue, you were the finest teachers?

You are so nostalgic,* Socrates. Honestly, if we said something last year would you bring it up now and be at a total loss to handle the issue at hand?

But the issue at hand is a difficult one—as is suitable for something said by wise men—and in fact what you said just now is especially tough: what exactly did you mean when you asked if I was "at a total loss to handle the issue at hand"? [c] Isn't it clear that it means I am unable to refute you? Please tell me just what is the sense of the phrase "at a total loss to handle the issue at hand"?

Actually, what you asked just now is much easer to handle, if you answer my questions.

Before you answer mine?

Are you refusing to answer me?

Well, this doesn't really seem fair.

Oh, it's fair alright.

According to what principle? Well, obviously this one: you have come to us as a pan-sophist with respect to arguments, [d] so you know when you ought to answer and when you ought not. So now you won't answer my question because you know you ought not.

Now you are just babbling to avoid answering my question. My dear sir, be persuaded and answer since you agree that I am wise.

It seems that I must answer since you are the master here. Ok, ask away.

Is it things that have minds or things that do not have minds that have sense?

Things that have minds.*

And do you know any phrase that has a mind?

Certainly not.

[e] So then why did you ask me just now what sense my phrase has?

My mistake. What was I thinking? Or maybe I was right to speak as if phrases have sense. Would you say that I made a mistake or not? Because if I did not make a mistake, then you did not refute me, despite being wise, and you are at a total loss to handle the issue at hand. But if I did make a mistake, [288a] then you were wrong to say that no one can make a mistake. Oh, and notice that I'm not talking about things you said last year. So it seems, Euthydemus and Dionysodorus, that you haven't been able to make any progress* with this old gem of an argument about the impossibility of error: as always, it appears to knock itself down at the same time as it knocks others down. Despite your amazing facility with words your craft has not yet been able to discover a way to stop that from happening.

Bravo, [b] you men of Thurii, or Chios, or wherever you want to say you are from, Ctesippus added. You have an amazing capacity for talking nonsense.

I was afraid that insults might start flying so again I tried to get Ctesippus to ease up and I said, Ctesippus, I'm going to say the same thing to you that I said to Clinias, which is that you don't know how amazing the wisdom of our visitors is, but they don't want to give us a serious demonstration of it. Instead they are imitating Proteus the Egyptian and bewitching us. [c] So let's imitate Menelaus and not let them go until they show us what they take seriously, because I think they will reveal something very fine when they start to take the discussion seriously. So let's beg, implore and pray to get them to show us their true colors. I'll take the lead again and handle the discussion like the person I pray they will show themselves to be. [d] I'll pick up where we left off earlier and do my best to go through what follows to see whether I am able to draw them out and by taking the discussion seriously myself, see whether they will finally pity me and be serious themselves.

Clinias, please remind me where we left off. I think it was when we finally agreed that we must love wisdom. Was that it?

Yes, that was it, Clinias replied.

And to love wisdom is to acquire knowledge? Isn't that so?

Yes.

Which knowledge will we acquire if we go about it correctly? [e] Isn't it simply this: the knowledge that will benefit us?

Yes, indeed, that is it.

And would it benefit us if we knew how to spot the places to mine huge quantities of gold?

Perhaps.

But didn't we prove earlier* that this knowledge would be worth nothing—not even if we could have all the gold in the world without digging—not even if we knew how to turn ordinary rocks into gold? [289a] Don't you recall we concluded that we would derive no benefit unless we had the additional knowledge of how to use the gold?

Yes, I remember now.

So if you know how to make something but not how to use it, your knowledge is of no benefit to you—and this applies to making money, and to the doctor's knowledge and so on?

I agree.

[b] And doesn't this give us clear indication that even if we knew how to make ourselves immortal, not even that knowledge would benefit us if we didn't also know how to use our immortality?

Yes, we did agree to all that.

Then, my fine young man, the knowledge we need is one that combines* making something, and using what is made.

So it seems.

So it is entirely unnecessary for us to become lyre-makers [c] or to acquire that kind of knowledge because the craft of lyre-making is entirely separate from the craft of lyre-using, isn't it? Aren't lyre players quite different from lyre-makers?

Yes, they are.

So obviously we don't need to become flute-makers for the same reason.

I think so.

Well, by the gods, should we learn the craft of speech-writing? Is that the knowledge that will make us happy if we possess it?

I don't think so, Clinias answered.

[d] Do you give some clear indication that this is not the knowledge we are seeking?

I've seen speech-writers who don't know how to use their own speeches—the very ones that they've written themselves—just like lyre-makers who don't know how to play the lyres they make. Other people are able to use speeches, but the speech-writers cannot. So clearly when it comes to speeches, the craft of making them is separate from the craft of using them.

That seems to me a sufficient indication that we wouldn't be happy by possessing the craft of speech-writing, although I had a sense that with speech-writing we were getting close to [e] the knowledge that we've been looking for. Whenever I talk with speech writers they seem beyond wise to me, and their craft seems lofty and divine. I suppose that after all this isn't actually surprising since speech writing is part of the enchanter's craft and it is inferior to that craft by only a little. [290a] Compare the two: the enchanter's craft allows you to charm snakes, spiders, scorpions and other wild animals, and even diseases; but on the other hand, the speech-writer's craft allows you to charm juries, legislative assemblies and other crowds. Doesn't it seem that way to you?

Yes, it does seem exactly as you say.

Well, then, where shall we turn to find the knowledge we are looking for?

I can't see a way forward.

I think I've found it myself.

What is it?

[b] The craft of an army general seems to me to be the one that—more than any other craft—would make us happy if we possessed it.

It doesn't seem that way to me.

Why not?

Well, the general's craft is a craft of hunting people.

And so?

And so like every hunting craft, it includes no more than hunting and catching. Once a hunter captures what he hunts, he isn't able to use his prey: people who hunt and fish turn their catch over to the cooks. [c] It's the same with geometers, astronomers and calculators. Actually, they are hunters too. Geometers don't create geometrical figures, they discover geometrical reality;* and they hunt only—they don't know how to use what they discover, instead they hand it over to the dialecticians,* and the dialecticians who aren't completely senseless know how to use them.

Well done, Clinias! You are indeed extremely fine and wise. Are these things really so?

Very much so. It's just this way with generals: [d] when they capture a city or an enemy camp, they hand it over to the politicians because they don't know how to use what they capture. It's just like the way that quail hunters turn over what they capture to the quail keepers. So if we need to find a craft that knows how to use what it acquires—whether by capturing it or making it—and if this is also to be the craft that makes us blessedly happy, then we have to look at some craft other than generalship.

CRITO. [e] What are you saying, Socrates? Did the lad really articulate such an argument?

SOCRATES. Don't you think so, Crito?

CRITO. By god, no I do not. I think that if he could say something like that, then he doesn't need Euthydemus—or anybody else—as a teacher.

SOCRATES. Then, god help me, was it Ctesippus who said it? I don't remember.*

CRITO. [291a] It doesn't sound like something Ctesippus would say either.

SOCRATES. Well, I definitely heard it, and it definitely wasn't Euthydemus or Dionysodorus who said it. Perhaps it was uttered by some divine presence.*

CRITO. Oh, yes, by god, that must be it, Socrates. But tell me, after this did you keep on looking for the craft you were searching for? Did you find it or not?

SOCRATES. [b] No, in fact, it was pretty ridiculous—we were like children chasing crested larks—every time we thought we had caught the craft, it slipped away. Why should I go through the whole, long story? We came to the royal craft and were examining it to see whether it was the one that creates and perfects our happiness but that's when we fell into a labyrinth: just when we thought we were at the end of our quest we got turned around and somehow ended up right at the beginning. [c]

CRITO. How did that happen, Socrates?

SOCRATES. Well, first of all, it seemed to us that the political craft and the royal craft were one and the same.

CRITO. Then what?

SOCRATES. Generalship and the other crafts hand over their works to the political craft as if only the political craft actually knows how to rule them all. So it seemed obvious to us that this was the craft we'd been looking for: it is the cause of right action in the city, [d] and—as Aeschylus said*—it sits alone at the stern of the city; it steers all things and rules all things and makes all things useful.

CRITO. Wasn't that the right idea, Socrates?

SOCRATES. You can judge for yourself if you want to hear was happened next, for we took up the investigation like this. Come now, the royal craft, which rules all the works of the other crafts, [e] does it have a function or produce any result* of its own? We said that yes, absolutely it does. Would you say the same thing, Crito?

CRITO. I would.

SOCRATES. Then what would you say that function or result is? For example, suppose I were to ask you about the doctor's craft: when it rules its entire domain, what function does it perform, or what result does it produce? Health, wouldn't you say?

CRITO. I would.

SOCRATES. And what about your own craft: farming? [292a] When it rules its own domain, what does it produce? Wouldn't you say that it provides us with food from the earth?

CRITO. I would.

SOCRATES. Then what about the royal craft? When it rules its own domain what does it produce? Perhaps you don't clearly see a way forward here.

CRITO. No, by god, Socrates, I don't.

SOCRATES. We didn't either, Crito. But at least you know this much: if it is the craft we are looking for, then it must be beneficial.

CRITO. Yes, very beneficial.

SOCRATES. Then it must provide us with something good, right?

CRITO. Necessarily.

SOCRATES. [b] And remember that Clinias and I agreed that nothing except knowledge is good.*

CRITO. Yes, I remember that.

SOCRATES. So what do we say about all the other results of the political craft, and there are many, for the political craft provides us with wealth, freedom and social cohesion? Don't we have to say that all these things are neither good nor bad?* If the political craft is to be beneficial to us and to make us happy, then doesn't it have to make us wise and knowledgeable?

CRITO. [c] Yes, that's correct; that follows from what you agreed to as you reported it.

SOCRATES. So the royal craft makes people wise and good?

CRITO. Is there any problem with that, Socrates?

SOCRATES. Well, does it make everyone good in every way? Does it give us every kind of knowledge, like shoemaking, carpentry and all the rest?

CRITO. Oh, I certainly don't think so, Socrates.

SOCRATES. [d] Then which knowledge *does* it provide us with, and what are we going to do with that knowledge? Certainly it cannot be the producer of any of the things we said are neither good nor bad, nor can it provide us with some other knowledge besides itself. Do we have anything to say about what it is and in what way it is beneficial? Do you have any objection to saying that with it we shall make other people good?

CRITO. None at all.

SOCRATES. Then in what ways will they be good and beneficial? Perhaps they are good and beneficial because they make other people good and beneficial. And then those other people are good and beneficial because they make still other people good and beneficial? [e] How many times are we going to plough the same ground?* We aren't getting anywhere in understanding how we are making people good; all we are doing is discrediting the political craft by making it seem empty. So as I was saying, we are no closer to understanding what that knowledge is that makes us happy; in fact, we seem more in the dark than ever.

CRITO. By god, Socrates, that's quite an impasse you reached.

SOCRATES. Yes, indeed, and when we reached this impasse, [293a] I gave an impassioned plea that our two visitors would save us as the Dioscuri* save sailors from drowning at sea. Clinias and I were going under for the third time* so I begged them to make every effort to help us and to show us what that knowledge is that will help us go through life well.

CRITO. What happened then? Was Euthydemus willing to show you something?

SOCRATES. How could he not? He started out in quite a magnanimous manner like this.

[b] Which would you prefer, Socrates, shall I teach you the knowledge that's confounded you, or shall I show you that you already possess it?

What?! Can you really do that? I replied.

Easily, said Euthydemus.

Then, by god, show me that I already have it; that's much easier than learning it at my advanced age.

Then tell me, he said, is there something that you know?

Oh yes, many things, but nothing very important.

Good. And do you think that it is possible for something both to be and not to be what it is?

[c] No, by god, I certainly do not.

And you definitely know something?

I do.

So you are knowing, since you know something?

Certainly, I am knowing-of-that-thing-I-know, I said.

That doesn't matter. Doesn't it necessarily follow that you know everything since you are knowing?

No, by God, since there are very many things I do not know.

Ah, then, said Euthydemus, but if you are not-knowing something, then you are not-knowing.

…not-knowing-that-thing, I quickly added.

But it is no less true that you are not-knowing. And since you just now said that you are knowing, [d] then by your own admission it turns out that you are both knowing and not-knowing at the same time.

Bravo,* Euthydemus! So how do I already possess that knowledge I've been seeking? Let me guess: since it is impossible both to be and not to be the same thing at the same time, if I know one thing I know everything since I can't be knowing and not-knowing at the same time, and since I know everything, I already have that knowledge I've been seeking. Is that what you are saying? Is this what it is to be wise?

[e] You are refuting yourself, Socrates.

But what about you, Euthydemus; aren't you in the same trouble? I won't worry if I'm in the same boat as you and your brother Dionysodorus. Tell me, don't you two know some things but not others?

Not at all, Socrates" said Dionysodorus.

What do you mean? Don't you know anything at all?

We certainly do.

[294a] Then you know everything, since you know something?

Of course! And you do too: if you know one thing, you know everything.

Oh Zeus! I said. This is amazing. Is it really true that every person in the world either knows everything or nothing?

Indubitably. They can't know some things but not others or they would be both knowing and not-knowing.

And so…?

…and so everyone knows everything, if he knows even one thing, Dionysodorus concluded.

[b] By the gods, Dionysodorus, it's clear to me now that you two are actually serious* about this, although it was not easy for me to get you to take us seriously. Do you two really know everything? For example, carpentry and shoemaking?"

Certainly, Dionysodorus said.

And you are able to mend shoes?

Yes, by God, and to stitch leather.

Well, what about other kinds of things? Do you know the number of stars in the sky, or the number of grains of sand in the world?

Certainly. Do you think we wouldn't agree to all that as well?

At this point Ctesippus took up the argument and said, By God, Dionysodorus, [c] give me a clear sign, a proof that will let me know that you are speaking the truth.

What proof shall I give you? asked Dionysodorus.

Do you know how many teeth Euthydemus has, and does he know how many teeth you have?

Isn't it enough for you to be told that we know everything?

No way, said Ctesippus. Just tell us this one thing to prove that what you say is true: if each of you says how many teeth the other has, and we count them and discover that you got the number right, then we'll believe you about all the other things.

[d] They thought he was mocking them and they weren't willing to go through with it, but they kept insisting that they knew every single thing Ctesippus asked them about. And Ctesippus was completely unabashed so that in the end there was nothing he didn't ask them about—even the most embarrassing things. They courageously stood their ground and affirmed that they knew everything—it was like watching wild boars standing their ground against repeated spear-thrusts. Finally, Crito, I was compelled by disbelief* to ask [e] Dionysodorus whether he knew how to dance.

Certainly I do, he answered.

And are you so advanced in wisdom that even at your age you can do that trick where the harlequin dances in circles and juggles machetes?

There is nothing, he said, that I cannot do.

And do you know it all now only, or do you always know?

Always.

Did you two know everything when you were children, right from birth?

They both affirmed that they knew everything from birth.

[295a] This just seemed unbelievable to us, so Euthydemus asked, You don't believe us, do you?

No, except that you two present the appearance of being wise.

Ah, but if you are willing to answer my questions, I will show that even you agree with these amazing things.

I will be happy to be refuted. For if it has escaped my notice that I am wise, and you can demonstrate that I have always known everything, what greater gift of Hermes could I ever discover in my entire life?

But you must answer my questions, he said.

[b] Ask and I shall answer.

Well, then, Socrates, said Euthydemus, are you knowing or not?

I am.

And when you know something, do you know it by means of that by which you are knowing?

By means of that by which I am knowing? I think you are talking about my mind: I know things by means of my mind; or is that not what you mean?

Aren't you ashamed of yourself, Socrates, answering a question with a question?

Well, what am I to do? I'll do as you say, but when I don't know what you are asking, do you want me to answer anyway without asking for clarification?

[c] Surely you have some understanding of the question.

Yes, I do.

Then just answer according to your understanding of the question.

But what if you ask the question with one thing in mind, and I think you mean something different and answer according to what I incorrectly think you are asking? Is it ok with you if my answer is entirely beside the point?

Oh, it's perfectly fine with me, though I suspect that in the end you won't be fine with it.

Well, then, by God, I won't answer until I find out what you mean.

You won't answer according to your understanding of the question because you are a stupid old fool!

[d] I could see that he was upset* with me for explicitly distinguishing claims when he wanted to capture me by entrapping me with words. This reminded me of Connus who gets upset with me when I don't comply with his requests, and consequently he pays less attention to my education as if I'm an ineducable. So since I had made up my mind* to be Euthydemus' student, I thought that I ought to comply with his requests so that he wouldn't think I was ineducable and refuse to teach me. So I said, If that seems to you the right way to do things, [e] Euthydemus, then that's the way they must be done. Your knowledge of discussion is much finer than mine, since I have only a layman's grasp* of the craft. So ask again from the beginning.

Again, you must answer whether you know what you know by means of something or not.

I do. I know things by means of my mind.

[296a] Not this again! You are answering more than I asked. I didn't ask you by means of what you know, I asked you only whether you know by means of something.

I did again answer more than was necessary, but that's because I'm only a student. Please excuse me. I will answer simply that yes, I do know what I know by means of something.

And do you always know by this means, or do you know by this means sometimes and by another means another time?

Always—*whenever I know*—it is by this means.

Won't you stop adding things on to your answers?

I'm just trying to be careful so that this "always" doesn't trip us up.

[b] It won't trip *us* up, Euthydemus said; if it trips anybody up, it will be *you*. Just answer the question: do you always know by this means?

Always, I said, since I have to drop the qualification* "whenever I know."

So you always know by this means. Next, are you always knowing some things by means of this and other things by means of something else, or are you always knowing all things by means of this?

By means of this I know all things that I know.

There you are doing it again, you are adding something in addition to what I asked.

Ok, then I retract the qualification "that I know."

No, no, don't take anything back; I don't need any help from you. [c] Just answer one more question: could you know all things without knowing everything?

It would be incredible if I did.

Ok, now you may add on whatever you wish, since you agree that you know all things.

It seems so, I said; "I know all things that I know" means that I know everything if we ignore the qualification "that I know."

So, therefore, Euthydemus continued, you have agreed that you always know—"by means of that by which you know," or "when you know," or however you want to phrase it. For you have agreed that you "always know" and that you "know everything." So obviously you knew when you were a child, [d] and when you were being born, and when you were being conceived. In fact, you knew even before you existed, and before heaven and earth came to be you knew all things, if you *always* know. And, by god, you always *will* know, and know *everything*, if I want it that way.*

May you wish it to be so, most honored guest, if what you say is really true. But I don't believe that your wanting it to be true is enough to make it true unless your brother here helps you out. Then, maybe, you have a chance. [e] On the one hand, I see that I'm no match for you when it comes to disputing about the claim that "I know everything"—as you put it—since your wisdom is so portentous; but what about a claim like "good men are unjust"? Please tell me, do I know this or not?

Yes, you certainly do know it.

Know what?

That good men are not unjust.

[297a] Oh, yes, of course, I've known that for a long time, but that's not what I asked. Where did I learn that the good *are* unjust?

Nowhere, said Dionysodorus.

So I do not know it, I said.

At this point Euthydemus interrupted and argued with his brother, You are ruining the argument! If you say that he does not know that the good are unjust, then he will be knowing and not-knowing at the same time! Dionysodorus blushed.

Wait a minute, Euthydemus, I said, [b] are you saying that your brother—who knows everything—just said something incorrect?

Dionysodorus quickly jumped in and asked, Am I really Euthydemus' brother?

Hold on a minute, Dionysodorus, first give Euthydemus a chance to teach me how I know that good men are unjust. Please don't begrudge me this lesson.

You're just changing the subject, Socrates, so that you don't have to answer my question.

Well, you can't really blame me, I said, since I'm no match for the two of you, so it doesn't take much to get me to try to change the subject. [c] I am far weaker than Herakles* who couldn't fight both the hydra—a sophist who, because of her wisdom would send up many arguments if one was cut off—and a crab—another kind of sophist that had come from the sea—very recently, I think—so that when he got annoyed with the crab pinching him on the left leg, he called his nephew Iolaus [d] to help him out— although I suspect that if my Iolaus showed up we'd both end up getting pinched.

When you've finally finished this epic tale of yours, Socrates, will you tell me whether this Iolaus was more Herakles' nephew than your own nephew?

I suppose that if I know what's good for me I'll answer your question, Dionysodorus, because I'm quite sure that you won't quit asking it. You are envious and you want to prevent Euthydemus from being the one to teach me that wisdom I seek.

Just answer the question, he said.

My answer is that Iolaus is more Herakles' nephew than mine [e] because he is not my nephew at all. My brother Patrokles is not his father—although my brother's name "Patrokles" sounds a bit like Herakles' brother's name "Iphicles."

So Patrokles is your brother?

Well, half-brother: we have the same mother but not the same father.

So he is your brother and he is not your brother?

…not by the same father, I repeated. Chaeredemus was his father; Sophroniscus was mine.

So Sophroniscus and Chaeredemus were both fathers?

[298a] No doubt about it: the former was mine, the latter was his.

So if you are talking about fathers, you'd say that Chaeredemus is other than father.*

Other than *my* father, I said.

Really? Being a father, how can he be other than a father? Or are you the same as a stone?*

I don't think so, but I'm afraid you'll show that I am.

So you are other than a stone?

Other indeed.

And since you are other than stone, you are not stone; just as you are not gold since you are other than gold?

Correct on both counts.

Therefore, Dionysodorus concluded, since Chaeredemus is other than a father, he is not a father.*

Apparently.

[b] Euthydemus broke in here and said, Because if Chaeredemus is a father, and Sophroniscus is other than Chaeredemus, then it will turn out that Sophroniscus is other than a father, so he's not a father, which makes you fatherless, Socrates!

Ctesippus took up the argument at this point and asked, But isn't it exactly the same with your father, Euthydemus? He is other than my father, isn't he?

Oh, no, not at all, replied Euthydemus.

So he's one and the same person?

Indeed, one and the same.

I'd be really sorry if that were true, moaned Ctesippus. [c] But go on. Is he my father only, or is he also the father of absolutely everybody?

Oh, he's the father of others too, or do you think that one and the same man can be both a father and not a father?

Well, actually, yes I did think that.

What? Is it possible for something to be gold and not gold, or for someone to be human and not human?

You're mixing apples and oranges* here, Euthydemus. Surely you must admit that it would be very strange if your father is the father of everybody.

But he is.

Well then is he the father of human beings only? Or is he also the father of horses and of all other living animals?

[d] My father is the father of absolutely all.

So your mother is also the mother of all?

Yes, indeed, the same goes for my mother.

And is she the mother of the sea urchins?

Yes, and your mother is too, Euthydemus added.

So that would make you the brother of piglets, puppies and guppies, said Ctesippus.

You are too.

Which would make your father a pig-dog-fish.

Yours too.

Dionysodorus jumped in here and said to Ctesippus, You will make all these same admissions if you answer my questions. Tell me, do you have a dog?

Yes I do, said Ctesippus, but he's a very bad dog.

Does he have puppies?

[e] Yes and they are just as bad as he is.

So your dog is definitely their father?

Oh, yes, I actually saw him mounting the bitch who bore the puppies.

Ok. And you admit that the dog is yours?

Yes.

So he's *yours*, and he's a *father*, so he's *your father*!* You're the son of a dog, and your brothers are puppies! Dionysodorus immediately asked his next question in order to prevent Ctesippus from getting in a reply, Tell me just one more small detail: do you beat your dog?

Laughing, Ctesippus said, Yes, by the gods, since I can't beat you!

So you beat your own father! Dionysodorus concluded.

[299a] There would be more justice in beating yours for ever getting it into his head to have such wise sons as you. No doubt* the man who sired the puppies and you has long enjoyed all the benefits of your distinctive brand of wisdom.

Ah, but you see, he doesn't need to have many good things, Ctesippus, and neither do you.

I suppose you don't either?

No, I don't. And neither does anyone. I'll show you why. Tell me, [b] Ctesippus, if you think it's a good thing for a sick person to drink medicine if he needs it. And do you think it's a good thing for a soldier to go to war armed rather than unarmed?

I do think so, yes, but I suspect that you are about to say something fine.*

Perhaps I am, but you won't find out without answering my question. Since you've agreed that it is good for someone to drink medicine when he needs it, doesn't it follow that it is good to drink as much as possible?* And wouldn't it be magnificent if the medicine were mixed with a wagon load of hellebore?*

That would be perfect, said Ctesippus, [c] if the one drinking it were as big as the statue at Delphi.

Furthermore, Euthydemus continued, since it is a good thing to be armed when you march off to war, a soldier ought to be loaded down with spears and shields—if being armed is a good thing.

Indeed, said Ctesippus, but you don't actually believe this, do you? Wouldn't you prefer just one shield and one spear?

Oh, for myself, yes indeed.

And is that how you'd equip Geryon and Briareus? Ha! I thought that you and your companion would have been smart enough to see that coming, seeing how you two both fight in armor.

Euthydemus was silent, [d] but Dionysodorus went back to the answers Ctesippus had given earlier and said, Gold. You think it would be good to have some, don't you?

Certainly, and a lot of it, too.

And would you say that we ought to have good things always and everywhere?

Absolutely.

And you agree that gold is good?

I have agreed to that.

Therefore, one ought to have it always and everywhere—especially inside oneself. [e] So wouldn't that person be happiest who had three talents of gold* in his stomach, a talent in his skull, and a gold stater in each eye?

Well, if we're still using words the way you did when you concluded that my dog was my father, then we can support your claim about having gold inside us with the case of the Scythians.* You know that they gild the skulls of their enemies and drink from them, so since these gilded skulls belong to them, we can use your logic to say that they drink for their own gilded skulls. In fact, they claim that the happiest and best men are those who have the most gold in their own skulls. And furthermore, since they gaze into their own gilded skulls as they drink from them, we could even say that they carry their own heads in their hands!

[300a] Euthydemus went on, And do these Scythians—and everybody else, for that matter—see things possible or impossible to see.*

Possible, obviously.

You too?

Me too.

And you see our clothes?

Yes.

So it is possible for our clothes to see.

Ha! Strangely so, said Ctesippus.

And what do they see?

Not much, or maybe you don't think their eyesight is too good. Anyway, you argue like someone who is sleepwalking—talking without saying anything.

[b] Here Dionysodorus spoke up and asked, But surely that's impossible; there's no talking of the silent,* is there?

No, agreed Ctesippus.

So by the same token, there's no such thing as a silence of the talking?

That's even less possible.

But whenever you talk about stones, wood or iron isn't that a case of talking of the silent?

Not when I visit the blacksmith's shop: when he works the iron he makes it sing and shout. Your wisdom didn't let you see that coming, did it? Try the other one now and tell me how there is a silence of the talking.

[c] I think Ctesippus was showing off because Clinias was watching.

When you are silent, asked Euthydemus, are you silent about everything?

I certainly am.

Well that's the "silence of the talking" because talking is among the "everything" you keep silence of.

And yet, answered Ctesippus, not everything is silent, is it?

Of course not, said Euthydemus.

Well, then, my good man, does everything talk?

All the talking things talk,* of course.

But that is not what I asked; I asked whether all things are silent or speak.

[d] Dionysodorus interrupted and said, Neither and both. Ha! I'm certain that you won't be able to do anything with that answer.

Ctesipppus burst out laughing, as he often does, and said, Euthydemus, your brother is having it both ways and has completely ruined the argument!

Clinias thought this was very funny too and he started laughing, so Ctesippus was very pleased with himself. Ctesippus is quite a clever rascal, and I think that he had picked up this very argument from Euthydemus and Dionysodorus because nobody else today has this kind of wisdom.

[e] At this point I asked Clinias, Why are you laughing at such excellent and beautiful* things?

But Dionysodorus answered, Have you ever seen a beautiful thing, Socrates?

I have seen many.

[301a] And are they the same as The Beautiful* or not?

Here I was completely at a loss, and I completely deserved it for making a fuss about Clinias laughing. But I answered and said that they are not the same as The Beautiful, although each of the beautiful things has some beauty present with it.*

Well, then, if a beautiful thing is beautiful because beauty is present with it, then are you an ox when an ox is present with you? I'm present with you now; does that make you Dionysodorus?

God forbid!

And can you explain to me how another thing becomes other by having The Other present to it?

[b] I calmly replied, That confounds you? You see, I was so eager to possess the wisdom of these two men that I was imitating it.*

How could I not be confounded—me and everybody else—at what is impossible?

What do you mean, Dionysodorus? Isn't The Beautiful beautiful, and isn't The Ugly ugly?

Beauty is in the eye of the beholder.

Ok, so in your eye, isn't The Beautiful beautiful* and The Ugly ugly?

Yes, it certainly is.

So The Same is the same and The Other is other? Surely you don't think that The Other is the same. [c] I would have thought that even a child wouldn't be confounded by the fact that The Other is other. I guess that you've deliberately skipped this topic because in everything else we've covered you two seem to me to be just like craftsmen completing their work to the last detail—you've carried out the discussion in fine style.*

Oh, so you know the sort of work that belongs to each craftsman? For example, do you know which craftsman pounds metal on the anvil?

I do. That work belongs to the blacksmith.

And how about the craftsman who shapes clay on the wheel?

That's for the potter.

And which craftsman slaughters an animal, skins it, slices up the meat and then roasts and stews it?

[d] That's the cook.

So if someone does the work that belongs to his craft, then he will act correctly?*

And you just said that the work belonging to the cook* is to slaughter and to skin?

Yes, I did. I'm afraid of what's coming next, so please go easy on me.

So if someone slaughters and skins the cook, then he will act correctly? He'll be doing the right thing by cutting the cook up into meaty bits, roasting them and tossing them into a stew? And the one who spins the potter on the wheel or pounds the blacksmith on the anvil will also be doing the work that belongs to each of the craftsmen?

[e] Oh, Poseidon! You are completing your wisdom! Will such wisdom ever come to me in such a way that I can truly claim it as my own?

Would you know the exact moment when it changed from simply being present with you to actually belonging to you as your own?

I would if you were willing to help me, I said.

So you think that you know what truly belongs to you as your own?

Unless you say otherwise, for from you I must begin,* and with Euthydemus I must end.

Alright, then, Dionysodorus continued, do you think that something truly belongs to you as your own when you control it [302a] and can use it as you wish? For example, you think that an ox or sheep is your own when you are allowed to sell it or to give it away or to sacrifice it to whichever god you choose, and if it isn't yours in that way, then it doesn't truly belong to you as your own?

Immediately I blurted out that he was certainly correct and that only things like this truly belonged to me as my own, because I knew something fine would result from this line of questioning and I wanted to hear it right away.

And you call those things alive that have a soul?

[b] Yes.

And you agree that only those living things are yours over which you exercise the sort of authority and control we just mentioned?

I agree.

At that point, Dionysodorus faked a solemn pause,* pretending that he was contemplating some profound matter and he said, Tell me, Socrates, do you have a Paternal Zeus?*

I immediately suspected where he was going with this argument, and I turned out to be exactly right. But I was really at a loss as to how I could escape; I felt like a fish that had already been caught in a net. All I could say in answer to his question was the truth: No.

Then you are a miserable excuse for a person, [c] and you aren't even a true Athenian,* if you have no Paternal Gods or shrines, then there is nothing decent or respectable about you.

Enough, Dionysodorus, don't go too far. Don't treat your pupil with such irreverent abuse. Of course I have altars and shrines, both Household and Paternal, just like every other decent and respectable Athenian.

Well what about these other "decent and respectable" Athenians? Do they have shrines to Paternal Zeus?

No, we are Ionians,* descended from Ion, and because Ion's divine father was Apollo, Athenians and Athenian colonists have a [d] Paternal Apollo.* We don't have a Paternal Zeus, but we do have a Household Zeus, a Tribal Zeus and also a Tribal Athena.

Fine, said Dionysodorus, whatever you call them, you've got an Apollo, a Zeus and an Athena?

Yes, we certainly do, I said.

And they are your gods?

They are our Ancestors and Lords.

Ok, but you agree that they are yours, right?

Yes, I have agreed that they are, though I'm worried about what's going to happen to me now that I've agreed.

And these gods are alive? [e] You've agreed that whatever has a soul is alive, so unless you are going to say that Athena has no soul, you must agree that she is alive.

Oh, yes, they do have souls.

Then they are alive?

They are alive.

And didn't you also agree that something alive is yours when you are free to sell it, give it away or sacrifice it to whichever god you choose?

Yes, I agreed, so there's no escape for me, Euthydemus.

Then tell me this, since you've agreed that Zeus [303a] and the other gods are yours, are you free to sell them, give them away and use them however you want, just as with the animals that are yours?

When he said that, Crito, I just lay there speechless as if the argument had knocked me out.

By Herakles, bravo! What a fine argument! shouted Ctesippus, as if he were rushing in to bring water and a towel to a boxer who had just lost the match.

Dionysodorus took a victory lap and asked Ctesippus, Is Herakles a bravo, or is Bravo a Herakles?

By Poseidon, I give up, said Ctesippus. What incredible arguments! The two are unbeatable!

SOCRATES. [b] At that point, my dear friend Crito, everybody present exploded with applause for the argument and the two men. Thoroughly entertained, we were all laughing and clapping until we exhausted ourselves. Up to that point, you see, it had been only those devoted to Euthydemus who had been cheering at the conclusion of each argument, but now it was almost as if the very pillars of the Lyceum were happily cheering for the two men.

I was ready to concede that [c] I had never seen anyone so wise, and I was totally enthralled by their wisdom so I turned myself to praise and extol them, and said, You two are a blessedly happy pair for having such an amazing nature that you have accomplished such a feat so quickly in so short a time. Your arguments have many other beautiful features, Euthydemus and Dionysodorus, but one in particular stands out as especially magnificent, and that is that you don't care at all about the majority of people, or prestigious dignitaries or the socially prominent; [d] you care only about people like yourselves.* I am certain that there are only a very few people like you who would tolerate* these arguments. Others won't understand them, and so I am certain that they would be more ashamed to refute others with such arguments than to have others use such arguments to refute them.

But there is another aspect of your arguments that will play well before a popular audience and that people will quite like. Whenever you say something outrageous like that nothing is beautiful* or good or white and so on,* or when you say that The Other isn't at all other, [e] you "sew up the mouths of men" as the saying goes. On it's own that might ruffle some feathers, but since you sew up your own mouths as well,* it's actually pretty amusing and nobody takes offense.

But the greatest thing is that you've got everything worked out so well that anybody can learn it in no time at all. I witnessed this first hand because I paid close attention to Ctesippus and I saw how quickly he was able to imitate you.* [304a] It is quite a fine thing that your proficiency can be picked up so quickly by others, but that makes it quite unsuited to public discussion. If you take my advice you'll be careful not to argue in front of a large group because they'll learn your maneuvers quickly and give you no credit at all. The best thing would be just to argue with each other in private, and if you do allow anybody else to join you, it should only be someone who has paid you a fee. [b] You'll give this same advice to your students too if you are sensible: they should never argue with anyone except you and each other. Rare items can fetch a high price, Euthydemus—although water is cheapest and best, according to Pindar.*

But come now, admit Clinias and me as students. We talked a little more after that but then we left.

So Crito, think seriously about joining us as students of these two men, [c] since they say they will teach anyone who will pay their fee and won't deny anyone because of their age or character. What's more, you'll be interested to hear that they say learning from them will in no way hinder you from making money.

CRITO. I certainly do enjoy a good discussion, Socrates, and I would love to learn something from them, but I'm afraid I am not one of those people you referred to when you said that Euthydemus and Dionysodorus care only about people like themselves.* [d] I'm actually one of those people who would rather be refuted by their arguments than refute others with them.

It's ridiculous for me to advise you, Socrates, but I'd like to report something that I heard. As I said earlier,* there were so many people gathered around you yesterday that I couldn't really hear what was being said. Anyway, as I was walking around, someone left your group and came up to me. He thinks himself to be very wise, and he's one of those clever men* who write speeches* for people to deliver at trials.

Crito, he said to me, why are you walking away? Don't you heed these wise men?

No, by god, I replied, I couldn't hear a thing because of the crowd, even though I stood as close as I could.

Well it really was worth hearing.

[e] What did I miss?

Oh, you would have heard the discussion of men who are the wisest among the current generation at this type of argument.

What did you learn from them, I asked.

I learned just what anyone learns when they listen to such fools making much unworthy ado about what is worth nothing at all.

Those are the words he used. Anyway, then I asked him, Isn't philosophy a pretty sophisticated pursuit?

Sophisticated! [305a] It's worthless nonsense if you ask me. If you had been there you would have been ashamed of your friend—it was revolting to see how willing he was to hand himself over to people who don't care at all about what's being talked about but cling to every word. And as I was just saying, it's knuckleheads like this who are the most influential people today. The fact is, Crito, that this entire business and everybody who wastes their time on it are pathetic and ridiculous.

Personally, Socrates, [b] I don't think he was right to condemn the entire business, and I don't think anybody else would be right to condemn it either. However, the willingness to carry on a discussion with such people in front of a large audience—I do think he was right to blame that.*

SOCRATES. Such men are amazing, Crito. But I don't yet know what to say in reply to his condemnation of philosophy. Tell me, this man who approached you, was he an orator, one of those clever men who does battle in the law courts; or was he a speech writer, someone who equips an orator and sends him into battle?

CRITO. [c] Oh, by god, he's not an orator at all; in fact I don't think he's ever appeared in court. But people do say that he understands the business, by god, and he's a clever man who writes clever speeches.

SOCRATES. Now I understand. Actually, I was about to say something about them myself. These are the men whom Prodicus describes as occupying the borderlands between the philosopher and the statesman.* They think they are the wisest people of all—and not just that they are in reality the wisest, but that they also appear to be the wisest to the majority of people, so that the only ones [d] standing in the way of their universal esteem are the philosophers. They believe that if they can put down the philosophers as worthless, then they can win the undisputed victory in the eyes of everyone for the reputation of being wise. They really do think themselves truly to be the very wisest people, so whenever they are tripped up in an informal conversation, they claim to have been discredited by Euthydemus and his group.

Their claim to wisdom has a certain plausibility: they are moderately familiar with philosophy,* and moderately familiar with statesmanship—[e] it's plausible to think that they have as much of each as they need, and by avoiding the risks that come with statesmanship and the disputes that come with philosophy, they enjoy the fruits of wisdom in safety and peace.

CRITO. Well what do you think about it, Socrates? Their view certainly does seem quite plausible.

SOCRATES. It's more plausible than true. [306a] It's not easy to convince them that when you are in between good and bad by having a little of both, although you are better than the bad, you are also worse than the good. Alternatively, if you are in between two good things, you are actually worse than both of them because you are not as useful as either of them is for achieving its own distinctive purpose. The only case where something in the middle is actually better than what it's in between is [b] when it's in between two bad things, because it isn't quite as bad as either of the things it shares in. So if philosophy and statesmanship* are both good, each one being good for its own distinctive purpose, then these clever speech writers are worse than both because they have only a little bit of both. If one is bad and the other is good, then they will be better than one, but they will be worse than the other. The only way they could be better than both is if philosophy and statesmanship are both bad. But I don't think [c] they will agree that they are both bad, or that one is bad and the other good. The truth of the matter is that they are worse than philosophers at achieving the distinctive purpose of philosophy, and they are also worse than statesmen at achieving the distinctive purpose of statesmanship; and so while they want to be thought of as being in first place, they are actually in third place.

But, Crito, we shouldn't be angry with them because of what they desire, although we do need to see them as they truly are. We should treat them with compassion, [d] and in fact we should be friendly to anyone who has anything at all intelligent to say and makes a robust effort to follow through on their line of thought.

CRITO. In any case, Socrates, like I've said before, I'm still at a loss as to what to do with my sons.* The youngest one is still small, but Critoboulos has already reached the age where I need to find someone who will do him some good. You know that I've made my children a very high priority; [e] I was careful about the woman I married so that my sons would have a noble lineage on their mother's side, and I've been careful about money so that they would be well off financially. But when I spend time with you, Socrates, I feel that I must be crazy to focus so much on these sorts of things and neglect their education. On the other hand, when I look at the people who profess to be effective teachers, I am appalled; to tell you the truth, Socrates, when I've considered their credentials I find them to be totally unsuitable. [307a] In the end I just don't know how to turn the lad to philosophy.

SOCRATES. My dear friend Crito, don't you know that in every business, the inferior are many and worthless while the superior are few and worth a great deal? Take gymnastics for example. Don't you think it is a fine thing? And the same with money-making, rhetoric and generalship?

CRITO. Yes, I certainly do.

SOCRATES. And have you seen that in each of these pursuits, [b] the majority of practitioners does a ridiculously poor job?

CRITO. Yes, indeed, by god, that's the truth.

SOCRATES. And is that going to make you shun them all and not entrust your son to any of them?

CRITO. No, that wouldn't be right at all, Socrates.

SOCRATES. Then don't do what you ought not do, Crito. Forget about those who practice philosophy— whether they are good or bad—and put philosophy itself well and truly to the test. [c] If philosophy seems to you to be a worthless pursuit, then turn absolutely everybody away from it, not just your sons. But if, on the other hand, it appears to you to be what I believe it to be, then pursue it and work at it with confidence,* as the saying goes, "both you and your children."*

APOLOGY

(SOCRATES' DEFENSE)

Setting: Athens, inside of the court of the Archon Basileus. The year is 399 BCE. Meletus has concluded his speech prosecuting Socrates for impiety and corrupting the youth.

Characters (in order of appearance):
Socrates (469-399; 70 years old, from a middle class family, not handsome at all; his name is traditionally pronounced "SOCK-ra-teez," though "so-KROT-ays" is closer to the original)
Meletus (probably around 20 years old, undistinguished poet; his name is traditionally pronounced "mel-EE-tuss," though "MEL-ay-toss" is closer to the original)

Dramatic Structure:
Prologue: Socrates intends to focus on the truth (17a1-18a6)
Statement of the Case: separation into two accusers (18a7-19a7)
Defense Part 1: against the Old Accusers (19a8-24b2)
Defense Part 2: against the New Accusers (24b3-28a1)
Defense Part 3: Socrates' divine mission (28a2-34b5)
Conclusion: how the jury should decide the case (34b6-35d8)
Socrates' Punishment: Socrates proposes a fine (35e1-38b9)
After Sentencing: Socrates' final address (38c1-42a5)

SOCRATES. [17a] I don't know* what impact my accusers had on you, men of Athens,* but they spoke so persuasively that I almost forgot myself.* However, almost nothing that they said is true. I was most astonished by one of the many lies they told: that was when they said that you have to be careful not to let yourselves be deceived by me, [b] as if I am a clever speaker.* That was their most embarrassing claim because it will soon be refuted when I show that I am in no way a clever speaker, unless by "clever"* they mean someone who speaks the truth. If that's what they mean, then I am indeed an orator, though not one who will sink to their level.

So as I just mentioned, my accusers have said almost nothing that is true. But from me you will hear the whole truth—though not in flowery language like theirs, by god,* [c] embellished with fancy words and phrases. You will hear what it occurs to me to say, without elaborate planning in advance, because I believe that what I say is right, and no one should expect anything else. It wouldn't be fitting for a man of my age to come before you like a child making up an elaborate story. So there is one thing I sincerely beg of you, please do not shout and interrupt* me if you hear me defending myself in the same language it has been my habit to use in the marketplace, at the money-changers' tables, and other places, where* many of you have heard me. [d] I'm over seventy years old and this is my very first appearance in court, so the style of speaking used here is foreign* to me. Now, if I were literally a foreigner, you would surely excuse me for speaking in the dialect I'd been raised to speak; [18a] so I make this request, and I think it's a fair one, that you disregard my manner of speaking—whether it is worse or better than you are used to hearing in court—and consider and pay attention to just this one thing: is what I say right or not; for this is the virtue of a juror, just as the virtue of an orator* is to speak the truth.

First, then, it is right for me to defend myself, men of Athens, against the false accusations brought by my first accusers; after that I'll deal with my later accusers. [b] Many people for many years have arisen to accuse me before you, though nothing that they say is true. I fear my early accusers much more than Anytus and his followers; he is dangerous enough, but these others are more dangerous: they got to many of you when you were children* and misled you and made false accusations against me, saying, "Socrates is a wise man, a deep thinker who inquires into the heavens and all things under the earth and can make the weaker argument stronger." [c] The people who gave me this reputation are the more dangerous accusers because whoever listens to them thinks that a man who inquires into such things cannot possibly acknowledge the gods.* On top of that, there are many accusers like this, and they've been making these accusations for a long time, talking to you when you were young and impressionable and when there was nobody around to come to my defense. The most frustrating thing of all [d] is that it is impossible for me to know or to state their names, unless one happens to be a comedian.* It is extremely difficult to deal with those who persuaded you out of malice and slander—not to mention the ripple effect when the people who were persuaded went and persuaded others: I can't bring them forward and cross-examine* them. I'm forced to shadow box, trying to refute someone who isn't even there to answer questions. So please appreciate the significance of this distinction I've drawn between my two sets of accusers: some are quite old, but others are new; [e] and bear in mind that I must first defend myself against the former because you have been listening to them for much longer.

Well, then, I must make my defense, men of Athens, [19a] and in the short time allowed try to remove from your minds the slander you were so long in acquiring. I wish for this result, if it is better for you and for me,* and even more I'd like my defense to be successful,* but I'm well aware of how difficult this task is. Let it be as god wills; I must obey the law and make my defense.

Let's start from the beginning: what is the original accusation [b] from which the slander against me arose, and on which, I suppose, Meletus relied when he brought his indictment against me? What did the original slanderers say? Let me put it as if I were reading an affidavit: "Socrates is a wrongdoer and a meddler who inquires into things below the earth and in the sky, he makes the weaker argument stronger, [c] and teaches others these same things." It's something like that. You've seen it yourselves in Aristophanes' comedy,* someone named "Socrates" is suspended in the air, talking about how he walks on air and spouting all kinds of nonsense that I don't understand at all. I mean no disrespect for such knowledge, if anyone is wise in such things—I don't want Meletus to bring me up on charges of slander—but I have no part in it. [d] In fact, I call most of you as witnesses: all those who have ever heard me talking—and there are many of you here today—speak up and tell* the others if you have ever heard me discussing* such matters, even a little bit. Once you realize that there is nothing to this allegation, you'll know that the other reports are just as false. If any of you has heard that I try to teach people, and expect a fee for doing so, it's simply not true.

[e] Not that there's anything wrong with that; in fact I think it quite admirable if someone actually could teach such things, someone like Gorgias of Leontini, or Prodicus of Ceos, or Hippias of Elis. Each of these three is able to go into any town at all and persuade the young men to abandon their fellow citizens in favor of him, [20a] and convince them to pay a fee and be grateful on top of all that—and keep in mind that these young men could spend time with, and learn from, any of his fellow citizens for free!

Come to think of it, I have heard that there is another wise man visiting here from Paros. I was talking with Callias the son of Hipponicus, who's paid more than anyone else in sophist's fees. He has two sons, so I asked, him, "If your sons were colts or calves, we'd be able to find and hire a supervisor for them [b] who would make them fine and good with respect to their own proper virtue; I suppose that would be a horse-trainer* or a rancher. But since they are human beings, whom do you intend to get to supervise them? Who is knowledgeable in this form of virtue,* I mean human and civic virtue? I'm sure you've thought about this because you have two sons. Is there such a person who is knowledgeable in this form of virtue?"

"Certainly there is," he said.

"Well then who is he? Where is he from and what's his fee for teaching?" I asked.

"Evenus of Paros," he said, "and he charges five minae."*

I thought Evenus a blessedly happy man [c] if he truly possesses this craft without charging an excessive fee.* If I knew such things I certainly wouldn't sell myself short. But I do not know them.

One of you might reply to this, "But Socrates, what, then, *do* you do? How do you explain these slanderous allegations? Surely they wouldn't have arisen if you were doing nothing out of the ordinary, you must be behaving differently from most people.* Tell us what it is [d] so that our opinion of you won't be misguided." That is a legitimate request, and I will try to show you what has caused this slander, and how I gained this reputation. Please hear me out; some of you might think I'm joking, but I assure you that everything I'm about to say is true.

It is nothing other than a sort of wisdom* that has caused me to gain this reputation. What sort? I suppose you'd call it "human wisdom,"* and I guess I have it. Maybe those other men I was just talking about—Gorgias, Prodicus and the rest—[e] have a wisdom that is greater than mere human wisdom—I'm not sure what to call it, but I certainly do not have it, and anyone who says that I do is lying and is slandering me. Now, please do not interrupt me in what I'm about to tell you, even if you think I am boasting, because this testimony does not come from me but from a most venerable source: the witness I call to testify about my wisdom—if it is any kind of wisdom at all—is none other than the god at Delphi.*

I suppose you know Chaerophon. [21a] He was a friend of mine since we were young, and a friend of yours as well because he shared your exile and return.* Well, you know what sort of person he was: very passionate about anything he started. He actually went to Delphi and dared to ask the oracle—again, I beg you, please do not shout out—he asked if there was anyone wiser than I.* The Pythia's answer was that no one was wiser. Unfortunately, Chaerophon has died, so he cannot give evidence, but his brother is here in court to testify to all this since he was an eyewitness.

[b] Please keep in mind my point in telling you this: I want to show you the origin of the slander about me. When I heard this I thought to myself, "What does the god mean? What is this riddle?* I am well aware that I am not wise in any way at all, so what could the god possibly mean in calling me the wisest person? Surely he's not lying; that isn't permitted* for the god." For a long time I wondered what it could mean, and reluctantly I set about the following sort of investigation.

I went to a man with a reputation for wisdom [c] to see if I could refute the oracle and say to it, "Look! This man is wiser than I, but you said that I am the wisest." I talked with this man—there's no need for me to mention his name, he's quite involved in politics—and he made quite an impression on me: he seemed to me to be the sort of person who appears very wise to many people, and especially to himself, but in fact is not. So I tried to show him that he thought he was wise when he was not. [d] That didn't go over so well with him or with the people standing around listening, so I left and thought to myself, "I am wiser than this man; neither one of us really knows anything fine and good, but he thinks he knows when he doesn't; I don't know any such thing, but at least I don't think that I do. So it seems that in this small way I am wiser: what I don't know, I don't think that I know."

After this, I went to a man who was thought to be even wiser than the first, but it turned out exactly the same way. [e] It was then I realized that I was making enemies.* I kept on talking like this with person after person although I was well aware of how unpopular I was becoming. This bothered me, and even made me a little afraid, but I had to take the god very seriously; I sincerely believed that I had to continue investigating the oracle's meaning, and that meant talking with everybody who [22a] had a reputation for knowledge.* And by the dog,* men of Athens—for I have to tell you the truth—what I found was remarkable. As I carried out my investigation in service to the god of Delphi, those with the greatest reputations seemed the most deficient, and those who were thought inferior turned out to be the more intelligent ones. I have to tell you about my journey—my "labors of Herakles" if you will—that resulted in* finding the oracle to be irrefutable.

After the politicians I went to the poets: the tragedians, [b] the dithyrambs* and the others. I assumed that in comparison with them, it would be obvious that I was the ignorant one. So I took up the poems they seemed to have worked on the most, and asked them what they meant, thinking that I would learn something worthwhile from them. It is shameful to speak the truth here, but that is what I must do: any of the bystanders could have explained the poems better than the authors themselves. It didn't take me long to realize that poets compose their poems not from wisdom, [c] but from some natural talent or divine inspiration, like a seer or a prophet who says many fine things but doesn't actually know what he's saying. I think poetic inspiration must be something like that, but because of their poetry they think that they are the wisest people when it comes to things other than poetry,* and they most certainly are not. So I left them thinking that I had the same advantage over them that I have over the politicians.

Finally I came to the artisans. [d] I was well aware that I didn't know anything, and I was sure I would find that they know many fine things. I wasn't disappointed. They know many things, and in those respects they are wiser than I. Unfortunately, it seemed to me that the artisans have the same fault as the poets: because of their skill they think they possess the greatest wisdom in other matters as well. This mistake casts a sort of shadow over their wisdom. [e] So on behalf of the oracle I asked myself whether I should prefer to be like them—sharing both their wisdom and their folly—or should prefer to stay as I am, lacking their wisdom, but free of their folly. Honestly, I had to say that I prefer to stay as I am.

This investigation [23a] has aroused a great deal of hostility against me, and this hostility has become a very grave burden. It is the source of the many slanders I've endured, especially the slander of being called "wise." Whenever I refute someone's claim to wisdom in a particular subject, the bystanders assume that I am wise in that subject matter. But the truth is, gentlemen, that god is wise, and in the oracle he is saying that human wisdom is worth little or nothing. It seems that he used my name, "Socrates," [b] only as an example, as if to say, "That person among you is wisest who—like Socrates—knows that in truth he is worth nothing* with respect to wisdom." This is why I still search for anyone that I think is wise, whether citizen or foreigner, and in accordance with the will of god I investigate him. When someone shows me that he is not wise, I show him that he is not wise, and in doing so I am helping god. It is because I am a servant of god that I have no free time to engage in politics or even my own business, [c] which is why I live in great poverty.*

On top of that, my investigations have created an additional source of hostility against me. There are many young men—especially those from wealthy families—who have a great deal of free time, and who like to follow me around listening when I examine people. In fact, they often imitate me and try their hands at examining others. I guess they find no shortage of people who think they are knowledgeable but who in fact know little or nothing, and who, instead of being angry with themselves, are angry at me [d] and say, "Socrates is an infectious disease and he's corrupting the youth." If you ask these people what I do, or what I teach, they don't have an answer because they are ignorant of what I do, so in order to avoid looking like complete idiots they simply repeat the stock allegations against all philosophers about "things below the earth and in the sky," and about "not believing in the gods" and "making the weaker argument stronger." I think these people just don't want to admit the truth, which is that they pretend to be knowledgeable, but in fact they know nothing. They are ambitious, [e] impassioned and numerous, and they speak forcefully and persuasively about me. For a very long time now they have filled your ears with vicious slander.

This slander is the basis of the allegations brought against me by Meletus, Anytus and Lycon. Meletus is angry on behalf of the poets, [24a] Anytus on behalf of the artisans and politicians, and Lycon on behalf of the orators. So, as I said at the start, I would be amazed if I could rid your minds of the slander against me that has had so long to grow, when I have such a short time to speak.

Well, there you have it, men of Athens; that's the truth. I haven't concealed anything large or small, or held anything back, although I know quite well that it is this very habit of speaking the truth openly that has raised so much hostility against me. But that very hostility is itself a clear sign that I'm telling you the truth: this really is the slander against me, and these really are the causes of that slander. [b] Whether you investigate now or later, this is what you will find.

That is my defense against my first accusers and the accusations they have made against me. Now I will defend myself against Meletus "the good and patriotic citizen," as he calls himself, and my later accusers.*

Let's take up Meletus' affidavit, which he presents as if it states a different set of accusations than what I've already discussed. It goes something like this:* "Socrates is a wrongdoer because he corrupts the youth,* and [c] he does not acknowledge* the gods the city acknowledges, but other new deities." Such is the complaint. Let's examine it point by point.

He says that I am a wrongdoer because I corrupt the youth, but I say that Meletus is doing wrong by pulling a sort of prank on the court, bringing someone up on charges that are a joke to him, things he's never taken seriously in his life. I'll try to make this clear to you.

Meletus, come here and tell us [d] whether you think it is extremely important for our young men to become as good as they possibly can.

MELETUS. I do.

SOCRATES. Then tell the jury who makes them better? Obviously you know because you care.* You say that you've found the one who corrupts them: me. Then you drag me into court and accuse me before the jury. So who benefits them? Tell the jury. What's the matter, Meletus, why the silence?* Don't you have an answer? Don't you see that you are embarrassing yourself and giving the jury a clear sign that I'm speaking the truth: you don't really care about the youth at all. Come on, tell us, who improves them?

MELETUS. The laws.

SOCRATES. [e] I didn't ask you *what* improves them, I asked you *who* improves them. So let me re-phrase the question: who improves the youth, given the fact that they know the laws?

MELETUS. These jurors, Socrates.

SOCRATES. What are you saying, Meletus, that these men are able to educate the young and improve them?

MELETUS. Certainly.

SOCRATES. All of them, or only some of them?

MELETUS. All of them.

SOCRATES. Well, by Hera, what an abundance of benefactors! But what about the audience? Do they improve the youth or not?

MELETUS. [25a] They do.

SOCRATES. And how about the members of the Council?

MELETUS. The Council members do too.

SOCRATES. And what about the members of the legislative assembly? Do they corrupt the youth or do they all improve them?

MELETUS. They also improve them.

SOCRATES. So every Athenian, with the sole exception of myself, makes the youth fine and good. I alone corrupt them. Is that what you are saying?

MELETUS. That is exactly what I'm saying.

SOCRATES. So by your reckoning I'm the one and only bad influence in Athens. Tell me this: do you think it works that way with horses? [b] Everybody improves them, but there's just one person who corrupts them? Isn't it completely the opposite? Isn't it just one person, or only a few who improve them: the horse-trainers? The many corrupt them, if they keep and ride horses without proper training, don't they? Isn't it the same, Meletus, with all animals? Obviously it is, whether you and Anytus admit it or not. It would be an extremely happy* state of affairs if just one person corrupted the youth and everybody else improved them. [c] You've made it clear to everybody, Meletus, that you have never actually thought carefully about the youth; you've revealed how uncaring you truly are, and you've shown that you've never cared about the things you drag me into court over.

Next, Meletus, tell us: is it better to live amongst fellow citizens who are honest or dishonest? Oh, come now, please answer; I'm not asking a hard question. Don't dishonest people always end up doing something bad to the people around them, and don't good people do good?

MELETUS. Yes, exactly.

SOCRATES. [d] And does anyone want to be harmed rather than benefitted by the people around him? Please answer the question; the law requires you to answer. Does anyone wish to be harmed?

MELETUS. No indeed.

SOCRATES. Ok, then, are you accusing me of corrupting the youth and making them more dishonest voluntarily or involuntarily?

MELETUS. Voluntarily.

SOCRATES. But then don't you see what you are saying, Meletus? At your young age are you so much wiser than I am at my age that you know that bad people always do bad things to those around them and good people always do good, [e] while I am such an ignorant fool that I don't realize how much of a risk I am running of being harmed by the people I corrupt—*voluntarily*, as you say? No, I don't believe you, Meletus, and I don't think anyone else will believe you. Either I don't corrupt the youth at all, or if I do, [26a] I do it involuntarily.* Either way, your accusation is false. Look, you don't haul someone into court for involuntarily making a mistake; you just point out to them that they are making a mistake. Obviously if I learn that I'm making a mistake I'll stop. But instead of showing me the error of my ways, you have deliberately avoided me, preferring to bring me to court instead, which is for people who need punishment not instruction.

You see, men of Athens, that what I said is clearly true: [b] Meletus has never cared about any of this.

Let's move on to the next allegation, shall we Meletus? Exactly how is it that, according to you, I corrupt the youth? Your official indictment seem to allege that I corrupt them by teaching them to acknowledge new deities instead of the gods the city acknowledges. Is that what you mean?

MELETUS. Yes, that is very much what I mean.

SOCRATES. Then for the sake of these very gods* we are talking about, Meletus, please clarify your allegation. There are two very different accusations you might be making, and I don't know which of the two you mean. [c] You might mean to say that I acknowledge the existence of some gods, and teach others to acknowledge them—in which case I acknowledge the existence of gods and so am not guilty of the charge of atheism*—but these gods are different from the ones the city recognizes. Alternatively, you might be saying that I don't acknowledge any gods at all and that I teach this to others. Which is it?

MELETUS. That's what I mean: you are a complete atheist.

SOCRATES. [d] Are you serious, Meletus? Doesn't everybody, myself included, believe that the sun and moon are gods?

MELETUS. No, by god, gentlemen of the jury.* Socrates says that the sun is a rock and the moon is dirt.*

SOCRATES. Meletus, do you think you are accusing Anaxagoras?* Are you so contemptuous of the jury that you think they are all illiterate and don't know that cheap editions* of Anaxagoras' books are available from every bookseller? [e] His doctrines are so distinctive that everybody would laugh at me if I tried to take credit for them. By god, Meletus, do you sincerely think that I don't believe any god exists?

MELETUS. No, by god, you don't believe in any gods at all.

SOCRATES. You are incredible, Meletus. In fact, I think I can show that even you don't really believe what you are saying. Men of Athens, Meletus seems to me to be one of those young zealots who has let his emotions run away with him. [27a] He's like a child with a riddle, "I wonder if I can fool Socrates and everybody else, hiding the fact that I'm joking around and contradicting myself?" Look again at the indictment; he almost comes right out and says, "Socrates is guilty of not acknowledging gods and of acknowledging gods." That's got to be a joke. So let's ask him what he means. [b] And please don't shout or interrupt me if I question him in my usual way.

Can someone acknowledge the activities of human beings without acknowledging human beings?

[Meletus objects to answering Socrates' questions.]*

Please make him just answer the question without raising objection after objection. Can someone acknowledge the activities of horses without acknowledging horses? Or acknowledge flute playing without acknowledging flute players?

[Meletus refuses to answer.]

No, obviously not. If you aren't going to speak, I'll have to give the answer myself. But answer this next question, [c] can someone acknowledge the activities of deities without acknowledging deities?*

[Officers of the court instruct Meletus to answer.]

MELETUS. No, it's not possible.

SOCRATES. Thank you for answering, although you answered only because the court compelled you to. Now, you yourself have said that I acknowledge, and teach others to acknowledge, the activities of deities—whether old or new—it's written down in your affidavit that I acknowledge the activities of deities. So it necessarily follows that I acknowledge deities, isn't that so?

[Meletus again refuses to answer.]

Of course it is; I'll put you down as agreeing since you don't answer. [d] Now, one more thing, we all hold that deities are gods or the children of gods, don't we?

MELETUS. Of course.

SOCRATES. Therefore, if I hold that there are deities—as you yourself admit—and if deities are gods, then you've got to be joking when you accuse me of holding that gods do exist and also that they do not. Even if deities are not gods themselves but are the children of gods—as in many myths where one parent is a god and the other is a mortal—who can believe in the children of gods without believing in gods? [e] That would be like believing in mules without believing in horses and donkeys. Either you drew up the indictment against me as a sort of test to see if we could guess your riddle or else you couldn't find any genuine crime to accuse me of. You can't expect anyone with even a bit of sense to agree that someone can believe in the activities of gods and deities without also believing in [28a] gods, deities or heroes.

There's no need to drag this out any longer, men of Athens. This is sufficient to prove that I am not guilty of what I've actually been indicted for. Unfortunately you know all too well that what I said earlier is true: a great deal of hostility from a great many people has grown up against me. I can escape the official charges, but what will catch me—if I am indeed caught—is not Meletus or Anytus or anything other than malice and slander. They've caught many good men before, [b] and I'm sure they will do so in the future; there's no chance that it will stop with me.

At this point, someone might ask, "Aren't you ashamed,* Socrates, for conducting your affairs in such a way that you are at risk of being put to death?" I would be right to answer as follows:

"You are wrong if you think that a man who is worth anything at all should weigh the risks of life or death. Rather, he should consider one thing and one thing only: whether he is doing what is right or wrong,* whether he is performing the deeds of a good man or a bad man. [c] On your account, the demi-gods who died at Troy would have been a worthless lot, including the son of Thetis. He scorned danger in comparison with disgrace when his mother—a god—said something like this to him when he was eager to kill Hector, 'Oh my son,* if you avenge the death of your companion Patroclus and kill Hector, then you shall die, for next after Hector, death is prepared for you.' When Achilles heard this, he made light of death and danger for [d] he was far more afraid of living a bad life and not avenging his friends. He replied, 'Then let me die next,* after bringing justice to the wrongdoer, so that I will not remain here a laughingstock beside the beaked ships, a worthless weight upon the earth.' Do you think he even considered death and danger?"

The truth of the matter, men of Athens, is this: when a man has taken his stand, whether he thinks it is best or he has been stationed by his commanding officer, there he must remain,* it seems to me, and face the danger weighing neither death nor anything else before shame. It would be hypocritical of me if, on the one hand, [e] I remained at my post risking death at Potidaea, Amphipolis and Delium,* where I had been stationed by my duly elected* commanding officer, but then on the other hand I deserted my post because I was afraid of dying when I had been stationed by god—as I believe that I have been—to lead a philosophical life and to examine myself and others. [29a] I really would be a hypocrite if I did that, and it would be right to haul me into court on the grounds that I didn't acknowledge the gods and I refused to obey the oracle because I was afraid of dying and I thought that I was wise when I was not.

To fear death is nothing other than to think oneself to be wise when one is not because it is thinking that one knows something that one does not know. People fear death as if they know it is the greatest of evils when in fact nobody knows if it is actually the greatest of goods for a human being. [b] Isn't this the most disgraceful kind of ignorance: to think that one knows what one does not know? Perhaps this is what sets me apart from other people, and if I am wiser it is only in this respect: I do not in fact know about the afterlife, and I don't think that I know about it. What I do know is that it is bad and shameful to do wrong and to disobey one's better,* whether god or man. Whenever I am confronted with things that I know to be bad, and things that, for all I know, are actually good, I shall always fear and flee the former, not the latter.

[c] Anytus told you that I would flee the city rather than appear before you and risk the possibility of execution. He was confident that you would not acquit me because he warned you that if you let me go your sons would be thoroughly corrupted by what Socrates teaches. Suppose you don't believe him and instead say to me,

"Socrates, we do not believe Anytus and so we will acquit you on the condition that you cease and desist your investigations, and that you stop doing philosophy; [d] if you are caught doing either, you shall die."

If you were to acquit me on those terms* I would say to you,

"Men of Athens, I am your devoted friend but I shall be persuaded more* by god than by you, and as long as I live and am able, I will not stop doing philosophy, exhorting you to pursue wisdom and showing you that you are not yet wise, saying in my usual way to everyone I happen to come across, 'My good man, since you are an Athenian you are a citizen of the greatest city, one with the highest reputation for wisdom and strength. So aren't you ashamed of yourself that you care so much about money, [e] fame and status but don't care about, or even consider, intelligence,* truth or the improvement of your soul?' If anyone disputes this and says that he does care I won't let him go; I'll question him, examine him and cross-examine him, and if it seems to me that he does not possess the virtue he claims to have [30a] I'll reprimand him for neglecting things that are most worthy of his attention and for focusing on trivialities. I'll do this for young and old, both foreigner and citizen, but even more so for citizens because you are more nearly related* to me. Know well that god commands me to do this, and I think that no greater good has ever come to you than my service to the god. For all I do is go around trying to persuade you, both young and old, that you should not care for your bodies or your possessions nearly as much as you care about [b] how your soul will be in the best condition possible, saying 'Virtue does not come from possessions, but from virtue* come possessions and all good things for human beings, both individually and collectively.'"*

Now if this message corrupts the young then so be it, but no one can claim that I say anything other than this. So believe Anytus or not. Acquit me or not. [c] I will not change course—not even if I have to die many times.

[There is an uproar in the court.]

Don't shout out and interrupt me, men of Athens; remember I asked you not to interrupt me but to listen because I think it will be to your advantage to hear what I have to say. I am about to say some other things that might make you shout out but please don't.

Know that if you kill me, being the sort of man that I am, you will be doing a greater harm to yourselves than to me. Meletus and Anytus won't harm me because they are not able to harm me; I don't think it is permitted* [d] for a better man* to be harmed by a worse. They might kill me, banish me or get me disenfranchised—they and others may think these to be great harms, but I do not. It is a much greater harm to do what Meletus is now doing: he's trying to get a man executed unjustly. So although you might think that I am making my defense on my own behalf, really I am speaking in defense of you to prevent you from making the mistake of [e] condemning god's gift to you.

If you kill me, you won't easily find another like me, someone who—to use a comical analogy—was attached to the city by god as a sort of gadfly on a sluggish horse who needs a good sting to get it moving. It seems to me that god put me in this city to perform that sort of function: rousing, persuading and reprimanding each one of you [31a] all the time and everywhere. You won't easily get another like me, and so if you take my advice, you will spare me. You might be annoyed with me and, like someone who is trying to take a nap swats at a fly that keeps waking him up, you might listen to Anytus and kill me. Then you could sleep the rest of your lives away unless god cares so much for you that he sends another like me to sting you awake again.

It should be obvious that I am the sort of person who is likely to be a gift from god to the city: [b] my life doesn't look like an ordinary human life. I've neglected my own career and finances for years, and instead I've always been concerned for you, coming up to each of you individually like a father or older brother urging you to care about virtue. You could make some sense of this behavior if I somehow turned a profit or charged a fee, but you can see for yourselves that as shameless as their accusations are, not even my accusers could be so shameless [c] as to trot out a witness willing to testify that I even once charged or asked for a fee. But I can give you a sufficient witness that I am speaking the truth: my poverty.

Perhaps you want to ask me why I haven't been politically active if I'm so civic-minded. In fact you've heard me mention the cause many times, [d] and Meletus even mocked it in his charges. Ever since I was a child, a godly and divine sign* has come to me, and whenever it comes it always tells me not to do what I am about to do, it never urges me to continue. This is what has opposed my entering into politics, and it seems to me that it has been right to do so: if I had entered politics long ago, then long ago I would have been executed and neither you nor I would have profited from it. [e] Don't be annoyed with me for speaking the truth. That man is beyond salvation who opposes you—or any majority—and prevents anything unjust and illegal* from happening. [32a] The man who fights for justice must live a private life and stay out of politics if he expects to be safe for very long at all.

I can give you very clear proofs that this, and not mere words but something that you respect: deeds. Listen to what has happened to me and you will know that I yield to no one contrary to what is right out of a fear of death, not even if I will be killed on the spot for not yielding. What I'm about to tell you might sound like the usual sort of boasting* you hear from defendants, but every word is true.

I have held political office only once: [b] I served as a member of the Council. Our tribe Antiochis* happened to be presiding when you resolved to try as a group the ten generals who failed to rescue the drowning men after the sea battle.* The trial was illegal, as you all came to see later, but at that time I was the only member of the executive committee to oppose you, I was the only one who voted against your doing something in violation of the laws. Public advocates were ready to impeach and arrest me, and you shouted out encouragement to them, [c] but I thought that I should take the risk and stand with law and justice rather than to join you in committing an injustice out of fear of prison or death.

That happened when Athens was still a democracy. When the oligarchy* was imposed, the Thirty summoned me with four others to the Rotunda* and ordered us to arrest Leon of Salamis so they could execute him. They gave many such orders to many other people because they wanted to implicate as many as possible in their crimes. [d] Then I showed by my actions, not only by my words, that—to put it bluntly—I don't care about death; what I do care very much about is that I avoid doing anything unjust or impious. Despite their power, that government was not able to frighten me into doing anything unjust. When the five of us left the Rotunda I simply went home; the others went to Salamis and arrested Leon.* They probably would have executed me for disobeying their orders, but the government soon fell. [e] There are many witnesses who can testify to all this.

How long do you think I would have lived if I'd stayed involved in politics while acting like a decent human being, always helping the just cause as one ought to do and making that my highest priority? Not long at all. [33a] Throughout my entire life I have been the same kind of person in public as I am in private: I yield to no one contrary to what is right.

I am no different when it comes to those who slander me and say that they are my students. I have never been anyone's teacher. But of course if someone wants to listen in on my conversations I never begrudge them that opportunity. And I certainly don't ask someone for money to talk with me and shut up if they don't pay. [b] Young or old, rich or poor, I'm equally happy to talk to anyone who is willing to answer my questions and listen to me. If some of them turn out to be honest people and others don't, it's not right to say that I am the cause: I have never taught anybody anything, and I've never even offered to teach anybody anything. If someone claims that he learned something from me in private, or that he heard me talking about something in private that I don't talk about openly and in public, you can be certain that he's not telling the truth.

You might wonder why some people enjoy spending so much time with me. [c] I've already told you* the answer: some people enjoy listening to me examine those who think they are wise but are not. It can be amusing. And as I said,* I have been ordered to do this by god: the order has come from oracles and from dreams and in every way that a person's divinely allotted portion* in life orders him to do anything.

This is all true, and it is easily tested. Because if I am corrupting the youth, [d] and I've already succeeded in corrupting some of the youth, then by now some of them must have grown up and figured out that when they were young I gave them bad advice. Surely they would come forward now to accuse me and make me pay for the harm I've done them. Or if they don't want to come forward themselves, their fathers or brothers or some other relative would come forward on behalf of the family and make me pay. But you see that no one has stepped forward, and there are plenty to choose from right here in the court.* [e] You are well acquainted with seven of the young men who have regularly joined in my conversations: Critobulus, Aeschines, Epigenes, Theodotus, Theages, Plato and Apollodorus—they are here in court today all except for Theodotus and Theages who are dead. They can provide evidence of my influence on them, or their relatives who are here can do so: the fathers of Critobulus, Aeschines and Epigenes are all here, [34a] and the brothers of Theodotus, Theages, Plato and Apollodorus are here. There are many others I could mention as well. Surely Meletus ought to have called at least one of them as a witness. In fact, he can do so right now; I'll yield my time* to him if he wants to submit evidence from one of these witnesses. You see it is quite the opposite: all these people are actually here to help me—the person who corrupted their son or brother according to Meletus and Anytus. [b] Obviously people I've corrupted would defend me, but those I didn't corrupt, as well as the fathers and brothers of those I allegedly corrupted have no reason to come to my defense except for the one reason that is right and just: they know that Meletus is lying and that I am telling the truth.

That is my defense, gentlemen. Some of you may be [c] annoyed with me for not putting on more of a show. You may think back to when you were on trial for a much lighter offense than what I am being charged with, and you threw yourself on the mercy of the court with tears streaming down your face begging the judges to have pity on you. Some of you actually brought family members, friends and even your own children into court* to get as much pity as possible. But I shall do no such thing, despite facing grave danger. Comparing my defense with the display some of you have made in court might annoy some of you and you may be tempted to cast your vote against me in anger. [d] If one of you does feel this way—I don't expect that you do, but if you do—the appropriate thing to say in reply is this:

"I do have a family. I wasn't born 'from oak or stone'* as Homer says. I have a family including three sons;* one is almost grown and the other two are children, but I will not bring them here to beg you to acquit me."

Why won't I do this? I do not think that I'm better than you, [e] men of Athens, and I'm not trying to put you down or dishonor you. It's also not about whether I fear death or not. It's really about protecting our good names—mine, yours and Athens'. I simply don't think it is admirable for a man of my age to do those sorts of things, especially when people have made up their minds—whether they are right or wrong to think so—that [35a] Socrates is an exceptional individual. Now, if one of you seems to be exceptional in wisdom, courage or any other virtue and he were to carry on like this it would be shameful. But I have often seen someone who appeared to be an amazing role model behave in exactly this sort of way, thinking that it would be a terrible thing to be killed—as if he would be immortal if you didn't kill him. These people seem to me to bring shame upon our city, so that any foreigner observing such a spectacle [b] would assume that even those Athenians with exceptional virtue—the people whom the Athenians themselves judge to be worthy of the highest political offices and the greatest honors—are no better than women.* If you have a reputation worth protecting, then you shouldn't behave like that; and if someone does behave like that, you shouldn't sit back and let them get away with putting on such a spectacle, you should demonstrate that you will much more easily convict someone who makes a laughingstock of the city than someone who keeps a dignified silence.

Aside from protecting our reputations, I don't think it is right [c] to seek an acquittal by begging; one ought to instruct the jury of the facts and persuade them of the truth. The jury does not sit to dispense justice by corruptly favoring particular individuals, rather, the jury's job is to decide whose case is just; and the oath they swore was not to render whatever verdict they liked, but to judge according to the laws. Defendants should not induce you to violate your oaths, and you should not accustom yourselves to violating your oaths—neither action is pious.

So do not expect me to behave in ways that I think are neither admirable, nor [d] just, nor pious, especially when impiety is the thing for which Meletus has brought me to trial. Clearly if I resorted to some of these shameful tactics to get you to violate your sacred oaths I would be trying to get you to stop acknowledging the gods, and my defense against Meletus' accusations would prove that his accusations are actually true. But they are not true, men of Athens, because I do acknowledge the gods, and not even one of my accusers does. I leave it to you and to god to judge my case in whatever way will be best for me and for you.

[Socrates is convicted by a vote of 280 to 220.]*

[Meletus asks for the death penalty.]

[e] I'm not upset, men of Athens, at this [36a] result—that you have condemned me—and for several different reasons, and this result that has resulted* is not surprising to me. But what is really amazing to me is the number of votes cast on each side: I didn't think that the vote would be so close*—if only thirty people had changed their vote, I would have been acquitted. So it seems to me that I've actually been cleared of the charges Meletus brought against me, and not simply cleared of the charges—it is obvious to everyone that if Anytus* and Lycon hadn't come forward to accuse me, [b] Meletus would have been fined one thousand drachmas for failing to secure a fifth of the votes.*

The man estimates that I deserve death. Well, then, what counter-estimate* shall I propose? Obviously the counter-estimate should be accurate, but what would be accurate? What do I deserve to receive or to pay: after all, I haven't exactly led a quiet life, but I also haven't really cared about what most people care about—making money, managing the family business, rising to high military or political office, involving myself in some political faction or caucus. I thought that [c] I was too principled a person to survive for very long if I lived that way. So I didn't choose that path; it wouldn't have done you or me any good. Instead I came to each of you privately and did you the greatest favor that, in my opinion, one person can do for another: I tried to persuade each of you not to care more about your possessions than about how you will become as good and wise as possible, and not to care about the city's possessions more than the city itself.* [d] What do I deserve to receive for doing you this great favor? Something good, if I must give an accurate estimate of what I truly deserve; and the benefit I receive should be suitable for a person like myself. So what befits a poor man like myself who is your benefactor and needs free time to exhort you? Nothing would be so appropriate for such a man as permanent maintenance in the Prutaneion. That is surely more appropriate for a man like me than it is for someone who wins at the Olympic games with a pair or a team of horses: he gives you only the appearance of being happy, I exhort you to achieve the reality.* [e] And besides, he doesn't need the food; I do. So if I must estimate the true value of what I justly deserve, [37a] I estimate this: permanent maintenance in the Prutaneion.

You might think that I'm a bit too full of myself to say this, like when I talked about not begging you to pity me. But that's not what I'm doing, men of Athens; rather, it's like this. I am convinced that I wrong no one voluntarily. Obviously I am not convincing you—we have such a short time to talk with each other. I'm sure that you would be convinced if you had a law like they have elsewhere,* that cases involving the death penalty cannot occur on just one day [b] but must take place over several days. But as things are, it isn't easy to dispel such great slander in such a short time.

Since I am convinced that I wrong no one, I'm certainly not going to wrong myself by saying that I deserve to suffer something bad. What do I have to be afraid of? The penalty Meletus proposes? I've already told you* that I don't know whether death is a good thing or a bad thing, so why should I propose an alternative that I know full well to be bad? Imprisonment? [c] Why should I live in prison, a slave to the Eleven?* A fine and imprisonment until I pay? That comes to the same thing because as I just said, I don't have any money to pay a fine.

Shall I propose exile? Perhaps you would accept that, but what a coward clinging to life I would have to be to propose it. Do you think I'm too stupid to figure out that if you, my fellow citizens, are unable to put up with [d] my exhortations and discussions, and you find them so burdensome and intolerable that you are trying to get rid of me, then others won't easily tolerate them? They most certainly will not. What a fine life* I would be leading at my age, driven out of one city after another, for I know quite well that wherever I go, the young men will listen to me as they do here: if I shoo them away, they will persuade their elders to drive me out of the city; [e] if I don't shoo them away, their fathers and relatives will drive me out of the city for the sakes of the young men.

At this point you might ask, "Socrates, if we drive you out, can't you just learn to shut up and mind your own business?" This is the most difficult thing of all to make some of you understand, [38a] because you'll think I'm being ironic and you won't believe me if I tell you that I can't keep quiet because then I would be disobeying god. You will believe me even less if I tell you that the greatest good for a human being is just this, to spend each day discussing virtue and the other things you hear me talking about and on which I examine myself and others: the unexamined life* is not worth living for a human being. This is true, gentlemen, though it is not easy to believe.

I am not accustomed to thinking of myself as deserving something bad. [b] If I had money, I would estimate my penalty at an amount that I could pay, since that won't harm me, but I don't really have any money, unless you are willing to estimate as much as I am able to pay. Perhaps I could pay you one mina of silver*—so that's my estimate.

[Plato interrupts.]*

Plato here, as well as Crito, Critobulus and Apollodorus are telling me to set the amount at thirty minae, and they will guarantee the amount. So that is the amount I estimate, and these men are sufficient to guarantee payment.

[Socrates is sentenced to death.]*

[c] You certainly have* saved some time by giving me a speedy trial instead of holding it over a period of several days.* But what you have gained because of it is the reputation among those who want to vilify Athens as being the city that is guilty of killing Socrates, a wise man—since those who want to disparage you will say that I am wise even if I am not. To those of you who condemned me to death I say that you would have gotten your wish if you had just waited for a little while: you can see for yourselves that I am an old man and death is not far off.

[d] And to these same people I say that although you may think that I was convicted because I failed to use arguments that would have persuaded you to let me go if only I had been willing to say anything and everything to secure my release, you are completely mistaken. I was convicted not because of any arguments I failed to use, but because I didn't have the audacity and shamelessness to address you in a way that would have given you great pleasure to hear; you would have loved to hear me weep and wail, doing and [e] saying many things that are unworthy of me, but which you are used to hearing from others. I did not think that I should grovel before you simply because I was in danger, and I have no regrets about my defense: I would much rather die as a result of this defense than live as a result of the other. In court as in war no one should [39a] stoop so low as to do literally anything to avoid death. Often it is obvious in battle that you can escape death by throwing your shield away and begging for mercy from your pursuers. In fact, you can usually find a way to escape death if you are shameless enough to do absolutely anything to avoid danger. It is not very difficult to escape death; what is more difficult to escape is vice, [b] because vice sneaks up on you much more quickly than death. Because of my age, I have been overtaken by the slower of the two pursuers, but my accusers have been overtaken by the quicker because they are clever and rush to judgment. I go to my death, convicted by you; but they go to injustice and evil, convicted by the truth. I accept my sentence, and they must accept theirs. Perhaps events had to unfold this way; I believe that things are as they should be.

[c] After saying that, I feel a desire to prophesy to you who condemned me, for I have reached the stage in which most prophesies arise:* when one is about to die. I say to you who have killed me that soon after my death a much harsher punishment shall come to you than what you have inflicted on me. You have done this thinking that by getting rid of me you could avoid being called to account for what you've done with your lives, but I say to you that your action will have exactly the opposite effect: there will be many people* [d] calling you to account, people I've been holding back without your noticing. They will be much harsher because they are young, and you will be even more annoyed with them than you are with me. If you think that killing people is the way to shut them up and prevent them from reprimanding you for not living as you should, then your reasoning is unsound. First, it is impossible to silence all criticism; but second, that is not the admirable response. The easiest and most admirable way to silence your critics is to remove the basis of their reproach: make yourselves the best people you can be. With that, I'm done prophesying to those who condemned me.

[e] To those of you who voted to acquit me, I'd be very happy to discuss what's happened while the officers of the court* are busy and I don't yet have to go to the place where I must die. Stay with me as long as it is allowed; nothing prevents us from talking with one another. [40a] Since you are all my friends, I want to show you the meaning of what has happened to me. Because, gentlemen of the jury*—for you are rightly and properly addressed as such—something amazing has happened to me.

I often experience a prophetic warning* that stops me whenever I'm about to go wrong, even in trivial matters. Well, what about now, when the result is what you have all witnessed, something that is generally thought to be the worst of all evils? [b] When I left home at dawn, when I came to court, and when I made each point I made in my defense, my divine sign never came to me. It has often stopped me from speaking, sometimes in mid-sentence, but in this matter it hasn't opposed anything I've said or done. How do I explain this? I'll tell you. I suspect that what has happened to me is actually a good thing, and that we are mistaken [c] when we think that death is bad. The clear proof of this is the fact that my usual sign didn't oppose me, and it would have opposed me if coming here wasn't going to result in something good.

Let's also consider in another way how much hope there is that death is something good. For death is one of two things:* either the dead are nothing and experience no sensations whatsoever, or it is a sort of transition or a migration of the soul from this place to another. If there is no sensation in death, [d] if it is like a dreamless sleep, then death would actually be like the profit one receives for an investment. I think that if you picked one night during which you slept so soundly that you didn't even dream, and you compared that with all of the other days and nights of your entire life, and you counted how many days and nights were better and more pleasant than that one night of dreamless sleep, [e] you'd probably be able to count them on the fingers of one hand, whether you are the Great King of Persia or just an ordinary individual. If death is like that, then I say it is pure profit; for if all of time is like that, then it is no different than that one night.

But if, on the other hand, death is like travelling abroad, and what they say is true, that all the dead are there, then what greater good can there be, gentlemen of the jury? [41a] If you arrive in Hades* freed from these so-called judges, and you find true judges—the very ones who are said to judge there:* Minos, Rhadamanthus, Aeacus, Triptolemus, and all the other demigods who lived righteous lives—that wouldn't be such a bad vacation, would it? Or think of it this way: what would you give to meet and talk with* Orpheus and Musaeus, Hesiod and Homer? If what they say is true, I would gladly die many times. [b] It would be amazing to spend my time there and to compare my own experience with Palamedes or Ajax or any other of the ancient heroes who died because of an unjust verdict. I don't think that would be unpleasant at all. But even greater than that, I would examine people there as I do here, and I would put them to the test to discover who among them is wise, and who thinks he is wise but isn't. How much would you pay, gentlemen of the jury, to examine the leader of the vast army that marched against Troy, [c] or Odysseus, or Sisyphus, or the myriad other men and women that could be mentioned? To spend time with them, to talk with them and examine them—wouldn't that be an extraordinary happiness? I don't suppose they would put me to death for such behavior the way people here do; after all, they are immortal and are far happier than we are—if what is said about them is true.

So, gentlemen of the jury, you must be of good hope in the face of death, and bear in mind this one truth: [d] it is not possible for anything bad* to happen to a good man either in life or in death, nor is a good man neglected by the gods. What has happened to me now is no accident; it's clear to me that it is better for me to die and to be freed from trouble.* This is why my divine sign didn't turn me away from court, and why I am not very angry* with my accusers, or with those who voted to convict me, although freeing me from my troubles was not their intention when they accused and convicted me—they thought they were harming me, [e] and for that they deserve to be blamed.

And yet I do have a favor to ask of them:* when my sons have grown give them what they deserve, give them grief in exactly the same way that I gave you grief if they seem to you to care more for money or anything else more than virtue, and if they think more highly of themselves than they deserve. Reprimand them, as I reprimanded you, for not caring about what they ought to care about, and for thinking that they are worthy when they are not. If you do this, [42a] then I will finally have received justice from you, as will my sons.

But now I must leave. I go to die and you to live. Which of the two is better is unclear to all but god.*

CRITO

Setting: Athens' jail. Before dawn.

Characters (in order of appearance):
CRITO (a contemporary of, and devoted friend to, Socrates; author of seventeen philosophical dialogues; he was wealthy and managed Socrates' money quite well; his name is traditionally pronounced "CRY-toe," though "KREE-tone" is closer to the original)
SOCRATES (469-399 BCE; from a middle class family, not handsome at all; his name is traditionally pronounced "SOCK-ra-teez," though "so-KROT-ays" is closer to the original)

Dramatic Structure:
Parodos: Crito urges Socrates to escape (43a1-44b5)
Episode #1: Crito's arguments for escape (44b5-46a8)
Episode #2: Socrates' reply to Crito (46b1-50a5)
Episode #3: the Laws' reply to Crito (50a6-54d1)
Exodos: Socrates recommends that they follow god (54d2-e2)

SOCRATES. [43a] Why have you come so early, Crito—or is it later than I think?
CRITO. Oh, no, you are quite right, it's still early.
SOCRATES. About what time is it?
CRITO. Almost sunrise; it's still mostly dark out.
SOCRATES. I'm surprised that the guard* let you in.
CRITO. He and I have gotten to know each other quite well over the past few weeks,* since I come here so often. Besides, I've done him a small favor.*
SOCRATES. Did you just arrive or have you been waiting here for a while?
CRITO. I've been here a little while.
SOCRATES. [b] Well, then, why didn't you wake me when you arrived instead of sitting here quietly?
CRITO. No, by god, Socrates, you were sleeping so soundly and peacefully that I just couldn't wake you. I wish that I could have as pleasant and restful a sleep as you obviously do. In fact, I have often thought that your way of life has given you a remarkably steady happiness,* but now I am even more amazed: despite being in such terrible circumstances you can still take things so easily and remain so calm.
SOCRATES. Actually, Crito, it would strike a wrong note* if a man who had lived to my age resented the fact that it was his time to die.
CRITO. [c] Well, I've seen plenty of other men your age who have had this sort of misfortune, and their age doesn't prevent them from resenting their lot.*
SOCRATES. True enough. But why have you come so early?
CRITO. I have terrible news, Socrates—I suppose it's not so terrible from your point of view, given what you just said, but it will be awful for all of your friends, and I was absolutely crushed when I heard it.
SOCRATES. What is it? Has the ship from Delos* arrived? [d] Is my reprieve over?
CRITO. No, it hasn't arrived yet, but I think that it will arrive today, judging from the reports of some people who have come from Cape Sounion* and left it there. It is clear from them that it will arrive today, and so it will be necessary, Socrates, for your life to come to an end.
SOCRATES. Then, Crito, may things turn out for the best. Whatever is dear to the gods,* let it be so. However, I don't think that the ship will arrive today.
CRITO. [44a] What do you base that on?

SOCRATES. I'll tell you. On the day after the ship arrives I will be executed.

CRITO. So say the authorities.*

SOCRATES. Then I don't think it will arrive today, but tomorrow. I am basing this on a dream I saw* while I was sleeping just now. I guess you made the right decision not to wake me up.

CRITO. What was the dream?

SOCRATES. It appeared as if some beautiful and enchanting woman [b] in a white robe came to me, called me by name and said, "Socrates, on the third day shalt thou reach fertile Phthia."*

CRITO. What a strange dream, Socrates.

SOCRATES. Although it's meaning seems perfectly clear to me.

CRITO. All too clear. But, my dear friend, there is still time for you to relent and be saved.* If you die, I will lose a companion the likes of whom I shall never find again. But that is not the only misfortune I will suffer: many people who don't know us well [c] will think that I just didn't care enough about you because I could have saved you if only I'd been willing to spend a little money. What reputation could be more shameful than that of being the sort of person who cared more about money than about his friends? Most people* will never believe that you refused to escape and were not willing to listen to us although we tried our best to persuade you.

SOCRATES. Oh, but, my dear Crito, why do you care so much about the opinion of most people? The people who are most reasonable are far more worthy of consideration, and they will believe that things were done exactly as they have been done.

CRITO. [d] Surely you can see that we must care about the opinion most people hold of us. The present circumstances make that abundantly clear: they can inflict on you not the smallest but the greatest harm if you are misrepresented to them.

SOCRATES. It would be wonderful if most people could do us the greatest harm, because then* then they could also do us the greatest good, and all would be well. But as things are, they can do neither, since they haven't the capacity* to make us intelligent* or stupid, they simply act however it happens* to occur to them to act.

CRITO. I suppose so, but tell me this, Socrates. You aren't worried, are you, that if we help you escape, then extortionists* will prosecute* me and the friends who help us, and that we will lose all our property, or have to pay a huge fine, or suffer some other penalty? Because if that is [45a] what you are afraid of, don't give it a second thought. We are doing the right* thing in trying to save you, and we'll run these risks—and even greater ones, if necessary—to keep you safe. Please don't argue with me, let's just leave right now.

SOCRATES. All that you say does weigh heavily on my mind, Crito, and much else besides.

CRITO. Forget it completely, Socrates. I've already made arrangements with people who are willing to rescue you from here and take you out of the country, and they did not charge much. Second, you've seen how easy it is to pay off extortionists; we can settle with them very cheaply. [b] Third, you already have my money at your disposal, and that will more than cover all the expenses, but if you are concerned about me and don't want to spend my money, we have several foreign friends who are more than willing to spend their money to help. Simmias of Thebes* brought sufficient funds with him just for this purpose, but we also have Cebes and very many others.

So as I said, Socrates, don't let your fears stop you from saving yourself. And don't let what you said in court* worry you—that you wouldn't know what to do with yourself if you lived as an exile. [c] There are so many places you can go where people will welcome you with open arms. If you want to travel to Thessaly, I have some well established ties there who will be thrilled to entertain you and even to sponsor you* if you want to settle down. You could have a very pleasant life in Thessaly.

In addition to all that, Socrates, I don't think it is right for you to do what you are doing, which is, essentially, to betray yourself at a time when you could actually save yourself. You are acting like your own worst enemy by trying to finish the job that your actual enemies began when they prosecuted you.

And what about your sons? You are betraying them too, [d] abandoning them when you should finish raising them, and should make sure that they get a good education. Without you, what will be their lot in life? They'll end up like all orphans do when they lose their father. If you are not going to take the trouble to raise your sons, then you shouldn't have had them in the first place; but since you have had them, you have a responsibility to see that they are raised and educated. You're not taking your responsibility to them seriously.

You ought to make the same choice that a brave and good man would make, since you have spent your whole life saying that we ought to care about virtue more than anything else in life. Really, Socrates [e] I am ashamed on your behalf, and also on behalf of us your friends. It's going to look as if we behaved like complete cowards in this whole affair. We let you get dragged into court when we could have avoided it;* and then of course there was the whole way in which your defense* was made, and now the crowning absurdity is that it will appear as if we let this opportunity to save you slip through our fingers [46a] because we were too frightened and cowardly to act boldly when the opportunity presented itself.

Socrates, please don't let all these things become shameful and disgraceful to all of us. Make your decision—actually, there is no time to decide, you should already have made up your mind—there is only one choice to make. We must act tonight, this very night; if we wait any longer then nothing will stop the inevitable. Listen to me, Socrates, please don't argue with me.

SOCRATES. [b] My dear friend Crito, your passionate concern for my welfare is really very admirable, if it is well directed. If it is not well directed, then it will be quite troublesome.

Let's carefully consider whether we ought to do as you say. I have always been the sort of person who is persuaded by nothing other than the reason* that seems best to me upon consideration. I cannot discard the reasons I have accepted in the past simply because of the lot that has befallen me—they don't appear to me in any different light now,* [c] and I sill honor and obey them as I always have. So if we don't have anything better to say on the matter in the present circumstances, you can be sure that I won't agree with you—not even if the majority of people you are so concerned about have the power to scare us like children with even more terrible consequences than we face right now, whether it be binding us in chains, or sending a plague of death* upon us, or confiscating our property.

Well, then, what is the most appropriate way to consider the matter? Perhaps we should first take up the argument you gave from the opinions of others. [d] In the past we have agreed that we ought to pay attention to some opinions and not to others. Were we right about that? Or was it all fine and good to talk like that when I wasn't about to be executed, but now that I am in real danger we can see that it was just idle talk, irresponsible and immature? I want to investigate this question with you Crito, and see whether our former agreement appears in quite a different light given my present circumstances, or it seems exactly the same regardless—whether we ought to ignore it, or obey it.

It has been said—by people who thought they were saying something important—that when it comes to the opinions that people hold, [e] we ought to hold some in high regard, but not others. By the gods, Crito, does this seem right to you? You are not facing the prospect of dying tomorrow, in all likelihood, [47a] and so your current circumstances won't skew your judgment. So consider: do you accept the claim that we must not honor all the opinions that people have, but only some of them, and that we must not honor the opinions of all people, but only the opinions of some people? What do you say? Is that right?

Crito: Yes, it is.

SOCRATES. We should value the worthwhile opinions and not the worthless* opinions?

CRITO. Yes.

SOCRATES. And the worthwhile opinions are those of intelligent people, while the worthless opinions are those of unintelligent people?

CRITO. Of course.

SOCRATES. Then what about the kinds of examples I've given in the past? [b] When a professional athlete is in training, does he follow the advice of everybody who offers an opinion, or does he pay attention only to that one person* who happens to be a doctor or a trainer?

CRITO. Only to the one.

SOCRATES. So he should fear the blame and welcome the praise of that one, but not of the many?

CRITO. Clearly.

SOCRATES. Therefore he should regulate his activity, his exercise, and his diet according to the opinions of the one person who is an expert* trainer, and not according to the opinions of everybody generally.

CRITO. That's true.

SOCRATES. [c] Then we agree on those points. Now, if he disobeys the advice of the expert trainer and rejects his opinions, and instead listens to the advice of the many who have no expertise, won't the result be bad?

CRITO. Of course.

SOCRATES. In the case of the professional athlete, what will be the bad result and what will be its extent? What will the wrong activities, exercises and diet affect?

CRITO. It will affect his body. He'll ruin his physical condition.

SOCRATES. Well said, Crito. Instead of belaboring the point and going through example after example, can't we just focus on the issue at hand: when it comes to what is just or unjust, fine or shameful, good or bad, should we listen to and follow the advice of the many [d] or the one—if there is one who knows the truth—and it is only the opinion of the one that we should be ashamed to ignore and fear to disobey, no matter how many others weigh in on the matter? Because if we do not follow his advice, then we will corrupt and damage the part of ourselves* that—as we have agreed in the past—is improved by justice and destroyed by injustice. Or is there nothing to this?

CRITO. No, I quite agree with you, Socrates.

SOCRATES. Then here's the next step. Suppose we actually do follow the advice of the person who doesn't know what he's talking about, and we completely ruin the part of ourselves that is improved by health and is corrupted by disease. In that case, would life still be worth living? [e] You agree that the part of us that is improved by health and is ruined by disease is the body, don't you.

CRITO. Yes, I do.

SOCRATES. Well, then, is life worth living when the body is completely ruined and debilitated?

CRITO. Not at all.

SOCRATES. Then is life worth living if we have completely ruined and debilitated the part of us that is mutilated by injustice and improved by justice? Or do we think that the part of us, whatever it is, [48a] that is affected by justice and injustice is less important than the body?

CRITO. Certainly not.

SOCRATES. It's actually more important, isn't it?

CRITO. Very much so.

SOCRATES. Then, my good friend, we should not pay any attention to what most people will say to us, but only to that one person who is an expert on justice and injustice, and to the truth itself. So we can conclude that your first point was not correct when you proposed that we pay attention to the opinion of most people regarding what is just or unjust, fine or shameful, good or bad.

Moving on to your second point, someone might well say, "But the majority can put us to death."

CRITO. [b] Yes, indeed, Socrates, that's obvious. It is quite true that someone might raise this objection to ignoring the opinion of the majority.

SOCRATES. But Crito, that objection doesn't seem to me to invalidate the argument we just went through. Look at it this way, do you and I still agree that the most important thing is not to live, but to live well?

CRITO. We do.

SOCRATES. And do we still agree that to live well, to live finely, and to live justly is all one and the same?*

CRITO. We do.

SOCRATES. Then from all that we have agreed we must conclude that the question before us is whether it is right for me to attempt to escape without having been released* by the Athenians. [c] If it appears* right, then we shall make the attempt; if not, then we won't. The questions you raised about money, reputation and raising my children bring in the kinds of issues that most people would raise. But most people would casually execute* someone and bring him back to life if they could without giving it a second thought. But you and I have no choice in the matter since the argument has chosen* for us. We must consider whether we would be doing the right thing to pay money to, [d] or exchange favors* with, the people who will get me out of here; and whether the escape itself, and everything that you and others do to aid and abet my escape is right, or whether in truth all these things would be wrong. If it appears that we would be wrong to do all these things, then we should not consider whether we will die if we remain here calmly, or whether we will suffer anything else at all—none of that should be considered before* the issue of whether we would be wrong to do it.

CRITO. That is well said, Socrates, but look to see what we should do.

SOCRATES. Let's look together,* my good friend. If at any point you have an objection [e] to something I say, make it and I will believe you. But if not, then please do not continue urging me to escape without being released by the Athenians. It really means quite a lot to me to act with your approval and not contrary to your will. So look to the beginning of the inquiry, be sure that it is satisfactory, and answer my questions [49a] according to your sincere beliefs.*

CRITO. I will try.

SOCRATES. Do we say that in no way must we do something wrong voluntarily? Or do we say that in one way* we ought to do something wrong voluntarily, but in another way we ought not? In the past we have often agreed that in no way is it good or fine to do wrong. Have these past few days drained us of all our convictions? Have we reached an age where we suddenly realize that all this time we thought we were having serious conversations about right and wrong [b] when in fact we were just being immature? Or is the truth exactly what we've always maintained that it is, regardless of whether most people agree with us or not, and regardless of whether the results are worse or better than what we've experienced so far: to do wrong is both bad and shameful for the wrongdoer in every way? Do we still say that or not?

CRITO. We do.

SOCRATES. Then we must not do wrong at all.

CRITO. Certainly not.

SOCRATES. So we must not even do wrong in return for being wronged, since we must not do wrong at all.

CRITO. [c] So it appears.*

SOCRATES. What else? Ought we do something bad,* or not?

CRITO. Surely not, Socrates.

SOCRATES. Then what about doing something bad in return for having something bad done to you? Most people would say that is right, but is it?

CRITO. Not at all.

SOCRATES. I suppose that is because there is no real difference between doing something bad and doing something wrong.

CRITO. That's true.

SOCRATES. Then we must not return wrong for wrong, or bad for bad, no matter how someone has treated us.

Think carefully, [d] Crito, and be sure that in agreeing to these claims you are not agreeing to anything contrary to your beliefs. I know that there are few people who believe this now, and few who will believe it in the future, and that between those who believe it and those who don't there can be no common counsel*—we must necessarily spurn each other's conclusions. So consider this carefully and see whether you share my view and agree with me that we should begin* our deliberation from this proposition, that it is never correct to do wrong, or to return wrong for wrong, or to do something bad to someone who has done something bad to us. Or do you reject this proposition as a starting point? [e] I have believed this for a long time and I still believe it; but if you think otherwise, tell me what you believe and teach me what I do not understand. If you stand by what we have just agreed, then let's move on to the next point.

CRITO. Yes, I still maintain this view and agree with you. What is the next point?

SOCRATES. Here's the next thing to say—or, rather, ask: should a man do what he has justly agreed to do, or should he cheat?*

CRITO. He ought to do what he justly agreed to do.

SOCRATES. But notice what follows from this. If we leave here [50a] without persuading the city to let us go, then won't we be doing something bad to the very last one we should ever do something bad to? Would we or would we not be abiding by our just agreements?*

CRITO. I have no answer to your question, Socrates, because I don't understand it.

SOCRATES. Consider it this way. Suppose that while I am sneaking away*—or whatever you want to call it—the laws* and the commonwealth* should come to us, stop us,* and ask,

"Tell me,* Socrates, what do you have in mind to do? Can you intend [b] by this action you are undertaking anything other than to destroy us the laws, and the entire city, as far it is up to you?* Or does it seem possible to you for that city to continue to exist and not be overthrown in which judgments that have been passed are without force* and are rendered null and void by private citizens?*

How shall we answer these questions, Crito, and others like them? Because there is a great deal that someone might say against destroying the law—especially if he is a politician*—and in defense of the view that duly rendered judgments are to be authoritative.

[c] Shall we say, "Yes, that is what we intend to do because the city has wronged us by not judging correctly* in our case." Is that what we shall say?

CRITO. Yes, by god, Socrates.

SOCRATES. Then what if the laws reply as follows?

"But Socrates, was that the agreement between you and us? Or did you agree to abide by the judgments that the city renders?"

And if we are surprised at this, they might go on to say,

"Don't be surprised, Socrates, just answer the question, since you are used to carrying on conversations by question and answer. Come now, what charge* [d] do bring against us and the city, that you are trying to destroy us? In the first place, is it not true that we gave you life, since it was through us that your father took your mother in lawful wedlock, and in this way you were born? Tell us, do you have any complaint to lodge against any of our laws having to do with marriage? Are you dissatisfied with any of us on the grounds that we are not excellently constructed?"

"I have no complaint," I should answer.

"Well, then, do you have any complaint to lodge against any of our laws having to do with the raising and the education of children, such as you yourself received? Do you think that any of us are not excellently constructed who advised* your father to educate you in [e] music and gymnastics?"*

"They are excellently constructed," I should answer.

"Very well, then. Now, since we have established that you were born, raised and educated by us, could you dare say, in the first place, that you are not our offspring and subject*—both you yourself and also your ancestors? And if that is so, do you think that you and I stand on a basis of equality* with respect to what is right, so that whatever we may do to you, you may do back to us? You and your father did not stand on a basis of equality with respect to what is right, nor did you and your master*—if you happened to have one—so that whatever they did to you, you could do to them in return, [51a] whether it be returning insult for insult, or blow for blow,* or anything like that. Do you think that it will be acceptable to treat your fatherland and the laws* this way, so that if we undertake to destroy you, thinking that it is right to do so, it will be equally right for you to undertake to destroy the laws and your fatherland as far as you are able? And will you—the true guardian of virtue*—say that in doing this you will be doing the right thing?

Or are you so clever* that you have overlooked the fact that in comparison with your mother and your father and all of your ancestors, your fatherland is more honorable, more to be revered, is holier, [b] and deserves even more respect from the gods and from every intelligent person; and that you ought to feel awe for your fatherland and be even more submissive and subservient when your fatherland is angry with you than when your father is angry with you; and that you ought either to persuade* it or do what it commands, and suffer in silence whatever it orders you to suffer, whether it be flogging or chains;* and if your fatherland leads you off to war to be wounded or killed, you must do all these things, and it is right for you to do them; and you must not give way, withdraw or abandon your post,* but in war, in court and everywhere you must do [c] what your city and your fatherland commands, or else persuade her with respect to what is just by nature; and to use force against your mother or father is not pious, and it is much more impious to use force against your fatherland?"

What shall we say in answer to these questions, Crito? Do the laws speak the truth or not?

CRITO. They seem so to me.

SOCRATES. And they might continue as follows.

"Then consider this, Socrates. Are we speaking the truth when we say that it is not right for you to try to do what you are now trying to do? For we brought you into existence, we raised you and educated you, and we gave a share of all the fine things we could [d] to you and to all the other citizens, but even so* by granting permission we publicly proclaim that any Athenian who wishes, may take his property and go wherever he wishes. Once he is a registered adult* and has seen us the laws and has seen how the affairs of the city are managed, if in any way we are not pleasing to him, he is free to leave. Not a single law prevents or forbids expatriation to one of our many colonies, or even to a foreign land, if he is not pleased with either the laws or the city; he may go [e] wherever he wishes and take his possessions with him.

On the other hand, whoever remains here having seen how we render judgments* and how, in general, public affairs are administered, we say that he has in fact agreed* to do what we command him to do, and that he is doing wrong in three ways if he does not obey us: he is not obeying those who brought him into existence and raised him, and third, after having agreed to obey us, he is neither obeying us nor persuading us* that we are doing the wrong thing [52a] despite being allowed the opportunity to do so and despite the fact that we never issue cruel commands—no, although we allow him two options, to persuade us or to do what we command, he does neither.

We tell you, Socrates, that these are the charges to which you will be liable if you do what you are thinking of doing. And among Athenians, you would not be the least liable to these charges, you would be the most liable."

Now, if I were to ask them, "Why would I be more liable to these charges than any other Athenian?" they might fairly answer that I have entered into this agreement more clearly than has any other Athenian.

[b] "Socrates," they might say, "we have an especially clear sign that we and the city have satisfied you: you would not have stayed here at home more than any other Athenian if you were not satisfied with us more than any other Athenian. In fact, you've never even attended the Olympic Games or any other festival outside Athens—although once your friends dragged you to the Isthmian Games*—and you never even went on a vacation abroad like most people. The only time you left Athens voluntarily was when we sent you somewhere as part of your military service. Other than that, not once did you feel the desire to know other laws, or to know what it was like to live in another city, [c] we and our city seemed sufficient to you. In fact, you were so thoroughly pleased with the city, and you were so eager to chose us and to agree to live as a free citizen in accordance with us that you decided to have your children here.

Furthermore, at your trial you could have proposed exile* for your punishment, in which case you could have done with the city's will what you are now proposing to do against it. But no—you put on a fine show of self-importance* saying that it didn't bother you if you had to die and you claimed that you would choose death rather than exile. Now it's a different story. Now you have no shame at contradicting your own principles, and you have no respect for us the laws, whom you are trying to destroy. [d] You are behaving like the lowest of slaves, trying to run away in complete violation of the contracts* and agreements you made that you would be a decent, law-abiding citizen.

Therefore, first answer us this: are we or are we not speaking the truth when we assert that you have agreed—in deed, though not in word—to live here in accordance with the laws?"

What shall we say to this, Crito? Can we do anything other than agree that they are speaking the truth?

CRITO. We must agree, Socrates.

SOCRATES. "Then we can draw no other conclusion," they would reply, [e] "than that you are violating the contracts and agreements you made with us. You are doing this despite the fact that your agreement was not made under compulsion,* you were in no way misled as to the content of the agreements, and you were not pressured into making the agreement in a hurry—you had seventy years to make up your mind, during which time you could have left us if you were not satisfied with us or if in any way the agreement with us did not seem to you to be just. But you preferred neither Sparta nor Crete—both of whom you have said on many occasions to have good laws*—nor any other [53a] Greek or foreign city. You have left the city less often than the blind, the lame and people with other disabilities leave. That shows how much more than any other Athenian you have been satisfied both with the city and also with us, the laws—who could possibly be pleased with a city and not its laws?

So, Socrates, are you going to abide by your agreements? You will if you are persuaded by us, and that way you will avoid looking ridiculous if you leave the city.

Consider it this way, Socrates. If you commit these offences and do what is wrong, what good will you actually do for yourself* and for your friends? [b] Because it is quite clear that your friends will risk being banished by the city and having their property confiscated.

As for you, suppose you go to one of the nearby cities—Thebes or Megara, for example, because they both have good laws. You will come to them as an enemy of the state, Socrates, and anyone who cares about their city will view you with suspicion and will think of you as someone who undermines the laws. You will also confirm the opinion of the jurors in your trial who thought you were guilty, [c] because anyone who undermines the law seems most of all to be a corrupter of the young and the innocent.

Will you, then, avoid these suspicions by avoiding cities with good laws that have decent, law-abiding citizens in them? But if you do that, will you have a life that is worth living? What kind of conversations can you possibly have with people in such cities? Wouldn't you be ashamed to use the same arguments that you used here—that nothing is more important for human beings than virtue, justice, law and order? How would it look [d] for such words to come from Socrates the fugitive?

Or will you avoid all these places and head out to Crito's associates in Thessaly? They don't care about law and order there. They will probably enjoy hearing the ridiculous story of how you snuck away in some silly disguise, dressed up like a sheepherder or whatever runaways wear, and maybe wearing makeup to change your appearance. Don't you think that everyone will gossip about you—the old man who probably hadn't long to live, [e] but who clung so greedily to life that he was willing to become one of the worst offenders against the law? Perhaps not, if you can avoid annoying people, but even so you will have to put up with a great many insults, groveling like a slave to everyone you meet. And what will you do there except attend every banquet you can, as if you are on a permanent vacation? Where will those arguments [54a] about justice and the other virtues be then?

But you want to live for the sake of your children so that you can raise and educate them. Think this through. After having made them exiles, you want them to have the benefit of an education in Thessalian dissolution and debauchery? Or perhaps you think they would be better off being raised and educated in

Athens while you are up in Thessaly? Surely your friends will take good care of your children. But don't you see: whether you are off in Thessaly or Hades* your friends will take good care of your children, [b] if they truly are your friends.

Therefore, Socrates, obey us—we raised you as a father raises his son. Do not care more about your own children, or your own life, or anything else, than you care about what is right, so that when you arrive in Hades, you will have all these arguments in your defense when you address those who rule. For while you are here it is clear that it will not be better, or more just, or more pious* for you to escape—either for yourself or for your friends—nor will it be any better when you arrive down there. Keep in mind that if you do leave, [c] you will leave as a man who was wronged not by the laws, but by men.* And if you escape so shamefully, returning wrong for wrong and violating the agreements and contracts you made with us, harming those you least ought to harm—yourself, your friends, your fatherland and us—we shall be angry with you while you live, and after you die our brothers in Hades will not receive you kindly, for they will know that you did everything you could to destroy us. [d] Do not do what Crito urges you to do; be persuaded by us."

Know well, my dear friend Crito, that this is what I seem to hear—just as those who celebrate the rites of the Corybantes* seem to hear flutes—and the sound of these arguments rings inside me, rendering me unable to hear anything else. So you should know that, as it seems to me now, if you speak against them, you will speak in vain.* Nevertheless, if you think you can do something more, speak.

CRITO. Socrates, I have nothing to say.

SOCRATES. Then let it go, Crito, and let us follow this course of action since in this direction god is leading us.

PROTAGORAS

Setting: Athens (for the discussion with the friend) and the opulent home of Callias (for the discussion with Protagoras). The date is probably before the outbreak of the Peloponnesian War, perhaps around 433. Socrates is about 36 years old, Protagoras is about 57.

Characters (in order of appearance):

FRIEND OF SOCRATES (unknown)

SOCRATES (469-399 BCE; from a middle class family, not handsome at all; his name is traditionally pronounced "SOCK-ra-teez," though "so-KROT-ays" is closer to the original)

HIPPOCRATES (unknown friend and younger neighbor of Socrates; his name is traditionally pronounced "hip-OCK-rah-teez," though "hip-oh-KROT-ays" is closer to the original)

DOORMAN FOR CALLIAS (unknown)

PROTAGORAS (c.490-420; the most famous of the Sophists; his name is traditionally pronounced "pro-TAG-or-us," though "pro-tah-GORE-oss" is closer to the original)

CALLIAS (c.450-370; wealthy aristocrat from a powerful Athenian family that retained the hereditary honor of Torchbearer for the Eleusinian mysteries; Callias was ridiculed for his extravagance, but he did serve effectively as general in the Corinthian War of 391/0, and as ambassador to Sparta; his name is traditionally pronounced "KAL-ee-ass," though "call-EE-oss" is closer to the original)

ALCIBIADES (451/0-404/3; son of a noble father and exceptionally noble mother, the family shared guest-friendship with a Spartan family, and his name is in fact Spartan; he was raised in the house of his famous cousin Pericles; extremely attractive, intelligent, capable and ambitious; he held important military roles for Athens, then Sparta, then Persia, then Athens again, and finally Persia where he was murdered; his name is traditionally pronounced "al-sib-BUY-uh-deez," though "al-kee-bee-AH-days" is closer to the original)

CRITIAS (c.460-403; from an aristocratic family; well educated, sophisticated and accomplished; cousin of Plato; in 404 he was one of the Thirty Tyrants to lead Athens after losing the Peloponnesian War, he was killed when the democratic faction took control of the city; his name is traditionally pronounced "KRIT-ee-us," though "kree-TEE-oss" is closer to the original)

PRODICUS (from the island of Ceos just off the southeastern tip of Attica, Prodicus was a contemporary of Socrates, and was primarily a teacher of rhetoric, but he gave naturalistic accounts of some religious myths and was probably an atheist; he served occasionally as a diplomat; "his name is traditionally pronounced "PROD-ick-us," though "PROD-ick-oss" is closer to the original)

HIPPIAS (from Elis in the northwest plain of the Peloponnesus; a little younger than Protagoras, he was a famous teacher and orator, author of many books on many subjects; his name is traditionally pronounced "HIP-ee-us," though "hip-EE-oss" is closer to the original)

Dramatic Structure:

Prologue I: Socrates meets his friend after talking with Protagoras (309a1-310a7)

Prologue II: Socrates asks Hippocrates why he wants to be Protagoras' student (310a8-314c2)

Parodos: Socrates and Hippocrates meet Protagoras (314c3-317e2)

Episode #1: Protagoras on the teachability of virtue (317e3-328d2)

Episode #2: Socrates and Protagoras on the unity of virtue (328d3-335c7)

Episode #3: Interpretation of a poem by Simonides (335c8-347a5)

Episode #4: Socrates and Protagoars return to the unity of virtue (347a6-361d6)

Exodos: Socrates and Protagoras agree to talk again later (361d7-362a4)

FRIEND. [309a] Where are you coming from, Socrates? I bet you were with the pack* following Alcibiades around. In fact I just saw him the other day and he is still quite a fine* man—though, between you and me, Socrates, "man" is the right word because his beard really is filling in.*

SOCRATES. What of it? Don't you agree with Homer when he says that [b] a young man is most beautiful when his beard is just filling in?*

FRIEND. So what's happening now? Have you just been with him? How is he treating you?

SOCRATES. Quite well, especially today—he came to my defense and said many things in support of my side.* I came from him just now, but I have something very surprising to tell you: although he was present, I paid no attention to him—in fact, I almost completely forgot that he was there.

FRIEND. [c] What? I can't imagine what could have driven a wedge between you two. Surely you haven't fallen for someone more beautiful in the city?

SOCRATES. Yes, I have; in fact, he's much more beautiful than Alcibiades.

FRIEND. Who? Is he Athenian or a foreigner?*

SOCRATES. A foreigner.

FRIEND. From where?

SOCRATES. Abdera.*

FRIEND. And you found this foreigner to be even more beautiful than the son of Cleinias?

SOCRATES. Yes, my friend, don't you think that the wiser man will appear more beautiful?

FRIEND. Oh, so it was some wise man that you were with today?

SOCRATES. [d] The wisest man alive, if you think the wisest man alive is Protagoras.

FRIEND. What are you saying? Protagoras is staying here in town?

SOCRATES. This will be his third day here.

FRIEND. And you just came here from being with him?

SOCRATES. [310a] Yes. I said many things and heard many things.

FRIEND. Tell us the entire conversation in detail, if you have the time. Please sit right here, my slave will get up and make room for you.

SOCRATES. Certainly. I'd be happy to talk if you'd be happy to listen.

FRIEND. We'd be very happy. Please tell us everything.

SOCRATES. Then we are agreed. Listen to this.

This morning before dawn, while it was still completely dark out, Hippocrates the son of Apollodorus, brother of Phason, [b] was knocking very loudly on my door with his cane. When someone opened the door he burst right in calling out for me very loudly.

"Socrates! Are you awake or still sleeping?"

I recognized his voice and answered, "Hippocrates, I'm up. What is so urgent?"

"Good news!"

"That's good to hear. What is it, and why have you come here so early to tell me?"

"Protagoras is here!" he announced loudly right in my ear.

"Oh, that. He's been here a day or two. Did you just find out?"

"Yes, by the gods! Just last night." [c] He groped around in the dark for my bed* and sat down near my feet. "Yes, it was just last night when I came back from Oenoë.* My slave Satyrus had run away—I meant to tell you that I was going after him but something came up and I forgot to let you know. Anyway, after I got back it wasn't until we had eaten dinner and I was about to go to bed that my brother finally told me that Protagoras had arrived in town. Well, I immediately got ready to come over and tell you, but then I realized that it was already very late at night. So as soon as I had slept off the fatigue of my travels yesterday I got up and immediately [d] came right over here."

It was obvious how enthusiastic and excited he was, so I teased him and said, "Why do you care? Does Protagoras owe you money?"

He laughed and said, "Yes, by the gods! That's it, Socrates: he is the only man who is rich in wisdom and he hasn't given me any of it."

"Well, by god," I replied, "if you give him silver and win him over, he'll make you a wise man."*

"By Zeus and all the gods [e] if that were only true! I wouldn't spare any of my money or any of my friends' money either! This is exactly why I've come to you: would you please talk to him* on my behalf? I'm too young to approach him myself, plus I've never seen him or even heard him—I was just a child when he first visited Athens.* Oh, Socrates, absolutely everybody praises him and says that he is the wisest speaker there is. Why don't we walk over there right now, [311a] he's sure to be inside still. I've heard that he is staying with Callias, the son of Hipponicus. Please, Socrates, let's go right now!"

"Oh, no, my good friend, we can't go there so early. Let me get out of bed and we'll go into my courtyard. We can spend some time there until daylight and then we can go to see Protagoras. He's sure to be there when we arrive, so don't worry."

So I got out of bed and we went into the courtyard. [b] In order to test the strength of his convictions about Protagoras I said to him, "Tell me, Hippocrates, you plan to go to Protagoras and pay him whatever fee he asks, but what sort of man do you expect to find when you meet him, and what sort of man do you expect to become once you've met him? I mean, suppose that you took it into your head to go to your namesake Hippocrates of Cos,* the Asclepiad,* and to pay him whatever fee he asked. In that case, what if someone asked you, 'What do you take that Hippocrates to be, Hippocrates, [c] so that you intend to pay his fee?' What would you answer?"

"I'd say that he is a doctor."

"And by paying his fee, what would you intend to become?"

"A doctor."

"And what if you decided to go to Polycleitus the Argive,* or to Phidias the Athenian,* and you planned to pay their fee? What if someone asked you exactly the same question, 'What do you take Polycleitus or Phidias to be so that you intend to pay their fee?' How would you answer them?"

"Sculptors."

"And by paying their fees, what would you intend to become?"

"A sculptor, obviously."

"Well, then," I said, [d] "you and I are going to Protagoras to pay his fee for you—if we have enough money to persuade him to take you on as a student, and I suppose that if we don't have enough we will impose on our friends to make up the difference. What if someone sees how intent we are on doing this and says, 'Tell me, Socrates and Hippocrates, what do you take Protagoras to be so that you intend to pay his fee?' [e] What will we answer? What other name do we hear applied to Protagoras? Phidias is a sculptor, and Homer is a poet, so what sort of man is Protagoras?"

"Sophist.* That's what people call him," Hippocrates answered.

"So it is as a sophist that we will pay him money?"

"Exactly!"

"Then how would we answer this follow-up question, [312a] 'And what sort of man will you become if you succeed with Protagoras?'"

When I asked him that the sun had risen and I could see quite clearly that he blushed. "If this case is like the other cases we've gone through, then obviously I would become a sophist."

"By the gods, Hippocrates, wouldn't you be ashamed to present yourself to Greeks as a sophist?"

"By god, Socrates, yes I would—if I have to say what I think."*

"But on the other hand, maybe this is not like the other cases.* Maybe the sort of education you hope to receive from Protagoras [b] is like the ones you received from your grammar teacher,* your music teacher and your physical education teacher. You weren't learning a craft from them as if you were going to take up grammar, music or gymnastics as a vocation; you were becoming an educated individual, as every free person deserves to become.*

"Yes, certainly, that's it, Socrates. That is the sort of education people get from Protagoras."

"Do you know what you are getting yourself into?" I asked him.

"What specifically are you referring to, Socrates?"

"You are about to hand your soul* over [c] to someone you call a sophist, in order to be trained* by him. But I would be surprised if you know what a sophist is, and if you don't know that, then you don't really know the person you'll be entrusting your soul to—in particular, you don't know if it is a good thing or a bad thing to hand your soul over to him."

"I think I know what a sophist is."

"Then tell me, what do you think a sophist is."

"I think that a sophist is just what the name says: someone who is knowledgeable in wise matters."*

"But you could say the same thing about painters and carpenters because they are knowledgeable in wise matters. [d] If we asked, 'In which wise matters is the painter knowledgeable?' I suppose we would say that painters are wise when it comes to painting likenesses—and so on with carpenters and the rest. So if we asked, 'In which wise matters is the sophist knowledgeable?' what should we answer? What business does he manage?"*

"I suppose we should say that he knows how to make someone a clever speaker."*

"Perhaps that answer is true, but it isn't sufficient because it raises a further question. On what subject does the sophist make someone a clever speaker? For example,* [e] when your kithara* teacher makes you knowledgeable about playing the kithara, doesn't he also make you a clever speaker about playing the kithara?"

"Yes."

"So then, on what subject does the sophist make you a clever speaker?"*

"Obviously on the subject that he knows."

"Quite likely. But what is it that he knows, and which he teaches his students?"

"By god, I have no answer."

[313a] After he said that I just had to ask, "But then do you know what sort of danger you are putting your soul in? Think of it this way. Suppose you had some reason to entrust the care of your body to someone, gambling on whether they would benefit or harm your body. Wouldn't you think long and hard about whether or not you should go through with it, and wouldn't you take several days to ask your friends and family for their advice? But today you are about to gamble with your soul, which is far more important than your body. Absolutely everything depends upon your soul: if things go well or badly for you it is all because of the good or bad condition of your soul.* But you haven't consulted with your father, your brother, [b] or any of your friends about whether you should entrust your soul to this foreigner who has just arrived. You admit that you heard only last night that he was in town and you come to me before dawn without even raising the question, let alone actually getting advice about whether you ought to entrust your soul to him. You are ready to spend all the money you have, and all of your friends' money as well, having already made up your mind to become a student of Protagoras despite the fact that you don't even know the man—as you yourself admit—you've [c] never engaged him in discussion, and you call him a sophist despite the fact that you don't know what a sophist is. That is the man into whose care you intend to entrust your very soul."

He heard me out and said, "So it seems, Socrates."

"Well, then, how about this, Hippocrates? Suppose we say that the sophist happens to be a sort of salesman dealing in food for the soul. That's the sort of person I think a sophist is."

"But what feeds the soul Socrates?"

"Learning, of course. And we have to be careful not to let any sophist cheat us when he praises what he has to offer, as sometimes happens with people who sell food for the body. [d] Grocers* don't know if what they are selling is good or bad for the body; they just recommend everything they have. And those who buy from them don't know any better—unless he happens to be a doctor or a physical trainer. It's the same with these people who travel from city to city selling learning: they recommend everything they have to offer and sell to anyone who wants to buy. Perhaps some of them don't know if what they are selling is good or bad [e] for the soul, and those who buy from them are probably just as ignorant—unless he happens to be a doctor of the soul.*

"Therefore," I continued, "if you happen to know what is beneficial or harmful to the soul, then it is perfectly safe for you to buy learning from Protagoras—or from anyone else. However, if you do not know what is beneficial or harmful to the soul, [314a] then watch out: you will be gambling with your dearest treasure.

"You see, Hippocrates, there is much more danger in buying learning than there is in buying bread. If you buy bread or wine from a salesman, you can put it in a bag, take it home, and before you eat or drink it, consult with someone who actually knows about food and drink. You can get their advice about whether you should consume what you bought or throw it out, and if you should consume it, how much you should consume and when. So there isn't much danger in buying things like bread or wine. [b] But you can't take away learning in a bag. Once you've paid for it, you take it into your soul and walk away having learned it—the damage or benefit has already been done.

"So we really should consult with our elders about this," I continued, "since you and I are too young to make such important decisions. But for now, let's stick with our plan and go hear the man. After we've heard him, we'll consider the issue of whether or not to become his students.* In fact, Protagoras isn't the only one there: [c] Hippias of Elis is also there, and I think that Prodicus of Ceos is too, as well as many other wise men.*

We agreed, and off we went. By the time we reached Callias' front door we were deeply involved in a conversation we'd gotten into on the way. We didn't want to break off the discussion before reaching a satisfactory conclusion, so we just stood there on Callias' porch talking to each other. I think that the doorman, a eunuch,* overheard us and [d] was irritated by the traffic of so many sophists coming and going. Finally we knocked on the door.

"Hmph!" he grunted. "More sophists. He's got no time for you." Then he used both hands to slam the door as hard as he could. We started knocking again and with the door still shut he said, "Gentlemen! Didn't you hear me say that he's got no time for you!"

"But, my good man," I said, "we have not come to see Callias, and we aren't sophists! Don't worry, [e] we just came to see Protagoras, we won't bother Callias at all. Just announce us." Reluctantly, he opened the door.

When we entered we saw Protagoras strolling along the portico.* With him I immediately spotted Callias, [315a] Paralus, and Charmides on one side of him, with Xanthippus, Philippides and Antimoerus on the other side.* Antimoerus is Protagoras' star pupil and he's learning the trade—he'll be a sophist soon. Following behind them, trying to hear what was being said, there was a large group of people that almost looked like a chorus line.* There were a lot of foreigners among them—Protagoras leads them around from city to city, charming* them with his voice like [b] Orpheus, and they follow the sound like men who are under a spell. There were some people from our country there as well. It was really funny to watch this chorus of dancers because they never got in Protagoras' way: whenever he turned around to walk back the way he had come, everybody on either side of him spun around as if on cue and took up their position to follow behind him again.

Then, to quote Homer, "after him I recognized"* Hippias of Elis [c] sitting in a chair on the opposite side of the portico. Seated next to him were Eryximachus, Phaedrus, Andron* and a lot of other foreigners, many of whom had come with Hippias from Elis. They seemed to be asking Hippias questions about nature, the heavens and astronomical matters, and he was answering their questions in detail.

Then, to quote Homer again, "next I saw Tantalus,"* [d] because Prodicus was there. He was in a room that Callias' father used as a storage room, but because of all the visitors Callias had converted it into a guest room. Prodicus was lying in bed wrapped in plenty of blankets and sheepskins.* Pausanias* was near him, and with Pausanias was a young man who seemed to me to possess [e] a fine and good* nature—his form certainly was very beautiful. I think I heard that his name is Agathon, and I wouldn't be surprised if Pausanias is in love with him. The two Adeimantuses were also in the guest room: the son of Cepis and the son of Leucolophides.* There were others there as well. From outside the room I couldn't quite hear what they were discussing, although I wanted to hear Prodicus—he seems to me to be a very wise [316a] and divine man.* Unfortunately for me, his voice is so deep and loud that it echoed in the room and I couldn't hear anything clearly.

We had only just arrived when in came 'Alcibiades the beautiful' as you call him—and I quite agree. Oh, and Critias* was with him.

So after we entered, Hippocrates and I spent a little time looking around, but then we went up to Protagoras [b] and I said, "Protagoras, this is Hippocrates. He and I have come because of you."

"Do you want to talk alone or with these others?" he replied.

"It makes no difference to us," I said. "You may decide once you've heard why we've come."

"Well, then, why have you come?"

"Hippocrates is an Athenian, he is the son of Apollodorus, his lineage is great and prosperous, and his own nature does not appear to be inferior to that of anyone his age. I think [c] he wants to establish a reputation for himself in the city, and he thinks that this is most likely to happen if you become his teacher. You decide whether or not to discuss this in private."

"You are right to be circumspect* on my behalf, Socrates. A foreigner like myself must be cautious when he arrives in a great city and tries to persuade the best of the young men that they will be greatly improved by associating with him, and by leaving their current mentors—whether they are close relatatives or not, old or young. [d] Some of these mentors may become jealous or even hostile, and they may end up plotting against the new foreigner in town.

"It is out of fear of this jealousy," he continued, "that the ancient practicioners of the venerable craft of sophistry have gone to great lengths to disguise their invidious craft. Homer, Hesiod and Simonides* disguised it as poetry. Orpheus, Musaeus and their followers disguised it as spirituality and prophecy. I have even noticed sophistry disguised as gymnastics, for example by Iccus of Tarentum* and [e] Herodicus of Selymbria*—as fine a sophist as any alive today. Music has been used as a disguise for sophistry by your own Agathocles as well as by Pythocleides of Ceos* and many others. All of these, as I said, were afraid of the jealousy they might provoke, and so they used their crafts as veils.

"I, however, [317a] do not agree with them," he declared, "because they failed to accomplish their goal: they failed to conceal their wisdom from the men who wield power in cities, which was the whole point of concealing the fact that they were all sophists. Of course they had some success with common men, who perceive nothing but simply repeat what powerful men say. Nevertheless, it is just as foolish to try to conceal what powerful men see quite clearly as it is for a slave to try to run away from a master who inevitably catches him. [b] In fact, the mere attempt to conceal what you truly are is going to provoke far more animosity because when people find out that you are hiding something, they inevitably suspect that there are other far more disreputable things that you are also hiding. I have taken the opposite road. I acknowledge openly that I am a sophist and I educate* people. I think that honesty is the better policy—it certainly is the safer option of the two. I've taken other precautions as well so that, god willing, I don't suffer anything terrible as a result of [c] admitting that I am a sophist.

"I have been practicing my craft for many years, and I have lived for many more.* In fact, I'm old enough to be the father of anyone in the room. So if you wish, I would be very pleased to discuss everything out in the open."

I suspected that Protagoras wanted to put on a fine show for Prodicus and Hippias, as if we had come to him like lovers* panting for their beloved, [d] so I said, "Why don't we call Prodicus, Hippias and everbody with them over here to listen to our conversation?"

"By all means," Protagoras agreed.

"Well, then," said Callias, "let's set the courtyard up like a council chamber so that we can all sit comfortably for the discussion."

Everybody was delighted at the thought of listening to wise men, so we all grabbed couches and benches and arranged them where Hippias was sitting because the benches were already there. While we were doing that, Callias and Alcibiades [e] went and got Prodicus up off his couch and brought him and everybody in his room out to join us.

When everyone was seated, Protagoras addressed me and said, "Socrates, now that we are all together, please tell everyone what you were saying to me just a moment ago on this young man's behalf."*

[318a] So I said, "I'll begin the same way I began earlier when I told you why I've come. Hippocrates here happens to want you to become his teacher, so he says he would be glad to learn what will result if you teach him, that's all."

Protagoras took it from there and said, "Young man, if I teach you, then on the very first day that you are instructed by me you will go home a better man than when you came. The very same will be true on the next day, and on the day after that, and so on: every day you will be better and better."

[b] When I heard that I said, "Protagoras, what you've said is obviously reasonable since even you, being as old and wise as you are, would become better and better each day if each day someone taught you something that you didn't already know. Don't give us that sort of answer. Here, let me give you an analogy. Suppose Hippocrates changed his mind and instead of you, he wanted that young man who has just come to town to be his teacher: Zeuxippus of Heraclea.* Well, Zeuxippus could tell Hippocrates exactly what you've told him, [c] that every day he'll get better and better. But suppose Hippocrates asked the follow up question, 'In what respect will I become better?' Zeuxippus would reply, 'Painting.' And if he went to Orthagoras of Thebes* to be his teacher, Orthagoras too could say what you said, that he would make Hippocrates better each day of instruction; and if Hippocrates asked in what respect Orthagoras would make him better, he would say 'Playing the flute.'* So now you, Protagoras, answer this same question: [d] if Hippocrates here takes you on as his teacher, and on the very first day that you teach him he goes away better than he was the previous day, and that happens every day of his instruction, exactly what will you make him better at doing, and in what respect will he be better?"

After he heard me out, Protagoras said, "What a fine question, Socrates! I enjoy answering fine questions. If Hippocrates becomes my student, he will not have the same experience that he would have if he chose any other sophist.* It's an absolute disgrace to see how other sophists treat young men. [e] After they have finally escaped learning the skills* they teach at school, most sophists force these young men to study more skills, teaching them arithmetic, astronomy, geometry and music."* I noticed that when he said this, he looked over at Hippias. "On the other hand," he continued, "if he becomes my student, then he will not learn anything other than the very thing he came to me to learn. The subject he will learn from me is good deliberation* for his own household—how he can best manage his own household, [319a] and good deliberation for his own city—how he can be as influential as possible* in both word and deed."

So I then asked, "Am I following you? Are you talking about the political craft, and are you claiming that you make men good citizens?"*

"That is precisely the claim that I make, Socrates."

"That is a fine skill to possess," I said, "if you actually do possess it. But there's no point in saying to you anything other than what I actually have in mind:* I don't think that the political craft is teachable,* [b] and yet when you say that you actually teach it, I have no basis for doubting it.* I owe you an explanation of why I think that this craft is not teachable and cannot be handed down from one person to another.

"Greeks say that Athenians are wise, and I go along with that,"* I began. "Now, I've noticed that when we meet together in the legislative assembly to consider some public building project, we send for professional builders to advise us. If we are considering building a ship, we call in the shipbuilders to advise us, and so on for every craft [c] that we think can be taught and learned. But when someone who isn't thought to be a skilled craftsman in the trade tries to advise us, the assembly won't listen to him no matter how handsome, wealthy or nobly born he is. He'll be laughed out of the meeting or shouted down until he either gives up, security hauls him away, or the President of the assembly rules him out of order. That is how Athenians conduct business when particular crafts are involved. However, when we are deliberating about [d] the management of the city, we let just anybody stand up and speak,* whether he is a carpenter, blacksmith, shoemaker, merchant, ship captain, rich or poor, upper class or lower class, and nobody objects like they do in examples I just mentioned: nobody accuses him of talking about a subject that he's never learned and that no one has ever taught him. Obviously the reason is that they think this subject is simply not teachable.

"On top of that," I continued, "it is not just that way [e] with affairs of state, it is the same when it comes to managing our own private affairs. Even the wisest and best of our citizens are utterly incapable of passing this virtue on to others. Pericles,* the father of these two young men here,* gave them a fine education in every subject that has teachers; [320a] but when it comes to his own wisdom, he doesn't teach it to them himself, nor does he hire someone else to teach it to them. Instead, they are left to graze just anywhere like sacred cattle* on the chance that they might somehow find virtue themselves. Or, if you like we can consider the case of Cleinias, the younger brother of Alcibiades here. Pericles is his guardian and he was afraid that Alcibiades would corrupt him, so he took Cleinias out of Alcibiades' house and placed him with his brother Ariphron to be reared and educated. But in less than six months he took him out of his brother's house, [b] at a complete loss as to what to do with him. I could go on with many examples of good men who were never able to improve members of their own families, or anybody else.

"Therefore, Protagoras," I concluded, "considering all this, I don't think that virtue is teachable. However, since I heard you say that it is, I'm not so sure. I suppose there is something in what you say because you've experienced many things, you've learned many things, and you've discovered many things on your own. So if you can clearly demonstrate to us [c] that virtue is teachable, please don't keep it to yourself, please show us."

"Oh, Socrates," Protagoras answered, "of course I will not keep it to myself. But do you want me to show you by telling you a story—as an older man might speak to a younger man—or by giving an account?"* Immediately many of those who where sitting there urged him to proceed in whatever way he wished. So Protagoras said, "I think it will be more enjoyable to tell you a story."

"Once upon a time there were gods, but no mortals. [d] When the allotted time arrived for mortals to come into being, the gods formed them under the ground by mixing earth, fire and other compounds of earth and fire. And when they were about to lead them into the light, they arranged for Prometheus and Epimetheus* to adorn them with the powers suitable for each. Epimetheus begged his brother to let him be the one to assign the various powers, "and once I've made all the assignments, you may inspect them." Prometheus was persuaded, and Epimetheus assigned the powers.

"On some he bestowed strength without speed, [e] and he adorned the weaker ones with speed. Some he armed with weapons, and to those without weapons he gave them a different nature so that they were not without the power to save themselves: to the ones he made small he gave wings so they could escape, or gave them the power of burrowing into the ground. Some he made large [321a] and their sheer size protects them. That is how he maintained a balance among creatures in his distribution of powers so that no species would be wiped out. After he made sure that they could avoid killing each other off entirely, he devised ways to protect them from the divinely ordained seasonal weather: he gave them thick hair and tough hides that protect them from the cold, provide a shield against the heat, and act like blankets when they bed down for the night. [b] He put hooves on the feet of some and on others he put thick skin without hair or blood.* Next, he provided different kinds of food for each kind of creature: to some he gave the green pastures, to others he gave the fruit of the trees, and to others he gave the underground roots. He did give other animals as food for some to eat, but he did not allow these to bear many children; instead, he allowed the animals that get eaten to bear many young so that their kind would not die out.

"Now, Epimetheus was not very wise, and he completely failed to notice [c] that he had lavished all the powers on the creatures that lack rationality.* The human race was left unadorned,* and he was at a loss as to what to do about it. While he was wondering what to do, Prometheus came to inspect the distribution of powers, and he saw that all the other animals were very well equipped in every way but human beings were naked, barefoot, without a bed and without weapons; and the allotted day had already arrived when human beings were to be led out of the earth and into the light. At first he too was at a loss as to how to provide for the salvation of human beings, [d] but then he stole from Hephaestus and Athena* their wisdom in technology together with fire—since without fire there is no way to acquire or use technology—and gave them to human beings. That was how human beings acquired the wisdom to stay alive, but they still did not possess political wisdom*—that was with Zeus. Prometheus was not allowed onto the Acropolis where the house of Zeus sits—and the guards* there are terrifying—but he was able to sneak into the [e] workshop shared by Hephaestus and Athena and steal the art of fire from Hephaestus, and all the other arts of Athena, and give them to human beings. This is why human beings [322a] are able to stay alive. Later, they say, Prometheus was brought to justice for stealing—all because of his brother Epimetheus.

"Since the human race has a share in the divine allotment,* and shares kinship with the gods,* a human being is the only kind of animal to acknowledge the gods, to make sacrifices to them and to erect statues in their honor. Second, because humans possess technological skill, they articulated names* and invented language, and they discovered how to build houses, to make clothing, shoes and beds, and how to make food grow from the earth. Thus adequately provided for, in the beginning [b] human beings lived scattered around—there were no cities.* In this condition they were being killed off by wild animals because they are stronger than human beings in every way. Their professional and technological skill was sufficient to provide them with food, but not to protect them from wild animals because they lacked the art of war, which is part of the political craft.* They did figure out how to band together* and to found cities, but when they banded together they wronged one another because they still did not possess the political craft. So again they were scattered and were in the process of being destroyed.

[c] "At this point, Zeus was afraid that the entire human race would perish, so he sent Hermes to bring them shame* and justice so that their cities would be well ordered, and they would be united by the bonds of friendship. But Hermes asked Zeus in what way he was to give shame and justice to human beings, 'Should I distribute these in the same way that Epimetheus distributed the technological skills? For example, one doctor is sufficient for many [d] who lack medical skill, and so on with the other professions. Should I distribute shame and justice in the same way, or should I givem them both to everyone?'

"'To everyone,' Zeus said, 'let all have a share in justice and shame, because cities could not exist if only a few people had a share of them like the other crafts. In addition, lay down a law from me that whoever is unable* to share in justice and shame is to be killed as a disease in the city.'*

"And that, Socrates, is why Athenians and others think that it is appropriate to be advised by only a few people when they are considering architectural virtue* or something that has to do with any of the other professions. If someone [e] without any professional expertise tries to advise them they won't even listen to him. You made this point, and it is quite a reasonable one, too. However, when it comes to [323a] political virtue, where it is necessary to follow justice and temperance, it is reasonable for them to listen to everybody because it belongs to everybody to have a share of this virtue* or else cities couldn't even exist. That, Socrates, is the reason.

"And just to make sure that you don't think you are being misled, and that everybody really does believe all men* have a share of justice and the other political virtues, consider this clear sign. With all the other forms of excellence it is just as you say: if someone claims to be an excellent flute player—or claims to have any other skill—when in fact he doesn't, people just laugh [b] or get angry with them and their family has to come and reprimand* him for behaving like a lunatic. But it's just the opposite when it comes to justice or some other political virtue. Imagine a situation where, instead of lying about having a skill that you don't actually have, you tell the truth about what a scoundrel you really are. Suppose that someone is actually unjust, everybody knows that he's unjust, and he comes right out and admits the truth: he's unjust. Well, ordinarily honesty about your shortcomings is considered a form of temperance, but in this case everybody would think he's a lunatic. They'll say that every man has to at least say that he is a just person, whether he is or not, and that its crazy to go around telling people that you aren't just. Obviously they think that [c] each person must have a share of justice, even if only a small one, in order to live among people at all.

"That is all I have to say about why it is reasonable to consider the advice of every man concerning this virtue, because of the belief that every man has some share of it. Next, I shall try to demonstrate that people think this virtue does not come by nature, nor does it come to us on its own; instead, they think that it is teachable and that whoever acquires it, does so by carefully cultivating it.

"To begin, think about bad traits that people have [d] by nature or by misfortune. No one is angry at them, or blames them, or teaches them or tries to correct them in order to change them when they have some problem like that—we just feel sorry for them.* For example, if someone is ugly, short or frail nobody is so foolish as to try to make them something they are not. I believe that we behave like this because everybody knows people have these attributes by nature or by chance, both the admirable attributes and the opposite ones. But on the other hand, any good attributes we gain by carefully cultivating them, by deliberate habituation,* or by instruction, [e] if someone lacks them and instead has the corresponding bad attributes, that is when we get angry at them, or we try to correct them, or we blame them. Injustice and impiety are clear examples, [324a] but to sum things up, this holds for every attribute that is opposed to political virtue. In the case of these vices everybody gets angry with you and blames you if you have them because the only reason you have them is that you learned them or you acquired them by deliberately cultivating them.

"In fact, Socrates, if you care to consider what effect correction can have on someone, that in itself will show you that everyone believes virtue can be acquired. If someone does something wrong, nobody corrects or punishes* them with one and only one thought in mind: they did the wrong thing.* That would be [b] retaliating without thinking like a wild animal. If you try to correct someone rationally, then you don't retaliate for the wrong that was done because you can't undo what has already been done.* Instead,* you must look to the future and make sure that the one you punish never does wrong again,* and that anyone who sees him punished will never do wrong.* If that is what you are thinking when you punish someone, then clearly you think that virtue comes by education: you are correcting someone in order to dissuade* them from ever doing wrong again. This opinion is held by everyone who [c] administers punishment either in their own private affairs or as a public office, and the Athenians above all—your fellow citizens, Socrates—administer punishment and corrections to those they believe have done wrong. Therefore, according to this account,* the Athenians are among those who think that virtue can indeed be acquired, and that it is teachable. Thus, it is perfectly reasonable for your fellow citizens to listen to the advice of blacksmiths and shoemakers on political matters, because they believe that virtue is teachable and can be acquired—as I have sufficiently demonstrated to you, Socrates, [d] as it seems to me.

"This still leaves the difficulty you raised about good men: why is it that these good men teach their own sons the subjects that have teachers, and make them wise in these subjects, but when it comes to the virtues that make them good men, they fail to make their sons better than anyone else? I will answer this question not with a story, but with an account.

"Consider it this way, Socrates. Is there or is there not some one thing in which all citizens must have a share [e] if there is to be a city at all? Upon this one point, and this one point alone, hangs the solution to the difficulty you have raised. For, suppose there is.* And suppose that this one thing in which all citizens must have a share is not carpentry, or pottery or blacksmithing or any of the technical crafts. [325a] Suppose, rather, that it is justice and temperance and piety—in a word, suppose that this one thing is virtue.

Now, suppose further that in addition to being the one thing that everyone must have a share in if there is to be a city at all, it is also something that everyone must display in their actions if they want to learn or to do anything else at all, and they should never do anything without doing it virtuously. And suppose further that whoever is without it—man, woman or child—must be instructed and corrected until the corrections have made them better people, or else if they do not heed their instruction, and are not rehabilitated by the correction, [b] they must be exiled from the city or executed as incurables. Suppose this is the nature of the situation we all face, but good men do not teach their sons to be virtuous—they teach them everything else but not virtue—think of how utterly absurd their behavior is. We have already demonstrated that these good men think that virtue is teachable—both in their private lives as well as in public life—so are we going to say that they don't bother to teach their own sons to be virtuous, or to cultivate the virtues in them? But when it comes to subjects that don't carry exile or the death penalty for those who don't learn them, those subjects they do teach their sons? Does it make any sense to say that although the penalty for not learning [c] or cultivating virtue is death, exile, the confiscation of one's property, or the utter ruin of one's entire family, despite all that good men don't teach their sons to be virtuous and don't take the greatest care possible to make sure that their sons grow up to be virtuous men? That is what we'd have to say, Socrates, if we accepted your view.

"No, Socrates. From the time when they are very small,* and for as long as they live, good men teach their sons to be virtuous and reprimand them when they do something wrong. As soon as a child can understand words, the nursemaid, mother, guardian* and [d] the father himself do everything in their power to make the child the best it can be. In both words and actions they teach and demonstrate to the child that this is right and that is wrong, this is admirable and that is shameful, this is pious and that is impious, do these things and don't do those things. Hopefully, the child learns these lessons willingly; but if not, they treat him like a piece of wood that has been bent and twisted out of shape: they straighten him out with warnings and beatings. When they've grown a little and are ready to go to school, they ask the teacher to be more concerned [e] that the child is well behaved than that he learns to read or to play the kithara. Of course that is exactly what his teachers do. But then, once they have learned all the letters of the alphabet and are starting to learn how to read—just as earlier they learned to understand speech—their teachers put works of the great poets on their desks and require them to learn various passages by heart. [326a] In these poets they find many admonitions and stories of great men from the past that have won everlasting praise and glory. These stories fill the young man's heart with jealousy and a fervent desire to imitate these great men. His kithara teacher does the same, first watching to make sure that the child conducts himself temperately and does not misbehave, but then when he is learning to play the kithara the teacher gives him works from the great lyric poets to learn while the teacher demonstrates [b] how to accompany the poems with music. He requires the students to learn the rhythms and harmonies* that are appropriate for young men's souls and make them more tame and civilized,* more disciplined and cooperative.* As a result, these young men are improved both in speech and in action. And keep in mind that all of human life requires us to be disciplined and cooperative. Next, they are sent to a physical trainer to improve their bodies and make them useful servants of their minds [c] so that they are not forced by their own physical weakness to act like cowards before the enemy or in any other situation.

"Those who are most able to provide such an education for their sons are the wealthy, and they provide the best teachers for their sons, start them early and educate them the longest. And even when they are finally let out of school that isn't the end of their education: the city itself takes up their education and makes them learn the laws of the land and live their lives in accordance with them—the laws serve as a sort of pattern for living [d] so that they don't just do whatever it occurs to them to do. It's like a child who is just learning to write: the teacher draws horizontal lines on the student's tablet and requires the child to write inside the lines. In a similar way the city traces outlines for living* in the laws derived from the great lawgivers of the past, and punishes or corrects anyone who strays outside the lines. We aren't the only ones who call our criminal justice system 'corrections' [e] because the laws are intended to guide us and we are called to give an account* of our actions when we go outside the law.

"Considering all this care that is focused on virtue both in private and in public life, are you surprised or confused about the teachability of virtue? You shouldn't be surprised. It would be much more surprising if virtue were *not* teachable?

"Why, then, do so many sons of good fathers end up so undistinguished? Listen and learn. The answer isn't surprising at all if what I've said up to this point is true, namely, [327a] that no one can be entirely unskilled in virtue if the city is to exist at all. If I'm right about this—and certainly I am—then we can compare virtue to any profession you might learn. For example, suppose that we couldn't possibly live together in a city unless each and every one of us played the flute to the best of his ability. In that case, each one of us would be teaching everybody else how to play the flute, and would never be shy about criticizing someone else's playing. That is just how things currently are with justice and the law: no one is ever shy about telling someone what the law is or telling them what they ought or ought not do. [b] We're all like professional carpenters advising other carpenters on how best to complete a carpentry job. After all, the justice and virtue of our fellow citizens is our best insurance policy. That is why everyone is eager to talk about and instruct others on both law and justice. So go back to my analogy: if everybody had to play the flute, then we'd all be teaching each other to play the flute, and we'd be correcting each other when anyone played badly. But in that case, Socrates, do you think that the sons of good flute players would necessarily be better at playing the flute than the sons of bad flute players? I think not. I think that whichever son is naturally well disposed towards playing the flute [c] will gain fame as a flute player, but whoever lacks natural talent will remain undistinguished. It often happens that the son of a good flute player isn't very good at it, and the son of a poor flute player is really good at it. But if everybody were always teaching and correcting each other, then even the poor players would be better than people who don't know anything about playing the flute. It's the same with justice and virtue.

"Take any person you think is unjust, but who was reared by laws and by human society, and he'll seem like an expert in the craft of justice compared with [d] a man who grew up without any education at all, without law courts, without laws, and without anyone compelling him to care about virtue. I'm thinking about the kind of wild savage that the poet Pherecrates* wrote about in his comedy at the Lenaea.* Do you remember how the chorus of misanthropes in that play left the city to live with the savages? If you found yourself among those savages you'd be more than happy to come back here and spend your time with the likes of Eurybatus and Phrynondas,* and you'd beg for the company of the scoundrels we have in the city.

[e] "The only difficulty, Socrates, is that you are being too picky. Everyone is a teacher of virtue, as far as he is able—but you say you can't find a single one! It's like having a son and then looking for someone to teach him [328a] how to speak Greek but not being able to find anyone who could do it. Or suppose you were looking for someone to teach carpentry to the son of a carpenter who had learned the craft from his own father, and from his father's friends in the craft. A carpenter can teach his son carpentry only as far as he is able to teach it, and it probably wouldn't be easy to find a better teacher if you are going to be really picky about learning the finer points of carpentry. But if you are only looking for someone to teach the basics of woodworking, it is easy to find lots of teachers.

"It's the same with virtue, and with everything else. If we happen to come across someone special [b] who can help us advance in virtue even a little bit, then we should gladly welcome* him. I think that I am just such a man, and that I am better than others at making people fine and good. The service I provide is worth more than the fee I charge, as my students will freely admit. In fact, it is for this very reason that I have devised a unique way of determining my fee: when someone learns from me, if he wishes he may simply pay my fee, [c] but if he doesn't want to pay me fee, he may simply go to a temple and make a sacred oath to the god stating how much my lessons were worth and donate that amount to the temple.*

"That, Socrates, concludes my story and my account showing that virtue is teachable, that Athenians believe that virtue is teachable, and that it is not surprising to find that the sons of good fathers are not always good, or that the sons of bad fathers are not always bad. After all, the sons of Polycleitus are nowhere near as good sculptors as he is, and they are about the same ages as Paralus and Xanthippus here, who are not nearly as great politicians as their father Pericles is. The same thing is true for every other craftsman. [d] Surely it is too soon to judge them because they are so young and there is great hope for them still."*

Protagoras stopped his speech after having made this display of such length and such quality. I was captivated* for quite a while and I kept looking at him as if he was going to go on talking, and I was eager to hear what he would say. But when I saw that he really was finished, I collected myself with a bit of difficulty, looked at Hippocrates and said, "Son of Apollodorus, I am grateful to you for urging me to come here today. It is simply tremendous [e] what I've heard from Protagoras. Up until now I thought that no one had developed a way of making people good, but now I am persuaded except for one small impediment,* which Protagoras will easily clear away since he's already expounded so many things.

"If you happen to hear any of our public speakers* talking about the subject you just addressed, Protagoras, [329a] you'd probably hear the same sort of speech you just made. In fact, you'd probably hear the same from Pericles or any other competent speaker. However, if you ask them a follow-up question they are just like books:* they have nothing to answer and nothing to ask. Even if you ask them about some small point they just made it's like striking a bell: you hit it once and it rings on and on with exactly the same note until you stop it with your hand. That's what orators are like; [b] you ask them a simple question and all they do is stretch out the point they've already made, droning on and on. But you are different, Protagoras. You've just made it clear that you are adept at delivering a long and beautiful speech, but you are just as adept at giving a succinct answer when questioned, and of waiting patiently for an answer when you question someone else*—abilities that few master. So since just one small point is lacking in order for me to have the whole picture, please answer this one question.

"Virtue is teachable, you say, and if anyone can persuade me of that, you can. [c] But there was one gap in your account and it surprised me, so I'd very much like you to close it. You said that Zeus sent justice and shame to people, and you repeated the claim* that justice, temperance, piety and all the others are, taken together, just one thing: virtue. That is the point I'd like you to go through more precisely. Is virtue just one thing although it has parts—the parts being justice, temperance, piety and so on—or it is just one thing with many different names—justice, temperance and piety [d] all being different names for one and the same thing?* That is what I yearn to know."

"But that's easy to answer, Socrates. Virtue is one thing, and those are its parts."

"But then," I asked, "are they parts of virtue in the way that the mouth, the nose, the eyes and ears are parts of a face, or in the way that the top, the bottom, and the sides are all parts of a single lump of gold? With the parts of a lump of gold there is no real difference between them, or between the parts and the whole, except that some parts are larger and some are smaller."

"The former, it seems to me, [e] Socrates. Justice and temperance are parts of virtue in the way that eyes and ears are parts of a face."

"Then is it possible to have some of the parts of virtue but not others; or if you have even one of them, do you necessarily have all of them?"

"Oh, no, it is possible to have only some of the virtues. Many men are brave but unjust, and some are just but not wise."

"So these are also parts [330a] of virtue," I asked, "courage and wisdom?"

"Oh, yes, indeed," Protagoras answered, "and wisdom is the greatest of the virtues."

"And each one of them is something different from each of the others?"

"Yes."

"And each one has its own unique power, just like the parts of a face? Because an eye is not an ear, and the power of an eye is not the same as the power of the ear. It's the same with all the other parts: each one has its own distinctive power that is different from the others. Is that the way it is with the parts of virtue? Is each one different from each of the others, [b] and each has its own unique power? Obviously it would have to be like that if it fits the pattern."

"Yes, Socrates, that's exactly how it is."

So then I said, "Then no other part of virtue is like knowledge,* and no other part is like justice, and it's the same with courage, temperance and piety?"

"Correct," Protagoras agreed.

"Well, then, in that case, let's consider what kind of thing each one is, and let's begin with justice. [c] Is justice a real thing* or not? It seems to me that is, but how does it seem to you?"

"It seems so to me as well."

"Then, what about this? Suppose someone asked us, 'Protagoras and Socrates, this real thing that you mentioned just now—justice: it is just or unjust?'* I would answer that it is just, but how would you vote on that issue? The same as me or different?"

"The same."

"So justice it exactly the kind of thing to be just—that's what I would say [d] in answer to that question. And you would agree?"

"Yes," he said.

"Then suppose this person next asked, 'And do you also say that there is such a thing as piety?' I think that we do say that."

"Yes, we do."

"I suppose his next question would be, 'And do you say that it too is a real thing?' Do we say that it is or not?" Protagoras agreed that we do, so I continued, "Then he'd ask, 'And is this real thing of such a nature as to be impious or pious?' That kind of talk bothers me so I would reply, 'Shh! You shouldn't even imply that piety could be impious. How could anything be pious [e] if piety itself weren't pious?' What about you, Protagoras? Would you give the same reply?"

"Yes, certainly."

"After we said all this, his next question would be, 'Then what about what you said just a little while ago? Perhaps I didn't hear you correctly. I thought you said that none of the parts of virtue are like any of the other parts.' I would reply that yes he did hear that correctly, [331a] but you were the one who said it, Protagoras, not me. He'd probably turn to you then and ask you directly, 'Is this true, Protagoras? Do you really say that no part of virtue is like any other? Is that your position?' How would you answer him?"

"Of course I would say that it is my position."

"Once we've agreed to all this, how would we answer his follow-up question, 'Therefore, piety is not the sort of thing to be just, and justice is not the sort of thing to be pious?* Doesn't this mean that justice is not pious, and piety is not just? And if that is true, don't we have to say that justice is impious, [b] and piety is unjust?'* How would we answer him? Personally, I would say that justice is pious and piety is just, and if you concede that point I would say that you agree. In fact, I would go so far as to say that justice and piety are one and the same thing—or at least that they are very similar to one another. Of all the virtues, these two seem most like one another: justice seems very much like piety, and piety seems very like justice. Is there any reason not to say this or does that sound correct to you?"

"I'm not entirely convinced that it's so simple, Socrates. [c] I can't agree that justice is piety and that piety is justice. I think there's a difference here, but what difference does it really make? If you want, let's have it your way: justice is pious and piety is just."

"No, Protagoras, I'm not interested in examining any 'if you want'* or 'if you think.' I want to put myself to the test* and I want to put you to the test. So let's not just have it my way or have it your way; I think our examination will be much better [d] if we leave the 'if you want' out of it."

"Fine," he replied. "Justice is in some way like piety. In fact, anything is in some way like anything else. There is a way in which white is like black, hard is like soft, and so on for all the pairs of opposites.

Earlier we said that each part of the face has its own distinctive power and that they are not like one another—well, they are also like one another in some way. [e] If you want, you can refute any claim that two things are not like one another by pointing out a different way in which they are like one another. But really, Socrates, it isn't right to call two things alike just because there is some respect in which they are like one another, or to call them unlike simply because there is some small respect in which they are not like each other."

That surprised me, so I asked him, "Are you saying that justice and piety are like one another in only some small respect?"

"Not exactly," [332a] he replied, "but I also don't think that things are exactly as you say they are."

"Well, if you find this topic tiresome we can switch to something else you said. Is there something that you call foolishness?" He agreed that there is, so I continued, "And do you say that it too is a real thing and that it is the opposite of wisdom?"

"I do believe that, yes."

"And when a person acts correctly and beneficially, does it seem to you that in doing so he is acting temperately or intemperately?"*

"Temperately," Protagoras said.

"And, of course, [b] they are acting temperately when they act with temperance?"

"Necessarily."

"So those who do not act correctly are, in doing so, acting foolishly and not temperately?"

"Yes."

"So these are opposites: acting foolishly and acting temperately?"

"Yes."

"And actions done foolishly are done with foolishness, and those that are done temperately are done with temperance?"

"That is correct."

"It's like actions that are done strongly are done with strength, and actions that are done weakly are done with weakness."

"Yes, that is also correct."

"And it would be the same with quickness and slowness: actions that are done quickly are done with quickness and actions that are done slowly are done with slowness?"

[c] "Yes."

"So can we generalize this and say every action that is done with one of a pair of opposites will be done in a similar way, and those actions that are done with the other member of the pair will be done in the opposite way?"

"I agree."

"Well, then, how about this? Is there such a thing as the beautiful?"

"Certainly."

"And is its opposite anything other than the ugly?"*

"No, that is it."

"And is there such a thing as the good?"

"There is."

"And is its opposite anything other than the bad?"

"No, that is it."

"And is there such a thing as a high-pitched voice?

"Yes."

"And is its opposite anything other than a low-pitched voice?"

"That is the opposite."

"And in any case of opposites, each is opposed to just one opposite, not many?"*

"Yes, that is correct."

[d] "Alright, then, let's sum up what we've agreed to so far. We've agreed that one thing has only one opposite, not more than one?"

"Yes."

"And we have agreed that when an action is done in an opposite manner, it is done with the opposite?"

"Yes."

"And we've agreed that what is done foolishly is done in an opposite manner to what is done temperately?"

"Yes."

"And what is done temperately is done by temperance, and what is done foolishly is done by foolishness?"

[e] "We have agreed to that also."

"Because if something is done in the opposite manner, it is done by the opposite?"

"Yes."

"The one is done by temperance and the other is done by foolishness?"

"And those two kinds of actions are done in opposite manners?"

"Yes."

"So they are done by opposites?"

"Yes."

"Therefore, foolishness is the opposite of temperance?"

"So it appears."

"And do you remember earlier we agreed that foolishness is the opposite of wisdom?"

"Yes, we did agree to that."

"But one thing has only one opposite?"

[333a] "Yes."

"Then, Protagoras, which claim shall we let go of? That one thing is opposed to only one thing? Or shall we give up the claim that temperance and wisdom are distinct parts of virtue, like the parts of a face, and that not only are they distinct from one another, they are actually quite dissimilar because they each have their own peculiar powers? Which shall we give up? They are not in harmony with one another, they do not accompany one another and they do not fit together. How could they possibly accompany one another if necessarily [b] each thing has only one opposite, not more, but foolishness—which is one thing—is the opposite of wisdom, but then again it is also the opposite of temperance as it seems. Isn't that how things stand, Protagoras?"

He didn't want to admit it, but he finally said, "Yes, it is."

"So temperance and wisdom are one and the same thing? And earlier it seemed that justice and piety pretty well* seemed to be one and the same thing."

"Let's not give up now, Protagoras, let's consider what remains for our investigation. Do you think that a person who acts unjustly [c] can be temperate insofar as he is acting unjustly?"

"Personally, Socrates, I would be ashamed to say 'yes,' but many people say that it is possible."

"Shall I pursue the inquiry with them or with you?"

"If you want," Protagoras said, "first carry on the argument with the many."*

"It makes no difference to me as long as you answer my questions on their behalf, whether you agree with them or not.* My main concern is to examine the issue at hand, although perhaps the one asking the questions and the one answering will also end up being examined as well."*

[d] At first Protagoras put on a show about how annoying the discussion* was, but ultimately he agreed to answer my questions. "Then let's start over: do you think that some people are acting temperately by acting unjustly?"

"Answering on behalf of most people, I would say yes."

"And to act temperately is to act with a sound mind* and to be sensible?"

"Yes."

"And to be sensible in this case you mean making a good plan to act unjustly?"

"Again, answering for most people, yes."

"And what do you mean here by a good plan to act unjustly? Would it be a good plan if things turned out well* or badly?"

"If they turned out well."

"Now, you do say that some things are good, don't you?"

"Yes, I do."

"And good things are the things that are beneficial to people?"

[e] "Yes, by god, and even if they are not beneficial to people I still call them good."

Protagoras seemed upset, contentious and a bit belligerent in answering questions.* When I noticed this I tried to ask my questions in a less confrontational way. "When you say that something is good without being beneficial, [334a] Protagoras, are you talking about things that are not beneficial in relation to human beings, or to things that are absolutely not beneficial at all? Do you say those kinds of things are good?"

"Certainly not.* But I do know of things that are of no benefit whatsoever to human beings—certain kinds of food, drink, drugs and many other things—but are nevertheless beneficial. You see some things don't benefit human beings but do benefit horses; some things are beneficial only to cows or to dogs. In fact, some things aren't beneficial to any animals but only to trees—and some things are beneficial only to the roots of trees and harmful to the new buds. For example, fertilizer [b] is good for all plants, but only when you apply it to the roots, if you put it on the new branches and foliage you'll destroy the whole plant. Also, olive oil is totally bad for all plants, and it is harmful to the hair of every animal except for human beings; for us it is an excellent hair tonic, and it is great for the rest of the body too. You see, what is good is so diverse and multifarious that what is good for the outside [c] of the body can be terribly bad if taken internally; that's why all doctors forbid their patients to take olive oil with their food except for a very small amount, just barely enough to make their food more appetizing and palatable."

When he finished the crowd cheered and applauded him for speaking so well, and I said, "Protagoras, I happen to be the sort of person who is apt to forget some things,* and if someone gives me a long speech [d] I lose track of what the argument is about. It's like if I were a bit hard of hearing you'd do me the favor of speaking to me in a louder voice than you use when you speak to others; so because I tend to lose track of the argument in long speeches, please cut your answers short so that I can follow."

"What do you mean by cutting my answers short?" he asked. "Do you want me to answer less than the question demands?"

"Oh, certainly not," I replied.

"Then my answers should be just as long as they ought to be?"

[e] "Yes," I agreed.

"Should my answers be as long as I think they should be, or as long as you think they should be?"

"I've heard, at any rate, that when you are teaching someone something, you can, if you wish, speak so long that the argument never ends, or so briefly [335a] that no one could cover the material more succinctly than you. So if you intend to carry on a discussion with me, please choose the latter method of brevity."

"Oh, Socrates," he replied, "I have participated in many debates,* and if I did what you are telling me to do, carrying on the discussion however my opponent told me to, I wouldn't have shown myself to be better than anyone, and the name Protagoras would not have become well known throughout Greece."

I knew that he wasn't pleased with himself [b] because of the way he had answered my earlier questions, and that he wouldn't willingly go along with answering any further questions that I would ask in the discussion, so I thought I really had no business remaining there with his associates. "Well, then, Protagoras," I said, "I don't want to continue the conversation in a way that is not acceptable to you, so when you would like to carry on the discussion in a way that I can follow, I would be happy to do so then. It is said about you—in fact, you say it yourself—that you can carry on a conversation with either long speeches or short statements, [c] since you are wise, but I'm not up to making long speeches, although I wish I had that ability. Since you have both abilities, you should make this concession so that we could continue our conversation; but since you aren't willing to do that, and there is somewhere that I should go* so I don't really have the free time to listen to long speeches, I'll be going—although I'm sure your speeches would be delightful to hear."

I stood up to leave, but as I was getting up Callias grabbed me with both hands: with his right he took my hand [d] and with his left he got hold of my old, worn out cloak and said, "We won't let you leave, Socrates, because if you go our conversation just won't be the same without you. Please stay with us. There is nothing I would rather hear than a discussion between you and Protagoras. Do us all this favor."

I stood there ready to go and said, "Son of Hipponicus, I always love your commitment to philosophy, [e] and now I do so more than ever. Honestly, I would like to do as you request, but you are asking me to do something that I am able to do. The way things are right now, it's like you are asking me to follow and keep up with Crison,* the runner from Himera, when he was in his prime, or to keep up with someone like Pheidippides who ran all the way from Marathon to Athens after we defeated the Persians.* [336a] Believe me, I am even more eager than you to keep up with Crison but I just can't, so if you want to see me running with him, you'll have to get him to slow down. I can't go any faster, but he can go slower. If you are eager to hear me and Protagoras, then he must answer as he did at the start: briefly and keeping to the question that is asked. [b] If he doesn't, then how will we hold a discussion? I thought that a discussion is a form of dialogue between people, and that it is very different from a public speech."

"But Socrates," Callias said, "it seems fair to allow Protagoras to carry on the dialogue with you in the manner that seems appropriate to him, and to speak in whatever way he wishes to speak, just as you are perfectly free to speak in whatever way seems appropriate to you?"

Alcibiades interrupted at that point and said, "Actually, no, Callias,* that does not seem fair. Socrates has just admitted that he is not in the same league as Protagoras when it comes to long speeches and he has conceded that match. But I would be surprised if he conceded to Protagoras when it comes to dialogue [c] or to the knowledge of how to give an argument and how to deal with an argument that is given by someone else. So if Protagoras is willing to concede that he's inferior to Socrates at discussion, then I'm sure Socrates will be satisfied.* But if he challenges Socrates, then he should carry on the discussion by question and answer, not by stretching his answers out into long speeches and dodging* the issue, [d] refusing to give an actual argument and rambling on so long that everybody forgets what the original question was. Because* Socrates won't forget what the issue is—I promise you that—never mind his joke about being a forgetful sort of person. So I think that Socrates' proposal is the fairer of the two, since each of us should express his own opinion on the matter."

After Alcibiades made his point I think that Critias spoke next. He addressed Prodicus and Hippias and said to them, "It seems to me that Callias [e] has taken Protagoras' side, and of course Alcibiades always wants to win at anything he's excited about. But there's no reason for us to choose sides between Socrates and Protagoras. Let's all come together and ask them not to break up our gathering here."

[337a] After he spoke, Prodicus responded, "Well said, Critias. People who attend such discussions as this should be fair but not equal*—the two are not the same. On the one hand, we should fair to them by hearing them both out; but on the other hand, we should not treat them equally because we should listen more to the wiser of the two, and listen less to the less knowledgeable of the two. I urge you both, Protagoras and Socrates, to agree with one another that you will argue [b] without fighting.* On the one

hand, friends can argue with friends while preserving the goodwill each has for the other; but on the other hand, disputants and enemies fight with one another. If we conduct ourselves in this way, then our gathering will be marvelous, and you two who speak will earn from those of us who listen acclaim without praise.* On the one hand, acclaim comes right from the heart without any deception; but on the other hand, praise is often given with empty words by liars who don't actually believe what they say. [c] And we who listen shall be gladdened without being pleased.* On the one hand, we are gladdened by learning something and by participating in some intellectual activity that is purely in the mind; but on the other hand, we are pleased by eating or by some physical activity that is purely in the body."

A great many approved of what Prodicus had said, and next to speak was the wise Hippias. "Gentlemen, all you who are present here today I consider to be family, friends and neighbors* [d] by nature, not by custom.* For people who are alike are family by nature, but custom is a tyrant that forces us contrary to nature.* Wouldn't it be a shame if we who understand the real nature of things, and are the wisest of the Greeks, and because we are the wisest are now gathered together in the Greek capitol of wisdom, in the greatest and most prosperous house of the city, and yet we show nothing [e] worthy of such great honor—instead we are at odds with one another like ordinary people. I implore and advise you both, Protagoras and Socrates, to be reconciled and agree to the terms that we your advisors recommend. [338a] Socrates, for your part, do not insist upon the form of dialogue that involves precise answers that are extremely brief if Protagoras finds it disagreeable: slacken the reigns a little to allow answers that are elegant and suitable for a magnificent man. And Protagoras, for your part, when you answer a question don't rig your speech with full sails and race ahead of the wind so far out to sea that you lose sight of land. Both of you should steer a middle course. Please heed my advice and select a moderator here who will act as a fair judge and arbitrator [b] for the appropriate length of your speeches."

Hippias' suggestion was agreeable to all* present, and everyone applauded him for making it. Callias said that he would not allow me to leave and he insisted that I select a moderator for the discussion. But I said that it would be inappropriate to select a presiding official for the discussion, because there were only three possibilities. "First, suppose the person chosen is inferior* to us. Well, obviously it would be inappropriate for an inferior to stand over and judge his superiors. Second, suppose that the person chosen is not our inferior but is just like us. Well, that wouldn't be right either because if he's just like us then he'll behave just like us [c] and be redundant. But the third option of choosing someone superior to us is also problematic. In truth, as it seems to me, it will be impossible to choose someone wiser than Protagoras, so what you would be doing is choosing someone who is not superior to Protagoras and declaring that he is. I personally would not consider it an insult to me, but it would a disgraceful insult to Protagoras.

"So here's what I'm willing to do," I continued, "to satisfy your desire to continue the conversation. If Protagoras is unwilling [d] to answer my questions, then I will answer his and at the same time I will try to show him how I think questions ought to be answered. Then, after I have answered as many questions as he wishes to ask, it will be his turn to answer my questions. That way, if he does not keep his answer focused on the question that I ask, all of us together will urge him—as you just urged me—not to ruin the discussion. [e] And there's no need to select just one person to act as a moderator because we all can moderate the discussion together."

My proposal sounded fine to everyone and so we agreed to follow it. Protagoras was very unwilling to go along with the proposal, but in the end he really had no choice but to agree to these terms. After he asked enough questions, it would be his turn to give short answers to my questions.

He started his line of questioning this way. "I believe, Socrates, that the greatest part of a man's education is to be skilled with words, [339a] and by that I mean primarily the ability to discern what is done correctly and what is done incorrectly in a poem, and the knowledge of how to explain the difference when asked for an account. And so the question that I want to ask you has to do precisely with the topic that you and I were discussing—virtue—but the only difference is that I'd like to ask about it in relation to a poem. The one I have in mind is by Simonides,* and in it he says to Scopas the son of Creon the Thessalian:

[b] Indeed,* it is difficult for a man to become truly good;
Foursquare in hands, feet and mind; complete without fault.

Do you know this poem or shall I recite it for you?"

"That won't be necessary," I said, "I do know it. In fact, I've paid special attention to that poem."

"I'm glad to hear it," Protagoras said. "In your opinion, would you say that this poem is well written and that it is correctly composed?"

"Certainly," I said, "both well written and correctly composed."

"But do you think that a poem can be well written if the poet contradicts himself?"*

"No."

"Then you need to take a [c] better look at this poem, Socrates."

"But, my friend, I have already examined it sufficiently."

"Then you know that later he says:

Nor do I think the judgment of Pittacus* to be in tune,
Although he was a wise man he said that it is difficult to be good.

Do you understand that it is the very same man who said this and also lines I quoted earlier?"

"I know."

"And do you think that these lines are compatible with those earlier lines?" Protagoras asked.

"They seem so to me," I said, although I was afraid* that he had a point. "Don't they seem that way to you?"

"How [d] can he appear to be consistent with himself when he says both things? First he says that it is difficult for a man to become truly good, but then just a little later in the same poem he forgets that: not only does he refuse to accept Pittacus' aphorism, he actually blames Pittacus for saying exactly the same thing he said earlier—that it is difficult to be good. Therefore, by blaming Pittacus for saying what he himself said, he is blaming himself; and so either the first claim or the second is incorrect."*

Many in the audience loudly applauded and praised Protagoras at this point, [e] and at first I felt like I'd been punched by a good boxer: I felt stunned and dizzy by the combination of his argument and all the shouting and clapping. But then I turned to Prodicus for help—to tell you the truth, I did that in order to buy myself some time and to give myself a chance to think about the poem. "Prodicus, Simonides is from your town [340a] so it is only right that you come to his defense. I call on you the way that Scamandrius called on Simois when he was being attacked by Achilles: 'Dear brother, let us together resist the might of this man.'* I call on you to help me prevent Protagoras from defeating Simonides. In fact, defending Simonides requires your particular area of expertise that allows you to distinguish between wishing and [b] wanting* as not being the same thing, in the way that you drew those fine distinctions earlier. Consider whether you agree with me because Simonides does not appear to me to contradict himself. But you give your opinion first, Prodicus: is it one and the same thing to become and to be, or are they distinct?"

"The two are distinct, by God" Prodicus said.

"And in the first quotation Protagoras gave, where Simonides expresses his own opinion, he says that [c] it is difficult for a man to *become* good?"

"True," agreed Prodicus.

"Then later, in the second quotation, where he disagrees with Pittacus, he's not disagreeing with the very same thing he just said—as Protagoras maintains—he's disagreeing with quite a different claim? Pittacus did not say that it is difficult to *become* good, which is what Simonides said; rather, Pittacus said that it is difficult to *be* good, which is not the same thing. So you see, Protagoras, if Prodicus is correct to say that being and becoming are not the same thing, then Simonides does not contradict himself. Perhaps

[d] Prodicus—and, in fact, a great many people—agree with Hesiod when he says that it is difficult to become good:

> The obstacle placed before virtue by the gods is sweat
> But once someone has reached the summit
> Then the path is easily trod, though before it was difficult."*

Prodicus approved of this, but Protagoras said, "Your correction, Socrates, makes a worse error than the one you are correcting."

"Then I've done a terrible job, it seems, [e] and am a ridiculous doctor since my treatment makes the disease worse."

"That is exactly how it is," Protagoras said.

"How so?" I asked.

"Simonides would have to be an idiot to say that it's easy to hold on to virtue—that is the hardest thing of all, as everybody agrees."*

"Then by god," I said, "it's fortunate that we have Prodicus here with us. I suspect that [341a] his wisdom is both divine and ancient;* perhaps it derives from the time of Simonides or even earlier. Although you have experience with many other forms of wisdom, Protagoras, you seem unexperienced in this one—unlike me: I can claim to have some skill because I am one of Prodicus' students.* So in this instance I think you don't understand that perhaps Simonides meant something different by the word 'difficult'* than you assume. It's like when Prodicus scolds me for using the word 'terrible' when I am praising someone—for example, if I say that Protagoras is a terribly wise man, he will ask me [b] whether I am ashamed of myself for calling something good terrible. He says that calling something terrible is saying that it is bad. At any rate, nobody says 'terrible wealth,' or 'terrible peace,' or 'terrible health;' but they do say 'terrible illness,' 'terrible war,' or 'terrible poverty.' So, what is terrible is bad. Perhaps Simonides, Prodicus and everybody from the island of Cos assumes that what is difficult is bad, or uses it in some way that you aren't familiar with. Since Prodicus speaks the same dialect as Simonides, let's ask him about it. Tell us, Prodicus, what did Simonides mean by [c] 'difficult'?"

"Bad," Prodicus answered.

"And that's why he criticizes Pittacus for saying that it is difficult to be good? It's as if he heard Pittacus saying that it is bad to be good."

"Can you think of anything else he could be saying?" Prodicus asked me. "Simonides is accusing Pittacus of not knowing how to distinguish words correctly—after all, Pittacus was actually raised on the island of Lesbos* and so he grew up speaking a foreign language."*

"Well, Protagoras," I said, "you hear what Prodicus has to say. [d] Do you have any reply?"

"You are quite wrong, Prodicus," he said, "I know quite well that by 'difficult' Simonides meant the same thing that we mean by that word; he didn't mean 'bad,' he meant 'not easy' and 'what takes much effort.'"

"I agree with you, Protagoras," I said. "That is what Simonides meant—and Prodicus knows it also, he was just joking and putting you to the test to see if you would be able to defend your view. Simonides did not mean 'bad' when he said 'difficult,' [e] and there is a clear sign of this in the very next line:

> God* only has this gift

Certainly he wouldn't say that it is bad to be good and then go on to say that this gift of being good belongs only to god. If he did say that, Prodicus would call him intemperate and a fraud.* But I'd like to tell you what I think Simonides meant in this ode* [342a] or poem—as you call it. So if you'd like to test my skill at interpreting poetry, I'll explain my view. But if you'd prefer to give your view I will listen."

"Go right ahead," Protagoras said, "if you wish." Prodicus, Hippias and the others urged me to explain my view.

"Very well, then," I said, "I shall try to explain to you what I think about this ode.* The most ancient philosophy in Greece is to be found on the island of Crete [b] and in Sparta—and in fact these are the very places where philosophy is the most prevalent. There also happen to be more sophists in Crete and Sparta than there are anywhere else on earth. Of course they deny this and pretend to be uneducated—as Protagoras said earlier* when he was talking about sophists—so that it isn't completely obvious how far they excel all other Greeks in wisdom. They pretend that their superiority lies in battle and courage* because they think that if their true superiority were known, then everybody would try to cultivate it. They've been quite successful at concealing this and deceiving Spartan sympathizers* in Athens, who imitate them by getting punched around in the boxing ring, [c] working out in the gymnasium and wearing those short capes that are fashionable in Sparta—thinking that Spartan superiority over all Greeks derives from these sorts of things. One way they conceal this is by expelling Spartan sympathizers and any foreigner living in their city when they want to consult with their sophists, because they get annoyed when they have to hold secret meetings. They also don't allow their young men [d] to travel to other cities in order to prevent them from forgetting what they learn at home. The Cretans do this also.

"In both places it is not only the men but also the women who think so much of their education. Here's how you'll know I'm telling you the truth that Spartans are the best educated in philosophy and in argumentation. Have a conversation with a completely ordinary Spartan and for much of the conversation [e] he will appear to be completely ordinary. However, at some point he'll toss in a word or compressed phrase that is absolutely devastating—like a dart right to the bullseye—and he'll leave you looking like you have the conversational skills of a toddler. That is why it has long been recognized, and is still recognized today, that being a Spartan sympathizer consists more in the love of wisdom than the love of athletics: the ability to make devastating comments like that reveals [343a] a complete education. Men like this include the famous Seven Sages:*

Thales of Miletus,
Pittacus of Mytilene,
Bias of Priene,
Solon of Athens,
Cleobulus of Lindos,
Myson of Chen, and
Chilon of Sparta.

All seven of these men were advocates, admirers, and students of Spartan education. In fact, you can see that their wisdom is just the terse sort of the Spartans by the short, memorable sayings of theirs [b] dedicated to Apollo and inscribed on the temple at Delphi: everybody says, "know thyself" and "nothing in excess."

"What is my point? I'm trying to show that this is the way of the ancient philosophy: brief and laconic.* It was in this form that the saying of Pittacus, 'it is difficult to be good,' which was acclaimed by the wise, was handed down from generation to generation. [c] Simonides wanted a reputation for wisdom, and he knew that he'd get it if he could defeat this saying, like a young boxer dethroning the reigning champion. It seems to me that his aim in this entire poem is to defeat Pittacus' famous saying.

"Let's all examine it together to see if what I say is true. It seems to me that if he actually intended to say that it is difficult for a man to be good, [d] then he wouldn't have started with 'Rather,' like this:

Rather,* truly it is difficult for a man to become good;

Starting with this word* makes no sense if we don't assume that he's setting up a contrast between himself and Pittacus, fighting against his view. On the one hand, Pittacus says that it is difficult to be good, but then on the other hand, Simonides argues against him saying* that it is not difficult to *be* good, rather it is difficult to *become* good.

"Next, when he uses the word 'truly,' he's not using it to modify 'good.' He's not distinguishing between being good and being truly good—as if [e] some people are truly good, and others are good, but not truly. That doesn't make any sense, and it doesn't sound like anything Simonides would say. He's using a figure of speech called 'hyperbaton'* in which two words that go together are separated by a word or phrase inserted between them. In this case, the word 'truly' is separated from the word 'difficult.'* We can get the sense of it if we think of Pittacus and Simonides in a dialogue like this:

PITTACUS. People, it is difficult to be good.

SIMONIDES. [344a] Pittacus, what you say is not true. It is not to *be* good, but rather to *become* good— foursquare in hands, feet and mind; complete without fault—that is truly difficult.

This puts the 'truly' in its proper place next to 'difficult,' and it also makes complete sense of the 'rather' because he is contrasting what he thinks is the truth with what Pittacus famously said.

"There are many other expressions [b] in the poem that show it is well constructed—it is quite a graceful and carefully composed work—but it would take a long time to go through all of them. Let's just go through the structure and intention of the poem as a whole, and I think we'll see that the entire poem is designed as a refutation of Pittacus' famous saying.

"A few lines later Simonides goes on almost as if he is giving an argument.

SIMONIDES. To become a good man is truly difficult, but at least it is possible for a short time. However, once someone has become a good man, to remain [c] in that state and to be a good man— which is what you are talking about Pittacus—that is impossible and inhuman. Only god has that blessing.

It is not possible for a man not to be bad
Whom unmanageable misfortune has knocked down.*

Who is he talking about here? For example, in managing a ship, who can get knocked down by unmanageable misfortune? Certainly not the passenger because you can't knock someone down if he isn't standing up.* [d] Passengers are not even trying to manage the ship, so if a storm wrecks it you cannot say that their efforts to manage the ship were ruined. But you can say that the pilot's efforts to steer clear of bad weather were ruined by the unmanageable storm, just as you can say that a farmer's efforts to grow a crop were ruined by unmanageable bad weather, and a doctor's efforts to heal a patient were ruined by unmanageable illness.* It is allowed by some that an honorable man may become bad.* For example, another poet said

But a good man is sometimes bad and sometimes honorable.*

[e] On the other hand, a bad man cannot *become* bad because he is always necessarily bad.* Therefore, when an unmanageable misfortune knocks down a resourceful, wise and good man, it is not possible for him not to be bad.

SIMONIDES. But you, Pittacus, say that it is difficult to be good. You are wrong: it is difficult to *become* good—to *be* good is impossible.

When things are going well, all men are good;
But when things are going badly, all men are bad.

[345a] Who is he talking about here? For example, in reading and writing, who is good and what is it for things to be going well? Obviously it's when the one who has learned how to read and write successfully reads or writes.* And what about treating the sick: who is good and what is it for things to be going well in treating the sick? Obviously it's when the one who has learned to treat sick people successfully treats sick people. But what does he mean when he says that all men are bad when things are going badly? Who could

become a bad doctor simply because things are going badly? Obviously someone who was not only a doctor but a good doctor, because only a good doctor can *become* a bad doctor by having things to badly. Those of us who aren't doctors at all cannot become any kind of doctor—or any kind of carpenter, or blacksmith, or weaver, [b] or anything like that—by having things go badly for us. And if we cannot become any kind of doctor by having things go well or badly for someone who is ill, then obviously we cannot become a bad kind of doctor by having things go badly.

"So only a good man can become bad,* either because of age, or because the work eventually takes its toll on you, or because of illness or some other affliction: the only way to change from doing well to doing badly is to be deprived of the knowledge you possess. A bad man cannot *become* bad because to become bad is to change from being good one day to being bad the next day; since a bad man is already bad, he cannot change from being good to being bad—he must become good before he can become bad.

"This is what the poem is referring to, [c] that it is impossible for a man to *be* good—to be *continuously* good. But on the other hand, to *become* good is possible, and then for someone who has become good to become bad is also possible. The ones who are good for the longest time are the best, and they are loved by the gods.

"Simonides said all of this against Pittacus. This is even more obvious in the next part of the poem. He goes on to say

> I shall not seek what can never be,
> Throwing away my life on an empty hope,
> Searching for an utterly blameless man
> Receiving his just deserts for his blameless life.
> But if I do happen to find such a man,
> I'll be sure to tell you all about him.

[d] The entire poem is a scathing attack on Pittacus' saying. Look at what else Simonides says.

> I praise and consider myself a friend to
> All who do nothing shameful, voluntarily,*
> For even the gods do not fight against necessity.

Here he's saying the same thing. Surely Simonides isn't so uneducated as to say that he praises those who don't do anything bad voluntarily because that would imply that he thinks there are some people who voluntarily do bad things. On the contrary, I think pretty much the same thing as Simonides here: [e] no wise man thinks that any human being voluntarily goes wrong or does something shameful or bad. Simonides knows perfectly well that everyone who does something shameful or bad does so involuntarily.* So he's not saying that he praises people who do nothing shameful voluntarily; the 'voluntarily' applies to himself: he's saying that he voluntarily praises people who do nothing shameful. He's contrasting voluntary praise with involuntary praise, praise that is given under compulsion.*

"Simonides thought that fine and good men are often compelled to praise and to befriend someone. [346a] For example, people are often forced to put up with being treated badly by their father or mother or even by their country. Men with no sense of honor or respect are more than happy to whine and complain and make all kinds of scandalous allegations about their own parents or their country. Of course they do this simply to avoid being condemned for neglecting their parents or for failing to carry out some civic duty. They exaggerate their complaints [b] and so add voluntary enemies to the ones they are compelled to put up with. Good men, on the other hand, keep their complaints to themselves and compel themselves to praise their parents and their country, even if they feel angry at them. Good men stay calm and reconcile themselves to the situation, forcing themselves to be friendly to, and to speak respectfully about, their own parents and their own country. I think Simonides often felt that he was praising and extolling some tyrant involuntarily, only because he had to. That's why he addresses Pittacus the way he does.

SIMONIDES. [c] It is not because I am overcritical that I find fault with you, Pittacus, since

I am satisfied as long as you aren't bad
Or too reckless. A man of sound mind* knows that
Respect for what is right benefits the entire community.
I don't pass judgment on any such man

'because I am not a judgemental person' is what he means.

Fools are too numerous to count

and so anyone who enjoys finding fault with others will never run out of people to find fault with. 'But in my view,' according to Simonides,

All are fine, as long as they are
Not mixed up with anything shameful.

[d] When he makes this last comment, he's not talking about mixing the fine and the shameful like mixing a little black paint into the white paint. That would be completely ridiculous. He simply means that he accepts people who are in the middle and doesn't blame people for not being perfect.

SIMONIDES: I do not seek a man who is wholly blameless, receiving his just deserts for his blameless life. But if I do happen to find such a man, I'll be sure to tell you all about him.

What he means here is that if the only people he praises are the people who are absolutely blameless, then he'll never praise anybody.

SIMONIDES: I am satisfied if someone is in the middle as long as he doesn't do something bad, because I praise and am a friend to all such people.

Here he uses [e] the Mytilenean dialect* because that's where Pittacus was from. And here is where the word 'voluntarily' belongs, because in such cases his friendship and praise is voluntarily given.

SIMONIDES: Voluntarily I praise and befriend all who do nothing shameful, that is the man I praise and befriend voluntarily, because there are some people I praise involuntarily. And so, Pittacus, if you didn't go to extremes [347a] but said only what is reasonable and true, then I would never blame you. But in fact you lie about something that is extremely important, and that is why I blame you.

"And so, Prodicus and Protagoras," I concluded, "that is what I believe Simonides was thinking when he wrote this ode."

Then Hippias said, "In my opinion, you've done quite well in expounding this ode. [b] I too have a good account of it,* and I'd gladly share it with you if you wish."

Alcibiades responded, saying, "Yes, Hippias, the next time we'll hear your account. But right now we really ought to follow through on what Socrates and Protagoras agreed. So if Protagoras has any more questions he'd like to ask Socrates, then Socrates should answer; but if he has no more questions, then it is Socrates' turn to ask questions."

I broke in and said, "I leave it to Protagoras to do as he pleases. But if it's alright with him, let's leave odes and poems out of it. [c] I'd like to complete our examination of the issue I raised at the start. Discussing poetry reminds me too much of common drinking parties.* Uneducated people cannot sustain an intelligent conversation with one another while they are drinking, and so instead of listening to each other they hire [d] flute girls and listen to them instead. But when the guests are all educated, fine and good men, you won't see any flute girls, dancing girls or harp girls. They are able to entertain one another without any of those immature diversions by carrying on an intelligent conversation, speaking and listening to each other in an orderly way, [e] even if they drink quite a lot.* If we are the kind of men most of us* claim to be, then we don't need any strangers to help our conversation, and we don't need poets. It is impossible to question poets about what they say.* When they are brought into a discussion, some will say that the poet had one thing in mind, but others will say that the poet had a different view, and they go on arguing about something that is impossible to prove either way.* Educated men avoid such conversations. [348a] Instead, they rely on themselves and talk with one another, putting one another to the test in turns. I think that you and I ought to follow their example, Protagoras. Let's set the poets aside and just talk to one another; let's put each other, and the truth, to the test.

"So, if you want to ask any further questions, then please go right ahead: I'm ready to give you answers. Or, if you wish, you can answer my questions; we were in the middle of discussing something,* and I'd really like to complete that discussion."

[b] After I said this, and a few other things along the same lines, Protagoras didn't state clearly which of the two alternatives he would choose. So Alcibiades spoke up, and looking at Callias said, "What do you think of Protagoras being unwilling to say clearly whether or not he'll answer Socrates' questions? Is that any way for a gentleman to behave in a gathering such as ours? I certainly don't think so, Callias. He should either continue the discussion with Socrates, or he should say definitively that he doesn't want to so that we know how things stand. That way Socrates can carry on his discussion with someone else, or we can switch to another topic and two other volunteers can debate it."

[c] It seemed to me that Protagoras felt ashamed of himself because of what Alcibiades had said, and because Callias—as well as almost everybody present—asked him to continue. So he reluctantly rejoined the discussion; he told Socrates to ask questions and that he would answer them.

So I said, "Protagoras, please don't think that I want to discuss with you anything other than the issues that always puzzle me—it is these issues that I want to investigate. I think there's a lot in what Homer said: [d] 'when two go together, one perceives before the other'.* We are all more resourceful in every thought, word and deed when we go together. 'But if one alone perceives,' he immediately goes around looking until he finds someone to show it to in order to confirm it.* The reason I'd rather discuss this with you than with someone else is that I think you are the best person* to inquire about the things [e] into which a reasonable man might reasonably inquire, and especially about virtue. Who other than you? It's not just that you think of yourself as being a fine and good man—many others are quite decent people, but they are not able to make others decent as well. Not only are you a good man, but you are able to make others good, and you have such faith in your ability that unlike others who conceal this skill from others, [349a] you come right out in the open and declare to all the Greeks that you are a sophist, and educator and a teacher of virtue, and you are the first to charge a fee for your instruction. Obviously I couldn't possibly neglect to call upon you to join me in this inquiry, and to engage you in question and answer.

"So now, I'd like to go back to what I asked you at first. There are some things I'd like you to remind me of,* and other things I'd like to delve into. [b] I think the question was this: wisdom, temperance, courage, justice and piety—are these five names for one thing, or does each one name a unique thing with its own distinctive capacity, each one being different from each of the others? You said that they are not different names for the same thing, but that [c] each of these names referred to a unique thing, and that all together they are the five parts of virtue—not like the parts of a lump of gold, which are all like one another and like the whole, but rather like parts of a face in which each part is unlike the whole, and unlike each other part, since each part has its own unique capacity. Tell me if you still maintain this view. If your view now is any different than it was earlier, that's perfectly fine with me, just tell me what you think now. I certainly wouldn't be surprised if you said that earlier [d] just to put me to the test."

Protagoras answered, "I say that these are five parts of virtue, and that four of them are fairly similar to one another, but that courage is very different from all the others.* You can tell that this is true because you will find many people who are extremely unjust, impious, undisciplined and stupid, but are also extraordinarily courageous."

[e] "Stop there," I said. "What you've said is worth examining. Do you say that courageous people are daring people,* or something else?"

"Yes, bold," he answered, "and ready to launch headlong into what most people fear."

"And do you also say that virtue is something fine, and that because it is something fine you offer yourself as a teacher of it?"

"Oh, yes, it is among the finest of things, if I'm not out of my mind," Protagoras agreed.

"But, then, is all virtue fine, or is only one part fine while another part is shameful?"

"It is wholly fine, as fine as possible."

"And do you know who [350a] dares to dive into wells?" I asked.

"I do. Divers."

"And do they dive into wells because they know how to,* or for some other reason?"

"No, that is it, because of knowledge."

"And which ones are daring when it comes to fighting on horseback: the cavalry or those who have never trained on horses?"

"The cavalry."

"And who is daring when it comes to fighting with a light shield: those who are trained in fighting with a light shield, or those who are untrained?"

"The trained ones," Protagoras answered. "It's the same in all the other cases, if that's what you are looking for, Socrates: the ones who know are more daring than the ones who don't know; and once they've learned, [b] they are more daring than they were before."

So then I asked, "Have you ever seen anybody who was ignorant of all these things, but was daring in each of them?"

"I have indeed," he said, "but they were excessively daring."

"And these daring people are also courageous?"

"But in that case, courage would be shameful—but these people are out of their minds."

"So what are you saying about courageous people? Aren't they daring?"

"Yes, I still say that."

[c] "But then these men," I said, "are daring, but they won't be courageous,* will they, because they are out of their minds? And on the other hand, the wisest people are the most daring people, and since they are the most daring, won't they be the most courageous? On this account, then, won't wisdom be courage?"

"You are not remembering very well what I said in anwer to your question, Socrates. When you asked me if the courageous are daring, I agreed. But I was not asked if the daring are courageous. If you had asked me that, I would have said that [d] not all of them are courageous. You have not demonstrated that I was incorrect to say that the courageous are daring.

"Next," Protagoras continued, "you show that those who have knowledge are more daring than when they were ignorant, and they are more daring others who are currently ignorant, and for this reason you think that courage and wisdom are one and the same thing. But you could use exactly the same sort of argument to conclude that strength and wisdom are the same thing. Here's how it would go.

> SOCRATES. Are the strong [e] capable?
> PROTAGORAS. Yes.
> SOCRATES. And are those who know how to wrestle more capable than those who do not know how to wrestle, and more capable than they were after they learned than before they learned how to wrestle?
> PROTAGORAS. Yes.*
> SOCRATES. So the strong are capable, and the capable are knowledgeable?
> PROTAGORAS. Yes.

SOCRATES. So strength and wisdom are one and the same thing.

But notice the flaw in your reasoning: I agree that the strong are capable, but I do not agree that the capable are strong. [351a] Capability and strength are not the same thing.* Capability can derive from knowledge, but it can also derive from passion or even from madness. But strength derives from nature and also from the nurture of the body.

"You can see exactly the same sort of thing with daring and courage: they are not the same thing; although courageous people are daring, not all daring people are courageous. Daring can derive from skill, [b] but it can also derive from passion or from madness—just like capability. But courage is like strength* because it derives from nature or from the nurture of the soul."

In response, I asked, "Protagoras, do you say that some men live well and some badly?"
He agreed.
"And is someone living well if they are living in distress or in pain?"
"No," he said.
"What if he lived his life pleasantly to the end? Do you think that living that way is living well?"
"Yes, I do think so."
"Therefore, [c] to live pleasantly is good, and to live unpleasantly is bad?"
"If you live enjoying fine things, not shameful things."
"What's that, Protagoras? Surely you aren't saying what most people say—that some pleasures are bad and some pains are good? I mean that insofar as something is pleasant, apart from anything other than pleasure that results from it, isn't it in that respect good? And isn't it similar with painful things; insofar as they are painful aren't they bad?"
"I don't think it's that simple, Socrates. [d] I don't think we can say that all pleasant things are good and all painful things are bad. I think it is safer to give the answer I've given my whole life: some pleasant things are not good, some painful things are not bad, and there is a third category of things that are neither good nor bad."
So I asked, "Well, what things do you call pleasant? Aren't they things that either produce pleasure, [e] or are pleasant in themselves?"*
"Certainly."
"That's what I'm asking about. Insofar as something is pleasant, isn't it good? I'm simply asking about the pleasure itself—isn't that good?"
"Well, to quote you, Socrates, 'Let's investigate the issue.' You claim that pleasure and good are the same thing. If that claim is shown to be reasonable, then we will agree to accept it. But if not, then we'll be at odds with one another on this point."
"Would you like to lead the investigation, or shall I?"
"Oh, it's only right that you should lead it; after all, you are the one who has put it forward."

[352a] "Perhaps we can shed some light on it this way," I began. "Suppose a doctor was trying to evaluate your physical condition. After looking at your face and hands he might say, 'Alright, please take off your shirt so that I can do a more thorough examination.' That's the sort of thing I'd like to do now to pursue our investigation. I've heard what you say about what is good and what is pleasant, but now I'd like to hear more. So I'm inclined to say, 'Alright, Protagoras, [b] please show me your thoughts on this: how do you think of knowledge?' Do you say what most people say about it? Most people think that it isn't strong, that it doesn't lead us, and it doesn't rule us.* They don't think of knowledge like that at all. Instead, they think that in many cases, someone with knowledge is not ruled by their knowledge but by something else—sometimes passion, sometimes pleasure, sometimes pain, and at another time desire rules him and often people are ruled by fear. [c] They think that knowledge is like a slave that is dragged around by all

these other things. Is that the way you think of knowledge, Protagoras? Or do you think that knowledge is something fine, and that it is able to rule a person, and that if someone knows* what is good and what is bad he will not be mastered by anything that will cause him to act contrary to what his knowledge commands him to do, and that intelligence* is sufficient to benefit us?"

"It seems to me just as you say, Socrates. In fact, [d] it would be particularly disgraceful for me to deny that wisdom and knowledge are the mightiest of all when it comes to human action."

"I think you've expressed the truth quite admirably, Protagoras. However, you know that most people do not agree with us. They say that many people know what's best to do, and are able to do it, but they aren't willing to do it, and instead they do something else. I've asked some of them what is responsible for this, and they say that in cases where someone is unwilling to do what they know is best, [e] they are overcome* by pleasure or pain, or they were mastered by one of the things I was just mentioning."

"Yes, well people say lots of false things, Socrates."

"Then help me to convince them and to teach them what is actually going on in these cases they describe as [353a] being overcome by pleasure, and not doing what you know full well to be the best thing to do. I suppose that if we simply told them that they are wrong they would probably ask us, 'But if this isn't actually being overcome by pleasure, then what is happening in these kinds of cases? Explain that.'"

"Why should we investigate what most people think?" Protagoras asked. "They say whatever happens to occur to them."

[b] "I think that this will help us to discover how courage is related to the other parts of virtue. So if you still think* that it is right for me to lead this investigation, then follow me and I will pursue the course that seems the best way to make things clear. But if you'd rather not, do as you like and I'll let it go."

"You're right, Socrates. Finish what you've begun."

[c] "Then, again, imagine that they ask us the question I just mentioned.

THE MANY.* We call this experience 'being overcome by pleasure.' What do you call it?

SOCRATES/PROTAGORAS. Listen, and Protagoras and I shall try to explain. When you talk about being overcome by pleasure*—for example, the pleasure of eating, drinking, or having sex*—you claim that someone knows they are doing something wrong,* but they do it anyway?

THE MANY. Yes.

SOCRATES/PROTAGORAS. In what way do you say that the action is wrong? [d] Is it wrong insofar as it produces pleasure, and is pleasant in itself;* or is it wrong insofar as it produces illness and poverty and has many other such results? I mean, suppose the action never produced any of these ill effects: would you still say that it is bad on the grounds that it produces pleasure in some way?

THE MANY. No. It is not bad because it produces pleasure. [e] It is bad because of its later results: illness and all the other things."

"Yes," said Protagoras. "I think that is what most people would say."

SOCRATES/PROTAGORAS. And by causing illness, it causes pain? And similarly with poverty: by causing poverty, it causes pain?

THE MANY. Yes.

SOCRATES/PROTAGORAS. So doesn't it seem to you, gentlemen, as Protagoras and I maintain,* the action is bad for no other reason than that it causes pain and it ends in [354a] our being deprived of some pleasure?

THE MANY. Yes.

SOCRATES/PROTAGORAS. What about the opposite* situation? When you say that some painful things are good, are you referring to activities like exercising, performing military service, and undergoing medical treatments like having wounds cauterized, having a limb amputated, taking medications, going without food and so on. Are these the sorts of things that you call good, but painful?

THE MANY. Yes.

SOCRATES/PROTAGORAS. In what way [b] do you say that these are good? Are they good insofar as they cause pain later, and are painful in themselves; or are they good insofar as they produce health and a robust body, the protection of the city, political power and wealth?

THE MANY. Yes. They are good because of those good results.

SOCRATES/PROTAGORAS. Well, then, what about these good results? In what way do you say that they are good? Are they good for any other reason than that they end in various kinds of pleasure, they provide relief from various kinds of pain, and they prevent* pain? Is there any other end result [c] you can point to as a basis for calling them good other than pleasure and pain?*

THE MANY. No."

"I agree that there isn't any alternative end result," Protagoras said.

SOCRATES/PROTAGORAS. "So you pursue pleasure as good, and avoid pain as bad?

THE MANY. Yes.

SOCRATES/PROTAGORAS. So you think that pain is bad and pleasure is good, since you call enjoyment* bad when it takes away greater pleasures than it gives, or when the pains it gives are greater than [d] the pleasures it gives. If there were any other end result you were using other than pleasure and pain to decide that a particular enjoyment is bad, then you'd be able to state what it is. But you can't identify anything other than pleasure and pain, can you?"

"No, certainly they can't," said Protagoras.

SOCRATES/PROTAGORAS. Furthermore, just as you can call an enjoyment bad, so also you can call a pain good. If a lesser pain frees us from greater pains, or it produces more pleasure than pain, then you call that [e] pain good, don't you? If there were some other goal* you were using as a standard to judge what is good and what is bad—besides the one I've been using—you'd be able to tell me what that goal is, wouldn't you? But you don't have any other goal to use as a standard, do you?"

"What you say is true," Protagoras agreed.

So I said, "I think they would then ask us a question."

THE MANY. "Why are you going on and on about this, looking at it from every angle?

SOCRATES/PROTAGORAS. Two reasons. First, it isn't easy to demonstrate what it is to be—as you put it—overcome by pleasures. Second, the entire demonstration depends upon this point. So you can still take it back [355a] if you have any reason to say that the good is something other than pleasure, or that the bad is anything other than pain. Are you content to live out your whole life in pleasure without pain? If that is enough for you, and if you have nothing else to say except that the good and the bad are whatever results in pleasure or pain,* then we can move on.

My claim is that if you accept this account of the good and the bad, then your assertion that people are often overcome by pleasure becomes ridiculous.* You assert that people often do something bad because they are driven and overpowered by pleasure, despite the fact that they know they are doing something bad, and it is possible for them to avoid doing it. [b] Similarly, you assert that often people are unwilling to do something good because they are overcome by the pleasure of doing something else. That these assertions are ridiculous will become perfectly clear if we stop using different words for the same things. 'Pleasure,' 'pain,' 'good,' and 'bad' sound like four things, when it appears that they are only two. Therefore, we ought to use just two names for them. First we'll use 'good' and 'bad;' next we'll use 'pleasure' [c] and 'pain.'

Let's begin with your scenario of a particular action that is in fact bad, and a man knows that it is bad, but he does it anyway.* Now, restricting yourself to just 'good' and 'bad,' please tell me why he does something he knows to be bad?

THE MANY. Because he is overcome.

SOCRATES/PROTAGORAS. Overcome by what? And remember, don't use 'pleasure' or 'pain' in your answer—substitute* 'good' for 'pleasure' and give your answer that way. So, again, you claim that he is overcome, but overcome by what?

THE MANY. He is overcome by…good, by god!

SOCRATES/PROTAGORAS. [d] I hope I'm not being rude, but that's ridiculous. You are saying that someone does something bad, knowing that it is bad, and he doesn't have to do it, but he does it anyway because he is overcome by something good.* Now, let's be clear: are you saying that the good is worthy of conquering the bad, or that it is not worthy of conquering the bad?

THE MANY. I suppose I have to say that it is not worthy, because otherwise this wouldn't be a case of someone going wrong, which is what we mean when we say that someone is overcome by pleasure.

SOCRATES/PROTAGORAS. Then in what respect is the good unworthy of overcoming the bad? Is it when one side is smaller and the other is greater, [e] or when one has fewer and the other has more?

THE MANY. I can't explain it any other way.

SOCRATES/PROTAGORAS. Clearly, then, your case of a man going wrong in choosing something bad because he is overcome by something good is a case of him choosing to do something that is more bad and less good than an alternative action that he could choose. That settles that.

Now let's use the other pair of words—'pleasure' and 'pain'—and consider the same scenario. So instead of talking about a man who does something 'bad,' we'll say that he does something 'painful,' knowing full well that it is painful, and he does it because he is overcome [356a] by something pleasant. And again, we'll say that the pleasure is not worthy of conquering the pain. But in what respect is pleasure unworthy of conquering pain? Can it be anything other than a matter of excess and deficiency in relation to one another? So when it comes to pleasures and pains, one alternative is worthy of conquering or overcoming the other alternative when the first is more, greater or larger than the second.

THE MANY. But there is another difference to consider, Socrates. Experiencing pleasure right now is very different from pleasure or pain at some later time.*

SOCRATES/PROTAGORAS. But surely they aren't any different with respect to pleasure or pain, and that's really the only distinction that matters, isn't it? Just like [b] an expert at weights and measures put the pleasures and pains in the scale, both the near and the far, to see which is more. If you are choosing between two pleasant options, then measure them both and the option with greater and more pleasures must be taken. If you are choosing between two painful options, then measure them both and the option with smaller and fewer pains must be taken. If you are facing an option with both pleasures and pains, then measure them all—both the present and the future pains and pleasures—and if the pleasures exceed the pains, then it must be done; otherwise, if [c] the pains exceed the pleasures, then it must not be done. Is there any other way to make the choice?"

I told Protagoras that I was sure they couldn't identify any other way to make the choice, and he agreed.

SOCRATES/PROTAGORAS. "Since this is so, please answer this next question. If you take two things of exactly the same size and place one near you and one far away from you, doesn't the near one look larger than the one that is far away?

THE MANY. Yes it does.

SOCRATES/PROTAGORAS. Obviously sounds are louder when they are close and quieter when they are far away, but isn't the same thing true when it comes to thickness and with number? Something thick won't seem quite so thick if it is far away, and a collection of things that looks like a lot when you see it up close will look like only a few things if the collection is farther away, won't it?

THE MANY. Yes.

SOCRATES/PROTAGORAS. Well, then, [d] suppose your whole life depended upon choosing the larger things and avoiding the smaller things. In that case, what would we look upon as our salvation in life: the *science of measurement,*[*] or the *power of appearance*? Think about it. The power of appearance makes us wander all over chasing illusions, changing our minds and regretting many of our choices and many of the things we've done. But the science of measurement renders appearances powerless by showing us the truth; [e] it gives our souls peace by allowing us to hold on to the truth, and it saves our very lives.

"What do you think, Protagoras? Once they had considered all this, would people agree that it is the science of measurement, and not the power of appearance, that saves us?"

"Yes, they would," Protagoras said.

"And what if saving our lives depended upon choosing an odd number or an even number, or there was a situation where it was absolutely necessary that we correctly choose more things rather than fewer things, whether they were right in front of us or far away? In those kinds of situations what would save us? [357a] Knowledge, right? And it would have to be a knowledge of measurement, wouldn't it, because that is the science of magnitude, both large and small. In fact, if we are dealing specifically with calculating even and odd numbers, then it would be arithmetic that would save us, wouldn't it? Don't you think people would agree with that?"

"Yes, I think they would."

SOCRATES/PROTAGORAS. "Well, then, gentlemen, since our salvation in life actually depends not on correctly choosing odd or even numbers, but on correctly choosing pleasures and pains—more and fewer, [b] greater and lesser, sooner and later—isn't it clear that we need to rely on measurement, which is the study of magnitudes telling us when one thing exceeds another, when it falls short of another, and when they are precisely equal?

THE MANY. Necessarily.

SOCRATES/PROTAGORAS. And since it is measurement, it is necessarily a science and a form of knowledge, isn't it?

THE MANY. Yes.

SOCRATES/PROTAGORAS. Now, exactly which science it is and exactly which form of knowledge it is we shall consider later. In order to answer the original question that you asked, all that Protagoras and I need [c] to demonstrate right now is that it is definitely a form of knowledge. Remember, Protagoras and I maintain that nothing is stronger than knowledge, and that when you have it, knowledge is always stronger than pleasure and everything else. But you said, to the contrary, that often pleasure is stronger even for a man with knowledge.[*] Do you recall what you asked us when we disagreed?

THE MANY. Yes. We asked you what you call this experience if you don't call it being overcome by pleasure.

SOCRATES/PROTAGORAS. [d] If we had told you the truth right away and said that we call it ignorance, you would have laughed at us. But now, if you laugh at us for giving that answer, you are also laughing at yourselves. You have agreed with us that those who go wrong in their choice of pleasures and pains—or good and bad, if you want to call them that—go wrong because they lack knowledge. In fact, you've even agreed that the particular kind of knowledge people are lacking when they make that mistake is measurement. And obviously when people go wrong because [e] they lack knowledge, they are going wrong because of ignorance.

So this is what being overcome by pleasure really is: the worst ignorance possible. And ignorance is precisely what Protagoras, Prodicus and Hippias say they cure. But because you don't think that ignorance is the problem, you don't accept these sophists as your teachers, and you don't send your children to them either. It is because you don't think that this problem can be solved by education—and because you care so much about money that you don't want to pay their fees—that is why you aren't doing well in your private affairs or when you participate in public affairs.

[358a] "That is what we should say to the many people who think that we can do what we know is bad because we are overcome by pleasure. And so with Protagoras, I ask you both, Hippias and Prodicus—you may consult together on this issue—do you think that what I've said is true or false?"

They both were completely convinced that my account was entirely true, so I continued, "You agree, therefore, that the pleasant is good and the painful is bad. Prodicus, I beg your indulgence here since I know that you like to distinguish different terms, but whether you call it pleasure, or delight, or enjoyment, or whatever you like, [b] I think you know what I have in mind, my friend." Laughing, Prodicus said that he agreed, and so did the others.

"Well, then," I asked, "what about this next point? All actions that are aimed at living our lives pleasantly and without pain are fine and beneficial, and if they are fine and beneficial, then aren't they also good?" They agreed to this also, so I asked, "Therefore, if what is pleasant is good, then whenever someone knows or believes* that there is an alternative to what he is doing that is better, [c] he won't continue doing what he's doing, instead he'll do what is better, won't he? Being overcome by oneself is nothing other than ignorance, and being master of your own actions is nothing other than wisdom." Everybody agreed to this.

"So then the next point is this: what is ignorance? Isn't it having a false opinion and being mistaken about something important?" They agreed. "And nobody voluntarily goes for bad things, or things they believe to be bad. [d] It simply isn't in human nature* willingly to go towards what is bad rather than towards what is good. Also, if it is necessary to choose between two bad alternatives, nobody chooses the greater if it is possible to choose the lesser." Everybody agreed to all of this.

"Then here's the next point. Is there something that you call fright or fear, and is it the same thing that I call fear? Prodicus, this question is for you. I'm referring to an expectation of something bad—whether you call it fear or fright." Protagoras and Hippias said that both fright and fear were an expectation of something bad; [e] Prodicus said that it was only fright, and that fear was different. So I said, "That's fine, Prodicus. My point is this: if the account I just gave is true, then will anyone be willing to go towards what he is afraid of, when it is possible for him to go towards what he is not afraid of? Based on what we've agreed to, isn't that impossible? We've agreed that if someone is afraid of something, then they think it is bad, and nobody goes for—or voluntarily accepts—what he thinks is bad." [359a] Everybody thought that was correct.

"Alright, then," I continued, "based on all this, Prodicus and Hippias, let Protagoras defend his first answer and prove that it is correct. I'm not talking about his very first answer when he said that there are five parts of virtue, that they are all different from one another, and that each one possesses a unique capacity.* I'm talking about his later answer, when he said that four of the virtues are fairly similar to one another, [b] but that one of them—courage—is very different from all the others.* He said that I would know he was right about this by the following clear sign:

'You'll find, Socrates, people who are extremely impious, unjust, intemperate and foolish, but are also extremely courageous. That is how you can be sure that courage is very different from the other parts of virtue.'

At the time I was surprised at this answer, but given everything that we've gone through since then, I'm even more surprised now. I asked him if he called courageous men daring, and he agreed that they are, but he added that they are also [c] ready to launch themselves into situations that others fear. Do you remember giving that answer, Protagoras?"

"Yes, I do," he said.

"So tell me: towards what are courageous people ready to lauch themselves? The same things that cowards are ready to launch themselves towards?"

"No."

"Then towards something different?"

"Yes."

"Do cowards go towards things that may be dared, but courageous people go towards things that are frightful?"

"People do say that," Protagoras answered.

"True, but that's not what [d] I'm asking. My question to you is what *you* say courageous people are ready to launch themselves towards? Are they ready to attack frightful things thinking that they are frightful?"

"But you have just proven that to be impossible," Protagoras pointed out.

"That is also true," I said. "If that proof is correct, then nobody goes towards what is frightful thinking that it is frightful, because we found that being overcome is simply ignorance."

"I agree."

"Then everyone goes towards what may be dared—both courageous people and cowards. [e] So the courageous and the cowardly go towards the same thing."

"But, Socrates, what cowards go towards is the complete opposite of what the courageous go towards. Courageous people voluntarily go to war; cowards do not."

"Is going to war fine or shameful?"

"Fine."

"And didn't we already agree that what is fine is also good?* Didn't we agree that all fine actions are also good?"

"That is true—and I have always believed this."

"And you have always been correct about this. [360a] But tell me this: is there anyone who does not voluntarily go to war since it is both fine and good?"

"Yes—cowards."

"And if it is both fine and good, then it is also pleasant?"

"I suppose we did agree to that,"* Protagoras said.

"So cowards do not voluntarily go to what they know to be finer, better and more pleasant than the alternative?"

"But if we agree to this we will completely destroy what we agreed to earlier."

"Well, what about a courageous person? Does he go toward the finer, better and more pleasant option?"

"Necessarily."

"So in general [b] can we say that when courageous people are afraid, their fear is not shameful, and when they are daring, their daring is not shameful?"

"Yes, that is true."

"And if they are not shameful, then aren't they fine?"*

"Correct."

"And if they are fine, then they are also good?"

"Yes."

"But on the contrary, the fear and daring of cowards, the bold and the insane is shameful?"

"I agree."

"And what explains why their daring is shameful and bad when the daring of courageous people is fine and good? Isn't it because their daring comes from ignorance and foolishness?"

"Yes, [c] that explains it."

"Then the next point is this: what do you call that which explains why cowards are cowards? Do you call it cowardice or courage?"

"I call it cowardice."

"But weren't cowards just revealed to be cowards because of their ignorance of what is to be feared?"

"They certainly were," Protagoras agreed.

"So it is because of this ignorance that they are cowards?"

"Yes."

"And you also agreed that cowardice is that because of which they are cowards?"

"Yes, I did agree to that."

Then I asked, "So cowardice is the ignorance of what is and what is not to be feared?" Protagoras simply nodded in assent, so I continued and asked, "And, of course, [d] courage is the opposite of cowardice?"

"Yes."

"And wisdom about what is and what is not to be feared is the opposite of ignorance* about them?" Again, he simply nodded his agreement, so I went on, "And ignorance about those things is cowardice?" He nodded agreement again, but this time only very reluctantly, so I drew the conclusion, "Therefore, courage is wisdom* regarding what is and is not to be feared, since wisdom is the opposite of ignorance?"

At this point, Protagoras wasn't even willing to nod his head, he just sat there in silence, so I asked him, "Won't you affirm or deny what I've asked?"

"Finish it yourself," he said.

"I have only one more question [e] to ask you, Protagoras. Does it still seem to you as it did at first* that some people are extremely ignorant, but extremely courageous?"

"You seem extremely eager to win,* Socrates, and just as eager for me to answer. So to make you happy I'll say that from everything that we've agreed to, it seems to me impossible."

"Really, Protagoras, my only aim in asking all these questions is to investigate virtue and above all to discover what virtue is. Because I know that if we can make it clear what virtue is, [361a] then we can reveal the truth about that issue you and I have gone on so long about—I've said that virtue is not teachable, and you've said that it is teachable. But the conclusion of our discussion seems to be mocking us and laughing at us. If it could speak, I think it would say something like this.

'How absurd you two are! Socrates, you started out saying that virtue is not teachable, but now you are completely contradicting yourself [b] by trying to prove that every virtue is knowledge—justice, temperance, courage, and so on—because that would be the best way to prove that virtue is teachable. Obviously, if virtue were anything other than knowledge—as Protagoras has been trying to say—clearly it would not be teachable. But now if it turns out that virtue is nothing but knowledge—as you have been urging, Socrates—it would be very surprising if turned out not to be teachable. And you, Protagoras—you started out by by asserting that virtue is teachable, but now you are completely contradicting yourself by trying to prove that [c] virtue is anything other than knowledge—which would mean that it couldn't very well be taught.'

"I don't know about you, Protagoras, but when I see that matters are in such a confused state as this, I can't wait to straighten everything out. What I would really like to do now is to make a thorough investigation of virtue, starting with the discovery of what virtue is. After we've figured out what it is, then we can consider whether or not it is teachable.

"I guess you could say that I don't want Epimetheus [Afterthought] to deceive us again and ruin our investigation [d] the same way he ruined us by neglect when he distributed powers to the various creatures.* I much prefer Prometheus [Forethought] in your story—I try to exercise forethought about my life, and that is why I spend so much time on questions like this. So as I said at the beginning, if you are willing, I would gladly investigate this with you."

But Protagoras responded by saying, "I commend your zeal for pursuing arguments, Socrates. [e] I like to think that I'm not bad at it myself,* but I am also the least envious person you'll ever meet. In fact I have often said that of all the people I've ever met, I admire you more than any—especially among those of your generation. And I declare that I would not be surprised if you become famous for your wisdom. But let's return to this topic another time—whenever you wish. But now it's time to turn to something else."

[362a] "Then that is what we must do, if it seems good to you. As for me, I mentioned earlier* that I have somewhere to go—I stayed so long as a favor to our fine host Callias."

Having said and heard all this, we left.*

MENO

Setting: Athens soon after the restoration of democracy in 404 BCE. Probably at a gymnasium.

Characters (in order of appearance):
MENO (a Thessalian, perhaps about 19 years old; his name is traditionally pronounced "ME-no," though "MEN-own" is closer to the original)
SOCRATES (469-399 BCE; from a middle class family, not handsome at all; his name is traditionally pronounced "SOCK-ra-teez," though "so-KROT-ays" is closer to the original)
SLAVE (Meno and Socrates call the slave "boy" so we know he is male, but the diminutive is probably more an indication of status than age)
ANYTUS (younger than Socrates; a wealthy Athenian who served as general in 409 but failed his mission and was prosecuted, he was found not guilty after bribing the jury; influential politician after the restoration of democracy in 403; one of Socrates' prosecutors in 399; his name is traditionally pronounced "an-NIGHT-us," though "AN-oo-toss" is closer to the original)

Dramatic Structure:
Episode #1: Meno asks Socrates whether virtue is teachable (70a1-79e6)
Episode #2: Socrates argues that learning is recollection (79e7-85b7)
Episode #3: Socrates argues hypothetically that virtue is teachable (85b8-89c4)
Episode #4: Socrates objects that there are no teachers or students of virtue (89c5-96c10)
Episode #5: Socrates replies that true opinion may be as useful as knowledge (96d1-100c2)

MENO. [70a] Can you tell me Socrates, is virtue* teachable? Or, if it isn't teachable, then do we acquire it by habituation?* Or, if we acquire it neither by habituation nor by learning it, then do people become virtuous by nature or in some other way?

SOCRATES. In the past, Meno, you Thessalians had quite a reputation among us Greeks for your horses and your wealth. In fact, you were considered quite a marvel for both. [b] But now, apparently, you've added wisdom* to your marvels. But I suppose this is especially true of the citizens of Larissa,* where your friend Aristippus* comes from. Gorgias* is responsible for this. When he arrived in Larissa, all the leaders of the Aleuad clan*—including your lover Aristippus—were seized by a passion* for wisdom. Then, of course, this passion spread through Thessaly. Gorgias is the one who got you people accustomed to giving impressive answers fearlessly to any question you are asked—just as if you actually know that the answers you give are true. [c] He leads by example in this, because he invites anyone who wishes to ask him anything they choose, and nobody goes away without an answer from him.

But here in Athens, my friend Meno, things are just the opposite. As far as wisdom goes, we're suffering from a sort of drought here; [71a] all the wisdom seems to have gone north to you. For example, ask your question to anyone from here and they'll laugh in your face and say,

"Stranger, I'm afraid that you've mistaken me for someone blessed by the gods if you think I know whether virtue is teacheable or in what way people come by it. I am so far from knowing whether virtue is teachable or not that I don't even know what virtue happens to be."*

[b] I'm in the same boat, Meno. I must plead intellectual poverty and blame myself for not knowing at all what virtue is. And if I don't know what virtue is, then how could I know what qualities it has?* Or does it seem possible to you for someone who doesn't know at all* who Meno is to know whether he is beautiful, wealthy and noble, or completely the opposite? Does that seem possible to you?

MENO. Certainly not. But tell me, Socrates, do you truly [c] not know what virtue is? Is that what we should report about you and your fellow Athenians when we get back home?

SOCRATES. Not only should you report that, my friend, but you should also report that in my opinion, I have never met anyone who knows what virtue is.

MENO. What? Didn't you meet Gorgias here?

SOCRATES. I did.

MENO. Didn't he seem to you to know what virtue is?

SOCRATES. My memory isn't excellent,* and so I really can't say now how he seemed to me then. Perhaps he does know, and perhaps you know what he says virtue is. So please remind [d] me what he says. Or tell me what you say—I suppose you share his view.

MENO. I do indeed.

SOCRATES. Well, then, forget about Gorgias since he isn't here. By the gods, Meno, what do you yourself say that virtue is? Please tell me and don't hide it from me. Here I was just saying that I've never met anyone who knows what virtue is and now you may be about to show me that I'm wrong about this because I've met both you and Gorgias, and you two both know what virtue is.

MENO. [e] It isn't difficult to say what virtue is, Socrates. First, if you'd like me to start with the virtue of a man it's easy. This is virtue for a man: to be competent at managing the city's affairs,* and in managing them to help his friends, to harm his enemies and to avoid being harmed himself. Second, if you'd like me to tell you what virtue is for a woman, it's not difficult to delineate them, because a woman must run the household well, preserving what is within and obeying her husband. Then, if you'd like, I could tell you what virtue is for a child—including the virtues of girls and the virtues of boys—and then there are the virtues of older men, the virtues of free men and the virtues of [72a] slaves. There are a great many other virtues as well, so I could keep on telling you what virtue is, because there is a virtue associated with every activity, every age, every profession—and I suppose it's the same with the vices.

SOCRATES. It seems I hit the jackpot, Meno. I was only looking for one virtue, but I've discovered that you are keeping a whole swarm of them. Well, let me stick with this image of [b] a swarm of bees. Suppose that instead of asking you what virtue is, I asked you what a bee is. You would say that there are many different kinds of bees. But what would you answer if I asked you this question: you say that there are many kinds of bees, and that bees differ from one another, but do they differ from one another insofar as they are all bees? Don't they differ from one another in some other respect—their beauty, size, or some other such quality?

MENO. I would say that insofar as they are all bees they do not differ from one another.

SOCRATES. [c] And what if I should ask this next question: then tell me, Meno, what is it that makes them all the same, that in which they do not differ from one another? You would be able to tell me?

MENO. I would.

SOCRATES. Then do the same for the virtues. Even if there are many different kinds of virtue, tell me that one form* they all share in common and on account of which they are all virtues. It is by looking at the form that you'll have an answer if anyone asks what virtue happens to be. [d] Or don't you understand my meaning?

MENO. I think I do understand, but I'd like a firmer grasp of the question.

SOCRATES. Well, go back to the answer you just gave about virtue. Is it only with virtue that we can say that there are different kinds for men, for women, and for all the others you distinguished? Or could we say the same thing about health, size or strength? Would you say that health for a man is one thing, but health for a woman is something different? Or, on the contrary, would you say that wherever health happens to be, it is just one form, [e] whether it is in a man or a woman or in anyone else?

MENO. It seems to me that health is the same* in a man and in a woman.

SOCRATES. Then what about size and strength? Will a strong woman* and a strong man be strong by the very same form and by the very same strength? That is what I mean by calling them the same: strength doesn't differ insofar as it is strength whether it be in a woman or in a man. Or do you think that it does differ?

MENO. No, I don't.

SOCRATES. [73a] Then does virtue, insofar as it is virtue, differ if it is in a man or a woman, an old or a young person?

MENO. It seems to me, Socrates, that this isn't like the other cases.

SOCRATES. How so? Weren't you just saying the virtue of a man involves managing the city well, and the virtue of a woman involes managing the house well?

MENO. I was.

SOCRATES. And is it possible to manage well a city or a household—or anything else for that matter—without managing it temperately and justly?

MENO. Certainly not.

SOCRATES. [b] And whoever manages something temperately and justly* will manage it with temperance and justice?

MENO. Necessarily.

SOCRATES. Then if they are to be good, both women and men need to be just and temperate?

MENO. Apparantly.

SOCRATES. What about old and young people? Can they be good if they are intemperate and unjust?

MENO. Certainly not.

SOCRATES. They can be good only if they are temperate and [c] just?

MENO. Yes.

SOCRATES. So all people are good in the same way, since they all become good in the same way?

MENO. So it seems.

SOCRATES. But they wouldn't be good in the same way if they didn't have the same virtue?

MENO. Certainly not.

SOCRATES. So since virtue is the same for all, try to remember what you and Gorgias say virtue is.

MENO. Well, if you are seeking an account [d] that applies to everyone, then what else could virtue be than to govern people?

SOCRATES. Yes, that is exactly the sort of account we must seek. But, Meno, is this virtue for a child or a slave? Does a virtuous slave govern his master, and would the one who governs be a slave?

MENO. No, I certainly don't think so, Socrates.

SOCRATES. No, that doesn't seem likely. But consider this. You say that virtue is to be able to govern, but shouldn't we add "justly and not unjustly" to this?

MENO. I think so, Socrates, because justice is virtue.

SOCRATES. [e] Is justice virtue, Meno, or it is one of the virtues?

MENO. What do you mean?

SOCRATES. Oh, nothing special; my point applies in other cases as well. For example, I would say that round is one of the shapes, not that it is is shape, because there are shapes other than round.

MENO. That is correct, Socrates, I see your point. I agree that justice is not the only virtue, there are others as well.

SOCRATES. [74a] What are they? Tell me what the other virtues are, as I would tell you the other shapes if you asked me.

MENO. Courage seems to me to be a virtue, and so does temperance, wisdom, magnificence,* and there are a great many others.

SOCRATES. Once again, Meno, in looking for just one virtue we've found many—though not in exactly the same way as before. Aren't we able to discover the one virtue that runs through them all?

MENO. I certainly can't do it, Socrates. [b] I just can't discern one virtue running through all the others, like in other cases.

SOCRATES. That's quite understandable. I'll try to move the discussion forward, if I can. You understand that what I'm asking applies to everything. For example, suppose someone asks you about the example I just mentioned: "What is shape, Meno?" If you were to answer "Round," then he would follow up with just the same question I asked you, "Is round shape, or one of the shapes?" I assume that you would answer, "Round is one of the shapes."

MENO. Certainly.

SOCRATES. [c] Because there are other shapes besides round?

MENO. Yes.

SOCRATES. And if he were to ask you what other kinds of shapes there are, you would tell him?

MENO. I would.

SOCRATES. Here's another example. Suppose someone asks you what color is and you mention white. He might then ask, "Is white color, or one of the colors?" I assume that you would answer, "White is one of the colors, because there are other colors besides white."

MENO. I would.

SOCRATES. And if he asked you to list other colors you would do so, [d] because there are many colors that don't happen to be white?

MENO. Yes.

SOCRATES. Then what if he continues to press the issue like I have been doing and asks you this. "We keep getting many, and that's not what I'm after. Since you call the many shapes by the one name 'shape,' even though the various shapes are quite opposed to one another, what is it that encompasses round no less than straight, and which you call 'shape'? [e] You agree, don't you, that straight is no less a shape than round?"

MENO. I do.

SOCRATES. And when you say that shape includes both straight and round, you are not saying that there's no difference between straight and round, are you?

MENO. Certainly not, Socrates.

SOCRATES. All you are saying is that round is a shape and straight is a shape, and neither one of them is more of a shape than the other. Is that correct?

MENO. That is true.

SOCRATES. Then instead of asking what it is to be round, or what it is to be straight, suppose I ask you what it is to be called by the name 'shape'? [75a] Try to answer that question. Imagine this, Meno. Suppose someone put this question to you, whether about shape or about color, and you responded, "I don't understand what you want, Socrates, I don't know what to say." He would probably be surprised at you and say, "Don't you understand that I am looking for that which is the same in all these cases?"* Or would you have nothing to say, Meno, if he should ask you, "What is it that is one and the same in round shapes, straight shapes, and all the other things that you call shapes?" Try to answer this question as a sort of exercise before you answer the same question about virtue.

MENO. [b] Why don't you answer it, Socrates?

SOCRATES. Ah, you're asking me to do you a favor?

MENO. I certainly am.

SOCRATES. If I do this favor for you, will you then answer the same question about virtue?

MENO. I will.

SOCRATES. Then I'll do my best. This will certainly be worth the effort.

MENO. Yes, it certainly will.

SOCRATES. Alright, then, I'll try to tell you what shape is. Consider whether you will accept this account: shape is the only thing that always accompanies color. Is that an acceptable answer, or would you like another one? I would certainly [c] be content with a similar account of virtue from you.

MENO. But that is a foolish* answer.

SOCRATES. What do you mean?

MENO. On your account, shape is what always follows color. Fine. But what if someone says that he doesn't understand what color is,* so that he is just as puzzled by shape. What do you think you would say to answer that question?

SOCRATES. I would tell him the truth. If the one asking the question is one of those wise men—an eristic* or a debater—I would say [d] to him, "My claim stands. If it is not correct, it is your job to refute it." But if, like you and I, we were having a friendly conversation, then I wouldn't be so brusque, I would answer in a manner more suited to dialectic than to eristic.* I suppose that what is more suited to dialectic is not only to speak the truth, but also to restrict the conversation to claims that the person being asked questions says that he knows.* That is how I will try to speak with you. [e] So tell me, do you call something an end, a limit, or an extremity? I mean these things all in the same way; I know that Prodicus* might draw fine distinctions between them, but you and I might well say that something has been limited or terminated. That's all I'm asking, nothing subtle.

MENO. Oh, yes, I understand what you mean.

SOCRATES. [76a] Good, then are you familiar with what geometers call a two-dimensional plane figure, and a three-dimensional solid figure?

MENO. Yes, I am quite familiar with them.

SOCRATES. Excellent! Then you should understand my account of shape. I say that in every shape, the shape is delineated by where the solid ends. Or to put it like a definition I would say that shape is the limit of a solid.

MENO. And what do you say about color, Socrates?

SOCRATES. That's a bit cheeky of you, isn't it, Meno? You are asking your elder to answer your questions when you aren't willing [b] to recall for him what Gorgias says about virtue.

MENO. I'll tell you about Gorgias after you tell me what you say about color.

SOCRATES. Even a blindfolded man could tell just by listening to you, Meno, that you are quite good-looking* and that many desire you.

MENO. Why is that?

SOCRATES. You speak in that very assertive way that charming people have of ordering everyone around. [c] But you've discovered my weakness for good-looking people, so I'll do as you ask.

MENO. Ha, ha. Yes, I do have you wrapped around my finger, Socrates.

SOCRATES. Would you like me to answer you in the style of Gorgias, which might be the easiest way for you to follow?

MENO. Oh, yes, of course I would appreciate that.

SOCRATES. Then do you and Gorgias agree with Empedocles that there are certain emanations or effluences* from things?

MENO. Definitely.

SOCRATES. And do you also agree that each of us has pores into which and through which these emanations flow?

MENO. Certainly.

SOCRATES. And that of these emanations, some are a good fit for our [d] pores, but others are either too large or too small for them?

MENO. Yes, that is true.

SOCRATES. And there is something that you call sight or the power of vision?

MENO. Indeed.

SOCRATES. Fine. Then, from these claims, "comprehend my meaning"* as Pindar says. Color is an emanation from shapes that is commensurate with sight and is perceptible.

MENO. I think that you have given an excellent answer, Socrates.

SOCRATES. Perhaps that is because it is put in terms with which you are well familiar. At the same time, I think you understand that from this statement about color, you could give a similar statement about sound, [e] smell and all the others.

MENO. Certainly.

SOCRATES. Well, it is quite a distinguished* answer to the question, Meno, and that may be why it appeals to you more than the statement that shape is the limit of a solid.*

MENO. Yes, Socrates, I do much prefer this one.

SOCRATES. But I am persuaded that it is not the better of the two.* And I think I could persuade you too if, as you told me yesterday, you didn't have to leave before the mysteries,* but could stay and be initiated.

MENO. [77a] But I would stay, Socrates, if you would tell me many such things.

SOCRATES. Then I shall try my best to do so, leaving nothing out, for your sake as well as mine. But perhaps I won't actually have too many such things to say. But come now, it's your turn. Try to fulfill your promise: speaking about virtue as a whole,* tell me what it is, and stop "making many out of one," as jokers say when they accidentally break something to pieces. Leave virtue whole and fully intact and tell me what it is. [b] I've already given you models for how to do this.

MENO. Then virtue seems to me to be just what the poet says: "to rejoice in what is fine* and to be able to achieve it." I agree with the poet. Virtue is desiring fine things and being able to acquire them.

SOCRATES. Then would you say that the one who desires fine things desires good things?

MENO. Undeniably.

SOCRATES. Well, are you saying that some people desire bad things and others desire [c] good things? Don't you think that all people desire good things?

MENO. No, I don't.

SOCRATES. So some people do desire bad things?

MENO. Yes.

SOCRATES. Are you saying that they desire bad things falsely believing that they are actually good, or that despite knowing full well that they are actually bad they desire them anyway?

MENO. I think that both happen.

SOCRATES. So you do think that some people desire bad things, knowing full well that they are bad?

MENO. Undeniably.

SOCRATES. But when you talk about desiring something, do you mean desiring to possess it?

MENO. Yes, [d] what else could I mean?

SOCRATES. Well, then, when someone desires something bad, knowing that it is bad, does he think that it will benefit him when he possess it, or does he know that it will actually harm him?

MENO. Again, both. There are those who think that bad things benefit them, and there are others who know that bad things will harm them.

SOCRATES. Tell me about the first group, about people who think that bad things benefit them. Do you think they know that the bad things they desire to possess are actually bad?

MENO. Oh, no, I don't think that at all.

SOCRATES. Ok, so isn't it clear that these people do not actually [e] desire bad things. They desire things that they think are good,* not knowing that in fact they are bad.

MENO. I suppose so.

SOCRATES. Then let's move on to the second group of people, the people who you say desire bad things, thinking that they will be harmed by possessing them. I suppose they know they'll be harmed by these things?

MENO. [78a] Necessarily.

SOCRATES. Don't they think that those who suffer harm are struggling* by as much as they are harmed?

MENO. That too is necessarily true.

SOCRATES. And aren't those who are struggling unhappy?*

MENO. I certainly think they are.

SOCRATES. Is there anyone who wishes to be struggling and unhappy?

MENO. No, I don't believe so, Socrates.

SOCRATES. Therefore, Meno, no one wishes for bad things, if no one wishes to be struggling and unhappy. Because what is it to be struggling except to desire bad things and then to get what you desire?

MENO. I suppose [b] that is true, Socrates. No one wishes for bad things.

SOCRATES. Next, didn't you say that virtue is wishing for good things and being able to acquire them?

MENO. Yes, I did say that.

SOCRATES. But now we've agreed that this desire for good things belongs to everyone, and so on this count no one would be better than anyone else. Is that so?

MENO. So it seems.

SOCRATES. So if one person is better than another, it would have to be on account of his superior ability to acquire good things?

MENO. Yes, certainly.

SOCRATES. So then your account of virtue would seem to be this: [c] the power to acquire good things.

MENO. I think that the way you just put it is entirely correct.

SOCRATES. Then let's examine this and see whether it is true, because it may well be. So, to be clear, you say that virtue is to be able to acquire good things?

MENO. I do.

SOCRATES. And by "good things" you mean, for example, health and wealth?

MENO. Yes, and also the possession of gold and silver, as well as social status and political power.

SOCRATES. And that is all? There are no good things besides these and things like them?

MENO. Yes. [d] I don't want to list them all, but these are the only kinds of things that are good.

SOCRATES. Well, then, virtue is to procure gold and silver. So says Meno, hereditary guest-friend* of the Great Persian King. But tell me, would you add to this that the procuring must be done in a just and pious manner, or is this irrelevant? If someone acquires gold and silver unjustly, would you still call that virtue?

MENO. Certainly not, Socrates.

SOCRATES. That would be vice, wouldn't it?

MENO. Entirely so.

SOCRATES. So it seems that the power to acquire things must be accompanied by justice, temperance, [e] piety or some other part of virtue, because if it is not, then it will not be virtue, despite the fact that it does succeed in acquiring good things.

MENO. How could it be virtue without any of these?

SOCRATES. Then what about the opposite sort of case. Consider someone who refuses to acquire gold or silver because it would be unjust or impious to do so? In that case, wouldn't the refusal to acquire count as virtue?

MENO. Apparantly.

SOCRATES. So virtue is no more the procurement of such good things than it is the refusal or the failure* to procure them. Instead, it seems that whatever you do with justice will be virtue, [79a] and whatever you do without justice, temperance, piety and so on, will be vice.

MENO. I think it is necessarily as you say.

SOCRATES. Didn't we recently say that each of these is a part of virtue: justice, temperance and so on?

MENO. Yes.

SOCRATES. Well, then, Meno, have you been playing games with me all this time?

MENO. What do you mean, Socrates?

SOCRATES. After asking you not to break virtue into pieces, and giving you models for how to do it, you ignored all this and you tell me that virtue [b] is the ability to procure good things with justice, and you say that justice is a part of virtue. Didn't you say that?

MENO. Yes, I did.

SOCRATES. What results from your claims is that virtue is this: to make sure that no matter what you do, you do it with a part of virtue. Justice, temperance, piety and so on, you say are parts of virtue.

MENO. What are you getting at?

SOCRATES. Just this. Although I asked you to tell me about virtue as a whole, you avoid this topic and instead tell me that each and every action is virtue as long as it is done with a part of virtue. [c] You are breaking virtue up into pieces again, and acting as if you had already told me what it is as a whole so that I understood what it is. It seems to me, my friend, that we have to go back to the beginning and ask again what virtue is, if we are going to say that every action that is done with a part of virtue is itself virtue. Aren't we led right back to the original question if we say that every action done with justice is virtue? Or don't you think this leads us back to the beginning? Do you think that even if someone does not know what virtue is, he may still understand what it is to be a part of virtue?

MENO. I don't think so.

SOCRATES. [d] In fact, if you recall, when I gave you my first answer to the question, "What is shape?" we rejected it because it referred to color, and we had not already agreed on what color is.

MENO. And we were right to reject it on those grounds.

SOCRATES. Then while we are inquiring about virtue as a whole, you don't make your point clear if you answer in terms of its parts, or in any way try to elucidate what virtue is by referring to virtues. [e] If you do that, you'll just have to face the same question again: what is virtue? Don't you agree?

MENO. Yes, you are quite right about that.

SOCRATES. Then answer again from the beginning, what do you and Gorgias say virtue is?

MENO. Oh, Socrates, even before I met you I heard [80a] that you are yourself puzzled,* and you make others puzzled as well. Now I can see for myself that you are bewitching* and enchanting me. Your incantations have thoroughly perplexed me. In fact, if you don't mind a joke at your expense, you look very much like the flat electric ray in the sea that stuns anyone who comes into contact with it. That is just the effect you seem to have had on me. Honestly, Socrates, [b] my very soul is stunned. It's almost as if I can't even move my mouth, I simply have nothing to say in answer to your question, despite the fact that I have delivered countless grand speeches on virtue to many people, and in my opinion they have been quite good speeches. But now I am utterly at a loss when it comes to saying what virtue is. It's probably a good thing that you don't travel to other cities because if you have this effect on people elsewhere you might be arrested as a sorcerer.

SOCRATES. Ah, that's very mischievous of you, Meno. You all but had me fooled.

MENO. What do you mean?

SOCRATES. [c] I know why you compared me to the electric ray.

MENO. Why do you think I did that?

SOCRATES. So that I would compare you to something, and since you are very good looking I would have to compare you with something quite beautiful. But I will not indulge you. Now, as far as your comparison goes, I will admit that I am like the electric ray as long as you say that it is just as stunned as it makes others; but if you don't admit that, then I cannot agree with you. When I cause others to be puzzled, it is not because I have all the answers*—on the contrary, I am more puzzled than anyone,* and that is why

I am able to make others [d] puzzled. So now in the case of virtue, I do not know what it is, and now that you've come into contact with me, you don't know what it is either, although perhaps before you met me you did know. Nevertheless, I would very much like to inquire with you and find out what virtue is.

MENO. But Socrates, how will you inquire into something when you admit that you do not know at all what it is?* Which of the things you don't know will you investigate? And even if you do happen to stumble upon the very thing you seek to find, how will you know that it is the very thing that you don't know?

SOCRATES. [e] I understand what you are saying, Meno. Do you see what sort of eristic argument you are bringing forward? It is impossible to inquire into what you know, or into what you do not know: you cannot inquire into what you know because you already know it so there's no point in inquiring; and you cannot inquire into what you do not know because you don't know what you are inquiring into.

MENO. [81a] Doesn't that seem like a pretty good argument, Socrates?

SOCRATES. Not to me, it doesn't.

MENO. Can you say why?

SOCRATES. I can. I have heard from both men and women who are wise in divine matters—

MENO. What sort of account did they give?

SOCRATES. A true and fine account, as it seemed to me.

MENO. Who did you hear from, and what did they say?

SOCRATES. I heard from priests and priestesses* who have taken great care to be able to give an account of their practices. [b] In fact, Pindar and many other inspired poets give the same account. What they say is this—consider whether you think that what they say is true.

They say that the soul of a person is immortal, and that at one time it is finished with life, which is called "death," but then at another time it is born again—the soul is never destroyed. That is why we must live as holy a life as we possibly can:

> For when Persephone* receives due recompense for wicked deeds
> Up again she sends the soul to see the upper sun once more.
> For nine years must the soul delay, and to Persephone repay
> Punishment all full and fitting, ere it can spring up again,
> [c] And so become a king renowned, or born a hero, vict'ry-crowned,
> Wisdom far surpassing all, fame forever without pall.

Therefore, because the soul is immortal and has been born many times, and has seen everything on earth and in Hades, there is nothing it has not learned. So it is not surprising that it should be able to recollect what it knew before about virtue and everything else. For since [d] all of nature constitutes one large family,* and the soul has learned everything, then as long as you are brave and never give up the search, there is nothing to stop you from discovering everything once you have recollected one thing—a process that we call "learning." To inquire and to learn is nothing but recollection.

So we should not be persuaded by that eristic argument. It will just make us lazy, and it appeals only to the indolent. This theory of recollection, however, [e] makes us inquisitive and diligent. I trust that it is true, and so I am willing to inquire with you to discover what virtue is.

MENO. Yes, Socrates, but what do you mean when you say that we do not learn—what we call learning is actually recollection? Can you teach me how this is so?

SOCRATES. Ha! I told you that you were mischievous, Meno. [82a] You just asked me to teach you something after I said that there is no such thing as teaching, only recollecting. You are trying to trick me into contradicting myself.

MENO. No, by god, Socrates, I swear that is not what I had in mind. I was just asking a perfectly natural question. If there is some way to demonstrate to me that what you say is true, please show me.

SOCRATES. It's not easy to do, but I'm eager to try for your sake. Please call over to us one of your many [b] attendants, whomever you wish, so that I may use him for my demonstration.

MENO. Certainly. [*To one of his slaves*] Come here.

SOCRATES. Is he Greek?* Can he speak Greek?

MENO. Oh yes. He was born in my house.

SOCRATES. Now pay close attention, Meno, and see whether he seems to be recollecting, or learning from me.

MENO. I will.

SOCRATES. Tell me, boy, do you know that a square figure is this sort of thing? [*Socrates draws a square in the sand.*]

BOY. I do.

SOCRATES. [c] So a square has 4 sides, and all of them are equal in length?

BOY. Certainly.

SOCRATES. And aren't these lines that I've drawn through the middle also equal in length?

BOY. Yes.

SOCRATES. Then a figure like this can be larger or smaller? Some squares are larger than others?

BOY. Certainly.

SOCRATES. So if this side is 2 feet long, and that side is also 2 feet long, how many square feet would the whole be? Think of it this way. Suppose that while this side is 2 feet long, this other side is only 1 foot long. In that case, wouldn't the whole thing be just 2 square feet?

BOY. [d] Yes.

SOCRATES. So then if the square is not 1 by 2, but 2 by 2, then its size will be twice 2?

BOY. It will be.

SOCRATES. So its size will be 2 times 2 square feet?

BOY. Yes.

SOCRATES. And how many are 2 times 2 square feet? Figure it out and tell me.

BOY. 4, Socrates.

SOCRATES. And could we have another figure like this one, with all its sides equal, but it is twice as large as this square?

BOY. Yes.

SOCRATES. And if it is twice as large, how many square feet will it be?

BOY. 8.

SOCRATES. Alright then, try to tell me how long [e] each side of that larger square will be. The sides of this square are 2 feet long, so how long will the sides be of the square that is double in size?

BOY. Obviously, Socrates, they will be double in length.

SOCRATES. [*Turning to Meno*] Do you see, Meno, that I have taught him nothing; I have asked him everything? At this point he thinks he knows how long the sides of an 8 square foot figure will be. Isn't that how it seems to you?

MENO. Oh, yes, that is how it appears to me.

SOCRATES. But in fact he does not know how long the sides will be?

MENO. No, he does not.

SOCRATES. He thinks that to double the amount of square feet in the figure, you have to double the length of the sides.

MENO. Yes.

SOCRATES. Now watch how his recollection works in connecting things together,* which is the way one ought to recollect.

[*Turning to the boy*] Tell me this. You say that by doubling the length of each side, [83a] the total amount of square feet in the figure will be doubled. Keep in mind that we are talking about a square, so if you double one side, you have to keep all four sides equal. If we do that, if we make all 4 sides double the length of the original square, do you still think that we will double the amount of square feet in the entire figure?

BOY. I do.

SOCRATES. So if we extend this bottom line by 2 extra feet, then it will be twice its original length?

BOY. Certainly.

SOCRATES. And if we do the same for all 4 sides, you say that it will be 8 square feet?

BOY. [b] Yes.

SOCRATES. Alright, then, let's draw the figure with 4 equal sides of 4 feet each. And you say the result will be 8 square feet?

BOY. Yes.

SOCRATES. Now take a look at the figure. Do you see in the upper left corner there are 4 small squares that all together are exactly the same size as our original square? And do you see the same in the upper right corner: 4 small squares that are together exactly the same size as our original square? Do you see that it is the same in all 4 corners of this larger square?

BOY. Yes.

SOCRATES. So what is the size of the whole thing? Is it 4 times as large as our original square?

BOY. Of course.

SOCRATES. And if it is 4 times as large, is it double the size of the original square?

BOY. By god, no.

SOCRATES. If it is not double in size, then how much larger is it?

BOY. 4 times as large.

SOCRATES. Therefore, [c] if you double the length of the sides, you do not double the size of the square, you quadruple it?

BOY. That certainly is true.

SOCRATES. And 4 times 4 is 16, so won't this larger figure be 16 square feet?

BOY. Yes.

SOCRATES. So how would we get a figure of 8 square feet? We only want to double the size of our original square, but here we actually quadrupled the number of square feet, didn't we?

BOY. Yes, we did.

SOCRATES. Well, suppose we cut this large square in half, right down the middle from top to bottom, and then we cut it again from left to right, horizontally in the middle. That would separate off the four corners, and each of those corners if 4 square feet, is that right?

BOY. Yes.

SOCRATES. And 8 is twice 4, but half of 16?

BOY. That is true.

SOCRATES. So to make an 8 foot square figure, the sides will have to be to be longer than the sides of our 4 smaller corner squares, but shorter than the sides of the entire 16 foot square figure? [d] Is that so?

BOY. Oh, yes, I do think it is so.

SOCRATES. Well said! You should always answer according to your sincere beliefs.* Now, tell me again, the 4 corners of our large square each have 4 square feet, and the sides are all 2 feet in length, is that correct? And the large square as a whole has 16 square feet, and the sides are all 4 feet in length?

BOY. Yes.

SOCRATES. So necessarily the figure with 8 square feet will have sides that are longer than the sides of our 4 foot square figure, but shorter than the sides of our 16 foot square figure?

BOY. Necessarily.

SOCRATES. [e] Then try to tell me how long you think the sides must be.

BOY. 3 feet.

SOCRATES. Ah, well, if it is to be 3 feet, then let's expand one of our corners by 1 foot on both sides. That way we'll have a square that is 3 feet long on all of its sides. Do you see that?

BOY. Yes.

SOCRATES. Therefore, if it is 3 feet on this side and 3 feet on that side, then will the whole thing be 3 times 3 square feet?

BOY. It seems to.

SOCRATES. And how many square feet is 3 times 3?

BOY. 9.

SOCRATES. And we are trying to double the number of square feet of our original figure. If our original figure was 4 square feet, then how many square feet do we want our new figure to have?

BOY. 8.

SOCRATES. So it turns out that we do not get an 8 square foot figure by making the sides 3 feet long?

BOY. Certainly not.

SOCRATES. Then how long does each side need to be in order to produce an 8 square foot figure? Try to be accurate, [84a] and if you don't want to state a particular number, you can just point to where* on our figure you think the sides need to be if we are going to create an 8 foot square figure.

BOY. By god, Socrates, I just don't know.

SOCRATES. [*Turning to Meno*] Do you understand what progress he has made on his journey of recollection? At first, he did not know the answer to the question—just as now he still does not know—but earlier he answered confidently as if he did know, and did not realize that he was in fact puzzled.* But now he realizes [b] that he's puzzled and that he does not know the answer to the question, and he does not think that he knows it.

MENO. That is true.

SOCRATES. So now he is actually better off in regard to what he does not know?

MENO. I think so.

SOCRATES. And have we harmed him by making him puzzled, and stunning him like an electric eel?

MENO. No, I think that we have not harmed him.

SOCRATES. In fact, haven't we actually done him some good with respect to discovering the truth? Now that he realizes his own ignorance, he is eager to inquire; but earlier he would have confidently asserted many times to many people* [c] that you double the size of the figure by doubling the length of the sides.

MENO. So it seems.

SOCRATES. Do you think that earlier he would have tried to discover the answer or to learn the truth, when he thought that he already knew the answer, but didn't, and before he became puzzled, before he realized his own ignorance and eagerly desired knowledge?

MENO. No, I don't think he would have, Socrates.

SOCRATES. So being stunned has actually been of some benefit to him?

MENO. I think so, yes.

SOCRATES. Now observe that from this puzzlement, he will discover the correct answer by inquiring together with me, although I will only ask questions; I will not teach him anything. [d] But you be on your guard and make sure that he does not make any discoveries because I taught him something or because I gave him any answers.* I will only ask for his sincere opinion.

[*Turning to the slave*] Tell me, do you understand that this here is our figure of 4 square feet?

BOY. I do.

SOCRATES. And we could add another one to it that is exactly the same size?

BOY. Yes.

SOCRATES. And we could add a third one that is exactly the same size as the other two?

BOY. Yes.

SOCRATES. And finally, what about this empty space here in the corner. Shall we fill it?

BOY. Certainly.

SOCRATES. So now we have 4 squares of equal size?

BOY. [e] Yes.

SOCRATES. And how much larger is the whole than each of the 4 parts?

BOY. 4 times as large.

SOCRATES. And we were supposed to create one that is only 2 times as large? Or don't you remember?

BOY. Oh yes, I do remember.

SOCRATES. Then what about this line that goes diagonally from one corner to the opposite corner? [85a] Does it cut this 4 square foot figure exactly in half?

BOY. Yes.

SOCRATES. Now what if we do the same thing with each of the three remaining squares? If we connect each of these interior diagonal lines, then wouldn't there be a new figure inside the large square?

BOY. There would be.

SOCRATES. Then think about this new figure inside the larger figure. How large is this new figure that we've drawn using the four diagonal lines?

BOY. I can't quite figure it out.

SOCRATES. Think about the diagonal lines cutting each of our 4 square foot figures. Has each diagonal line cut each of the 4 square foot figures in half? Or is it not exactly half?

BOY. Oh, yes, each diagonal has cut each corner square exactly in half.

SOCRATES. And if the new figure that we have drawn using these four new diagonal lines has cut each of the 4 corner squares exactly in half, then how many half squares does it contain?

BOY. 4.

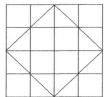

SOCRATES. And what about each of the 4 corner squares? Each one of them has been cut exactly in half, so how many half squares does each corner square contain?

BOY. 2.

SOCRATES. And what is 4 in relation to 2?

BOY. Double.

SOCRATES. Now can you tell me how large this new figure is? [b] If it is double the size of each corner square, and each corner square was 4 square feet, how many square feet are there in this interior figure?

BOY. 8.

SOCRATES. Which of these lines produced the 8 square foot figure?

BOY. These ones that are diagonal.

SOCRATES. These four lines that cut each of the 4 square foot figures in half?

BOY. Yes.

SOCRATES. The experts call this line a "diagonal" because it runs diagonally from one corner to the opposite corner. So can we say that it is possible to create a square that is exactly twice the size of a smaller square by using the diagonal?

BOY. Yes, certainly, Socrates!

SOCRATES. What do you think, Meno? Did he answer any question that I asked him with an opinion that was not his own?

MENO. [c] No. Each opinion was his own.

SOCRATES. And as we said a little while ago he did not know the solution to the problem I posed?

MENO. That is true.

SOCRATES. And these opinions were inside him,* weren't they?

MENO. Yes.

SOCRATES. So someone who doesn't even know that he doesn't know something can still have true beliefs about the very thing that he doesn't know?

MENO. I think so.

SOCRATES. Right now these opinions have just been stirred up in him like a dream. However, if he is asked these same questions often and in different ways, understand that in the end [d] his knowledge of these matters will be no less accurate than anyone's.

MENO. So it seems.

SOCRATES. Therefore, without anyone teaching him, simply by being asked questions he will gain knowledge, retrieving knowledge from within himself?

MENO. Yes.

SOCRATES. And to retrieve knowledge from within oneself is to recollect?

MENO. Certainly.

SOCRATES. And the knowledge that he now has—either he acquired it as some particular point in time, or else he has always had it?

MENO. Yes.

SOCRATES. And if he always had it, then he has always known it; but if he acquired this knowledge at a particular time, it was not during this lifetime—or [e] has someone taught him geometry? But notice that what is true of this particular geometrical knowledge is also true of all geometrical knowledge, and in fact it is true of anything that can be learned. So, is there anyone who has taught him everything that can be learned? It is only right that you should know the answer to this question since he was born and raised in your household.

MENO. I know that no one has ever taught him.

SOCRATES. And yet he has these opinions, doesn't he?

MENO. I cannot deny it, Socrates.

SOCRATES. And if he did not acquire these opinions in this lifetime, [86a] then obviously he learned them at some other time?

MENO. Clearly.

SOCRATES. And this other time was when he was not a human being?

MENO. Yes.

SOCRATES. So if there are true opinions inside of him both when he is and when he is not a human being—true opinions that need only to be awakened in him to become knowledge*—then won't his soul have learned these things for all time?* Since it is clear that for all time he either is or is not human.

MENO. Clearly.

SOCRATES. [b] Therefore, if the truth about reality is in the soul always, then the soul would be immortal. The result is that the one who happens not to know something right now—that is, there is something that he has not yet recollected—he should have confidence, and should try to inquire and to recollect.

MENO. I think that is really well said, Socrates, though I don't know exactly how it can be true.

SOCRATES. And I too think it is well said, Meno, although I cannot draw all these conclusions definitively. Nevertheless, for the proposition that we are better, braver and less slothful if we think that we ought to inquire into what we do not know than if we think that [c] we cannot possibly discover what we do not know, and hence that we should not even inquire into what we do not know—for this proposition I will fight for as long as I am able, both in word and in deed.

MENO. This too seems to me quite well said, Socrates.

SOCRATES. Well, then, since we agree that we must inquire into what we do not know, do you wish to work together to discover what virtue is?

MENO. Yes, I'd like that very much. But, Socrates, I would also very much like to inquire into, and to hear from you about, the question I asked at the beginning. As we seek to disover what virtue is, are we taking it to be something that is teachable, [d] or is it something that people acquire by nature or in some other way?

SOCRATES. If I were in charge of this inquiry, Meno, then I would not consider whether virtue is teachable before I discovered what it is. However, since you are not even trying to control yourself—no doubt because you are a free man*—instead you are trying to control me, and succeeding quite well, I shall go along with you. What else can I do? It seems that we must [e] inquire into some of the qualities virtue has without having found out first what it is.

Suppose you loosen the reigns on me just a bit and allow us to investigate whether virtue is teachable or not by using a hypothesis. By "using a hypothesis" I mean the sort of thing that geometers use when they consider a question in geometry. For example, suppose someone asks whether a given area* can be inscribed as a triangle in a particular circle. [87a] In that case, a geometer might give this sort of answer.

"I do not yet know if that area can be so inscribed. However, if you allow me to make use of a hypothesis I think that we may make some progress. Let's hypothesize that when we apply the area in question to a particular line, the area falls short by a particular proportion. If that hypothesis is true, then we can draw certain conclusions; if that hypothesis is not true, then we can draw different conclusions. So if you allow me to use a hypothesis, [b] we can make some progress."

Shall we proceed this way with virtue? Since we don't know what it is, and we don't know what qualities it has, let's consider the question of whether it is teachable or not by using a hypothesis.

We might start along the following lines: what sort of thing would virtue be in the soul if it were teachable, and what sort would it be if it were not teachable? First, then, would virtue be teachable if it were similar to or different from knowledge?* I suppose we could talk about recollection instead of knowledge—as we were just saying—but [c] let's not worry about the exact term used. Or perhaps this is too obvious: nothing other than knowledge is taught to human beings, is it?

MENO. I think that is correct.

SOCRATES. And if virtue is a kind of knowledge, then clearly it would be teachable.

MENO. How could it not be teachable in that case?

SOCRATES. So we quickly answered that question: if virtue is of one sort, then it is teachable, otherwise it is not.

MENO. Quite right.

SOCRATES. Well, then, after this it seems that we ought to consider whether virtue is knowledge, or has something to do with knowledge.*

MENO. [d] Yes, I think that we must consider this next.

SOCRATES. And do we say that virtue is a good thing? Do we hypothesize that virtue is itself good?

MENO. Certainly.

SOCRATES. So if something that is separate from knowledge is good, then perhaps virtue is something separate from knowledge. But if nothing is good that is not encompassed by knowledge,* then we are correct to suppose that knowledge is part of virtue.

MENO. Yes, that is so.

SOCRATES. And in fact [e] it is by being virtuous that we are good?

MENO. Yes.

SOCRATES. And if we are good, then we are beneficial, since all good things are beneficial. Isn' that so?

MENO. Yes.

SOCRATES. And virtue, in fact, is beneficial?

MENO. That necessarily follows from what we've agreed.

SOCRATES. Then let's consider which things benefit us. Let's take them up individually. Health, strength, beauty and wealth—we say* that these, and things like them, are benefits, [88a] don't we?

MENO. Yes.

SOCRATES. But don't we also say that these very things sometimes harm us? Or do you disagree?

MENO. No, I don't disagree at all. These things do sometimes harm us.

SOCRATES. Then let's find out what is leading us* when they benefit us and when they harm us. Isn't it when correct use* is leading that they benefit us, and when correct use is not leading they harm us?

MENO. Certainly.

SOCRATES. Next, let's consider which things benefit us with respect to the soul. Do you acknowledge each of these as being a genuine quality of the soul: temperance, justice, courage, discernment,* memory, magnificence, and all that [b] sort of thing?

MENO. I do.

SOCRATES. From this list, consider the ones that you think are not knowledge, but are something other than knowledge, and tell me whether or not you think that sometimes they are harmful, and sometimes they are beneficial. For example, what about courage? Suppose courage is not intelligence* but is something like recklessness. When someone is reckless and acts senselessly, won't he be harmed; but if he acts thoughtfully and intelligently, doesn't he benefit?

MENO. Yes.

SOCRATES. Isn't it the same with temperance and discernment? Learning and training with sense* is beneficial, but without sense it is harmful?

MENO. Certainly, [c] very much so.

SOCRATES. Therefore, the bottom line here is that all these endeavors and endurances of the soul bring about happiness if they are being led by intelligence, but if they are led by thoughtlessness they bring about the exact opposite. Is that correct?

MENO. So it seems.

SOCRATES. From this it follows that if virtue is one of these qualities of the soul, and if it is necessarily beneficial, then it must be intelligence, since all of the qualities of the soul when taken themselves by themselves* are neither beneficial nor harmful. It is only by the addition of [d] intelligence or thoughtlessness that they become beneficial or harmful. So according to this argument, virtue must be intelligence because it is beneficial.

MENO. I think that is correct.

SOCRATES. Then what about all the other things we were talking about just now: wealth and things like that are good sometimes,* but sometimes they are harmful. So isn't it the same as with the qualities of the soul: intelligence makes them beneficial by leading them, but thoughtlessness makes them harmful when it leads? So also [e] when it comes to wealth and so on, when the soul uses them correctly and leads them correctly, it makes them beneficial, but if it doesn't do so correctly, then it makes them harmful?

MENO. Certainly.

SOCRATES. And an intelligent soul leads us correctly, but a thoughtless soul leads us astray.

MENO. That is so.

SOCRATES. Therefore, we say that this is so in all cases: for human beings, all things depend upon the soul, and the soul itself depends upon intelligence, [89a] if these things are to be good. According to this account, what is beneficial would be intelligence. But do we also say that virtue is beneficial?

MENO. Certainly.

SOCRATES. Intelligence, then, is virtue;* either the whole of it, or a part of it?

MENO. I think that is very well put, Socrates.

SOCRATES. And if that's the way it is, then people would not be good by nature.

MENO. I don't think they would.

SOCRATES. [b] I agree. In fact, I would guess that if people were good by nature, then we would have people who knew how to recognize them when they are young. Once they had pointed out one of these young people who is good by nature, we would guard them on the Acropolis,* protecting them even more than we protect our gold so that no one will corrupt them. Of course we would go to such great lengths to protect them because when they came of age they would be a tremendous benefit to our city.

MENO. You are probably right about that, Socrates.

SOCRATES. So since good people are not good by nature, [c] then they must learn to be good?

MENO. I think that follows necessarily. In fact, Socrates, it is clear that according to our hypothesis, if virtue is knowledge, then it is teachable.

SOCRATES. Perhaps, by god. But were we right to agree to that hypothesis?

MENO. Just now it seemed right.

SOCRATES. Yes, but if the idea is sound, then it will seem right not just now, but also in the future.

MENO. [d] Why do you say that, Socrates? Do you have some particular reason to be concerned about or to doubt our hypothesis that virtue is knowledge?

SOCRATES. I'll tell you what I'm thinking, Meno. I do not doubt that virtue is teachable if it is knowledge. However, consider if you think there is reason to doubt that it is in fact knowledge. Tell me this: if something is teachable—not just virtue, but anything at all—then aren't there necessarily both teachers and students of it?

MENO. I think so.

SOCRATES. [e] And conversely, if there were neither teachers nor students of something, would it be reasonable for us to surmise that it is not teachable?

MENO. That is true, but don't you think that there are teachers of virtue?

SOCRATES. Oh, I have often done everything I could to see if anyone teaches virtue, but I have been unable to find any. I have even enlisted many others in my search whom I thought to be quite experienced in the matter.

[Anytus enters]

Well, it's a fine thing that Anytus has just joined us. Let's make him a partner in our inquiry. [90a] It seems likely that he will be a good partner in this search because, in the first place, his father Anthemion is wealthy and wise. And it wasn't just some stroke of good luck that made Anthemion wealthy, nor was his wealth simply given to him—as Polycrates' money was given just recently to the Theban Ismenias.* Anthemian earned his wealth through his own wisdom and hard work. In the second place, Anytus himself has a reputation for being a decent, law-abiding citizen who doesn't act as if he is superior to others, and is neither pompous nor offensive to others. [b] Third, it seems that many Athenians think that he has raised and educated* his son well since they select Anytus for the highest offices.* That is just the sort of person one ought to join when looking for teachers of virtue—to find out if are are any, and if so, who they are.

So Anytus, join us in our search—myself and your guest-friend Meno. We are looking to see who would be teachers of this subject. For example, if you wanted Meno to become a good doctor, [c] to which teachers would you send him? Wouldn't you send him to doctors?

ANYTUS. Of course.

SOCRATES. And if you wanted him to become a good shoemaker, you'd send him to shoemakers?

ANYTUS. Yes.

SOCRATES. And likewise in other cases?

ANYTUS. Of course.

SOCRATES. Now, tell me one thing further about these examples. We say that if we want Meno to become a doctor, then the right thing to do is to send him to doctors. But what exactly do we mean when we say, "the right thing to do is to send him to doctors"? [d] Are we saying that we would be well advised to send him to those who claim expertise in medicine rather than to those who do not, and to those who actually charge a fee for practicing medicine, and who declare themselves to be teachers of anyone who wishes to learn?*

ANYTUS. Yes.

SOCRATES. Does the same hold true for playing the flute and everything else like that? [e] Wouldn't we be fools to refuse to send someone who wanted to learn to play the flute to those who claimed that they taught people the skill and charged a fee for their services, and instead bother people who don't even claim to teach the skill, and who don't even have one student whom they've taught the skill we want them to teach? Wouldn't that be completely unreasonable?

ANYTUS. Yes, by god, that would be utterly stupid.

SOCRATES. Well said. So now perhaps I can get your help [91a] in advising your guest-friend Meno here. A while ago, Anytus, he was telling me* that he wanted the wisdom and virtue by which people govern their households and city well, take good care of their parents, and know when to welcome someone—either a citizen or a foreigner—and when to turn them away, and to do all this in a way that is worthy of a good man. [b] To whom should we send him so that he can learn all this correctly? Isn't it clear from the argument we gave just now, that we should send him to those who claim to be teachers of virtue, and who declare that they are willing to teach all Greeks who want to learn, and who charge a fixed fee for their lessons?

ANYTUS. Who are you referring to,* Socrates?

SOCRATES. You know that there are people who are called "sophists."

ANYTUS. [c] Herakles!* Socrates, bite your tongue! I sincerely hope that no relative or friend of mine, either from this city or another, is ever seized by such a madness as to hand themselves over to one of them to be ruined. It is obvious that they ruin and corrupt everyone who associates with them.

SOCRATES. What do you mean, Anytus? Are you saying that, of all the people who claim to know how to do some good, the sophists are so different from all the others that not only do they provide no actual benefit—as do the others—[d] but they harm and corrupt those who are handed over to them as students? And on top of that, they openly expect to be paid for doing this. I don't have enough evidence to trust you* on this, Anytus.

I know that just one man, Protagoras, has earned more money for teaching this particular brand of wisdom than Phidias* and ten other sculptors combined—and you know what unrivaled works of beauty he has created. What you are saying is truly shocking. Suppose that what you are saying about these sophists were true of shoemakers or weavers. Imagine people handing over old shoes or clothing to be repaired by them, but instead of repairing them, they actually ruined them and made them worse than they were before. [e] There is no way that they could conceal what they had done, and they'd be run out of business, reduced to poverty and they'd quickly die from hunger. But according to you, Protagoras fooled all of Greece because he was corrupting the people who associated with him, and he was sending them away in worse condition than when they came to him, and he managed to pull this scam for forty years—I think he died at about age seventy and that he'd been practicing his craft for forty years. And it's not just Protagoras: [92a] there are many others, some of whom were born before him but are still practicing their craft today. Shall we follow your account and say that either they knowingly deceived and ruined the young men who came to them for improvement, or that they themselves didn't realize what harm they were doing? In other words, do you really think that these men—whom some consider to be the wisest of all people—are actually insane?

ANYTUS. They are far from insane, Socrates. The young people [b] who pay their fees are the insane ones; and even more insane are their parents who are supposed to be looking out for them but hand their children over to them. But the maddest of all are the cities that allow these people in* and don't drive them out immediately—no matter whether they are foreigners or citizens.*

SOCRATES. Has a sophist wronged you, Anytus? Why are you so opposed to them?

ANYTUS. No, none of them has ever wronged me, by god. I've never given them the opportunity to wrong me or anyone close to me.

SOCRATES. So you have no experience with these men at all?

ANYTUS. None whatsoever, and I hope it stays that way.

SOCRATES. [c] You surprise me, Anytus. How can you say whether something is good or worthless when you have no experience with it at all?

ANYTUS. Easily! And anyway, I know who these people are, so it doesn't matter whether I do or do not have personal experience with them.

SOCRATES. Perhaps you are a seer,* Anytus. I'd be surprised if there was any other way for you to know that what you just said about them is in fact true. However, we are not trying to discover who would ruin Meno [d] if we sent him to them—perhaps you are right about the sophists. Instead, please do your family friend here the favor of telling us to whom we could send him, in such a great city as Athens, so that he could become virtuous in the way I was just describing.*

ANYTUS. Why don't you tell him?

SOCRATES. But I already did tell him who I supposed* are teachers of virtue—you said I was wrong, and perhaps [e] you are right. So now it's your turn. Tell us which Athenian Meno should go to. Name anyone you wish.

ANYTUS. Why should you hear just one name? Any of the fine and good* Athenians he happens to meet, and whose advice he follows, will do him more good than any sophist will.

SOCRATES. Did these fine and good people just spontaneously become fine and good; and are they able to teach something that they never [93a] actually learned?

ANYTUS. I expect that they learned from the previous generation, which was also fine and good. Don't you think that there are many fine and good gentlemen in our city?

SOCRATES. I think so, Anytus, and it seems to me that there are many good statesmen here,* and that there are no fewer now than there have been in the past. But have these good men been good teachers of their own virtue? That is the issue before us. We are not asking whether there are good men here now or in the past; [b] we are asking whether or not virtue is teachable. In order to answer that question, we are considering whether good men—those living now or earlier—know how to transmit to another person the virtue that makes them good men, or whether virtue cannot be transmitted to or received from another person. That is what Meno and I have been considering for a while. So let's follow your lead. Wouldn't you say that Themistocles* [c] was a good man?

ANYTUS. I would indeed—an exceptionally good man.

SOCRATES. Therefore, if anyone was ever a teacher of his own virtue, he was?

ANYTUS. Yes, I think so, if he wanted to teach it.

SOCRATES. But don't you think that he wanted others to be fine and good, and most of all his own son? Or do you think that he was jealous of his own son and so he deliberately [d] refused to impart to him the virtue that made him a good man? Haven't you heard that Themistocles taught his son Cleophantus to be a good horseman? Well, at least he could stay upright on a horse and accurately throw a javelin while riding.* And he could do many other amazing things that Themistocles taught* him: Themistocles made him wise in all that can be learned from good teachers—haven't you heard our elders tell these stories?

ANYTUS. Yes, I've heard them.

SOCRATES. So no one could accuse the son of having a bad nature?

ANYTUS. [e] I suppose not.

SOCRATES. Well, have you ever heard any one of our elders—or anyone younger, for that matter—say that Cleophantus was just as wise and as good as his father, and in the same ways that his father was wise and good?

ANYTUS. Certainly not.*

SOCRATES. Then should we believe that Themistocles only wanted his son to be educated in horseback riding and things like that, but not in the particular kind of wisdom he had that made him a good man— when it comes to virtue, he didn't care to make his own son any better than his neighbors, assuming that virtue is teachable.

ANYTUS. By god, perhaps you are right about that.

SOCRATES. Well, that's the sort of teacher of virtue Themistocles turns out to be—a man whom you agree was among the best men of his time. [94a] Let's consider another: Aristides,* the son of Lysimachus.* Or don't you agree that he was a good man?

ANYTUS. Oh, I most certainly do think he was a good man.

SOCRATES. Aristides gave his own son—also named Lysimachus—the finest education of all Athenians, in as many subjects as there are teachers. Does it seem to you that he made his son a better man than anyone else? I suppose you've actually met Lysimachus and have seen the sort of man he is.

Or, if you wish, [b] let's consider Pericles*—a magnificently wise man. You know that he raised two sons: Paralus and Xanthippus.

ANYTUS. I do.

SOCRATES. Then, as you know, he taught them horsemanship so that they were inferior to no Athenian. Plus, he taught them music, wrestling, and everthing else that takes skill* so that, again, they were inferior to none. But did he not want to make them good men? I think that he did want to make them good men, but perhaps virtue is not teachable.

Please don't think that this applies to just a few careless* Athenians who haven't taught their children to be virtuous. [c] Bear in mind that Thucydides* raised two sons, Melesias and Stephanus. He educated them very well and made them the finest wrestlers in Athens. One son he placed with Xanthias and the other with Eudorus, both were considered the finest wrestlers of their time. Don't you recall?

ANYTUS. I did hear that.

SOCRATES. Well, isn't it clear that Thucydides would never have [d] spent his money teaching his own sons those things but neglect to teach them the very things that would have made them good men— assuming that virtue is teachable—when this would have cost him absolutely nothing. Perhaps Thucydides was a common man* who didn't have a lot of friends among Athens or her allies?* But he was a member of a great and venerable family and he had tremendous influence both in the city and among other Greeks. So if he was too busy with political matters to teach his sons personally, and if virtue is teachable, then he surely would have found those who could teach his sons and turn them into good men, [e] no matter whether those teachers were Athenians or guest-friends living here in Athens. So, my friend Anytus, perhaps virtue is not teachable.

ANYTUS. Socrates, I think you speak ill* of people too easily. I would advise you, if you are willing to listen to me, to be discreet. Perhaps in other cities it is easy to do ill* or good to people; [95a] but here in Athens it is much easier.*

[Anytus leaves]

SOCRATES. Meno, Anytus looks angry, and I'm not surprised. He thinks I'm slandering these men, and he considers himself to be one of them. If he ever comes to know what it is to slander someone,* then he'll stop being angry, but right now he doesn't know.

Anyway, tell me, Meno, don't you have some fine and good men in Thessaly?

MENO. Certainly.

SOCRATES. [b] Are they willing to take on the responsibility of teaching the young? Do they agree that they are teachers and that virtue is teachable?

MENO. By god, Socrates there is no agreement in Thessaly on those issues. Sometimes you'll hear someone say that virtue is teachable, but then at other times they say it is not.

SOCRATES. Can we call them teachers of virtue if they don't even agree that virtue is teachable?

MENO. I don't think so, Socrates.

SOCRATES. Well what about these sophists who are the only ones to make this claim for themselves? Do you think they are teachers of virtue?

MENO. [c] Actually, Socrates, I admire Gorgias so much precisely because I have never heard him claim to teach virtue. In fact, he laughs at others who make that claim for themselves. He simply claims to be able to make people clever speakers.*

SOCRATES. So you don't think that the sophists are teachers of virtue?

MENO. I'm not sure what to say, Socrates. I'm like most people, sometimes I think they are, sometimes I think they are not.

SOCRATES. Are you aware that it is not just you and the politicians who sometimes think that virtue is teachable, but sometimes think it is not? [d] The poet Theognis* says the same thing.

MENO. In which poem?

SOCRATES. In the elegiac lines* where he says:

> And beside them drink and eat, and with them
> Sit, and please them, whose power is great.
> Good things from the good you will learn*; but if with the bad
> [e] You associate, you will ruin whatever intelligence you have.

You see that in these lines he's saying virtue is teachable?

MENO. So it appears.

SOCRATES. But a few lines later he changes his mind and says something like this*

> If a man could create good sense and instill it into another,
> Often would such a man earn huge fees.
> Never from a good father would be born a bad son,
> [96a] If he heeds the words of the wise. But by teaching*
> You will never make a bad man good.

Do you see that here he says exactly the opposite* of what he said about the very same topic?

MENO. So it appears.

SOCRATES. What a sorry state of affairs this seems to be, Meno.* Can you name anything other than virtue where those who claim to be teachers of it are denied by others to be genuine teachers of it, and some deny that they even know the subject at all—in fact, [b] some claim that they are actually the opposite of experts in the field: they claim that these self-professed experts are actually the worst people at what they claim to teach? On top of that, people who are agreed to be fine and good sometimes say that the subject matter is teachable, but sometimes they say that it is not teachable. When any subject matter is in such a state of confusion, can anyone be said definitively to be a teacher of it?

MENO. No, by god, I don't think so.

SOCRATES. Well if the sophists are not teachers of virtue, and those who are agreed to be fine and good aren't either, then is nobody a teacher of virtue?

MENO. It seems so.

SOCRATES. [c] And if there are no teachers, there are no students?

MENO. I think it is as you say.

SOCRATES. And didn't we agree* that if there were neither teachers nor students of something, then it was not teachable?

MENO. We did agree to that.

SOCRATES. And we haven't been able to find teachers of virtue anywhere?

MENO. That is so.

SOCRATES. And if there are no teachers, then there are no students?

MENO. So it seems.

SOCRATES. Therefore, virtue would not be teachable?

MENO. [d] It seems not, if we've carried out this inquiry properly. So now I really wonder, Socrates, whether there are in fact any good men at all, or how men can come to be good.

SOCRATES. I'm afraid, Meno, that you and I are rather negligent* in our education: you haven't learned enough from Gorgias, and I haven't learned enough from Prodicus. So now we really need to think about the sorry state we are in, and inquire into who can make us better than we are. [e] The reason I say this is because in thinking over our inquiry so far, it occurs to me that all this time we've been overlooking something fairly obvious. We've been assuming that only knowledge can lead us correctly and allow us to do the right thing. Perhaps this oversight is why we've found it so difficult to discover how men come to be good.

MENO. What do you mean, Socrates?

SOCRATES. I mean that good men are bound to be beneficial, aren't they? [97a] Were we right to agree* that it wouldn't be any other way?

MENO. Yes.

SOCRATES. And were we also right to agree that they would be beneficial if they led us correctly in whatever we were doing?

MENO. Yes.

SOCRATES. Where I think we went wrong was when we agreed that someone couldn't possibly lead us correctly if they lacked knowledge*.

MENO. What do you mean?

SOCRATES. I'll explain. If someone knows the road to Larissa*—or to wherever you want to go—and he actually goes there and leads others there, wouldn't we be right to say that he leads correctly and well?

MENO. Certainly.

SOCRATES. [b] But what if someone had a true belief* about which is the correct road to Larissa, although he had never actually been there, and didn't know which was the correct road to take? Wouldn't he still lead you there correctly?

MENO. Certainly.

SOCRATES. So as long as he has a true belief about what the other person knows, he won't be any worse a guide to Larissa than the one who knows the way, because his belief about which road to take is true?

MENO. Yes, I suppose he won't be a worse guide.

SOCRATES. So when it comes to doing the correct action,* true opinion is just as good a guide as knowledge. This is what we were overlooking in our discussion just now about what virtue is. We were assuming [c] that knowledge is the only guide to correct action, but true opinion does just as well.

MENO. So it seems.

SOCRATES. So true belief is no less beneficial than knowledge?

MENO. Yes, Socrates, but there is a difference. The one with knowledge will always be successful; the one who has only true belief will be successful sometimes, but other times he won't be.

SOCRATES. What do you mean? Won't the one who always has true beliefs always be successful as long as his beliefs are true?

MENO. That seems necessary. So now I wonder,* Socrates, [d] since true belief makes us just as successful as knowledge, why is knowledge valued so much more than true belief? On what grounds are they distinguished so sharply?

SOCRATES. Do you know why you wonder at this, or shall I tell you?

MENO. By all means, tell me.

SOCRATES. It is because you haven't paid attention to the statues of Deadalus.* Or don't you have any in Thessaly?

MENO. What do you mean?

SOCRATES. If you don't fasten them in place, they'll run off and escape you; but if you tie them down they'll stay.

MENO. [e] So what are you saying about true belief and knowledge?

SOCRATES. His statues aren't very valuable if you don't tie them down because, like runaway slaves they won't stay with you for long. But if you tie them down they are worth a great deal because they are quite fine works. Why am I telling you this? The statues of Daedalus provide a good analogy for true beliefs. True beliefs are very fine things, and they do us lots of good for as long as they remain with us. [98a] The problem is that they don't remain with us for long. They escape the soul and so they aren't worth much until you fasten them down by figuring out what is responsible* for their being true. This is just what recollection is, Meno, as we agreed earlier.* When we tie down our true beliefs, two things happen: first, our true beliefs become knowledge, and second, they become stable. This why knowledge is valued so much more than correct belief, and it is also why knowledge and true belief are different from one another: knowledge is true belief that has been tied down.

MENO. By god, Socrates, that sounds quite reasonable.

SOCRATES. [b] Yes, it does seem reasonable, Meno, and that's why I assert that it is true—not as if I actually know that it is true, but because it is reasonable. However, to say that true belief and knowledge are distinct from one another seems to me to be more than just reasonable. In fact, if there is anything that I would claim to know—and this includes very few things—I would say that this is one thing I know.*

MENO. Quite correct, Socrates.

SOCRATES. And am I also correct to conclude that if true belief guides us in performing some action, the results will be no worse than if knowledge guides us?

MENO. Yes, I think that is also true.

SOCRATES. [c] Doesn't it follow, then, that an action done because of a true belief is no less successful, and no less beneficial, than an action done because of knowledge? And doesn't it also follow that a man with true belief will be no less successful, and no less beneficial, than a man with knowledge?

MENO. Yes, that is so.

SOCRATES. And we agreed that a good man is beneficial?

MENO. Yes.

SOCRATES. So then it is not only because of knowledge that men are good and are beneficial to their cities—if, indeed, there are men who are good and beneficial to their cities—but also because of true belief. But neither of these is natural to human beings: [d] neither knowledge nor true belief. Or do you think that either of them is a natural endowment?

MENO. No, I don't think so.

SOCRATES. Therefore, since they are not in people by nature, then people would not be good by nature.

MENO. No, they wouldn't.

SOCRATES. And since people are not good by nature, the next thing we have to consider is whether they can be taught to be good.

MENO. Yes.

SOCRATES. And we decided that if virtue is knowledge, then it is teachable?

MENO. Yes.

SOCRATES. And we also decided that if virtue is teachable, then it is knowledge?

MENO. Certainly.

SOCRATES. [e] And did we also say that if there are teachers of virtue, then virtue is teachable, but if there are no teachers of virtue, then virtue is not teachable?

MENO. We did agree to that.

SOCRATES. And haven't we agreed that there are no teachers of virtue?

MENO. Yes we have.

SOCRATES. So haven't we agreed that virtue is not teachable, and it is not knowledge?

MENO. Certainly.

SOCRATES. But we have agreed that virtue is good?

MENO. Yes.

SOCRATES. And also that being led correctly is both beneficial and good?

MENO. Certainly.

SOCRATES. [99a] Now, are we agreed that only these two things lead us correctly: true opinion, and knowledge? If someone has either of these two, then he will lead us correctly? Some result might occur correctly by chance, but that doesn't come about by human leadership. If some result comes about correctly by human leadership, it does so only by these two: true belief, and knowledge?

MENO. I think so.

SOCRATES. And since virtue is not teachable, it would not be knowledge?

MENO. It appears not.

SOCRATES. [b] So we have eliminated knowledge as one of the two possible things that make men good and beneficial when it comes to political action. It isn't knowledge that leads us correctly in political action.

MENO. I suppose not.

SOCRATES. So it isn't because of some wisdom, or because they are wise, that Themistocles and the others that Anytus was talking about lead the city. This would also explain why they aren't able to make others like they are: it isn't because of knowledge* that they lead the city.

MENO. It seems just as you say, Socrates.

SOCRATES. Therefore, if they do not lead the city by knowledge, then the only alternative remaining is that they lead the city by good judgment.* [c] It is by good judgement that these political men lead the city correctly, because as far as knowledge is concerned, they are no different from prophets or seers.* They say many true things because they are inspired, but they don't actually know that what they are saying is true.*

MENO. You may be right about that.

SOCRATES. Therefore, Meno, do these men deserve to be called divine? They say and do many great things correctly, but they don't understand exactly why they are correct?

MENO. Yes, that's it.

SOCRATES. So are we correct to call all of these divine: [d] prophets, seers and poets? And are we correct to say that great statesmen are not the least of those who are divine and are inspired, and that they are possessed by the gods when they say many great things and accomplish many great deeds despite the fact that they don't actually know that they what they say is true, and what they do is good?

MENO. Certainly.

SOCRATES. After all, Meno, it is an expression among women to call good men divine, and when the Spartans praise good men they say, "A divine man was he."

MENO. [e] That seems correct, Socrates, though perhaps Anytus here would be upset by it.

SOCRATES. That doesn't worry me, Meno. We'll talk things over with him soon enough. If we have conducted this entire inquiry well, then virtue does not come by nature or by teaching, but by divine dispensation, [100a] and those who receive it don't actually understand it if there is no statesman who is able to impart his expertise to others.* If there were such a statesman, then he might fairly be described as being the sort of man among the living as Homer says Teiresias was among the dead, because he says that

Teiresias was the only one in Hades in full possession of his faculties, all the others were mere "flitting shadows."* In the same way, here among the living, a statesman with understanding would be a true man of substance among shadows with respect to virtue.

MENO. I think you've put it in the finest way possible, Socrates.

SOCRATES. So, Meno, based on this argument, we think that whoever becomes virtuous, acquires virtue by divine allotment.* However, we cannot be certain of this conclusion until we attempt to discover what virtue is itself by itself,* before asking in what way people become virtuous.*

But now it is time for me to go, and time for you to persuade your guest-friend Anytus of these things that you have been persuaded of so that he won't be quite so angry. If you succeed in persuading him, you will be benefitting Athens.

PHAEDO

Setting: the home of Echecrates in Phlius, west of Corinth, near Nemea on the Peloponnesus. A group of philosophers has gathered to hear from Phaedo how Socrates died.

Characters (in order of appearance):

ECHECRATES (perhaps a younger contemporary of Plato, a Pythagorean philosopher from Philus; his name is traditionally pronounced "eh-KECK-ra-teez," though "eh-KEH-krot-ays" is closer to the original)

PHAEDO (perhaps a contemporary of Plato, from Elis north of Olympia he came to Athens as a prisoner of war and became a follower of Socrates; he wrote two Socratic dialogues and established a philosophical school in Elis; his name is traditionally pronounced "FEE-dough," though "FY-doan" is closer to the original)

SOCRATES (469-399 BCE; from a middle class family, not handsome at all; his name is traditionally pronounced "SOCK-ra-teez," though "so-KROT-ays" is closer to the original)

XANTHIPPE (probably much younger than Socrates, but older than Plato; her name means "Golden Horse" and probably indicates that she was from an aristocratic family; her name is traditionally pronounced "zan-THIPP-ee," though "ksan-THIPP-ay" is closer to the original)

CEBES (probably younger than Socrates, a Pythagorean philosopher from Thebes and a follower of Socrates; his name is traditionally pronounced "SEE-bees," though "KEB-ays" is closer to the original)

SIMMIAS (probably younger than Cebes, a Pythagorean philosopher from Thebes and a follower of Socrates; his name is traditionally pronounced "SIM-ee-us," though "sim-EE-os" is closer to the original)

CRITO (a contemporary of, and devoted friend to, Socrates; author of seventeen philosophical dialogues; he was wealthy and managed Socrates' money quite well; his name is traditionally pronounced "CRY-toe," though "KREE-tone" is closer to the original)

Dramatic Structure:

Prologue: Echecrates asks Phaedo about the day Socrates died (57a1-58c5)
Parodos: Phaedo describes the scene and who was present (58c6-59c7)
Episode #1: Socrates' initial case for the immortality of the soul (59c8-85b9)
Episode #2: Simmias and Cebes express doubts about Socates' case (85b10-91c5)
Episode #3: Socrates' concluding case for the immortality of the soul (91c6-107b10)
Episode #4: Socrates' myth of the afterlife (107c1-115a8)
Exodos: the death of Socrates (115b1-118a17)

ECHECRATES. [57a] You yourself,* Phaedo, were actually present with Socrates on the day when he drank the hemlock mixture* in prison? You didn't just hear about it from someone else?

PHAEDO. I was there myself, Echecrates.

ECHECRATES. Then what did he say before he died? And how did he meet his end? I would really like to hear because no one from Phlius ever vists Athens anymore, and we haven't had a visitor from there in a long time [b] who could give a clear account of what happened except for the fact that he drank the mixture and died. Aside from that, we haven't really heard anything.

PHAEDO. [58a] Then you haven't even heard how his trial went?

ECHECRATES. Yes, we did get a report about it, but we wondered why he died so long after* his trial. Why was that?

PHAEDO. Coincidence.* It just so happened that the day before his trial, the Athenians had decorated the stern of the ship that they send to Delos.

ECHECRATES. What ship is that?

PHAEDO. The Athenians claim it is the very ship that Theseus sailed* to Crete, leading the seven boys and seven girls to be sacrificed to the Minotaur.* [b] As the story goes, when Theseus set sail, the Athenians prayed to Apollo that if the "Twice Seven" were saved, they would send a sacred embassy every year to his shrine on Delos. Well, Theseus did save the "Twice Seven," and also himself, and so to this very day, once every year they send a sacred embassy to Delos. Now, they have a law that says once this begins the city must remain pure and cannot carry out any executions until the ship returns from Delos, which can sometimes take a while if the winds are not favorable. [c] The mission is said to begin when the priest of Apollo decorates the stern of the ship, and—as I said—this happened the day before Socrates' trial. That is why Socrates spent so much time in jail between his trial and his death.

ECHECRATES. [d] And what about the circumstances of his death, Phaedo? Tell me everything: what was said, what was done, which of his companions were with him—or didn't the authorities allow him any company? Did he die alone without his friends?*

PHAEDO. No, not at all. In fact, he had quite a few friends with him.

ECHECRATES. Please tell us* every detail, unless you don't have enough time right now.

PHAEDO. I do have time now, and I'll try to give you a complete account. I am always delighted to remember Socrates, whether I am telling others about him or listening to the stories that others have to tell about him.

ECHECRATES. Well, Phaedo, your audience is just as delighted to hear about Socrates as you are. So please do your very best to tell us absolutely everything as accurately as you can.*

PHAEDO. [e] Honestly, Echecrates, I felt very strange when I was there. You know the mixture of sorrow and compassion you feel when you are with a loved one who is dying? Well, I didn't feel that because both in his speech and in his general demeanor Socrates was just so happy. He met his end fearlessly and nobly. Somehow it just seemed perfectly clear that he was going to Hades* in accordance with divine providence, [59a] and that if anyone would fare well there, he would. That is why I didn't exactly feel sad, the way you would expect to feel when you are mourning someone's death; but I also didn't feel the usual pleasure we felt when we expected to have a philosophical conversation with Socrates—which in fact we had. It's hard to explain, but I felt a very strange and uncanny mixture of pleasure and pain when I contemplated the fact that he was actually about to die. Everyone present was in pretty much the same state, laughing one moment and crying the next, especially Apollodorus—[b] you know how emotional he is.

ECHECRATES. Oh, yes, I certainly do.

PHAEDO. He was a complete mess, and the rest of us weren't much better.

ECHECRATES. Who happened to be present, Phaedo?

PHAEDO. A number of Athenians were there, including Apollodorus,* whom I just mentioned. But Critobulus and his father Crito were there, as well as Hermogenes, Epigenes, Aeschines, Antisthenes, Ctesippus of Paeania and Menexenus. Plato, I think, was sick.

ECHECRATES. Were there any non-Athenians there?

PHAEDO. [c] There were three Thebans there: Simmias, Cebes and Phaedondas; and there were two Megarians: Euclides and Terpsion.

ECHECRATES. Weren't Aristippus and Cleombrotus* there?

PHAEDO. No. Someone said that they were in Aegina.

ECHECRATES. Was anyone else there?

PHAEDO. I think that was everyone.

ECHECRATES. Then tell me what you all discussed.

PHAEDO. I will try to relate everything to you from the beginning.

[d] First of all, in the days before his death, we had been in the habit of visiting Socrates: we would gather early in the morning at the courthouse where his trial had been held because it was next to the jail. We would wait around together until the jail opened, which was never early. When it opened, we would go in and spend the whole day with him.

On the day that Socrates died we gathered even earlier than usual because [e] when we had left the evening before we learned that the ship had arrived from Delos. We agreed then and there that we would all gather very early the next morning. We arrived, and the guard who usually greeted us came out and told us to wait outside until he said it was alright to enter. "The Eleven,"* he said, "are removing Socrates' chains and are arranging for him to die this very day." It wasn't long before he came back and told us that we could enter.

[60a] We entered and saw Socrates unbound, and Xanthippe*—you know her—holding his son and sitting beside him. Well, when Xanthippe saw us she cried out the sort of thing women tend to say, "Oh, Socrates! This is the last time your friends will speak to you, and you to them!" Socrates looked at Crito and said "Crito, have someone take her home." Crito had some attendants lead her home crying and beating her breast.*

[b] Socrates sat up on his bed, bent his leg and started massaging it where he had been shackled. While he was rubbing it he said, "How strange a thing is that which men call 'pleasure' and how surprisingly it is related to its opposite: pain. They don't seem to want to be present to a man at the same time, and yet if a man pursues one of them* it's almost certain that the other won't be far behind, as if the two were joined at the head. [c] It seems to me that if Aesop had considered it, he would have composed a story* about how god wanted to end their feud and reconcile them but since that was impossible he sewed their heads together, which is why, to this very day, when one one of them visits you, the other follows. That is just what seems to be happening to me now: the pain in my leg from the shackle has gone, and now the pleasure has followed right behind it.

Cebes jumped in* and said, "By god, Socrates, I'm glad you just reminded me of something. [d] People have asked me to find out about your compositions based on some of Aesop's stories, and also about the hymn* to Apollo that you've written. Just yesterday Evenus asked me what you were thinking in composing these pieces since you arrived here when you've never composed anything before. So if you want me to have an answer ready for Evenus* when he asks me again—and I'm sure that he will—what should I tell him?"

"Tell him the truth, Cebes," Socrates answered. "I am not trying to rival his compositions, [e] which I know full well would not be easy to do. I am putting my interpretation of certain dreams I've had to the test, and at the same time purifying myself if I am at fault* for not heeding the dream's repeated command in this way. Let me tell you about it.

"The same dream* often haunted me in my past life before my trial—it appeared differently in different dreams but it always conveyed exactly the same message: 'Socrates, heed the Muses!'* At the time I thought that the dream was urging me to continue doing exactly what I was already doing, [61a] and that, like fans at a race who encourage the runners to keep running, the dream was urging me to continue practicing philosophy, which is the greatest of the arts inspired by the Muses. But now, after my trial, while the festival of the god has delayed my death, I thought that perhaps I should heed the Muses in a more conventional way, just in case my repeated dream was commanding me to compose what most people think of as something inspired by them. I certainly don't want to violate the command.* So just to be on the safe side, before I depart [b] I've worked on a couple of compositions to ensure that I've obeyed my dream. First I wrote a hymn to the god whose festival was being observed. After my hymn to the god, it occurred to me* that a poet needs to tell stories and not come up with arguments* if he's to be a real poet, and since I'm no storyteller,* I simply took something from Aesop* that I knew and turned that into a poem.

"That is what you should tell Evenus, Cebes. And tell him 'Farewell' from me and that if he is wise he will follow me quickly,* [c] since it seems that I am going away today—the Athenians command it."

Here Simmias broke in, "What a farewell message to Evenus that is, Socrates! I'm well acquainted with him and I hardly think that he would willingly comply with such advice."

"But isn't Evenus a philosopher?"* asked Socrates.

"Yes, I suppose he is," answered Simmias.

"Then of course he'll take my advice, as will anyone else who is worthy of the name 'philosopher,' though he probably will do no violence to himself, since they say it is not permitted."* When he said this he sat up, [d] put his feet on the ground, and remained there for the rest of the discussion.

Cebes then asked him, "How can you say that, Socrates? On the one hand it is not permitted to do violence to oneself, but on the other hand a philosopher will wish to follow someone who is dying?"

"What's this, Cebes? Haven't you and Simmias already learned about this as students of Philolaus?"

"Not clearly,"* Cebes answered.

"I myself have only heard about it from others, but I don't mind telling you what I've heard.* In fact, [e] it seems quite appropriate for someone who is about to depart for the other side to tell stories about departing to the other side, and to consider what we think about it. What else should we do between now and sunset?"

Eager to hear what Socrates had to say, Cebes asked, "What reason do they give for denying that it is permitted to kill oneself? I've heard that before, Socrates; in fact, I heard it from Philolaus when he was living here in Phlius, and I've heard it from others too, but what I've never heard is a clear reason why we ought never kill ourselves."

[62a] "Then I'll try my best to tell you what I've heard," Socrates replied. "It may well be surprising to you* if suicide is the one and only act that is unconditionally impermissible. In other words, even if a man is in terrible circumstances where it is better for him to die than to go on living, although it is permissible for someone else to put him out of his misery it is not permitted for him to do the deed himself."*

"By Zeus,* you've hit the nail on the head" exclaimed Cebes—though he fell into his own dialect when he said it, making us all smile.

[b] "It does seem unreasonable if we put it like that," continued Socrates, "but perhaps there is a reason for it. The secret doctrine may be that 'All mortals are stationed on guard duty,* and so under no circumstances may they desert their posts.' Profound as it may be,* I'm not sure that I could explain or defend it, but this much does seem well said, Cebes, that there are gods who take care of us,* and that we human beings count as one of the possessions of these gods. Doesn't it seem so to you?"

"Oh yes, it does seem like that to me," Cebes agreed.

[c] "And wouldn't you be angry with one of your possessions if it killed itself without any indication from you that you wanted it to die? Wouldn't you punish it if you could?"

"Yes, I certainly would."

"Then perhaps it is not unreasonable that it is impermissible to kill oneself* unless god sends some necessity like the one that is before me."

"That seems likely," Cebes agreed. "But then a problem arises for the claim you just made when you said that philosophers will take the prospect of death so lightly. [d] How can they take that attitude if, as you say, god cares about us and we are his possessions? We can reasonably infer that intelligent people will be troubled at the prospect of leaving the service of such a caretaker—who is clearly the best there could possibly be. Surely intelligent people will not think that they can take better care of themselves if they are set free. An unintelligent person might think that he ought to escape [e] from his master without stopping to think that a good master is not one to run away from, but to stay with for as long as possible—to run away from such a master is totally irrational. A sensible person will want to stay with the better caretaker. But this seems to be the exact opposite of what you said, Socrates, because it entails that the prospect of death will be troubling to intelligent people and attractive to fools."

Socrates seemed delighted by Cebes' conscientiousness. He looked at us and said, [63a] "Cebes always scrutinizes arguments and is never easily persuaded by what someone says."

"Yes, that's true," Simmias agreed, "but I do think he has a good point in this case. Why would wise men* flee those who truly are their better masters, and be so easily rid of them? In fact, Socrates, I think that Cebes is really directing his argument at you personally because you don't seem troubled at all by the fact that you are about to leave us and the good rulers of your life who are, as you agree, gods."

[b] "You have every right to make this allegation," Socrates said. "And so I think that I must make my defense against it, just as I did in court."

"Yes, you must," Simmias agreed.

"Well, then, I shall try to make a more persuasive argument to you than the one I made to the jury. You see, Simmias and Cebes, it would be wrong for me not to be troubled about death unless I thought that when I die, I shall first meet other gods that are wise and good, and then I shall meet men who have died and are better than the men here.* You need to understand that [c] I do hope to arrive among good men— although I would not assert this with absolute confidence, nevertheless if there is anything I am confident about it is that I shall arrive among divine and good masters. So because I do believe this, I am not troubled, I am hopeful that there is something for those who have died, and that—as the old saying goes—it will be much better for the good than for the bad."

"Socrates, you are going to share your thoughts on this before you leave us, aren't you?" asked Simmias. "You aren't going to keep them to yourself, are you? [d] Surely this confidence of yours is a good common to us all, and so if you persuade us that you are right to be hopeful in the face of death, then you will have achieved your goal of presenting a more successful defense to us than you did to your jury."

"I'll do my best," Socrates said. "But first let's find out what Crito has been trying to say."

Here Crito finally spoke up and said, "It's just that the person charged with giving you the hemlock mixture has told me that you really ought to speak as little as possible before drinking it. He says that talking will raise your body temperature, which will diminish the effectiveness of the mixture. [e] If that happens, you may have to take a second or even a third dose."

"That's fine," Socrates said, "just tell him to go ahead and prepare two or three doses."

"I figured you'd say that, Socrates," Crito replied. "But he's been bothering me for a while."

"Ignore him," Socrates continued. "I'd like to give you, my judges, the reason why it seems to me suitable* for a man who has really spent his life in philosophy* to be confident [64a] in the face of death, and to be hopeful that when his life is complete he will win the greatest of goods on the other side. And so, Simmias and Cebes, I shall try to say how this might be so.

"Non-philosophers seem unaware of the fact that those who correctly devote themselves to philosophy are practicing nothing other than dying and being dead. And if this is true, then it would be strange if they are troubled at the arrival of the very thing for which they have been eager their whole lives, and which they have eagerly been practicing for a long time."

Laughing, Simmias exclaimed "By Zeus, Socrates, [b] you made me laugh—and I was really in no mood for laughing just now. I think that most people*—and that includes my fellow Thebans—would completely agree that philosophers are a moribund lot and they are well aware that death is exactly what they deserve."

"And what they say would be true, Simmias," Socrates replied, "except for the claim that they are well aware of what philosophers deserve. In fact they do not understand in what way philosophers are dying, nor do they understand what makes philosophers worthy of death, or what kind of death they deserve. [c] So let's leave others out of it* and simply talk amongst ourselves.

"Do we think that there is such a thing as death?" Socrates began.

"Certainly," replied Simmias, taking up the argument.

"And is death anything other than the escape of the soul* from the body? This is what it is to be dead, isn't it, for the body to become separate from the soul, itself by itself,* and for the soul to become separate from the body, itself by itself? Is death anything other than this?"

"No, that is exactly what it is," Simmias agreed.

"Then, my friend, consider whether you agree with me on another point, [d] because I think it will advance our inquiry if you do. Does a philosophical man seem to you to care about the supposed pleasures of food and drink?"

"Very little, Socrates."

"And what about the delights of Aphrodite?"

"Certainly not," Simmias answered.

"And what about the other ways in which we serve the body? Will such a person make these high priorities? I mean things like expensive clothing and shoes and other ways of decorating the body. Will a philosopher value such things, or will he tend to overlook them, [e] making due with the bare necessities?"

"A true philosopher will disdain such things."

"So, then, on the whole," Socrates continued, "it seems to you that a philosopher does not occupy himself with such matters, but as far as he is able he divorces himself from his body and directs his attention to his soul?"

"Yes, it does."

"Then isn't it clear that, first in these respects, [65a] more than any other human being the philosopher manages to tear the soul away from its partnership with the body?"

"So it seems."

"And aren't there many people who will think that the one who takes no pleasure in such things, and doesn't indulge in them, has a life that is not worth living? Won't they say that someone who doesn't care about the pleasures of the body already has one foot in the grave?"

"True."

"Then what about the acquisition of genuine intelligence? Is the body an empediment or not if it is made a partner in an inquiry? [b] Here's what I mean. Do we derive any truth from seeing and hearing, or are the poets* right to repeat that we neither see nor hear anything accurately? And if these two bodily senses are neither accurate nor clear,* the other senses must be less so since they are inferior to these, don't you agree?"

"Yes, certainly," Simmias said.

"Then when does the soul reach the truth? Obviously it is deceived by the body whenever it tries to investigate something by means of the body."

[c] "That's true."

"So if anything real ever becomes clear to the soul, then it is in reasoning that it does so?"

"Yes."

"And I suppose that the finest reasoning of the soul occurs when it is not distracted by sights or sounds, pleasures or pains—when the soul becomes in the highest degree itself by itself, it bids farewell to the body, and as far as it is able it reaches out to touch reality without relying on the body as a partner."

"All that is so."

"So here too the soul of the philosopher, more than any other, [d] disdains the body, flees from it, and seeks to be itself by itself."

"It seems so."

"Then what about these sorts of things, Simmias: do we say justice itself* is something or nothing?"

"By Zeus, Socrates, of course we say that it is something."

"And what about beauty itself* and goodness itself?"

"Of course."

"And did you ever see any of these with your eyes?"

"Not at all."

"And did you ever touch any of them with any of the other bodily senses? My question applies to all of these forms,* for example magnitude, health, strength and, in a word, to the reality that each of these happens to be. [e] Do we observe what is truest* about them through the body, or is it rather like this: we come closest to actually knowing these real beings if we do our utmost to train ourselves to think about each one in itself as accurately as possible?"

"Certainly by thinking," Simmias agreed.

"Therefore," concluded Socrates, "isn't the man with the purest knowledge of each thing the one who approaches it by thought itself—as opposed to approaching it with a veil of visions in his thoughts, [66a] or by dragging some other perception in with his reasoning? More than anyone else he strives to hunt down each of the real beings—pure and pristine, itself by itself; and he does so by thought—pure and pristine, itself by itself. More than anyone else he is freed from the shackles of eyes and ears and, in a word, the entire body, because when soul partners with body there is no tranquility for the soul, and the body prevents the soul from possessing either intelligence or the truth. If anyone can succeed in attaining reality, Simmias, isn't this the one?"

"How marvelously you express the truth, Socrates!"

[b] "From all these considerations, then, we must conclude that genuine philosophers will say something like the following to each other.

'There is a danger that we will be led off the track in our hunt for the true and real beings: as long as we have the body and it contaminates the soul we shall never attain our goal: the truth. The body keeps us busy with countless tasks for the simple necessity [c] of food; and if we happen to fall sick, that further impedes our hunt. Lusts and desires and fears and phantoms of every kind fill our heads with complete nonsense to the point where we are barely able to think at all. War, battle and discord are the fruits of the body and its desires. Every war* that has even been fought has arisen over the possession of wealth, [d] and the necessity of possessing wealth is all because of the body, in whose service we are enslaved. It is because of all this trouble that we have no time* for philosophy. The crowning touch to all this is that even if we do manage to get some time for study, the body interrupts us at every turn. It complains and diverts our attention and distracts us so that we are unable to focus on the truth.

'Thus it is shown that if we are ever going to have any pure knowledge, [e] then we must be free from the body and we must focus on our studies with the soul itself. Only then, so it seems, will we achieve what we desire and what we declare we love: wisdom.* Only when we are dead will we achieve this, as our argument indicates, not while we are alive. For if pure knowledge* is not possible for us with the body, then there are two alternatives: either the possession of knowledge is impossible for us, or it is possible only when we are dead, [67a] for then and only then will the soul be separate from the body, itself by itself. While we yet live it seems that the nearest we can approach to knowledge is by reducing our association and partnership with the body to the bare necessities of life, not filling ourselves with its nature but keeping ourselves pure from its contamination until god himself frees us from it. And it is reasonable to conclude that when we have been released from the foolishness of the body, we shall be pure, we shall be with those who are pure, and through ourselves [b] we shall know all that is pure and true. It is forbidden for the impure to touch the pure.'

"I think that is the sort of thing that all lovers of learning will think and will say to one another. Do you agree, Simmias?"

"Entirely."

"Then," said Socrates, "if this is true, my friend, there is every reason to hope that when I reach my journey's end, there if anywhere I shall possess that for the sake of which we have devoted so much of our lives. [c] Therefore I march under orders to a foreign land. But there is just as much hope for another man, provided that he has prepared his thinking by purifying it."

"There certainly is."

"Purification is what we have long said it to be: maximal separation of the soul from the body so that the soul is accustomed to being itself by itself, collecting its thoughts and regaining* its composure from all over the body, making itself perfectly at home—as far as possible—both for the present and [d] the future, released from the body like a prisoner freed from jail."

"Yes, that is certainly true."

"Death is what we call the release and separation of the soul from the body?"

"Indeed," Simmias said.

"Releasing the soul we declare to be the greatest desire of true philosophers, and it is only philosophers who desire this release and separation of the soul from the body?"

"So it seems."

"And so you see that what I said at the beginning* is true: it would be ridiculous for a man [e] who has spent his entire life trying to live as close as possible to a state of death to be troubled when death itself draws near to him."

"Yes, I see now that it would clearly be ridiculous," Simmias agreed.

"In reality, then, true philosophers practice dying, and so of all human beings, they fear death least. Consider it this way. If a true philosopher scorns the body in every way and desires to hold his soul itself by itself, and then he achieves exactly this condition, wouldn't it be completely irrational for him to be troubled or afraid? [68a] Shouldn't he actually be glad to be going to a place where he would finally achieve the intellectual state he had longed for all his life, and where he would finally be rid of what had been holding him back?

"In fact," continued Socrates, "think of all those who have willingly gone to Hades itself in the hope that there they might see and be with the one for whom they long—a lover, a wife or a child* who had died. How, then, can the one whose true love is wisdom,* [b] and who has every reason to hope that he shall be united with his beloved in Hades and nowhere else—how can such a person be troubled when he dies? Won't he go there gladly? We must think that he will, my friend, if he is really a philosopher. He will fervently believe that he will be purely united with wisdom there and nowhere else. If things really are as I have just described them, then wouldn't it be completely unreasonable for such a person to fear death?"

"Completely, by Zeus," Simmias said.

"Therefore, if you see a man who is troubled at the prospect of death, isn't that a clear sign that he is not [c] a wisdom-lover* but a body-lover? In fact, won't such a man also be a money-lover or an honor-lover or both?"

"Oh, yes, he certainly will."

"Then consider a further point, Simmias. If philosophers are the ones who are least troubled at the prospect of death, then won't philosophers be the ones who are most appropriately described as courageous?"

"Ah, yes indeed, Socrates."

"And what about temperance—or at least what is commonly called temperance, which consists in not being excited by desire but downplaying it and maintaining your composure? Isn't that characteristic only of those who downplay the body and live their lives in philosophy?"

[d] "Necessarily," Simmias said.

"Now, if you wish, let's compare the courage and temperance of philosophers with the courage and temperance of non-philosophers. I think you'll find them quite strange."

"How so, Socrates?"

"You are aware that all others think of death as a great evil?"

"Certainly."

"Fear of a greater evil* is what makes the brave among them face death—when they do face death."

"So it is."

"Therefore, it is by fear and by being afraid that all are courageous—except, of course, for the philosophers. But isn't it unreasonable to say that someone is courageous because of fear and cowardice?"*

[e] "Completely unreasonable."

"And what about those among them who maintain a kind of composure? Isn't this parallel to the case of courage: aren't they temperate because of intemperance?* You and I will say that this is impossible, but isn't this exactly what the superficial notion of temperance entails? They restrain themselves from indulging in some pleasures only because they are afraid of missing out on other pleasures they desire, and the lure of those other pleasures is too powerful* for them to resist. So although they say that [69a] intemperance is to be ruled by pleasures, nevertheless they are able to control some pleasures only because they are controlled by other pleasures. That is what I was just saying: in a way, they are temperate because of intemperance."

"So it seems."

"Oh, my good friend, Simmias, these kinds of exchanges lead us no closer to virtue: giving up one pleasure simply to gain a greater pleasure, accepting one pain simply to avoid a greater pain, facing one fear because you're driven by terror. This is not the correct sort of exchange to be making for the sake of virtue; it's like trading some coins for others. Wisdom is the only correct coin,* and we ought to exchange all these others for it.* [b] It is when pleasures, pains and fears are all exchanged for wisdom, and when all this buying and selling is done wisely, that we have the reality of courage, temperance, justice* and all the virtues together with wisdom, regardless of whether we add or subtract the pleasures, pains, fears and so on. It is when these pleasures, pains, fears and so on are taken separately from wisdom and exchanged for one another that we have a mere shadow of virtue that is in reality fit only for a slave:* it lacks the real substance and truth of virtue. In reality, true virtue is a sort of [c] purification* from all this sort of thing, and temperance, courage, justice and wisdom itself are all a kind of purification.

"I suppose," Socrates continued, "that those who established initiation rites for us were not simpletons, but were in fact giving us riddles when they said that those who are unitiated and uncleansed are stuck into the mud* when they reach Hades, but when those who have been both initiated and cleansed arrive in Hades, they dwell with the gods. I recall a line from one of their hymns that says,

celebrants are many, worshippers are few.*

[d] "In my opinion, these 'worshippers' are the true philosophers, and through my whole life I have done everything in my power to be counted among them. Whether my efforts have been successful I shall soon know, god willing.

"That is my defense,* Simmias and Cebes, of why it is reasonable for me to be neither grief-stricken or troubled at the prospect of leaving you and my masters* here. [e] I think that there on the other side I shall find good masters and good companions, just as I have found here. I hope that my defense to you has been more persuasive than was my defense to the Athenian jury."

After Socrates said that, Cebes took up the conversation and said, "Socrates, what you've said about virtue and wisdom seem to me quite excellent. [70a] However, what you've said about the soul will not be believed by many people. A common view is that when the soul is released from the body it ceases to exist, because on the very day that someone dies their soul is destroyed and annihilated. They say that when the soul is released from the body it is immediately scattered upon the wind like a dying breath or a puff of smoke.* Of course, if somehow it could be kept together itself by itself, and remain separate from all the troubles associated with the body that you mentioned,* then we would indeed have a great and beautiful hope [b] that what you say is true. But it will take more than just a little exhortation and credulity to accept both that a person's soul exists after death and that it retains the power of thought."

"True, Cebes," replied Socrates, "But what do you propose that we do? Shall we continue our conversation* and see whether or not my view is reasonable?"

"I would be delighted to hear what you think about it, Socrates."

"Then I suppose that nobody listening to us [c] could accuse me of babbling on about trivial things—unless, of course, he happens to be a comic poet.* So, then, if it seems good to you, let's examine the issue.

"Maybe we should consider it this way. Either the souls of those who have died are in Hades, or they are not. The first alternative is reminiscent of that ancient account* according to which the souls in Hades arrived there from here, and that they come back again when they are born here after being among the dead. If that is how it works—the living are born again from the dead—then wouldn't it necessarily follow that* [d] the souls of those who have died are in Hades? Obviously they could not be born again if they hadn't already been, and this would be sufficient proof of the conclusion, if it is sufficiently proven that the living can come from nowhere other than from among the dead. Of course, if the second alternative is true, then we would need an entirely different account."

"Yes, certainly," Cebes agreed.

"Well, then, the easy way* to learn this is not to focus exclusively on human beings, but to consider all animals and plants. In fact, let's take absolutely everything that becomes* [e] and look to see whether all things come to be in any other way than opposites from opposites, for everything that happens to have an opposite. For example, the noble is the opposite of the shameful,* the just is the opposite of the unjust, and so on for countless other cases. So let's investigate whether everything that comes to be necessarily does so in no other way than from its opposite. For example, when something becomes larger, doesn't it necessarily become larger from something that was smaller earlier?"

"Yes."

"So if something becomes smaller, doesn't it come to be smaller later [71a] from something that was larger earlier?"

"It is so," agreed Cebes.

"And doesn't something become weaker later after being stronger earlier, and doesn't something become faster later after being slower earlier?"

"Certainly."

"And doesn't something become worse from being better, and more just from being less just?"

"How could it be otherwise?"

"So we've made this point sufficiently,* namely, that all things come to be in this way: opposites from opposites?"

"Certainly."

"Next, isn't there something else to notice here? In all these pairs of opposites, aren't there actually two ways of becoming? [b] Doesn't the first become the second in a different way than the second becomes the first? For example, when something smaller becomes larger don't we say that it *grows*, and when something larger becomes smaller don't we say that it *shrinks*?"

"Yes."

"And similarly with separating and combining, cooling and warming, and so on with all the others? Even if we don't actually have a name for a specific kind of becoming, isn't it always necessarily this way: each opposite comes to be from the other by its own specific process?"

"Certainly," Cebes said.

[c] "And, of course, being awake has an opposite, namely, being asleep. So doesn't being alive have an opposite?"

"Certainly."

"And it is…"

"…being dead," Cebes answered.

"So if these are opposites, then they must come to be from one another, and there must be two processes of becoming between them?"

"How could it be otherwise?"

"I'll tell you about one of the two pairs I just mentioned, and you tell me about the other. Being asleep and being awake are opposites, we come to be asleep from being awake,* [d] and we come to be awake from being asleep, and the process of coming to be asleep we call *falling asleep*, while the process of coming to be awake we call *waking up*. Does that make sense?"

"Certainly."

"Then you give me a similar account of life and death. You do say that death is the opposite of life, don't you?"

"I do."

"And they come to be from one another?"

"Yes."

"Then what comes to be from the living?"

"The dead."

"And what comes to be from the dead?"

"I must agree," Cebes said, "it is the living."

"So, living beings—including living people—come to be from what is dead?"

[e] "It appears so."

"And so our souls are in Hades?"*

"So it seems," Cebes agreed.

"Now, one of these two processes is fairly clear: becoming dead is clear isn't it?"

"Certainly."

"We can't stop there, waiting for the other shoe to drop, can we? Doesn't nature need a process of becoming that is the complement of dying?"

"Entirely so."

"Then what is it?"

"Coming back to life."

"And if there is such a thing as coming back to life, [72a] it would be the process of passing from death into life, wouldn't it?"

"Certainly."

"So we are agreed on this point also, that the living come to be from the dead no less than the dead come to be from the living. This being so, it seems to me that we have a clear indication that the souls of the dead must exist in some place from which they come to be alive again."

"It seems to me also that this follows necessarily from what we have agreed."

"Look at it this way, Cebes," Socrates continued. "I think we were not wrong to agree to all that. If the pendulum* never swung back again to complete the cycle, [b] if all becoming went in a straight line like a rock that simply rolls downhill and never back up again, then at some point all becoming could end, everything could come to rest in exactly the same state."

"What do you mean?" Cebes asked.

"Oh, it's not difficult to understand what I mean. Suppose for example that people fell asleep but the process never reversed itself to complete the cycle. [c] That would ruin the whole point of the story about Endymion* because he wouldn't be the only one who was permanentely asleep—we'd all be that way. That would be one way to avoid the perpetual succession of opposites on which our argument has been based. Anaxagoras* provides a quite different way: suppose that opposites did not succeed opposites, but that opposites were permanently compresent with one another: 'all things together,' as he says. But whichever way we go—whether death succeeds life without any return cycle, or death is already present with life, [d] everything ends up dead. There would be nothing that was simply alive. I suppose you might try to imagine life coming to be from something other than death, but without the return cycle even that source of life would eventually be exhausted and, again, everything ends up dead."*

"Indeed, every single thing would be, in the end, dead. I think that every point you've made is true, Socrates."

"I think so too, Cebes. We have not been led astray on any point: coming back to life is real, the living really do come to be from the dead, and dead souls continue to exist."

[e] At this point, Cebes took up the argument and said, "In fact, Socrates, we can add the argument that you often give according to which what we call learning is in fact recollection.* If that is true, then necessarily what we are now recollecting we learned at an earlier time, [73a] but that would be impossible if our souls did not exist somehow prior to being born in human form. This would seem to prove the immortality of the soul."

Before Socrates could reply, Simmias broke in and asked, "What arguments are those? Remind me because I can't recall them very well right now."

"Well, first of all," Cebes answered, "there is the astonishing fact that just by asking someone questions it is possible to get them to come up with the correct answers themselves, if the questions are put well. They wouldn't be able to do that if they didn't already have within them knowledge of the correct answer. Second, [b] the clearest possible proof of this comes when you lead someone to see the truth by using diagrams and things like that."

"And if you're not persuaded by those arguments," Socrates added, "see whether you agree if you consider it in the following way. Right now you are skeptical that what is called learning is actually recollection?"

"I wouldn't exactly say that I'm skeptical," answered Simmias, "I suppose I just need to experience what we are talking about: recollection. Actually, what Cebes said did remind me and I am almost persuaded. But I would really like to hear the argument you just referred to."

[c] "I'll gladly explain it. We are agreed that if someone recollects something, then they knew it at some previous time."

"Certainly," Simmias agreed.

"Then are we also agreed that recollection is involved in a different way of knowing something? What I mean is this. Suppose you see something, or you hear it, or perceive it by one of your other senses, and instead of coming to know only it,* you also come to think about something else such that the knowledge of the second thing is distinct from the knowledge of the first thing. In that sort of case wouldn't we be right to say that the thought of the second thing is a form of recollection?"

[d] "What do you mean?"

"For example, the knowledge of a person is not the same thing as the knowledge of a lyre."

"Certainly not."

"Well, you know how a lover feels when he sees the lyre that his beloved used to play, or the cloak that he used to wear. He comes to know the lyre by perception, but in thought he grasps the form of his beloved who played the lyre, and that is recollection. It's like when someone sees Simmias he often recollects Cebes, and there are many more examples that could be given."

"Oh, yes, indeed, by Zeus, there are lots of examples of that," Simmias agreed.

[e] "And it's a sort of recollection, isn't it, especially when you are reminded of something that you haven't thought about in a long time?"

"Certainly."

"Well, how about cases like this? Is it possible for someone to see a picture of a horse and then recollect a person they saw riding a horse? Or what about seeing a picture of a lyre and recollecting a person they heard play a lyre? And isn't it possible for someone to recollect Simmias when they see a picture of Cebes?"

"Oh yes, indeed," Simmias answered.

"And, of course, it is possible to recollect Simmias when you see a picture of him?"

[74a] "It is."

"So from all these examples can't we infer that there are cases of recollection when the thing recollected and the thing perceived are similar and also when the two are not similar to one another?"

"Yes, that does follow."

"Now, in a case where someone recollects something similar to what he perceives, won't he necessarily have an additional experience? Isn't he bound to consider whether the thing he perceives completely measures up to the thing he recollects?"

"That is necessary."

"And do we say that there is such a thing as equality?* I'm not talking about one stick that's equal to another stick, or one stone that's equal to another stone, or any such thing. I'm talking about something else that is beyond all these things:* equality itself.

[b] "Yes, by Zeus, we do indeed say that there is such a thing," Simmias said enthusiastically.

"And do we know what it is?"

"Certainly."*

"Where did we get our knowledge of it? Didn't we get it from seeing the sorts of things I just mentioned, equal sticks and stones and things like that? Wasn't it from these that we thought of that other equality? Or doesn't equality seem to you to be something other than these? Consider it this way. Don't equal sticks or equal stones sometimes appear equal to one* but appear not equal to another, although they remain the same?

"Certainly."

[c] "But the equals themselves* have never appeared unequal to you, or has equality ever appeared to you to be inequality?"

"Never, Socrates."

"Then these equal sticks are not the same as equality itself?"

"It certainly does not appear so."

"And yet it was these equal sticks that put you in mind of equality itself, and you derived your knowledge of equality itself from them—despite the fact that equality itself is different from them?"

"That is entirely true."

"Of course, equality itself may or may not be like these equal sticks."

"Certainly."

"But that makes no difference, does it? Whether they are similar or not, as long as seeing these [d] puts you in mind of the other, we necessarily have a case of recollection, don't we?"

"Very much so."

"Then don't we necessarily have an additional experience in this case? Aren't we bound to consider whether these equal sticks and those equal stones and so on actually measure up to equality itself, or do they somehow fall short of it?"

"They fall short by quite a bit."

"Suppose someone looks at something and thinks, 'This thing that I'm looking at wants to be [e] like some other thing, but it cannot measure up, it falls short and is inferior.' Doesn't this claim necessarily imply that such a person knew beforehand* the other thing that he's using to measure what he's looking at, and in comparison with which he notices that what he's looking at comes up short?"

"Necessarily."

"Isn't our experience of equal sticks and equality itself just like this?"

"Yes, exactly."

"Doesn't this necessarily imply that we knew equality [75a] some time before we first saw equal things and thought to ourselves, 'These are striving to be like equality but they are falling short'."

"It does indeed imply that."

"And are we also agreed that there is nowhere else that we could have derived this knowledge of equality? It is only by seeing or touching or in some other way perceiving equal things that we consider equality? I'm treating all the senses as being basically the same."

"And they are the same for the purposes of our argument," Simmias added.

"So in fact it must be from the senses and from the senses alone that [b] we think all the equal things we perceive are striving for equality but falling short of it? Is that what we are saying?"

"Yes, that is correct."

"So before we began to see or hear or in some other way perceive equal things we must already have grasped knowledge of what equality is. Otherwise we would not have been able to refer the equal things we perceive to equality and notice that they are striving for, but failing to attain, equality.

"That follows from what we've agreed."

"But we've been seeing and hearing and using our senses from birth,* haven't we?"

"Of course."

[c] "But didn't we already agree that we must have had the knowledge of equality before we we began to use our senses?"

"Yes."

"So it seems that we must have had it before we were born."

"That follows."

"And if we acquired this knowledge before we were born, and hence had it when we were born,* then at birth and before we were born didn't we already know the equal, the greater, the lesser and all such things? Don't forget that our discussion is not restricted to equality, but is also about beauty itself, [d] goodness itself, justice itself, holiness itself and everything that we ratify in our discussions with the "itself" seal of approval. Necessarily we acquired the knowledge of all these before we were born?"

"That is true."

"And if on each occasion that we have acquired this knowledge we do not forget it, then on each occasion we are born knowing it and we continue to know it through our whole life. For this is what it is to know something: having acquired knowledge, to hold on to it and not to lose it—or wouldn't you say that to forget is to lose knowledge?"

[e] "Oh, yes, that is correct."

"But what if we acquired various kinds of knowledge before we were born and then lost them? At some later time we might use our senses on particular things and recover the different kinds of knowledge that we had before. In that situation, wouldn't what we call learning actually be recovering our own knowledge? Wouldn't we be correct to call this recollection?"

"Certainly."

[76a] "That's because we found it is possible to perceive something—either by seeing it or hearing it or using some other sense—and to think of something else that we have forgotten, comparing what we see to what we forgot, whether the two are similar or dissimilar. So there are two possibilities: either we are all born knowing these things and we know them through our whole lives, or else we are not born knowing them but come to know them later by a process that we call 'learning,' but which is in fact recollecting."

"Yes, those are the only two alternatives, Socrates."

"Which do you choose, Simmias? Are we born knowing, [b] or do we later recollect knowledge we acquired earlier?"

"I can't decide, Socrates."

"What about this: when a man knows something, is he able to give an account* of it or not?"

"It is entirely necessary that he is able, Socrates."

"And is everyone able to give an account of the things we are talking about?"

"I wish they were," Simmias said. "But I very much fear that tomorrow at this time no human being alive will be worthy of doing so."

[c] "So you think that not everybody knows these things?"

"No."

"Then they are recollecting them when they learn them?"

"Necessarily."

"When did our souls* acquire knowledge of them? After we were born as human beings?"

"Surely not."

"Then before?"

"Yes."

"Then, Simmias, our souls existed before they were in human form, and they existed separately from these bodies, and they possessed intelligence."

"Unless they acquired this knowledge at the moment they were born, Socrates. We haven't considered this possibility."

[d] "Good point, my friend. But at what other time could we possibly lose it? We have agreed that we have it before we are born and that we do not have it after we are born. At what other time could we possibly lose it? Or do you want to suggest that we gain and lose it in the very same instant?"

"Oh, certainly not, Socrates, forget I mentioned it."

"Then is this how things stand, Simmias? If these things that we are always talking about really do exist—the beautiful, the good and all such things—and if we refer all of our perceptions to them, [e] discovering in the process not only that they existed before we discovered them but also that in discovering them we are actually recovering our own knowledge,* then doesn't it necessarily follow that just as they existed before we were born, so also our own souls existed before we were born into this human form? If they do not exist, then our discussion has been a complete waste of time.* Isn't this how things stand? Necessarily if they exist, then our souls existed before we were born; and if they do not exist, then our souls did not exist before we were born."

"Marvelous, Socrates!" exclaimed Simmias. "The discussion has taken an auspicious turn. I see now that it is with the very same necessity [77a] that our souls existed before we were born, and that these realities you speak of exist. Nothing is more manifestly clear to me than the reality of all these sorts of things we've been talking about—beauty, goodness and the rest. In my view, the point has been sufficiently proven."

"But what about Cebes? Is he satisfied with this argument?"

"Suficiently, I think," answered Simmias, "despite the fact that you won't find a more resolute doubter of arguments than Cebes. But I think that he is entirely convinced that our souls existed before we were born. [b] But the question remains, Socrates, will they continue to exist after we die? Cebes' concern* still stands: many fear that when someone dies, their soul is scattered to the winds and meets its end. Even if the soul came together and existed somewhere else before it was born into a human body, what prevents it from disintegrating and coming to an end once it leaves the body?"

[c] "Well said, Simmias," Cebes added. "It appears that we have been given only half of the argument that we need. It has been proven that our souls existed before we were born, but now we need an additional proof that they continue to exist after we die if the argument is going to be complete."

"But it has been proven," Socrates said, "if you put this argument together with* the argument we agreed upon just a short while ago that everything living comes to be from the dead. [d] If the soul exists beforehand, and necessarily when it enters the realm of the living and is born it comes from nowhere other than from death and from being dead, doesn't it necessarily follow that it continues to exist after it dies since at some point it will have to be born again? That proves what you just asked about.

"However," Socrates continued, "I think that you and Simmias would like to continue this conversation. Perhaps you share a fear common among children that when the soul leaves the body the wind literally blows the soul away and [e] scatters it to the four winds, especially if it's blowing really hard."

That made Cebes laugh, and smiling he went along with Socrates' joke, "Then since we are so afraid, Socrates, try to convince us—or rather, convince the frightened child in each of us—that we shouldn't be afraid of death as if it were some kind of bogeyman."

"The way to handle your inner child," Socrates advised, "is to sing to him every day. Charms will ease his fears."

[78a] "But where shall we find someone good at charms* since you won't be here tomorrow?"

"Greece is large," Socrates answered, "and good men are in it—and there are many good men in foreign lands. You ought to travel through them all seeking good charmers, sparing no expense; do whatever it takes because there is no more auspicious quest upon which you could embark. But most of all, you ought to seek them amongst yourselves:* I don't think you will easily find anyone better able to do this than you."

"We will do as you say, Socrates," Cebes replied. "But if it is alright with you, [b] let's go back to the point where we left off."

"Certainly, I'm happy to return to that point."

"Wonderful!"

"Then I think these are the sorts of questions we should ask ourselves," Socrates continued. "What kinds of things are liable to be dispersed? What sorts of things should we fear will be dispersed, and for what sorts of things needn't we fear dispersion? After we settle that, we can ask which kind of thing the soul is, and decide whether we should be confident about, or afraid for, our own souls."

"That is true," Cebes answered.

[c] "Compounds and things with composite natures, aren't these the sorts of things that are liable to suffer dispersion* into their component parts? And uncompounded things are not likely to suffer that fate?"

"That seems right."

"So isn't it reasonable to conclude that if something remains as it is without changing, then it is uncompounded; but if it does not remain the same, if it changes, then it is composite?"

"It seems so to me."

"Then let's go right to those very things we've talked about, [d] the ones we ratify with the honor of being "itself" when we indulge in our usual style of question-and-answer: equality itself, beauty itself and so on. Is each of those always itself, or is each always different? Is it even possible for any of them to change? Or is each one of them always exactly what it is, itself by itself, uniform, remaining constant, and never in any way altering in the slightest in any respect?"

"Each is constant, necessarily," said Cebes, "remaining itself."

"And what about the many particular beautiful things, for example, beautiful people, beautiful horses, [e] beautiful clothing or anything else like that? Or we could consider the many particular equal things that are only called 'equal' because of their relation to equality itself. Do they remain constant, or are they entirely the opposite; do they never remain the same* as each other or as themselves, and in a word, are they in no way constant?"

"That is exactly correct," Cebes agreed, "they are never constant."

[79a] "These you can touch and see and perceive with all of your other senses, but those unchanging things cannot be grasped in any way except by rational thought, they are unseen and invisible?"

"That is entirely true."

"Then shall we posit two kinds of beings: some are visible and others are unseen?"

"We shall posit them."

"And the unseen things are always constant, but the visible things are never constant?"

"Let us posit that also."

[b] "And how about us? Are we not, on the one hand, body, but, on the other hand, soul?"

"Of course."

"Then to which kind of being is the body more similar, and more closely related?"

"To the visible, in every way," Cebes replied.

"And what about the soul? Is it visible or unseen?"

"Unseen—at least by human beings, Socrates."

"Oh, yes, indeed we are talking about what is by nature visible to human beings. You aren't thinking about visibility to anyone other than human beings, are you?"

"No, just to human beings."

"Then what do you say about the soul? Is it visible or invisible?"*

"Not visible."

"So unseen?"

"Yes."

"Therefore, the soul rather than the body is more like the unseen, and the body rather than the soul is more like* the visible?"

[c] "That is entirely necessary."

"Now, didn't we say a while ago* that when the soul employs the body to inquire about something, either by seeing or hearing or by using some other sense—because inquiring through the senses is what it means to use the body for inquiry—the soul is dragged by the body through what never remains the same and grabs onto them, wandering around dazed and confused like a drunken man trying to keep from falling down?"

"Yes, exactly."

[d] "But when it inquires itself by itself, it crosses over to what is pure and immortal, to what always is and remains constant. And because the soul is of a kindred nature with these, when it is finally able to be itself by itself, it remains with them always, finally at rest from its wanderings, remaining constant and unchanging even as it touches constant and unchaning reality. Isn't this the experience called wisdom?"

"That is beautifully put, Socrates, and completely true."

"So, then, based on what we said before and what we've just agreed to now, [e] which kind of being would you say the soul is more like, and more related to?"

"After the way you've handled the subject I'm sure that everybody—even the slowest of learners—would agree that the sould is wholly and entirely more like what remains constant than it is to what does not remain constant."

"And the body?"

"It is more similar to what does not remain constant."

"We can look at this this way also. Whenever the soul and body are together, [80a] nature prescribes that the body should be ruled and obey, and that the soul should rule and be master. On this analogy, which would you say is more like the divine, and which is more like the mortal? Don't you think that that the divine is by nature the one suited to rule and to lead, while the mortal is suited to be ruled and to obey?"

"I certainly do."

"Which is the soul more like?"

"Clearly the soul is like the divine, and the body is like the mortal."

"Consider, then, Cebes, whether everything we've said means that [b] we can draw the following two conclusions. On the one hand, the soul is most like what is divine, immortal, intelligible, uniform, indissoluble, and remains constant. But on the other hand, the body is most like what is human, mortal, multiform, unintelligible, dissoluble and never remains constant. Do we have any objections, my friend, or does that conclusion stand?"

"No, we have no objections."

"Then in that case, isn't it entirely fitting for the body to be quickly dissolved, but for the soul to remain entirely undissolved, or very nearly so?"*

[c] "Of course."

"But you realize, don't you, that although it is fitting* for the body to dissolve quickly, in fact decomposition does not set in immediately? When a human being dies, the visible part, the body—which we call the corpse—remains visible, and although it is fitting for the corpse to be dissolved, to decompose and to be dispersed, in fact it remains for quite some time. This is especially true if the body was healthy and died in the winter. In fact, if the body is embalmed or mummified as they do in Egypt it remains intact for a very long time, and [d] parts of it, like the bones, sinews and such, are even said to be immortal."

"Yes."

"But the soul, the unseen part, departs for another realm, one that is noble and pure and unseen: the true Hades. There the soul is in the presence of the good and wise god,* and there, god willing, my own soul shall go. Now, since the soul is like this by nature, do we agree with those who say that when it separates from the body it is immediately dispersed and destroyed? [e] Far from it, my friends. The truth is much more like this. Suppose a soul departs in a state of purity, without dragging anything of the body along with it, because in life it did not form a partnership with the body but instead it shunned the body and gathered itself into itself and made this its constant practice. Could this be anything other than a soul that has correctly practiced philosophy, [81a] and in doing so practiced to face death calmly—in other words, it practiced dying."

"I agree entirely."

"Then if it is in that condition when it dies, won't it depart for that which is like itself—to the unseen, divine, immortal and wise realm? And when it arrives there, won't it be happy since it will finally be freed from its wandering, its foolishness, its fears and wild desires and all the other human ills: 'truly to dwell with the gods for the rest of time,' as is said of initiates.* Is that what we shall say, Cebes?"

"Yes, by god, we shall."

[b] "But what if a soul that is impure and polluted* is freed from the body? This soul has been a full partner with the body and has both served and loved it. Such a soul has been bewitched by the body's desires and pleasures to the point that it thinks nothing is true except what is in bodily form, what can be touched or seen, eaten or drunk or used to procure the delights of Aphrodite. Things that are intelligible and choiceworthy to philosophy are difficult or impossible for it to see with the eyes of the body and so it has grown accustomed to fearing them, fleeing them and hating them. [c] When such a soul is separated from the body and is itself by itself, can it possibly be pure?"

"There's no way that it could be."

"Quite the opposite, in fact, I think that bodily form will entirely suffuse it because it has cohabited and intimately associated with the body. Because of this continual association with the body, and because it has lavished such attention on the body, it will have grown almost to the point of being united with the body, won't it?"

"Certainly."

"I'm sure that this must be a tremendous burden on a soul—to be united to the visible, and to be so earthen and heavy. A soul like that must be so weighed down that even after death when it has been freed from the body it is dragged back into the visible world by fear of the unseen and fear of Hades. You know they say that [d] souls of the dead meander among the tombstones in graveyards, and some even claim to have seen these shadowy phantoms—just the sort of apparition* that such a soul would produce: it was set free in an impure state, and because it shared in the nature of the visible, after death it is still visible."

"That seems fitting, Socrates."

"It does seem fitting, Cebes—not for the souls of the good, but for the souls of the bad who are compelled to wander such places to pay the penalty for nurturing their souls so badly. And they must continue to wander until [e] their incessant desire for the bodily form again shackles them to bodies. And it seems fitting that each soul will be shackled to the sort of body that corresponds to what it cared most about in life."

"What sorts of bodies do you have in mind, Socrates?"

"For example, those who were not careful when it came to hunger, thirst or lust but actually indulged their appetites will be shackled to the body of a donkey [82a] or some other such wild animal. Don't you think that sounds about right?"

"That certainly does sound appropriate."

"Those who preferred to live by injustice, robbery or tyranny will find themselves shackled to the bodies of hawks, buzzards or wolves.* Can you think of more suitable destinations for them?"

"No doubt about it they'll end up in those kinds of bodies."

"So obviously in each case a soul will go to a body that is suited to what it cared about most in life?"

"Oh, yes, that's obvious."

"If we turn to the happiest of souls, those who will head to the best of places, they will be the souls that have taken care to train themselves in the personal and social virtues,* [b] which are called temperance and justice. I'm referring to those who have developed good habits by careful training, but without engaging in philosophy or theoretical inquiry."

"Why are they the most happy?"

"Because it will be only fitting for them to return in the body of a civilized and social animal like a bee, wasp or ant. From there obviously they would return as human beings and would become respectable people."

"That seems fitting."

"But none may join the gods who has not lived a philosophical life* and departed [c] with a pure soul; this is permitted only for those who love learning.* It is for the sake of joining the gods,* my friends Simmias and Cebes, that those who correctly practice philosophy do not indulge any desires of the body, they maintain self-control and do not surrender to them. They don't live this way out of fear that they will drain their financial resources or fall into poverty—like those who love money—nor do they life this way out of fear that they will gain a bad reputation or be dishonored—like those who love status and power."

"No, that wouldn't be appropriate for them, Socrates."

[d] "No, by Zeus. That is why all those who care for their own souls happily bid farewell to those who live their lives in service to their bodies. Those who serve the body do not know where they are going, but those who care for the soul gladly follow where philosophy leads them, proceeding in freedom and purity."

"How do they do that, Socrates?"

"I'll tell you. Those who love learning know that [e] when philosophy seizes them, their souls are completely shackled to the body and they're stuck with it. So when they investigate reality they cannot do so with the soul itself by itself: they are compelled to stumble around in ignorance, studying reality like prisoners looking at the outside world through the bars of a jail cell. Philosophy sees that the most terrible thing about this imprisonment is that the bars locking a man in are forged from his own desires, [83a] and so philosophy gently encourages the soul and tries to set it free, pointing out that any investigation that is carried out through the eyes will be full of fraud, and that any investigation through the ears or through any of the bodily senses will be equally fraudulent. Philosophy then persuades the soul to withdraw from all these senses, using them only insofar as they are absolutely necessary, and to gather itself into itself and to muster only its own forces, placing its own trust in nothing other than [b] itself—philosophy convinces the soul that it must remain itself by itself if it is going to understand any real thing itself by itself, and that it must believe there to be no truth at all in what it consider through other means since it is just going to be different in something different.* What the soul sees by itself is intelligible but unseen, while what it sees by other means is perceptible and visible.

"Now, the soul of the true philosopher," Socrates continued, "believes that it must not resist this attempt to free it, and so as far as it is able it resists pleasures and pains, desires and fears. At this point, the soul has calculated that anyone who indulges an intense pleasure, pain, desire or fear not only suffers the obvious bad consequences—[c] illness, poverty and so on—but in addition also suffers the ultimate and greatest of all incalculably* bad results."

"And what is this terrible result?" asked Cebes.

"To be compelled to believe that whatever caused the intense pleasure or pain is the truest and most manifestly clear* being there is. This happens especially with things that are visible, don't you agree?"

"Certainly."

[d] "Isn't it in this sort of experience more than any other that the soul is bound to the body?"

"How so?"

"Because each pleasure or pain is like a nail that fastens the soul so tightly to the body that the soul almost takes on bodily form, and it believes that whatever the body says is true actually is true. So because the soul believes whatever the body believes,* and enjoys whatever the body enjoys, the soul is compelled to take on the same character as the body, and even finds its nourishment in whatever nourishes the body. That is why it cannot arrive in Hades in a pure state; it is so full of the body that it must depart and immediately fall into [e] another body where it grows like a seed growing in the dirt. It has no share in what is pure, uniform and divine."

"Nothing could be more true," Cebes said.

"That is why those who love learning in the right way are called brave and decent by many, or don't you agree?"

[84a] "Oh, yes, I do agree."

"The soul of a philosophical man would calculate the way I just indicated. He would not think that once philosophy had set him free from pleasures and pains he ought to hand himself right back over to those very pleasures and pains, undoing all the work he had just done—like Penelope* unweaving by night what she wove during the day. No, the philosophical man thinks that he ought to work at calming the tempest of feelings, following reason and continually keeping a clear head so that he may contemplate what is no mere matter of opinion: the truth and the divine, [b] nourishing his soul with only this. He thinks that he ought to live as long as there is life within him,* and when his life is complete he shall be freed from all human troubles and shall depart to be with his own kind. So my friends Simmias and Cebes, a soul that has been nurtured like this, and has worked very hard in this way, has nothing to fear: he won't be terrified that when his soul leaves his body, his soul will be torn apart, or scattered by the winds, or that it will simply vanish into thin air."

[c] Silence held us all for a long time after Socrates said that. He seemed to be meditating upon the account he had just given—which is just what most of us were doing. Cebes and Simmias had a short conversation with one another, and seeing them talking Socrates asked, "What are you two talking about? Do you think I've left anything out? Certainly if you'd like to go through the issues thoroughly there are many points where someone might ask questions or have doubts. Of course, I have nothing to say if you two are considering something else, but if you have any difficulty with what I've said, please don't hesitate to voice your concerns [d] and explain them fully—especially if you think that something better can be said on the subject. And please take me along with you if you think you can make some progress with my help."

Simmias spoke up and said, "I'll tell you the truth, Socrates. For a while now both Cebes and I have had a particular problem in mind and each of us has been urging the other to express it because we really want to hear how you will deal with it. But we hesitate to bring it up because we don't want to be disagreeable, especially under the present circumstances."

Socrates gently laughed when he heard this and he said, "I am surprised at you, Simmias. [e] How difficult would it be to convince others that I'm really not troubled by my present circumstances when I am unable to persuade even you? You seem to be afraid that here at the end of my life my disposition is suddenly going to change and I will no long be eager to hear objections and discuss things further. I suppose you think that I'm not as good a prophet as swans. You know that they sing [85a] throughout their lives but when they perceive that they must die they sing even more, and they sing the most beautiful song they've ever sung. They are rejoicing because they are returning to the god they serve. People have completely misrepresented this phenomenon because of their own fear of death—they say that the swan's song is a lament sung in pain at the prospect of death. They have failed to reason this out properly because no bird sings when it is hungry or cold or suffering in any way—not even the nightingale, the swallow or the hoopoe, all of whom are falsely said to sing lamentations. No, I don't think any of them [b] sing out of grief, including swans. But I do think that swans are prophetic, they are, after all, servants of Apollo. And so because they see in advance how good it will be in Hades, they sing and rejoice on that day more than on any other. I consider myself to be a fellow servant with the swans, consecrated to the same god, and I believe that I have received a prophetic power from our master that is no worse than theirs. As a result, I have no more sorrow at leaving this life than they have. So you ought to ask me any question you want; we will talk for as long as the Eleven* permit it.

"That was beautiful, Socrates. Ok, then I'll tell you the problem I have, [c] and Cebes will explain what he does not accept in what you've said. But before I begin, I want to emphasize something that I think you probably agree with: to know with certainty* the kinds of things we are discussing is either impossible or very difficult in this life, but even so we must never surrender—we must put such claims to the test in every way we can until we have exhausted every possibility. We must do one of two things: either we must know the truth—by learning it from someone or by discovering it ourselves—or else, if that proves to be impossible, we must choose the best and most difficult to refute of all the accounts people have put forward [d] and cling to it like a liferaft, sailing through the storms of life. Those are our only two options if we are unable to sail through life in a more solid, more seaworthy vessel, steering clear of all the dangers by means of some divine doctrine.* So I am not ashamed to ask my question—you've invited me to do so, and I would regret it in the future if I failed to ask you when I had the chance. Because, you see, Socrates, Cebes and I have been considering what you've said and I do not think that you have sufficiently made your case."

[e] "Perhaps that is the truth, Simmias," Socrates agreed. "So tell me, in what way do you think I have failed to make my case sufficiently?"

"Here's my concern, Socrates," Simmias continued. "You've said that the soul is not a body, and that it is invisible, beautiful and divine. But all that is true of what musicians call the tuning* of a lyre.* [86a] The lyre itself and the strings are bodies, they are composed of earth and are by nature mortal, but the way that they are tuned is not itself a body, but the attunement of the lyre can be quite beautiful and even divine. Now, what if someone takes a well tuned lyre and smashes it—breaks it and cuts the strings? They could say about the tuning what you just said about the soul, namely that it is impossible for the tuning to have perished, and so it must still exist. They might say that no one could possibly destroy the tuning—which is divine and immortal—before the lyre and strings perish—which are material and mortal. [b] Socrates, I'm sure it has occurred to you that we think* the soul is to the body what a tuning is to a lyre: just as a lyre has strings that must be properly tuned to one another, so also the human body is in a way a tuning of the moist and the dry, the cool and the warm, and so on for all the pairs of opposites. [c] All of these must be in the right measure, and they must be well blended with the others. So, obviously, if the soul is a sort of tuning of the bodily strings, then if these strings are stretched to the breaking point, or are loosened way too much, because of illness or injury, then necessarily the soul must immediately be on the verge of destruction—even if it had been a divine attunement. That's just how it is with any instrument capable of producing harmonies—in fact, it holds true in any craft that involves carefully balancing and blending various elements with one another. And if the tuning is broken or falls apart somehow, then what remains of the body will endure for some time [d] until it is burned up or it just decomposes. What can we say in response to this theory that the soul is a blending of what constitutes the body, and that in what is called 'death,' the soul is the first thing to perish?"*

For a moment Socrates just looked at Simmias with that peculiar expression of his, then he smiled and said, "Simmias is quite right to raise this objection, and he clearly has a really good grip on the issues. If someone is ready with an answer, go ahead and give it. But it seems to me that we should first hear what objection Cebes wants to raise. [e] That way we'll have plenty of time to consider our response, because once we've heard them out, then either we should agree with them,* if they seem to be singing in tune, or else we'll have to figure out some way to defend our view. So come, then, Cebes, tell us what your concern is."

"Ok, I'll tell you," Cebes replied. "It seems to me that we remain right where we were a while ago,* [87a] and that the objection I raised still applies. Let's separate the issue of the existence of the soul prior to birth from the existence of the soul after death. I do not retract my agreement with you on the existence of the soul prior to birth: I agree that you proved your case on that point earlier. But I don't think that anything you've said proves that the soul continues to exist after death. Mind you, I do believe that the soul is something stronger and more enduring than the body—that is a point on which I disagree with Simmias. In my view, the soul is vastly superior to the body in every way. I realize that my view sounds incoherent: how can I say that the soul is more enduring than the body, but deny that the soul continues to exist after death [b] when I plainly see that the remains of the body continue to exist for some time after death? See if there is something in my answer. I'm going to use an illustration like Simmias did.

"Imagine that an old tailor dies, but someone says, 'Actually, the man has not been destroyed—he is still safe and sound.' When asked to give proof of this astonishing claim he shows the cloak that the tailor had worn for years—one he'd made himself.* [c] Obviously this won't convince anyone, but he might then ask, 'Which of these two kinds of things is the more enduring: a human being or a cloak that has been worn day in and day out for years?' When he hears the answer 'a human being,' he will conclude that the tailor is safe and sound, since he is more enduring than his cloak, and his cloak is still safe and sound."

Continuing his objection, Cebes said, "I am not persuaded by this argument, Simmias. Hear me out. Obviously the person who gives this argument is being silly. The tailor who makes and wears many cloaks over the course of his entire life is going to outlive many of them, [d] except for the very last one. But this does not entail that a human being is feebler or more delicate than a cloak.

"We can apply this same reasoning to the soul and the body. We might well say that the body is weaker and more delicate and that the soul is more enduring. So perhaps the soul wears out many bodies* over the long course of its existence. In fact, we can see that this is true within the course of just one long life: for the body is continually wearing out and losing energy so that [e] unless the soul continually weaves and re-weaves the body by replenishing food and water, the body would die very quickly. Therefore, it is necessarily true that when the soul perishes, it is wearing its final garment—its final body. Without its soul, the body reveals its inherent weakness and it begins to decay.

"So the comparative strength and durability of the soul does not entail that [88a] it survives after the body has died. In fact, we can take this a step further. Let's grant even more than you granted in your objection, Simmias. Let's allow that the soul existed before birth, and in fact has gone through many births and deaths because it is more durable than the body. But even if we accept all this, it still does not follow that the soul does not suffer in this repeated process of death and re-birth. At some point, it may suffer a final death* that it does not survive. [b] But of course no one knows which death and dissolution of the body will bring about the destruction of the soul because we cannot perceive the destruction of the soul. If this is all correct, then we are fools* to be confident in the face of death unless we can prove that the soul is deathless and indestructible.* If a man cannot prove this about the soul, then necessarily when he faces death, he will fear that when his body dies, his soul will be completely annihilated."

[c] This made us all extremely uncomfortable*—as we all admitted to each other later—because we had all been completely convinced by Socrates' earlier arguments, but now Simmias and Cebes seemed to have torn all that down, leaving us with nothing but chaos and disbelief. And we felt this not only about the arguments in the past, but also about future arguments as well: we felt completely worthless as judges of arguments, and that perhaps the issues were inherently undecideable.

ECHECRATES. By the gods, Phaedo, I'm feeling exactly what you all felt. Once I heard you recount the objections of Simmias and Cebes [d] I thought to myself, 'How can I ever trust an argument again? The arguments that Socrates gave were so persuasive but now they've been completely discredited.' When you went through the theory that the soul is a sort of attunement of the body you reminded me of how impressed I have been by that theory for quite some time now. So now I feel as if I have to start over from the beginning* and try again to find some argument to persuade me that when someone dies, their soul does not also die. So please, by god, tell me how did Socrates continue the discussion? [e] Was he visibly upset like everybody else or not? Did he calmly support his position in response to the objections, and if so, how successful was he? Please tell me everything in detail, as clearly as you can.

PHAEDO. I have often been amazed by Socrates, but I never admired him more than at that moment. [89a] Of course it's no surprise that he had something to say, but what was so admirable was that, in the first place, he was so pleased to listen to the two young men who were arguing against him. He listened to them kindly and respectfully. But second, he accurately perceived just what a profound effect the objections had on all of us. So third, instead of simply launching into a philosophical response to the objections, he took the time to heal us: he saw that we looked like defeated soldiers who dropped their shields and ran from a battle, so he rallied us and got us turned in the right direction so that we were ready to follow him into the fray, considering the argument once again.

ECHECHRATES. How did he manage to do that?

PHAEDO. I'll tell you.

I happened to be sitting to Socrates' right [b] on a low stool beside him so that he was above me and his right hand was near my shoulder. Well, at this point he gently touched my head and started playing with my hair, twirling some of my locks between his fingers. He often used to do this to tease me* for wearing my hair long.

"Tomorrow," Socrates said, "perhaps you will cut your beautiful hair,* Phaedo."

"I suppose so, Socrates," I said.

"Don't."

"Why not?"

"Today you and I shall both cut our hair if this argument dies and we are not able to bring it back to life. [c] Remember that famous oath the Argives swore after losing the town of Thyrea* to the Spartans: they cut their hair short and swore that no man could wear his hair long until they had won back Thyrea. Let's swear a similar oath: we will both cut our hair if we are unable to win back our account* from Simmias and Cebes."

"But Socrates, they say that not even Herakles* could handle two opponents at once."

"Then call on me as your Iolaus while there is still daylight."*

"Oh, yes, I certainly do call for your help, but not as Herakles calling for Iolaus—I am your Iolaus calling for help from Herakles."

"Whatever. But first, there is something that we must be very careful about."

"What is that?"

[d] "We must beware of turning into what I call 'misologists.'* Nothing worse can happen to us than to become the sort of people who hate rational inquiry. In fact, I can tell you just how misology arises because it does so in just the same way that misanthropy arises. The first step in becoming a misanthropist is to place implicit trust in someone when you don't have a sufficient understanding of what you are trusting

them to do—you just assume that everything this person says is true, that all his advice is sound,* and that he is utterly reliable. The second step is taken soon after that, because you quickly realize that you placed your faith in a scoundrel and that he was entirely untrustworthy. After that happens a few times—especially when [e] it is some relative or friend who disappoints you—and you find that trusting people just leads to angry disagreements with them, you end up hating everybody and thinking that there isn't a single honest or trustworthy person in the world. Have you seen this happen?"

"Oh, yes, I certainly have," I answered.

"But isn't it shameful to be a misanthropist? Isn't it clear that misanthropists are trying to deal with people without knowing the first thing about them, [90a] which is that very few people are extremely good and very few people are extremely bad: most of us are in the middle, aren't we?

"What do you mean, Socrates?"

"For example, isn't it rare to find an extremely tall person or an extremely short person? Or how about an extremely large dog or an extremely small dog, or anything else like that? Or think of extremely fast and extremely slow runners, or extremely shameful and extremely admirable people, or people with extremely light or extremely dark complexions. Haven't you noticed that when you measure people on some such spectrum, it is rare to find someone at either extreme, most of us are somewhere in the middle?"

"Oh yes, that is definitely true."

[b] "So if we held a competition in being bad, very few people would excel?"

"Probably," I said.

"Probably indeed. Although if we held a competition in being bad not among people but among arguments we may well find very many that excel. But that's not the point I wanted to make; I was just filling out the example to make sure that you understood what I was saying. My main point is this: misology begins the way that misanthropy begins—with the combination of implicit trust and insufficient understanding. If you trust that an argument is entirely sound and that its conclusion is perfectly true but you don't sufficiently understand arguments, then you might soon change your mind and decide that it's conclusion is actually false. You might do this again and again, changing your mind about an argument— sometimes the conclusion is true,* sometimes it is false. In fact, [c] some people have devoted quite a lot of attention to contradicting arguments,* and they think that they have achieved the pinnacle of wisdom: in their minds, they alone comprehend that no argument whatsoever is sound or firm, and absolutely everything is constantly in flux, never remaining the same for any length of time but like the strait of Euripus* they turn this way and that way constantly."

"Yes, that is certainly true."

"So, then, imagine this scenario, Phaedo. [d] Imagine someone who has encountered arguments whose conclusions sometimes seem true but sometimes seem false, and instead of laying the blame on himself* for his own lack of skill with arguments, out of annoyance he blames the arguments themselves. Now, suppose further that in fact there is an argument that is reliable, it's conclusion is true, and it can be comprehended. How sad will it be that this person completely misses this opportunity for knowledge and truth because he has come to hate all argumentation, and he spends the rest of his life condemning reason?"

"By Zeus, that would be very sad."

"Then our primary duty, Phaedo, is to be very careful that [e] we do not allow into our souls even the suspicion that no argument is sound. Much rather should we be ready to accept that the lack of soundness is in ourselves, and that we need to redouble our efforts to face the issue bravely and to reason soundly. This is important for you and the others for the sake of your futures, [91a] but it is also important for me as I face my death, since I am at risk in this situation of loving victory more than loving wisdom. You know how those boorish people carry on a dispute: they don't think about what the truth actually is, instead they only think about how to make those present accept whatever position they have put forward—that's the only thing they really care about. I suppose that I'm like that too because I am eager to convince you all that what I'm saying is true, but I'm unlike them because this is only my secondary concern: my primary concern is to convince myself that the view I've put forward is the truth. [b] Here is how I'm calculating the consequences, my friend—and by the way, notice how selfish I'm being. If my view happens to be true, then it's a good thing that I believe it. But if I'm wrong and there's nothing after death, then the only bad result is that for this brief time I'm living in a sort of fool's paradise, falsely believing that my soul will go somewhere wonderful after I die. On the positive side, this fool's paradise of mine will spare you the pain of listening to me weep and moan about dying.

"So there you have it, Simmias and Cebes," Socrates continued. "That is how I am prepared to meet the argument ahead, and if you take my advice, [c] you'll focus much more on the truth and ignore the fact that it is Socrates who is making the argument. If you sincerely believe that what I say is true, then agree with me; but if not, then oppose me with every reasonable argument you have so that in my enthusiasm I don't deceive you, like a bee leaving its sting in you before it dies.

"So, let us proceed to consider the objections that Simmias and Cebes have raised. First of all, remind me of what you said just in case I've forgotten something. Simmias, didn't you say that you are skeptical and afraid that the soul is destroyed before the body because it is a sort of tuning of the body, [d] despite the fact that the soul is more divine and more noble than the body? Cebes, didn't you agree with me on this point, that the soul lives longer than the body, but from this you said it does not follow that the soul cannot be destroyed: after wearing out many bodies it is possible that the soul will be destroyed when it leaves its final body. In fact, haven't you given a new definition of death, Cebes? Earlier we defined death as the separation of the soul from the body, but now you seem to be saying that death is the destruction of the soul—since the body is constantly being destroyed and re-built by the soul. Are these the issues to be considered, Simmias and Cebes?"

[e] They both agreed that they were.

"And do you reject all of the earlier arguments or only some of them?"

"Some we accept, but others we reject," they replied.

"Well, what about the argument that what we call learning is actually recollecting, [92a] and that therefore the soul had to exist before it was shackled to the body?"

"I was very impressed by that argument," said Cebes. "It convinced me when you gave it, and I still hold to it more than to any other view on the matter."

"Same here," said Simmias. "I was just as impressed as Cebes, and I'd be very surprised if I ever change my mind on that point."

"But, my Theban friend," Socrates pointed out, "you'll have to change your mind if you still want to maintain that an attunement is a composite thing and the soul is an attunement that results from the various tissues of the body being held in a sort of tension with one another. Surely you cannot say that [b] the tuning exists prior to the things that are tuned."

"Oh, not at all, Socrates," Simmias said.

"But don't you see, you are saying exactly that when you say that the soul exists before it takes on human form and enters a human body—in effect, you are saying that the soul is composed of things that don't exist yet. This doesn't fit with the analogy you gave: the lyre, strings and even [c] the notes all exist before the attunement exists. The tuning is the last to arrive, and the first to be destroyed. How can you harmonize your two positions?"

"I don't think I can," Simmias said.

"But if you say that the soul is a kind of tuning, then what you say about the soul should be consistent with what you say about the lyre, shouldn't it?"

"Yes it should."

"Then it seems you must sing a different tune. Since you cannot accept both claims, which one do you choose: leaning is recollection or the soul is a tuning?

"Learning is recollection. [d] I accepted the view that the soul is a tuning without proof, simply because it seems likely and somehow fitting, which is why so many people believe it. But I realize that arguments which rest on premises that are likely can be misleading, and that if we don't guard against them we can be totally deceived—in geometry* and everything else. The proof that learning is recollection, however, rested on a hypothesis that deserves to be accepted. It was agreed that before it enters the body, the soul exists just as those beings that we honor with the title of being 'itself by itself.'* [e] I am convinced that I have accepted this correctly and with sufficient grounds. So necessarily I must reject the view that the soul is a tuning, even if I myself was the one to put it forward.

"Consider it this way, Simmias," Socrates continued. "Do you think that a tuning, [93a] or any other composite thing, can be in any condition other than that of its components?"

"There's no way that it could be."

"Nor can it act or be acted upon in any way other than its components act or are acted upon?"

"No."

"So then, the tuning doesn't lead, it follows the strings that are tuned."

"Yes."

"So it is entirely impossible for a tuning to be moved, or to make a sound, or to do anything contrary to its component parts?"

"Yes, that makes sense."

"Alright, I'll return to this point later.* But for now, let's consider another point. Each tuning is a tuning insofar as it is tuned."*

"I don't understand what you mean," Simmias said.

"For example, if a musician tunes one lyre more fully* or more completely than he tunes another lyre— [b] supposing that is possible—then the attunement of the first lyre will be fuller or more complete* than the second."

"Certainly."

"But is the soul a matter of comparative degree like this? Can one soul be more fully or more completely a soul than another? Can one soul be less fully or less completely a soul than another?"

"No, not at all."

"By Zeus, let's not give up. Don't we sometimes say that one soul is intelligent, virtuous and good, and that another soul is stupid, vicious, [c] and bad? And isn't it sometimes true to say this?"

"Yes, sometimes it is true."

"Well, what will those who posit that the soul is an attunement say about such things as virtue and vice in the souls? Is each of these an additional attunement, or lack of attunement, within the soul? Does a good soul have two attunements: one is the soul itself, and the second attunement is the goodness of the soul? So a bad soul will have only one attunement:* itself? Its badness consists in the fact that it lacks the additional good attunement that the first soul possesses?

"I really couldn't say, Socrates. But obviously those who maintain this view must say something like that."

[d] "But we just agreed that no soul can be more or less of a soul than another. And this is the agreement* that one attunement is no more or less an attunement than another, and that one attunement is not an attunement to a greater or lesser degree than another. Isn't that right?"

"Certainly."

"And what is not more or less an attunement was not more or less tuned? Isn't that so?"

"It is."

"And if one thing was no more or less tuned* than another, then can it be attuned to a greater or lesser degree than the other? Or are they both attuned to an equal degree?"

"To an equal degree."

"And since one soul cannot be more or less of a soul than another soul, [e] neither one can be more or less tuned than the other?"

"That is so."

"Since this is so, one cannot possess or lack attunement to a greater degree than the other?"

"There's no way that it could."

"Since this too is so, if virtue is an attunement and vice is a lack of attunement, then is it possible for one soul to be virtuous or vicious to a greater degree than another soul?"

"No, it couldn't."

[94a] "On the contrary, Simmias, if we reason correctly, don't we have to conclude that no soul is bad if it is an attunement, because an attunement, since it is entirely this itself, namely an attunement, is never a lack of attunement to any degree?"

"Yes."

"So no soul, since it is entirely a soul, is bad?"

"How could it be, given what we've already agreed."

"And from this it follows that all souls of all living beings are similarly good, if every soul is similarly by nature this itself, namely a soul."

"It seems so to me, Socrates."

"And do you think that conclusion is right? [b] Would we have reached this conclusion if our hypothesis that the soul is an attunement were correct?"

"There's no way we would."

"Alright, then, let's consider another point. Of all that is in a human being, would you say that anything other than the soul rules, especially if the soul is intelligent?"

"No, I wouldn't."

"And does the soul submit to the passions of the body or does it resist them?* For example, aren't there cases where someone feels hot and thirsty but his soul resists the urge to drink? And don't we sometimes resist the urge to eat despite being hungry?* Don't we see countless examples [c] of the soul resisting the passions of the body?"

"Yes, we certainly do."

"But didn't we agree just now* that if the soul is an attunement, then the soul follows the strings* that are tuned, it doesn't lead them or act contrary to them? The tuning doesn't oppose the tightness or loosness of the strings, the ways that the strings are plucked, or any of the conditions of the component parts of the instrument that has an attunement. Is that correct?"

"Yes, we did agree to that. How could it be otherwise?"

"But doesn't the soul act in exactly the opposite way? Doesn't it actually lead all those things of which it is composed? [d] Doesn't the soul resist all these passions to some degree our whole life through, and master all of them to some degree? Don't we sometimes punish our bodies with harsh and painful treatments like exercise and medicine? And don't we also employ milder means, encouraging ourselves for good behavior and discouraging ourselves from bad behavior? Have you ever noticed that in a way we speak to our desires, fears and passions as if they were other people? Odysseus from Homer's *Odyssey* is a good example of this. Remember that the night before Athena helped him avenge the wrong done to his household Homer says,

> He struck his chest and rebuked his heart with these words,

> [e] 'Endure, my heart; worse you've endured.'*

"Do you think that Homer would have written those lines if he thought that the soul was merely led around by the passions of the body instead of leading them and actually mastering them? Didn't he think that the soul was a far more divine thing than an attunement of the body's components?"

"By Zeus, Socrates, I do believe that you are right about that."

"Therefore, my good friend, we completely reject the theory that the soul is an attunement, [95a] since that view is incompatible with the divine poet Homer, and also with our own agreements."

"That is true."

"Very well, then," Socrates continued, "it seems that the Theban goddess Harmony* has been sufficiently favorable to us. So, Cebes, let's see if we can come up with an argument that will earn the favor of Cadmus."

"At this point," Cebes said, "I expect that you will discover just such an argument. Your argument against the theory that the soul is an attunement was astonishing. When Simmias originally raised his objection, [b] I didn't think that anyone could refute it. But then I was amazed to see that it couldn't even withstand your first argument. So as I said, at this point I won't be surprised if the argument of Cadmus suffers the same fate."

"Oh, my good friend, please, now is not the time for boasting—overconfidence can blind us to some of the details and, as you know, the devil is in the details. But, be that as god wills; let us advance like Homeric heroes into the fray and test our mettle against your argument.

"What you ask for," Socrates continued, "is, in short, a proof that the soul is [c] immortal and indestructible. We need to prove this in order to show that the philosopher who is confident in the face of death, and who believes that he will fare better on the other side if he lives a philosophical life than if he lives some other kind of life, isn't being foolish or stupid. Now, it's not enough to prove that the soul is strong and godlike and that it existed before we were born as human beings. As you pointed out, this does not prove the immortality of the soul, it proves only that the soul has a long history that we cannot easily measure, and that before it was born into this world as a human being it existed, it knew some things, and it did many things. In fact, [d] being born into a human body may be the start of its dissolution—acquiring a body may be like acquiring a deadly disease: we live a life of hardship and in the end we are utterly destroyed in what is called 'death.' Furthermore, you argue that it makes no difference if the soul is born into a human body once or many times—you'd have to be a fool not to fear death if you do not know, and cannot prove, [e] that the soul is immortal. I think that is your position, Cebes. I've restated it to make sure that we've left nothing out, and to give you the opportunity to make any additions or corrections."

Cebes replied, "No, Socrates, there is nothing I wish to add or to change. You've summed up my position accurately."

Socrates was quiet for a while after this, and he sat there thinking to himself. Finally he said to Cebes, "It is no small thing you seek. To discover the proof you are after, we need to consider coming to be and passing away in general—in short, we need to discuss generation and corruption. [96a] If you like, I'll tell you about my own personal journey in considering this vast topic, and if anything I say seems useful to you, we'll see if it helps us with your concern."

"Oh, yes, Socrates, I would very much like to hear what you have to say."

"Listen, then, and I'll tell you. When I was young* I was extremely interested in the form of wisdom that is called 'natural science.'* I thought it would be most impressive to know what is responsible* for each thing: why each thing comes to be,* why each thing passes away, and why each thing exists.* [b] I kept casting about indecisively, starting with questions like these:

Are those people* correct who say that a living body coalesces when hot and cold cause earth to congeal into a milky slime that provides nourishment?

Is it blood by which we think,* or is it air or fire? Or is it something else entirely; is it actually the brain* that enables us to perceive things with our senses—hearing, seeing, smelling and so on—and is it these sensations that enable us to remember and to form beliefs, and then finally is it these memories and beliefs that enable us to gain knowledge?

If that is how these kinds of things are generated and come to be, then how do they corrupt and pass away?

What about the earth and everything in the heavens?"*

[c] I pursued these investigations but in the end decided that I was pretty worthless at it. In fact, I can actually prove to you that I'm no good at that sort of inquiry. I had reached the point in my studies where I thought—and others did too—that I knew the answers to some of these kinds of questions. But then something very odd happened: it was almost as if I had gone suddenly blind so that I unlearned everything I had recently thought I knew. For example, why does a human being grow? I thought it was obvious to everyone that we grow by eating and drinking, [d] so that from the food we eat flesh is added to flesh, bone is added to bone and so on, each part receiving what is appropriate to it, and in that way a small person becomes larger. That is what I thought back then; doesn't it seem reasonable enough?"

"It does to me," Cebes replied.

"But consider this. Are there cases where you would say that one man is taller than another by a head, [e] or that one horse is taller than another horse by a head? Back then I thought that was a perfectly reasonable thing to say. Or better yet, these examples are even clearer. I used to think that ten was more than eight because of the two added to the eight, and that a two foot rod was longer than a one foot rod because of the additional one foot on the first one?"

"And what do you think of those now?"

"By god, Cebes, now I have to say that I do not know* how one man can be taller because of a head, or how ten can be greater because of two. This way of talking just gets me confused now: if we add one to one, is it the original one that suddenly becomes two, [97a] or is it the two ones combined that both turn into two when you combine them? Suppose you have one olive and I have one olive: we have one and one. But now if we move them closer together, at some point we say, 'Aha! Two olives!' I am so confused by this: how does simply moving the olives closer together explain the fact that there are two? Or what if we took one olive and cut it in half: how many halves would there be? Two! So bringing together causes there to be two, [b] and the completely opposite act of separating apart also causes there to be two. In fact, not only am I confused about the cause of two, I can't even figure out one. Why does one come to be? Why does one pass away? Why does one exist? I can no longer persuade myself that the way I used to answer these questions is correct. So I've whipped up my own approach that I'll tell you about in a moment.

"To continue my story, one day I heard someone reading from a book, [c] and he said it was the book of Anaxagoras. The passage he read was this: 'mind is the cause and regulator of all things.' I was absolutely delighted with this cause: it just seemed so appropriate for mind to be the cause and leader of all things. Here's what I thought.

'If this is so, then in organizing everything, mind organizes each thing in the way that it would be best for it* to be. So if someone wanted to discover the cause of something—why it comes to be, why it passes away, and why it is—he should try to discover in what way it would be best for that thing to be, [d] to act or to be acted upon. From this theory it follows that whether you are inquiring into yourself or into anything else, you need consider nothing other than what is best, and what is the highest good—by doing so you will necessarily study the entire spectrum, for the knowledge of what is good is one and the same as the knowledge of what is bad.'

"While I was thinking this through, I felt so glad that in Anaxagoras I had found a like-minded person who could teach me about the causes of things. I thought he would tell me first whether the earth is flat or round.* [e] Second, he would explain the cause of the earth's shape, why it necessarily had to be that shape, and in his explanation he would refer to what is better, indicating why it is better for the earth to be the shape it is than to be some other shape. Third, if he said that the earth is in the center of the cosmos* I assumed that he would explain why it is better for it to be there than to be anywhere else. If he could make all this clear to me, [98a] I made up my mind that I would never seek any other kind of cause. I was prepared to learn about the sun, the moon, the stars, their various speeds in relation to one another, their revolutions and all the changes they go through, how they act and how they are acted upon, and how all of this is for the best. Because he said that all things are arranged by mind, it never occurred to me that he would appeal to any other cause than to say that it was best for things to be exactly as they are. [b] I thought that when he gave the cause of each particular thing, and for things as a whole, he would also explain how it is best for each thing to be as it is, and how it is best for things as a whole to be arranged as they are. With high hopes I got hold of his books as soon as I could and read them immediately because I was so eager to know what is best and what is worst.

"Well, my friends," Socrates continued, "my hopes were all dashed to pieces when I read his books. He never actually appealed to mind as a cause that [c] sets things in order. Instead, the only causes he appealed to were air, aether, water and many other absurd things. Anaxagoras seemed to me to be like a man who argues as follows:

'Everything that Socrates does, he does because of his mind. So first, the cause of his sitting is that his body is composed of bones and sinews. On the one hand, bones are hard and are separated from one another by joints. On the other hand, sinews [d] can be tightened or relaxed, and together with the flesh and skin they surround the bones and hold them together. Next, because the bones are able to swing freely in their joints, when the sinews tighten and relax in various ways, Socrates is able to bend his various limbs. That is the cause of Socrates' sitting here bent in these ways.'

"We could give similar causes for my talking with you now, citing as causes sounds and air and hearing and countless [e] other things—completely ignoring the true cause: it seemed to the Athenians that the better course of action was to convict me, and because of this it seemed to me that the better course of action was to sit right here, because it is more just for me to obey the court. By the dog,* [99a] these bones and sinews would be in Megara or Boeotia right now if I didn't think that it was more just and more right to obey the just commands of my city than to run away and desert my post like a coward. It is absurd to say that my bones and my sinews are the causes of my remaining.

"Of course someone might well say that without my bones and sinews I couldn't do what I think is the right thing. Quite true. But to cite these as the causes of my doing what I do, saying that I act with my mind [b] but do not deliberately choose what seems to me the better course of action, is to give a hopelessly facile explanation—that is a simple failure to distinguish the cause of an action from the necessary conditions for the cause to be effective. People who cite these necessary conditions as causes look to me like people clumsily working in the dark: they apply the name 'cause' to things it doesn't belong to. So one of them says that the earth stays beneath the heavens because the earth is caught in some kind of whirlpool.* Another says that the earth is flat like a baker's kneading board, and that it floats on a column of air.* [c] They never look for a power that keeps things in their place because it is best for them to be in that place, and it never occurs to them that such a power would be divine. Apparently they think that they will find an Atlas that is more powerful, more immortal and more comprehensive than this. Truly, they give no thought to the good, which embraces all and binds all.

"I would gladly be the student of anyone who could teach me about such a cause," Socrates continued, "but since I'd been deprived* of my teacher, and since I couldn't discover it myself or learn it from anyone else, I've embarked upon a second sailing.* [d] Would you like me to show you this alternative, Cebes?"

"Oh, yes, Socrates, I'd like that very much" replied Cebes enthusiastically.

"At this point, I ended my investigation into why each thing comes to be, why each thing passes away, and why each thing exists. After that, it seemed that I ought to be careful not to suffer the affliction that often occurs to people who investigate the sun during an eclipse—sometimes they ruin their eyesight if they look at it directly instead of looking only at reflections of the sun in water [e] or on some other surface. I thought about this, and I was afraid that my soul would be blinded if I looked at things with my eyes and tried to grasp them with my senses. So I took refuge in argumentation;* it seemed to me that the best thing to do is to investigate the truth of things in arguments. Perhaps my analogy isn't exact:* [100a] studying the truth of things by examining arguments isn't exactly like studying the sun by looking at reflections of the sun on vaious surfaces, but anyway, that is how I set out in my second sailing. In each case, I lay down as an hypothesis* the account* that I judge to be the most sound.* Next, whatever is in agreement* with that hypothesis I lay down as being true, and whatever disagrees with it I lay down as being false—whether I am considering causes or anything else. That is a very brief account of how I proceed, but I'd like to make it clearer to you because I suspect that you don't fully understand what I mean."

"No, by Zeus," Cebes said, "not exactly."

[b] "Actually, I'm not saying anything new. I've mentioned it before in our conversation today, and I've mentioned it in other conversations—in fact, it seems I never stop talking about it. I hypothesize that there is a form of the beautiful itself by itself, and a form of the good and the large and all the others.* That is my starting point, and from it I will try to show you the kind of cause that I have focused my attention on. If you agree with me that these forms exist, then I hope to discover, and to demonstrate to you, why the soul is immortal."

[c] "Yes, I do agree with you," Cebes said, "so please proceed."

"Then consider whether you see things as I do on this next point. I think that if anything other than the beautiful itself is beautiful, then it is beautiful for no other reason than that it participates* in the form of the beautiful. That is how I see it in all cases. Do you agree with such a cause?"

"I agree."

"That is why I do not understand, and cannot learn, those other causes cited by those wise men. If someone tells me [d] that something is beautiful because of its bright color or its shape or anything else like that, I just let it go—all those things confuse me. This is what I maintain openly, simply and perhaps foolishly:* nothing other than beauty itself makes something beautiful, whether by being present with the beautiful thing, or associating with it in some way—or however it comes to be with the beautiful thing. I don't insist on any particular way of saying how beauty itself comes to be with the beautiful thing, but I do say that it is by beauty that all beautiful things are beautiful. This seems to me to be the safest answer I can give to myself or to anyone else; this answer will never let me down if I hold onto it, [e] the safe answer for myself or for anyone else is simply to say that it is by beauty that all beautiful things are beautiful. Doesn't it seem that way to you?"

"It does."

"And it is by the large itself that large things are large, and larger things are larger; and by the small itself that smaller things are small?"

"Yes."

"Then you would not agree if someone said that one man was larger than another 'by a head,'* and that the smaller man was smaller 'by a head.' [101a] Wouldn't you rather insist on saying that anytime one thing is larger than another, it is larger by nothing other than largeness itself, and it is on account of the large itself that it is larger? And wouldn't you similarly insist that when one thing is smaller than another, it is smaller by nothing other than the small itself, and it is on account of the small itself that it is smaller? And wouldn't you insist on all of this out of fear that you'd immediately run into contradictions if you said anything else? For example, if you say that one man is larger than another 'by a head' and the other man is smaller than the first 'by a head' you'd be saying that the very same thing that makes one man larger makes another man smaller. On top of that, since a head is actually a rather small thing, [b] you'd be saying that it is by something small* that something is large—which is ridiculous. Aren't those the kinds of contradictions you'd fear?"

Lauging, Cebes said, "Yes I would."

"And so you'd also be afraid to say that two is responsible for the fact that ten is greater than eight instead of saying that the greater itself is responsible for that fact? And the same goes for saying that a two foot length is longer than a one foot length by half its own length, instead of saying that the long itself is responsible for that fact?"

"Certainly."

"What if one is added to one, or one is divided into two? [c] You would beware of saying that it was the addition or the division that was responsible for there being two, wouldn't you? Surely you would declare openly that you know of no other way for each thing to come into being than for it to participate in its appropriate form of being. So in this case, nothing other than the number two is responsible for the generation of two things or two parts of one thing, and if anything is going to become two it will have to participate in the number two—just as something will have to participate in the number one if it is to be one. You will let go of all these other things like divisions and additions and other such refinements, leaving them for people wiser than you. [d] Aware of your inexperience with such complications, you'd be 'afraid of your own shadow' as the saying goes—you would stick with your safe hypothesis and answer accordingly.

"However," Socates continued, "if someone focuses* on your hypothesis itself, you will let them go without an answer until you've considered what follows from your hypothesis, and whether those consequences cohere with one another or not. When you needed to give an account of your hypothesis, you would give it in exactly the same way: you would lay down whatever higher hypothesis seems best [e] until you arrived at something adequate.* You wouldn't throw everything into confusion like those people who love to argue just for the sake of arguing by asking about the hypothesis and its consequences simultaneously*—not if you want to discover something about reality. Of course, people who love arguing don't care about the truth; they are pleased with themselves as long as they can throw everything into confusion. However, I think that if you are a philosopher, [102a] you will follow the procedure I've laid out."

"Nothing could be more true," Simmias and Cebes said at the same time.

ECHECHRATES. By Zeus, Phaedo, how reasonable! That would be clear even to people who aren't very smart.

PHAEDO. Yes, exactly, and that's how it seemed to everyone present.

ECHECHRATES. And to everyone not present, who are hearing it now for the first time. What was said after that?

PHAEDO. I think it went like this.

After all this was granted, [b] and it was agreed that the forms exist and that everything called by the name* of a form participates in that form, Socrates asked this question.

"If you agree to all this, then what do you say about the following sort of case? Suppose that Simmias is larger than Socrates, but smaller than Phaedo. In that case, would you say that both largeness and smallness* are in Simmias?"

"Yes, I would," Cebes agreed.

"However, you would not agree that in this case the sentence 'Simmias exceeds Socrates' is the most perspicuous way to express the truth, would you? [c] Simmias does not exceed Socrates by his nature—that is, simply by being Simmias—but by the magnitude that he happens to have.* And he does not exceed Socrates simply because Socrates is Socrates, but because of the smallness Socrates has as opposed to the largeness that Simmias has."

"True."

"And, of course, Simmias is not exceeded by Phaedo simply because Phaedo is Phaedo, but because of the largeness that Phaedo has in relation to* the smallness that Simmias has?"

"That is so."

"So that is how Simmias is said to be both small and large—he is in the middle because he is both. His largeness exceeds Socrates' smallness, [d] but his smallness is exceeded by Phaedo's largeness." That made Socrates laugh, and he added, "I seem to be speaking like a book, but things are as I say, aren't they?"

"Yes, they are," Cebes agreed.

"I'm putting it this way because I want you to see things as I do. It seems to me that in the first place, largeness itself will never be simultaneously large and small.* But in the second place, the largeness in us* will never admit smallness in its presence, and it won't agree* to being exceeded. So when smallness—the opposite of the largeness in us—approaches, one of two things must be true: either the largeness in us flees and departs,* [e] or else by the time smallness arrives the largeness in us has been destroyed.* It will not be willing to stay or to allow smallness in its presence so that it becomes something other than what it was. For example, I am willing to stay and to allow smallness in my presence and still be what I am because I am not a large man. But the large itself will never dare to be small. Similarly, the smallness in us will never be willing to become or to be large. The same is true with all opposites: as long as it is what it is, one opposite will never become or be its own opposite: [103a] when its opposite approaches, it either departs or is destroyed."

"That seems entirely correct to me," Cebes said.

At that point someone else* spoke up—I don't exactly recall who it was—and said, "By the gods, aren't we now saying exactly the opposite of what we agreed earlier?* Didn't we agree that the larger comes to be from the smaller, and the smaller from the larger? In short, an opposite comes to be only from its opposite. But now it seems to me that we are saying this never happens."

Socrates turned his head toward the speaker and listened carefully. [b] "Your memory is strong, but you failed to notice that there is one difference between what we said then and what we are saying now. Then we said that one contrary thing* came to be from another contrary thing, for example,* a larger thing comes to be from a smaller thing. But now we are saying that an opposite itself can never become its own opposite, for example, the form of the large itself never becomes the form of the small itself—whether we are talking about the large in us or the large in nature. Earlier, my friend, we were talking about things that have the opposites, and we were calling them by the names of the opposites they possessed. But now we are talking about the opposites themselves—those opposites which, when they are in things, give their names to the things they are in, [c] as, for example, when we call a large tree large. What we are saying now is that these opposites themselves—not the things the opposites are in—would never be willing to come to be from one another."

Turning to Cebes, Socrates asked, "Did our friend's comment raise any concerns for you?"

"Oh, no," Cebes replied, "I have no concerns about that issue. However, I cannot deny that I have many concerns."

"Then we are all agreed on this point at least," Socrates continued, "an opposite itself never comes to be its own opposite."

"Entirely so," Cebes agreed.

"Then consider whether you agree with me on this next point. Do you agree that hot is something, and cold is also something?"

"I do."

"And is hot the same thing as fire, and is cold the same thing as snow?"

[d] "By Zeus, no I certainly do not agree with that."

"Because the hot* is not the same thing as fire; and the cold is something other than snow?"

"Yes."

"I think you will also agree to my next point. Snow will never accept the hot—not as long as it remains snow. There's no such thing as hot snow. That phrase we used a little while ago* applies to this case: when the hot approaches, the snow either departs or is destroyed."

"Certainly, I agree with that."

"And it's the same with fire, isn't it? When cold approaches, fire will either depart or be destroyed, won't it? It wouldn't dare receive the cold and remain what it is: there's no such thing as cold fire."

[e] "That is true."

"Therefore, it is not only the form itself that is always worthy of its own name. There are cases like fire being hot and snow being cold where something always has the form's character* whenever it exists. Maybe my point will be clearer with another example. The form of the odd itself must always be worthy of its own name, don't you agree?"

"Certainly."

"But is the form of the odd itself the only thing like this? That is my question. Or is there something else [104a] that is not identical to the form of the odd itself, but nevertheless is always rightly called odd in addition to its own name, because by nature it can never exist without being odd? The number three* is one of many examples I could give of this. Think about it: wouldn't you agree that in addition to always being worthy of the name 'three,' the number three is also always worthy of the name 'odd'? And isn't this true despite the fact that the number three is not identical to the form of the odd itself? By their very natures three, five and half of all numbers, [b] although they are not identical to the form of the odd itself, nevertheless are always odd. Similarly, two, four and the other half of all numbers are always even despite the fact that they are not identical to the form of even itself. Isn't that so?"

"Of course."

"Then please observe what I'm trying to make clear; it is this. It is not only the opposites that refuse to accept one another. In addition, there are things that, although they are not opposites of one another, nevertheless they are always opposed.* It seems that these additional things do not accept a character* that is opposed to what they are in themselves. Instead, when the opposed form approaches, [c] either it is destroyed, or it departs. Shall we not say that three would rather die or suffer any other fate than to become even while remaining three?"

"Certainly," agreed Cebes.

"So three and even* are always opposed to one another, although they are not opposites of one another? I mean, even is the opposite of odd, not three, isn't it? And three isn't the opposite of anything: it isn't the opposite of two, for example, is it?"

"Certainly not."

"So it isn't only opposite forms that will not remain when its opposite approaches, there are other things that are opposed and will not remain when whatever it is opposed to approaches."

"Entirely true."

"Then would you like us to define what sorts these are, if we are able?"

"Yes, absolutely."

[d] "Won't it be the sort of thing that, when it takes hold of something,* not only does it compel whatever it takes hold of to take on its own distinctive character, but it also always compels that thing to take on the character of one of a pair of opposites?"

"How do you mean?"

"It's like the example we were just discussing. You know that when the character of three takes hold of something, it compels that thing to take on the character of three and also the character of odd."

"Certainly."

"What we maintain in a case like this, is that as long as* one character has compelled something to take on one of a pair of opposite characters, that opposite character can never come to that thing."

"No, it cannot."

"And when the character of three compels something to take on the character of three, it also necessarily compels it to take on the character of odd?"

"Yes."

"And the opposite of odd is even?"

"Yes."

[e] "And the character of even never comes to three."

"Certainly not."

"Three has no part in even."

"No part whatsoever."

"So three is not-even."

"Yes."

"Earlier* I said that I would define the sorts of things that, although they are not opposites, nevertheless they will not accept something that is an opposite. The example we've been considering is three: although three is not the opposite of even, nevertheless it will not accept the even and it brings to bear the opposite of even against it. We could say the same thing about two and odd, [105a] fire and cold and many other examples. See if you define this sort of thing in the following way. Refusing to accept one of a pair of opposites is not restricted exclusively to the other member of the pair: there is also the case of that which brings one of a pair of opposites with it when it approaches something—because that which comes bearing one opposite will never accept the other opposite. Recall the example I've been using; there's no harm in hearing many examples. Five will not accept even, and ten will not accept odd—although ten is twice five. Despite the fact that ten is not not an opposite of anything, nevertheless [b] it will not accept odd. Or consider the case of fractions: one-and-a-half and other such numbers, or one-half and one-third and fractions like that are all opposed to the character of the whole despite the fact that none of them are the opposites of anything. Do you follow these examples, and do you agree with me about them?"

"Yes, indeed, I follow you, and I certainly do agree with your account."

"Then let's go back to the beginning. Now you don't have to answer my question using the same word that I use. Here, follow my lead. Earlier* I pointed out that I am inclined to give very safe answers to certain kinds of questions; for example, if someone asks what makes a beautiful thing beautiful, I think it's safe to say that beauty is what makes a beautiful thing beautiful—and notice that I use the same word in my answer that was used in the question. Well, now that we've just gone through this point about opposites, I have a new safe answer. If someone asks me by what coming into a body that body will be hot, [c] I no longer have to stick with my earlier simple, and possibly foolish, answer that it will be hot by heat coming to be in it; now I can give the more sophisticated answer that fire will make it hot. Similarly, if someone asks me by what coming into a body that body will be ill, I won't say that it is illness, but fever.* And if someone asks me by what coming to be in a number that number will be odd, I won't say that it is oddness, but one.* Do you think that you grasp my view sufficiently?"

"Yes, quite sufficiently," Cebes answered.

"Then answer this question: by what coming into a body that body will be alive?"*

"Soul."*

[d] "And this is always so?"

"How could it be any other way?"

"Therefore, when soul takes hold of something, it brings life to that thing?"

"It does."

"And is there an opposite of life?"

"There is."

"What?"

"Death."

"Therefore, soul will never accept the opposite of what it always brings to something? Doesn't this follow from what we've already agreed?"

"Yes, it certainly does."

"Then, do you recall this other point we made? What name do we give to something that will not accept the character of even?"

"Odd," Cebes replied.

"And what names do we give to things that will not accept the characters of just or musical?"

[e] "Unjust and unmusical."

"Well, then, what do we call something that will not accept the character of mortal?"

"Immortal."

"Therefore, soul will not accept the character of mortal?"

"No."

"Therefore, soul is immortal?"

"Yes, soul is immortal."

"Well, then, shall we say that this has been proven? Or how does it seem to you?"

"Yes, indeed, it has been sufficiently proven, Socrates."

"Then what about this next point, Cebes? If odd was necessarily indestructible, [106a] then would three necessarily be indestructible?"

"How could it not be?"

"So if the un-hot were necessarily indestructible, then whenever someone brought heat to snow, the snow would depart without melting, because the other two alternatives are impossible: it couldn't stay and become hot, and since it is un-hot it could not be destroyed."

"That is true."

"We could say the same thing about the un-cold, couldn't we? If the un-cold were indestructible, then when someone brought cold to a fire, the fire would depart without becoming cold, because the other two alternatives are impossible: there is no such thing as cold fire, and if un-cold is necessarily indestructible, then fire would be indestructible."

"Yes, that follows necessarily."

[b] "Therefore, don't we have to say the same thing about the immortal? If the immortal is also indestructible, then it is impossible for soul to be destroyed when death approaches it. Doesn't it follow from what we've said that soul will never accept death and will never be dead, just as three will never be even, odd will never be even, fire will never be cold, and the heat that is in fire will never be cold? Of course, someone might raise the following objection.

'We have already agreed that odd cannot become even when even approaches it. [c] But what is there to prevent the odd from simply being destroyed, and even taking its place?'

"In reply to this objection we cannot actually claim that odd is not destroyed, since in fact odd is not indestructible. However, if we did agree that odd is indestructible, then we could contend that when even approaches, odd and three depart. In fact, we could make the same contentions about hot and fire if we agreed that hot is indestructible. Isn't that so?"

"Certainly," Cebes agreed.

"Therefore, the same holds true now in the case of the immortal. If we agree that the immortal is also indestructible, then soul will be both immortal [d] and indestructible. But if we do not agree that the immortal is indestructible, then we'll have to find some other argument."

"Oh, there's no need to look for another argument, Socrates. Nothing could escape destruction if the immortal, which is eternal,* accepted destruction."

"Then I think everyone will agree that god, the form of life itself, and anything else that is immortal is never destroyed."

"By god, Socrates, everyone will agree to that—including the gods."

[e] "So if the immortal is indestructible, then soul would be indestructible if it is immortal?"

"That is entirely necessary."

"Therefore, when death approaches, the mortal part of a human being dies; but the immortal part withdraws, because it is indestructible. The immortal part withdraws from death."*

"So it seems."

"Soul is immortal, then, and [107a] indestructible. Our souls shall indeed be in Hades."*

"I certainly have nothing to say against this conclusion, and I have no doubts about your arguments. But if Simmias or someone else has something to say, he should speak up. If anyone wants to hear or to say anything about the matter, I don't know if there is any better time than the present."

"I don't have any doubts about the argument," Simmias said, "but given the magnitude of the issues we are discussing, [b] and given the fact that I have such a poor opinion of our ability to discern the truth about them, I must admit that I'm still doubtful about what we've said."

"Well said, Simmias. And even if our first hypotheses are credible to you two, nevertheless you should still examine them more carefully. If you analyze them sufficiently, I think that you will follow the reasoning more carefully than anyone, and if the truth becomes clear to you, there will be nothing left for you to seek."

"That is certainly true, Socrates," Simmias replied.

[c] "But the point it is right for us to keep in mind, my friends," Socrates went on, "is that if the soul is immortal, then we ought to take care of it, not only in the present, which we call 'life,' but for all time. In fact, after the argument we've just been through, the danger of neglecting our souls would seem to be quite terrible. You see, if death is complete obliteration, then it is a godsend to bad people,* because when their body is destroyed, their bad souls are destroyed with them. But since we've seen that the soul is immortal, [d] there is no escape from our own badness, and there is no salvation for the soul, except for us to become as good and as intelligent as possible. The soul goes to Hades having nothing except its education and training, which, we are told, are either the greatest benefits or the worst detriments to a soul from the moment it arrives there.

"The story goes like this," Socrates continued. "When each man passes away, the guardian spirit* allotted to him while he was living takes him by the hand* and leads him to a certain place. Once there, those who have been gathered must submit themselves to judgment.* Then they must proceed to Hades [e] following the guide appointed to lead them from this world to the next. There they receive their due* and remain for their due amount of time until another guide brings them back here in many long cycles* of time.

"But this journey," Socrates said, "is not like the one described by Telephus* in Aeschylus' play of that name, [108a] because he says that one simple road leads to Hades. It seems to me that the road isn't simple, and that there isn't just one. If there were just one simple road you wouldn't need a guide because nobody would get lost on the way. I think that the road to Hades has lots of double and triple forks* in it. The offerings we see left at crossroads are clear signs of that.

"On the one hand, a soul that is well-behaved and intelligent follows its guide and is not disoriented* by its circumstances. But on the other hand, the soul that yearns to have a body—as I was saying before*—haunts its own corpse for a long time [b] and remains in the visible realm. But finally, after putting up a tremendous fight and suffering terribly, its duly appointed guardian spirit leads it away by force. Now, when a soul reaches the meeting place where the other souls are, if it is impure because of its impure acts—murder or some other injustice souls like that commit—all the other souls turn their backs on it and flee, no one wants to associate with such a soul, and no guide wants to lead it. [c] So it wanders alone, lost and disoriented, until a certain amount of time passes, and then finally it is carried by necessity to its proper place. But the pure souls of those who conducted themselves with decency have gods for companions and guides, and they easily find the places that are appropriate for them.

"And that's not all," Socrates went on. "Earth* has many amazing regions. Someone has persuaded me that the usual accounts do not do justice either to its nature or to its size."

[d] "Really?" Simmias asked. "I too have heard many accounts of the earth, but they are all more or less similar, and apparently nothing like what has persuaded you. I'd like to hear it."

"It certainly doesn't take the craft of Glaucus* to tell you what I've heard, Simmias," Socrates answered, "but to prove that it is true would be much more difficult and would take far more than the craft of Glaucus. I don't think that I'm up to that task, and even if I did know that it was true, I don't think the life that is left to me is long enough to go through it all. [e] But there's no reason I can't tell you what I believe about the character of the earth and its regions."

"I'll be content with that," Simmias answered.

"Well then," Socrates went on, "the first thing I've been persuaded of is that if the earth is round like a ball* and at the center of the heavens, [109a] then it doesn't need air, or anything else like that, to keep it from falling. The fact that the earth itself is in a state of equilibrium,* together with the fact that it is in the center of the heavens, so that the heavens are exactly the same in all directions, is enough to hold the earth in place. For a thing that is in equilibrium and is placed in the center of something homogeneous cannot incline in one direction more than any other and so it will remain in place. This was the first point on which I was persuaded."

"And it is quite correct," said Simmias.

"The second point is that the earth is immense. The region where we live, [b] between the Pillars of Herakles* and the Phasis river is only a very small part of the earth. All the people who live around the Mediterranean Sea are like ants or frogs living around a little pond, and there are many other people who live in many other regions. You see, the region in which we live is basically just a pit into which water, mist and air has collected, like sediment that sinks to the bottom. In all directions there are many such pits of every shape and size. The earth itself is where all this sediment has filtered down from, and so it is actually pure—as pure as the heavens in which it fixed, just like the stars. So the earth is situated in pure aither,* [c] which is what most people who talk about such things call it.

"Of course it escapes our notice that we are living in one of these pits. We think that we are living on the surface of the earth. It's like if someone lived on the sea floor: from his perspective, he would think that he lived on the surface of the Mediterranean. He would look at the sun and stars through the water, and what we think of as the sea, he would think of as the heavens. [d] And because he has neither the speed nor the power that it takes to swim up through the water, he would never make it to the surface, poke his head out and see just how much purer and more beautiful our realm is than his. He would never actually see our realm with his own eyes, or hear about our realm from anyone who had seen it.

"We are in that same sort of situation. We think that we live on the surface of the earth, but in fact we live at the bottom of a sea of air,* which we call the heavens, assuming that the stars actually move through the air. [e] And because we have neither the speed nor the power that it takes to fly up through the air, we can never make it to the surface. But if one of us ever did make it to the top, or somehow generated wings and could fly up there, he would be able to poke his head out and see what is up there—like fish who sometimes poke their heads above the surface of the water and look at us. If his nature could handle the sight, he would know the true heavens, and the true light, [110a] and the true earth.

"For this earth, these rocks, and this entire region is tarnished and corroded. Just think of how the salty sea water eats away at everything so that nothing worth speaking of can grow in it, and virtually nothing can achieve a fully perfect form. It's all just hollowed out caves, and sand and worthless mud and muck. Even where there is solid land there is nothing to compare with the beautiful features of our realm. Well, in the same way, the beauty of the realm above us would be vastly superior to the beauty we see here.

[b] "In fact, Simmias," Socrates continued, "if it is a fine thing to tell a story,* then it is worth hearing what things happen to be like on the true earth and in the true heavens."

"Oh, yes, Socrates, we would be very glad to hear your story," Simmias replied.

Socrates then told us this story. "First, it is said that if you saw the earth from above, it would look like one of those balls that are made from twelve pieces of leather, each piece a different color. But in comparison, the colors here are like the samples of colors that painters use. [c] From high above the earth you'd see that each color is brighter and purer than the colors we are used to. One part is an amazingly beautiful deep sea purple, another is pure gold, another is whiter than the purest chalk or the whitest snow.

The earth is composed of these and other colors that are more numerous and more beautiful than the colors we see. This is because each pit in the earth that is filled with water and air [d] glistens with its own color, and so the entire earth looks like a beautiful, shining rainbow of brilliant colors.

"It is in such a beautiful rainbow that living things grow—trees, flowers and fruits that are just as colorful as the earth itself. Also the mountains and the stones shimmer in every hue. Actually, the precious gems that we have—carnelian, jasper, emerald, and so on—are shards of those stones. [e] On the true earth, every stone is precious, but even more beautiful than the stones we have down here. What is responsible for this is the fact that the stones there have no impurities; they are not tarnished and corroded by the salty sea air and the decay that mars and corrupts everything down here, including the land, the stones, the plants and the animals. No, the true earth is adorned with pure gems, and also with gold and silver, [111a] and all the precious metals. They are right out in the open, large, abundant and everywhere you look. Blessed are those who gaze upon such a sight.

"In addition to animals, there are many people living there. Some live inland, but others live by the air just as some of us live by the sea. Others live off the coast on islands surrounded by air.* In a word, what sea and air are to us, [b] air and aither are to them. They have seasons, but theirs are far more temperate than ours are, so they never get sick and they live much longer than we do. Their senses are vastly superior to ours: in sight, hearing, intelligence and so on they surpass us to the same extent that air surpasses water in purity, and aither surpasses air. They also have sacred groves and temples for the gods, and the gods actually dwell in them. [c] So they have communion with the gods through oracles, prophecies and visions. They see the sun, moon and stars as they really are, and their blessedness is just as splendid.

"Such is the nature of the earth as a whole, and of what surrounds the earth. Inside the sphere of the earth there are many regions like the pit in which we live, but they are of all shapes and sizes. Some of these pits are much deeper and wider than ours, some are deeper but not as wide, [d] and others are shallower but wider. Under all of these pits there are many channels that interconnect with one another. Some of them are very broad but others are quite narrow. Water flows through some of them, and the torrents mix with one another creating an incredibly vast river that flows forever with both cold and hot water. Fire flows through others and when they mix they create an immense river of fire. There are also rivers of mud and lava [e] like in Sicily.* Each region is periodically filled by each of these rivers as a pulsation circulates the fluids through the entire earth. The nature of this circulation is as follows.

"One of the earth's chasms* is [112a] larger than all the others, and its opening* goes right through the whole earth. Homer refers to it when he says: 'Very far off,* the deepest gulf beneath the earth.' He's referring to what he and many poets call Tartarus. All the rivers I've just described flow into Tartarus and then out again, taking on different tastes and colors* depending upon which lands they flow through. [b] What is responsible for the continual flowing of these rivers is that there is no basin into which they all empty, so they pulsate and swell up and down. The air and wind does the exact same thing because they follow the liquids when they flow to the other side of the earth and when they flow back to this side. It's like when someone breaths continuously inhaling and exhaling, except that when the winds are sucked into Tartarus and then expelled by the flowing rivers they create terrible gales and tempests. [c] When the water flows to what is from our perspective the lower side of the earth, it fills the streams there as if it was being pumped into them. Then the water leaves that side and returns to our side, filling the streams here. On each side, once the streams have been filled, the water flows along its own courses and makes all the springs, ponds and seas. From there the water seeps back down [d] under the earth. Some of it takes a very long journey through many different lands, but some of it makes only a very brief trip; in the end, all of it ends up back in Tartarus. The water always flows back into Tartarus at a point below where it was blown out earlier, some closer, some farther. Some re-enter Tartarus from the same side they left, some re-enter on the opposite side. Some coil all the way around the earth like a giant snake, and others make the complete circuit several times before plunging back down into Tartarus. [e] And, of course, once the water flows down into Tartarus at the center of the earth, it does not flow beyond that point because then it would be flowing uphill.*

"The rivers I've been talking about so far are numerous, large and varied. But among them, four are special. Ocean is particularly large and it flows around the earth in a circle.* Opposite this river is the Acheron, which passes through deserts [113a] and then flows under the earth and pools in the Acherusian lake. This is the lake where most of the souls of the dead go, and after they've stayed there for their allotted portion of time—for some it's a long time, for others it's shorter—they are sent back up again to be born as living creatures. The third river comes out between these two, and near where it comes out there is a vast area that is completely on fire. There it creates a sea that is larger than our Mediterranean, but because of the fire it is full of boiling water and mud. [b] From there it snakes around all roiling and muddy, and among other places it comes near the Acherusian lake, though it does not empty into the lake. From there it twists and turns until it finally pours down into Tartarus. This is the Pyriphlegethon river, and wherever you see lava flows on earth, they come from this river. Just as the river Ocean has an opposite—the river Acheron, so also the Pyriphlegethon has an opposite—the river Cocytus.* This river first flows through a terrible and wild region that is all a sort of dark blue color, [c] which is what people refer to when they say that something looks "stygian." The Cocytus then flows into a lake that is known as Styx, and it gains terrible powers* there. From there it continues beneath the earth and flows around in the opposite direction of the Pyriphlegethon, which it passes near the Acherusian lake, and continues its circuit, mixing with no other waters, until it empties into Tartarus on the opposite side from the Pyriphlegethon. [d] That is the nature of the four rivers.

Those who have died are led to a certain place by their guardian spirits. First they must submit themselves to trial, and they are judged as to whether they have lived well and piously or not.

"Those who are found to have lived lives in the middle—neither especially holy nor especially unholy—are led to the river Acheron. There they embark upon boats that take them to the Acherusian lake where they dwell and are purified.* If anyone has committed an injustice, he is absolved by paying a just penalty. If anyone has done good deeds, [e] he is rewarded in proportion to his worth.

"Those who are found to be incurable because of the magnitude of their faults,* or because they have done many very sacrilegious* things, or have blood on their hands because they have wrongly and violently killed many people, or anything else like that, their appropriate allotment casts them into Tartarus. From there they never depart.*

"Those who are found to be curable, though greatly at fault, either because they attacked their own father or mother [114a] in a moment of blind rage but feel tremendous regret for what they did and try to make up for it the rest of their lives, or they've actually committed homicide in such a state,* must fall into Tartarus.* After they've been there for a year, a wave throws them out: those who committed homicide are cast into the Cocytus river, and those who committed crimes against their father or mother are cast into the Pyriphlegethon. Both rivers carry them near the Acherusian lake. At that point, those in the Pyriphlegethon shout and call out to the parents whom they outraged, begging [b] to be allowed out of the river and into the lake, and pleading for their parents to accept them. Those in the Cocytus do the same with those whom they killed. If they succeed in persuading someone, then they leave the river and their troubles are over. But if not, the river carries them back to Tartarus and they have to go through the whole cycle again until they succeed in persuading someone they wronged in life. That is the judgment imposed on them by their judges.

"Those who are found to have lived lives of exceptional piety are set free from these places in the earth. [c] They are released as if from a prison. They go up and live in pure homes above the earth. Among these are the people who have been sufficiently purified by philosophy, and for the rest of time they live unencumbered by bodies. They continue on to even finer dwellings, which would not be easy to describe even if we did have sufficient time.

"You see, Simmias, this is why we must make every effort in life to participate in virtue and intelligence. We have every reason to hope that our efforts will be rewarded, and the reward is quite beautiful.

[d] "It would not be appropriate for a man of intelligence to maintain firmly that these things are exactly as I have described them. However, if we have seen that the soul is immortal, then it seems to me quite appropriate for a man of intelligence to suppose that something like this is true about our souls and their future abodes—for it is a fine supposition indeed. In fact, one ought to speak these things as if they are a sort of charm, which is why I made my story so long.

"So for the sake of these things a man ought to have confidence for the condition of his own soul if, [e] on the one hand, during his life he has let go of the pleasures and adornments of the body as foreign to him, thinking that they will do him more harm than good, and if, on the other hand, he has been eager to learn and to adorn his soul not with something foreign to it, but with its own proper adornments: temperance, [115a] justice, courage, freedom and truth. In such a condition a man can confidently await his journey to Hades.*

"You will journey there another day, Simmias, Cebes, and all you others, but now to speak like an actor in a tragedy, 'my fate calls to me.' It is time for my bath—I'd rather bathe before drinking the hemlock and spare the women the trouble of having to bathe a corpse."

[b] After he said this, Crito asked, "Very well, then, Socrates, what instructions do you have for me or for these others gathered here, either about your children or about anything else. Or is there anything at all that we can do for you?"

"The only thing you can do for me, Crito, is just what I have always asked of you, it's nothing new: take care of yourselves and act in accordance with the principles I've affirmed, even if you don't completely agree with me. Because it won't do anyone any good if you completely agree with me [c] but fail to live your lives according to these principles."

"We are very eager to do so, Socrates," Crito assured him. "But do you have any particular requests regarding how we will honor you in your funeral rites?"

"No, do as you wish—if you can catch me and I don't escape you," Socrates said laughing. Then looking at us all peacefully he said, "My friends, I can't seem to persuade Crito that I am this Socrates—the Socrates who is talking with you now and who carefully arranged all the arguments I've just gone through. He thinks I am that Socrates—the one [d] who, in a little while, will be a corpse, and he's asking about how to treat me at my funeral. I have gone to great lengths to prove that after I drink the hemlock, I will no longer be with you—I shall have departed and joined the ranks of the blessed. Apparently he thinks I was talking merely to comfort you and myself. So, please, make a guarantee to Crito about me—the opposite of the guarantee he gave about me, because he guaranteed to the city that I would remain* in Athens if they spared me the indignity of jail while we awaited the return of the ship from Delos. Please guarantee to Crito that I will not remain here when I die; [e] I will be gone. Perhaps this will make it easier for him. When he sees my body burning or being buried he will not be upset on my behalf, thinking that I am suffering terribly, and he won't say at the funeral that it is actually Socrates that he is laying out, accompanying to his grave, or burying. You know well, my good friend Crito, that speaking imprecisely is not only discordant, but can also produce bad effects on souls. Please, my friend, you mustn't say that you are burying me; you will only be burying my body—and to answer your question, [116a] deal with my remains however you think proper."

When he said this he went into another room to bathe. Crito went with him but told us to stay where we were. So we waited and talked with each other about everything we had heard from him. We also couldn't help expressing what a great misfortune had befallen us: we all felt as if our father was being taken from us and that for the rest of our lives we would feel like orphans. [b] He bathed, and then his children were brought to him. Two were small at the time, but the third was bigger. The women of his household had arrived and he talked to them in Crito's presence. He gave them some instructions and then sent the women and children away. Then he came back to us.

By this time it was almost sunset—he had spent quite a lot of time inside.* He came in freshly bathed and sat down with us, but we didn't get to talk much before the servant of the Eleven* came and stood [c] in front of him.

"Socrates," he said, "usually when I give someone the order to drink the mixture they get angry with me, and I have to remind them that I'm simply following orders. But I'm sure that you won't be angry with me. During your confinement I've known you to be the most decent, the kindest and the best man ever to come here. I know that you won't be angry with me because you know who is truly responsible for this. Well, now, you know what message I came here to give you. [d] Fare well, Socrates, and try to bear easily what must be done." As he said this he turned away and left, crying.

Looking up at him Socrates said, "Fare well to you also. We shall do what must be done." Then turning to us he said, "What a fine man he is. The whole time I've been here he's dropped in to talk with me and keep me company. He's been very considerate, and you saw how tears came to his eyes as he was leaving. He is quite an admirable man. But come now, Crito, let's obey him. Bring me the hemlock, or if it has not been mixed yet, have the man prepare it."

[e] "But Socrates," Crito replied, "I think the sun is still a little above the mountains, it hasn't quite set. Also, I think that others have drunk the mixture quite late after the order was given, sharing wine and a meal with their companions. In fact, I've even heard of people taking the time to have sex one last time before drinking the poison. Please don't hurry; we still have some time left."

"It's reasonable for others to behave that way, Crito," Socrates replied, "because they think they have something to gain by it. But it's not reasonable for me to do that because [117a] I don't think I have anything to gain by any of that. I would only make myself ridiculous in my own eyes, clinging to every last second of life when there is nothing left. Come, then, my friend, please do this for me."

When he heard that, Crito nodded to the slave standing beside him, and the slave went out to get the man who would administer the mixture. After a while they came in with the hemlock prepared. When he saw the man, Socrates said to him, "Well, then, my friend, since you know about this sort of thing, tell me what I should do."

"Just drink it and walk around until [b] your legs feel heavy," the man told him. "Then lie down and the mixture will take effect." He then offered the cup to Socrates, who took it calmly.

Then, Echecrates, fearlessly and without hesitation or change of expression he looked the man right in the eye* and asked, "Am I allowed to pour a libation from this cup?"

"Actually, Socrates," he answered, "we prepare only as much as we think is necessary."

[c] "I understand," Socrates said. "At least I am allowed to—and I ought to—pray to the gods that my journey be a fortunate one. So that is my prayer. May it be so." He was perfectly calm, cool and collected, and he drank the entire cup.

Up to then, most of us had managed to hold back our tears, but when we saw him drinking the hemlock, and especially when we saw that he finished the whole cup, we could do so no longer. I hadn't the strength to hold back the tears that then started pouring down my face. I buried my face in my cloak and wept for myself—not for him—because of the terrible thing that was happening to me: [d] my friend was being taken from me. Crito had gotten up and left the room before me because he couldn't stop from crying. Apollodorus had broken down before the rest of us, but when he actually cried out in grief, the rest of us did too—all except for Socrates.

"What are you doing, my friends? One of the reasons I sent the women away was to avoid [e] just such an inauspicious din. It is said that one ought to die hearing encouraging words. Please control yourselves and remain calm." When he said that we were ashamed of ourselves and we managed to stop crying.

Socrates walked around and when his legs felt heavy he followed the instructions and laid down. Then the one who had given him the mixture examined his legs and feet. He squeezed Socrates' foot very hard and asked if he could feel it. [118a] Socrates said that he could not. Then he squeezed Socrates' calf and showed us that he was growing cold and stiff. He touched Socrates again and said that when it reached his heart* he would be gone. When the cold reached his stomach, he took the veil from his face—which had been covered until then—and uttered his final words: "Crito, we owe Asclepius a rooster.* Be sure to give it to him; don't neglect it."

"I will," Crito replied immediately. "Is there anything else you'd like to say?"

Socrates didn't answer. Soon after that he moved a little, and the man who had given him the hemlock removed the veil and we saw that his eyes were fixed. Seeing this, Crito closed his eyes and his mouth.

Socrates completed his life that way, Echecrates. He was our friend, and of all the men of his generation, he was the best, the wisest, and the most just.*

NOTES ON CHARMIDES

153a1 ["Potidaea"]: the Potidaean campaign could be considered the final straw that broke the camel's back and sparked the Peloponnesian War. Socrates says that when he performed his military service at Potidaea (and at Amphipolis and Delium) he followed orders and remained at his post despite the fact that his life was in danger (*Apology* 28d10-29a1). Alcibiades served with Socrates at Potidaea, and according to him Socrates withstood the hardship of the campaign better than anyone, and that he even saved Alcibiades' life (*Symposium* 219e5-220e7). Thucydides describes the campaign of 432-30 BCE at 1.56-67, 2.70. The Athenians won the initial skirmish (though a hundred and fifty Athenian soldiers were killed, including the general) and the Potidaeans withdrew inside the city walls. The Potidaeans held out too long (some residents ultimately resorted to cannibalism, 2.70). It is possible that Socrates did not return to Athens until the summer of 429, and so he may have spent around three years there.

153a4 ["the Queen"]: the shrine was south of the Acropolis, but we know nothing else about it. As the wife of Zeus, Hera is the Queen of the gods (*Homeric Hymn to Hera* 12.1-2; Bacchylides, *Ode* 19.21-2), so it is possible that this was a shrine to her.

153b4 ["that battle"]: after the successful siege of Potidaea, the Athenians decided to subdue Potidaea's allies in the region. With a force of two thousand hoplites (heavily armed foot soldiers with spears and swords) and two hundred cavalry Athens marched north to Spartolus and won the first engagement, forcing the Chalcidian hoplites to retreat. Unfortunately, the Chalcidian cavalry and peltasts (light armed foot soldiers with javelins) were successful and caused a panic among the Athenian troops. Only four hundred and thirty Athenians survived—all the Athenian generals were killed (Thucydides 2.79).

154a3 ["beautiful"]: when Socrates mentioned "beauty," he used the Greek word "*kallos*," but here Critias answers using "*kalos*," and then immediately switches back to "*kallos*." These words are used more then fifty times in the *Charmides*. Both words mean "beautiful," e.g. Athena is described as beautiful (*kalē*) at *Odyssey* 13.289 and Ganymede is described as the handsomest (*kalleos*) mortal man on earth (*Iliad* 20.235). The difference is that *kallos* seems normally reserved for the physical beauty of people (both mortal and immortal) and things (e.g. garments, ships, honeycombs), while *kalos* has at least two additional main uses. It can describe a favorable quality of something, e.g. a "fair" wind (*Odyssey* 14.253), "genuine" silver (Xenophon, *Memorabilia* 3.1.9), "auspicious" sacrifices (Aeschylus, *Seven Against Thebes* 379). It can also be used in a moral sense to refer to an honorable, noble or virtuous individual (*Odyssey* 17.381; Xenophon, *Memorabilia* 1.1.16). The opposite of *kalos* in the moral sense is *aischros* (see note on 155a5 and note on 158c6 below).

154a4 ["find out"]: *eisesthai* from *oida*; this could be translated as "know," but Socrates' cognitive terminology is overworked in the *Charmides*. *Oida* is used well over two dozen times and primarily refers to knowing something in the sense of seeing it. However, this can also include mental perception, as when we say today, "Oh, I understand, I see what you are saying". In addition to *oida*, Socrates uses *gignōskō* over two dozen times. *Gignōskō* is knowing something by seeing it, but it refers also to perceptual discrimination or discernment, and so it can mean "to judge" or "to think." Socrates uses *manthanō* about a dozen times in the *Charmides*, and it means to "learn" by study or practice. It can also refer to noticing something, or to having learned it, and so to understand it. The verb *epistamai* and its related noun *epistēmē* are used well over a hundred times in this short dialogue. At 165c4-d6 Socrates gives medicine and building as forms of *epistēmē*, and he assumes that each has (i) a distinctive subject matter and (ii) a useful point (a *telos*, compare 165c10-d2 with 173b2, b5 and d6). The primary notion associated with *epistēmē* is knowledge by acquaintance, e.g. practice, and professional skill. It is not at all clear that Socrates intends to distinguish any of these different Greek words sharply, so I think it is wrong to use a one-to-one correspondence when translating them into English. In particular, I think it is bound to be more misleading than helpful to translate "*epistēmē*" with the English "science," because Socrates certainly did not have the same conception of "science" that we have today. See also note on 165c5 below.

154a5 ["admirers," also at 154c4]: "*erastai*" is related to "*erōs*," and so refers to someone with an erotic passion for someone. The word applies indifferently to heterosexual and homosexual contexts (they assumed that *erōs* is essentially the same phenomenon in both contexts; we might compare it to the modern idea of a "libidinous desire"). The ancient Greeks did not think that *erōs* was unnatural, degenerate or perverted, although they well understood that erotic passion can be intense and that it can provoke undisciplined people to behave very badly, but it was the bad behavior and weak character that was condemned, not the underlying *erōs*. "*Erastēs*" was also used in an extended sense that did not necessarily imply any specifically sexual desire. It is certainly possible that some of the young men Critias refers to here did have a homosexual desire for Charmides, but others probably were just "star struck" by this wealthy, aristocratic, and stunningly handsome young man, and wanted to be in his entourage.

154b9 ["white line in white marble"]: it may be that Socrates' father, Sophroniscus, was a stonecutter or sculptor, and so perhaps Socrates had heard this proverb from childhood. Obviously, a white line in white marble will be nearly invisible, and so stonecutters marked white marble that was to be cut using string dipped in red ochre. Perhaps we shouldn't press this proverb too far, but the trouble with the white line is not that it is necessarily inaccurate, but only that it requires more attention to follow it. Socrates is not saying that he is an unreliable detector of beauty, just that it is not always easy for others to appreciate the beauties that he marks off as being beautiful.

154c8 ["statue"]: Antisthenes of Athens (c.446-c.360) once asked a beautiful young man who was posing as if for a sculptor, "If a bronze statue could speak, on what would it pride itself most?" "It's beauty" was the reply. To which Antisthenes said, "Then aren't you ashamed to take pride in the very same thing which an inanimate object would take pride in?" (Diogenes Laertius, *Lives of the Philosophers* vi.9). Socrates is compared to a peculiar kind of statue at *Symposium* 215b3, 216e6 and 222a4.

154d7 ["Herakles"]: the Roman "Hercules." This exclamation was common, especially in wrestling schools because Herakles was the patron demi-god of wrestling.

154d8 ["a small thing"]: there is probably a deliberate innuendo here. Greeks exercised naked, and there could be a prurient element in older men watching the spectacle (Theognis 1335-36). The innuendo takes the next step in the prurience of Chaerephon and the others, because the most intense focus of Greek homosexual desire was the penis of the beautiful boy, and the ideal penis was short and thin, i.e. it was a small thing. Whether or not Plato intended this innuendo, he clearly is making this "small thing" a turning point in the conversation. Socrates originally asked about two things in the youth: wisdom and beauty. Critias, Chaerephon and the others have focused on bodily beauty and forgotten all about wisdom—beauty in the soul—treating wisdom as if it is a trivial concern next to physical beauty.

154e1 ["soul"]: the *psuchē* makes a human being or an animal alive. Loss of the *psuchē* is associated with loss of consciousness (*Iliad* 5.696) and loss of life (*Iliad* 16.505). Homer associates the *psuchē* with blood (*Iliad* 14.518), but Plato associates it with breath (*Cratylus* 399d10-e3). Although a ghost is often an "*eidōlon*" or a "*phantasma*," it can also be a *psuchē* (e.g. *Iliad* 23.65). In the *Republic* (cf. Book IV) we should probably think of the *psuchē* as what gives us a psychology and makes us the people we are. Since virtue is in the *psuchē*, our voluntary decisions are in the *psuchē*, so whatever is connected to voluntary decisions (e.g. beliefs, intentions, emotions, desires, memories, hopes, and so on) are in the *psuchē*. Frequently "mind" or even "intellect" seems the correct translation, but this can create a confusion with *dianoia* at 157c9, so whenever possible I keep "soul" for *psuchē*. The exceptions are at 160a1, 160a8 and 160b4 (see note on 160a1 below).

154e7 ["discussion"]: as a deponent verb, *dialegomai* means literally to "talk through" (it is used also at 155a5-6, 155c7, 159b4, 170e6). It can refer to a simple conversation, a discussion on a particular topic, or even an argument over an issue. Plato uses it in a special sense at *Republic* 5.454a5, cf. 6.511b5, c5 ("dialectic"). There may be another innuendo here (see note on 154d8 above) because Aristophanes sometimes uses this word as a euphemism for sexual intercourse (Aristophanes, *Ekklēsiazusae* 890, *Plutus* 1082). But again, if it is Socrates' intention to make this innuendo, he is doing so in order to turn the minds of his friends from Charmides' body to his soul.

155a3 ["Solon"]: Solon was an Athenian politician, lawgiver and poet (c.638–c.558 BCE). Plato gives us the earliest explicit reference to "Seven Sages," of which Solon was one (*Protagoras* 343a, *Timaeus* 20de, though the canon was probably formed decades before Plato's birth). In the *Critias*, Plato has Critias tell the story of Atlantis, a story that was brought to Athens by Solon (cf. *Critias* 108d5). Plato has Diotima refer to Solon as the father of Athenian law (*Symposium* 209d7; cf. *Republic* 10.599e3, *Laws* 9.858e3). Plato also has several of his characters quote Solon's poetry (Nicias at *Laches* 188b3-4, Laches at *Laches* 189a4-6, and Socrates at *Lysis* 212e3-4 and *Republic* 7.536d1-3).

155a5 ["shameful," also at 159d2]: *aischros* is the opposite of *kalos* (see note on 154a3 above). Typically, a young woman of the upper class would not need a chaperone because she was never allowed to be in any situation where a chaperone would be called for; but young men often were.

155b1 ["Boy"]: Critias' attendant (*akolouthos*) is not called a "*doulos*" (the generic term for a slave), and yet Critias calls him "boy" (*pais*) without using the "*Ō*" of polite direct address, so it is clear that this attendant is indeed a slave.

155b2 ["healer"]: *iatros* is the normal word for a doctor, but in Socrates' day there was no medical profession legally empowered to issue or revoke medical licenses. So the Greek word "*iatros*" covered everyone from the most professional Hippocratic to the traditional and well-meaning "herbalist" and the most unscrupulous "snake oil peddler." Our understanding of this word affects whether we think Critias is outright lying to Charmides, and hence, by going along with the lie, Socrates is himself lying to Charmides. Our view here will also be influenced by what we suppose Charmides' medical complaint consisted in. Literally, he complained about "weakness," and "weariness with respect to his head." Charmides might be suffering from hangovers due to intemperate carousing with his friends. Socrates may well honestly believe that he has a remedy for such headaches, and that the cure recommends discussing the value of temperance.

155b6 ["remedy" also at 155c8, 155e3, 155e6, 155e7, 157b2, 157c5, 158c1, 158c2; see also *Laches* 185c5, 185c8]: a *pharmakon* is a potion (a *pharmakotribēs* is someone who grinds and mixes either drugs or dyes). If the potion is intended to heal someone, then it is "medicine;" if intended to harm, it is "poison" (cf. *Odyssey* 4.230). A *pharmakon* can have magical effects (e.g. turn men into swine, *Odyssey* 10.233-43); however, Plutarch speculates that Helen's bewitchment of the wine at *Odyssey* 4.220 consisted simply in her charming words (Plutarch, *Symposiacs* 1.1.4).

155c5 ["at a loss," also at 156b2, 167b7, 169c3, 169c5; see also *Laches* 194c1]: Socrates uses the verb *aporeō*, related to the noun *aporia* (169c6, 169d1, "confounded"; see also *Laches* 194c4, 194c5, 196b2, 200e5). The adjective *aporos* can refer to a literal dead end, a place with no way out or an impassable or difficult obstacle. Logically, a refutation can put you in *aporia* if you see no way to defend your claim. Here Charmides' beauty puts Socrates in a temporary *aporia*, but later Socrates' logic will put Charmides in *aporia*, which they hope will also be temporary.

155d2 ["surged"]: there is a play on words here that isn't easy to capture. At 155d1, when Socrates describes Charmides as he gets ready to ask his question, he uses the verb *anagō*, i.e. to set sail or put out to sea. The word that I translate as "surged" (i.e. *perirreō*) means to "flow around," as when the sea flows around a ship leaving a harbor.

155d3 ["my noble friend"]: Socrates directly addresses the person to whom he is narrating this entire dialogue. Perhaps Plato hoped that his readers would feel Socrates is speaking to them, and that they would actively engage with the ideas and arguments in the dialogue—as if they are part of the on-going discussion.

155d3 ["cloak"]: a *himation* is an outer garment that was usually worn over a *chiton* (males) or *peplos* (females). It was draped over one's clothing like a shawl and could be worn in a number of different ways. Occasionally men wore it without a *chiton* underneath, but in that case it would probably be referred to not as a "*himation*" but as an "*achiton*" (e.g. Xenophon, *Memorabilia* 1.6.2). So probably this scene is very tame: what is inside Charmides' *himation* is just his *chiton*, and the titillation is probably similar to when a heterosexual male sees an attractive woman's blouse after her jacket has blown open a bit by a slight breeze. Socrates' discomfort lasts until about 156a9.

155d4 ["wise"]: *sophia* can refer to four different states. (1) Skill: a skilled carpenter is *sophos* in the ways of carpentry. (2) The shrewdness of judgment associated with expertise or with sagacity. The "Seven Sages of Greece" were called *sophoi*, and their bits of sage advice were quoted often (e.g. Solon of Athens said "moderation in all things;" Chilon of Sparta said, "Do not desire what is impossible;" Bias of Priene said, "Most men are bad"). (3) The learning that comes with instruction and education (*sophia* is like *mathia*—from which we get "math"—but *sophia* tends to be speculative, *mathia* deductive). (4) The subtlety, cleverness and ingeniousness that can entail deviousness or scheming craftiness. It needn't be difficult to keep these senses separate, but a character like Odysseus can suggest a connection between (1) craft and (4) craftiness, a demagogue can suggest a connection between (2) shrewdness and (4) deviousness, and a sophistic lawyer can suggest a connection between (3) education and (4) scheming. The contrary of *sophia* is *amathia* (e.g. 22e3).

155d5 ["Cydias"]: Plutarch associates Mimnermus, Cydias, and Archilochus. Mimnermus was a 7th century elegiac poet and Archilochus was a 7th century lyric and elegiac poet (Plutarch *De faciae quae in orbe lunae apparet* 19). Plutarch is referring to poets who wrote on solar eclipses, so we can assume that Cydias wrote at least one poem about a solar eclipse.

155e3 ["I did"]: perhaps Socrates is lying. He says "*epistaimēn*" from "*epistamai*" and if he is claiming to be an expert medical doctor (cf. 165c4-d6, 171a8-c2) then he is knowingly affirming a falsehood. Alternatively, he may not be sharply distinguishing "*epistamai*" from other forms of knowledge, and if he does indeed know of a good cure for a hangover (in an informal sense of "know"), then he may be telling the truth.

155e5 ["charm"]: Homer mentions a charm used to stop bleeding (*Odyssey* 19.457). According to Xenophon, Socrates once quoted the song used by the Sirens as a charm to lure Odysseus to his destruction (*Odyssey* 12.184, *Memorabilia* 2.6.10). Hippocrates associates charms with medical charlatans (*On the Sacred Disease* 1). At 157a4-5 he says that his charms are *kaloi logoi*, "beautiful words" or "fine arguments." In the *Phaedo*, Cebes implies that Socratic arguments are charms (78a1-2).

155e8 ["no benefit"]: Socrates uses *ophelos* here and at 175b2, where he uses it as the opposite of *anōphelēs*, which is literally the opposite of *ōphelimos*, so probably Socrates is using *ophelos* and *ōphelimos* interchangeably. The idea of being benefitted becomes crucial at the climax of the dialogue where it appears as if all the benefits to human beings are provided by the various particular crafts, e.g. doctors make us healthy and builders make us homes. If temperance is a form of knowledge and is beneficial, then what particular benefit does it provide us with (174e3-175b2)? However, at *Euthydemus* 280d4-7 Socrates argues that you get no benefit (*ophelos*) from a good thing unless you use it (and use it correctly, 280e3-4). Good medicine is no benefit to you if you don't take it as the doctor prescribed. From this point of view, we should notice that Socrates does *not* say that without the charm, the leaf is not an analgesic, he says that it is no *benefit*. An analgesic that makes it easier for you to continue your intemperate ways may decrease some of the pain you experience, but it may simultaneously make your life much worse, and so may not ultimately be a real *benefit* to you.

156a3 ["persuade me"]: if Socrates were a doctor, he might reasonably expect a fee for treating Charmides. Socrates never asks anyone for money (this was a point of pride for Socrates, cf. *Apology* 19d8-20c3, 31b5-c3, 33a5-b8, *Euthyphro* 3d6-9, *Hippias Major* 300c9-d2). Because Critias is present as chaperone, there is no suggestion of any shameful sexual exchange—and anyway, Socrates seems spectacularly uninterested in sex (cf. *Symposium* 216c4-219e5). Perhaps Socrates is being sincere about his motives at *Charmides* 166c7-d6 and *Apology* 25d8-e4. See also note on 157c1 below. The notion of proceeding without Socrates' consent returns at the end of the dialogue (176c7-d5).

156b2 ["power"]: Socrates uses the noun *dunamis* here and at 168b3, 168b5, 168d1, 168d2, 168e5, 169a3. He uses the verb *dunamai* at 156b3, 171b11, 173d5, 175b3, 175d2. See note on *Laches* 192b1.

156d4 ["my charm"]: Perhaps Socrates is compounding an earlier lie by changing his story (see note on 155e3 above). However, puzzling out the true meaning of an enigmatically brief claim is a theme in the *Charmides* (e.g. 162b8, 163b1-c8, 164d3-165b4, and *ainigmatōdesteron* at 164e6). Socrates has no objection to using language with unexpected significance, as long as you go on to clarify your meaning (163d1-e2).

156d5 ["Zalmoxian doctor"]: Herodotus mentions a Thracian god (*daimōn*; Socrates' Thracian uses *theos*) named Salmoxis or Gebeleïzis (*Histories* 4.94.1). Herodotus goes on to say that the Greeks who live in the region believe that they have, in effect, debunked Salmoxis' scam. They claim that Salmoxis is just a human being who started building an underground chamber while he told people that he and his companions would not die, but would pass over to a wonderful place where they would be immortal. Once the chamber was finished, he lived in it for three years, until he was sure that everybody thought that he had died, at which point he came back out, thus "proving" that he could cheat death (4.95). This story is rather insulting to the Thracians, and so Herodotus politely takes no definite position on it (4.96.1). Strabo gives a different version, using the name "Zamolxis" (Strabo, *Geography* 7.3.5).

156e6 ["originates in the soul"]: there are two main problems here. First, the eyes are component parts of the head, which has other components in addition to the eyes; however, the human body does not seem to be a component part of anything more comprehensive. Second, it is not clear how "the person as a whole" (*panti tō anthrōpō*) is different from "the body" (*tō sōmati*) or from "the soul" (*tēs psuchēs*). Obviously we don't have enough to speculate on Zalmoxian medical theory (Socrates does not claim to be a Zalmoxian doctor), but we can see that Socrates is using these medical enigmas to get Charmides to agree to two points: (1) a seemingly localized problem like a headache may well have root causes that are not similarly localized, and (2) medical problems may stem from character problems, e.g. lack of temperance (157a5-6). So perhaps by "the body," he means the various parts of the body (e.g. eyes, feet, lungs, liver); by "the person as a whole" he means the various parts connected properly into the human form; and by "the soul" he means the life, i.e. the living human person including the moral character as well as the past, present and future stages of one's life.

157a6 ["temperance"]: "*sōphrosunē*" is a compound of three parts: (1) the "*sō-*" prefix is related to the noun "*sōs*" (safe and sound, alive and well) and to the verb "*sōzō*" (to save, to preserve, to keep alive); (2) the "*-phro-*" middle is related to the noun "*phrēn*" (heart, mind, will) and to the verb "*phroneō*" (to understand, to be wise, to think, to know, to will); and (3) the suffix "*-sunē*" turns the word into an abstract noun. Hence, *sōphrosunē* can refer to being of sound mind, i.e. sanity as opposed to insanity (*mania*, e.g. Xenophon, *Memorabilia* 1.1.16); but it can also refer to prudence as opposed to stupidity and imprudence (e.g. Homer, *Odyssey* 23.30). But in Plato, it probably means something like self-control or moderation (see Aristophanes, *Clouds* 962; Plato, *Symposium* 196c; and Aristotle, *Nicomachean Ethics* 3.10). I think that Plato deliberately wrote the incidents at 154c3-8 and 155c5-e3 to provide a clear example of *sōphrosunē*: Socrates does not allow a sudden, strong desire to derail his mental purpose. So I agree with Cicero's choice to translate *sōphrosunē* into Latin with *temperantia*, from the verb "*temperāre*," which means to divide or proportion duly, to mingle in due proportion, to combine properly. A blacksmith "tempers" a steel sword to make the blade tougher: tempered steel can be struck with great force without fracturing or breaking. Imagine having a soul as tough as tempered steel: no threats or pains could make you give up your purpose, and no temptations could divert you from accomplishing your goal.

157b5 ["error"]: *hamartēma* can be used to impute moral culpability, and so "fault" may be a better translation, but we don't know enough of the Thracian's view to know if he blames doctors for this oversight. His claim that "if the whole is not in good condition, then it is impossible for any part to be in good condition" does not contradict his claim that "the proper treatments of many [though not all] illnesses have escaped the Greek doctors." He may believe that Greek doctors can successfully ameliorate many conditions without actually putting the whole in a completely good condition—this entails that there is something left to be desired in their treatments, not that there is nothing at all to recommend them. For a closely related word, see note on 171d6 below.

157e3 ["Athenian families"]: this extended emphasis on Charmides' noble lineage (157d9-158b4) is interesting. Many scholars read the *Charmides* in light of the terrible and brief rule of "The Thirty Tyrants" imposed upon Athens at the end of the Peloponnesian War. They held power for only about a year (404-403), but they managed to execute about 1,500 alleged political enemies in that brief time. Critias was one of the leaders. Charmides also participated in the government with his uncle, but we are not sure of the role he played. Critias and Charmides were both killed in the battle when the democratic faction took back control of the government. It is not clear how (or whether) these events should affect our interpretation of this dialogue. The emphasis on Charmides' lineage may suggest that Plato is reflecting on traditional assumptions about what qualifies someone to wield political power: is noble birth sufficient?

158a1 ["virtue"]: *aretē* is often best translated as "excellence." It can have both moral and non-moral uses. Dogs, horses and farmland all have their own distinctive *aretai* (see note on *Apology* 20b6). In Homer, *aretē* often refers to brave deeds. Often "skill" is a good translation because it does not imply moral excellence (as at Laches 184c2), but I try to reserve "skill" for *technē* (craft), or *mathēma* (something learned). Often in Plato *aretē* refers to five moral virtues: courage, temperance, justice, piety, and wisdom.

158b6 ["sufficiently temperate"]: there is a confusing pleonasm here. The issue of whether temperance is in ("*parestin*," b5) Charmides suggests that temperance is all-or-nothing: either it is in you or it isn't. However, "sufficiently temperate" ("*sōphrōn hikanōs*," b6) suggests that temperance is a matter of degree. Should we understand the latter as (a) a vague repetition of the former, (b) an alternative to the former, or (c) a deliberate obfuscation because Socrates disavows knowing what temperance is (165b5-c2)?

158b7 ["Abaris the Hyperborean"]: literally, Hyperboreans are people who live beyond ("*huper-*") the north wind ("*boreas*"), i.e. far north. Herodotus mentions Abaris at 4.36, and says only that he allegedly travelled around the world carrying an arrow and eating nothing. He was legendary as a healer. The arrow is a symbol of Apollo, the deadly archer who strikes from afar and kills with plague (Homer, *Iliad* 1.43-52). Of course, the god of illness is also the god of healing.

158c6 ["sense of shame"]: the adjective *aischuntēlos* is related to the noun *aischunē*, which can be a synonym for *aidōs*. A sense of shame is also a sense of honor, i.e. it restrains us from doing anything dishonorable. Apollo says that *aidōs* is both a great benefit and a great harm for human beings (Homer, *Iliad* 24.44-45): it benefits us by restraining us from doing things we ought not do, but it harms us when concern for what others think of us restrains us from doing something we ought to do. Socrates may complicate this at *Apology* 28b3 and 28c3 by distinguishing between (a) what one *is* ashamed of and (b) what one *ought to be* ashamed of: (a) may be good in some circumstances, bad in others, but (b) can only do us good. See note on 160e4 below).

158c7 ["considerate"]: Socrates uses litotes, he says that Charmides' answer was "not low-born" (*ouk agennōs*). The meaning is something like "dignified," because it has associations with Charmides' aristocratic lineage, but today associations with the upper class are often thought to entail an unseemly arrogance, which is not what Socrates has in mind at all. Alternatively, "tactful" might be appropriate, but today this is often associated with being manipulative or calculating, which is, again, not at all what Socrates has in mind.

159a4 ["Does that seem reasonable?"]: this final question is typical of a Socratic interrogation. Socrates makes a point, sometimes explaining it, giving examples, evidence or reasons for thinking that it is true, and then asks whether his interlocutor agrees. Our view of Socrates' approach—or "the Socratic method," if there is such a thing—will be shaped by how seriously we think Socrates intends these questions. Are they (a) *pro forma*, and intended to force his interlocutor down the path he is creating, or (b) sincere, and intended to offer his interlocutor the opportunity to disagree, ask for clarification, draw a distinction, and so on.

159b1 ["he hesitated"]: Some people feel that Socrates is unfair to Charmides on the grounds that he peppers the poor lad with rapid-fire questions. But it is clear both here and at 160e2 that Socrates puts no pressure on Charmides to answer his questions: Socrates allows him all the time he wants before answering (in fact, he himself asks for time to think before he answers questions put to him, see 165c2). This is in stark contrast with the eristic method of the sophists Euthydemus and Dionysodorus (see *Euthydemus* 276c2).

159b5 ["calmness"]: the adjective *hēsuchos* and the abstract noun *hēsuchotēs* (= *hēsuchia*) refers to silence, stillness or rest. Since Charmides refers to "participating in a discussion" (*dialegomai*) he can hardly mean to say that temperance is keeping completely silent and saying nothing. I suspect that we are in the right ballpark if we associate Charmides' *hēsuchotēs* with the Roman *gravitas*, i.e. a solemn weightiness and sobriety that eschews just the sort of skittish frivolity associated with energetic young men Charmides' age.

159c1 ["fine things"]: "fine" translates *kalos*. See note on 154a3 above. At *Laches* 192c8 Socrates asks whether courage is fine (*kalos*) and good (*agathos*). Notice that when Charmides says that temperance is a kind of calmness, Socrates does not contradict him. This makes sense, given that Socrates claims not to know what temperance is (165b5-c2). But then how can he argue one way or the other with Charmides? This auxiliary belief that temperance is fine provides the key:

Step 1: temperance and calmness are one and the same thing.

Step 2: temperance is fine.

Step 3: calmness is fine.

Step 4: calmness is not fine (as illustrated by the many examples).

By denying that he knows what temperance is, Socrates denies himself of the authority to say whether or not all temperate actions are calm. However, he does not deny himself (or Charmides) the authority to say whether every calm action is fine. Socrates' use of auxiliary claims allows him to put proposals to the test despite the fact that he denies that he knows what the virtue is.

159c3 ["correctly"]: literally, Socrates asks about writing "the same kind of letters" quickly or calmly. Clearly his point is not that writing quickly is fine even if what you write is gibberish. Greek children learned writing by copying what the instructor wrote, so Socrates is contrasting the students who have no trouble doing this—and so are among the first to complete the exercise accurately—with those students who do have difficulty with the exercise.

159c11 ["matial arts"]: the *pankration* was like modern "mixed martial arts." Boxing, wrestling and kicking moves were all allowed, including twisting bones out of their sockets or breaking them, and strangling your opponent to unconsciousness. No weapons were allowed, and in Athens (but not Sparta) biting and gouging were not allowed. Today we might ask about Tai chi, a martial art that is often practiced by moving very slowly and calmly. Socrates does not deny that some calm actions are indeed fine (160b9-d3), but even one counter-example refutes a universal claim.

159d2 ["embarrassing"]: *aischros* is the opposite of *kalos* (see note on 154a3 above).

160a1 ["intellect"]: Socrates uses "*psuchē*" here and below at 160a8 ("intellectual") and 160b4 ("mind"). See note on 154e1 above.

160d8 ["Put this all together"]: Socrates uses the verb *sullogizomai*, which could be translated as "syllogize" or "calculate." In Aristotle, a "syllogism" involves deductive reasoning, e.g. "all A's are B, and all B's are C, so all A's are C" (*Prior Analytics* 1.21). Socrates is reversing this procedure: given that Charmides is praised as temperate (C), speculate on the cause (B) of this praise, and then speculate further on what could produce this cause (A). We have reason to call this a "hypothetico-deductive method," and the supremely grand conclusion we might try to draw from this is that Socrates has invented "the scientific method."

160e4 ["ashamed"]: Charmides uses the verb *aischunō* and the related adjective *aischuntēlos*, and then quite naturally speculates that what causes *aischunē* is *aidōs* (see note on 158c6 above).

160e9 ["good"]: the inference from *kalos* to *agathos* is not necessarily as obvious as Socrates and Charmides take it to be, since *agathos* may imply that an action is good for the agent himself, while *kalos* may imply that the action benefits someone else (cf. Aristotle, *Rhetoric* 1.9.1366a36-b1, 1366b36-1367a4). Socrates also draws the inference from *kalos* to *agathos* at *Protagoras* 359e4-8. It is a little less controversial to assume that courage is both *kalos* (*Laches* 192d8) and *agathos* (*Laches* 194d4) without inferring the latter from the former.

160e11 ["not good"]: as with "*hēgēsōntai mē ōphelimon*" at *Republic* 10.607e5, the negation applies to the noun ("it produces what is not good"), not the verb ("it does not produce what is good"). Most translators overlook the fact that Socrates and Charmides are taking seriously the "ye shall know them by their fruits" pattern of reasoning established by Socrates at 160d5-e1. Socrates is about to use Homer to show that modesty can produce a result that is not good, and so given the admission here, it will follow that modesty cannot be good.

161a4 ["Homer"]: *Odyssey* 17.347. This is an exact quotation.

161b6 ["minding your own business"]: literally, "doing the things of oneself." Obviously I cannot translate this literally because "doing your own thing" means something quite different in modern English. Probably the phrase was used to identify the opposite of a "busybody" (*polupragmōn*, literally "doing much;" or *periergia*, literally "working around/beyond," 161d11). But whereas being "meddlesome" or a "busybody" in English refers primarily to prying into the affairs of others and it is uniformly considered a character flaw, the relevant Greek conception splits into three related meanings. If the leading idea is "much" (from *polu-*) or "excel" (from *peri-*), then a *polupragmōn* or *periergos* person is either (a) diligent, thorough, curious or inquisitive (which can be quite admirable), or (b) someone who goes too far and wastes effort on a task (which can be shameful). But if the leading idea is "around" (from *peri-*), then a *polupragmōn* or *periergos* person is someone who (c) wrongly involves himself in the affairs of others ("poking his nose around"). Theophrastos (Aristotle's successor at the Lyceum; c.371–c.287 BCE) wrote about the *periergos* as someone who presents himself as kind-hearted but who doesn't actually provide any help; he eagerly undertakes projects beyond his ability, e.g. he will gladly offer to guide you through a forest even if he doesn't actually know the way (*Characters* 14). In *Lovers*, Socrates contrasts philosophers with dilettantes who are overly curious about, and dabble or meddle (*polupragmenounta*) in, many areas of study (137b1-6). All three senses are combined in later Greek to describe superstitious people who seek super-human knowledge they ought not pursue (Plutarch *Alexander* 2.5; *Acts of the Apostles* 19:19).

161e8 ["produce some definite result"]: building and weaving produce products (e.g. garments and built structures), but medicine restores the body to a state of health, so "product" is not the right translation of "*ergon*" here. Socrates makes this explicit at 165c10-166b6 below.

162b5 ["to know"]: *gignōskō* refers to knowledge or recognition by perception, observation or reflection, and hence to judge, to determine, to decide or to understand, to think. Charmides denies knowledge at b9 with the word *oida*, which is probably the most common word for knowledge. *Oida* is closely related to *horaō*, which refers to visual perception, so to say "Oh, I know what you are saying" is like "Oh, I see what you are saying." Here and elsewhere Plato treats *oida* and *gignōskō* as interchangeable (e.g. *Meno* 71b4-6).

162b6 ["what he meant"]: this may be the second time that Socrates has gone along with someone's pretense (i.e. if he was merely pretending that he had a remedy for Charmides' headaches). If we agree with Alcibiades' view of Socrates (*Symposium* 216e2-5), then we may think that Socrates is playing his usual game of irony and laughing at his interlocutors. But if we take Socrates' own view of himself (if he is not being ironic at *Apology* 37e5-38a6), then going along with the pretenses of others is part of his usual and sincere epistemic restraint: a correct guess of his does not amount to knowledge, and Socrates does not profess to know what he does not know.

162e9 ["make something"]: probably he has in mind 161e7-8 where he asked Charmides about doctors, builders and weavers producing some definite result (see note on 161e8 above). However, there he used "*prattein*," and here he uses "*poiein*." The difference matters to Critias (see 163a10-12). Allowing for the looseness of living languages, neither Socrates nor Critias is abusing Greek. "*Praxis*" and "*poiēsis*" are semantically close enough that it is not an abuse of language to slide between the two (e.g. Xenophon, *Memorabilia* 2.8.5-6—conducting business, or achieving your objective, is the production of an object if you happen to be a builder or weaver); but of the two, "*poiēsis*" is more closely associated with the production of an object (e.g. Homer, *Iliad* 1.608), so Critias is just as within his linguistic rights to distinguish the two as is Aristotle (*Nicomachean Ethics* 6.4.1140b6).

163b4 ["Hesiod"]: *Works and Days* 311. The point Critias is about to make is attributed to Socrates by Xenophon (*Memorabilia* 1.2.56-57).

163b8 ["working in a brothel"]: Socrates did not mention either of these last two. It is Critias' view that they belong in the same category as the things Socrates did mention, but what category would that be? I suspect that the distinction he is assuming is that between the liberal arts and the illiberal arts, where the latter are for people who must work to earn a living, and the former are for those who hire and manage people who must work to earn a living.

163c2 ["nothing fine about it"]: notice that right away there is a significant difference between Critias' approach to temperance and Charmides' approach. Calmness, modesty and minding one's own business are not moral properties—they can all be explained in non-moral behavioral terms. In effect, Charmides was trying to give "reductive definitions" of temperance, "reducing" the moral property of being temperate to a non-moral, and non-evaluative, property. It is not clear that such an approach can possibly be successful. On the other hand, by introducing the moral, and evaluative, notion of what is "fine" (*kalos* in its moral sense; see note on 154a3 above) into his own account of temperance, Critias seems to be defining one moral property in terms of another moral property (and one evaluative property in terms of another). If Charmides' approach may be doomed to failure (if no collection of non-moral properties can fully account for any moral property), Critias' approach may be doomed to vacuity (if defining one moral property in terms of another requires that the second moral term be further defined, which threatens circularity or an infinite regress). See note on *Phaedo* 101e1.

163d4 ["Prodicus"]: at *Euthydemus* 277e3 Socrates quotes Prodicus as saying that one must learn "straightness concerning names," which probably means "correctness of terms" (see also *Cratylus* 422c3-4). Prodicus of Ceos was a contemporary of Socrates, and was primarily a teacher of rhetoric, but he gave naturalistic accounts of some religious myths and was probably an atheist. He took part in several diplomatic missions, and used these as opportunities to find students willing to pay his fees. He is mentioned many times in Plato's dialogues.

163d6 ["what meaning you are giving it"]: John Locke famously complained about what he called "affected obscurity," which consisted in "either applying old words to new and unusual significations; or introducing new and ambiguous terms, without defining either" (*An Essay Concerning Human Understanding* 3.10.6). He was renewing a Socratic demand. The sophistic approach would be unacceptable to both Locke and Socrates (see *Euthydemus* 295b7-c9).

163e1 ["'*doing*' good things"]: on this one line of Greek text, Socrates uses both "*poiēsis*" and "*praxis*," two words famously distinguished by Aristotle (*Nicomachean Ethics* 6.4.1140b6). Here is where they leave behind the notion of "minding one's own business" in the sense of not being a busybody, and instead focus on actions that produce good results. Below, at 163e8-11, Critias allows himself to continue to use "*poiēsis*" (which I translate there as "making"), though he immediately switches to "*praxis*" (which I translate there as "doing").

164b1 ["for himself"]: the fact that the needy man's modesty is not good for the needy man himself entails that modesty cannot be temperance (161a2-10). Socrates persists in assuming that temperance is self-beneficial (because it is good), and also beneficial to others (because it is fine).

164b8 ["when he is not?"]: it is possible to heal someone without benefitting them if, e.g., it is possible that the patient is better off dead (cf. *Laches* 195c7-d9).

164d5 ["inscription at Delphi"]: in the sixth century BCE three maxims were literally inscribed into a wall of the temple of Apollo at Delphi (in the *pronaos*, so that one would see them as one entered; Pausanias, *Description of Greece* 10.24.1): "know thyself" (*gnōthi seauton*), "nothing in excess" (*mēden agan*), and "oaths bring ruin" (*enguē para d' atē*). Probably "know thyself" was originally understood to mean something like "never try to exceed your mortal limitations."

165a3-4 ["Oaths bring ruin"]: compare today's "a verbal contract is worth the paper it's written on." Sometimes people dispute the exact terms and implications of an oath, and even whether the oath was actually sworn or not. Such disputes can create tension between friends or family members or even ruin relationships. Perhaps it is prudent to swear oaths sparingly.

165b8 ["I do not know"]: Socrates uses "*eidenai*" from "*oida*" (see note on 154a4 above). "*Epistēmē*" is about to be used quite a lot, and nobody in the dialogue bothers to say whether or not more than one conception of "knowledge" is meant. I should point out that neither here nor anywhere else does Socrates affirm the absurd claim "I know that I do not know anything."

165c4 ["kind of knowledge"]: this sentence is a translator's worst nightmare. The first "knowledge" translates Plato's *gignōskein*, while the second translates "*epistēmē*" (see note on 154a4 above). This is the very first instance of "*epistēmē*" in the *Charmides*, and from here to the end of the dialogue this word is very important, which suggests that it should be translated differently from the other words that can mean "knowledge." But I think that "science" is more misleading than helpful (although the first use of the verb *epistamai* was at 155b6 where Critias asked Socrates if there was any reason he couldn't pretend that he "knows" a remedy for headaches—and this does seem to suggest a professional sort of understanding). If Prodicus wrote a treatise on Greek epistemic words, neither Socrates nor Critias seems to have read it (Socrates takes a step in this direction at *Euthydemus* 277e3-278b2).

165c7 ["knowledge of oneself"]: "*heautou*" is a direct reflexive that refers back to the chief word of the sentence or clause in which it occurs (usually the subject of the sentence or clause). However, it is masculine, so Critias must be referring to the man who obeys the Delphic command to "know thyself" by knowing *him*self (Socrates again uses "himself" at 167a1). He is not saying the temperance knows *it*self, but he will say that soon ("*heautēs*" at 166c3 is feminine, and refers either to the explicit "*epistēmē*," or the implicit "temperance," both of which are feminine nouns in Greek). Later Critias suggests that "knowledge knows itself" can be equivalent to "a man knows himself" (see 169d9-e5).

166a3 ["What you say is true"]: it is not clear how much Socrates is conceding here. At most, Critias has caught Socrates in a false assumption, if by "*ergon*" (at 165d2 and d5, and emphasized by Critias at 165e7, e8 and 166a1) Socrates means "product," i.e. a physical item. Building and weaving produce physical items; calculation and geometry do not. But I don't think Socrates means "*ergon*" in this way, because his very first example is medicine, which does not produce a physical item, rather it puts a pre-existing item (i.e. the body) in a specific state (i.e. a healthy state). Calculation does not put a physical object in a specific state, but it does, nevertheless, have a specific result, i.e. the number resulting from the calculation (e.g. 4 as the sum of 3 and 1). So I generally translate "*ergon*" as "result," not "product." Socrates does not press this issue here, because his first concern is that all the crafts he can think of have subject matters that are distinct from the craft itself, and upon which the craft operates. "Can a craft have itself as its subject matter?" is the question that will occupy them until 169d5.

166b9 ["just the same"]: at *Phaedrus* 265c8-266b1 Socrates distinguishes two ways of proceeding with an issue. One sees distinct things under one form (e.g. foxes and coyotes are both canines), and the other divides a single form into distinct kinds of things (e.g. canines include both foxes and coyotes). If one ought to proceed in both ways, then Critias is wrong to object to Socrates' procedure as he himself has characterized Socrates' procedure. Also, notice that Socrates has just given what we might call an "inductive argument" for a universal claim about knowledge; several arguments below also seem to be inductive (cf. Aristotle claims that Socrates is responsible for introducing two things: universal definitions and inductive arguments, *Metaphysics* 13.4.1078b17-19).

166c1 ["of other forms of knowledge"]: why does Critias add this? Perhaps Socrates' question at 166e4 below is driven by the fact that Critias has just modified his account of temperance. You can't analyze an account that keeps changing.

166c4 ["just now denied"]: probably Critias has in mind 165b5-c3 where Socrates claimed that he was inquiring into the truth because he does not know what the truth is (he may also be remembering what Socrates said to Charmides at 161c5-6). Critias assumes that the following is an exclusive disjunction: either (1) Socrates is inquiring into the truth of the matter, or (2) Socrates is trying to refute Critias. Socrates replies (166c7-d6) that this is not an exclusive (cf. heads or tails) disjunction, but an inclusive (cf. soup or salad) disjunction.

166e2 ["what comes out"]: I find Socrates' use of *ekbainō* (step out) curious. A refutation seems to be a dead end, i.e. a place with no further steps to take. If we take "*ekbainō*" seriously, then it suggests that in Socrates' view, at least some refutations do provide us with a step forward.

166e7 ["For example"]: this sentence is not in Plato's text. I add it because this is the point in the dialogue where beginners start to get lost, and I don't want that to happen. In my defense, what I have Socrates say in this sentence is clearly the sort of thing he has in mind (see 171c4-9), and it is exactly the sort of thing he does tend to add (as we just saw at 164a9-c3).

167a1 ["only the temperate man"]: Socrates treats answers to his "what is it?" question as being or entailing bi-conditionals. If temperance is analyzed as self-knowledge, then self-knowledge is what temperance is, so that *all and only* self-knowledgeable people are temperate.

167a9 ["third time's a charm"]: literally he says, "the third is for the savior." At a symposium, the first libation was poured to Zeus and the Olympians, the second to the heroes, and the third to Zeus the Savior. Plato also refers to this practice at *Republic* 9.583b2 and *Philebus* 66d4. The first consideration of the view that temperance is self-knowledge was 165b3-166a2; the second was 166a3-c3.

167e1 ["desire"]: *epithumia* is naturally associated with pleasure, and it can be contrasted with *boulēsis* (translated as "wish" at 167e4 and often elsewhere), which is naturally associated with what we think is good. Since Socrates mentions *epithumia* and *boulēsis* separately, we might assume that he thinks it is possible to have a desire (*epithumia*) for something that we anticipate will be pleasant, but that we simultaneously think is bad for us, and hence something for which we do not have a wish (*boulēsis*). But if he thinks that this is possible, then his later dream that wisdom can truly rule our lives must have come through the gate of ivory (see note on 173a7). Alternatively, if his dream came through the gate of horn, then we are misunderstanding something about human psychology is we think it is possible for a wise person to wish for something they do not desire. See note on *Protagoras* 340a8-b1.

167e1 ["not a desire for pleasure"]: Socrates is not denying the possibility of a desire for desire (or, below, a wish for a wish, or a love of love). He is simply pointing out that, e.g., normally when we say that S desires x, we assume that S sees something pleasant in x. Hence, if it is possible to find a desire itself pleasant, then it is possible to have a desire for a desire. In other words, if you can't see anything pleasant in x, then you will have a very hard time convincing Socrates that any attitude you have towards x counts as desire.

169b4 ["I divine"]: the verb *manteuomai* is related to the noun *manteia*, which refers to the power of divination (e.g. determining the will of the gods by the examination of the entrails of sacrificial animals), and also to the noun *mantis*, which refers to a diviner, seer or prophet (see 173c3 below). Socrates' use of this word is extremely interesting because many scholars question the status of the additional claims Socrates brings into his refutation. For example, Socrates himself points out that his very first refutation of Charmides depended upon the claim that temperance is among the fine things (160d1-2). Neither Socrates nor Charmides claimed to *know* that temperance is among the fine things. At *Cratylus* 411b4 Socrates uses *manteuomai* for an idea that has just popped into his head, but he takes it very seriously, so while it is something less than knowledge, it is also more than a mere guess or a baseless conjecture. (It is also worth comparing Aristotle's use of *manteuomai* at *Rhetoric* 1.13.1373b7, which also seems to refer to something that is less than knowledge, but more than a guess).

169c3 ["confounded"]: see note on 155c5 above.

169d1 ["concealing"]: at *Cratylus* 395b6 Plato uses this same verb (*epikaluptō*) to say that the name "Atreus" hides its etymology. Xenophon uses this word to explain why one ought not track the hare while snow is falling: the snow *conceals* the hare's tracks (*On Hunting* 8.1). Socrates is saying that Critias is covering his tracks. Is Plato imputing to Critias deliberate intellectual dishonesty? See also how Critias responded to Socrates' earlier refutation at 165a8-b3. How we interpret these passages can affect how we think Plato is treating Critias in this dialogue, e.g. do we think that Critias pointed out a genuine problem in Socrates' assumptions at 165ee-166a2, or was he failing to understand Socrates' actual point?

169d6 ["touched on earlier"]: at 167a1-2.

170b12 ["know that he knows"]: this question makes my translator's head explode. Socrates uses three different Greek words for knowledge in this one short sentence: how will he know (*oida*) that he knows (*gignōskō*) by means of this knowledge (*epistēmē*). It is not clear whether he has 3, 2 or only 1 kind of knowledge in mind (compare *Euthydemus* 277e3-278b2).

170c9 ["to know *that* you know, not *what* you know"]: this sentence is all that Socrates actually says here; I've added the preceding two sentences because Socrates is being highly abstract, compressed, and elliptical. We might put his point here by saying that in medical school doctors learn which medicines cure which illnesses, but if temperance is the knowledge of knowledge, then it is temperance that tells you that what you learned in medical school actually counts as *knowledge*. But even if this sounds as if it makes sense, Socrates is about to argue that it does not (see 171a11–c2).

170d5 ["to discern"]: at 167a1-8 Socrates and Critias agreed that the ability to discern who does and who does not have the knowledge they profess to have is an important consequence of the kind of self-knowledge they are considering. Upon consideration, they cannot support this claim. See also *Laches* 189e1.

170e10 ["only the temperate person"]: they agreed to this at 167a1-8.

171c2 ["a true doctor"]: Critias' notion that a good manager of doctors does not need to be a doctor himself, and hence doesn't need to study medicine in addition to studying management, is similar to Protagoras' notion that he can teach people to be good citizens without teaching them arithmetic, astronomy, geometry and music (see *Protagoras* 318d9-319a2; see note on *Protagoras* 318e5). Plato argues that those who wield political power must be well educated on a broad range of fundamental sciences (cf. *Republic* 7.525a9-531d4).

171d6 ["a mistake"]: *hamartētos* is closely related to *hamartēma* (see note on 157b5 above) and also to *hamartia*, which is used at 171e7 ("error," see note on 171e7 below). A "mistake" is in between a "wrong" (*adikēma*) and a "misfortune" (*atuchēma*). If I deliberately burn your field to ruin your crop I do something *wrong*, and you are right to sue me in court to pay you for your loss. If I do a careful and controlled burn of the stubble in my field and as a result of some unforeseeable accident your field catches on fire despite my taking all reasonable precautions, it's a *misfortune* and insurance should take care of it. In between those two kinds of cases are mistakes: if I innocently burn part of your field thinking that it is my field, then I make a *mistake*. This is more than a misfortune because I truly am responsible for the burning of your field (and perhaps I should have been more careful); but it is less than doing something wrong because I really didn't intend any harm to your field, I really did think I was burning my field. I don't really deserve to be punished for a *mistake* the same way I deserve to be punished for doing something *wrong*, but I should take responsibility for my mistake and compensate you for your loss. (Aristotle distinguishes *hamartia* from *hamartēma* as an "essential mistake" as opposed to an "accidental mistake," e.g. a poet makes an essential mistake when he makes a poetic mistake, e.g. violates a rule of the meter, and he makes an accidental mistake if he describes something inaccurately, e.g. poetically describing horses as moving in ways that they do not move in reality; *Poetics* 25.1460b15-22). Also, in the Christian bible, *hamartia* is typically translated as "sin").

172e7 ["error"]: *hamartia*. Socrates may be overlooking a very serious problem: even if you never make a *mistake*, it does not necessarily follow that you never make an *error*. I may make absolutely no mistakes in preparing to cut a piece of marble according to the specifications I was given, but if someone without my knowledge and beyond my control interferes, then my cut may not be the correct one: I may make an error (the wrong cut) without making a mistake (I did everything correctly). Some troubles are unforeseeable and beyond our control. Socrates may overlook exactly the same point at *Euthydemus* 281a1-282a6.

172a3 ["happy"]: *eudaimōn*. The inference is far more obvious in Greek than in English. "*Eudaimōn*" begins with the prefix "*eu-*" which is the adverb from *agathos* ("good"), and is the same word that Socrates just used twice (at 172a2 and a3) when he spoke of actions being done "well." The "*-daimōn*" part refers to the gods, and so a "*eudaimōn*" person is someone whose life includes all the rich blessings the gods can bestow upon a mortal. Primarily Greeks thought of things like health, property, wealth, status, family, friends, honor, power and virtue as blessings of the gods. I hesitate to translate "*eudaimōn*" as "happy," because in English "happy" often refers to a transient feeling of pleasure, which is most definitely not what "*eudaimōn*" means. This word occurs below at 173e6-7, e8, e10, and 174a11. At 176a5 it is used with *makarios* (176a1), which may simply be a synonym, although it may also be used to indicate a more glorious kind of happiness.

172b4 ["learn more easily"]: if you must be a doctor in order to recognize other doctors, and hence, to manage doctors effectively, then the super-ordinate craft of the manager will require much study. The expert manager will need something like encyclopedic knowledge of many crafts (a "second order" knowledge of "first order" crafts). If politics involves managing all crafts, then politicians will need to have an extremely demanding education. Critias is well educated, but not *that* well educated. The "learn more easily" standard is much more readily met.

172b7 ["weaker and less efficient"]: because Socrates disavows knowledge, perhaps he would put his own refutations in this category (see his self-deprecating remarks at 175a9-b2 and 175e6). But we cannot definitively say that this is what he means, because he doesn't say what someone learns if he "learns the knowledge of the thing he learns." On a formal interpretation, when you learn the *knowledge* of what you are learning, you are also learning the formal features of knowledge, e.g. the use of precise definitions of basic terms so that you may think clearly, as well as how to employ the principle of non-contradiction so that you may think consistently. On a content-based interpretation, when you learn the *knowledge* of what you are learning, you are also learning specific strategies for discovery, proof and explanation. In my opinion, the real difficulty of this passage is not what Socrates says (it is only a suggestion), but Critias' agreement without asking for clarification: what exactly does Critias think he is agreeing to?

172c4 ["empty handed"]: literally he says that perhaps they inquired to "no benefit" (*ouden chrēston*). Surely he does not mean that the investigation has been worthless or a waste of time: the issues they have broached are quite interesting and have laid the foundation for very worthwhile research (see his comment on the "great man" at 169a1-2). His "*ouden chrēston*" comment derives from the next problem he sees, and which he gets Critias to see, finally, at 174b10-175a8. Investigating the knowledge of knowledge seems to be a dead end; perhaps instead they should focus on the knowledge of good and bad.

172c5 ["paradoxical result"]: compare 167c4 and 168a10. Here Socrates has in mind a different paradox that he is about to explain. Socrates typically sees a problem in advance, and then leads his interlocutor to see it also. Is he "setting them up to fail" in an objectionable way, or is he genuinely offering them the opportunity to prevent the problem from arising by noticing something along the way that he hasn't noticed?

172e4 ["By the dog"]: Socrates uses this expression at *Phaedo* 98e5; *Cratylus* 411b3; *Gorgias* 461a7-b1; *Republic* 3.399e5, 8.567d12, and 9.592a7. It is a bit peculiar, but in *Wasps* Aristophanes has the character Sōsias swear "by god" (*ma Di'* on line 76) and then swear "by the dog" (*ma ton kun'* on line 83), so Socrates wasn't the only one to use this expression, and it probably was not seen as objectionable. At *Gorgias* 482b5 Socrates exclaims, "By the dog, the god of the Egyptians," so perhaps he's swearing by Anubis, the Egyptian god who guides the souls of the dead from this life to the afterlife. Perhaps there is deep significance here, but it may also be nothing more than a colorful turn of phrase. It certainly would not have been perceived to be any form of blasphemy or religious heterodoxy.

173a7 ["gate of horn"]: at *Odyssey* 19.562-67 Penelope tells Odysseus (in disguise as *Aithōn* the beggar) that dreams coming through the gate of horn actually come to pass (the pun is that "horn" is *keras*, and "come to pass" is *krainō*), but dreams coming through the gate of ivory are deceitful (the pun is that "ivory" is *elephas* and "deceive" is *elephairomai*). Her dream is fulfilled. By contrast, the deceitful dream Zeus sends Agamemnon is not said to pass through any gate at all (*Iliad* 2.16-19; it is met with suspicion at lines 80-81 and it almost leads to the complete destruction of the Greek force).

173c3 ["divination"]: cf. *Laches* 195e1-196a3.

174b11 ["in a circle"]: at 163e10-11 Critias defined temperance as "the doing of good things." Does Plato think that the circle is worthless or pointless? In other words, even if they were closer to the truth at 163e10 than they are here, was the discussion in between worth having? See note on 166e2 above.

174e1 ["it will include"]: Critias favors a principle of transitivity, so that if A manages B, and B produces x, then A may be said to have produced x. Socrates argues that transitivity holds only if the superordinate managerial craft possessed by A includes the sub-ordinate craft possessed by B (see note on 172b4 above, and note on 174e5 below).

174e5 ["a while ago"]: at 171b7-c9. Again (see note on 172b4 above), if temperance is not going to require the comprehensive study of all craft knowledge, then its scope will have to be quite restricted.

175a9 ["I was right"]: at 172c2-6.

175b3 ["real things"]: see also 166d2-6 and 169a1-7. On the idea that a lawgiver gives real things names see *Cratylus* 388e1-389a3. It is difficult to deny that Socrates is a "realist" in the sense that he believes the virtues exist independently of our beliefs about them, our concepts of them, and the language we use to discuss them. He is not a "subjectivist" or a "cultural relativist" about the virtues, which would make sense if he is inventing what we think of today as the science of human behavior (psychological science).

175b6 ["we granted"]: at 169d2-4.

175c1 ["we conceded"]: at 172c6-d2.

175c7 ["nothing more unreasonable"]: the pinnacle of Socratic wisdom is to eschew false pretentions to knowledge (*Apology* 23a3-c1).

175e1 ["being most temperate"]: some scholars have argued that there is a "Socratic fallacy" in inferring that you have no right to use term T if you cannot provide an adequate definition of T. This certainly is a fallacy, but if it is Socratic, then Socrates himself violates it here: all admit that they have failed to define temperance, but Socrates nevertheless still refers to temperance with seeming confidence. Of course, one might think that Socrates is being ironic: it is possible to argue that Charmides' inability to define temperance *proves* that he is not in fact temperate, and Socrates knows it (cf. 158e7-159a7). On the other hand, Socrates claimed that if temperance is in Charmides, then it gives Charmides some perception of it, from which he can form an opinion about it. Socrates did not say that it would be easy to form a true opinion of temperance that would hold firm upon examination; such an opinion might well take some time to develop.

175e4 ["has turned out"]: the present participle "*ousan*" indicates that Socrates is not looking to the future to find out whether using the charm will prove beneficial; it already appears to have had no effect, which entails that Socrates thinks he's actually used the charm already. But where? Also, he does say "if" (*ei*), so perhaps he is allowing that there may still be some hope for the charm to take effect.

176c8 ["under orders"]: the dialogue ends very playfully with a role-reversal. At the beginning, Charmides was the object of erotic attention, and the one to be seduced, but now he is the one making Socrates submit to his desires. There is a similar reversal at *Symposium* 217a2-219d2. Also, portraying himself as a soldier under orders (as if Critias is his commanding officer) reminds us that Socrates himself has just returned from the battle at Potidaea. And finally, the issue of Socrates' consent recalls the question of persuading Socrates to tell Charmides about the charm ("persuade me" at 156a3).

NOTES ON LACHES

178a1 ["You have seen"]: the *Gorgias*, *Hippias Minor* and *Ion* also begin after a demonstration. The *Euthydemus* actually includes a demonstration, but Euthydemus and Dionysodorus are portrayed as having given up teaching how to fight in armor and instead teach virtue (*Euthydemus* 273c2-d9). Sparta had a mandatory system of public education that focused on athletics and martial arts (for both boys and girls). In Athens, education was voluntary by hiring private tutors. Stesilaus is the name of the man who just put on the demonstration (183c8); Laches is familiar with him and has quite a low opinion of him (183c8-184a7).

178a4 ["speak freely"]: although *parrhēsia* can refer to a vice (an unrestrained tongue, *Phaedrus* 240e6), it can also refer to a great privilege among Athenians (*Republic* 8.557b5; Euripides, *Hippolytus* 422), and together with *isēgoria* (the equal right to speak in the legislative assembly) is almost identical with democratic freedom (Polybius, *Histories* 2.38.6). Slaves lack the right of *parrhēsia* when speaking to their masters, and so to speak one's mind honestly and openly is a sign of being a free person. Lysimachus repeats the verb at 179c1-2 (Socrates uses it with Charmides at *Charmides* 156a9-b1), and Laches uses the noun at 189a1. See also *Gorgias* 487a3, b1. *Parrhēsia* is important later for Christians (e.g. Acts 2:29).

178b3 ["knowledgeable"]: here I translate the aorist infinitive of *gignōskō*, although I think the aorist participle of the same word is used in the sense of judgment immediately afterwards.

179a2 ["Thucydides"]: not the famous historian.

179a6 ["teenagers"]: a *meirakion* was under the age of 21, but older than a *pais*. Lysimachus and Melesias were given excellent educations when they were *paides* (cf. "paedagogy"), but their education did not continue (*Meno* 93e11-94a7, 94b8-e2). In the *Meno*, Socrates uses Lysimachus and Melesias—together with the children of Themistocles and Pericles—as evidence that virtue is not teachable (94e2). Assuming that Anytus is correct to say that the best way to teach virtue is to follow the advice of any fine and good Athenian you happen to meet (*Meno* 92e3-6), then the failure of these fine and good Athenians to teach their own children virtue seems to entail that virtue is not teachable.

179b1 ["you both have sons"]: Demosthenes refers to a scoundrel named Melanopus, the son of someone named Laches, but we cannot be sure that this is the Laches of Plato's dialogue (*Against Timocrates* 24.127). Nicias had a son named Niceratus (*Laches* 200d1, he was named after his grandfather, Nicias' father; *Gorgias* 472a5-6) who was well regarded. Unfortunately, his great family wealth is probably what caught the attention of the Thirty Tyrants, who had him put to death (probably in 404 BCE). Nicias' son is mentioned as being present at the discussion in the *Republic* (1.327c2).

179b7 ["messmates"]: according to an old sailor's maxim, "a messmate before a shipmate, a shipmate before a stranger;" Greeks seem to have had a similar view (cf. Aeschines, *On the Embassy* 2.22). In the Classical Period, it seems to have been the custom to eat only two meals each day: a light lunch (or "brunch," *ariston*), and a substantial dinner (*deipnon*) in the evening. It was not uncommon for men to dine together in dining-rooms with the same group of men dining together on a regular basis—as in military practice.

179c3 ["admirable"]: the word *kalos* can refer to physical beauty, and so can be a synonym for *kallos* (e.g. *Charmides* 153d4). The difference is that *kallos* seems normally reserved for the physical beauty of people (both mortal and immortal) and things (e.g. garments, ships, honeycombs), while *kalos* has at least two additional main uses. First, it can describe a favorable quality of something, e.g. a "fair" wind (*Odyssey* 14.253), "genuine" silver (Xenophon, *Memorabilia* 3.1.9), "auspicious" sacrifices (Aeschylus, *Seven Against Thebes* 379). Second, it can also be used in a moral sense to refer to an honorable, noble or virtuous individual (*Odyssey* 17.381; Xenophon, *Memorabilia* 1.1.16). I often translate it as "fine," since I think this word is ambiguous in English in roughly the way "*kalos*" is ambiguous in Greek. The opposite of *kalos* in the moral sense is *aischros*.

179d1-2 ["the affairs of others"]: here Lysimachus appears to draw the line between minding your own business and minding someone else's business so that it includes your own sons, but nobody else's. If that is what Lysimachus intends, then he assumes that "one's own business" is not entirely selfish, though it doesn't include very many others. "Minding one's own business" is considered as a possible answer to the question "what is temperance?" in the *Charmides* (at 161b3-164d3). In the *Republic*, Plato's "Noble Lie" is deliberately designed to get people to think of and care for their fellow citizens as members of their immediate family (3.414b8-c2, 414d1-415c7, 415d3-4). In fact, Plato argues that "*idiōsis*" ("isolation" or "privatization") is a chief cause of dissolution in a city, when fellow citizens do not say "mine" and "not mine" in unison (5.462a9-c5). Notice also that "*idiōsis*" is the opposite of *koinōnia* ("partnership" or "fellowship"), which Lysimachus is about to propose establishing between himself, Melesias, Laches and Nicias (see note on 180a1 below).

179d7 ["make them the very best"]: the heroic warrior Achilles was given the following command by his father Peleus, "Always be the best, and be pre-eminent over others" (*Iliad* 11.784; Glaucus' father Hippolochus gave him this same advice, 6.208). In the *Iliad* this clearly expresses an aristocratic value. In democratic Athens of the 5th century, it would be alarming for Lysimachus and Melesias to express the same value, since, e.g., equality under the law (*isonomia*) and the equal right of speaking in the *Ekklēsia* (*isēgoria*) were important democratic values. Perhaps they mean only that they want their children to be the best that they can be, not that they want their children to rule over other Athenians.

179e2 ["fight in armor"]: *hoplomachia* is the art of fighting heavily armed, i.e. with a *hoplon* (a heavy round shield), greaves, breastplate, helmet, spear and short sword. The "hoplite" phalanx formed the core of Greek armies. The primary abilities needed by the hoplite soldier were (1) to be able to march at different speeds while remaining in formation (since different soldiers can have different natural strides) and (2) to march straight forward (since the soldiers in the right-most file tend to veer rightward so that their unprotected right sides are not directly presented to the enemy, and the soldiers to their left tend to veer rightward to gain protection from the shield that the soldier to his right is holding in his left arm; Thucydides 5.71.1). The sword was a secondary weapon and was normally not used at all. In the *Laws*, Plato includes *hoplomachia* as part of military training for young men and women, but he also includes music, dance, and wrestling as well as archery, light armed fighting, tactics and maneuvers, encampment and cavalry training (*Laws* 7.795d-796d, 813c-814b).

180a1 ["partnership"]: *koinōnia* is the opposite of *idiōsis* (see note on 179d1-2).

180c2 ["town"]: Athens comprised 139 "towns" (*dēmoi*). Some were very small (we might call them "villages" or "hamlets" but some were quite large. Some time after 508 BCE Cleisthenes reformed the Athenian population, grouping various numbers of towns into "districts" (*trittues*), and grouping one district from the Shore, one from the City, and one from Inland to form a "tribe" (*phulē*). There were 10 tribes, and so with 3 districts in each tribe there were 30 districts. (Before the 8th century BCE the *phulai* may actually have been extended families or clans). Cleisthenes' main purpose in doing this was probably to break down traditional power blocks, and encourage the democratization of political power. Official enrollment in your town (which would be your father's town, regardless of whether you actually lived there or not) when you turned 18 years old guaranteed you Athenian citizenship, with all the rights, privileges, duties and immunities pertaining thereto. The 139 towns were traditional, and so it is likely that in all but the largest of them, you were at least acquainted with every family in it. Each town (and each tribe) had its own political organization to oversee its financial, military, and religious affairs.

180c4 ["training of young men"]: it must have been galling to Plato that his mentor was charged with "corrupting the youth" (*Apology* 24b9) when no Athenian had spent more time and thoughtful consideration into the proper training of young men.

180d1 ["music"]: literally, *mousikē* referred to the arts of the Muses, and so included both "music and lyrics" in today's sense. Since Homer and Hesiod sang beautifully about a wide range of topics (e.g. history, theology, military science, ethics, politics), a "musical" instruction could also include a wide range of topics. So Greek education in *mousikē* is the origin of what we call "arts and letters" or "the liberal arts." In the *Republic* Plato seems to distinguish three branches of education: *grammata* (i.e. basic literacy, reading and writing; 3.402a7-b3), *gumnastikē* (physical, athletic and military training; 3.403c9-d5), and *mousikē* (everything else). Probably they did not rigidly separate prose and poetry (the earliest analysis of prose rhythm is Aristotle's *Rhetoric* 1408b21-1409a21).

180d1 ["Damon"]: Damon developed an "ethos theory" of rhythm, i.e. that certain rhythms are associated with (or even help to produce in people) certain states of character (*Republic* 3.400b1-c5). In fact, Plato seems to accept Damon's theory that the forms of music allowed in a city can have a great impact on its political, social and legal order (4.424c5-6). Later in the *Laches*, Socrates says that he, Nicias and Damon are "associates" (*hetairoi*)—this could mean that they are friends or acquaintances, but it may mean that both Socrates and Nicias have actually been Damon's students (197d1-3; see also Nicias' defense of Damon at 200b5-6). But we must bear in mind that the study of "music" typically included the study of lyrics, i.e. poetry (see previous note). This was a cause for concern among many. Plato's *Protagoras* claims that Agathocles used music as a screen to conceal the other things he was teaching (*Protagoras* 316e1-3). He doesn't say what those other things are, but Plutarch says that he was ostracized from Athens because of the influence he had with Pericles, and because he used music as a screen to hide the fact that he was urging Plutarch in the direction of tyranny (Plutarch, *Pericles* 4.1-2). To this day there are those who fear that the study of the liberal arts will have politically pernicious effects.

180d7 ["son of Sophroniscus"]: Athenians typically identify one another with a name, a patronymic and a town of origin, e.g. "Socrates the son of Sophroniscus from the town of Alopece." Often if you knew two of the three, you could guess the third, so it is not an especially surprising coincidence that Lysimachus knew of, and was friends with, Socrates' father.

180e1 ["you owe it to me"]: *dikaios* means "just" or "right." The related noun *dikaia* refers to the virtue of justice, which is a main concern of Plato's *Republic*. *Dikaios* occurs here and at 181c2, 181d3, 189b4, 192d6, 200d5, and 200e4.

181a4 ["by Hera"]: it was uncommon to swear by Hera. "By god" or "by Zeus" were far more common. In fact, of the thirteen principle deities (the twelve Olympians plus Hestia), Hera is the only who is never invoked in an oath in any surviving comedy (or fragment thereof). It is, therefore, interesting that Socrates himself swears by Hera six times in Plato's dialogues: *Apology* 24e9, *Hippias Major* 287a2, *Gorgias* 449d5, *Phaedrus* 230b2 and *Theaetetus* 154d3. The fact that Lysimachus swears by Hera is evidence that this was a practice peculiar to Alopece, but we do not know why that would be so. Perhaps there was an important temple to Hera there.

181b1 ["country"]: what Laches says in Greek is more elegant since he says that Socrates is a credit not only to his "*pater*" (father) but also to his "*patris*" (fatherland). Since WWII, however, "fatherland" has taken on quite a different connotation than it had in Socrates' day.

181b1 ["Delium"]: in 424 the Peloponnesian War had been dragging on for eight years. Historically, Greeks expected a "war" to be settled in one afternoon: the disputing parties sent their armies against one another, and whoever won the battle, won the war, and won the dispute. For a war to last eight years was unthinkable—until it happened. The Athenians thought they could end it by fomenting democratic revolutions in Boeotia (militarily and strategically important allies of the Spartans), and by mounting a surprise invasion. The Boeotians discovered the plan and had time to send a strong army against the Athenians and defeated them. According to Alcibiades, Socrates helped his friends to mount a solid, defensive retreat, and he was able to save Laches' life (*Symposium* 220e-221b). See Thucydides 4.91-96. Obviously this detail is an interesting one to mention in a dialogue whose main topic is courage.

181d7 ["one of you two"]: from 181d8-184c8 we get a pair of speeches, pro and con. Thucydides regularly pairs speeches like this in his history of the Peloponnesian War. While this approach might seem, in one way, "fair to both sides," at the same time the two speeches can appear to cancel one another out: both sides can seem "equally reasonable" in the sense that reasons are presented for both sides. If that happens, on what are we supposed to base our ultimate decision? Not reason, it might appear. Socrates' initial response is at 186d3-187b5. Perhaps his secondary response is at 190d7-199e12. If so, then the secondary response leaves something to be desired, though it may be the best we have (compare *Charmides* 172b1-8).

182a2 ["horsemanship"]: horses remained status symbols long after service in the cavalry ceased to be the privilege of the upper classes. Generally, horses were not work animals, and so their upkeep demanded disposable income. First and foremost a "free man" did not have to work for someone else to earn a living: he provided for himself and his family from his own resources. One had to be able to do this to afford the full panoply of hoplite armor and weaponry.

182a3 ["this great contest"]: the Peloponnesian War.

182a7 ["broken formation"]: the primary goal of phalanx warfare is to break the enemy's formation, because that is when a hoplite soldier is at his most vulnerable. The movie cliché in which two armies run at each other and engage in multiple one-on-one battles—like a massive outdoors barroom brawl—is ludicrous. See also note on 179e2 above.

182c6 ["more daring and more courageous"]: Nicias will later suggest that there is a close connection between courage and daring (194e11-199e12). "Daring" (*tharseleos*) could also be translated as "bold," "confident" or "audacious;" the core idea seems to be that of not hanging back to play it safe, but launching an attack (which could be "bold" or "audacious") although doing so puts you at risk (which may require "confidence"). It occurs here and at 194e12-195a1, 195c1, 195e6, 196d2, 198b3, b6, 198c3, 199b1, b3, b9, and 199c6.

183c7-8 ["extremely unlucky"]: this comment is at odds with the previous two suggestions, i.e. (1) men like Stesilaus avoid battle like cowards, and (2) if they really were experts in military conflict, they would have made names for themselves in battle (cf. "those who can't, teach"). So Laches is clearly being ironic here (as he is elsewhere).

183d5 ["spear-sword"]: this is the earliest occurrence of the word "*dorudrepanon*." When it refers to a weapon, "*doru*" refers to a spear (or to only its shaft). A *drepanon* is a curved blade, e.g. a scythe for mowing grass (Homer, *Odyssey* 18.368), a blade for pruning vines (Plato, *Republic* 1.333d3), or a scimitar (Herodotus, *Histories* 5.112.2). So a "*dorudrepanon*" is a spear with a curved blade attached to it. We might call it a "halberd," but that would make it sound as if it was a normal weapon, and to the Greeks it was nothing of the sort. In theory, a spear with an additional curved blade could be used not only to stab enemy soldiers, but also to hook and unseat soldiers on horseback, or to cut sails and rigging of enemy ships (cf. Strabo, *Geography* 4.4.1). However, Greek warships stowed rigging, sails and masts before battle, so at sea a *dorudrepanon* would be useful only against merchant ships or transports. Perhaps more obviously to Greeks, a *dorudrepanon* would be useless (or counter-productive) to a hoplite soldier in a phalanx, since the scythe blade is likely to get caught on the shield or armor of either friend or foe, and, more importantly, it must be wielded with two hands (a hoplite needs to hold his shield with his left arm).

183d7 ["fell out"]: *apebē* can mean "occurred," but it can also mean "disembarked," which is clever because the event that occurred almost resulted in Stesilaus falling overboard.

183e2 ["the other ship's tackle"]: others translate "*skeuos*" as "rigging" because it was easier to capture a cargo ship if you cut its sails or the ropes that held the sails aloft. So other translators are attributing to Stesilaus a sensible stratagem. If we stick with what Laches actually says, then we must assume either that Stesilaus tried to snag the rigging, missed and got his weapon stuck in the ship's cargo, or else he was deliberately trying to snag the cargo and pull it overboard for later retrieval—neither of these scenarios reflect well on Stesilaus, especially given the actual outcome.

184b5 ["reckless"]: Laches uses the comparative ("*thrasuteros*"), so perhaps "emboldened" is a better translation, but I don't want to confuse Laches' *thrasus* here with Nicias' *tharseleos* at 182c6 (see note above). Nicias will later suggest that there is a close connection between courage and daring (194e11-199e12), but he sharply distinguishes courage and recklessness (197c1).

184b7 ["vilified"]: perhaps "slandered" would be a more accurate translation because Plato has Laches use the word "*diabolē*," which was, in Plato's view, one of the main causes of the prosecution and execution of Socrates (see *Apology* 18d2, 19a1, b1, 20c5, 20d4, 20e3, 21b2, 23a2, 24a3, 28a7-8, 37b2). Also, I think that this sentence is clear enough on its own so that there was no need for Plato to have Laches add the next sentence—again I suspect that Plato has Socrates' unfortunate demise in mind: at *Meno* 92e3-95a1 Anytus seems to embody the attitude Laches describes here.

184d5 ["the majority"]: cf. *Crito* 47a2-d6. Many scholars focus on Socrates' criticism of following the majority and infer that he opposes democracy and supports oligarchy. The inference is invalid. What makes the majority inadequate judges is not that they are many as opposed to few, but that they lack knowledge (*epistēmē*, *Laches* 184d8) or intelligence (*phronēsis*, *Crito* 47a10). So if Socrates' activity as gadfly—stinging *hoi polloi* into taking their own values more seriously (*Apology* 30e5, and see note on 20c8)—ever becomes successful, and the populace at large becomes intelligent and knowledgeable, then Socrates would be an ardent supporter of democracy and of consulting the majority on important issues. Plato's dim view of democracy results not from a dim view of the working classes, but because he thinks that the majority of people, regardless of their lineage, are largely uneducable (see the "Noble Lie" at *Republic* 3.414b8-e6).

184e4 ["In all likelihood"]: "*eikos*" is a participial form of "*eoika*," which means "to look like," "to seem," or "to befit." So the participle means "like," "seemly" or "probable." Often (especially in philosophical writings) it means "reasonable," and some translators go that way here—making Melesias sound confident and logical. But I am uncertain about this character. Plato gives him only 7 lines to speak in the entire dialogue, totaling a mere 17 Greek words. The last thing he says is, "What do you mean?" (or "I don't understand"). I feel that he is cagey, either because he is intimidated by being in the company of Nicias and Laches (who are far more accomplished and respected than he is), or because knows he's not as smart as Socrates, or perhaps because he is inclined to believe the popular slander against Socrates (cf. *Apology* 18e5-19c1) and fears that he's being set up to be verbally tricked and embarrassed.

185c5 ["ointment"]: *pharmakon*, see note on *Charmides* 155b6. An obvious answer to Socrates' question here is "both," because a *pharmakon* can be either medicine or poison, but his point is still reasonable because you won't know what to do with the medicine (or poison) unless you first know whether you wish to heal or to harm the eyes.

185d10 ["that for the sake of which"]: Socrates does not deny that an expert in horses is also an expert in bridles, but he does not insist upon it. An expert in horses considers only bridles that can be used on horses, not hypothetical bridles that are too large, too small, too heavy, or too frail to use on a real horse. An advisor who considers bridles *for the sake of horses* can ignore these more exotic bridles.

185e2 ["souls"]: *psuchē*, see note on *Charmides* 154e1.

185e4 ["training"]: *therapeia* (from which we derive "therapy") is service or attendance (a *therapōn* is an attendant, a *therapaina* is a handmaid; the abstract noun *therapeia* is used in religious contexts for acts of worship or service to the gods, but it is also used for medical treatment). Obviously it would be anachronistic to say that Socrates is looking for a "pediatric psychologist" or an expert in "developmental psychology," but he clearly is suggesting that there is a need for something like medical science of the human *psuchē*.

186a8 ["they have good souls themselves"]: all Socrates says is that they are "good" (*agathos*), and in theory this could mean that they are good teachers. However, he uses *agathos* again at 186b4-5 in reference to the product of the training he expects of these people. If we accept the legitimacy of the command, "physician, heal thyself!" then we are warranted in rejecting the credentials of someone who claims to be able to make souls good, but who himself lacks a good soul.

186b7 ["accusations"]: Socrates was accused of, among other things, corrupting the youth (*Apology* 23d1-2, etc.). The charge must have been galling to Plato.

186c3 ["Sophists"]: *sophistēs* is related to *sophia* (see note on *Charmides* 155d4). The primary sense is that of being a master of one's craft, and expert practicioner, and is applied to poets, musicians, and seers.

Solon, as one of the famous "seven Sages," was called a *sophistēs* (Herodotus 1.29.1, Isocrates Antidosis 15.235). In the late 5th century it was applied to itinerant teachers of grammar, rhetoric, mathematics and politics like Protagoras, Gorgias and Prodicus. In the 2nd century CE Lucian refers to Jesus of Nazareth as a *sophistēs* (*De morte Peregrini* 13).

186c4 ["fine and good"]: "*kalos te k'agathos*" is a stock expression (cf. 187a8), perhaps it is a bit like "a decent, upstanding young man" in English. It could be used with or without specifically moral implications; it could be used with or without specifically aristocratic implications. It could express purely generic or vague approbation. It is naturally opposed to "*phaulos*" (e.g. at 187a7) which primarily describes something as being of little or no worth (and this can be meant in a moral or aristocratic sense, or not).

187a2 ["free time"]: *scholē* is leisure, rest or ease. Literally, a "scholar" is someone who doesn't have to work for a living, and has the time to sit around studying and discussing issues that may not be directly related to earning an income.

187b1 ["the proverbial Carian"]: The Carians were from southwest Asia Minor (modern day Turkey) near Halicarnassus (they believed they were indigenous to the region, but the Greeks believed they had migrated there from the nearby islands—the absence of prehistoric remains could be interpreted as support for the Greek view). Carians often served as mercenaries, and so were used militarily when Athenians wanted to protect their own soldiers. Socrates is saying that Laches and Nicias should not use the children of Lysimachus and Melesias like the modern day "guinea pigs" in their first experiment.

187b8 ["a pithos"]: I've kept the word "pithos" because in English there really is no equivalent. A Greek *pithos* could stand 5 feet tall, and filled with oil or wine could weigh well over a ton. Often they were elaborately decorated and were stunningly beautiful works of art. Obviously making a *pithos* was reserved for master potters, not beginners.

187c3 ["Obviously"]: I take a perverse pride in my translation of this sentence. Unlike Socrates, whose long sentences are long because they express complex though coherent thoughts; Lysimachus rambles.

187d1 ["educated"]: the boys are teenagers, and so they already had the traditional education provided by families of means, i.e. reading, writing, music (including the poetry of Homer and Hesiod), and gymnastic training. Traditionally, no more education was expected, so Lysimachus' offhand comment here suggests changing attitudes towards education among the Athenian upper classes. No wonder Sophists flocked to Athens, happy to charge fees for "higher education."

188a3 ["put to the test"]: *basanizō* is used here and at b5 below. Literally, it means "to rub on the touchstone." Rub gold on a touchstone and it leaves a mark (gold is a relatively soft metal); rub fool's gold (iron pyrite) on a touchstone and it leaves no mark. This was a traditional metaphor used when torturing slaves for information—without torture, a slave can be expected to say whatever his master wants him to say; torture was thought to be the only way to get the truth out of a slave (perhaps because a slave who testifies against his master will be punished by his master unless the slave gave that testimony under duress, and hence cannot be blamed). Plato uses this word at *Republic* 2.361c5-6 for a situation in which a man's commitment to justice is painfully put to the test. Alcibiades poignantly describes being put to the test by Socrates at *Symposium* 215e1-216c3.

188b3 ["Solon"]: one of the famed "seven sages." Nicias is referring to Fragment 10 of Solon's poetry.

188b5 ["horrible or horrific"]: Plato gives Nicias a very clever phrase, "*aēthes oud' au aēdes.*" Most translate this as "unusual or unpleasant," using the repeated "un-" to capture the near identity of "*aēthes*" ("out of character") and "*aēdes*" ("distasteful"). But in fact Socratic interrogation is unusual, and many find it quite distasteful—we must not overlook the fact that the word he uses twice for being "put to the test" by Socrates is the same word in Greek for being tortured. Nicias is not denying the obvious, he is saying that despite the fact that Socratic interrogation is torturous, it's not all *that* bad, so don't be a wimp—it'll be good for you.

188c4 ["not one but two"]: Laches begins by saying that his view is "*haplous*" (single, simple) and then says it is not "*haplous*" but "*diplous*" (double, compound). One way of translating this makes him sound like an idiot (e.g. "I have one view of discussion, or, rather, not one view, but two"). But (a) he's not an idiot, (b) the view he is about to express can legitimately be expressed as one view (i.e. one's deeds ought to match one's words) or as two views (i.e. (i) it is good for one's deeds to match one's words, and (ii) it is bad for one's deeds not to match one's words), and (c) what Laches says accurately exploits an ambiguity in the word "*haplous*" since "simple" can mean "single" as opposed to "double," but it can also mean "plain" as opposed to "fancy." Laches' view is rather humble and unsophisticated, though it could be expressed as two sides of the same coin.

188c7 ["virtue"]: *aretē*, see notes on *Charmides* 158a1 and *Apology* 20b6.

188d6 ["Ionian"]: today we distinguish between major and minor keys (or scales); the Greeks distinguished at least half a dozen (the most common names are the four listed here by Laches). In the *Republic*, Plato suggests that music in the different keys had different effects on the soul, and therefore we ought to be very careful about which kinds of music we allow children to hear since their souls are still being formed. He seems to have thought that the Dorian and Phrygian modes fostered endurance and confidence, respectively, and in his ideal city he outlaws all other keys (*Republic* 3.399a3-c6). Aristotle seems largely to agree with Plato, (especially about the affects of the Dorian and Phrygian modes; *Politics* 8.5.1340b3-5), though he does not think the other modes deserve to be outlawed. It may be that the Dorian mode originated in the Greek world and that the others derive from outside the Greek world, but it reflects race-based assumptions to think that the Greek mode is especially connected with courage (and, hence, that the others are not). See 193d11 below.

189c1 ["no one"]: there is a triple negative in the Greek. It is not ungrammatical and so it cannot possibly be rendered in ordinary English. To me, Socrates sounds genuinely humbled at being so highly praised.

189e3 ["know"]: in both the abstract statement (189e3-7) and the concrete example (190a1-5) Socrates uses two different words for knowledge, and it is not at all clear whether he intends them to be interchangeable, or whether each means something significantly different. In both cases, the first knowledge-word is "*epistēmē*," which could refer to expertise, e.g. medical expertise, and so in some contexts it can be translated as "science" or "scientific knowledge" (see note on 193b5 below). Also in both cases the second knowledge-word is "*oida*," which is a very common word for knowledge (it is used over thirty times in the *Laches*) and primarily refers to knowing something in the sense of seeing it. However, this can also include mental perception, as when we say today, "Oh, I understand, now I see what you are saying." So, for example, at 190c10 below, I translate "*oida*" as "grasp."

190b8 ["what virtue is?"]: he is not concerned with defining the word "virtue" (i.e. *aretē*), or with giving an analysis of their concept of virtue (they may have quite different conceptions of virtue from one another). Clearly Socrates thinks that there is something to the following: what sight is to the eyes, and what hearing is to the ears, virtue is to the soul. Here again (see note on Charmides 158a1), Socrates seems to be trying to invent the scientific study of the human *psuchē* ("psychological science" we might call it).

190c4 ["Therefore"]: it is highly unusual for Socrates to claim to know what virtue is. An alternative interpretation would emphasize the word "therefore." On this view, his claim here is purely conditional, i.e. if we claim to be advisors on adding virtue to souls, then we know what virtue is, given that we couldn't be advisors on adding virtue to souls if we did not know what virtue is.

190e5 ["remain in formation"]: notice that Laches defines a moral property in non-moral behavioral terms. We might call this a "reductive analysis" of courage, "reducing" the moral property of being courageous to a non-moral, and non-evaluative, property. It is not clear that such an approach can possibly be successful: how could any collection of non-evaluative properties ever fully capture all there is to an evaluative property? Nicias brings an explicitly evaluative term into his account, but this raises a different problem. See note on 195c12 below.

190e7 ["I am to blame"]: on one interpretation, this is mock humility; Socrates is being ironic. Alternatively, Socrates is being sincere because he genuinely is sensitive to the way that one person can say something with one thing in mind, but someone else hears it and has a completely different idea about it (see *Euthydemus* 295b7-c9). On this interpretation, Socrates did put his question badly because he failed to put it in a way that gave Laches the same idea in answering that Socrates had in asking.

190a8 ["fleeing as well as pursuing"]: Xenophon noted that the Persian cavalry could manage to keep their horses running away, while they turned and shot arrows at their pursuers (*Anabasis* 3.3.10). The Greeks though of "Scythians" as horse-riding barbarians in the north and east. Neither Socrates nor Laches attribute to the Scythians what the Romans called "Parthian tactics" (the Parthians are from the north of what is now Iran, near the Caspian Sea): they would engage the enemy, feign a retreat, and then at a certain signal, turn on the enemy and kill them off.

191b3 ["author of rout"]: *Iliad* 5.223 (where Aeneas himself is speaking) = 8.107 (where Diomedes is speaking, after he and Sthenelus took Aeneas' horses, 5.318-30). However the description of Aeneas as "author of rout" occurs only at 8.108, so clearly Plato has 8.107-8 in mind.

191c1 ["battle of Plataea"]: in 479 Spartans, Athenians, Corinthians and others stood against the Persian army (a year after the Athenians had defeated the Persian navy in the Battle of Salamis, and Xerxes had fled back to Persia leaving his army in the capable hands of his most trusted general Mardonius). Herodotus does not describe the Spartans as employing the tactic Socrates mentions (*Histories* 9.30-84). Perhaps Plato has in mind the Spartan use of this ploy at Thermopylae (*Histories* 7.211.3). The fact that Laches does not correct Socrates and say that the tactic was used at Thermopylae in 490 rather than at Plataea in 479 suggests to me that this was simply a mistake on Plato's part. It could be used as evidence for thinking that Plato wrote this dialogue when he was quite young.

191d7 ["desires or pleasures"]: probably we should remind ourselves that the primary, literal meaning of the Greek *andreia* is "manliness." Greek sexists would call a man "soft," "effeminate" or "womanly" if he gave in to certain desires or if pleasure overcame his resolve.

191e10-11 ["the same in all these cases?"]: compare *Euthyphro* 6d9-e6 and *Meno* 72a6-d1. Sometimes this is called Plato's "one over many" assumption (cf. *Republic* 10.596a5-b4). Aristotle thinks that Plato takes this principle too far (*Nicomachean Ethics* 1.6). See notes on *Phaedo* 100b6-7 and 102b2.

192a3 ["playing the kithara"]: the kithara was the major instrument of professional and public performance. It is a member of the lyre family (distinguished from the lyre by its box-shaped soundbox as opposed to the round soundbox of the lyre), not the harp family (distinguished from the harp by having two arms of equal length joined by a crossbar from which the strings are strung to a bridge and attached to the face of the soundbox). The strings were plucked with the fingers or struck with a plectrum (made of horn, bone, or wood; ancient Greeks never used a bow). The word "kithara" is the root of the modern English "guitar." Socrates took kithara lessons late in life (*Euthydemus* 272c1-5).

192b1 ["capacity"]: *dunamis* occurs here, at b6 and at 194c3 ("up to the task"). *Dunamis* is often translated as "power," but not in the sense of "strength" or "might" (which would be *kratos*), and not in the sense of "force" (which would be *bia*). Aristotle argues that virtue involves both *dunamis* and decision (*prohairesis*): two people can have the same *dunamis* for exaggeration, but only one of them actually is an exaggerator because he decides to exaggerate (*Nicomachean Ethics* 4.7.1127b14).

192c8 ["intelligent"]: *phronēsis* has to do with the *phrēn*, i.e. the heart or mind as the seat of the passions, the appetites or the mind as involving perception, thought, imagination and in general one's wits as in the English phrase "keep your wits about you." So a person who is *phronimos* is of sound mind, is sensible, intelligent, prudent or has practical wisdom. Here I would prefer to translate *phronēsis* as "prudence," because the word probably suggests intelligent regard for one's own welfare, but today we tend to think of "prudence" as meaning "caution," or as referring to a very narrow self-interested concern that doesn't involve concern for others—neither of which is suggested by *phronēsis*. We could also translate *phronimos* as "wise," in which case we could say that Socrates is about to distinguish between "wise endurance" and "foolish endurance." However, it is probably best to reserve "wise" and "wisdom" for *sophos* and *sophia*, respectively. *Phronēsis* also occurs at 193a7 and 197e2. The related adverb *phronimōs* occurs at 192e3 and 193a4, and the related adjective *phronimos* occurs at 192d10, 192e1, and 197c1.

192d1 ["harmful and bad?"]: normally you'd expect the opposite of "fine and good" (*kalos te kai agathos*) to be "shameful and bad" (*aischros te kai kakos*). Instead, we get "harmful and bad" (*blaberos kai kakourgos*). On top of that puzzle, both *blaberos* and *kakourgos* can mean "harmful." The solution to the latter also solves the former: *kakourgos* means "harmful" in the sense of working mischief, behaving like a knave, a thief or a criminal, which is quite shameful. See note on 193d1 below.

192d8 ["because"]: *epeidēper* with the indicative (and also the particle *ara*) is causal, so Socrates is drawing a conclusion, not stating a hypothetical connection. This is important because many scholars argue that Socrates is not entitled to assert "courage is fine" as a fact; it is *merely* something that they have agreed to. Our view here will be influenced by, among other things, our answers to these two questions: (a) are there moral facts in something like the way that there are facts about speed (Socrates' illustrative case at 192b1-3)? and (b) are Laches and Socrates cognitively capable of detecting the fineness of courage? If we answer "no" to either of these questions, we will be inclined to think that Socrates is *not* entitled to assert "courage is fine" as a fact. If we answer "yes" to either of these questions, then we will not be thus inclined without additional evidence.

192e1 ["what exactly we need to be intelligent about"]: Laches has not used the phrase "intelligent endurance," he has merely agreed to Socrates' use of it. The phrase could mean any number of different things; e.g. perhaps "intelligent endurance" is different from "enduring in an intelligent action;" intelligence can be related to or distinct from skill, prudence, wisdom and other cognitive virtues; intelligence might help us to avoid things that are harmful to ourselves, to others, or to both. Some scholars argue that Socrates commits the fallacy of ambiguity. But perhaps not. In a case where Al has suffered significant—though not total—hair loss, my claim that "Betty is dating Al" may refute your claim that "Betty does not date bald men," depending upon your notion of baldness. In response to my pointing out that Betty is dating Al, you might reply, "I stand corrected," or, "Yes, but I distinguish between *bald* and *balding*; Al is only balding, not bald, so my claim is not refuted." Whether Socrates' arguments refute Laches' notion depends upon what his notion is. The *fallacy* of ambiguity is the *illicit* switching of meanings; Socrates' use of *phronēsis* is permitted both by ordinary Greek usage of the word, and by Laches' own notion of the word. If Socrates is exploiting the semantic looseness of the word, he is not doing so *illicitly*. The eristic of the Sophists clearly exploits the semantic looseness of ordinary words (e.g. *Euthydemus* 275d3-277c7, with Socrates' analysis at 277e2-278b2). The difference with the Socratic *elenchos* is that Socrates never prevents someone from drawing any distinction they like, as long as they say what they are doing (compare *Euthydemus* 295b2-296c7 with *Charmides* 163d5-7). Both elenchos and eristic can spur someone to make explicit distinctions they've taken for granted implicitly (or had never considered), but only eristic illicitly creates ambiguity in order to exploit it. (See also note on 194d2 below).

193a6 ["strategically superior position"]: it is possible that this paragraph is a sly reference to the battle of Mantinea in 418. According to Thucydides, a thousand Athenian hoplites under the command of Laches joined the Argive alliance (*History of the Peloponnesian War* 5.61.1). Seeing the Spartan army advance, the Argive alliance immediately took up a strong tactical position. Although they were at a tactical disadvantage, the Spartans marched to within javelin range of the Argive alliance. Surprisingly, the Argive army did not attack, and for one reason or another the Spartans retreated to safety (5.65.2-3). The Argive alliance did not pursue them. Angry, the rank and file among the Argive alliance blamed their generals for poor leadership because they failed to order the attack when they clearly had the advantage (5.65.5). Compounding their apparent error, the Argive alliance abandoned their position of strength and camped in the plain. When battle finally came, the Spartans won, and Laches was among the dead. As if this weren't enough to suggest that Plato has this terrible defeat in mind, Thucydides' famous editorial comment on the battle is that "although the Spartans were inferior in skill, they were superior in courage" (5.72.2). Later in the *Laches*, it is possible that Plato inserts a sly comment about the battle in which Nicias lost his life (see note on 199a2).

193b2 ["unintelligent endurance"]: Socrates did not say anything about the thought processes of the enemy; he treats that as irrelevant. Whether the enemy in these circumstances simply charges into battle without thinking things through at all, or he did think things through and incorrectly thought he had the advantage, or correctly thought he was at a disadvantage but charged anyway, in any case he would be guilty of "unintelligent endurance" (though, if we wished, we could verbally distinguish at least three different ways to describe these three different forms of "unintelligent endurance").

193b5 ["knowledge of horsemanship?"]: *epistēmē* could be "expertise," and that might be a better translation here because Socrates and Laches both assume that *epistēmē* of horsemanship is not mere "textbook knowledge" as we might say today: someone with *epistēmē* of horsemanship actually knows what he's doing on a horse and is therefore a skilled rider. Plato's epistemic vocabulary is problematic enough (e.g. what exactly is the relationship between *phronēsis* and *epistēmē*?) that I try to minimize the confusion by translating *epistēmē* as "knowledge" whenever possible. According to Diogenes Laertius (3rd century CE), Plato distinguished three kinds of *epistēmē*: (1) *poiētikē*, which creates things that are visible, e.g. architecture and shipbuilding; (2) *praktikē*, which acts but does not create anything visible, e.g. playing the harp; and (3) *theōrētikē*, which reasons and knows but neither creates nor acts, e.g. geometry (*Lives of Eminent Philosophers* 3.84).

193b10 ["craft?"]: according to Diogenes Laertius, Plato distinguished three kinds of *technē*: (1) that which gathers raw materials, e.g. mining, woodcutting; (2) that which fashions raw materials into new things, e.g. carpentry; and (3) that which uses things that have been fashioned, e.g. playing the harp (*Lives of Eminent Philosophers* 3.100).

193c7 ["what he thinks"]: Socrates regularly encourages his interlocutors to say only what they sincerely believe (cf. *Crito* 49d1; *Euthydemus* 275e4-6, *Protagoras* 331b8-d1; *Gorgias* 495a5-b6, 500b5-7; *Republic* 346a3-4; *Theaetetus* 154c7-e6). This sharply distinguishes Socrates' *elenchos* from the *eristic* of the Sophists (cf. *Euthydemus* 275e3-6, 295b2-e3).

193d1 ["shameful and harmful?"]: at 192d1 they said that unintelligent endurance is harmful and bad (see note on 192d1 above).

193d10 ["I do not"]: Laches now sees the same point made at *Protagoras* 349e8-350c5.

193d11 ["Dorian mode"]: see 188d6 and note above.

194a5 ["courage is endurance"]: Socrates' claim here is one reason why some scholars think that the ultimate failure of the dialogue is due to the fact that they so quickly gave up on endurance as being courage, and that clues in the dialogue indicate that he does indeed agree with this analysis. Other scholars think that Nicias' upcoming comment about something Socrates himself once said (194c8-9) indicates that Socrates believes courage to be a form of wisdom or knowledge. Other scholars think that the dialogue does not suggest that any particular analysis of courage is correct. What do you think?

194c2 ["lost at sea"]: Socrates uses three related words: the verb *aporeō*, the adjective *aporos*, and the noun *aporia* (which is also used at 196b2 and 200e5). Literally it means to be without means or resources. So in general it means to be at a loss, puzzled, or to have failed. The Socratic *elenchos* seems deliberately to lead his interlocutor into *aporia*; the question is, why? Is Socrates skeptical that definitive answers to his questions can ever be found? Does he believe that being puzzled wakes people out of a sort of dogmatic slumber (cf. *Apology* 30e5; *Theaetetus* 155d2-4)? Being refuted certainly gave Laches a sort of "fire in the belly" to figure things out and get things clear in his head (*Laches* 194a6-b4).

194c8 ["defining"]: sometimes the verb *horizō* is used when someone is distinguishing different meanings of related words (cf. *Charmides* 163d7), but it is also used when distinguishing different kinds of things regardless of what words are used to name those things (cf. *Charmides* 171a5, a9, 173a9). The word "lie" and the phrase "stretch the truth" have different meanings, but they both refer to deliberately making a false claim. Similarly, the words "courage" and "bravery" have different meanings ("courage" means having heart, and "bravery" means acting with bravado) but they may both refer to the same state of the soul sought for by Socrates, Laches and Nicias in the *Laches*. It is not immediately clear whether Nicias is offering to define the Greek word *andreia*, or thinks he knows which *dunamis* of the *psuchē* the word refers to.

194c8 ["I heard from you"]: some scholars take this as evidence that Socrates endorses the view of courage Nicias is about to defend—or at least that he endorses some such view.

194d2 ["ignorant"]: Socrates continues to use knowledge-related words according to ordinary conventions, without drawing distinctions, and without trying to make ordinary speech terminologically tidy. Here he does not oppose *sophos* with *asophos*, he simply follows the custom of opposing *sophos* to *amathēs*. The opposition allows for quite a wide range of meanings; when opposed to *sophia*, *amathia* can mean "stupid," "boorish," "ignorant," "discourteous" or "perverse" (and, of course, each of those words could be parsed into yet finer distinctions). Some scholars argue that Socrates commits the fallacy of ambiguity (e.g. illicitly switching from being "good" to being "good at"). But perhaps not. Socrates' use of these words does not violate ordinary linguistic practice, and from Nicias' responses it is clear that he is not violating Nicias' own notions of what he means. If ordinary usage and Nicias' own thinking could be improved by drawing a few distinctions, then arguments like Socrates can suggest both why and how it would be reasonable to draw them. This would help to separate elenchos from eristic: the former exploits ambiguity to indicate why and how drawing distinctions is reasonable; the latter exploits ambiguity in order to win wars of words. (See also note on 192e1 above).

194e4 ["flute playing"]: an *aulos* was a wind instrument; a common variety used a reed, and so was like a modern oboe; others did not and were like a modern flute; some attached a bag to allow for more continuous play, and so were like modern bagpipes; some had double pipes and so were unlike any modern instrument. Some scholars argue that Socrates commits the fallacy of ambiguity here, since flute playing does not seem to be "wisdom" but "expertise" or "skill." However, both are included in the Greek "*sophia*," so Socrates' use of flute playing here is not illicit—at least not with respect to ordinary usage. Whether it violates Nicias' notion is up to Nicias to say. If Socrates' use of "*sophia*" is permitted both by ordinary usage and by Nicias, then it is not clear that he is guilty of *illicitly* switching meanings in his argument (a necessary condition for committing the *fallacy* of ambiguity). If Socrates' use of "*sophia*" is licit, but a problem arises, then Socrates' argument has helped to reveal a hidden problem in ordinary usage, and in Nicias' thinking.

194e8 ["knowledge"]: Nicias introduced his idea using *sophos* and here Socrates switches to *epistēmē*. Nicias could insist on distinguishing the two (see the distinction Critias draws at *Charmides* 163b3). He does not. Nicias switches to *epistēmē* at 195a1 and Laches casually switches back to *sophia* at 195a4; then at 195c7 Nicias switches to *oida*, then back to *epistēmē* at c11, then to *gignōskō* at e5, and even to *phronimos* at 197c1. Clearly, when Socrates inserted *epistēmē* for *sophia*, he did not violate Nicias' or Laches' notion of what Nicias meant. These five words certainly can be used with distinct meanings, but they are all in the same semantic ball park of an elevated cognitive condition. These changes in terminology, therefore, are not illicit (and so nobody is committing a fallacy); they are simply ways for Plato to keep his prose from becoming monotonous.

195a7 ["without insulting him"]: Socrates is sensitive to the interpersonal dynamics of refutation, and he tries to prevent conversations from degenerating into personal attacks (cf. *Euthydemus* 288b3, *Gorgias* 457c4-458b3). This separates the Socratic elenchos from the sophistic eristic, since Sophists quite freely insult people as a way to gain victory (e.g. *Euthydemus* 302b8-c3).

195c12 ["better"]: here Nicias introduces an explicitly evaluative term. If this is the first attempt in the *Laches* to give an evaluative analysis of courage, then it is similar to 163c2 in the *Charmides*, i.e. it is the point where the dialogue shifts away from considering "reductive" analyses of the virtue in question. This raises a dilemma. On the one hand, (1) all reductive accounts of moral virtue seem doomed to failure if no collection of non-moral (or, at the very least, non-evaluative) properties can fully account for any moral property. But on the other hand, (2) analyzing one moral property in terms of other moral properties seems to require a further analysis of these other moral properties. Two problems might arise here: (2a) the analysis of these other moral properties might lead right back to the original moral property we were trying to analyze, in which case the account is ultimately circular; alternatively, (2b) the analysis of these other moral properties might lead to still further moral properties in an infinite regress. In theory, there may be two solutions to this theoretical dilemma that faces any analysis of moral terms. First (the "foundationalist" answer), we might find some moral properties that stand in no need of analysis. Second (the "coherentist" answer, see note on *Phaedo* 101e1), we might analyze morally evaluative terms in non-moral but evaluative terms, e.g. along the lines Plato sketches at *Republic* 4.444d3-e2: virtue is to the soul (*psuchē*) what health is to the body. If Socrates is pursuing this second solution, then we might say that he is in the process of inventing the scientific study of human psychology, or is inventing the scientific notion of mental health, the virtues being healthy states of the human *psuchē*, and the vices being forms of mental disorder (e.g. courageous people are psychologically better than cowards at coping with dangerous situations).

195d1 ["more excellent"]: Nicias has twice used *ameinon*, which is the comparative of *agathos*. Here he switches to *kreitton*, which is the comparative of *kratus*, meaning "strong" or "mighty," and in Homer is an epithet of the god Hermes (*Iliad* 16.181, 24.345, *Odyssey* 5.49). Dying nobly in battle is the most dramatic example of the sort of thing Nicias has in mind. Given the choice of dying nobly in battle, knowing that honors and benefits to one's family will accrue thereby, or of being saved by a doctor only to live as a wounded invalid and a drain on the resources of others, many Greeks would choose the former without hesitation.

195e1 ["seers"]: a *mantis* is a diviner who purports to be able to interpret divine signs of future events. The word occurs ten times in the *Laches* (here and at e3, e4, e5, e9; 196a3, a5; 196d5; 199a2, a3). See note on 199a2 below.

196b5 ["lawyers"]: Laches does not say "lawyers" because the Athenian legal system did not permit legal representation in the way our system does. Each litigant had to represent himself. It was a common complaint, then, that slick talkers could win regardless of whether they were in the right. Aristophanes lampoons this in his comedy *Clouds*, and he makes Socrates a teacher of such unscrupulous verbal tricks.

196e1 ["Crommyon sow"]: many species of wild pigs can be quite large and quite dangerous. According to an old Greek myth, the Athenian hero Theseus killed a very dangerous sow (or, according to some versions, boar) that lived near the town of Crommyon (between Corinth and Megara, northwest of Athens). Strabo says that the sow was the mother of the more famous Calydonian boar (*Geography* 8.6.22).

196e8 ["monkey"]: Plato did know of baboons (*Theaetetus* 161c5), which can be quite fierce. However, *pithēkos* normally means "monkey" or "jackanapes" (e.g. Aristophanes, *Acharnians* 907). I think Socrates' point is that common sense holds lions, bulls and stags to be quite ferocious, lethal, and courageous, while the silly monkey who runs away whenever startled is quite the opposite. Notice that Socrates is, in a sense, not neutral: just as Socrates uses the Greek epistemic vocabulary in ordinary ways with ordinary semantic looseness, so also he readily appeals to common sense and proverbial wisdom. He does not, however, dogmatically preserve customary ways of speaking or thinking—he is happy to entertain serious proposals that custom is in error.

197c6 ["Lamachus"]: an Athenian general who quickly earned a reputation for bravado. In 425 he was lampooned by Aristophanes as full of bluster (*Acharnians* 572), but after his death Aristophanes paid tribute to his heroism (*Frogs* 1039). The Syracusan invasion was so large that the Athenians appointed three generals to lead it: Alcibiades, Nicias and Lamachus. In typically bold fashion, Lamachus urged the others to focus an immediate strike on Syracuse, but his colleagues believed that they should first secure friends on the island. Given the disaster that followed, perhaps Lamachus had been right. Lamachus was killed in action, shortly followed by Nicias.

197c9 ["true Aexonian"]: we don't know what this means. There are two problems. First, it sounds like Laches feels insulted and is biting his tongue so that he doesn't insult Nicias back, but it's not clear that he should feel insulted. Most translators have Nicias say that he calls Laches, Lamachus and others wise *since in fact* (*eiper*) they are courageous. That's no insult. Alternatively, *eiper* could mean "*if* in fact," which isn't exactly an insult, but it could be a good natured jibe. The second problem is that Laches was actually from the town of Aexone, so he literally was a "true Aexonian." One ancient commentator thought that Aexonians were generally considered to be too abusive, another thought they were considered too proud. My guess is that the former is correct: Laches has an insult to hurl at Nicias, but to do so would just feed the stereotype that Aexonians are always hurling insults at people.

197d3 ["Prodicus"]: see note on *Charmides* 163d4. On Damon, see note on *Laches* 180d1 above.

198b6 ["causes fear"]: obviously this is important. "What is to be feared" could be taken in a non-causal sense, e.g. "that which *ought to be* feared" or "that which is *of a nature* to be feared." Events in the past that are of a nature to be feared are often studied by military experts in order to learn from the past, but events in the past do not *cause* fear in the present because they are over and done with. See note on 199c4 below.

198c3 ["bad things"]: this phrase is a bit lame in English; many translate *kakos* here and below as "evil," but that word has connotations in English that *kakos* lacks in Greek. *Kakos* is as generic as its natural contrary: *agathos*. I think that this is the crucial claim in the upcoming argument. If it is possible that in some cases it is better for a person not to recover from an illness (195c11-12), then in some cases it may be better for a general to lose a battle. In that case, generalship is not the knowledge of victory and defeat in battle, it is the knowledge of good and bad in battle.

199a2 ["a law"]: the fact that there was a *nomos* establishing that the general outranks the seer (*mantis*) indicates that this rule was not a mere "decree" (*psephisma*) voted on by the *Ekklēsia*. Xenophon took the military role of the *mantis* quite seriously (*Anabasis* 1.7.18-20; 4.5.4; 5.2.9; 5.5.3; 5.6.29; 6.1.23-24; 6.4.13-16; 6.5.2-9; 7.8.10-11; *Cyropedia* 1.6.2; 3.3.34, 63; *Hellenika* 2.4.18-19; cf. 3.3.4-11, 7.2.21-23) despite knowing full well that signs admitted of different interpretations and that generals could exploit this fact for their own ends (compare *Hellenika* 3.2.24 with 4.7.4). On the other hand, Thucydides seems to treat the *mantis* as irrelevant in comparison with military science (compare 6.69.1 with 6.69.2), and occasionally as disreputable and extremely dangerous (8.1). Thucydides blames Nicias' most crucial error in judgment on the fact that he was "too superstitious" (*agan theiasmō*, 7.50.4): instead of taking his final opportunity to flee Sicily and save the Athenian army, he chose to obey the seers, who interpreted the lunar eclipse as indicating that they should wait three times nine days. The delay led to the worst defeat of the war, to Nicias' death, and perhaps made Athens' loss to Sparta inevitable.

199b1 ["isn't it?"]: Socrates is going very slowly—and is even repetitive—in this entire argument. I suspect that this is a deliberate attempt to allow Nicias or Laches to figure out where the argument is headed before he explicitly draws the conclusion.

199b4 ["future good things"]: to be completely accurate, at 198c3-4 they also allowed that not-bad things are to be dared. But this is not relevant to the point Socrates is about to make.

199c4 ["a third"]: it has been argued that Socrates' conclusion is invalidly drawn on the grounds that he commits the fallacy of false analogy. You might argue that courage is not analogous to other forms of knowledge because it is essentially focused on the future, while other forms of knowledge are not. However, this allegation is not available to Nicias because he has already agreed that all forms of knowledge are temporally inclusive. To avoid Socrates' conclusion, therefore, he must either retract that admission (something he is certainly free to do), or retract his claim that courage is a form of knowledge. More importantly, it seems false to say that courage is restricted to the present and future. A crucial part of training for a courageous general involves "Monday-morning-quarterbacking" past battles to discern what ought to have been feared and what ought to have been dared. I think that this explains why Nicias goes along so quickly with the modification Socrates is about to make to his view. We are always free to imagine ways of avoiding Socrates' inferences—in fact, I assume that Plato hoped his readers would do precisely that—but then we must also imagine how Socrates might reply to our gambits. See note on 198b6 above.

199d9 ["to take"]: "to take" and "to provide" (e1) imply successful action, not mere ability. Socrates often appears to assume that virtue is sufficient for happiness (*Apology* 30c6-d5, 41c8-d2; *Crito* 48b8-9; *Charmides* 173d3-5, 174b11-c3). Here he suggests a reason: if the possession of one virtue implies the possession of all virtue, then no vice could possibly prevent one from successfully accomplishing the good one knows to be achievable, and so one will achieve it.

199e1 ["about what is good and about what is bad"]: if you know what is good and what is bad and you happen to be in the barroom, then observers will call you "temperate;" if you happen to be in a court of law, observers will call you "just;" if you happen to be in a temple, they will call you "pious;" and so on.

200a2 ["such great hope"]: given Laches' earlier comments (especially at 197c2-9), it seems clear that he does not mean this sincerely—he is being ironic (which Nicias accurately perceives).

200c2 ["a wise one"]: this comment is curious. It could be intended as another ironic barb, but I wonder if Nicias' previous comment has actually softened Laches' attitude a bit.

201a3 ["spreading this around"]: education was for young people, and so it looked ridiculous for older men to be sitting in a classroom (cf. *Euthydemus* 272c1-d3).

201b1 ["Homer"]: here Socrates paraphrases *Odyssey* 17.347. At *Charmides* 161a4 he quotes the line exactly.

201c5 ["god willing"]: the singular was not uncommon and did not signify monotheism—the Greeks were polytheists. Plato ended other dialogues with Socrates mentioning god (e.g. *Apology* 42a5, *Crito* 54e2, *Republic* 10.621c7, cf. *Phaedo* 117b3-c5, *Phaedrus* 279b8-c3, *Theaetetus* 210c7). No doubt it was galling to Plato that his mentor was tried and executed partly on grounds of impiety or atheism (*Apology* 23d6, 24b9-c1).

NOTES ON EUTHYPHRO

2a2 ["Lyceum"]: see *Lysis* 203a1, *Euthydemus* 271a1, *Symposium* 223d10 (and also probably *Phaedrus* 229a1, since an Athenian might walk to the Lyceum by way of the Ilissus river). Although Socrates did frequent the agora (central square and marketplace, e.g. *Apology* 17c8), Plato more often associates him with gymnasia and wrestling schools, which often served as school grounds (e.g. *Charmides* 153a4, *Laches* 178a1). Euthyphro's *neōteron* might simply be "new," but (a) the word can suggest something calamitous (e.g. Herodotus 5.106.1), and (b) whatever it is has brought Socrates to the King's Porch, which in itself suggests something bad.

2a4 ["King's Porch"]: the court of the King's Porch tried cases of homicide, deliberate wounding, and cases connected with religion (e.g. the right to claim a priesthood, disputes about the duty to perform a sacrifice, and impiety).

2a4 ["like I am"]: at 9c9-10 Euthyphro expresses the hope that he will persuade his jury, and so this conversation is taking place before both Socrates' and Euthyphro's proceedings.

2a6 ["indictment"]: Euthyphro used *dikē*, and Socrates contrasts *dikē* with *graphē*. Informally, Socrates is correct to contrast the two: roughly, a *dikē* is a private case (technically a *dikē idia*), that was regarded as not concerning the community at large (e.g. a dispute between brothers over an inheritance); a *graphē* was the most common type of public case (technically a *dikē dēmosia*), that was regarded as concerning the community. Athens had no public prosecutors, and so it was up to private individuals to initiate public cases. See note on *Apology* 36b1.

2b7 ["know"]: *gignōskō*, see note on *Charmides* 162b5. Socrates cannot mean that he's never met Meletus, because he would have met him at the preliminary inquiry (*anakrisis*) when the *basileus* determined what crime was being alleged.

2b9 ["Meletus"]: scholars have speculated on who this might be, but no definite conclusion can be reached. On Greek names see note on *Apology* 33d8.

2c3 ["understood"]: Socrates uses the perfect tense of *gignōskō* (see note on 2b7 above) though he does explicitly add the qualifications "as he claims" (*hōs phēsin* at 2c4 and 3a2) and "perhaps" (*kinduneuei* at 2c5 and *isōs* at 2d4). Certainly Socrates would deny the unqualified versions of the claims (*Apology* 24c4-d1). Perhaps this is irony, but if Euthyphro is the intended audience, the irony is lost on him (see his response at 3a6-9). Perhaps the intended audience is the reader, giving us the guilty pleasure of laughing at, and hence feeling superior to, Meletus as the butt of Socrates' ridicule. Alternatively, Socrates' qualifiers are there (1) to bracket Meletus since the issue, and the political priorities he enunciates in this paragraph, are things he really does take seriously, and (2) to promulgate his own view that knowledge is the only proper basis for certain actions (cf. *Apology* 29a4-6), since on his own, Euthyphro may not have inferred that Meletus presumes himself to *know* that he is doing the right thing by indicting Socrates. See note on 12a5 below.

2c4 ["young people are corrupted"]: Meletus' allegation began with the claim that Socrates did not acknowledge the gods whom the city acknowledges—clearly a religious offense, which is why his indictment was lodged with the King (and not the Archon or the Polemarch). Without this religious allegation, it is not clear that Socrates could have been prosecuted at all, since it is not clear that there was a law in Athens against corrupting the youth. See notes on *Apology* 24b8, 24b9 and 24c1. It is interesting that Socrates puts the final charge first, and then (at 3b1-3) interprets the religious allegation(s) as explaining it.

2c6 ["ignorantly"]: see *Apology* 25d5-26a7.

2c8 ["mother"]: this could be an insult that confirms Socrates was ironically insulting Meletus at 2c3. Alternatively, he may simply be expressing what he says at *Apology* 26a1-4. In the *Crito* Socrates takes seriously the analogy of the laws with our parents, e.g. 50e3-4.

2d2 ["care"]: the Greek word for "care" is *melō*, so the first syllable matches the first syllable of "Meletus." Perhaps Socrates is deliberately playing on this similarity, cf. *Apology* 24d3-9.

2d3 ["young plants"]: cf. *Republic* 2.377a12-b3 (cf. 376e3-4). Also, in Aeschylus' *Eumenides* Athena says that she loves the Athenians as a gardener loves her plants (*Eumenides* 911-12). If Plato's account of education in Books 2-4 of the *Republic* can be called the first European treatise on "developmental psychology," then Socrates could be called the "father of developmental psychology," cf. *Laches* 180b7-d3. At the very least we can be fairly certain that Plato found the allegation that Socrates corrupted the youth galling.

3a7 ["heart of the city"]: the *hestia* is literally the hearth of the home, but it is often used metonymously to refer to the whole house itself. The goddess of the hearth, Hestia, received the first sacrifice (*Cratylus* 401c9-d3). Euthyphro admires Socrates, and this relationship between the two of them should influence how we understand this dialogue. For example, if Socrates treats Euthyphro ironically, then the irony is probably not intended in a mean-spirited way—it is probably intended as a friendly joke that Euthyphro himself will easily notice and perceive as an inducement to greater self-reflection (cf. *Apology* 30e1-31a1). Alternatively, the relationship between the two of them might be reason to deny that Socrates is speaking to his friend ironically.

3b3 ["acknowledge"]: *nomizō* can refer to belief, but we should not assimilate Greek paganism to later conceptions of "religious faith." If we define religion as a distinctive set of beliefs and practices consciously chosen by people to the exclusion of alternative beliefs and/or practices, then the Greeks did not have any religion at all. It wasn't until the rise of Christianity that Greek cult practices were thought of as a religion. Greeks had ritual traditions and traditional stories about gods, but the rituals were the more important of the two by far. If the correct actions (e.g. libations) are not performed in the correct ways (e.g. pouring a small amount of wine into the sea) at the correct times (e.g. before embarking on a voyage), and the circumstances are not auspicious (e.g. someone audibly curses while the libation is being poured), then the wrath of the relevant god may be provoked and serious consequences may result (e.g. a shipwreck). This emphasis on orthopraxy rather than orthodoxy led the Greeks to be highly syncretistic in two ways: (1) travellers in foreign lands would continue to perform their own rituals, but they would also perform the rituals of the people in whose lands they travelled (on the assumption that the local gods demanded respect), and (2) they readily identified their own gods with foreign gods, assuming that their god was called by a different name in distant places. So Meletus faced a dilemma in drawing up his charges: religious heteropraxy would be clearly illegal, but Meletus could not prove such a charge against Socrates (see, e.g., Xenophon, *Memorabilia* 1.1.2); on the other hand, he might convince some jurors that Socrates was guilty of religious heterodoxy (jurors might lump Socrates in with "those egghead atheists") but heterodoxy was not clearly illegal. *Nomizō* is ambiguous in the right way for his purposes, and I think that "acknowledge" is about as ambiguous in English.

3b5 ["divine sign"]: see *Apology* 40b1 and note on *Apology* 31d1. Xenophon offers the same speculation as Euthyphro (*Memorabilia* 1.1.2-3) and he offers a reasonable defense of Socrates. No doubt this played some role in Meletus' allegations (see *Apology* 31d1-2), but the main concern was deeper (see *Apology* 19a8-c5, cf. Aristophanes, *Clouds* 627).

3d1 ["jealousy"]: *phthonos* is ill-will or malice, often as a result of envy or jealousy. Euthyphro's references to *phthonos* and slander (*diaballō*) are remarkably similar to Socrates' opening use of both at *Apology* 18d2. Again (see note on 3b5 above), Socrates and Euthyphro share some important viewpoints, and so their expressions of friendship seem genuine (see note on 3a7 above).

3d8 ["charging a fee"]: Socrates emphasizes this point at *Apology* 19d8-e1 and 33a8. This is important to him for the reason he states here, but probably more so because of his disavowal of knowledge (cf. *Apology* 22e6-23b4): he cannot charge a fee for teaching what he knows about virtue if he knows nothing about virtue.

3e3 ["seers"]: a *mantis* is a diviner who purports to be able to interpret divine signs. Athens had a law establishing that the general outranks the seer (*Laches* 199a2). Perhaps this grants the seer less authority than Xenophon thought he should have (*Anabasis* 1.7.18-20; 4.5.4; 5.2.9; 5.5.3; 5.6.29; 6.1.23-24; 6.4.13-16; 6.5.2-9; 7.8.10-11; *Cyropedia* 1.6.2; 3.3.34, 63; *Hellenika* 2.4.18-19; cf. 3.3.4-11, 7.2.21-23), but perhaps allows him more authority than Thucydides thought he should have (compare *History of the Peloponnesian War* 6.69.1 with 6.69.2, see also 8.1). Thucydides blames general Nicias' most crucial error in judgment on the fact that he was "too superstitious" (*agan theiasmō*, 7.50.4): instead of taking his final opportunity to flee Sicily and save the Athenian army, he chose to obey the seers, who interpreted the lunar eclipse as indicating that they should wait three times nine days. The delay led to the worst defeat of the war, to Nicias' death, and perhaps made Athens' loss to Sparta inevitable. Socrates' attitude toward seers may be a bit closer to Xenophon's than to Thucydides': in addition to trusting his divine sign, he seems to believe in a prophetic dream at *Crito* 44a10-b4, and he seems to believe in his own prophetic power at *Apology* 39c1-3. Perhaps he is being ironic in these other passages, and so perhaps he is ironically insulting Euthyphro here by calling him a *mantis*. Alternatively, he is sincere in all three passages and does not disparage Euthyphro for being a *mantis* (there is no reason to think that what Euthyphro is about to say derives from his *manteia*). What we think Socrates' attitude towards Euthyphro is can influence or be influenced by what we think Socrates' attitudes are towards Ion (in the *Ion*) and Hippias (in the *Hippias Minor*).

4a12 ["rightly"]: there was no law against prosecuting your own father, but doing so could easily be considered an unholy or impious act. A surviving relative of a homicide victim had a duty to prosecute the killer, so if Euthyphro's father had killed a member of a different family, then a member of the deceased's family would be the one to initiate the lawsuit, not Euthyphro.

4b9 ["right"]: this seems quite close to Socrates' own view expressed at *Apology* 28b8-9. But Euthyphro's impartiality seems to exceed Socrates' (cf. *Apology* 30a4). Also, Socrates' view seems more in line with Athenian legal practice, which suggests a greater reverence for law (cf. *Apology* 32b1-c3, 35c2-5, *Crito* 51a7-c3).

4c1 ["pollution"]: *musaros* (adjective related to the noun *miasma*) is the opposite of *hagnos* ("sacred") and so means profane, polluted, defiled, impure or stained (e.g. from sex, birth, death, blood, homicide). *Miasma* was thought to be infectious and so many customs, rituals and laws developed to protect people from contracting it. E.g. temple functions were often carried out by virgins (pre-pubescent boys and girls) so that people who entered would not contract *miasma*. Murder trials were held in a space without a roof so that nobody involved would contract *miasma* if the accused turned out to be guilty (Antiphon, *On the murder of Herodes* 5.11). Those with *miasma* were liable to divine disfavor (e.g. the infliction of physical illness, shipwreck, economic loss or other disasters), and such disfavor could spread to the entire community—hence the communal interest in doing everything possible to keep all citizens free from *miasma*. In Athens, a deathbed pardon from a homicide victim gave the guilty party immunity from prosecution; otherwise the blood of the victim demanded prosecution or the *miasma* would spread. This distinguishes Socrates' from Euthyphro's attitude towards doing what is right (see note 4b9 above): Socrates associates obeying the law and doing what is right with justice; Euthyphro associates them with ritual purity.

4c4 ["Naxos"]: the largest of the Cyclades islands southeast of Athens in the Aegean.

4c8 ["Interpreters"]: the Interpreters were a traditional board whose members were from old noble families, and who interpreted the unwritten, traditional laws governing rituals and ceremonies (e.g. Demosthenes, *Against Evergus and Mnesibulus* 47.58; see also Aeschylus, *Eumenides* 609). There is no doubt that Euthyphro's father had both the legal right, and the ritual duty, to bring the killer of his slave to justice (cf. Antiphon, *On the murder of Herodes* 5.48). However, Athenian law regarding homicide was ancient and complex (e.g., see notes on 4d4, 4d7 and 4d9 below); it was prudent of Euthyphro's father to consult the religious counselors on the proper procedure. Obviously imprisoning the killer outside was not optimal, but because his *miasma* (see note on 4c1 above) was contagious he could not have been kept indoors, and if he had been allowed to flee the *miasma* would remain un-expiated.

4d4 ["killed him"]: Athenian law (religious and secular) disregards intent except in homicide. Unintentional homicide is committed, e.g., when you hit someone without intending to kill them, but they die from the blow; or you give someone a love potion to drink and it kills them (Aristotle, *Magna Moralia* 1.16.1188b29-38). Euthyphro's father could be thought to be guilty of unintentional homicide (Athenians did not recognize "negligent homicide"), but such cases were tried at the Palladium, not the King's Porch. See note on *Protagoras* 324a7.

4d7 ["prosecuting my father"]: if the employee were a slave, then Euthyphro had the right to prosecute whomever killed him—but alleged killers of slaves were tried at the Palladium (Aristotle, *Constitution of Athens* 57.3), not the Kings' Porch. So the employee had probably been a free hired hand, but in that case the responsibility of prosecution falls to his closest male relatives, not to Euthyphro. However, it is not clear that any law prohibited Euthyphro from prosecuting such a case (see note on *Apology* 36b1); perhaps the employee's relatives took the same view of the matter as Euthyphro's father. We do not know at what stage Euthyphro's case was: if he was only just initiating it, then the *Archon Basileus* could reject it on the grounds that the facts as presented by Euthyphro indicate that the death of the employee was not homicide (see Antiphon, *On the Choreutes* 6.41-43 and note on 4d9 below). If his father argued that the killing of the employee was lawful (see note on 4d4 above), then the case would be heard at the Delphinion, not at the King's Porch.

4d9 ["killed with impunity"]: the Greeks permitted killing in a wider range of cases than we do today, e.g. you could kill a man you caught having illicit sex with your wife, mother, sister, daughter, or concubine you kept for the sake of having free children. If a man had been exiled for committing homicide but was found within Athenian territory, he could be killed with impunity. Also, you could kill any thief robbing you by force or by dark of night. A reasonable Athenian might have thought that the employee's prior actions were such that it was permissible for Euthyphro's father to kill him outright.

4e2 ["holy"]: *hosios*. While "piety" (*eusebēs*) refers primarily to the feeling of awe, shame, fear, worship, reverence or honor (see note on 5c9 below); "holy" refers primarily to what is sanctioned by the law of god or nature (see note on 6e10 below). When *hosios* describes a person, it can mean either that he is ritually pure or that he is devout or pious. Probably Socrates is using *hosios* in the latter sense, so that it is synonymous with *eusebēs*, so I usually use "piety" for *hosios*. At 12e1-4 Socrates switches between *hosios* and *eusebēs* as if they are synonymous.

4e7 ["something impious"]: as described, Euthyphro's case raises several interesting legal puzzles (see notes on 4c8, 4d4, 4d7, 4d9). It is not obvious that Euthyphro's father would be found guilty of any crime under Athenian law (Socrates' summary of it at 9a2-8 is not unfair and it is not at all obvious how an Athenian jury would decide it). But Socrates does not raise any legal questions, or any questions of justice. He focuses exclusively on piety, partly for the reason he is about to mention, but also, I think, because he has noticed exactly the sort of thing that gets his philosophical engine going. With Laches he notices that standing fast is both courageous and not courageous (*Laches* 190e4-191c5); with Charmides he notices that calmness is both temperate and not temperate (*Charmides* 159b7-160d4); here he notices that Euthyphro's action is both pious (as Euthyphro claims) and impious (as Euthyphro's relatives claim). Scholars call this the problem of the "compresence of opposites," or "the F and not-F problem."

5a3 ["wonderful"]: *thaumasios* describes something as exceeding expectations, e.g. exceedingly good or admirable, or simply as being different from the norm, and hence extraordinary or strange. Literally, Socrates addresses him as "wonderful Euthyphro." Socrates is going along with Euthyphro's claim to be exceptional. Perhaps he is ironically (or sarcastically) criticizing Euthyphro for making just the sort of false pretention to knowledge that it is Socrates' divine mission to reveal (cf. *Apology* 23a5-b4). However, since he has not yet heard Euthyphro out, he may be sincerely pursuing an "innocent until proven guilty" course—since he disavows expertise he is hardly in a position to identify experts and non-experts prior to putting someone's self-avowed expertise to the test (6b2-4, cf. "anyone I think is wise" at *Apology* 23b6; see also *Charmides* 162d7-e5, 165b5-c2; *Laches* 190c4-6; *Euthydemus* 273d5-275a7). Indeed, Socrates' refutational method is deliberately designed to allow non-experts to expose false pretentions to knowledge (*Charmides* 166c6-d6).

5c7 ["impiety"]: *asebeias* occurs here and at 12e3; in both places it derives from Meletus' indictment. It is clearly related to *eusebēs* (5c9, 12e4 and e6) and *asebēs* (5c9, 14b6). Both are related to the verb *sebomai*, (*Crito* 51b2), meaning to feel awe or shame before, and so to fear, worship or revere, or more generally to honor.

5c9 ["the pious"]: *to eusebēs*; the definite article turns the adjective into a noun, thus turning an attribute into the name of a class of things, or of a particular abstract thing. Socrates clarifies this a bit here and at 6d9-e6, but his clarifications raise further philosophical questions that are explored by both Plato and Aristotle.

5d1 ["one and the same"]: cf. *Laches* 191e10-11. Socrates speaks of "the pious" as if it is a real thing and not simply as if the word "pious" has a meaning, or that we have some notion, idea or concept of "piety." Also, the phrase "one and the same" seems to imply that "the pious" that is in Euthyphro (if he is pious) is not simply similar to, but is numerically identical to "the pious" that is in Socrates (if he too is pious), so that "the pious" can be wholly in two or more discrete locations simultaneously. Hence, Socrates seems to accept realism and reject nominalism about universals (on universals, see note on *Meno* 77a6). He is not looking for the meaning of the word "piety" (*hosios*), nor is he trying to discover Euthyphro's notion or conception of piety: he is looking for a single real property. E.g. to "what is the swift?" Socrates does not answer, "the quick" or "the high velocity," he answers "the capacity (*dunamis*) that accomplishes much in little time" (*Laches* 192b1). This is a reductive account of "the swift" in the sense that it dispenses with facts about speed and instead refers to distinct facts to account for why certain statements about swift actions are true. One important question to ask about Socrates in the *Euthyphro* is whether he is looking for a reductive account of the real universal "the pious."

5d3 ["like itself"]: how is piety like impiety? Perhaps he means that universals, unlike particulars, are free from the compresence of opposites: a particular stick can simultaneously be equal (in length to one stick) and unequal (in length to another stick), but the equal cannot simultaneously be equal and unequal (*Phaedo* 74b7-9). If this is what he means, then perhaps Aristotle was wrong to draw a sharp distinction between Plato's and Socrates' theory of forms (*Metaphysics* 1.6.987a32-b10, 13.9.1086a37-b11, cf. 13.4.1078b12-1079a4). Alternatively, he may mean that impiety is self-predicating, i.e. impiety has the property of being impious. This sounds odd, and it may be odd, but perhaps he means only that impiety explains why impious things are impious, and so is itself the real property in virtue of which impious things are impious.

5d4 ["character"]: *idea* is a noun formed from the infinitive *idein*, which is "to see," so an *idea* is literally something seen, however it often refers to the outward appearance of something, and in some cases refers to a *mere* appearance as opposed to a reality. But its two main uses are to refer to (1) the shape or form of something (and so *idea* could be a synonym for *schēma* or *morphē*), or to (2) a kind, sort or species of thing (and so *idea* could be a synonym for *genos*). Given what Socrates says below at 12c3-e4, the latter seems his more likely assumption (cf. Plato's association of *genos* and *eidos* at *Sophist* 267d6-7). *Idea* is, of course, the word that gave rise to the phrase "Plato's theory of Ideas." Socrates uses *idea* here and at 6d11 and 6e3. See note on 6d11 below. See also note on *Phaedo* 104b9.

5d6 ["Entirely so"]: Euthyphro's answer seems facile. If we are to assume that he really does understand the question Socrates just asked, then we should compare him with Simmias in the *Phaedo* (e.g. at 65d4 and d6). But if he does understand the question, then why does he give the answer he's about to give, which is not to the point (as Socrates indicates at 6d1-e6)? Perhaps Euthyphro's answer truly is facile because he presumes to know things that he does not in fact know. See also note on 5d10 below.

5d9 ["to prosecute the wrongdoer"]: Socrates and Euthyphro consider four accounts of piety, as follows:

(1) piety is to prosecute the wrongdoer (5d8-6e9)
(2) piety is what is acceptable to (all) the gods (6e10-11b5)
(3) piety is a species of the just (11e4-14a10)
(4) piety is knowledge of prayer and sacrifice (14a11-15c10)

6a2 ["swallowing his sons"]: Hesiod, *Theogony* 459-506. Traditional Greek stories about the gods contain many scandalous actions, up to and including outright war (e.g. the Titanomachy between Titans and Olympians, the later Gigantomachy between a group of Gaia-born creatures and the Olympians, and, of course, the gods take different sides in the war between the Greeks and the Trojans). Using these stories literally as precedents could be taken seriously (Aeschylus, *Eumenides* 640-643), or used as a joke (Aristophanes, *Clouds* 904-6). I suspect that Euthyphro's references to traditional stories can be compared to what is today sometimes called "Biblical literalism" among Christians: some Greeks may have taken his view seriously, while others may have been disdainful of them.

6a8 ["difficult to believe them?"]: perhaps Socrates is contradicting what he says at *Phaedrus* 229c6-230a6, where he appears to accept traditional stories about the gods. Alternatively, Socrates may be expressing concern only about attributing unethical behavior to the gods (cf. Isocrates, *Busiris* 11.38-40). Plato clearly thought that the stories Euthyphro just referred to were false and that they should not be told to children (*Republic* 2.377e6-378a6). At the very least, it sound incongruous to draw the sacred/profane distinction, but then admit that the gods themselves do profane things.

6b2 ["I should concede this point"]: Socrates' point here is plainly reasonable, but scholars overlook the fact that it undercuts claims of alleged "Socratic irony." Of course, defenders of "Socratic irony" can always say that Socrates is making *this* claim ironically. Whether that makes the case for Socratic irony stronger or weaker is up to the reader to decide.

6c2 ["Great Panathenaea?"]: every year Athens held a civic festival for its patron deity Athena; every four years the festival was extended, included athletic and musical competitions open to all Greeks, and during which the sacred mantle was brought to the statue of Athena on the Acropolis. The embroidery depicted scenes from the Gigantomachy (not to be confused with the Titanomachy) when the monsters born from Gaia fought with the Olympians for mastery of the cosmos. Plato refers to the sacred mantle at *Republic* 2.378c3 and he condemns the sort of stories depicted on it as impious (378c8).

6c4 ["we say"]: Socrates normally assumes that inquiry is a cooperative endeavor, not a contest (cf. *Crito* 48d8-e1, *Laches* 190c4, *Charmides* 166d4-6). See also note on 11e4 below.

6d3 ["You said"]: at 5d8-9. Though, to be fair to Euthyphro, he did go on to generalize, adding "to prosecute a wrongdoer." Euthyphro cited what we could call a "maxim" for his action (see note on *Crito* 46b5), and he even indicates that he has in mind a universal because he indicates what property many different particular prosecutions share in common. However, since actions other than prosecutions can be pious, Socrates' objection is legitimate.

6d11 ["form"]: *eidos* is difficult to distinguish from *idea* (see note on 5d4 above). *Eidos* refers to something that is seen and so can refer to the shape or form of something, e.g. the shape of the human body (a beautiful body or a good physique) or a geometrical shape. It can also refer to a class or kind of thing, and hence to the nature of a thing. This is the only place in the *Euthyphro* where Socrates uses *eidos*. Because both *eidos* and *idea* are related to a verb for seeing (the non-extant *eidō*), we might suppose that Socrates assumes these real universals are sensible (i.e. can be perceived by our physical senses, cf. *apoblepōn* at e4), and it almost seems perverse of Plato to say that they are not perceivable (*Timaeus* 51d5). Aristotle points out that Plato thought the forms were non-sensible, but he does not definitely say what position Socrates took on this issue (*Metaphysics* 1.6.987a32-b10).

6e5 ["is such"]: *toioutos* is a demonstrative pronoun of quality, answering the question "*poios;*" (of what sort?). Socrates does not use any word for resemblance here. This might be used as evidence that the "characters," "forms" or "paradigms" Socrates has in mind are not the Platonic forms of the *Phaedo* or the *Republic*. Perhaps here forms are paradigms only because of the role they play in knowledge and explanation: if x is pious, then we can know that x is pious only if we know what the form of piety is, because the form of piety explains why x is pious. Plato distinguishes degrees of perfection (e.g. *Republic* 10.597a5), which is compatible with the notion (nowhere explicit in the *Euthyphro*) that sensible particulars resemble perfect paradigms (cf. *Parmenides* 132d1-4), and also with the notion that sensible particulars participate to varying degrees in perfect paradigms (cf. *Parmenides* 131a4-e7).

6e10 ["dear to the gods"]: *prosphilēs* literally means dear or beloved, but in actual use it was often merely a florid way to say that someone was acceptable (e.g. Thucydides 5.40.3) or popular (Herodotus 1.123.1). This is clearly a reasonable analysis of the Greek conception of piety: the feminine noun *hosia* can refer to divine law, and so the adjective *hosios* can refer to what is permitted by divine law, and hence to what is acceptable to the gods (see also note on 5d2 above). What is *anosios* is profane and unacceptable to the gods (e.g. Sophocles, *Antigone* 1071; Antiphon, *On the murder of Herodes* 5.84). *Prosphilēs* is used only three times in the *Euthyphro* at 6e10, 7a1 and 8b2. Socrates' casual switch from *prosphilēs* to *theophilēs* (see note on 7a6 below) suggests that he is treating these two words as synonyms.

7a6 ["dear to the gods"]: when rain extinguished the fire that was intended to kill Croesus, Cyrus concluded that Croesus must be a good man and *theophilēs* (Herodotus 1.87.2). At *Philebus* 39e10-11 Socrates says that a just, pious and good man is *theophilēs*. Places favored by a god can be described as *theophilēs* (e.g. Pindar, *Isthmian* 6.66). The *–philēs* can refer to love (e.g. when it is used in reference to family members) or to friendship, and so someone who is *theophilēs* is either loved by god, or a friend of god; "dear to god" seems sufficiently ambiguous in English, though sometimes "loved by the gods" fits the context. *Theophilēs* is often contrasted with *theomisēs* (7a7, 7a8, 8a5, 8a12, 9c6, 9c8), and Plato says that no one swears by god falsely if he does not want to be "most hateful to god" (*theomisestatos, Laws* 11.917a1). *Theophilēs* is used in the *Euthyphro* at 7a6, 7a7 (twice), 8a5, 8a12, 9c8, 10d10, 10d12, 10d13, 10e5, 10e6 (twice), 10e10, 11a1 (twice), 11a2 (twice), 15c2.

7a7 ["hated by the gods"]: Euthyphro distinguished the pair of contradictories "dear to the gods" and "not dear to the gods;" but Socrates substitutes the pair of contraries "dear to the gods" and "hated by the gods." Unlike contradictories, contraries leave open a middle ground between them—in other words, Socrates' formulation allows for the possibility of things that are neither pious nor impious. This seems more reasonable than Euthyphro's distinction, and Socrates' distinction fits better with Euthyphro's notion that the gods make war on each other. In other words, Socrates has helped Euthyphro avoid a couple of problems with his formulation.

7b8 ["how many teeth"]: the text could be translated "which of two numbers is greater." Probably he does not have in mind a situation where two people are disputing about whether 3 is greater than 2, but whether there are more of *these things* than *those things*. I've adapted *Euthydemus* 294c4-10 where such a dispute about quantity might arise and be settled by counting.

7c12 ["don't have an answer"]: perhaps Socrates is rushing Euthyphro, not allowing him time to think. But compare *Charmides* 159b1-2 and 165b5-c6 with *Euthydemus* 276c2. Perhaps we are to understand that Socrates paused here to allow Euthyphro time to think. In Plato's indirect dialogues (like the *Charmides* and *Euthydemus*) in which the fictional conversation is being recounted later, the narrator can describe pauses in the conversation; but in his direct dialogues like the *Euthyphro*, Plato does not add "stage directions."

7d2 ["good and bad"]: Xenophon mentions Socrates' contrast with arithmetic, measuring and weighing, but according to him, Socrates used this contrast to distinguish what humans can discover on their own and what they can discover only through divination (*mantikē, Memorabilia* 1.1.9). At least two other intentions are possible. First, Socrates may be drawing the objective-subjective distinction, indicating that we already have cognitive means to reach objective truth with respect to number, size, and weight but not yet with respect to normative properties like justice, admirability and goodness. The implication may be that a proper answer to the question "What is piety?" will involve something about which we have the cognitive means to reach objective truth. Second, he may be drawing the reduction-antireduction distinction (see note on 5d1 above). The implication may be that a proper answer to the question "What is piety?" will be reductive in the sense that it will eliminate normative—and hence disputed—terms like "good" or "just" and instead will use only non-normative—and hence undisputed—terms like "2 feet" or "3 pounds." Compare *Alcibiades* 126b8-d7, *Charmides* 166a3-b6, *Protagoras* 356c4-357e8, *Republic* 7.524a6-526c7, and *Philebus* 55e1-56c11.

7e9 ["the very same things"]: e.g. some gods may think "it is just for Zeus to rule us," while others will think, "it is unjust for Zeus to rule us" (cf. *Republic* 5.462c3-9).

8a4 ["the gods"]: Socrates is not fallaciously inferring that all of the gods both love and hate the same thing, he is validly inferring that the very same things will be loved by some gods, but hated by other gods. The phrase "*hoi theoi*" may be translated as "the gods," but in Greek it does not necessarily mean "all the gods."

8a7 ["pious and impious"]: this seems to come as a surprise to Euthyphro, though my mythology students see the point quickly; e.g. Artemis may kill you for having sex (cf. the myth of Actaeon), but Aphrodite may kill you for not having sex (cf. the myth of Hippolytus), and so sex is both pious and impious.

8b4 ["Hera"]: Hera cast her son Hephaestus out of Olympus and in revenge he sent her a golden throne with hidden chains that held her fast when she sat on it. Hera may frown upon children punishing their parents while Hephaestus may think it is acceptable in some circumstances. Zeus punished his father Kronos, who had punished his own father Ouranos. What will Kronos think of sons punishing their fathers? Perhaps he will reason casuistically thus: "I was right to punish my father in circumstances C1, but Zeus was wrong to punish me in circumstances C2." These myths, and the critique of legal arguments Socrates and Euthyphro are about to give, highlight not only a flaw in Euthyphro's previous analysis of piety, but also the tendency to use reasoning about universal moral principles (e.g. the wrongdoer must be brought to justice) as a way to conceal self-serving rationalization.

8c7 ["go on to argue"]: perhaps there are circumstances in which Callicles (cf. *Gorgias* 482c4-486d1) and Thrasymachus (cf. *Republic* 1.338c1-339a4) might make such an argument. E.g. Callicles might argue that superior individuals will occasionally violate conventional notions of justice, but that they ought not be punished for these transgressions (cf. *Gorgias* 483e1-484a2). Such a possibility raises especially profound questions, and some scholars take the fact that such issues are raised in the *Gorgias* and *Republic*, but not in the *Euthyphro*, as evidence that the latter was written earlier in Plato's philosophical development.

8d6 ["when"]: in 403 BCE there was an amnesty in Athens that was part of the settlement with Sparta, allowing the democratic faction to remain in control of the city after it defeated the oligarchs (*Constitution of Athens* 39). So a successful legal defense of a guilty person could be that he committed his crimes in 404.

8d8 ["Then"]: *oukoun* here is an adverb that, in questions, invites assent to an inference. E.g. when added to the verb "to think" means "surely you think, don't you, that...." Socrates assumes that the inference from human behavior to divine behavior is not merely valid, but obviously so. Xenophanes of Colophon (c.570-475 BCE), with whose philosophy Plato was familiar (*Sophist* 242d4-5), held that if horses could paint, they would depict the gods as horses. Socrates' assumption here does not entail, but is compatible with, the view that the traditional Greek depictions of the gods in stories and in art is mere anthropomorphism.

9c1 ["good speaker"]: I admit that my translation here is tendentious. Perhaps he means that the jury will listen to him if he speaks the truth, but I suspect he means that in order to get a jury to listen to you, it is important to tell them what they want to hear. I think he believes that a typical Athenian jury can be compared to children who are more inclined to listen to the dietary recommendations of a confectioner than those of a pediatrician (cf. *Gorgias* 521e2-522a7).

9c7 ["defined"]: *horizō* is a verb that refers primarily to dividing, separating or marking out a border (this verb is also used at 9d5). Socrates is not referring to defining words (see note on 5d1above), which he associates with Prodicus (cf. *Charmides* 163d1-4). At a bare minimum, Socrates wants an *eidos, idea* or *paradeigma* that accurately marks off the boundary of piety, i.e. it collects all the pious things (e.g. people and actions) and it collect only pious things: in other words, piety and the *eidos* of piety must be coextensive. Being coextensive, however, will not satisfy the condition of explanatory adequacy he insists upon at 6d9-e6 (see note on 6e5 above). In a particular room the predicate "is wearing a T-shirt" is coextensive with the predicate "is wearing jeans" if everyone in the room who is wearing jeans is also wearing a T-shirt, and *vice versa*; but there is no explanatory connection between the two predicates since it is possible to wear a T-shirt with chinos, and it is possible to wear jeans with a polo.

9d8 ["by adopting it"]: *hupotithēmi* is closely related to the root of the English "hypothesis." At this point Socrates has reason to conclude that Euthyphro does not know what he claimed to know. But he gives Euthyphro—as he gives others—more than one chance.

10a2 ["loved by the gods because it is pious"]: in a Christian context we might ask whether (a) "thou shalt not kill" is right because God commands it, or (b) God commands it because it is right? See note on 10d6 below.

10b1 ["because someone is carrying it"]: Socrates is using active and passive forms of the same verb, but his point is not verbal. He is not saying that the passive form of the verb was historically derived from the active form. He is applying the expectation of explanatory adequacy he emphasized at 6d9-e6 (see note on 6e5, and compare note on 9c7 above). A modern example may help. In 1957 Rogers and Hammerstein's *Cinderella* aired on CBS Television. In it the Prince sings to Cinderella, "Do I love you because you're beautiful, or are you beautiful because I love you?" Which way the explanatory connection works makes a tremendous amount of difference.

10b7 ["someone sees it"]: the claim "the chair is being seen" logically entails the claim "someone is seeing the chair." Socrates is not looking for a mere logical entailment, he is looking for an explanatory connection: if I am the one seeing the chair, it is false to say that I acquire the property of seeing the chair because the chair has the property of being seen by someone—as if the chair's being seen has to reach out to someone nearby and make them see it. Rather, it becomes true that the chair is being seen only when someone has the property of seeing it.

10d6 ["the gods love it because it is pious"]: Socrates and Euthyphro do not discuss the alternative, which may be relevantly similar to the view of William of Ockham (c.1285-1349 CE). In the context of Christianity we might ask whether (a) God commands, "thou shalt not kill" because it is just, or whether (b) "thou shalt not kill" is just because God commands it. Socrates and Euthyphro's view is similar to (a), but Ockham may be committed to (b), partly because he believes that the will of God is free, and that freedom is incompatible with any form of determination (e.g. determination of the will by right reason). Ockham's view is often called "voluntarism," i.e. the will is not determined by the greater good as presented by right reason. The view of Socrates and Euthyphro (as well as St. Thomas Aquinas, c.1225-74, and Francisco Suarez 1548-1617) is often called "intellectualism," i.e. the will is determined by the greater good as presented by right reason. Aquinas and Suarez defend the freedom of God's will by citing the freedom of creation: if God chooses to create human beings, then God has no further choice but to command "thou shalt not kill;" but since God freely chooses to create human beings, God freely chooses to command "thou shalt not kill" (if God had wanted to command "thou shalt kill," then God would have chosen to create only savage creatures, not human creatures).

10e5 ["simply because"]: here and earlier I have added the word "simply" to help make the point clearer. To say that the gods love piety because it is pious implies that piety has some positive form or character (*eidos* or *idea*, 6d11) that explains why the gods love it (and justifies their loving it). But the category of god-loved things includes more than just piety (e.g. the smell of burnt offerings, the Olympian games, a clean temple), and there is no positive form or character they all share in common other than the fact that the gods love them (just as all the things that are being carried have no positive form or character in common except for the fact that they are all being carried).

10e9 ["the exact same thing would be true of both"]: Socrates' formulation lends itself to a quasi-mathematical representation. Let "P" stand for the form of piety, and let "GL" stand for the form (if it is a form) of the god-loved (i.e. loved by all the gods). Euthyphro's current hypothesis, then, is: P = GL. If the two are indeed one and the same thing, then they can be substituted for one another *salva veritate*. However, we find:

P is loved because it is has the property of being P, [true],

GL is loved because it has the property of being GL, [false],

and also,

GL is loved just because the gods love it, [true],

·P is loved just because the gods love it, [false].

The fact that both pairs have one true and one false claim entails that P ≠ GL. Socrates appears to be using "Leibniz' Law" (aka "the indiscernibility of identicals," see also *Protagoras* 355b3-c1) millennia before Leibniz. This law fails in some contexts, so it is worth considering whether this is one of those contexts.

11a7 ["essence"]: this may be the first use of the philosophical distinction between *ousia* and *pathos*. To state the *ousia* of a thing is to answer Socrates, "What is it?" question, and so presumably he thinks that an *ousia* is a form, character or paradigm (see notes on 5d4, 6d11 and 6e5 above). A *pathos* does not answer the "What is it?" question, but this covers a wide range of properties. Since Socrates doesn't explain this distinction, probably we should not attribute a complex view to him here.

11c1 ["Daedalus"]: legendary artist, craftsman and inventor most famous for the wings he designed for himself and his son Icarus. But this story probably arose quite late (an Athenian vase painting from about 560 may be of Daedalus and Icarus flying). The oldest traditions associate him with Hephaestus, the divine smith, whose works are described as *daidaleos*, i.e. "curiously wrought." For example, when Thetis comes to ask for new armor for her son Achilles, Hephaestus is busy making twenty tripods with wheels that will roll themselves (*automatoi*) into the assembly of the gods when they are needed (*Iliad* 18.368-79; cf. Aristotle, *Politics* 1.4.1253b33-37). The weird image of bronze artifacts moving themselves about "automatically" captured the Athenian imagination, and so in numerous 5th century satyr plays and comedies Daedalus was portrayed as a sculptor of living statues. Socrates uses this same analogy at *Meno* 97d6-e5 (see note on Meno 97d6). See also *Hippias Major* 281d9-282a3, *Republic* 7.529d7-530a1, *Laws* 3.677d1-6. Why does Socrates say that Daedalus is his ancestor? If he means this literally, then perhaps this supports the tradition that Socrates' father was a sculptor or stone-cutter. Socrates' claim at *Apology* 22c8-e1 is not inconsistent with the family business being stone-cutting or statuary if Socrates himself proved unworthy of carrying on the family trade and so handed the management of his financial affairs to Crito (as was claimed by Demetrius Phalereus c.350–c.280 BCE). Alternatively, Socrates may be making a humble joke (cf. *episkōptō*, 11c2) at his own expense: with Daedalus, works wander in circles; with Socrates, words wander in circles.

11e1 ["gold of Tantalus"]: Tantalus was a mortal son of Zeus and the king of Lydia in Asia Minor, rich in mines. He was the father of Pelops, the grandfather of Atreus and the great grandfather of Agamemnon and Menelaus. Today he is mostly associated with having committed some crime against Zeus (different versions of the story mention different crimes, some more lurid than others) and his tantalizing post-mortem punishment in the underworld (Homer, *Odyssey* 11.582-592; Plato, *Hippias Major* 293b6; *Gorgias* 525e1). In Plato's day he was often associated with great mineral wealth (cf. Isocrates, *To Philip* 5.144). Socrates compares Prodicus to Tantalus at *Protagoras* 315c8-d1. Plato derives his name from *talanteia*, i.e. "swaying," referring to the rock swaying over his head according to one account of his punishment (*Cratylus* 395e1); or from *talanton*, accusative masculine singular adjective from *talas*, i.e. "wretched" (e2).

11e4 ["pay close attention"]: this clause is not in the text; I've borrowed it from *Laches* 197e6-8. There are some structural similarities between *Euthyphro*, on the one hand, and both *Charmides* and *Laches* on the other hand. In the latter two dialogues the examination of a particular virtue is handed off from one interlocutor to a second, and the second is intellectually more sophisticated than the first. I think that Plato is doing the same sort of thing here (and perhaps also at *Crito* 48d8). See also note on 6c4 above.

12a1 ["all pious things are just"]: this passage (11e7-12a2) may be one of the most influential passages in all of Plato for in it he succinctly lays out all four of the "categorical propositions" on which syllogistic logic is based. This is especially significant because syllogistic logic formed the basis of all higher learning for many centuries. The four "categorical propositions" are: (1) universal affirmation (e.g. all humans are animals), (2) universal negation (e.g. no humans are horses), (3) particular affirmation (e.g. some animals are horses), and (4) particular negation (e.g. some animals are not horses). If you see that horses and humans are species under the genus "animal," then you can see the connection between syllogistic logic and taxonomy (cf. the modern distinction of living beings into kingdoms, phyla, classes, orders, families, genera and species). Taxonomic reasoning is a natural corollary of the use of *idea* (see note on 5d4 above) and *eidos* (see note on 6d11 above).

12a5 ["your great wealth of wisdom"]: perhaps this should be read as virtually dripping with irony, or even sarcasm (see note on 2c3 above). Alternatively, because Socrates himself denies being wise (e.g. 2c5-6), he is in no position to say who is and who is not wise (cf. *Charmides* 165b5-c2) so he takes confident claims to wisdom at face value unless and until they are decisively refuted (though it is not clear what will count as the decisive refutation of a confident claim to wisdom by someone who admits that they lack wisdom, cf. *Charmides* 172b7-8). In the *Euthydemus* Socrates repeatedly treats the sophists Euthydemus and Dionysodorus with this same deference, and so the question of whether he is being sarcastic or sincere arises there as well.

12a8 ["the poet who wrote the lines"]: from *The Cypria*, allegedly by Stasinus (allegedly a younger contemporary of Homer himself). Since Homer's *Iliad* narrates events near the end of the Trojan War, and the *Odyssey* focuses on Odysseus, later poets couldn't resist filling in all the gaps. Eventually "The Epic Cycle" was complete: ten works in all ending with *The Telegony* (in which Odysseus' son by Circe, Telegonus, unknowingly kills his own father and then knowingly marries his father's wife, Penelope; while Odysseus' son by Penelope, Telemachus, knowingly marries his father's former divine lover, Circe); the cycle begins with *The War of the Titans* (starting with the original mating of Gaia and Ouranos). *The Cypria* was probably composed by the end of the 7th century BCE, and it begins with Zeus' decision to thin the human population of Gaia by war—all the ensuing suffering, then, is part of Zeus' cruel plan, which is probably the point of the lines quoted by Socrates (see note on 6a8 above).

12b10 ["fears and recoils"]: Socrates contrasts *aideomai* and *aischunō* with *phobeō* and *diedō*. While it is not impossible to draw subtle distinctions between the members of each pair, it is easy to see that Socrates is employing a chiasmus, i.e. in the first pair the more poetic term occurs first, followed by the more prosaic term; in the second pair the more prosaic term occurs first, followed by the more poetic term. He treats both pairs as synonyms.

12c6 ["one kind"] *morion* occurs here and at 12d2; it is closely related to *meros*, which occurs at 12d5, d6, d8, e1, e5, e8. Literally it means "part" as opposed to "whole," e.g. a section of land (Thucydides 7.58.2) or part of an army (2.39.3). The thought of dividing justice into parts is probably related to the thought of dividing nature at its joints (*Phaedrus* 265e1-2) and also to the taxonomic divisions in the *Sophist* (cf. 219c7, 220b10 etc.) In the *Sophist* it is clear that *meros* is related to *genos*, e.g. 220b4, to *eidos*, e.g. at 219c2, and to *idea* at 235d2, but not to *paradeigma* (see 218d9, 221c5, 226c1-2, 233d3, 235d7, 251a7.

12d10 ["evenly divisible by two"]: actually Socrates defines even numbers as "not scalene, but isosceles." We find this definition nowhere else, so perhaps it was invented by Socrates or Plato. A scalene triangle has no sides of equal length, an isosceles triangle has two sides of equal length, so this seems to be a mnemonic for the more standard definition I give in the text.

12e7 ["attending"]: *therapeia* primarily refers to what used to be called "paying court" either to gods or mortal kings and potentates. So it can mean "worship" or rendering service in the expectation of receiving favors from the ones in power. It also had a medical use and so can mean "therapy," "treatment" or "cure." Finally, it referred to the way that we tend animals by feeding, watering, cleaning them, protecting them from predators and so on. It is in the first sense, i.e. "paying court," that *therapeia* seems an appropriate word to use for the way that Greeks tended the temples of their gods, keeping them clean, leaving fresh fruit or flowers by the statue of the god and so on (cf. note on *Protagoras* 354b7). But if justice towards our fellow human beings is *therapeia* in this sense, then it would seem to follow that justice is a mercenary affair: we treat others justly only to help ensure that they treat us justly in return, so that if they do not treat us justly in return we may infer that we have no good reason to continue to treat them justly.

13c12 ["in order to clarify"]: sophists like Euthydemus and Dionysodorus may well have used the ambiguity of *therapeia* as a refutation of Euthyphro's claim (cf. *Euthydemus* 275d3-277c7, with Socrates' analysis at 277e2-278b2). The difference with Socratic argument is that Socrates never prevents someone from drawing any distinction they like, as long as they say what they are doing (compare *Euthydemus* 295b2-296c7 with *Charmides* 163d5-7).

13d10 ["function"]: *ergon* can mean product, but it does so because it refers primarily to work. The work of a carpenter is to produce products, but the work of a doctor is to heal. "Result" is often a good translation. To assume that every craft has an *ergon* is not to assume that every craft produces a product, see *Charmides* 165c4-166b6.

14a9 ["sum them up?"]: etymologically there is an obvious answer to Socrates' question, i.e. *eudaimonia* (usually translated as "happiness"). Literally *eudaimonia* refers to a life filled with all the blessings that god can bestow upon a mortal. Surely it would not be unreasonable to suggest that the virtue of piety (as well as, or together with, the other Greek cardinal virtues of courage, temperance, justice and wisdom) plays an important role in giving us fine and good lives (cf. *Charmides* 171d1-172a3; *Euthydemus* 282a1-6). Of course, this answer would raise more questions than it answers, but perhaps a full discussion of piety will inevitably raise those questions.

14a11 ["a moment ago"]: at 9b4-5.

14c1-2 ["you were so close"]: Euthyphro was close when he referred to saving one's family and the common good (14b4-5), but he turned away by turning vague ("ruins and destroys everything") instead of saying more specifically what would constitute saving "families and the common goods of cities."

14c3 ["I would have learned"]: some scholars argue that Socrates says this ironically—there is no answer to the question because the question rests on the false assumption that the virtue of piety can reasonably be compared with ordinary crafts (cf. *Charmides* 174a10-175a8). Others think that Socrates does take this comparison seriously (cf. *Laches* 198d1-199a5), and so think that the dialogue was indeed on the verge of identifying what piety is. Some scholars even suggest that Socrates has a particular answer in mind, e.g. the point of his own service to god expressed at *Apology* 23a5-c1, 29e3-30c1. But Socrates' own service is almost unique to him (*Apology* 30e1-7). I suspect that Socrates thinks they need to pursue Euthyphro's notion that piety plays an important role in one's own individual good as well as the good of one's family and in the common good as a whole—which substantially broadens any inquiry into one particular virtue (cf. *Gorgias* 507a5-c7).

14c9 ["to ask for something"]: Greeks did offer prayers of praise and thanksgiving, but thanks can be given for blessings bestowed, and praise can express admiration of those who bestow blessings upon us. The mercenary conception of piety Euthyphro expresses seems compatible with a conventional outlook. Many intelligent people are conventional thinkers, and so in my opinion some scholars go too far in criticizing (and ridiculing) Euthyphro's intellect.

14d5 ["miss anything"]: literally Socrates says that he doesn't want anything Euthyphro says to "fall to the ground." This phrase probably refers to wasted shots, i.e. arrows that miss their targets and hence fall to the ground (cf. Aeschylus, *Agamemnon* 366). This could be dripping with irony to the point of biting sarcasm, e.g. "I would hate for a single pearl of your great wisdom to slip through my fingers." Alternatively, Plato is making sure that Socrates enunciates an important principle of inquiry: people who think in purely conventional terms don't pay close attention to what is said because they tend to hear only what they expect to hear. In this case, Euthyphro seems to have forgotten Socrates' earlier argument that the gods love piety because it is pious, and that piety is not pious simply because the gods love it (compare 15c5-6 with 10d6-7). In other words, Socrates' argument was a "wasted shot."

14e3 ["skill"]: *technikos* (skillful, workmanlike, artistic) occurs here and at 15b10 in connection with Daedalus. However, at 11e1 Daedalus was said to have "wisdom" (*sophia*). Also, *technikos* here is taking the place of "knowledge" (*epistēmē*) in 14d1 above. Either Socrates is being sloppy, or he is equivocating, or he is assuming that *sophia*, *epistēmē* and *technē* are connected somehow.

14e6 ["commerce"]: in Sophocles' version, Ajax seems to have a mercenary attitude towards the gods because he assumes that reverence for the gods is appropriate only if we need their help (*Aias* 762-69). Athena punished him severely for saying that he did not need her help. We should also note that modern scholars have trouble distinguishing ancient attitudes toward magic and sacrifice: both have the goal of securing blessings or avoiding affliction.

15a10 ["as I just said"]: at 14b2 (and b6, untranslated).

15b1 ["part of justice"]: this phrase does not occur in the Greek; I am borrowing it from 12e5-8 because that is where Euthyphro expressed the analysis of piety that they are still considering. If we lose sight of the fact that they are still attempting to identify piety as a species of justice, then we may think that Socrates is about to commit the "fallacy of accident," i.e. from the claim that piety has the accidental property of being loved by the gods fallaciously inferring that piety is essentially identical to the god-loved. But in fact he is committing no such fallacy: he is offering Euthyphro one final opportunity to avoid falling back into his previous conception of piety as what is dear to the gods. Euthyphro's only hope is to distinguish worshipping and venerating the gods, and hence gratifying them, from (i) benefitting them (which he has just done, 15a5-6), and also from (ii) being dear to them (which he refuses to do, 15b4-5). The root of the problem is precisely what Socrates indicated at 14c3 (see note above), i.e. instead of pursuing his notion of piety as playing a role in achieving one's own good, the good of one's family, and also the common good of the city (14b4-5), i.e. *eudaimonia*, Euthyphro turns away (at 14b5-7) to the utterly conventional notion that the gods punish us for irreverence. From 14b8 on Socrates simply has to go through the motions of pointing out the moral bankruptcy of conventional theology (for example, compare the story of Athena and Ajax mentioned in the note on 14e6 with Socrates' incredulity at 6a6-c4).

15b8 ["wander away"]: see 11b6-e1.

15b11 ["earlier?"]: see 6e9-7a1.

15c12 ["give up the quest"]: *apodeiliaō* comes from *deilia* which is timidity or cowardice. Since Euthyphro is about to leave, Socrates' use of this word here can be interpreted as a preemptory charge of intellectual cowardice on Euthyphro's part. In other words, it is *not*—as many scholars say—that Euthyphro is unintelligent; rather, in Plato's view, although Euthyphro will dare to assert some unconventional views, ultimately he sticks with safe, conventional assumptions about piety.

15d3 ["Proteus"]: immortal Proteus of Egypt, aka "old man of the sea," possessed the knowledge of how Menelaus might make his way home. But in order to get the truth out of him, Menelaus had to grab him and hold on, which wasn't easy because Proteus tried to escape by turning himself into a lion, then a snake, a leopard, a boar, rushing water and a tree (but not fire, as his daughter had warned). Finally Proteus tires, asks Menelaus who revealed how he could be captured, and what Menelaus needed. Proteus answered all Menelaus' questions, and more (Homer, *Odyssey* 4.382-569). See also *Euthydemus* 288b7, *Ion* 541e7.

15d5 ["you would never have dared"]: Socrates is well aware that people are often guilty of having false pretentions to knowledge (*Apology* 23a5-c1) so perhaps Socrates is being ironic here. Alternatively, because Socrates disavows knowledge of what piety is, he may be in no position to pass judgment on Euthyphro, especially after so brief an examination. Socrates is not so arrogant as to deny that some may indeed have greater wisdom than he possesses (*Apology* d9-e2).

15e4 ["time for me to leave"]: there are at least three possible explanations for Euthyphro's abrupt departure: (i) he simply wants to get away from Socrates, (ii) he has just been summoned to the trial against his father and he goes through with his prosecution, and (iii) Socrates' reminder about the wrath of the gods and the condemnation of mortals has finally convinced him not to go through with the prosecution. Plato could have disambiguated the ending, but he did not.

NOTES ON EUTHYDEMUS

271a1 ["talking to"]: *dialegō* can refer to a conversation (e.g. *Phaedo* 98d6; Herodotus, *Histories* 3.50.3), but the "*dia-*" prefix can indicate a more pointed discussion, e.g. an examination or interrogation (e.g. Herodotus, *Histories* 3.51.1). Plato sometimes uses this word to refer to a special form of "dialectic" (e.g. *Republic* 511c5). I avoid translating this word as "dialectic" since it is never certain that Plato means it in that sense in the *Euthydemus*. Here is every place where the verb is used, so you can decide for yourself whether any of these uses should be translated as "dialectic:" 271a1, 273b4, 274b8, 275b6, 275c3, 283b9, 284e5, 295e2, 301c4, 304a2, 304a6, 304b2, 304b6-7, 304e1, 305b2. Perhaps 301c4 is a good candidate for using "dialectic."

271c3 ["the colony at Thurii"]: probably founded in 443. This "panhellenic" colony was initiated by Pericles and included volunteers from ten different Greek cities. It was intended to be a model city with a democratic constitution. It included some of the greatest intellectuals of the time (including the historian Herodotus and the sophist Protagoras). Unfortunately, it didn't take long for the "panhellenic" cooperation to break down: the Athenians were taken out of power, many were exiled, and the Delphians took over the leadership of the colony.

271c6 ["*Pan*-sophists!"]: Socrates returns to this point near the end of his discussion with Euthydemus and Dionysodorus (see note on 301c4 below).

272c5 ["Elder Educator"]: it's not entirely clear what is so funny about this name. Socrates does not claim to be a poor student or that he is a bad kithara player (on the kithara, see not on *Laches* 192a3), the joke simply seems to be about his age. So perhaps the joke turns on the typical view of a teacher as older than the student, so if the student is an old man one would expect the teacher to be ancient. If that's what the joke is about, then Socrates' solution to bring other old men along as students would be designed to break down the assumption that students are always young, and teachers are always older than their students. This would fit well with the end of the *Laches* (cf. *Laches* 201a2-5).

272e4 ["divine sign"]: see *Apology* 31d1, 40a4, 41d5-6, *Phaedrus* 242b8 and *Republic* 6.496c4. (See also *Theages* 128e5, but scholars dispute whether Plato wrote *Theages*; and see Xenophon *Apology* 12-13). This "divine sign" could simply be an unexplained feeling or inclination, and since Socrates couldn't explain it, he assumed it was from god. The references at *Euthyphro* 3b5 and *Theaetetus* 151a4 omit "*sēmeion*" ("sign"), and so in theory it is possible that Socrates is literally referring to a specific god that intervenes in his life. The fact that Socrates uses the word "*daimonion*" is probably irrelevant, since his phrase "*daimonia kaina*" at *Apology* 24c1 seems equivalent to his "*kainous...theous*" at *Euthyphro* 3b2, so that "*daimonion*" and "*theos*" are used synonymously. The "*phonē*" ("voice") at *Apology* 31d3 could be used as evidence that Socrates believed that a divine being actually spoke to him. This could be used as evidence that Socrates suffered from auditory hallucinations (and so could be a symptom of a sleep disorder, a lesion on the brain stem, schizophrenia, etc.); alternatively "*phonē*" could be analogical. Later, Christians literally demonized the pagan *daimōn*: in the Christian scriptures, "*daimones*" is used only in reference to the Gerasene demoniac (i.e. at Matthew 8:31, named "Legion" at Mark 5:9). This explains why the Christian Clement of Alexandria (c.150-c.215 CE) thought that Socrates was guided by a demon, a fallen angel who stole part of the truth and gave it to humans (philosophy is this partial truth; see *Stromata* 1.17).

273e2 ["gift of Hermes"]: also used at 295a8. This phrase is typically used for something that is remarkably good luck; we might call it a "godsend." Hermes was the messenger of Zeus, so perhaps there is more to Plato's use of this word than simply its vernacular tone. It may simultaneously be connected to the concepts of happiness (*eudaimonia*, *makarios*, e.g. 280b6, b7, d3, 282e3; 290d7) and success (*eutuchia*, e.g. 279c7).

273e7 ["as divine"]: i.e. when he asked them to be "gracious" or "propitious" (*hilaos*). This word was indeed used of divine favor, which is why I've also kept Socrates' references to Zeus and Hermes. Some will think that Socrates is being ironic here. If not, then he's probably just taking them at their word (cf. e2-4) and giving them the benefit of the doubt in a sort of "innocent until proven guilty" approach, i.e. accept that they are telling the truth unless and until they demonstrate otherwise). See note on 294d8 below.

274c1 ["his beloved Clinias"]: the dual passions of Ctesippus for virtue and Clinias is a fascinating detail. Homosexual desire is indicated by Plato's language (*erastēs* at 274b5, c5 and *paidika* at c3).

275a6 ["love wisdom"]: Socrates uses the verb *philosopheō* (also at 282d1 and 305c7), and so Socrates is literally asking the brothers to teach Clinias "to philosophize." The noun "*philosophia*" is used at 275a1, 288d8, 304e7, 305b6, 305d1-2, 306b2, 306c4, 307a2, and 307b7.

275b4 ["corrupt him"]: corrupting the youth was one of the charges brought against Socrates (*Apology* 24b9).

275e1 ["say what appears to you to be true"]: this is known as Socrates' "Sincerity Requirement," see also *Laches* 193c7; *Crito* 49d1; *Protagoras* 331b8-d1; *Gorgias* 495a5-b6, 500b; *Meno* 75d6, 83d2; *Republic* 346a; and *Theaetetus* 154c7-e6. Neither Euthydemus nor Dionysodorus express a sincerity requirement.

276a1 ["the wise are the ones who learn"]: "*hoi sophoi*" can refer to the intelligent or the knowledgeable: the "wise" learn because the intelligent learn, but the "wise" do not learn because those who already have knowledge are not said to learn what they already know. Aristotle would classify this as a fallacy of equivocation (*homonumia*; *Sophistical Refutations* 4.165b30-166a7). Aristotle explicitly refers to Euthydemus at 20.177b12, quoting a famous argument of his that does not appear in Plato's *Euthydemus* and is too compressed to be clear to us without the original context. So although there are several places in *Sophistical Refutations* where Aristotle might have been relying upon Plato's *Euthydemus*, it is also possible that he relied on independent sources.

276c3 ["dictates a passage"]: Greek education typically involved imitation, memorization and repetition (cf. *Protagoras* 325e-326a). A teacher would recite a line, or several lines, from Homer's *Iliad* or *Odyssey*, for example, and then expect the students to write down exactly what he had recited.

276d8 ["what they know or what they do not know"]: at *Meno* 80e1-5 Socrates refers to an "eristic argument" (sometimes called "the paradox of inquiry") that is similar, i.e. inquiry is impossible because we cannot inquire into what we know (since we already know it) nor into what we do not know (since we wouldn't know it even if we discovered it).

276e3 ["first question seemed fine"]: Socrates uses the adjective *kalos*. This could be irony, or outright sarcasm. Alternatively, Socrates thinks that learning to deal with the fallacy of equivocation is a beneficial exercise (cf. "games for students," 278b2).

276e9 ["learners learn what they do not know"]: Aristotle may have this passage in mind at *Sophistical Refutations* 4.165b30-34. This is another fallacy of equivocation (*homōnumia*): Aristotle says that "to learn" can mean "acquire knowledge" or "to understand by using knowledge." However, at *Rhetoric* 2.24.3 Aristotle analyzes this as a fallacy of composition: if you know each component (each letter of the word), then you know the composite (the word). Perhaps this is the analysis Aristotle suggests at *Sophistical Refutations* 4.166a32-33.

277b6 ["to learn is to acquire knowledge"]: this is the first of two important steps in this argument (for the second, see note on 277c2 below). Here Dionysodorus defines a crucial term. This is not only how to avoid being tripped up by the fallacy of equivocation, it is also a good way to mark distinctions that could be important, but might go unnoticed (cf. *Sophist* 218e2-221c3).

277c2 ["people who acquire something?"]: this is the second of two important steps in this argument (for the first, see note on 277b6 above). Here the definitional connections Dionysodorus draws begin to be converted to the types of propositions that are used in syllogistic reasoning. The syllogism Dionysodorus constructs is:

1. No acquirer is a possessor.
2. All knowers are possessors.
3. So: no acquirers are knowers.
4. All learners are acquirers.
5. So: no learners are knowers.

277d1 ["a third time"]: in Greek wrestling matches, the first person to knock his opponent down three times was the winner. Plato has made it clear that for these sophists, intellectual discussion is a game and the point is to win (cf. 273c4-9, 275e3-6, 276c1-3, 276d9-e2, 277b3-5). This is definitive of eristic.

277d7 ["Corybantic mysteries"]: the Corybantic celebrants set the initiate on a throne and danced ecstatically around him the way the divine Corybantes were said to have danced around the infant Zeus, or around the infant Dionysus to the flute-playing of Marsyas. Socrates makes a similar point about poets at *Ion* 533e5-534b6. At *Apology* 22b6-c3 Socrates says that when he examined poets, he discovered that any of the bystanders could explain their poems better than the poets themselves could: the poems are excellent but the poets don't actually know what they are saying when they write them. Compare also *Laws* 7.790d-791b where Plato defends the Corybantic rituals using his own psychological theory and not the theology professed by the Corybantics themselves. Socrates here may be saying that what Euthydemus and Dionysodorus are doing is excellent even if they themselves don't actually grasp what is excellent about it. See also *Symposium* 215e, *Phaedrus* 253a, *Republic* 3.399e.

277e3 ["language is a precision instrument"]: literally Socrates quotes Prodicus as saying that one must learn "straightness concerning names," which probably means "correctness of terms" (cf. *Cratylus* 422c3-4). Instead, I quote my own personal Prodicus, i.e. Dr. Frederick Peachy (my Greek instructor at Reed Colleged). Dr. Peachy frequently told us that "language is a precision instrument" when we struggling students would complain about the complexities of the Greek participle.

278b6 ["you would be able to play these games"]: Socrates does not say that this is the *only* thing you will be able to do if you learn them, since obviously that's false. If you learn these games then it will be more difficult for others to play them on you, as Socrates himself will demonstrate (e.g. 295b1-c9).

278c4 ["the promise"]: made at 275a3 and narrowed down by Socrates at 275a5-7.

278c5 ["protreptic wisdom"]: literally, "protreptic" means "turning toward." A "protreptic" speech is a speech of exhortation, urging the audience to turn towards something in particular. Aristotle's lost work *Protrepticus* was a short treatise urging young people to turn to, and study, philosophy. At 275a5-7 Socrates asked the two brothers to get Clinias to turn towards wisdom and virtue.

278e3 ["wishes"]: *boulomai*. It is not clear whether Socrates distinguishes *boulomai* from *epithumeō* (see notes on *Charmides* 167e1 ["desire"] and *Protagoras* 340a8-b1). He did just use *epithumeō* at 278d4 (translated as "I'd like"), but *epithumeō* (as well as the related noun *epithumia*) is entirely absent from the following discussion (i.e. 278e3-282d3). Does this imply that in Socrates' view, we can understand human behavior, or human virtue, by considering wishes alone, not desires; or does he assume that if we consider wishes, we have *ipso facto* considered desires?

279d6 ["wisdom is success"]: it is hard to deny that Socrates is indeed claiming that wisdom and success (*eutuchia*) are one and the same thing. Both this claim and his argument for it have drawn serious criticism. There are four main issues. (1) What does Socrates mean by "*eutuchia*" (success, good fortune, or luck)? (2) Does he really mean that wisdom and success are one and the same thing, so that simply by being wise you are necessarily successful (i.e. even if you never actually act wisely, and so never actually succeed at any task)? Or does he mean what he says at 280b2-3, i.e. that if you have wisdom, you don't need any *additional* source of success like divine assistance, or good luck, because your wisdom on its own guarantees success? (3) Should we take his qualification at 279e6 ("as a general rule," *hōs epi pan eipein*) as applying to the entire argument, so that he is not really saying that wisdom and success are one and the same thing (e.g. a wise doctor can cure any patient no matter how bad their condition), but only that the wise are usually more successful than anyone else (e.g. a wise doctor has a better chance than anybody else of curing a patient)? (4) Does he really intend to be asserting a claim that "any child knows"? If so, then why is any argument at all needed? If not, if he intends a stronger claim, then is his argument valid? See also note on 281b1 below.

280e3 ["correctly or incorrectly?"]: literally "*orthōs*" is an adjective that means "straight" as opposed to "bent" (e.g. standing up straight as opposed to sitting down, *Iliad* 23.271). Metaphorically it can refer to a norm, in which case it means "normal" as opposed to "deviant" (e.g. genuine as opposed to fake, *Republic* 341c9; morally right as opposed to morally wrong, *Republic* 540d6; true as opposed to false, *Protagoras* 359e8). Since Socrates is trying to convince Clinias to care about wisdom and virtue (275a1, a6, 278d3), we are on the horns of a dilemma at 280e3: either by "*orthōs*" he means moral correctness, in which case his inference that Clinias ought to care about virtue will be valid but this premise will assume what he is trying to prove; or else "*orthōs*" means only a generic correctness, in which case his premise does not assume what he is trying to prove, although his inference will be questionable. Compare *Meno* 88a4-5.

281b1 ["correct and successful"]: this passage suggests that we should translate "*eutuchia*" as "success" (see note on 279d6 above). Here Socrates uses both "*to orthōs*" (281a8) and "*katorthousa*" (281b1) to indicate what *epistēmē* produces. The "*kat-*" in "*katorthousa*" strongly suggests doing something through to completion, e.g. not merely drawing up a perfect plan for making a well-tailored suit, but actually producing a well-tailored suit that looks and fits perfectly.

281b3 ["achievement of their goals"]: this passage is difficult to translate because of "*eupragia*" (at 281b3). On the one hand, "*eupragia*" (= "*eupraxia*") seems to be a synonym for "*eutuchia*" (cf. Herodotus, *Histories* 7.49.4) in which case the inference here is unobjectionable, though redundant. On the other hand, if Socrates is not being redundant but is drawing a new conclusion, then (i) we must reject "successful" as the correct translation of "*eutuchia*," and (ii) we must question whether Socrates' inference here is valid. At *Protagoras* 344c6-d5 Socrates appears to accept that there are such things as unmanageable disasters that can prevent the successful completion of tasks like piloting a ship, growing crops or healing a sick person (see note on *Protagoras* 344d5). Does that contradict his point here?

281b8 ["a smart man"]: here I translate "*nous*" as "smart" (I translate it as "mind" at 272b2, 272e2, 282d2; "pay attention" at 272d8, 273b6, 283a2, 303e7; "intend" at 274a7; "sense" at 287e1). There are three problems with this passage. (1) How are we to translate "*nous*"? If we use "intelligence," then how are we to translate *phronēsis* (281b6, 281d8, 306d1)? If Socrates has not lost sight of his mission to turn Clinias to virtue and the love of *sophia*, then why is he bringing up *nous* and *phronēsis*? Is he using them all synonymously? Are the latter two approximations of *sophia* that somehow fall short? (2) In my translation, the question is about which of two men would benefit "more." However, the word "*mallon*" is ambiguous: "x *mallon* y" can mean "x more than y" or it can mean "x rather than y" ("x and not y"). (3) The great Neoplatonist philosopher and scholar Iamblichus (c.245-c.325 CE) claimed that "*noun echōn*" was not in Plato's original text. Most editors follow Iamblichus, thinking that the contrast Socrates wants to draw is between a stupid man with many things and a stupid man with few things, not between a stupid man with many things and a smart man with few. I see no reason to question the text. First, Socrates has no interest in suggesting to Clinias that it can be ok to be stupid as long as you have few possessions: surely he doesn't want Clinias to think that it is ok to be stupid under any circumstances. Second, the number of possessions is not Socrates' main concern, so the many/few contrast would be a red herring. The stupid/smart contrast, however, is clearly related to his concern to convert Clinias to virtue and the love of *sophia*: people typically think that many possessions makes you *eudaimōn*, so the contrast between a stupid person with much, and a smart person with little is directly relevant to the priorities Socrates would like Clinias to develop (it's not what you have, but whether you deal with what you have intelligently that matters most).

281d4-5 ["in themselves good by nature"]: it is not clear if this phrase is referring to a special kind of goodness, or a special way of being good, or if it is simply asking whether these things are good. At d6 Socrates uses the word "if" (*ean*), so we might think he is claiming that things like money and good looks have a special kind of goodness: *conditional goodness*. However, at e3-4 he seems to say that "conditional goodness" isn't a way of being good, rather a thing that has mere conditional goodness is not itself good at all, but the wise use of it is good. The issue of whether anything other that knowledge is good arises in the *Meno* (see note on *Meno* 87d6-7).

282b6 ["anything honorable"]: see the speech of Pausanias at *Symposium* 180c4-185c3, especially 184b5-e4; and see also *Phaedrus* 230e6-241d1. Greek courtship—both heterosexual and homosexual—typically involved a gift, e.g. the lover might offer the beloved a quail, goose, dog, or lyre. The context is intended to be playful, romantic seduction, but it is all too easy to disparage it as a shameful form of exchange. The idea that the beloved would be willing to do anything for the lover in exchange for wisdom will bring to some minds the thought of sexual favors, but given Socrates' attitudes expressed at *Lysis* 211d8-e8 and *Symposium* 218d6-219e3, we should consider the possibility that by saying "anything *honorable*," Socrates does not have sexual favors in mind here.

283b2-3 ["encouragement to virtue"]: of course, what we get is more sophistry (see note on 283d2 below). So this passage could be irony or sarcasm. However, Socrates did just say that what they got was amazing "in a way" (*tina*); perhaps it was amazing in a different way than he expected, and perhaps it was an encouragement to virtue in a different way than he expected. If the study of logic is important to wisdom, and if wisdom is important for virtue, then perhaps the study of logical fallacies is important for virtue.

283b10 ["not taking it seriously"]: Socrates pointed this out at 278b2-c5. Perhaps he's being ironic, saying things that he doesn't really mean, but if so, he's really sticking with the pretense. If he does intend these comments ironically, the irony is clearly lost on Crito, so the irony can only be intended for the reader to catch, but what would the point of that be? An alternative is that he is treating these sophists the way he describes treating all self-proclaimed wise people at *Apology* 21b-23b (see especially 23b4-7), i.e. he treats them as "innocent until proven guilty," or rather "wise until proven unwise." See also note on 285a5 below.

283d2 ["to become who he is not"]: thus begins the "fallacy of dropping the qualifier" or, as Aristotle puts it, the fallacy connected to using an expression absolutely or in a certain respect (*Sophistical Refutations* 5.166b38-167a21). An Ethiopian, for example, is black in a certain respect (his skin is black), but he is not black in a different respect (his teeth are white); so if you drop the qualifications and use absolute expressions then you can say that the Ethiopian is black and not-black, which sounds like a contradiction (*Sophistical Refutations* 5.167a12-15). Aristotle also explicitly mentions the sort of fallacy Dionysodorus uses here, since it is easy to slide between "not to be something" (e.g. a dog is not a man) and "not to be" absolutely (i.e. not to exist). For another explanation of this fallacy, see note on 284a6 below.

283e2 ["Thurian visitor"]: because they were exiled from the city of Thurii (271c3). Ctesippus brings up their association with Thurii again at 288b1. This may be perfectly polite, but perhaps Ctesippus is subtly reminding them that they are exiles—which a bit rude, but true.

283e9 ["saying something"]: the coming argument is a bit clearer in Greek than in English, at least grammatically. Perhaps the argument commits the fallacy known as "amphiboly," which turns not on the ambiguity of a word, but on the ambiguity of grammar. For example, consider the claim "speaking of the silent is possible." If the genitive case (i.e. "of the silent") is the "objective genitive," then silence is the object of what is being said, e.g. we can say things like, "he is keeping silent;" but if the genitive is the "subjective genitive" then silence is the subject of the speaking, i.e. silence is actually speaking (which sounds like a contradiction). Shakespeare has a famous example: "The duke yet lives that Henry shall depose" (*Henry VI Part 2*, Act 1, Scene 4, line 30): is Henry the subject or the object of the deposition? At *Euthydemus* 283e9 there may be an amphiboly in the Greek phrase "saying something:" if "saying" is a "success verb" (like "convincing"), then "saying something" is expressing a fact; but if "saying" is an "attempt verb" (like "trying to convince"), then "saying something" can merely be representing something as if it is a fact—the latter can be a lie, the former cannot. This amphiboly is more appealing in Greek than in English.

284a3 ["saying something real"]: yes, this is weird; it's slightly less weird in Greek, but that's only because it is even more vague in Greek (if you can imagine that). The real difficulty in understanding this argument is the fact that we really shouldn't just dismiss it outright. Plato is drawing on the philosophy of Parmenides; e.g. "what is there to be said and to be thought must necessarily be, since what is something is, but what is nothing is not" (Parmenides, Fragment 6, lines 1-2), and "for without what is, in all that has been said, you will not find thought, for there neither is nor will be anything other than what is" (Parmenides, Fragment 8, lines 35-37). It's not clear what these doctrines mean, nor is it clear—at this point in the *Euthydemus*—whether or to what extent Euthydemus and Dionysodorus are familiar with them. For all we know—again, at this point in the dialogue—these two sophists may be as wise as they claim to be and may understand Parmenidean philosophy. Plato himself was concerned with the philosophical issues implicated in this passage (cf. *Sophist* 236d9-245e5).

284a6 ["really is true"]: unless there are solid Parmenidean reasons to support this inference (see note on 284a3 above), then here is where the argument turns on an ambiguity. The verb "to be" has three prominent uses: (1) predicative (e.g. "to be heavy"), (2) existential (e.g. "To be, or not to be, that is the question," Shakespeare, *Hamlet* Act 3, Scene 1, line 56), and (3) veridical (i.e. "it is true"). If I lie and say that the book is heavy knowing that it is light, then I am saying something that "is" (is-predicative), but from this it does not follow that I am saying something that "is" (is-veridical).

284c1 ["accomplishing something"]: see *Charmides* 163b1-2 where Socrates asks Critias whether *poein* and *prattein* are the same. Both of these words are quite common, and both have wide ranges of meaning. They are much closer in meaning than "do" and "make" are in English. E.g. at *Odyssey* 1.250 Homer uses a form of *poein* to mean "accomplish" (when he says that Penelope was not able to accomplish, or bring about, an end to the suitors' revels); and at *Odyssey* 19.324 Penelope uses a form of *prattein* to say that anyone who bothers Aithōn the beggar will accomplish nothing in her palace. Both are primarily "success verbs" (see note on 283e9 above), but both can be used as "attempt verbs" as well (compare Xenophon's use of a form of *poein* at *Memorabilia* 1.3.1 and his use of a form of *prattein* at *Memorabilia* 3.8.1). Both words are ripe for close etymological, semantic and conceptual analysis, and so again (see 278b2 and 283b10) we are left to wonder if Euthydemus and Dionysodorus are using this argument as a lure to deeper analysis (which they will undertake after their fee has been paid), or if they are indulging in pure sophistry.

285a5 ["quibble about the word"]: Socrates clearly identifies the fallacy of ambiguity here, sliding from is-predicative (to be something or other) to is-existential (to be—period, i.e. to exist); see note on 284a6 above. The question is whether Socrates is being ironic in still taking seriously the possibility that Euthydemus and Dionysodorus are doing something more interesting than arguing fallaciously. If he is being sincere in the following eight lines (285a6-b5), then he is deliberately taking them at their word in a sort of "innocent until proven guilty" attitude; the proposition that these sophists are as wise as they claim to be is treated as an hypothesis to be put to the test: "if you truly are as wise as you claim to be, then you can turn Clinias to virtue and the love of wisdom; so if you prove unable to turn him thus, it will be clear that you are not as wise as you claim to be" (see note on 283b10 above). At 286d12 Socrates asks about their intentions (they slyly avoid answering the question).

285c1 ["guinea pig"]: literally he says that he will play the Carian. He makes a similar reference, and a similar point, at *Laches* 187b1. Carians were mercenaries, and so you'd send them into dangerous situations to spare your own troops. If these sophists aren't as wise as they claim to be, and they totally botch the job—turning Socrates vicious and foolish instead of virtuous and wise—then they've only lost one old man whose life is nearly complete, which is not as bad as ruining a young man before his life has really begun. This casts an interesting light on Socrates' repeated confidence in Euthydemus and Dionysodorus (e.g. 271c5-6, 273e1-274a4, 277d6-e3, 278c2-5, 282d4-e2, 288b6, 288c3-4, 303b7-c3)—as if he is saying, "These two are wise so we should be their students; but if they are not wise, let's protect the young ones." Can Socrates sincerely intend to say, "they are wise, but perhaps they are not"?

285e9 ["express or define"]: "*logos*" has many meanings in Greek, so it is ripe for the fallacy of ambiguity. It is etymologically connected to the verb "*legō*" which can simply refer to the ordinary act of talking. However, both can also refer more narrowly to the act of *defining* something, saying *what it is*. This specific kind of *logos* is the primary focus of Socrates' investigations in, e.g., the *Charmides* (what is temperance?), *Laches* (what is courage?), *Euthyphro* (what is holiness?). Plato was deeply concerned about finding the correct *logos* for his entire career (cf. *Meno* 97e-98a, *Theaetetus* 208c-210b).

286a2 ["we just proved"]: the reference is probably to 284c2-3, but this is not exactly what they proved (if, indeed, they proved anything) there. At 284c2-3, Euthydemus concludes that "no one speaks what is not (*mē ont'*)" but at 286a2 Dionysodorus claims that "no one says things as they are not (*hōs ouk esti*)." What Euthydemus concludes appears to rule out, e.g., speaking the Lernaean Hydra (since it is a mythological creature and isn't real); but what Dionysodorus claims rules out, e.g., saying that the horse is in the barn when it is actually out in the field. The "*gar*" (i.e. "because" at 286a2) is important: Dionysodorus isn't exactly asking Ctesippus to remember what they concluded, he's asking Ctesippus to remember what they concluded, and what (allegedly) follows from what they concluded.

286b4 ["a different definition of a different thing"]: this argument may be Plato's first draft of an argument he gives at *Cratylus* 429d1-430a5 (and following) and *Theaetetus* 200b1-5. It was probably a deliberate choice on Plato's part to have Dionysodorus flub the parallel: to complete the parallel accurately, this final possibility would involve Dionysodorus giving one definition of a thing, and Ctesippus giving a different definition of *the same thing*. That *would be* a contradiction between the two of them.

286c2 ["followers of Protagoras"]: probably Plato has in mind Protagoras' famous saying, "man is the measure of all things," because Plato interprets this claim as an expression of infallibilism (cf. *Theaetetus* 152a2-8).

286c3 ["before Protagoras"]: the Heracliteans (cf. *Theaetetus* 152e3).

286c4 ["refutes itself!"]: cf. *Theaetetus* 170a6-171c7.

286e2 ["possible to refute"]: cf. 272b1. One might suppose that to refute a claim is to show that it is, in fact, false. So if no claim is, in fact, false, then no claim can possibly be refuted.

286e9 ["a bit thick"]: this passage is ironic if Socrates is claiming that he is unintelligent (or stupid, *pachus*, cf. Aristophanes, *Clouds* 842) because he is about to ask an extremely intelligent question. However, Socrates qualifies his claim with "*pōs*," i.e. "in a way." Compare the anecdote about Euripides giving Socrates a copy of Heraclitus' book (filled with such aphorisms as "all things are in motion, nothing is still," *Cratylus* 401d5): when asked what he thought of it Socrates replied, "What I understood is excellent, and I think the parts I didn't understand are excellent too, but it would take a Delian pearl diver to get to the bottom of it" (Diogenes Laertius, *Lives* 2.5.22). Socrates consistently has trouble with nostrums and bromides (cf. *Charmides* 162a10-b2): if the author isn't a simpleton or fool, the clever saying cannot simply be dismissed as empty, but the precise content isn't easy to discern. If the contrast Socrates has in mind in this passage is marked by the word "naïve" (i.e. *phortikōteron* at e10), then he is not contrasting someone intelligent with someone unintelligent; rather, he is contrasting something sophisticated with something vulgar or common. The "naïve" (*phortikon*) question he asks (at 287a6) is intelligent, but driven by the plain old common sense notion that mistakes are possible.

287a2 ["to go wrong or make a mistake"]: *hamartanō*; see *Theaetetus* 189b12-c4, where Socrates also connects false belief with making a mistake. This word can refer to innocent mistakes (e.g. throwing a spear at a target and missing, Homer *Iliad* 5.287) or to guilty mistakes (e.g. acting wrongly or immorally, Homer *Iliad* 9.501). See notes on *Charmides* 157b5, 171d6 and 171e7.

287a8 ["what have you come here to teach?"]: compare *Theaetetus* 161d3-162a3.

287a9 ["just a little while ago"]: i.e. at 273d8-9, cf. 274d7-275a2.

287b3 ["nostalgic"]: literally Dionysodorus calls Socrates a Cronus. Cronus was Zeus' father, and so the yearly celebration of Cronus (i.e. the "Cronia") was a celebration of the "the olden days" before Zeus brought in the law and order associated with social constraints. E.g. during the Cronia, slaves were freed from their regular duties and were permitted to say anything they wanted to their masters.

287d7 ["minds"]: *psuchē*, see note on *Charmides* 154e1.

288a3 ["make any progress"]: perhaps Socrates is revealing that he was being ironic earlier when he called himself "a bit thick" (see note on 286e9 above). Alternatively, Socrates reveals here that he was genuinely keeping an open mind, and giving the two brothers the benefit of the doubt, in case they actually had something new to say about this puzzle.

288e4 ["prove earlier"]: i.e. at 280d1-281a1, though gold was not mentioned.

289b5 ["one that combines"]: this continues, without solving, a puzzle raised by their earlier agreements. At 281e3-5 they agreed that only wisdom is good and only ignorance is bad. If we take that literally, then we might think that to be happy (*eudaimōn*) we need only wisdom—a penniless wise person would not only be happy, but would be just as happy as a wealthy wise person, as long as he is just as wise. But then at 282a3-4 Socrates says that we will be happy by using things and using them correctly, which seems to imply that we do need something besides wisdom to be happy. Here at 289b5 he is consistent with what he says at 282a3-4: the wisdom that allows us to use things correctly actually does need things to use correctly, it won't make us happy on its own. What, then, are we to say about the things that are used correctly? Are they actually good when they are used correctly because they contribute to our happiness, so that wisdom is not the only good thing; or can they contribute to our happiness without actually being good, so that wisdom truly is the only good thing?

290c3 ["geometrical reality"]: it is quite surprising for such a sophisticated and abstract thought to be expressed by Clinias, who has, so far, seemed affable but unimpressive. Clinias is expressing a version of what has come to be called "Platonic realism" about mathematical entities. For example, consider the sentence, "7 is prime." This looks like a straightforward subject-predicate claim like "Socrates is Greek." If in fact Socrates is Greek (the sentence is true), then Socrates really exists, and he really has the property of being Greek. So if "7 is prime" is true, then 7 really exists and it really has the property of being prime. If this is the correct, then numerical and geometrical facts are discovered in something like the way in which new lands and new species are discovered (cf. *Republic* 7.527b7-8).

290c5 ["the dialecticians"]: it's not clear whom Clinias means. The verb *dialegō* can refer simply to a conversation, as when Odysseus is alone and talks to his own heart (*Iliad* 11.407). Obviously Clinias has something more specialized in mind. At *Philebus* 17a3-5 Socrates distinguishes dialectic from eristic, but doesn't explain how they differ. At *Cratylus* 390c10-d5 Socrates defines a dialectician as someone who knows how to ask (cf. 398d7-8) and to answer questions, and he says that the dialectician is the one who supervises the lawgiver (cf. *Statesman* 285c8-d6). At *Sophist* 253d1-e6, the Visitor identifies the dialectician as the one with taxonomic knowledge of real kinds (cf. *Statesman* 287a3-4 and *Philebus* 265d3-266c1), who alone has a pure and just love of wisdom (cf. *Philebus* 276e4-277a4). Dialectic and the dialectician have quite an exalted status in the *Republic* (cf. 7.533c7-d4).

290e4 ["I don't remember"]: is Socrates being sincere? It's not clear what the point of lying to Crito would be. If he is being sincere, then probably Plato thought this comment enhanced the verisimilitude of the dialogue; after all, can we really expect Socrates to remember word-for-word everything he's reported to Crito up to this point? Plato quite liked the trope of second- and third-hand stories that make reading the dialogue like peeling back the layers of an onion. Perhaps the *Symposium* is Plato's masterpiece: the speech of Diotima is recounted by Socrates, whose speech—together with the other speeches—is recounted by Apollodorus many years after the alleged event. The Neo-Platonists developed interesting allegorical interpretations of these different levels, but I suspect that these interpretations tell us more about Neo-Platonism than about Platonism. In the case at hand, I think that Plato has Socrates call his memory into question for at least three reasons: (1) to give Crito a line that indicates there is something remarkable in what Clinias (or whoever) said (see note on 290c5 above); (2) to suggest to the reader that it is not who said it, but what was said that is more important (Socrates engages Crito on the issue starting at 291d5; and perhaps Plato hopes the reader will engage with the ideas similarly); (3) to remind the reader that memory is important (and perhaps more important than you think, cf. *Meno* 80d-81e).

291a4 ["divine presence"]: or a "Higher Power" (see *Sophist* 216b4). It is odd for Crito to reject Socrates' account of who said what, because he couldn't get close enough to hear anything clearly (271a3). Did Socrates lie in how he just represented Clinias? Is he now being ironic with Crito by mentioning some divine presence? Alternatively, he may be suggesting that Clinias outdid himself with divine help, as Homer says that at a particular point in a difficult battle, Patroclus was "equal to a god" (*daimoni isos*, *Iliad* 16.786).

291d2 ["as Aeschylus said"]: see Aeschylus, *Seven Against Thebes* line 2.

291e1 ["produce any result"]: *apergazetai ergon*. The language at *Charmides* 165c4-166b6 is remarkably similar (see especially 165d2 and 165e1). It is worth considering whether these passages from different dialogues shed any light on one another.

292b1 ["nothing except knowledge is good"]: technically, they agreed that nothing except *sophia* (wisdom) is good (at 281e3-5), so Socrates seems to be treating *epistēmē* and *sophia* as referring to the same thing. On the claim that nothing except knowledge is good, see note on 289b5 above.

292b7 ["neither good nor bad?"]: cf. 281d2-e1.

292e3 ["plough the same ground?"]: literally Socrates asks if they are to become "Corinthus Divine," and he makes it clear that this was a proverbial phrase. A scholiast on the passage says that it derived from an argument made by ambassadors from Corinth to Megara—originally a Corinthian colony—after the Megarians broke its ties with Corinth. I suppose the argument went something like this:

C: You should re-establish ties with Corinth.

M: Why?

C: Because we are your founders.

M: So? Why should that give you authority over us?

C: Well, surely you should obey Corinthus Divine, who founded Corinth.

M: Look, if we don't recognize your authority over us, then why should we care about who allegedly has authority over you?

In other words, the appeal to Corinthus Divine is a repetition that adds no new consideration. Pindar uses the same proverbial saying in *Nemean* 7.104-105 where he compares it to ploughing the same ground three or four times—once is sufficient, the additional ploughings add nothing to the original.

293a2 ["the Dioscuri"]: literally, "sons of Zeus" (Castor and Polydeuces, a.k.a. Pollux). *Homeric Hymn* 33 is to the Dioscuri, and it specifically mentions that when wind and waves threaten to sink a ship, but the sailors gather in the prow and promise to sacrifice white lambs to them, the Dioscuri fly to them and save them by calming both wind and waves.

293a3 ["the third time"]: he literally refers to a third wave, but the idea is the same as ours today that the third time a drowning person sinks under the water is the time he actually drowns. If Socrates is serious about the number three, then I suspect the three "waves" are: (1) the consideration of the craft of speech writing (i.e. 289c6-290a5), (2) the consideration of the craft of generalship (290b1-d8, cf. 290a7), and (3) the consideration of the royal craft (291b1-292e5). But there are other possibilities.

293d2 ["Bravo"]: literally, according to the manuscripts he says to Euthydemus, "as the saying goes, 'you say every fine thing'." Perhaps the traditional saying is like Solon's phrase describing someone who completes his life to the end with all going well (Herodotus, *Histories* 1.32.5)—which is a bit, as we say today, Pollyanna. This perfectly suits what Socrates says in this paragraph: if we believe Euthydemus' argument, then Socrates has nothing to worry about since he knows everything; the latter seems too good to be true, so it's hard to believe Euthydemus' argument (exactly like what Socrates says at 294a4-6). An ancient scholiast disagrees with the manuscripts, and claims that the phrase (in his altered version) was often used ironically, so an alternative interpretation of this passage is that Socrates is being ironic (or sarcastic).

294b2 ["you two are actually serious"]: at 273d3 Euthydemus said that they were no longer serious (*spoudazō*) about teaching how to succeed in military and legal conflict. Socrates took this to mean that they are serious about virtue and the love of wisdom (273d5-9, 275a5-7), so he is surprised when they appear not to take either subject seriously (283b8-10, 288b7). He tries to get them to be serious (288c1-d4), but they continue not to take the discussion seriously (292e8-293a6). Here, at long last, Socrates seems to have gotten them to take things seriously. Both Heraclitus and Parmenides were well known for making paradoxical claims quite seriously—and possibly in contradiction to one another; e.g. Heraclitus, "life and death, waking and sleeping, young and old, these are one and the same, for these having changed become those, and those having changed become these" (Fragment 88); Parmenides, "coming to be is extinguished, and perishing is unheard of" (Fragment 8, line 21). Perhaps Socrates is treating Euthydemus and Dionysodorus ironically (or even sarcastically), or he is offering them every opportunity to show that they are like Heraclitus and Parmenides, i.e. that there is serious philosophical content behind their startling claims.

294d8 ["compelled by disbelief"]: this seems to be a turning point in the dialogue (cf. 295a1 and the new resistance Socrates puts up at 295c8-9). Up to now Socrates has been speaking—perhaps ironically—as if Euthydemus and Dionysodorus are the experts they claim to be (see note on 273e7 above). Here he clearly and explicitly disbelieves something they say. But if Socrates has been ironic with the two brothers up to this point, it is unclear why he would stop here, or why he would stop at all.

295d1 ["see that he was upset"]: alternatively, Socrates says that he "knew" Euthydemus was upset, but *gignōskō* refers primarily to sensory perception (to come to know by perceiving something to be true). Socrates is a perceptive interlocutor (cf. 277d2, 288b3, 294d1) and he seems aware that how we speak to someone can affect how forthcoming they are (cf. 285a2), and perhaps their willingness to continue a conversation at all (cf. *Gorgias* 522e-527e, *Euthyphro* 15e-16a). If we are inclined to interpret Socrates ironically, then we might also think that his speech is often calculated not to express his sincere opinion, but for the effect it is likely to have on his interlocutor (i.e. he is manipulative). Alternatively, if he is not being ironic, then he is sincerely committed to the position he expresses elsewhere (cf. *Apology* 23ab), since he does not claim to be wise, he is in no position to declare others to be wise or ignorant (cf. *Charmides* 165b), so he takes them at their word if they profess their own wisdom until they prove themselves to be ignorant.

295d5 ["I had made up my mind"]: when did he make up his mind to be Euthydemus' student? The whole conversation got going when the brothers declared that they were experts on virtue and were the finest and quickest teachers of virtue (273d8-9). Socrates expressed doubt about the truth of their claim, but he asked them to demonstrate their expertise by persuading Clinias to love wisdom and to care about virtue (275a5-7). Now it seems that Socrates is the student, so we should ask whether wisdom and virtue is still the subject matter. Probably we should infer than when Socrates became the student, Socrates had finally accepted that the two brothers are not the experts on virtue that they claim to be, but instead they do possess an expertise worth studying, i.e. the eristic that Socrates mentions to Crito on the next day (272a8-b1, b10).

295e2 ["layman's grasp"]: this could be ironic; Socrates' precision and facility with distinctions can easily seem superior to Euthyphro's fallacious tricks. But he just said that he had made up his mind (pluperfect) to be Euthydemus' student, and this would justify deliberately assuming that his own grasp of discussion is inferior to Euthydemus' grasp. Of course, his decision to be Euthydemus' student could also be interpreted as ironic, but he reported his decision to Crito: why would Socrates be ironic with Crito about that decision, especially when he seems to be perfectly in earnest about it (272b1-4, c7-d3, 304b7-c5). A similar question arises at the beginning of the *Apology* when Socrates claims not to be a *deinos* speaker (*Apology* 17b1): if by "*deinos*" he means something like "intelligent," then he is being ironic; but if by "*deinos*" he means something like "sophistic," then he is being sincere.

296b2 ["drop the qualification"]: see note on 283d2 above and note on 300c6 below.

296d4 ["if I want it that way"]: there is a stark contrast here with Ctesippus' argument at 294b11-c10. Ctesippus employs what we might call "clear sign" (*tekmērion*, 294c1) reasoning that is well designed to break the connection between (i) the claim that is concluded, and (ii) the will of the individual who is invested in which claim is concluded. If Ctesippus' test had been carried out and Dionysodorus' claim had stood the test, it would have been unreasonable to dismiss the conclusion on the grounds that Dionysodorus wanted his claim to stand. With Ctesippus' test, there is a parallel to what is sometimes called "the miracle argument" for scientific realism: roughly, it's no miracle if your conclusion survives a test because you choose to maintain it regardless of the test results; but under some circumstances the verification of a conclusion is so improbable that either the conclusion is true, or the verification was miraculous. Euthydemus' arguments do not work that way. With Euthydemus, there is a direct connection between (i) the claim that is concluded and (ii) the will of the individual who is invested in which claim is concluded.

297c1 ["weaker than Herakles"]: this may be ironic, although the two brothers have in fact reached the conclusions they've wanted again and again—they are focused on winning, and that's exactly what they are doing. Herakles is the Roman Hercules. Herakles' mother was Alcmene, and his father was Zeus; Alcmene's mortal husband was Amphitryon, and by him Alcmene bore Iphicles, and Iphicles later became the father of Iolaus. So Iolaus was Herakles' nephew on his mortal mother's side. The second of Herakles' famous twelve labors was to slay the many-headed Lernaean Hydra. Unfortunately, whenever he lopped one head off, more would grow in its place. So Iolaus helped: after Herakles lopped off a head, Iolaus cauterized the wound so no heads could re-grow. At this point, Hera sent a crab to distract Herakles, so he stepped on it and crushed it.

298a2 ["other than a father"]: this is the fallacy of transferring an attribute from an accident to a subject (Aristotle, *Sophistical Refutations* 5.166b28-37). Stated as a syllogism, the argument would look like this:

1. Chaerephon is other than Sophroniscus
2. Sophroniscus is a father
3. So: Chaerephon is other than a father.

This syllogism can appear to be valid: e.g. if Sophroniscus is sick and Chaerophon is not, the conclusion "So: Chaerophon is other than sick" would be true, but that doesn't follow from the fact that Chaerophon is other than Sophroniscus, it follows only from the fact that Chaerophon isn't sick right now (though he may be sick tomorrow). This is the hallmark of an invalid argument: the conclusion may be true, but it isn't necessarily implied by the premises.

298a3 ["same as a stone"]: cf. *Gorgias* 494a8, b6-7; *Symposium* 198c4-5.

298a8 ["not a father"]: there is an amphiboly (syntactic ambiguity) here, because "a father" can either be a definite description (referring to a particular father) or an indefinite description (referring to the class of fathers). Chaerophon is "not a father" if "a father" is being used as a definite description for Sophroniscus, but from this it does not follow that Chaerophon is "not a father" in the sense that he not a member of the class of fathers (Aristotle, *Sophistical Refutations* 24; Aristotle considers several different ways to analyze related fallacies). Judicious use of this fallacy can yield hilarious results, as we are about to see.

298c6 ["mixing apples and oranges"]: literally he says "you are not joining thread with thread, as the saying goes." With a negation, the saying implies that someone is improperly joining things that don't belong together.

298e5 ["*your father!*"]: we can call this a "fallacy of composition," but Aristotle discusses this together with the fallacy of transferring an attribute from an accident to a subject (see note on 298a2 above).

299a2 ["No doubt"]: Ctesippus' language is noticeably similar to what Ajax says ironically about Telamon (father of Ajax and Teucer by different mothers): "No doubt Telamon, your father and mine, will receive me with a smile and kind words when I return without you" (Sophocles, *Ajax* 1008-10). In context, he clearly means the exact opposite. Ctesippus is being ironic (or sarcastic) here.

299b4 ["something fine"]: *kalos* is often used ironically (or sarcastically). For example, in Aeschylus' *Eumenides*, after insulting and threatening the Eumenides (179-197), Apollo taunts them to boast about their *kalos* privilege, when he clearly means that their job is repellent and awful. Ctesippus is probably being ironic (or sarcastic) here.

299b7 ["as much as possible?"]: it's not clear why Euthydemus draws this inference. Perhaps his fallacy is this: from "it is good to drink the prescribed dose" he infers that "it is good to drink," which contradicts "it is not good to drink," which he will fallaciously infer from "it is not good to drink more than the prescribed dose." Alternatively, he may think it goes without saying that "if some is good, then more is better;" in which case the issue here may be related to Plato's concern with *pleonexia* (cf. *Republic* 2.359c5; *Gorgias* 492d-494a, 505a). Two parallel options are available to explain the next fallacy about going to war armed.

299b8 ["hellebore"]: "Go fill yourself with hellebore" was a jocular rebuke (Aristophanes, *Wasps* 1489). According to Hippocrates, hellebore could cause convulsions in a healthy person (*Aphorisms* 4.16) and it could form part of a helpful laxative (*On Regimen in Acute Diseases* 7). Hellebore was most known as a cure for insanity, and so "go drink hellebore" is a way of saying, "you're insane" (Aristophanes, *Wasps* 1489).

299e1 ["three talents of gold"]: a talent of gold is almost 26 kg (57 lbs). For comparison, the modern day "Good Delivery" bar of gold is roughly 250 mm (10 inches) long, 70 mm (2.75 inches) wide and 30 mm (1 inch) high, and it weighs almost half a talent (12 kg). By volume, two Good Delivery bars (about 1 talent) would be about 885 cubic centimeters. So 3 talents of gold would be about 2,655 cubic centimeters, and since a normal human stomach holds only about 2,000 cubic centimeters, you couldn't fit 3 talents of gold in there. However, since a normal human brain has the volume of around 1200 cubic centimeters, you actually could fit 1 talent of gold inside a human skull—though, obviously, it would have to be empty to begin with. A gold stater is a gold coin, and you could fit two gold staters in your eyes, though I do not recommend it.

299e4 ["the case of the Scythians"]: cf. Herodotus, *Histories* 4.65; Strabo, *Geography* 7.3.7 (Strabo mentions the Scythians drinking from the skulls of their enemies, but he doesn't mention gilding the skulls).

300a2 ["possible or impossible to see"]: Aristotle gives a related example of an amphiboly that works in Greek because the nominative and accusative neuter of the demonstrative pronoun *houtos* are spelled in exactly the same way. The fallacy, then, turns on shifting illicitly from the accusative (x is seen) to the nominative (x sees). See *Sophistical Refutations* 4.166a9-11.

300b1 ["talking of the silent"]: in the Greek phrase "*sigōnta legein*," the "*sigōnta*" can be the subject (nominative) or object (accusative) of the verb, and so it can mean that a silent thing is speaking (nominative) or that someone is speaking about a silent thing (accusative). Aristotle gives this analysis of this amphiboly at *Sophistical Refutations* 4.166a12-14.

300c6 ["All the talking things talk"]: here Euthydemus violates two restrictions he placed on Socrates at 295b6-296b8, i.e. (1) answer the question that was asked, and (2) do not add any qualifications to the answer. Ctesippus has caught him in a trap of his own making: if he doesn't escape by violating the restrictions he placed on Socrates, then Ctesippus will catch him in the following contradiction: "something talks and does not talk." He'll get "something talks" from "not everything is silent," "something does not talk" from "not everything talks," and then he'll use the fallacy of combination used at 298e5 to put those two together fallaciously.

300e1 ["excellent and beautiful"]: Socrates could mean this ironically. At 299b4 I translated "*kalos*" as "fine" (and argued that Ctesippus was using it ironically), but here I translate it as "beautiful" because the upcoming argument may be related to Plato's theory that there is a form of The Beautiful. Alternatively, Socrates has said that he wants to be a student of the two brothers, and if he means that sincerely, then presumably it is because he genuinely sees something excellent and beautiful in what he hopes to learn from them.

301a1 ["The Beautiful"]: this is not an ordinary Greek expression, so Dionysodorus is deliberately introducing a special notion. At *Hippias Major* 286d1-2 Socrates raises the question, "What is The Beautiful?" This seems related to his question, "What is The Pious?" at *Euthyphro* 5d7 (and probably also related to the question, "What is temperance?" at *Charmides* 159a10, and his question "What is courage?" at *Laches* 190e3). It is clear what the many beautiful things are that Socrates has seen (e.g. a beautiful statue, a beautiful woman), but what is "The Beautiful"? Is it the *definition* of beauty? At *Euthyphro* 6d9-e6 he says that in asking about "The Pious" he is looking for an *eidos* (form), *idea* (character) or *paradeigma* (paradigm, exemplar), and so philosophers have come to speak of Socrates' "theory of forms" or "theory of ideas." According to Aristotle, Plato's "theory of forms/ideas" was different from Socrates' theory because Plato "separated" the forms (Aristotle, *Metaphysics* 1.6.987a32-b10; it is disputed what Aristotle meant by this). It is not clear from this short passage whether they are discussing Plato's, Socrates', or someone else's "theory of forms/ideas."

301a4 ["some beauty present with it"]: this raises the famous "Problem of Participation." In what sense can a form/idea be "present with" a particular? The Greek word "*pareimi*" is perfectly ordinary (e.g. Menelaus was "present" at the Trojan War; Homer, *Odyssey* 4.497). Plato's preferred word for the relation a form bears to its particulars is "participation" (*metechō*, e.g. *Republic* 5.476c9-d3; or *metalambanō*, e.g. *Phaedo* 102b2). But he does occasionally use "*pareimi*" (e.g., *Lysis* 217d4, *Republic* 6.509b7). Plato worries about the Problem of Participation at *Parmenides* 131a-e.

301b2 ["imitating it"]: perhaps the imitation consists in two things. First, Socrates is willing to embrace claims that sound not just perplexing, but impossible (301a2-b4 with 294e2-295a3). Second, Socrates uses the same word (*aporeō*, "confounding") to describe Dionysodorus that Euthydemus used in describing Socrates at 293b2 (it's also used at 275d6, "at a loss," and 301c1). The noun *aporia* occurs at 292e6, 293a1, 301a2, 306d3. It is interesting to note that *aporia* is a well known effect of Socratic dialogue (see *Charmides* 169c6, d1; *Laches* 194c5, 196b2, 200e5; *Lysis* 216c5-6; *Hippias Major* 286c5, 298c6, 304c3; *Meno* 80a4, 84c5; *Protagoras* 324d2).

301b5 ["The Beautiful beautiful"]: this raises a famous "Problem of Self-Predication." While it sounds ok to say that the form of The Good is itself good, and the form of The Beautiful is itself beautiful, does it make sense to say that the form of The Large is large, or that the form of The Equal is equal (see *Parmenides* 131c-e; see also note on *Phaedo* 102d6)? In addition to the Problems of Participation (see note on 301a4 above) and Self-Predication, there is one more problem for forms that is raised at *Parmenides* 131e-132b; it has come to be called the "Third Man Argument" but in the *Parmenides* it is the "Third Large Argument." Roughly, the argument is this: if there is necessarily a form F over every group of f things, e.g. a form of The Large over a group of large things; and if Self-Predication is true so that the form of F is an f thing, then we can form a new group (the original group of f things together with the form of F), and there must be a form F2 over this new group. If F2 is also an f thing, then we'll need an F3 and so on. Aristotle brings up this problem at *Sophistical Refutations* 22.178b37-179a11.

301c4 ["in fine style"]: I'm pretty sure that Plato intends two puns here simultaneously. The phrase "in fine style" translates one word: *pankalōs*. The first pun derives from the "-*kalōs*" part of the word, since this means "beautiful," and they've just been using "beautiful" in their discussion. The second pun derives from the "*pan-*" part of the word, since this means "all," and Socrates began the *Euthydemus* by calling the two brothers "*Pan*-sophists" (271c6; see note on 271c6 above). It is interesting, therefore, to see that Socrates is still willing to use the "*pan*" adjective to describe them when he has just indicated that they've left one thing out (but see 301e1-2).

301d2 ["he will act correctly"]: Dionysodorus seems to ignore the possibility of a craftsman knowing how to act correctly, but choosing not to, e.g. because he doesn't have a desire to act correctly. Perhaps it's a simple oversight, but some scholars have argued that Socrates deliberately holds the view that when it comes to virtue, knowledge alone is sufficient for correct action, so that no non-cognitive states are required for correct action (e.g. compare *Charmides* 173a7-d5 with *Euthydemus* 281b2-4).

301d3 ["belonging to the cook"]: the amphiboly here is much more impressive in Greek than in English because in the Greek phrase "the cook to slaughter and skin," "the cook" can be the subject or the object of both verbs. Obviously Socrates agreed to the idea that the cook is the subject of the slaughtering, but Dionysodorus attributes to him the view that the cook is the object of the slaughtering. Compare the Shakespearean example in the note on 283e9 above.

301e8 ["from you I must begin"]: Socrates is using a classical poetic structure here. Nestor uses this when addressing Agamemnon (*Iliad* 9.97) and it is also used on line 17 of the first Homeric *Hymn to Dionysus*.

302b3 ["faked a solemn pause"]: Socrates uses the word "*eirōnikōs*," the adverb from the noun "*eirōneia*," which is the root of the English word "irony." According to Aristotle, *eirōneia* is the contrary of *alazoneia*, which is overstatement or boastfulness; hence *eirōneia* is understatement or self-deprecation (*Nicomachean Ethics* 2.7.1108a22). Hermogenes seems to use the verb *eirōneuomai* in the sense of "feign ignorance" in referring to Cratylus (*Cratylus* 384a1). Three different people charge Socrates with behaving *eirōnikōs* (*Republic* 1.337a4, *Gorgias* 489e1, *Symposium* 216e4), but the first two are openly hostile to Socrates, and the third is unreliable (to say the least). In the *Apology*, Socrates rejects a specific allegation that he speaks *eirōnikōs* (*Apology* 38a1). More generally, *eirōneia* refers to dissimulation, pretending to be something you are not. Given what Dionysodorus is about to argue (see note on 302b5 below), he is clearly not feeling genuinely solemn—quite the opposite, in fact; so Socrates' allegation of *eirōneia* in Dionysodorus is well founded. It is worth asking whether the end of Plato's *Sophist* is relevant here: the Eleatic Stranger's final definition of the sophist includes the *eirōneia* of pretending to know things that he doesn't know (*Sophist* 268a7, c8, cf. 267e10-268a4). Are Dionysodorus and Euthydemus the only ones speaking *eirōnikōs* (i.e. in a boastful way), or is Socrates also speaking *eirōnikōs* (i.e. in a self-deprecating way)?

302b5 ["Paternal Zeus?"]: Greek polytheists not only had many shrines to many different gods, they also had many shrines to many different aspects of a single god; Zeus, Apollo and Athena provide numerous examples. A shrine to "Liberator Zeus" was erected by the Greeks at Plataea after they defeated the remnants of Xerxes' army in 479 BCE. Athens had a shrine to "Civic Zeus" as a protector of the city, but they also had a shrine to "Civic Athena" because she was believed to be the actual founding god of the city. On the Acropolis there was a shrine to "Victory [*Nikē*] Athena" to celebrate her role in securing military victories for the city. At Bassae on the Peloponnesus there was a shrine to "Helper Apollo" for his role in healing and keeping (some) people safe from plague. According to Aristotle, the third question a candidate for Archon was asked in his examination prior to taking office what whether he had shrines to "Paternal Apollo" and "Household Zeus," and where the shrines were located (the first two questions were about his paternal and maternal lineage; the remaining questions were about his family tombs, whether he treated his parents well, paid his taxes and did his military service; *Athenian Constitution* 55.3). See also note on 302c1 and note on 302d1 below.

302c1 ["true Athenian"]: this really is a serious set of insults Dionysodorus is hurling at Socrates—the sort that could lead an Athenian to throw a punch (cf. Demosthenes, *Against Konon* 54.17). See note on 302b5 above: saying that an Athenian lacked a Paternal Apollo would be like saying that he beats his own mother, cheats on his taxes and dodges military service because he's a coward. These were all serious allegations and could lead to serious legal, political, social, religious and financial sanctions. For Plato's original audience, the discussion with Euthydemus and Dionysodorus is reaching a verbally shocking climax.

302c7 ["we are Ionians"]: though divided politically, the Greeks thought of themselves as a distinctive group of people ("*Hellēnes*" as opposed to "*Barbaroi*"), united by language, inter-marriage, shared customs, cults and so on. They also recognized four sub-groups of *Hellēnes*, i.e. Dorians (e.g. Crete,

Sparta), Ionians (e.g. Miletus, Ephesus), Aeolians (e.g. Thessaly, Boeotia), and Achaeans (e.g. Argos, Mycenae). The Athenians believed themselves to be descended from Ion, founder of the Ionians, and so Ion's divine father, Apollo (see Euripides, *Ion* 64-75), was their Paternal God. Honoring one's ancestors was extremely important in Greek religion and culture, and honoring one's *divine* ancestors was especially important.

302d1 ["Paternal Apollo"]: see note on 302b5 above. The Paternal Apollo and Household Zeus were as important as the family tombs. The Tribal Zeus and Tribal Athena were almost as important, but all four of these shrines honored indissoluble family ties of one sort or another.

303d1 ["people like yourselves"]: "the majority" is the phrase "*hoi polloi*," made famous in the 19th century, and pronounced like "hoy puh-LOY" (uttered with a disparaging tone). Socrates regularly disregards the views of *hoi polloi* (cf. *Apology* 20c8, 25b4, 36b7; *Crito* 44c6-7; *Laches* 184e2). "Prestigious dignitaries" (*hoi semnoi*) were mentioned by Socrates earlier (279a6). Socrates calls midwives *semnai* (august, reverend) because they care about their reputation and so refuse to act as matchmakers lest they be slandered as "procurers" (*Theaetetus* 150a3). He also employs a form of inquiry that disregards the dignity (*semnoteron*) of its subject matter since it's only concern is the truth (*Sophist* 227b4, *Statesman* 266d7). Socrates contrasts his own form of refutation with that practiced by Polus partly on the grounds his form does not, while that of Polus does, pay special attention to the opinions of the "socially prominent" (*dokountōn*, *Gorgias* 472a2). Hence, by "people like yourself" he could be including himself, although what he is about to say sounds as if he has in mind quite a small group of people that does not include himself.

303d3 ["tolerate"]: Socrates uses the verb *agapaō* here and at 306c8. Obviously we should not associate it with the Christian concept of *agapē* (see note on *Protagoras* 328b1). "Feel affection for" or "be contented with" is probably the main idea of this verb, but given the fact that Socrates is about to issue a warning (304ab), I think rather that Socrates is using this word the way he uses it at *Republic* 2.359a8, i.e. to be content with someone or something.

303d7 ["nothing is beautiful"]: at 301b3-4 Dionysodorus rejected the "Problem of Participation" (see note on 301a4 above): if you have an ox present with you, that doesn't make you an ox, so even if the form of The Beautiful is present with you, that doesn't make you beautiful. Hence, nothing is beautiful, not even The Beautiful; and nothing is other, not even The Other (hence Dionysodorus would also reject the "Problem of Self-Predication," see note on 301b5 above). At *Sophist* 251b6-c2 the visitor mentions people who don't want to make one out of many, or many out of one, and so reject the "Problem of Participation" but not the "Problem of Self-Predication" (they refuse to say that the man is good, but they will allow that The Man is man and The Good is good).

303d8 ["or white and so on"]: this addition is curious because The White never came up in the previous discussion. At *Philebus* 53a2-c2 he uses The White as an example (*paradeigma*, c3), and he says not only that it is white, but that it is beautiful and true. The "and so on" raises the issue of "The Extent of the Forms." Socrates has no trouble recognizing The Just, The Beautiful and The Good; he has some doubt about The Human, The Fire and The Water; he completely rejects the existence of The Hair, The Mud and The Dirt (*Parmenides* 130b7-d9). Elsewhere he has no trouble with The Bee (*Meno* 72a8-c4), The Shuttle (*Cratylus* 389d2) and The Bed (*Republic* 10.596b4). He gives a resolution to this issue at *Republic* 7.523a5-524d5 (of course, whether this resolution is satisfactory is disputed).

303e3 ["sew up your own mouths as well"]: see 286c4.

303e7 ["he was able to imitate you"]: see 300d7-9.

304b4 ["according to Pindar"]: see *Olympian* 1.1 and 3.42. In both places the claim that water is best is the first step in what has come to be called a "priamel," i.e. a triad setting up foils to highlight the poet's real focus. In Olympian 1 the triad is that water is best, gold is the supreme form of wealth and the sun is the brightest of all stars; this is the backdrop against which we should see how important a victory at the Olympian games is. At the end of Olympian 3 the triad is that water is best, gold is the most honored possession, and Theron of Akragas (for whom the ode was written) has achieved maximum excellence. "Water is best" was often quoted (e.g. Aristotle, *Rhetoric* 1.7.14.1364a28).

304c8 ["people like themselves"]: see 303d1. At 303d4-5 Socrates said that some people would be more ashamed to refute others with such arguments than to have others use such arguments to refute them.

304d4 ["As I said earlier"]: see 271a1-4. This explicit reminder that Crito tried to listen to the conversation the day before is not in the Greek text, it's my own addition to help orient the reader.

304d6 ["clever men"]: it is interesting to note that Socrates denies being a "clever" (*deinos*) speaker (*Apology* 17b3).

304d6 ["write speeches"]: in Athenian law courts, both plaintiff and defendant had to deliver his own speech—there were no lawyers. You could hire someone to write a speech for you, but you had to deliver it yourself in court, and you couldn't simply read the speech or the jury wouldn't believe you at all. It is possible that Plato does not have any specific speechwriter in mind here, though scholars love to speculate (e.g. several think that Plato is attacking Isocrates).

305b3 ["right to blame that"]: Crito's judgment combines three repeated Platonic themes. First, Crito is concerned about appearances (cf. *Crito* 45d8-46a2, 46c6-8); second, by associating with disreputable people Socrates is assumed to be just as disreputable (cf. *Apology* 19a-20c); third, there is the ominous insinuation of a threat to Socrates (cf. *Meno* 94e3-95a1).

305c7 ["the philosopher and the statesman"]: surely it is no accident that Plato's *Sophist* and *Statesman* seek to define the sophist and statesman in relation to each other, and also in relation to the true philosopher (cf. *Sophist* 217a3). But is the "clever man who writes clever speeches" a fourth kind of individual, or one of the three?

305d8 ["moderately familiar with philosophy"]: cf. *Gorgias* 484c5-485a5, 487c6-d2. I suspect that this is the context in which Socrates (and Plato) understood Pericles' famous claim that Athenians cultivate "philosophy without effeminacy" (Thucydides, *The Peloponnesian War* 2.40.1).

306b2 ["philosophy and statesmanship"]: Plato notoriously argues in the *Republic* that philosophers must become kings, or kings must become philosophers (5.473c11-e2), and that the study of philosophy and the study of politics are related (5.474b3-c3).

306d2 ["my sons"]: Crito had four sons (Critoboulos, Hermogenes, Epigenes and Ctesippus; Diogenes Laertius, *Lives of Eminent Philosophers* 2.12.121). Critoboulos and Crito were present at Socrates' trial (*Apology* 33d9-e1), and they were two of the four people who urged Socrates to increase his counter-proposal for his punishment once he was found guilty (Plato and Apollodorus were the other two, *Apology* 38b6-7). Crito, Critoboulos, Hermogenes and Epigenes were present at Socrates' death (*Phaedo* 59b7-8).

307c3 ["with confidence"]: cf. *Apology* 26a1-4. This issue was discussed in the Middle Ages under the paired questions, "Whether an erring conscience binds?" and "Whether an erring conscience excuses?" St. Thomas Aquinas answers "yes" to the first question and a qualified "no" to the second (*Summa Theologiae* IaIIae q.19 aa.5-6), and this sets up a possible "damned if you do, damned if you don't" scenario. (1) If your conscience tells you that an action is wrong, but you do it anyway, then you are guilty even if the action was in fact not wrong (you deliberately did something you sincerely believed to be wrong); and (2) if your conscience tells you that an action is not wrong, and so you do it, but it is in fact wrong, then you may be guilty because you might be to blame for the mistake your conscience made (you should have known better). Socrates' position here seems the same: as long as you put something "well and truly" to the test, then you are bound to follow what your reason tells you is the right course, and if you are in fact taking the wrong course, you are excused: if you made a truly good faith effort to discover the truth, you cannot be blamed for making a genuinely innocent error. This issue is interesting and important for its own sake, but it is especially important for Socrates: he regularly disavows *knowing* which course of action is right and which is wrong, but he can claim to have made a truly good faith effort to discern which is which.

307c4 ["both you and your children"]: cf. *Republic* 2.372b6, *Laws* 7.804d5.

NOTES ON APOLOGY

17a1 ["men of Athens"]: Socrates calls them "men of Athens" and not the more usual "gentlemen of the jury." See notes on 18a5, 26d4, and 40a2: Socrates distinguishes genuine jurors from those who are jurors in name only.

17a2 ["know"]: *oida*, a very common word for knowledge that does not imply any particular expertise. Among other things, Socrates is famous for his epistemic humility, i.e. true human wisdom is to know how little wisdom you truly have (see 23b2-3). It is appropriate that his very first claim in the *Apology* is that there is something in particular that he does not know.

17a3 ["forgot myself"]: Socrates almost forgot himself because the man Meletus described in his speech bore little resemblance to the real Socrates. "Persuasively" translates "*pithanōs*" (used here and at 23e1-2). This word can have two very different connotations. It can simply mean "credible," i.e. a reasonable argument; but it can also carry the implication of "*merely* persuasive," i.e. specious or misleading, deliberately designed to produce a false impression (as in, "a likely story," uttered sarcastically).

17b1 ["as if I am a clever speaker"]: sophists like Gorgias of Leontini claimed to be able to teach people to be clever speakers (*Meno* 95c4, *Protagoras* 312d7). Though Socrates was eager to meet and speak with such sophists, he could not be considered one of their students, with the sole exception of Prodicus (see *Charmides* 163d3-4, *Meno* 96d5-7, *Protagoras* 341a4, *Cratylus* 384b2-c1).

17b3 ["clever speaker"]: if he means that he will not do anything that other orators do, then he's either lying or being ironic. There are at least seven parallels (some close, some not so close) with speeches by Lysias, Isaeus, Isocrates and Aeschines in this Prologue alone: (1) blaming his accuser for using believable falsehoods (Lysias, *On the Property of Aristophanes* 19.3; Isaeus, *Aristarchus* 10.1), (2) denying that he is a clever speaker (Lysias 19.1, 2; Isaeus 10.1), (3) asking pardon for his manner of speaking (Isocrates, *Antidosis* 15.1, 179), (4) pleading unfamiliarity with courts of law (Isocrates 15.38), (5) requesting an impartial hearing (Lysias 19.2,3), (6) pleading for the jury not to shout out (Aeschines, *On the Embassy* 2.24), and (7) pleading old age (Isocrates, *Panathenaicus* 12.3). Alternatively, Socrates may be sincere: perhaps (1) Meletus did in fact make false accusations that sounded quite plausible, (2) Socrates refuses to make similar use of plausible falsehoods, (3) Socrates knows that the *elenchos* he plans to employ against Meletus (24c9-28a1, cf. 27b1-2) is his usual way of speaking, but is unusual in court, (4) although he may have attended trials before, he has never been either a prosecutor or a defendant, (5) he correctly believes that some jurors are prejudiced against him, (6) he's attended jury trials before and knows that sometimes the jury is unruly and (correctly, cf. 30c2) anticipates that they will be shocked by some of his claims, and (7) he's 70 years old. The parallels between Lysias, Isaeus, Isocrates, Aeschines, Socrates, and, no doubt, others of whom we are unaware, may be due largely to the fact that they were all reasonably intelligent, and all planned to deal with very similar conditions, i.e. an Athenian jury trial (cf. 32a9-10).

17b4 ["unless by 'clever'"]: see *Protagoras* 341a7-b5 where he says that Prodicus has to correct him when he uses this word. It is curious that at the beginning of his defense, Socrates notes that the same word may have two quite distinct meanings. He is also about to make the point that there are two different ways of understanding the nature of oratory and the proper function of an orator. He will also point out an ambiguity in the idea of being "wise," and a major part of his defense will turn on this ambiguity: he vehemently and repeatedly denies being "wise" in one sense (e.g. 18b7) but he explicitly affirms that he is "wise" in a different sense (e.g. 20d9). Socrates is relying on a certain level of intellectual agility on the part of his audience so that they will understand and not be confused by several different ambiguities.

17b8 ["by god"]: there is no reason to think that Socrates is a monotheist. Solon famously used the singular "the divine" (Herodotus, *The Histories* 1.32.1) and "god" (Herodotus 1.32.9) without offending traditional polytheist sensibilities. Socrates easily switches between the plural and the singular (e.g.

compare 35d5 with 35d7; compare *Phaedo* 63b7 with 106d5; also compare *Phaedo* 106d5 with 106d9). Socrates (like Solon) sometimes uses the singular as a vague reference to divine power (28e4, 35d7, 42a5). Often, as here, the singular is used as a colloquial oath for emphasis (26d4, 26e3, 26e5, 35d1, 39c5), but sometimes the singular refers to a particular god (e.g. Hera at 24e9; Apollo at 21b3, 21e5, 22a4, 23b5, 30a5-7, 30e1, 31a6-7; cf. *Phaedo* 85b5). Socrates sometimes uses the singular of *theos* to refer to his "divine sign" (40b1, see note on 31d1 below), but he treats this as an exceptional phenomenon. On Socrates' peculiar use of the exclamation "by the dog" see note on 22a1 below, and note on *Charmides* 172e4.

17c9 ["where"]: Socrates uses the word "*hina*" to mean "where," which is legitimate, but a little peculiar. Plato does this in several places, and not only in the *Apology*, so it looks colloquial. If this is correct, then Socrates is demonstrating the very point he is making, i.e. there is nothing fancy in his language: he will speak ordinary, colloquial Attic Greek.

17d1 ["shout and interrupt"]: Socrates puts this plea at the end of his long sentence; for clarity, I've moved it earlier. The decorum of modern courts was not maintained in ancient trials. They violate his request at 30c2, and probably earlier. See also 20e4, 21a5, 27b1. Cf. 27b4-5 where Meletus is the one who interrupts the proceedings, and 38b6 where I think there's an indication that Plato himself interrupted the proceedings.

17d3 ["foreign"]: This could be irony: he could be claiming that he knows nothing of public speaking or that he's never heard a formal, well-organized legal defense, both of which are surely false. Alternatively, he could be claiming that the way people speak in court is alien to him in the sense that he never speaks that way, especially since he's never been a litigant before. Socrates' typical way of speaking is to carry on a dialogue, so a legal monologue is indeed alien to him. His normal way of talking with people (his "native dialect," so to speak) sneaks in during the interrogation of Meletus (24c4-28a1).

18a5 ["virtue of an orator"]: compare 40a2. Socrates' point is not that *morally* good jurors focus on whether the defendant says what is right, and that *morally* good orator speaks the truth (though he certainly believes both); rather he is making what we might call the more technical points that (1) the function of a juror involves primarily looking to see whether the defendant says what is right (and not, e.g., whether you feel sympathy for him or for his children, cf. 34c3-4, 38d9-e2), and (2) the function of an orator is to speak the truth. Many agree with the first claim, but I think most people assume that (2) is false: many think that oratory is a form of persuasion, which uses the truth only when the truth happens to be persuasive. See notes on 17a1, 26d4, and 40a2.

18b5 ["when you were children"]: Socrates may have in mind the stage of his life represented by Plato at *Phaedo* 96a6-100a8, i.e. when he was young and fascinated by people like Anaxagoras of Clazomenae (500-428).

18c3 ["acknowledge the gods"]: on "acknowledge," see note on *Euthyphro* 3b3. *Theos* occurs more than 50 times in the *Apology*. Often there is no special significance to the singular "god" as opposed to the plural "gods" (the generic exclamation, "by god" or "by Zeus" is used by Socrates at 17b8 and 26e3, and by Meletus at 26d4 and 26e5). The very last word in the *Apology* is *theos*.

18d2 ["comedian"]: Aristophanes (c.455-c.386) created a ridiculous character named "Socrates" in his *Clouds* (see note on 19c2) who speculated about the heavens and about what is under the earth, and who claimed to be able to make the weaker argument stronger. *Clouds* was produced in 423, the same year that *Connus* by Ameipsias was produced ("Connus" was the name of Socrates' music teacher, see *Euthydemus* 272c2). *Connus* also had a ridiculous character named "Socrates" in it, and this may have been the funnier of the two plays since it took second place in the comedic competition, leaving Aristophanes to third place. In 421 Eupolis probably also had a ridiculous "Socrates" in his *Flatterers*.

18d5 ["cross-examine"]: witnesses were never cross-examined in Athenian courts, but a defendant was permitted to question the prosecutor. Socrates' cross-examination of Meletus at 24c4-28a1 is intended to get his prosecutor to refute his own case and to undermine his own credibility. Here Socrates imagines calling his earlier slanderers before the court as if they had prosecuted him as Meletus has done.

19a3 ["better for you and for me"]: this is an appeal to self-interest—Socrates' own self-interest in being found innocent of all charges, and the self-interest of the "men of Athens" he is addressing. Two questions arise: (1) how is it in the self-interest of his listeners to have the slander removed from their minds, and (2) does Socrates ever appeal to anything other than, or at odds with, self-interest as a sufficient reason for action?

19a4 ["I'd like my defense to be successful"]: according to Hermogenes (present both at Socrates' trial and his death, cf. *Phaedo* 59b7-8), Socrates actually did not want his defense to succeed: he wanted to die and be spared the woes of old age (Xenophon *Apology* 8; see note on *Phaedo* 61b8). So either Plato is contradicting Hermogenes, or Plato is putting a lie in Socrates' mouth. This is important for our understanding of Plato's *Apology*: from start to finish Socrates makes it clear that there are certain things he will not do to secure his release; why is that? If you could avoid death by doing something you find distasteful, shouldn't you compromise a bit? Since Socrates doesn't compromise, does he actually want to be found guilty and then be executed? If so, why? Is he terrified of old age? Is he deliberately trying to become a sort of martyr for philosophy? See note on 41d4 below.

19c2 ["Aristophanes' comedy"]: Aristophanes' *Clouds* was produced in 423 BCE, when Socrates was about 46 years old. See note on 18d2 above.

19d2 ["speak up and tell"]: we have records of two other Attic speakers (Andocides and Demosthenes) asking some members of the audience to instruct the others based on what they have personally witnessed. This could be evidence that Socrates is very well aware of orator's tricks and that he is employing them. So this passage could be evidence that Socrates was lying at 17b3 and d3 (see notes on those passages). But this isn't much of a trick; it actually seems a pretty natural thing to do, especially if you know that you are right, and many of the jurors know full well from their personal experience that an allegation is plainly false. (Also, Demosthenes wrote after Socrates' death, so it could not have influenced him, and Andocides was by no means a professional orator; in fact, the similarity of Socrates' turn of phrase here and Andocides' phrases in a few speeches could be interpreted as indicating that both men were being genuine).

19d5 ["discussing"]: *dialegō* can refer to anything from an informal conversation to a formal discourse, debate or argument (see notes on Euthydemus 271a1 and 290c5). This matters because depending upon our assumptions and translations, it is possible that *Phaedo* 96b9 (see note) makes a liar of Socrates here.

20b2 ["horse-trainer"]: at *Charmides* 163b8 Critias seriously misrepresents the down-to-earth examples Socrates tends to give. His use of such examples may be part of what he was referring to at 17c8 when he said that he would use the same language he typically uses.

20b6 ["this form of virtue"]: *aretē* is used here and at 18a5, 20b2, 20b4, 29e5, 30b3, 31b5, 35a3, 35b1, 38a3, and 41e5. Because *aretē* has both moral and non-moral uses (see note on *Charmides* 158a1), Socrates could be committing a fallacy of ambiguity here. If so, this is one of the "clever" moves he said he wouldn't use. This can support an ironic interpretation of Socrates. Alternatively, he might sincerely believe that virtue is a matter of healthy or normal development. "Virtue" for a colt will involve developing speed and a spirited character, as well as establishing a position in the social hierarchy of the herd. "Virtue" for a human being will involve developing strength and a courageous but pious attitude, as well as establishing good social relations based on justice and self-control. Plato, Aristotle and St. Thomas Aquinas accept something like this view of moral virtue as a human excellence. It is not absolutely out of the question that Socrates takes the comparison of young humans with young horses seriously.

20b9 ["five minae"]: the basic unit of weight for Greeks was the obol. In theory, the value of a coin was determined by its weight (though its composition mattered a great deal, e.g. an obol of gold could be more valuable than an obol of copper). 6 obols made a drachma; 100 drachmai made a mina; 60 minae made a talent. But this is misleading, because there was considerable variation in weight standards over time, as well as from city to city; and, of course, the value of money depends upon the cost of goods and services.

In Socrates' day, a juror earned three obols for each day on which he sat to try a case. This was less than an able-bodied day-laborer would earn in a day. So in theory, a juror would have to serve a thousand days (almost three years) to earn five minae. That sounds like a lot, but it was about the cost of one *oiketēs* (a house slave), of which there were many in Athens. Also, the five minae charged by Evenus is small compared with the one hundred minae paid to Zeno of Elea by two different individuals (Plato, *Alcibiades* 119a). Protagoras was said to have been the first to charge one hundred minae (Diogenes Laertius, *Lives of Eminent Philosophers* 9.8.52), and this implies that others followed suit; so again, Evenus' five minae should probably not be considered excessive. See also note on 38b5 below.

20c1 ["excessive fee"]: literally, an "out of tune" fee, but the connotation is one of ostentation as opposed to modesty. Instead of vulgar excess, the fee is restrained. This may be a pointed comment: how much would you pay to make your sons' bodies healthy? How much more would you pay to make their souls virtuous? See *Crito* 47d7-48a4. Paying five minae in exchange for virtue might be like giving someone bronze in exchange for gold (see *Symposium* 219a1). Scholars assume that Socrates is speaking of Evenus ironically, i.e. by calling him a blessedly happy man who does not charge an excessive fee he means that Evenus is a scoundrel who charges too much for the worthless sophistry that he peddles. Nothing in the text explicitly indicates that Socrates means anything other than what he says; in fact, it is clear from what Socrates does say that he has not yet met, talked with or examined Evenus, so he is in no position to pass judgment on him—to do so would be for Socrates to believe that he knows something he does not in fact know.

20c8 ["most people"]: *hoi polloi* (see note on *Euthydemus* 303d1). This phrase can refer to "the majority" as a statistical norm. This is the point being made by the hypothetical objection: shouldn't the statistical norm be the real norm for behavior? If you set yourself apart from the crowd, aren't you just asking for trouble? (Socrates uses this phrase again at 25b4 and 36b7; Socrates and Crito use it several times, beginning at *Crito* 44c4).

20d7 ["wisdom"]: *sophia*, see note on *Charmides* 155d4.

20d8 ["human wisdom"]: here and at 20e1 and 23a7 Socrates appears to distinguish two different kinds of wisdom: human and divine. He never explains the difference. Two salient possibilities are that he is (1) distinguishing two different objects of knowledge (the gods know truths we cannot know), or (2) two different ways of knowing (the gods have routes to knowledge that we lack, or they know things in ways that we cannot, e.g. perhaps they know with certainty whereas all human knowledge is undermined by some degree of uncertainty).

20e8 ["god at Delphi"]: divination (seeking extraordinary knowledge by interpreting omens or dreams, etc.) was at the very heart of ancient Greek religious experience. An important part of ritual animal sacrifice involved inspecting certain organs for divine signs. Consulting oracles at sites sacred to a god or hero was a very common form of divination. We know of about twenty oracles throughout the Greek world (and this does not include the many healing oracles that were primarily, though not exclusively, medical), but the most famous and most respected was the oracle at Delphi (which was believed to be located at the precise geographical center of the world). We have recovered a number of question-tablets (inscribed in lead) from the oracle of Zeus at Dodona and we know that they usually sought a "yes" or "no" answer (e.g. "Will my wife conceive a son?"). The oracle at Delphi was called "the Pythia" because Apollo (the "god at Delphi") killed a dragon (or snake, *drakaina*) on the island, and instead of burying her he let her body rot (the Greek word for "rot" is *puthō*; *Homeric Hymn to Apollo* 3.363-374).

21a1 ["your exile and return"]: Socrates is referring to the end of the Peloponnesian War, when Sparta installed an oligarchic government. Supporters of the democracy fled the city, organized, and within a year returned, defeated the oligarchs, and restored democracy. Socrates remained in the city, and he mentions the danger he was in by doing so at 32c3-e1.

21a7 ["anyone wiser than I"]: there was probably a commotion at this—if Socrates did indeed say it. Xenophon reports that the oracle said only that Socrates was "more free, just and temperate" than anybody else (*Apology* 14), avoiding the word *sophōteron* ("wiser") which Plato attributes to Socrates.

21b4 ["What is this riddle?"]: it is not an insult to the oracle to suspect that it is not to be taken at face value. The Greeks believed that the access mortals had to immortal knowledge was limited. Perhaps the most famous case was when Croesus, King of the Lydians, asked the Pythia whether he should wage war against the Persians, to which the answer was that if he did attack, he would destroy a great empire (Herodotus 1.53.2-3). Unfortunately it never occurred to him that this answer was a riddle: the great empire he would destroy would be his own (1.86.1).

21b6 ["permitted"]: *themis* usually refers to what is laid down or firmly established as being lawful, customary, right or just. It can also have a weaker sense, referring to what is fitting or appropriate; but it can also have a stronger sense by referring to an absolute law that cannot be violated. So "*ou...themis*" could be translated as saying that it is not fitting for the god to lie, or that it would be wrong or illegal for the god to lie, or that it is literally impossible for the god to lie. See also note on 30c9 below, and see *Phaedo* 61c10.

21e2 ["enemies"]: *apechthomai* has a subjective aspect (feelings of hatred) and an objective aspect (being someone's rival or hostile opponent, regardless of how you feel about them personally). Most translators focus on the subjective feelings and use something like "hate" or "resentment" here. I used the understatement "didn't go over so well" to translate this same word at 21d1 above. Here Socrates is explaining the origin of the slander against him (21b1-2) so I think he is talking about having objective enemies who want to harm him (regardless of how they feel about him), while at the same time showing that he wasn't in the wrong.

22a1 ["knowledge"]: the oracle was about "wisdom" (*sophia*), not "knowledge" (*eidenai*, from *oida*). Here and elsewhere Socrates is not picky about the words he uses.

22a1 ["by the dog"]: this is probably an example of Socrates speaking how it occurs to him to speak, rather than trying to use more formal rhetorical language (see note on 17c9 above). It is not an uncommon expression for Socrates (see *Phaedo* 98e5; *Cratylus* 411b3; *Gorgias* 461a7-b1; *Republic* 3.399e5, 8.567d12, 9.592a7). It is slightly odd, but in *Wasps* Aristophanes has the character *Sōsias* swear "by god" (*ma Di'* on line 76) and then swear "by the dog" (*ma ton kun'* on line 83), so Socrates wasn't the only one to use this expression. At *Gorgias* 482b5 Socrates exclaims, "By the dog, the god of the Egyptians," so perhaps he's swearing by Anubis, the Egyptian god who guides the souls of the dead from this life to the afterlife. Perhaps there is deep significance here, but it may also be nothing more than a colorful turn of phrase. It certainly would not have been perceived to be any form of blasphemy or religious heterodoxy.

22a7 ["resulted in"]: translators disagree about Socrates' use of "*hina*" here. Technically it introduces a "purpose clause" (or "final clause") answering an assumed "for the sake of what?" or "because of what?" question. Most translators follow suit and make this express Socrates' deliberate intention: he is deliberately seeking to prove that the oracle is irrefutable. But this is at odds with what he just said, i.e. that he set out to refute the oracle. So I agree with Burnet: the comparison with the labors of Herakles (i.e. the Roman Hercules) attracts the "*hina*" into functioning as an "object clause" after a verb of effort: it expresses the end result of his tremendous labors; he tried to refute the oracle with Herculean effort, and failed, so it must be irrefutable and hence worthy of being believed. The Russian nihilist Dimitri Ivanovich Pisarev (1840-68) allegedly once said, "Smash everything. If you strike out and destroy something, then it deserved to be destroyed; whatever survives the attack deserves to survive. In any event, you can do no harm." To a social conservative, Socrates' behavior can seem nihilistic and dangerous: he refutes even venerable opinions of venerable individuals (cf. *Meno* 94e3-95a1).

22b1 ["dithyambs"]: we don't know the etymology of this word, but it refers to a genre of choral hymn that predates the tragedies by at least several centuries. In Socrates' day, a dithyrambic choir consisted of 50 males, and each of the ten Athenian tribes entered both a men's and a boy's choir into the annual competition (which totals 1,000 singers; clearly this was an important part of the culture). The dithyrambs were sung in honor of Dionysus.

22c5 ["things other than poetry"]: my favorite example is Hesiod, *Works and Days* 646-662. The poet pontificates about maritime trade although he admits that he sailed only once in his life, and he took just about the shortest trip one can make and still legitimately claim to have been on the sea. He's qualified to lecture others on the topic not because of his experience, but only because the Muses taught him to sing wonderful songs (line 662).

23b3 ["worth nothing"]: this deflationary interpretation of the oracle is consistent with conventional Greek values. According to Xenophon, after defeating The Thirty in 403 BCE, Thrasyboulos warned the tyrants to "know themselves" (in accordance with the famous Delphic inscription, "know thyself") in the sense that they should be wary of over-estimating themselves. Socrates' interpretation of the oracle probably resonated with the jury.

23c1 ["great poverty"]: *"penia muria"* could be translated as "infinite poverty" or "incessant poverty." Socrates also claims to be poor at *Cratylus* 384b2-c1. It is possible to interpret this as manipulative irony to secure the sympathy of some jurors (especially if we think he is claiming to be literally destitute). We know that in mid-life he had enough money to serve as a hoplite in several campaigns (hoplites had to supply their own weapons and armor, which were not inexpensive). Another explanation, however, presents itself in this very sentence: he does not attend to his own family business (perhaps stonecutting; cf. 31b2-3). Perhaps we should understand this together with the claim of the Greek orator Demetrius Phalereus (c.350– c.280 BCE) who said that Socrates owned his house and had seventy minae invested with Crito (Plutarch *Aristides* 1.9). Perhaps Socrates simply handed over to Crito the management of his family finances and devoted himself full time to his philosophical service to the god, so his annual income from his own activities was precisely zero. We certainly get the impression from Plato's *Phaedo* that Socrates took it for granted that Crito would manage his mundane affairs (cf. *Phaedo* 60a, 63d, 115b-e, 118a).

24b5 ["later accusers"]: see 18a7-e4 and note on 18d2.

24b8 ["something like this"]: Socrates could have had Meletus' sworn statement read aloud in court. The fact that he does not further suggests that he doesn't think the official charges are really what he has to worry about (see note on 24b5 above). We have two versions that claim to represent Meletus' statement accurately: Xenophon, *Memorabilia* 1.1.1 ("Socrates is guilty of not acknowledging the gods whom the city acknowledges, instead he brings in other new divinities, and he is guilty of corrupting the youth") and Diogenes Laertius, *Lives of Eminent Philosophers* 2.5.40 (identical to Xenophon's version except that Diogenes uses a different word than Xenophon does for "brings in").

24b9 ["corrupts the youth"]: we have no evidence that there was a law against "corrupting the youth." Aeschines refers to laws protecting the *sōphrosunē* ("temperance," or, perhaps "morals") of boys (*Against Timarchos* 1.7), but those were probably sexual in nature (cf. 1.10) and there is never any question of this with Socrates. Socrates was probably charged with violating the law against sacrilege (*asebeia*)—which is why his case was tried by the *Basileus*—and the charge about corrupting the youth was added on by Meletus (or Anytus) to make the charges appear more substantial. We have two accounts of what were allegedly the original version of the charges (see note on 24b8 above) and in both the charge of corrupting the youth is the second charge. The fact that Socrates puts it first may indicate that he takes this charge more seriously. Plato proposes a statute against corrupting the youth at *Statesman* 299b8-c6.

24c1 ["acknowledge"]: see 18c3 and 26c3. "Gods" translates *theous*; "deities" translates *daimonia* (which occurs here and at 26b5, 27c1, 27c5, 27c6, 27c8, 31d1, and 40a4). Socrates' *"daimonia kaina"* at *Apology* 24c1 seems equivalent to his *"kainous...theous"* at *Euthyphro* 3b2, so probably he is using *"daimonion"* as a synonym for *"theos"* (see also *Republic* 2.382e6 and Herodotus 5.87.2; this synonymy is explicitly rejected by Christians, see 1 Corinthians 10:20-21). See note on 31d1 below. There is a vague use of the related *daimōn* to refer to unexpected changes of fortune that are out of our direct control, leaving it open as to whether it was some specific god that caused it, or some other entity or force that is in some sense beyond us (cf. Pindar *Pythian* 3.107-11). The use of *daimonion* in the charges could have been intentionally vague in order to make the charge easier to prove, and harder to refute.

24d4 ["you care"]: see note on *Euthyphro* 2d2.

24d7 ["silence?"]: if you think that Socrates is asking rapid-fire questions at Meletus without giving him an opportunity to answer, then you may think he is being unfair, or that he is using a sophistic trick (just the sort of thing he said earlier that he will not do, cf. 17b4). Alternatively, the word "silence" probably indicates that he actually paused and allowed Meletus to think before answering the question. This also seems to happen at 25b6, c6 and d2.

25b7 ["happy"]: *eudaimonia* and *eudaimōn* (25b7, 36d9, 41c4, 41c5) are traditionally rendered "happiness" and "happy" respectively, but this is problematic. "Happy" is etymologically related to "happen" and can refer to a fortuitous event or random accident. *Eudaimonia* is almost the opposite because it suggests the deliberate favor (*eu-*) of divine powers (*-daimonia*, see note on 27c1 below). "Fruition" or "flourishing" might be more accurate, since Greeks think of *eudaimonia* in terms of full and complete success of all our natural inclinations (e.g. health, status in the community, wealth, personal virtues, family and friends). The connection Socrates is making with horse training is perfectly relevant to the Greek notion of *eudaimonia*, since it is connotes "being all that you can be." If you think that experiencing a transitory and trivial feeling of pleasure is "happiness," then "happiness" is the wrong translation of *eudaimonia*.

26a1 ["I do it involuntarily"]: on the assumption that no one does wrong voluntarily see note on *Protagoras* 345e3-4.

26b8 ["these very gods"]: this phrase in itself could be thought to refute Meletus' allegation. Perhaps Plato and a few others in the audience and jury noticed.

26c3 ["atheism"]: see 18c3 and 24c1.

26d4 ["gentlemen of the jury"]: here Meletus uses the traditional and respectful phrase that Socrates scrupulously avoids using until 40a2. See notes on 17a1 and 18a5 above, as well as note on 40a2 below. Socrates is about to reveal Meletus' apparent respect as empty, or even cynical (cf. "contemptuous" at 26d7).

26d5 ["moon is dirt"]: Socrates regularly said prayers to Helios (*Symposium* 220d3-5); and according to both Plato and Xenophon he regularly participated in both domestic and civic sacrifices (Plato, *Euthydemus* 302c4-5; Xenophon, *Memorabilia* 1.1.2). This was commonplace among Athenians, but it seems they never actually had any rituals or sacrifices for the sun or the moon. A line in Aristophanes' *Peace* indicates that this was a well-known distinction between Greeks and "barbarians," because only "barbarians" actually sacrificed to the sun and moon.

26d6 ["Anaxagoras?"]: I suspect that Socrates paused after this line to allow the laughter to subside. The reference to Anaxagoras elegantly disposes of Meletus' allegation of atheism. See notes on 18b5, 18c3, and 27c1. As Socrates has said all along, there is nothing to Meletus' charges except the old joke from Aristophanes' *Clouds*; plus, the worries about people like Anaxagoras is a few decades out of date.

26d10 ["cheap editions"]: this passage is interesting for several reasons. It suggests that the ability to read was normal for a citizen at the time. It also suggests a lively book trade, and that then as now people were interested in controversial books. Socrates actually says that the highest you'd expect to pay for one of Anaxagoras' books is a drachma (not a large sum, see note on 20b9 above). Booksellers paid no royalties to authors: they could sell anything they could copy. Plus, they didn't pay for advertising or distribution: they just paid to have a bunch of copies made and then sold them at whatever price they could get for them. Notice also that Socrates mentions the possibility of taking credit for someone else's ideas: plagiarism and publishing go hand-in-hand.

27b4 ["Meletus objects"]: the Greek text does not contain anything that I have put in square brackets. These are my own "stage directions" based on what Socrates says and how he reacts.

27c1 ["deities without acknowledging deities?"]: literally, Socrates asks whether it is possible to acknowledge the activities of *daimonia* without acknowledging *daimones*. On *daimonion*, see note on 24c1 above. *Daimōn* (plural *daimones*) occurs here and at 27c8, 27d1, 27d4, 27d5, 27d7, 27d8, and 28a1. *Theos* comes in at 27d1 (and occurs over 50 times in the *Apology*). The Greeks had no sacred scriptures or canonical theology: there simply is no such thing as "*the* Greek view of the gods." (In fact, scholars dispute whether we should even refer to "Greek religion" at all; perhaps we should refer to "Greek religions" in the plural, or simply to "Greek cult practices and traditional stories.") Etymologically, "*daimōn*" means "divider" or "allotter," and should perhaps be thought of as whatever determines your "lot in life." Homer uses "*daimōn*" as well as "*theos*" to refer to the Olympian gods (e.g. *Iliad* 1.222). Hesiod says that when the "golden race" died out, they became "holy *daimones*" and to this very day they keep watch over us (like guardian angels. Plato develops this idea in a very influential way (e.g. *Republic* 10.620d-e). When the behavior of a regular human being is surprising, he can be addressed in the vocative, "*Ō Daimonie!*" At 27d1 Socrates says that a *daimōn* is either a *theos* or a child of a *theos*. (In the Christian Gospels, "*daimones*" is used only in reference to the Gerasene demoniac at Matthew 8:31, named "Legion" at Mark 5:9). Although *daimonion*, *daimōn* and *theos* could be distinguished from one another, it is perfectly permissible in ordinary Greek to run them together indiscriminately as Socrates does here. Perhaps by including "*daimonion*" in his charges, Meletus thought his allegations would be easier to prove; but if so, he clearly miscalculated, because as Socrates easily demonstrates here, the ordinary vagueness of that word actually makes it easy for Socrates to refute the charges.

28b3 ["ashamed"]: the adjective *aischros*, the noun *aischunē*, and the verb *aischunō*: may be translated as "embarrassing," "shameful," "ashamed," "disgrace," "shame" and so on (17b1, 22b5, 24d8, 28b3, 28c3, 28d10, 29b7, 29d9, 35a3, 35a8). *Aischros* is the opposite of *kalos* (fine), and is similar to *aidōs* (not in the *Apology* or *Crito*, but it is used at *Euthyphro* 12b1-c6); the difference is that *aidōs* is associated with community standards of propriety and the opinions others have of you, whereas something *kalos* is right or correct—despite what people may think (something *kalos* is admirable whether or not anyone actually admires it). At *Iliad* 24.45 Apollo says that *aidōs* is both a great benefit and a great harm to people (perhaps he means that concern for our reputation can restrain us from doing what we ought not or encourage us to do what we ought, but peer pressure can also have exactly the opposite effects). When *aischros* is used as the opposite of *kalos*, (e.g. *Apology* 35a3, cf. *kalon* at 34e3), it is not morally ambiguous in the way that *aidōs* is ambiguous (see 28b3 and c3 where Socrates seems to distinguish between (a) what one *is* ashamed of and (b) what one *ought to be* ashamed of).

28b9 ["right or wrong"]: this claim seems in tension with his later claim that property comes from virtue (see note on 30b3 below). There are at least two options. If we start with 25d10-e4 and 30b2-4, then we might think that in Socrates' view, virtue is necessary for acquiring or maintaining anything valuable in life at all, so that without virtue we would be leading a life in which we would be better off dead, with the result that the risk of death never justifies giving up virtue (thus the compatibility with 28b5-9). Alternatively, if we start with 28b5-9 we might think that in Socrates' view, virtue is by itself more valuable than all the other goods we can possibly have in life so that a shorter life with virtue is necessarily better than a longer life without virtue, although in most normal situations virtue will also produce numerous side benefits (e.g. fewer hangovers and lawsuits), with the result that virtue will (normally) pay off in material ways (thus the compatibility with 25d10-e4 and 30b2-4).

28c6 ["Oh my son"]: *Iliad* 18.95-96. This is not an exact quotation (judging by the text of the *Iliad* we have), but it's close. Perhaps Plato deliberately changed the passage to allow Socrates to fill in the necessary context and give the quotation the emotional power it deserves. Some read this passage in the *Iliad* as revealing that Achilles actually has two alternatives open to him: if Hector lives, then Achilles will live a long but undistinguished life; if Hector dies, then Achilles will die soon after with tremendous glory. Achilles says as much at *Iliad* 9.410-16, although this doesn't square with the usual accounts of someone's fate ("fate" is not dependent upon choice, effort or action), nor does it square with the other accounts of

Achilles' fate (e.g. *Iliad* 1.352, 416-18). Since Socrates is comparing himself to Achilles, the question about Achilles is now relevant to Socrates: does Socrates think his fate is dependent upon his choices, or does he believe that his fate is sealed regardless of what he chooses to do? See note on 28d2.

28d2 ["Then let me die next"]: *Iliad* 18.98-104. Again (see note on 28c6 above) the quotation is not exact, but it's close. Two important things are missing. First, at this point in the *Iliad* Achilles seems to assume that he has a single fate that is not dependent upon his choices (18.101). Second, Socrates skips the tremendous regret Achilles expresses for not saving Patroclus, and for being the indirect cause of the deaths of so many Greeks (18.98-99, 102-3). Stripped of those elements, Socrates' quotation makes the decision seem almost like an accounting decision, "Which is the greater disvalue, death or injustice?" to which Socrates answers, "injustice." The accounting approach seems independently suggested by the use of "*hupologizomai*" ("weigh," at 28b6 above and 28d9 below).

28d8 ["there he must remain"]: the claim seems clear but extreme. Is he saying that "I was just following orders" justifies or excuses any behavior no matter how unjust? Part of the trouble is with the examples he gives. We know that at Delium Socrates did not remain at his post: he retreated (*Laches* 181b1-4, *Symposium* 220e7-221e1). Does retreat violate the principle he enunciates here? Athens recognized three specific offences that constituted legally actionable cowardice: (1) failure to perform military service, (2) throwing away one's shield, and (3) deserting one's post ("*lipotaxia*"). Socrates' retreat at Delium doesn't count as any of these, so perhaps by "there he must remain," he is simply affirming that one must never *wrongfully* desert one's post. But this threatens to turn his apparently extreme claim into the empty truism "it is wrong to act wrongfully." If there is substance in his claim, then probably it derives from his insistence that the risk of death does not tip the balance. But if death does not, then what does tip the balance? See also note on 29b6 below, and also note on *Crito* 50e4.

28e1 ["duly elected"]: Athenians took democracy seriously. Most political offices were appointed by lot so that each person had an equal chance of being appointed—their democracy was direct by participation, not indirect by representation. Generalship was one of the few exceptions: generals were elected by popular vote, and individuals could be re-elected, so being a general was one of the few ways for an individual to gain prominence (this is how Pericles managed to gain so much personal influence for so long). Hence, under democracy generals were directly answerable to the people for their military decisions (unlike, e.g., in a monarchy where generals answer directly only to the king and not to the families of the soldiers who lose their lives). This is relevant to the case of the ten generals Socrates mentions at 32a9-c3.

28e2 ["Potidaea, Amphipolis and Delium"]: no matter which battle of Amphipolis Socrates fought in, he lists these three out of chronological order: either the list is Potidaea (432), Delium (424), Amphipolis (422); or it is Amphipolis (437-6), Potidaea (432), Delium (424). According to the first order, Socrates fought at Amphipolis when he was about 47 years old and the general (Kleon) took only about 1,200 soldiers. Probably a 47-year-old would not have been conscripted unless it were truly necessary, in which case we would expect an army larger than 1,200. So probably the second order is correct.

29b6 ["disobey one's better"]: that it is bad and shameful to do wrong might seem to go without saying. But that it is bad and shameful to disobey one's superior is questionable: does Socrates mean to assert that "I was obeying orders" automatically justifies or excuses any behavior at all? Perhaps this comment is to be understood in the same way as his "there he must remain" claim (see note on 28d8 above, and also note on *Crito* 50e4), i.e. because it is possible to retreat without being guilty of throwing away your shield, it is possible to fail to do what your commanding officer told you to do without being guilty of disobeying orders. If this is not going to degenerate into a truism, then Socrates must be assuming that the individual has a substantial burden of critical and self-critical reflection upon one's orders, the law, the will of the gods, what is right, and what one ought to do.

29d2 ["on those terms"]: an Athenian jury simply voted "guilty" or "innocent;" there was no such thing as a conditional verdict. There are at least two possibilities here: (1) Socrates is imagining the jury doing something illegal, in effect trying to legislate from the jury box; or (2) Socrates is imagining them telling him that they think he's actually guilty, but they'll vote "innocent" this time, warning him that if there's a second offense, no Athenian jury will be lenient.

29d3 ["persuaded more"]: "*mallon...ē...*" can be "x more than y" or "x instead of y." I think that Socrates means "x more than y" because he is willing to accept that there are good grounds for being persuaded by the men of Athens—it is just that (in this case?) there are better grounds for being persuaded by the god. In addition, "*peisomai*" can be "I shall be persuaded" or "I shall obey." The possibility of civil disobedience is clearly raised by the latter; the former doesn't rule out that possibility, but it doesn't clearly raise it. I think the English translation ought to be as ambiguous as the Greek text.

29e1 ["intelligence"]: perhaps Socrates is using *phronēsis* as if it is synonymous with "wisdom" (*sophia*), but perhaps he is only using it as a related intellectual virtue. *Phronēsis* could be "prudence," because it often suggests intelligent regard for one's own welfare, but today we tend to think of "prudence" as meaning "caution," or as referring to a very narrow self-interested concern that doesn't involve concern for others—neither of which is suggested by *phronēsis*. Often it is best translated as "wisdom," but it is probably best to reserve that word for *sophia*.

30a4 ["more nearly related"]: the "young and old, both foreigner and citizen" might be taken to suggest a duty of impartiality, but this seems contradicted by his preferential treatment of fellow citizens on the grounds of consanguinity (or social, political and economic interdependence). Perhaps his view here is related to the view he expressed at 25d10-e4.

30b3 ["from virtue"]: scholars who are shocked to hear Socrates say that property (or money!) comes from virtue choose to look past the obvious parallelism of the Greek text to a more complex grammar, i.e. "from virtue, property and all the other things become good things for people." This is grammatically possible, but surely 25d10-e4 removes all the potential shock value: if harming your neighbors turns them into thieves, they'll probably take *your* property first; so it stands to reason that if you are virtuous and improve your neighbors, you protect your own property from being stolen by them. (See also 31d8-e1 where Socrates has an opportunity to express a self-denying altruism but still keeps his own self-interest in view). It has been argued that because Socrates claims to be poor (23b9-c1) he cannot seriously affirm that virtue makes you rich; but notice that (a) he does not say *how much* property (or money) comes from virtue (perhaps it is just enough to live), (b) Socrates puts his poverty down to his unique service to the god (without which he probably would have had more money), and (c) he never claims to be a virtuous person. See note on 28b9 above.

30b4 ["both individually and collectively"]: he cannot mean "both in private life and public life" because he is about to argue that virtue most definitely does not pay off in public life—at least not in contemporary Athens (31d7-32a3, 32e2-33a1). His idea is that an individual's virtue contributes to his or her own individual prosperity, and the virtue of a good community contributes to the prosperity of the entire community (see 36c5-d1).

30c9 ["permitted"]: *themiton* is related to *themis* (see note on 21b6 above, and see *Phaedo* 61c10). A better man can no more be harmed by a worse man than the god can lie.

30d1 ["better man"]: Socrates is indeed claiming to be better than Meletus and Anytus. He does not claim to be more virtuous, just better (though, if he did claim to be more virtuous than they are, he might mean only that he is closer than they are to being virtuous, though none of them are actually virtuous). Probably the only thing he has in mind is what he says at 22e1-5.

31d1 ["godly and divine sign"]: "godly" translates *theios*; "divine" translates *daimonios*. Probably this is pleonasm and not a distinction between two grades of divinity (compare the switch from "*daimoniou*" at 40a4 to "*theou*" at 40b4). Socrates refers to his "*daimonion sēmeion*" ("divine sign") at *Euthydemus* 272e3, *Phaedrus* 242b8 and *Republic* 496c4, and Meletus mocks it (see 31d1, 40a4, 40b1; see also *Euthyphro* 3b1-6). Unfortunately, "*daimonion*" can be an adjective (as in "divine sign") or a noun (i.e. "a deity"), so "*daimonion*" without "*sēmeion*" at *Euthyphro* 3b5 and *Theaetetus* 151a4 could be "the divine [sign]," or "the deity" (see also Xenophon, *Memorabilia* 1.1.2 and *Apology* 13). Euthyphro's comment seems to suggest that Socrates' "divine sign" was so well known that the "*sēmeion*" often went without saying. Xenophon gives us a peculiar alternative, combining the adjective "*daimonios*" not with the neuter *sēmeion*, but rather with the feminine *phōnē* ("voice," Xenophon, *Apology* 12). Our manuscripts of Plato's *Apology* have "*phōnē*" at 31d1, but it does not fit well grammatically so it was probably a later addition (it was probably copied by accident from 31d3). In the *Theages*, Socrates refers to "*hē phōnē hē tou daimoniou*" (which could be translated as "the voice of the god," 128e5), but the *Theages* was probably not written by Plato, which makes it odd that at *Apology* 40a4 we have "*hē tou daimoniou*." Grammatically the sentence makes sense without this phrase and Burnet thinks it was a later addition, but Burnet seems too worried about the criticism of Socrates made by the Christian Clement of Alexandria (c.150-c.215 CE), who claimed that Socrates was guided by a demon, a fallen angel who stole part of the truth and gave it to humans (philosophy is this partial truth; see *Stromata* 1.17). But Xenophon argues plausibly that there is nothing religiously suspect in Socrates referring to a divine voice (Xenophon, *Apology* 12-13; and Socrates clearly refers to the "*phōnē*" at 31d3). We also need not take the idea of a "voice" literally (auditory hallucinations can be symptoms of schizophrenia, mania and various psychotic disorders): because the divine sign gives Socrates a sense of warning, it is natural to compare it to a vocal warning. Notice that Socrates also believes in prophetic dreams (*Crito* 44a6-b4, *Phaedo* 60e1-61b1).

31e4 ["unjust and illegal"]: "*adika kai paranoma*" combines issues of justice and law. *Paranomos* (31e4, 32b4, cf. 32b6) can refer to (1) violating a particular statute (*nomos*) or decree (*psēphisma*), (2) a non-specific offense that we might today call "breach of the constitution," or (3) behavior that is unrestrained and hence "lawless" (e.g. drunken brawling). Unfortunately this ambiguity is important because we are not certain that Athens had a law (*nomos* or *psēphisma*) that explicitly mandated individual trials or explicitly forbad group trials—this is directly relevant to the case of the ten generals (see note on 32b3). Around 415 BCE (nine years prior to the case of the ten generals) we have records of two cases known as "*graphē paranomon*" in which someone had proposed either a law or a decree that someone else thought contravened an existing law or decree. At this time it could be difficult to establish whether there actually was a law or decree that was relevant to the new proposal, which is, in part, why the Athenians decided in 410 to produce an exhaustive and definitive account of all law, and literally inscribe it in stone. It took them six years to complete the task, but thenceforth legal cases could be brought only on the basis of the inscribed laws. Unfortunately, only bits of the stone remain. In 403/2 BCE, after the restoration of the democracy, Archinus proposed a new legal procedure called "*paragraphē*," which would allow someone accused of a crime to sue his accuser if he thought the accusation was itself illegal.

32a8 ["boasting"]: "vulgar and forensic" would be a more literal translation. Gorgias accuses Socrates of using "vulgar arguments of demagogues" (*Gorgias* 482e3), and Socrates describes himself as speaking like a "vulgar" man in stark contrast with the sophistic fallacies of Euthydemus and his brother (*Euthydemus* 286e10). But probably what Socrates is referring to is that defendants typically portray themselves to the jury as pillars of the community (see Demosthenes, *On the Peace* 5.4).

32b2 ["Antiochis"]: in Socrates' day, the Athenian population was divided into ten "tribes" (*phulai*; this word could also be translated as "races" or "unions," it refers to a group of people). Some Greek populations were divided into tribes before the 8th century BCE, and it may well be that they were based on family connections (so perhaps "clan" wouldn't be too misleading a translation for the early *phulai*). But around 508 BCE Cleisthenes reformed the Athenian tribes so that there were ten of them. Athenian tribes were formed by geographical divisions. They thought of Athenian territory as naturally divided into three regions: Shore, City, and Inland. Each region was then sub-divided into ten "sections" (*trittues*). A tribe was formed by combining three sections: one from the Shore, one from the City and one from the Inland region. Since each region had ten sections, there were ten tribes. The tribes were a useful way of organizing the population and fairly distributing burdens: e.g. when an army was to be mustered, each tribe supplied its own brigades. Each tribe organized itself with its own officials and sanctuaries. An oracular pronouncement from Delphi instructed the Athenians to name their tribes after heroes (Pausanias 10.10.1).

We know nothing of the hero Antiochis except that he was the son of Herakles and Meda (the daughter of Phylas, King of the Dryopians; Diodorus Siculus 4.37.1; Pausanias 1.5.2) Herakles took Meda after killing Phylas for committing some impiety against a temple of Apollo.

32b3 ["the sea battle"]: the naval battle of Arginusae occurred in 406 BCE near the island of Lesbos (off the coast of Asia Minor, modern day Turkey). This battle is an excellent example of what we call the "fog of war" (see Xenophon, *Hellenkia* 1.6.27-35), and the legal battle afterward is an excellent example of what we should call the "fog of law" (see Xenophon, *Hellenika* 1.6.36-7.35). The sea battle was prolonged and messy, but the Athenians won. After the victory, the ten generals decided to send forty-seven ships to rescue the Athenians who had fallen into the sea, and the rest of the fleet would pursue the remaining Spartan fleet. Unfortunately a storm arose and they couldn't leave the shore, so virtually all of the men in the water died. Only six of the ten generals returned to Athens and in a legally complicated and disputed sequence of events they were found guilty of failing to rescue fallen soldiers and were executed. (In a democracy, generals are directly accountable to the people for their military decisions; in a monarchy they are directly accountable only to the King). Soon afterward the Athenians changed their minds and legal complaints were filed against those who had pressed for the execution of the generals. Four of the five escaped before they could come to trial and the ringleader was saved by the amnesty after the restoration of the democracy, but he was hated by all and he died of starvation (we don't know the details, but perhaps he sought sanctuary in a temple to protect himself from an angry mob, and he didn't dare set foot out of the sacred precinct, which resulted in his starvation). On Socrates' role in this trial see also Xenophon *Memorabilia* 1.1.18 and 4.4.2.

32c4 ["the oligarchy"]: in the spring of 404 BCE the highly effective Spartan general Lysander successfully blockaded Athens, forcing it to surrender. He then installed a governing board of thirty prominent Athenians who had long sought to restore the Athenian oligarchic form of government. They came to be called the "Thirty Tyrants" (although the Greek word "*turranos*" was normally used to describe a usurper). Critias the son of Callaeschrus was a leading member (he was also a friend of Socrates and of Alcibiades, and a relative of Plato's on his mother's side; he is a character in Plato's *Charmides* and *Protagoras*). They may have executed as many as fifteen hundred people as enemies of the state. In the spring of 403 a democratic faction attacked them and won (Critias was killed in the battle). A more moderate board of Ten replaced the Thirty, but negotiations with Sparta allowed the full democracy to be restored by autumn. As part of the deal, a formal amnesty was issued for all except the Thirty (and a few of their allies) in order to prevent a wave of revenge killings and legal prosecutions.

32c5 ["Rotunda"]: the Rotunda (*tholos*, 32c5, d5) was a circular building with a conical roof on the west side of the Agora (marketplace). Under the democracy it was a dining hall for the executive committee (*Prutaneis*). I can't help but think that when the Thirty summoned Socrates here his meeting with Critias—his (former?) friend—was extremely tense. I speculate that they summoned him to the Rotunda to create a friendly and informal atmosphere, and that they didn't literally order Socrates to arrest Leon of Salamis, rather they suggested that there was serious evidence against Leon and it would be a service to Athens for Socrates and the four others to bring him to justice. If so, Socrates saw through the ploy and knew exactly what they were doing.

32d6 ["arrested Leon"]: Leon was, in fact, executed. From Xenophon's account he was an honorable man who fled to Salamis precisely in order to avoid being arrested by the Thirty. There was no crime that he could be charged with so he wasn't even given a trial—they simply killed him (Xenophon *Hellenika* 2.3.39; Andocides *On the Mysteries* 94). Someone named Meletus was one of the four who arrested Leon (probably not the same Meletus who prosecuted Socrates), and because of the Amnesty, Leon's children were barred from prosecuting Meletus (and the others) for the wrongful arrest and death of their father.

33c1 ["already told you"]: see 23c2-7.

33c5 ["as I said"]: see 23b4-c1.

33c6 ["allotted portion"]: *moira* is usually translated as "fate" (as The *Moirai* are "The Fates"). It's root notion is that of portion or allotment. The expression "my lot in life" gets the sense. Apportionment can implicate fairness, as when someone is concerned that they have not received their fair share. So there is a wide spectrum of meanings possible here: Socrates could be implying that he was fated to behave as he has behaved (and so, perhaps, by implication, cannot be blamed since no one can avoid their fate); or he could be saying that it is right and proper for him to do what he does; or he could simply be saying that this is the lot that has befallen him (perhaps almost at random).

33d8 ["here in court"]: Socrates' catalog of associates at 33c7-34b5 employs a practice that is unfamiliar to us. Athenians typically identify one another with a patronymic and a town of origin, e.g. "X the son of Y from the town Z." Add a few of these together and you quickly get a passage that, to the modern eye, is a confounding jumble of unpronounceable names. It would not have sounded that way to the jurors (or looked that way to Athenian readers), many of whom would have been personally familiar with some (or all) of the people named. Socrates points out about a dozen familiar faces right there in the courtroom and he issues a direct challenge to Meletus along these lines, "If you say that I corrupt the youth, then *name one*."

34a5 ["yield my time"]: normally witnesses simply swore to the truth of the written depositions they had already submitted to the court before the trial. This passage seems to indicate that if the defendant agreed to give some of his allotted time to the prosecutor, novel testimony could be given. In *For Polystratus*, Lysias catches his opponent in a lie and offers to yield his time to allow his opponent to bring a witness who will prove that he wasn't lying: his opponent doesn't take the offer and no doubt the implication was not lost on the jury (Lysias 20.11).

34c3 ["your own children into court"]: Aristophanes lampooned this in 422 (the year after *Clouds*; see *Wasps* 976); it is mentioned by Lysias (*For Polystratus* 20.34) and Hyperides (*For Euxenippus* 41). Xenophon suggests that the practice was illegal (*para tous nomous*, *Memorabilia* 4.4.4), but we have no corroboration for such a law, and given what Socrates has said about obeying the law (32b6) he surely would have mentioned that the practice was illegal as an explanation for why he refused to do it.

34d5 ["from oak or stone"]: *Odyssey* 19.163. Again (see note on 28c6 and note on 28d2 above) Plato's quotation is not exact, but it's close. The quotation is from Penelope when she is interviewing a new beggar in her palace, a man who happens to be her long-lost husband in disguise: Odysseus. What she says is, "Tell me your family, where you are from. Surely you are not from some legendary oak or from a rock." This is a colorful way to ask someone if they know their lineage (e.g. whether they were orphaned at an early age). Consanguinity seems important to Socrates (see note on 30a4).

34d6 ["three sons"]: the word for the oldest son (*meirakion*) indicates that he has not reached his twenty-first birthday (cf. *Phaedo* 116b1-2). According to Xenophon, the name of the oldest son was Lamprocles (*Memorabilia* 2.2.1). This is interesting because typically the oldest son is named after his father's father, and Socrates' father was named Sophroniscus. It is likely, then, that Lamprocles was named after his mother's father, which means that Xanthippe was from a more noble family than Socrates (which is supported by her very name: the "-hippe" ending is associated with horses, which were for the upper class because they were not work animals). The youngest son was still small enough to sit on his mother's knee (*Phaedo* 60a2-3). Socrates may have married Xanthippe when he was around 50 years old. If he had other living children from an earlier marriage he probably would have mentioned them.

35b3 ["women"]: Socrates thinks that women can be just as admirable as men (cf. 41c1-2), so the sexism he expresses here is not a universal insult to women. He seems to be assuming the traditional sexist view that women are weaker than men, and in particular, that they are morally weaker, i.e. they give in to temptation and crack under duress more readily than men.

35d8 ["280 to 220"]: we know of an Athenian trial at around the same time as Socrates' that had a jury of 500 (Isaeus, *Dicaeogenes* 5.20). This raises a question because we have evidence that in the 5th century Athens appointed ten different jury panels at the beginning of each year, and that the total number of jurors was probably 6,000. Probably the panels were all the same size, which means they all had 600 men assigned to them. My guess is that they deliberately planned on having a hundred "alternates" to account for absentees and to make sure that 500 votes were cast. Substantial changes were made to the system of jury allocation in the 4th century, so inferences from 4th century juries to 5th century juries are uncertain (e.g. some trials in the 4th century may have had an odd number of jurors, e.g. 201, 501, 2501). Diogenes Laertius says that 281 more jurors voted guilty than innocent, which would mean that the vote was 391 to 110 (if he was assuming a jury of 501). Clearly that contradicts Plato's version of the vote. Probably Diogenes meant to say that 281 jurors voted guilty.

36a2 ["result that has resulted"]: my translation is fairly literal, and although this expression wouldn't have sounded as bad in Greek as it does in English, I want the sentence to sound awkward. Not only does Socrates use the word for "result" four times in one sentence, but the sentence is ungrammatical: it is an "anacoluthon." Plato employs a similar anacoluthon at *Republic* 331b1-5 (using *sumballetai*, as he does here) where the effect is to give the reader a sense of spontaneous conversation. If that's what he's doing here, then perhaps we should see the break down in Socrates' grammar as a sign of nonchalance. But I rather suspect that it is a sign of emotion: he's feeling a jumble (*sumballetai*) of emotions, and although it doesn't disrupt his composure, it does violence to his grammar. Compare *Charmides* 155c5-e8 where Plato portrays Socrates as emotionally affected without losing his composure.

36a5 ["so close"]: based on what he says next, it is clear that he expected to be convicted by a very large margin simply because of the influence of Anytus. He is surprised that he won over so many people by his defense. This could be evidence that he was not actually trying to get acquitted, but it could also be interpreted as indicating how influential he thought Anytus was.

36a9 ["Anytus"]: in 399 Anytus was a leading politician, and a powerful defender of the newly restored democracy. In the *Meno*, Plato suggests the source of Anytus' antipathy towards Socrates: Socrates disputes the claim that all of the "fine and good" men of Athens can teach the youth virtue far better than any sophist can (see *Meno* 92e3-6 and Anytus' warning to Socrates at 94e3-5a1). Meletus expresses Anytus' view, though far more crudely, at *Apology* 25a9-11. Compare this with Xenophon's speculation that Anytus didn't like Socrates because Socrates criticized Anytus' decision to have his own son take over the family tanning business (Xenophon, *Apology* 29).

36b1 ["a fifth of the votes"]: Athens had no public prosecutors, so it had to rely on private individuals to prosecute crimes against the state (e.g. embezzling public funds, taking bribes while in office, treason, desertion from the army, or the maltreatment of orphans). To encourage people to take on such cases, Athens made successful prosecutions profitable in some cases; e.g. if you successfully sued someone for smuggling goods into Athens without paying customs duties, you were allowed to keep half of the goods forfeited, or half of the fine the smuggler had to pay the state. Unfortunately, this solution caused the opposite problem: when financial rewards are available, too many people start prosecuting public cases. This opens the door to abuse, as when someone lodges a legal complaint, but drops it if you pay him a certain amount of money. Obviously that's extortion. Repeat offenders who abused the role of public prosecutor were called a very rude name: "fig revealers" (in Greek *sukophantēs*, "sycophants;" we're not sure exactly what this meant or why it was considered very rude). Punishments were instituted to curb the abuse of the role of public prosecutor; e.g. if a public prosecutor dropped a case after filing it, or failed to receive a fifth of the votes when it went to trial. According to Lysias, a man named Agoratus was successfully prosecuted on the charge of being a sycophant and he was fined ten thousand drachmae (Lysias, *Against Agoratus* 13.67).

36b4 ["counter-estimate"]: today we think of criminal action as deserving "punishment," and we tend to think that to punish someone is to make them suffer (e.g. by corporal punishment or by imprisonment). But the root of "punish" is the Greek word "*poinē*" which should be thought of as "satisfaction:" the wrongdoer must make satisfaction to those she or he has wronged. The typical form that "satisfaction" took was monetary payment, and so the penalty is expressed as an estimate of value (in Greek, the value is put into the genitive case: the genitive of price). This paves the way for an ambiguity that runs through this passage, and it's almost a pun: the punishment Socrates "deserves" depends upon the "value" of what he has done, and since in Socrates' view he has performed a very valuable service to Athens, he is "worthy" of a great reward (the three words I just put in quotation marks are all legitimate translations of the Greek word Socrates uses: *axia*).

36c8 ["the city itself"]. This passage has greater parallelism in Greek; a more literal translation would be (in part): "not to care more for the things of yourself than yourself…and not to care more for the things of the city than for the city itself." He is stating in a compressed form the point he made at 29d7-30b4.

36d9 ["the reality"]: in all likelihood the expression here is a deliberate play on a famous line by Aeschylus, "For he does not wish to appear to be the best, but to be the best" (*Seven Against Thebes* 592). Plato gives a rough paraphrase of this line, explicitly attributing it to Aeschylus, at *Republic* 361b7-8. I have taken a serious liberty in my translation because of this allusion: the actual text could be translated as, "he makes you seem to be happy, but I make you to be happy." That is a bold claim indeed, and it isn't supported by anything he's said before. What is compatible with what he's emphasized is that he does everything he can to re-direct peoples' attention away from the external trappings of happiness and towards the inner reality, to virtue in the soul. Notice that Socrates assumes there to be some important connection between being a good and wise person (36c7) on the one hand, and, on the other hand, being happy (*eudaimōn*). See note on 25b7 above.

37a8 ["they have elsewhere"]: e.g. at Sparta (cf. Thucydides, *The Peloponnesian War* 1.132.5; Plutarch, *Apophthegmata Laconica* 217a, *Of Alexandridas*). Suggesting that Spartan law was superior to Athenian law in this regard probably didn't win Socrates any friends on the jury.

37b6 ["already told you"]: at 29a4-b6.

37c2 ["the Eleven?"]: Athens selected eleven people annually to handle cases of alleged default on a loan from the city, and also to control the jail. They had authority over the archers who were slaves of Athens (the city itself owned them), and who were the closest thing they had to a police force. In certain kinds of cases (i.e. *ephēgēsis*), the Eleven actually arrested people and brought them to jail, but they also had the authority to conduct a summary execution of a criminal caught red-handed and who admitted his guilt.

37d4 ["fine life"]: clearly Socrates believes this would be the opposite of a fine life—it would be a shameful life. He is being sarcastic. If sarcasm is a kind of irony, then he is clearly being ironic here, but he is not being *eirōnikos* because he is not dissembling: he is not pretending that such a life would be fine, he is saying it sarcastically. Socrates denies being *eirōnikos* at 38a1.

38a5 ["the unexamined life"]: it is important to notice that Socrates qualifies this famous claim, i.e. it is only for human beings that the unexamined life is not worth living. Socrates refers to examining people seven times in the *Apology*, i.e. at 18d5, 23b5-c8, 28e5-6, 29e5, 33c3, 38a5 and 41b5-c3.

38b5 ["one mina of silver"]: see note on 20b9 above. Xenophon claims that Socrates absolutely refused to offer a counter-estimate for a penalty, and that he prohibited his friends from offering one on his behalf, saying that to do so would be an admission of guilt (Xenophon, *Apology* 23). According to Diogenes Laertius, Socrates offered to pay a mere 25 drachmae, but he also records that Eubulides says he offered 100 drachmae (which is precisely one mina; Diogenes Laertius, *Lives of Eminent Philosophers* 2.41). According to Herodotus, two minae was the ransom for a Peloponnesian prisoner of war (Heroduts, *Histories* 6.79.1); Aristotle says that one mina was considered a fair ransom for a prisoner of war (Aristotle, *Nicomachean Ethics* 5.7.1134b21-22). Philip of Macedon charged three or even five minae for his prisoners (Demosthenes, *On the False Embassy* 19.169).

38b5 ["Plato interrupts"]: this claim is not in the text, but surely he, Crito, Critobulus or Apollodorus vocally urged Socrates to increase the amount from one to thirty minae. In fact, I suspect that by this point in the trial Plato had been trying to get Socrates' attention for some time because the sentence at 38b1-5 meanders and is redundant, as if Socrates is distracted. Xenophon's claim that Socrates forbade his friends to name a fine might suggest that they were vehemently doing precisely that. According to Iustus of Tiberias (1ˢᵗ CE), Plato actually climbed up on the speaker's platform and began addressing the crowd but was shouted down—this is extremely unlikely (Diogenes Laertius, *Lives of Eminent Philosophers* 2.41).

38b9 ["sentenced to death"]: a separate vote on the penalty was conducted using wax tablets; a long line in the wax was a vote for the harsher penalty, a short line was a vote for the lighter penalty. This method was abandoned in the 4ᵗʰ century; instead they voted for the penalty in the same way they voted for guilt or innocence. If we can believe Diogenes Laertius, the imposition of the death penalty garnered even more votes than the guilty verdict (he says that it garnered 80 additional votes; assuming a jury of 501—as Diogenes seems to do—this would mean that the tally was 471 to 29 (see note on 35d8b above), or 361 to 139, or 291 to 210—if he meant that the gap between the votes increased from 60 to 80, Diogenes Laertius, *Lives of Eminent Philosophers* 2.42). In any case, some people who voted "not guilty," voted for the harsher of the two penalties. It is well worth considering both the legality and the justice of bifurcating the *liability* phase of a trial (guilt or innocence) from the *penalty* phase of the trial (punishment or the assessment of damages). It is one thing to estimate the just deserts of someone you believe to be innocent, and quite another to consider punishing someone given that they have just been found to be guilty.

38c1 ["You certainly have"]: Xenophon also records a speech Socrates gave after the verdict was announced (Xenophon, *Apology* 24; and again, Xenophon's account of the speech is very different from Plato's). As far as we know, Athenian legal procedure makes no provision for such a speech, though it doesn't forbid the convict from continuing to talk. This final speech could be pure Platonic fantasy (and Xenophon may have included a speech here simply because Plato did), but see note on 39e2 below.

38c1 ["several days"]: see 37a6-b2 and note on 37a8 above.

39c3 ["most prophesies arise"]: at *Phaedo* 84e3-85b9 Socrates compares his prophetic abilities with those of swans who, allegedly, sing a final song just before dying. The traditional view is that they sing because they are sad, but according to Socrates, they are servants of Apollo, and when they foresee that they will soon return to him, they are happier than they have ever been, and so they burst into song. Aeschylus portrays the traditional view: Clytemnestra compares Cassandra to a swan who sang her final song (*Agamemnon* 1444-47; her "swan song" was gloomy indeed, see 1322-30). In the *Iliad*, both Patroclus (16.851-54) and Hector (22.356-60) utter dying prophesies. Xenophon attributes to the Persian King Cyrus the view that both when we are asleep and when death is near, the soul is free of the body and hence it is most divine and most able to see the future (*Cyropaedia* 8.7.21). According to Sextus Empiricus, Aristotle held a very similar view (*Against the Mathematicians* 9.20-23). Cicero too held such a view (*De Diviniatione* 1.63).

39c8 ["there will be many people"]: as with most prophesies, it is not easy to say whether this was fulfilled. On the one hand, after Socrates' execution Plato and other followers of Socrates may have fled to Megara (Diogenes Laertius, *Lives of Eminent Philosophers* 2.10.106; 3.1.6). On the other hand, Plato didn't stay away: he returned to Athens and founded his philosophical school, the Academy, which (in some form or other) trained philosophers for almost a millennium. Also, tradition held that Socrates was succeeded by ten philosophers, the so-called "*Socratici viri*," chief of whom was Plato. Athens' legacy certainly owes far more to the critical and self-critical inquiry of Socrates than to the anti-intellectual and highly selective traditionalism of Anytus or the vapid religious boosterism of Meletus. According to Diogenes Laertius, soon after Socrates' death the Athenians regretted what they had done, so they honored Socrates with a bronze statue, exiled Lycon and Anytus, and executed Meletus (*Lives of Eminent Philosophers* 2.43). We have no record of Socrates being pardoned posthumously, but pardons were extremely rare in Athens (probably because nullifying a jury verdict seemed to them an anti-democratic thing to do, e.g. the sort of thing an aristocrat, king or tyrant might do).

39e2 ["officers of the court"]: see note on 38c1a above. Normally, when the sentence was announced, it was immediately carried out. However, the day before Socrates' trial the sacred ship had been decorated and sent off to Delos to celebrate an annual ritual to Apollo (see *Phaedo* 58a6-c5). The city had to remain pure until the ship returned, and since executing a criminal incurred ritual impurity, no executions could be held until the ship returned to port. Apparently the winds were not favorable and so the ship took several weeks to complete its round trip (*Phaedo* 58a10-c5). It is likely that nobody (not even Meletus) anticipated that Socrates would be executed—at most they probably thought he would be exiled (cf. 29b9-c5)—and so the officers of the court had to discuss how to proceed. Those who voted for execution may not have been interested in hearing anything more from Socrates (cf. 37e3-4), but if you've ever attended a large public gathering, you know that it can take quite a while to exit. Socrates' mention of a prophesy might have turned a few heads also. And finally, Socrates certainly had a great many friends and devoted followers who would stay with him, and listen closely to him, until he was led away. So in my opinion it is not implausible to think that Socrates did deliver a post-sentencing speech like this.

40a2 ["gentlemen of the jury"]: this is the first time Socrates uses this phrase (see notes on 17a1, 18a5, and 26d4). He uses this phrase again at 40e7, 41b8 and c8. "*Dikastai*" actually means "judges;" Athenian trials didn't have "judges" in our modern sense—the members of the jury judged the case.

40a4 ["prophetic warning"]: see note on 39c3.

40c5 ["one of two things"]: there are, of course, more than two possibilities. Socrates considers death as (1) a lack of associates combined with a lack of consciousness, or as (3) the presence of both associates and consciousness, which means that he ignores the intermediate possibility of (2) a lack of associates but the presence of consciousness. Option (2) is the possibility of becoming a ghost: unable to move on, and yet unable to make meaningful contact with others (e.g. many Greeks believed in a *taraxhippos* at Olympia, the ghost of a chariot racer who died in competition and who continues to startle horses, often causing terrible accidents). This possibility seems not to occur to Socrates, and it casts in high relief the fact that virtually all of the portraits we have of Socrates show him surrounded by people, deeply engaged in meaningful conversation.

41a1 ["Hades"]: the Greek Hades is not the same as the Christian Hell. Hell is a place of punishment for sinners (or simply banishment from the presence of God), whereas Hades is a vast underground cavern where the souls of the dead collect, almost like fog seeping down through cracks in the soil. There are a few stories of exotic punishments (e.g. Sisyphus and Tantalus), but they are exceptions. The god Hades is nothing like Satan, Lucifer or The Devil in Christian theology. In Greek polytheism, Hades is the brother of, and hence is on a par with, Poseidon and Zeus. However, while there were many rituals to honor Poseidon and Zeus, there were none for Hades (no sane person worships or even invokes the god of the underworld).

41a3 ["said to judge there"]: This set of four names is peculiar. Homer's Elysian plain (*Odyssey* 4.563) is where fair-haired Rhadamanthus dwells, while Hesiod's isles of the blessed (*Works and Days* 171) contains no mention of Rhadamanthus; they are instead ruled by Kronos. Neither is a dwelling for the dead. Pindar may be the first to blend these two together, and to make them an abode for the dead (*Olympian* 2.65-77). Aside from this passage and *Gorgias* 523e8-524a1, we have the trio of Minos, Rhadamanthus, and Aeacus only in Demosthenes (*On the Crown* 18.127; written in 330 BCE, fourteen years after Plato's death). The addition of Triptolemus (a prince of Eleusis, instructed by Demeter) is not only unexpected, it is problematic: Triptolemus *replaces* Minos on some Attic vases (presumably because Athenians resented Minos and his yearly demand of seven youths to be sacrificed to the Minotaur). Burnet has suggested that Triptolemus is included here to help make the Orphism (see note on 41a6 below) more palatable to Athenians by associating it with a local hero, and with the Eleusinian mysteries. Alternatively, he's simply being cavalier with traditional myths that contradict one another: at *Phaedrus* 229b4-230a7 Socrates shows that he is exceptionally familiar with traditional stories, but that in his view to "know thyself" is far more urgent than to figure out which Greek myth about the afterlife is closer to the truth.

41a6 ["meet and talk with"]: unlike the previous list of four names, this list is utterly canonical. These four set the standard for Greek poetry. Homer and Hesiod are closely associated as the fathers of epic poetry; Musaeus is closely associated with Opheus, and the two of them are at the heart of "Orphism" (see note on *Crito* 44b2).

41d1 ["anything bad"]: a stronger claim than the one he made at 30c9-d1. Perhaps this contradicts his claim at 25c5-e4 that wicked people always do bad things to their neighbors: the word "always" might imply that they do so whether their neighbors are good or bad. Also, it is because he believes that he doesn't deserve anything bad that Socrates is reluctant to recommend exile or a fine for his punishment (37b4, 38a8-b1), and this might imply that he thinks these would be bad. Advice that corrupts the young is bad (33d3, 34a8), and since he seems to accept the possibility that he might have corrupted some youth (cf. 25e6-26a4, 34a2-6), perhaps he also accepts the possibility that he did indeed do something bad to good men (though he could protest that the young are neither good nor bad, yet). People think that death is the worst thing, but they may be mistaken (29a4-b1, 40a7-8, 40b6-c1), although Socrates doesn't rule out the possibility that it is indeed the worst thing, or at least a bad thing. Socrates does not think that either death or disenfranchisement are actually bad, but he does think that trying to have a man executed unjustly is bad (30d1-5). At 28b5-9 Socrates says that when we act we shouldn't consider life or death or anything other than whether we are acting like good or bad people (cf. 28c8-d1). Are his claims all mutually consistent?

41d4 ["freed from trouble"]: no doubt it was this sort of comment that led Hermogenes to conclude that Socrates didn't actually try to get acquitted because he wanted to escape the troubles of old age (see note on 19a4 above). Burnet disagrees and thinks the "trouble" refers to the never-ending "labors of Herakles" (22a7). Alternatively, he could simply be referring to all the things living people have to do besides philosophy (e.g. eating, working, bathing, sleeping). Plato is clearly opposed to what is today called "Extraordinary Life-Sustaining Treatment" (ELST) i.e. medical procedures administered to terminally ill patients and designed to delay death (*Republic* 3.406a5-b8). But we commit the fallacy of false dilemma when we infer support for suicide from a rejection of ELST: what we today call "palliative care" is a third alternative. Probably some version of the third alternative is what Socrates has in mind at *Phaedo* 61b7-c10 (see note on *Phaedo* 61b8).

41d7 ["not very angry"]: I follow Burnet here, but most translators have Socrates say that he is not angry at all. The actual result is not bad for him, but they did try to harm him, so they can't be let off the hook completely. Socrates used the same phrase (i.e. "*ou panu*") at 19a5 when he said that the difficulty of his task did *not entirely* escape his attention, and that was litotes for the claim that he was quite well aware of the relevant fact. There is no litotes here. He used a closely related phrase (i.e. "*oute panu*") at 39d6 when he said that the jury was *not entirely* able to silence criticism.

41e1 ["ask of them"]: surely he wouldn't mind if the jurors who voted to acquit him reprove his sons if they need it, but I suspect that he especially wants the jurors who convicted him to do this so that they finally learn the importance of what Socrates tried to do for them. Perhaps then his service to god would not have been in vain.

42a5 ["to all but god"]: the very first thing Socrates says in the *Apology* is that there is something he does not "know" (*ouk oida*, 17a2). The very last word out of his mouth is "god" (*theos*). Should we say that the *Apology* begins with doubt and ends with faith?

NOTES ON CRITO

43a6 ["guard"]: Greeks (and Romans) typically did not use imprisonment as a punishment, and so "holding cell" or "jail" is probably the best way to to describe Socrates' location, and we probably should not refer to the guard as a "prison guard." On why Socrates was there, see note on *Apology* 39e2.

43a7 ["past few weeks"]: during his confinement, a group of Socrates' friends regularly gathered at dawn by the courthouse, which was next to the holding cell, and when the gate was opened, they would go inside and spend the whole day with Socrates (*Phaedo* 59d1-7).

43a8 ["small favor"]: *euergeteō* is vague. Perhaps Crito gave him some money (a bribe), but it could be any form of kindness, favor or benefit. See also note on 48d1 below.

43b7 ["happiness"]: *eudaimonizō* is the verb related to the noun *eudaimōn*. See note on *Apology* 25b7.

43b10 ["strike a wrong note"]: *plēmmelēs* literally means "out of tune," but it was used metaphorically for an error or fault (see "mistake," *plēmmeleia*, at *Apology* 22d8). But in what sense does his age make it "out of tune" for him to resent death? One possibility is that a man of his age should welcome death as a release from the pains associated with aging. This would be in tune with Xenophon's view that Socrates deliberately tried to get convicted so that he would be given a quick death, and so be spared the woes of old age (Xenophon *Apology* 8; see note on Plato *Apology* 19a4; see also *Apology* 41d4 and the note on that passage). Alternatively, by *plēmmelēs* Socrates means "unseemly," i.e. he has had more than his fair share of life and it would be greedy or cowardly to crave more or to fear the inevitable (see *Crito* 53d7-e1).

43c3 ["lot"]: *tuchē* is more often "fortune" or "chance." It is related to *tugchanō*, which is "to happen" or "to befall." It refers to an actual outcome, to what in fact results. It is not incompatible with a fatalistic sense of inevitable future events, but it does not imply it either. *Tuchē* is perfectly compatible with the modern situation in which we say that someone's "fate is in her own hands," i.e. what results depends upon her choices and actions. Socrates uses this word at 43d7, and at 46b8.

43e9 ["Delos"]: see *Phaedo* 58a6-c5, and note on *Apology* 39e2.

43d3 ["Cape Sounion"]: the southernmost tip of Attica. An important sanctuary of Poseidon was there, and the location was of strategic importance.

43d8 ["dear to the gods"]: the concept of what is "dear to the gods" is important in the *Euthyphro*, e.g. at 8b1-6, 15b1-c10.

44a4 ["the authorities"]: Crito does not answer "yes" because he hopes to convince Socrates to escape. The Eleven had jurisdiction over the jail (see note on *Apology* 37c2). Socrates also uses *kurios* at 50b8 (contrasted with *akuros* at b4), which is reason to think that Socrates assumes the Eleven to have just as legitimate authority over him as the laws have.

44a6 ["dream I saw"]: my translation is literal, rather than using the modern phrase "dream I had" because the difference may be significant. Socrates may believe that in dreams we literally have a form of perception similar or equivalent to sight. See *Apology* 33c5 and *Phaedo* 60e2.

44b2 ["fertile Phthia"]: this is almost an exact quotation of *Iliad* 9.363, where Achilles is planning to leave the war and take his plunder home. This is an important passage in the *Iliad*, so it is worth considering whether a literary analysis of this line illuminates Plato's text. The idea that while we live on earth we are in exile from our true home was Orphic, and some scholars seek to find Orphic influence in Plato's thought. For Plato's own account of Orphism, see *Republic* 2.364b2-365a3.

44b6 ["relent and be saved"]: it seems that before this day Crito had already tried to persuade Socrates to escape. I think this corrects the false impression we might have of Crito when he couches Socrates' escape as being all about Crito's welfare—his arguments about Socrates' welfare have already fallen on deaf ears, so his only hope is to try a different line of argument.

44c4 ["Most people"]: *hoi polloi* (see notes on *Apology* 20c8 and *Euthydemus* 303d1).

44d7 ["because then"]: the inference rests on the assumption that one and the same power can produce opposites. Sophocles' chorus affirms such a principle at *Antigone* 365ff. Aristotle claims that a craft is a capacity for opposites (*Metaphysics* 9.5.1048a7-11). Such a principle causes the final difficulty in the *Hippias Minor* at 375e9-376c1. It may be important that wisdom (*sophia*) is at issue in the *Hippias Minor*, but not here: here Socrates is considering the possibility that if *hoi polloi* might, without wisdom, do us the greatest harm then it could equally, without wisdom, do us the greatest good. He seems to treat this as idle speculation.

44d9 ["capacity"]: *dunatos* occurs here and at 46a2; the related verb *dunamai* occurs at 46b7, 51a5 and 54d5; the related noun *dunamis* occurs at 46c4. See note on *Laches* 192b1.

44d9 ["intelligent"]: the adjective *phronimos* is related to the noun *phronēsis*. See note on *Apology* 29e1. On Socrates' point here, see also *Apology* 30c6-d5.

44d10 ["happens"]: *tugchanō* is the root of *tuchē* (43c3, 43d7); it occurs here and at 45d2, 47b3, 49b5, 50e8, 52a8. The verb simply means "to happen" or "to occur" or "to befall by lot." So it could refer to random chance, but surely Socrates is not saying that *hoi polloi* act randomly. His point is simply that they do what it occurs to them to do, and "the chips fall where they may," as the modern saying goes.

44e3 ["extortionists"]: *sukophantēs*, see note on *Apology* 36b1.

44e4 ["prosecute"]: it was illegal to harbor exiles who had illicitly returned (Demosthenes *Against Polycles* 50.49), so perhaps there was a law against aiding and abetting escape from jail.

45a1 ["right"]: the adjective *dikaios* can refer narrowly to justice or widely to righteousness or to doing what is right. The word is used more than two dozen times in the *Crito*.

45b4 ["Simmias of Thebes"]: Simmias and Cebes are prominent in the *Phaedo*. Because Socrates mentions that in Thebes they were both "with Philolaus" (*Phaedo* 61d7), and Philolaus (c.470-390) wrote what may have been the first book by a Pythagorean, scholars are eager to find Pythagoreanism in the *Crito*.

45b7 ["said in court"]: see *Apology* 37c5-e2.

45c2 ["sponsor you"]: Crito says that he has *xenoi* in Thebes who will keep Socrates safe. This is much more than saying that he has "friends" in Thebes. Non-citizens have no rights, privileges or immunities, and so technically, a non-citizen cannot sue a citizen if the citizen cheats or even robs the non-citizen (though the maltreatment of strangers was generally believed to be a religious offense, and a sign of bad character).

45e4 ["we could have avoided it"]: Crito could have arranged for Socrates to flee Athens prior to the trial. Of course, this would have been illegal, but probably not entirely unexpected—even by Socrates' accusers.

45e5 ["your defense"]: see notes on *Apology* 19a4, 41d4 and 43b10.

46b5 ["reason"]: a *logos* that is the result—as Socrates puts it here—of *logizomenos* is a rule, principle or law. In English we might call it a "maxim" since it specifies the description under which I choose to do it. E.g. I choose to take a shower under the description "efficient way to get clean," and not under the description "a way to go from dry to wet and then back to dry." In that case, my maxim is "I shower to get clean efficiently," which identifies my reason for taking a shower. Under the description "abandoning my children" Socrates would not choose to stay in jail, he would escape with Crito; but under the description "obeying the law" Socrates would choose to stay in jail. Since Socrates has lived his whole life by the maxim "obey the law and god, and do what is right" (cf. *Apology* 28b5-29ee, 32a9-33a5), it is going to take quite some *logizomenos* to get him to abandon it now.

46b8 ["different light now"]: "obey the law" is a maxim that can be held in varying degrees of respect by different people, or by the same person in varying degrees in varying circumstances. Socrates here seems to assume that a superior maxim will not be so conditionally respected (see note on 49d3). A similar thought is important in the moral philosophy of Immanuel Kant (1724-1804), *Critique of Practical Reason* 1.1.1 Definition and Remark.

46c5 ["sending a plague of death"]: Socrates uses *epipempō*, which is sometimes used of the gods when they let loose upon mortals some terrifying punishment, as Hades did in Euripides' *Phoenician Women* 811. The juxtaposition of the melodramatic *thanatous epipempousa* with the mundane *chrēmatōn aphaireseis* (confiscate our property) could be a dig at Crito, implying that he cares too much about money. But that would be odd if indeed Socrates handed his finances over to Crito to manage (see note on *Apology* 23c1): it might be hypocritical of Socrates to trust Crito to look after his money, and then criticize him for being careful about his money. I suspect the juxtaposition is intended for humorous effect: Socrates is nonchalant in the face of death.

47a7 ["worthless"]: *ponēros* often means "wicked" in a moral sense but it can be used in a non-moral sense, just as the English "ne'er-do-well" and "good-for-nothing" can imply immoral laziness or morally neutral uselessness. Similarly, there is a moral and a non-moral use of *chrēstos* (useful or beneficial). Here Socrates clearly has in mind the non-moral senses of both words. Probably Socrates uses *ponēros* and *chrēstos* in their moral senses at *Apology* 25c6 (cf. *Apology* 33b4).

47b2 ["one person"]: Socrates seems to be relying on the contrast between the one and the many. If so, then we might suspect that his political inclinations are oligarchic or monarchic, certainly not democratic. Alternatively, if his emphasis is on intelligence, then he seems to be assuming that few people are intelligent. This too could lead him in the direction of oligarchy or monarchy (e.g. if he assumes that the many cannot be well educated, cf. *Republic* 3.414b8-415c7); however, it could lead him to urge the many to study so that they become worthy of democracy (e.g. *Apology* 29d2-30b4, 30d5-31b5, 36c5-d1, 38a1-6, 41e1-42a2).

47b10 ["expert"]: *epaïō* refers to hearing or listening, or more generally to perceiving or feeling. It can imply understanding or expertise (it is used also at 47c3, 47d9, 48a6). Plato does not use it very often, though it makes for an interesting contrast with the far more common *oida*, whose root refers to seeing, not listening.

47d4 ["the part of ourselves"]: at *Gorgias* 503d6-505b12 and *Republic* 4.444d13-e2 Socrates draws the parallel that health is to the body as justice is to the soul (*psuchē*).

48b8 ["one and the same?"]: Socrates does not say that these three *mean* the same thing; they do not. Perhaps he is saying that these three are identical to one another in something like the way that water is identical to H_2O. This identity thesis would mean that Socrates has anticipated the Cynics and Stoics. But this "identity thesis" would be extremely controversial and it is not at all clear that he has sufficiently justified it. To live well is to be happy (*eudaimōn*, *Euthydemus* 278e5-279a3, 280b6), and the Greeks typically assumed that *eudaimonia* has numerous components, e.g. noble birth, power, wealth, property, status, family and friends. Alternatively, Socrates might intend a "reciprocity thesis" according to which (i) to live well one must live finely and vice versa, and (ii) to live finely one must live justly and vice versa, and so (iii) to live well one must live justly and vice versa. Though weaker than the identity thesis, the reciprocity thesis would still seem clearly false to an ordinary Greek: a wealthy aristocrat might be considered *eudaimōn* even if he is not particularly just. Perhaps Socrates' earlier equation that health is to the body as virtue is to the soul is supposed to explain his view here: you cannot live well, finely or justly if you soul is ruined; and if your soul is in excellent condition, then you will live justly, finely and well. (So, e.g., a corrupt but wealthy aristocrat may have the external trappings of *eudaimonia*, but the corruption of his *psuchē* entails that he continually fails to derive any substantial benefit from his material advantages).

48b12 ["released"]: *aphientōn* (from *aphiēmi*, to set free, to discharge, to send away). Socrates is not imagining a pardon (which would be *aidesis*. Pardons were allowed only in cases of unintentional homicide, and they could be granted only by relatives of the deceased (or fellow phratry members if no relatives were alive). Socrates must have in mind an annulment of the jury verdict, and the only body which had power to do that was the Athenian people itself, operating through the *Ekklēsia*. For an example, see Xenophon, *Hellenika* 1.5.19. So when Socrates imagines being "released by the Athenians," he is being quite literal: he is imagining a meeting of the *Ekklēsia* in which his trial is discussed and a majority vote to annul the verdict in his case, which would be a very public, and resounding, vindication of his cause.

48c1 ["appears"]: *phainomai* (also at 48d3) is ambiguous between a doubtful and a confident assertion, e.g. "he gives the impression of being honest" (though he may not be), as opposed to "he has been revealed to be honest." I hope that "appears" is as ambiguous in English. However, the dialogue so far is a reconsideration of conclusions they have drawn earlier (46b6-8, c6-d7, 47a13-b3). Even at the end of the *Crito* Socrates is still willing to consider the possibility that he's drawn a conclusion that merely appears true but is not (54d2-7). In court he was willing to admit the possibility that he is ignorantly corrupting the youth (*Apology* 26a1-4). We might think this is problematic: if you admit that your conclusion may be wrong, can you act as if it is right? Socrates' behavior would be justified by the medieval doctrine that "an erring conscience binds" (cf. St. Thomas Aquinas, *Summa Theologiae* IaIIae q.19 a.5): if escaping is the right thing to do, but he falsely believes that it is the wrong thing to do, and he does it anyway, he is doing the right thing, but doing it wrongly (he's doing what he believes to be wrong, and that in itself is morally objectionable). See note on 48c7 below.

48c5 ["casually execute someone"]: cf. *Apology* 24c6, 37a8, 38c1. Consider also the (in)famous Mytilenean Debate (Thucydides 3.36-49). After defeating the rebellion of Mytilene, Athens voted to execute the entire male population of the city and to enslave all the women and children. The next day they changed their minds. Socrates is perhaps being a bit unfair by saying that Athenians do this sort of thing "with no thought" (*oudeni xun nō*)—Athenians debate almost everything, though perhaps on occasion they act precipitately.

48c7 ["the argument has chosen"]: my translation here is quite literal. Socrates portrays the *logos* as seizing them or taking them in its grasp (*haireō*). The argument has binding force. This supports the suggestion I made in the note to 48c1 above that we can understand Socrates' view here as relying on the assumption that "an erring conscience binds."

48d1 ["favors"]: *charis* is etymologically related to the English word "charity," but here it seems to be a euphemism—possibly for "bribe." See note on 43a8 above.

48d5 ["before"]: literally *pro* means "before" either spatially or temporally. Non-literally it refers to priority, but the priority of x over y can entail "x *more than* y" or "x *and not* y." Is Socrates saying that death is not a consideration at all, or that it is at best a secondary consideration (if it is secondary, the next issue would be whether it could combine with other considerations to override the wrongness of the action)? Compare *Apology* 28d9.

48d8 ["Let's look together"]: Socrates normally assumes that inquiry is a cooperative endeavor, not a contest (cf. *Euthyphro* 6c4, *Laches* 190c4, *Charmides* 166d4-6). See also note on *Euthyphro* 11e4.

49a1 ["your sincere beliefs"]: cf. 49c11-e8. Socrates regularly expects his interlocutors to express their sincere beliefs, and not, e.g., admit something they don't believe simply in order to avoid embarrassment. See *Laches* 193c7, *Protagoras* 331b8-d1, *Gorgias* 495a5-b6, 500b, *Republic* 1.346a3-4, *Theaetetus* 154c7-e6.

49a5 ["in one way"]: see notes on 46b5 and 46b8 above. Perhaps Socrates is envisioning Crito saying that if they focus on the escape from jail as breaking the law, then in that way they ought not do it; but if they focus on the escape as Socrates' way to fulfill his duty to raise his own sons, in that way they ought to do wrong (i.e. break the law) voluntarily. His first and final questions in this paragraph, then, propose that if it is wrong for them to escape, then it is wrong for Socrates to raise his own sons after having escaped (though it does not entail that Socrates would be right to abandon his sons after having escaped).

49c1 ["appears"]: see note on 48c1. Keep in mind that "appears" is ambiguous in Greek: here Crito could be saying "it seems to be true, but it might not be" or "it has been revealed that in fact it is true."

49c2 ["do something bad"]: *kakourgeō* can mean "injure," but it would be highly objectionable for Socrates to say that we must never injure anyone since he himself admirably performed his military service on at least three occasions. We may safely assume that he either did injure some enemies, or he was ready, willing and able to do so. It would be far less objectionable for Socrates to be using *kakourgeō* in its more general sense of doing something evil, wicked or vicious. Just as in English "bad" can mean *morally* bad, and "wrong" can mean *morally* wrong, so also in Greek *kakourgeō* can refer to doing something *morally* bad, and *adikeō* can refer to doing something *morally* wrong. That Socrates and Crito are taking *kakourgeō* and *adikeō* synonymously is further shown by the absence of *kakourgeō* from 49d7-9 (cf. *Euthyphro* 3a8).

49d3 ["no common counsel"]: so the principle "return wrong for wrong" is not a universally accepted principle. Socrates highlighted other principles that are not universally accepted at *Euthyphro* 8b1-6 (see note on 8b4). It is interesting that when the Laws consider the principle "we may violate our just agreements," they immediately extend the principle from Socrates to all "private citizens" (50b4). It will illuminate Socrates' view if we can discern similarities or differences with Immanuel Kant's "Formula of Universal Law" for the categorical imperative: "act only in accordance with that maxim through which you can at the same time will that it become a universal law" (*Grounding for the Metaphysics of Morals*, Section II). See note on 46b8.

49d6 ["we should begin"]: *archō* can refer to an opening gambit, like an initial claim that can be retracted later, but here Socrates seems to take it as a governing or ruling principle that is foundational for the entire discussion, a "first principle."

49e7 ["cheat?"]: *exapataō* means to deceive, beguile, cheat, swindle, or lie as Odysseus beguiled the Cyclops by lying and saying that his name was "No Man" (Homer, *Odyssey* 9.414; see also Xenophon, *Anabasis* 5.7.6), and as buyer or seller might try to cheat one another in the marketplace (Herodotus 1.153.1; see also Thucydides 5.42.2). *Exapataō* is a morally loaded term: in anger, Achilles accuses Agamemnon of being a cheater for granting but then taking back Briseis, and he describes Agamemnon as "clothed in shamelessness" (Homer, *Iliad* 9.371-2). I'm sure that Plato used a form of *exapataō* precisely because of this passage in the *Iliad* since it occurs only 8 lines after 9.363, which Socrates partly quoted at 44b2. Socrates really is asking the no-brainer, "Is it morally ok to cheat?" Obviously not, because cheating is morally wrong (*adikos*) and morally bad (*kakos*).

50a3 ["just agreements?"]: see note on 52e1 below.

50a7 ["sneaking away"]: although *apodidraskō* is often used of slaves running away from their legal owners (Plato, *Protagoras* 310c3; Xenophon, *Anabasis* 1.4.8) and soldiers deserting the ranks (Xenophon, *Anabasis* 5.6.34), it is not necessarily morally loaded in the way that *exapataō* is. E.g. Maiandrios escaped the slaughter at Samos not by fighting his way out or by running/sailing faster than the Persians, but by sneaking away unnoticed (Herodotus 3.148.1). However, here I think Socrates does have in mind the morally loaded sense. I think this for three reasons: (1) a morally justified "escape" (like that of Maiandrios) would not require the qualification "or whatever you want to call it," which implies that he realizes his use of *apodidraskō* is tendentious; (2) Socrates is sensitive to the fact that how we describe an action is important when deciding whether or not to choose it (see note on 46b5 above); and (3) at 48d3-5 he reiterated the principle he announced at *Apology* 28d6-10 which seems to entail that escaping without an annulment of his verdict duly voted by the *Ekklēsia* (see note on 48b12 above) would indeed be tantamount to desertion. If I am right, then Socrates is implying that Crito's use of *apeimi* at 44c4, obligingly allowed by Socrates at 48e3 and 49e9, was a euphemism. (Cf. Demosthenes, *Against Androtion* 22.56).

50a8 ["laws"]: Socrates personifies the laws of Athens and imagines them directly addressing him. Aeschines would later do something similar: he imagines the lawgiver (*nomothetēs*) as directly addressing (*dialegomai*) the individual to whom the laws apply (*Against Timarchos* 1.18). Demosthenes also describes the situation in which the laws lay a duty upon someone as the laws (*nomoi*) addressing (*dialegomai*) them (*Against Macartatos* 43.59).

50a8 ["commonwealth"]: *to koinon tēs poleōs* is not the "Constitution," since Athens did not have a Constitution in the modern sense. Perhaps it is the implicit "constitution," including the laws, legal principles, practices and precedents in Athens. This phrase can refer to the government as an institution or to the public authorities as a body (cf. Herodotus 3.156.2, 5.85.1, 8.135.2; Isocrates, *Helen* 10.36;

Thucydides 1.90.5, 2.12.2, 5.37.1). It may refer to Athens as an autonomous political entity, and so "State" might be a good translation (cf. Herodotus 1.67.5; Aristophanes, *Assembly Women* 208; Antiphon, *Second Tetralogy* 3.2.3; Xenophon, *Cyropaedia* 2.2.20). I've used "commonwealth" because I think that it is suggestive of all the above, but indeterminate enough to allow the reader to decide in context what Socrates is referring to, if he does have any determinate conception in mind.

50a8 ["stop us"]: Burnet and others take *epistantes* to mean "standing over" since there is a grammatical parallel with *Symposium* 192d3. *Ephistēmi* certainly can be used of visions in dreams that appear to hover (e.g. Homer, *Iliad* 10.496; Herodotus 1.34.1), so Socrates may be asking Crito to envision the personified laws of Athens hovering before them as they exit the jail. But given what the laws are about to say, they are clearly calling a halt to the escape, at least temporarily. Since he is about to draw an analogy between the laws and our parents (50e2-51c4), perhaps a relevant situation for comparison is children sneaking out through the window of their room in violation of their parents' curfew, when their parents open the door, see what's going on, stop them and ask them to explain and justify their escape.

50a9 ["Tell me"]: I find it odd that "laws" (*nomoi*) is plural, but "commonwealth" (*koinon*) is singular, and whoever is questioning Socrates and Crito refers to itself in both the singular (*moi* at 50a9) and the plural (*hēmas* at 50b1). Also, it seems to me that this singular and plural entity speaks peremptorily to Socrates (though they are not brusque or rude), so I have tried in my translation to make them sound distinctive and august.

50b2 ["as far as it is up to you?"]: there is an ambiguity here that can make a great deal of difference to our evaluation of Socrates' arguments. (1) *to son meros* might mean "as far as you are able," in which case we might think that Socrates is primarily concerned about the terrible consequences of civil disobedience, e.g. if one person disregards his sentence, respect for the law generally will be undermined, threatening general anarchy. (2) *to son meros* might mean "for your own part," in which case we might think that Socrates is primarily concerned with how he lives his own life, even if his disobedience is not infectious and does not threaten to undermine law abiding behavior in others. In other words, Socrates may be concerned about (1) general outlawry, or about (2) being an outlaw himself. I've tried to make my translation ambiguous. Compare *hoson dunasai* (as far as you are able) at 51a5.

50b4 ["without force"]: the authority to vacate a judgment is rightly constrained in every functioning state, but in democratic Athens it was especially jealously guarded. To vacate a judgment under the democracy necessarily suggested that the people were not being allowed to do as they wished, which necessarily suggested an attempt to overthrow the government. While today we might think anarchy was the threatened result, Athenians would probably have feared that some sort of oligarchic coup lay behind any attempt to render the authority of the democracy null and void.

50b4 ["private citizens?"]: an *idiōtēs* is a person with no special authorization. In political or legal contexts this can be a person who is not a magistrate of any kind (and is not even a juror). In professional contexts this can be an untrained person, a layman. In more general contexts it can be a generally unskilled or uneducated person, which is the root of the English word "idiot."

50b7 ["politician"]: Socrates may be using *rhētōr* almost in the disparaging way that Demosthenes uses it at *Against Timocrates* 123-124.

50c2 ["not judging correctly"]: *ouk orthōs...ekrinen* could refer either to procedural or to substantive injustice, so the reply is either that the trial was unfair (they violated proper procedure) or simply that the jury reached the wrong verdict (they found an innocent man guilty, despite following proper procedure). How we interpret this makes a great deal of difference to how we understand the Laws' response. It is hard to see how a "just agreement" can bind us to obey unfair trials, but it is easy to see how a "just agreement" can bind us to obey fair trials conducted by fallible human beings. 54c1 may imply that only substantive injustice is being considered.

50c9 ["charge"]: *egkaleō* can be used as a legal term for bringing formal, legal charges against someone for a specific offense. Socrates used this verb twice in the *Apology* i.e. at 26c5 and 27e5. Just as Socrates was on trial for his life because of the offenses alleged by Meletus, so also the personified laws of Athens portray themselves and the *polis* as being on trial for their lives, and they'd like to know what the charges against them are.

50d8 ["advised"]: *paraggellō* can be "command," but Athens had no law explicitly requiring that parents educate their children in "music and gymnastics" (see note on 50e1 below). Aeschines refers to laws regulating the upbringing of children, but we have no details (*Against Timarchus* 1.7). Our main source of information about Athenian education comes from Plato in the *Protagoras* and *Republic*, but the practices he describes seem voluntary, and depended upon the parents paying fees to the teachers they chose to hire. We do know two things: it was not illegal for parents to expose a child (though they could not directly kill it), and a son was legally absolved of the duty to care for his father if his father neglected to teach him a craft or a trade, or had prostituted him.

50e1 ["music and gymnastics?"]: *mousikē* and *gumnastikē* describe, for Plato, a well-rounded education that will produce—as we say today—a sound mind and a sound body. *Gumnastikē* could include games, general physical training and even some military training. *Mousikē* covered any art over which the Muses presided, but basically covered letters (reading and writing), arithmetic, playing a musical instrument (usually a lyre), and poetry. Poetry, however, included any subject touched on by Homer.

50e4 ["subject"]: *doulos* is usually opposed to *eleutheros* ("free"), in which case it means "slave" (e.g. Thucydides 8.28.4; in support of this translation see note on 51b5 below). But *doulos* can also be opposed to *despotēs* ("master"), in which case it can still mean "slave," but because *despotēs* can refer to an employer (cf. note on 50e8 below), *doulos* can refer to an employee. When Demaratos, the deposed King of Sparta, advised Xerxes, he said that "although Spartans are free men (*eleutheroi*), they are not free in all respects: the law is their master (*despotēs*), and they fear it more than your subjects fear you; they do whatever it commands, and it always commands the same thing: it forbids them to run from battle no matter how many men they fight, but to remain at their battle station and either conquer or be destroyed" (Herodotus 7.104.4-5). This sentiment is surprisingly close to views expressed by Socrates both in the *Apology* (e.g. 28d6-10) and in the *Crito* (e.g. 48c6-d5). Plato later expresses the view that the *dēmos* is the slave (*douleuō*) of the laws (*Laws* 3.700a3-5). So Socrates' use of *doulos* here might be (1) taken literally, i.e. citizens are literally slaves of the law, and so have no (or few) rights whatsoever against the authority of the state (in Athens, probably masters were not legally permitted to kill their slaves; slaves were permitted to take asylum at the Theseion and ask to be sold to a new master; and no one other than the slave's lawful owner could beat him); or (2) taken figuratively, i.e. citizens are not slaves but free (cf. 51c8-d5), and yet all—including every government official—are subject to law as their highest authority. If Socrates intends (2), then here we may have the earliest European expression of the principle known today as "the rule of law" (unless we can attribute this principle to Pittacus of Mytilene, see note on *Protagoras* 339c3, or to the Spartans, on Herodotus' authority; see note on 51a2 below; for a less ambiguous Platonic affirmation of the rule of law see *Laws* 4.715a8-d6, cf. the inevitable ruin that follows when the sovereign is above the law, 9.874e7-875c3). On (1) it is difficult to see how citizens can have any duty whatsoever to justice or to god (can a slave have more than one master?). On (2) citizens obviously have duties to law, justice and god, though it may not be clear how to settle cases in which these authorities seem to issue incompatible commands.

50e5 ["equality"]: the later Cynic philosopher Hipparchia uttered a famous argument that expresses the sort of equality Socrates has in mind here: "whatever it is not wrong for Theodorus to do, it is not wrong for Hipparchia to do; but it is not wrong for Theodorus to hit Theodorus, so it is not wrong for Hipparchia to hit Theodorus" (Diogenes Laertius 6.97). The more obvious parallel is that in Greek families, parents might speak to their children in harsh ways that it would be wrong (because impious) for their children to speak to the parents; and parents may strike their children, but it would be shockingly wrong for children to strike their parents. In a hierarchy, what is right is not equal between individuals at different levels.

50e8 ["master"]: a *despotēs* can be an owner, as the owner of a horse is the horse's "master" (Xenophon, *On the Art of Horsemanship* 4). But the head of a household is its *despotēs* without being the owner of everyone in the household (Xenophon, *Constitution of the Lacedaimonians* 7.4). The vagueness of reference is complicated by the fact that Greeks tended to assimilate the manual labor of slaves, free wage-earners and craftsmen (Aristotle, *Politics* 8.2). Here, because Socrates is a native Athenian citizen, it would be highly inappropriate for the laws to insinuate that Socrates might have been a literal slave at some point in his life; more likely they are simply referring to the fact that he did physical labor for some period of his life (e.g. he probably worked in his father's stone cutting business, if indeed that was the business of his father).

51a1 ["blow for blow"]: the violation of cultural norms when a son beats his father (and worse, threatens to beat his mother) is the turning point in Aristophanes' *Clouds* 1321-1511.

51a2 ["your fatherland and the laws"]: *patris* is literally "of [one's] fathers," i.e. the land of one's fathers, one's country or nation. Modern translators are reluctant to use "fatherland" because the Nazi's used it, but obviously Socrates was not a Nazi. We risk misunderstanding Socrates if we mistranslate this word. In Athens, the extended patriarchal family (*phratra*) controlled access to inheritance and civic rights; and each family had a sanctuary to Zeus *Herkeios* (Zeus of the front court of the home) and Apollo *Patrōos* (Apollo of the fathers). "Fatherland," therefore, indicates the basis of one's own standing and rights as an individual, but it does so by reference to one's patriarchal family, the state, and the gods. While an Athenian certainly could consider the problems that might arise if god, justice and law contradicted one another, it wouldn't be surprising if an Athenian failed to consider such a possibility. Notice that Socrates attributes his incarceration and imminent execution to his fatherland and the laws. He does not attribute them to the magistrate that presided at his trial, nor to the jury that convicted and sentenced him, nor to the guard that kept him in his cell. This suggests that in Socrates' view, Athens is under the "rule of law" (see note on 50e4 above).

51a6 ["true guardian of virtue"]: Socrates is implying that for him to escape from jail would make him a hypocrite after some of the claims he made during his trial, e.g. *Apology* 29b9-30c1.

51a7 ["clever"]: *sophos* is often used (especially by Socrates) with respect, and so it means "wise," but here he portrays the laws as being sarcastic with him, and insulting him with the old slander (cf. *Apology* 18b17). This entire paragraph is one sentence in Greek, so I have kept it as one sentence in English.

51b3 ["persuade"]: are the laws allowing disobedience itself to be a form of persuasion (like "civil disobedience" today), or would they accept only successful persuasion without disobedience? Cf. suppose your father gives you a bedtime of 9pm and you try to persuade him to let you stay up an extra half hour: do the laws allow you to stay up past 9 only if your father explicitly grants you permission to do so before 9, or do they allow you to persuade your father with a peaceful "protest" by staying up after 9 against his bedtime command, hoping that he will relent? See note on 51e6 below.

51b5 ["flogging or chains"]: the laws go too far here (and perhaps elsewhere in this sentence) because Athenians did not sentence Athenian citizens to being flogged or whipped, and they did not put them in chains (although convicted thieves could be sentenced to the stocks). Slaves could be flogged or whipped, and whips were associated with tyrants. If Socrates is not being deliberately hyperbolic, then this phrase supports the view that his use of *despotēs* (e.g. 50e8) implies a servile view of the citizen under law.

51b8 ["abandon your post"]: see note on *Apology* 28d8. In what sense is a retreating soldier innocent of abandoning his post? Perhaps Socrates' assumptions about obedience to law are not as strict as they appear to be. Compare Cicero's attitude toward keeping promises at *De Officiis* 3.24.93-25.96 (especially his distinction between obeying the letter as opposed to the intention of an agreement). Compare also Aquinas' attitude toward keeping the precepts of the Decalogue at *Summa Theologiae* IaIIae q.100 a.8 (these precepts are "indispensable" and so must be obeyed under all circumstances because they contain the intention of the lawgiver, so, e.g., we may never steal or commit murder; therefore the children of Israel were not stealing when they took the spoils of the Egyptians because such taking was in accord with the intention of the lawgiver; and Abraham was not planning murder in planning to kill his son because such planned killing was in accord with the intention of the lawgiver, *ad* 3). In general, non-teleological rules like algorithms may be easy to interpret and apply, but it may be difficult to know when they should be dispensed with; teleological rules may be difficult to interpret and apply since the intention of the rule-maker may be obscure, but such rules may be "indispensable." The worst-case-scenario is when a rule is simultaneously treated as non-teleological, but indispensable, e.g. consider the rule "follow orders" when your current orders (O) involve doing something wrong; a morally responsible non-teleological interpretation of O will judge that O is to be dispensed with under the circumstances, since it would be wrong to obey it; a teleological interpretation of O will be that although O appears to command doing something wrong, it does not, since the intention of O was to enjoin only right action (in the way that the planned killing of Isaac is not planned murder, taking the spoils of the Egyptians was not stealing, and retreating is not a violation of the rule that you should never "abandon your post").

51d1 ["but even so"]: *homōs* introduces a limitation or an unexpected qualification, e.g. Sarpedon grieved to see Glaucus leave the battle wounded, "even so" (*homōs*) Sarpedon did not forget to fight (*Iliad* 12.393): his grief leads us to expect that Sarpedon will flag in his military ardor, but quite the opposite happens. Here in the *Crito*, *homōs* may seem out of place: allowing citizens to leave Athens at will seems a natural extension of the generosity just mentioned. But the *homōs* is important: the Greeks did not have a tradition of Christian selfless giving, expecting nothing in return (e.g. Luke 6:35). For the Greeks, gift-giving helps to seal a mutual relationship between two people such that the receiver is, in some sense, beholden to or in the debt of the giver. Friendship involves reciprocity (cf. Aristotle, *Nicomachean Ethics* 8.14). The laws are implying that because they have given citizens so much, citizens owe much in return, and yet despite this fact, they allow citizens to leave, giving no return on the investment the laws have made in them. Some scholars attribute to Socrates a "love it or leave it" attitude; perhaps that is accurate, but his intention is to express the loaded opposition between being grateful and being ungrateful.

51d3 ["registered adult"]: normally male sons of citizens were officially enrolled as citizens at the age of 18 (Aristotle, *Constitution of Athens* 42.2; Aeschines, *Against Timarchus* 1.18). Officially they were then eligible to serve in public life (hence, metaphorically making a return on the investment that had been made in them).

51e2 ["render judgments"]: in the *Apology* Socrates says that some jurors convicted him with ill intent (41d7-e1), and he disagreed with the Athenian law that held capital trials on a single day and not, as in Spartan law, over several days (37a5-b1). But he never claims to be surprised by either fact (e.g. he never says anything like, "If only I had known that juries could behave so badly, I would have left Athens years ago!"). Socrates does not hold the laws responsible for the substantive injustice done to him (see 54b8-c1).

51e3 ["in fact agreed"]: Socrates uses *ergon*, implying the distinction between "word and deed" he relied on at *Apology* 32a5. In modern law, *de facto* agreements can be binding, e.g., in domestic partnerships that are not legal marriages.

51e6 ["neither obeying us nor persuading us"]: see note on 51b3 above. This claim is odd: I can understand (a) "having agreed to obey us, you do not obey us," and I can understand (b) "having agreed to obey us or persuade us, you neither obey us nor persuade us," but I have trouble with (c) "having agreed to obey us, you neither obey us nor persuade us." Is the option of persuading the laws implicit in the original agreement to obey them, or is persuasion never conceived of as an alternative to obedience (e.g. the persuasion must be successful and prior to the opportunity for disobedience)? How are we to understand the explicit reference below to "two options" (*duoin*, at 52a2)?

52b5 ["Isthmian Games"]: manuscripts disagree on this reference to the Isthmian Games. Greeks, like Romans (and like many modern cultures), were sports fanatics. Greeks loved to travel to the Panhellenic athletic contests, i.e. the Olympian Games (at Olympia in Elis, northwest of Sparta), the Pythian Games (at Delphi, northwest of Athens), the Nemean Games (west of Corinth), and the Isthmian Games (east of Corinth). I find it hard to believe that in all his years, Socrates was never dragged to one of these enormously popular festivals. The troubling evidence is at Plato's *Phaedrus* 230c6-e4, which suggests that unless he was called up for military service, Socrates stayed at Athens, i.e. he stayed literally inside the walls of the city.

52c4 ["proposed exile"]: see *Apology* 37c4-38a8.

52c6 ["self-importance"]: literally *kallōpize* means "to beautify the face." In effect, the laws are calling Socrates a hypocrite if he escapes now, since if he does then it will turn out to have been an empty show when at his trial he proclaimed, roughly, death before dishonor (e.g. *Apology* 30c1). Perhaps it is worth comparing Socrates' attitude with the story that closes Herodotus' *Histories* (roughly, it is better to rule with honor in a harsh land than to be a slave in exile in a soft land; Herodotus 9.122), with Achilles' choice at *Iliad* 9.411 (a short life with honor or a long life without it), and his regret at *Odyssey* 11.489-91 (better to serve on earth than to rule in Hades).

52d2 ["contracts"]: *sunthēkē* occurs here for the first time in the *Crito* (it also occurs at d8 and 54c3). *Asunthēkos* is "breach of contract." Perhaps my translation goes too far, since *sunthēkē* can refer to a convention, agreement, compact or treaty. The reference to a slave running away is odd, since slavery was not a contractual relationship (Solon outlawed debt slavery). I think the laws' point is not that runaway slaves are in breach of contract, but that they disregard the rule of law.

52e1 ["compulsion"]: the law of contracts in Athens was that any agreement made voluntarily (and hence, without compulsion) in the presence of witnesses was valid (Plato, *Symposium* 196c2-3; Demosthenes *Against Phaenippus* 42.12, *Against Evergus and Mnesibulus* 47.77, *Against Dionysodorus* 56.2; Dinarchus, *Against Philocles* 3.4). Hyperides adds that the agreement must be a just one: if it is an unjust agreement it is not valid (*Against Athenogenes* 3.13). It did not matter if the agreement was oral or written (though, obviously, a written agreement can be produced in court).

52e6 ["good laws"]: at *Hippias Major* 283e9 Socrates says that Sparta has good laws. Plato says that the laws of Crete are closely related to those of Sparta (*Laws* 3.683a2). The laws are about to say that both Thebes and Megara have good laws (53b5), but they seem to imply that Thessaly does not have good laws (53d3-4).

53a9 ["for yourself"]: why does Socrates have the laws ask this question? At 48b11-c2 Socrates said that if escape appeared to be the right thing to do, then they would do it, but if it appeared not to be the right thing to do, then they would not do it. If he has concluded that escape is not the right thing to do, then isn't the argument over? Why add the consideration of self-interest? He did say that "the most important thing is not to live, but to live well" (48b5-6), and he said that living well and living justly was one and the same thing (48b8-9). Is he contradicting himself here, suggesting that if the wrong course of action is in his self-interest, then perhaps he will intentionally do what is wrong? Perhaps the crucial word was "appears" (see note on 48c1). Perhaps the case the laws have given so far does make it "appear" that it would be wrong for Socrates to escape, but because Socrates and Crito also believe that the right course of action is always in the agent's self-interest, a separate consideration of Socrates' self-interest will help to confirm (or disconfirm) the result that the laws' arguments appear to support so far.

54a8 ["Hades"]: see note on *Apology* 41a1.

54b7 ["pious"]: in his trial Socrates seems to have assumed that self-interest, law, justice and god all recommend the same course of action (cf. 25d8-26a7, 29b6-7, 30b2-4, 32b8-c1, 33c4-7, 35c2-5). While this is controversial, it is not quite as controversial as we might think today. In Athens, laws did not contain definitions, and the commands of god typically required interpretation (21b4). So if in a given instance it appeared that self-interest, law, justice and god appeared to recommend incompatible courses of action, it would not be unreasonable to ask whether one was properly interpreting or applying all of these standards accurately, e.g. we might sensibly ask, "Is the law unjust, or are we simply misunderstanding the law, justice or both?"

54c1 ["by men"]: this agrees with Socrates' account in the *Apology* (see 41d5-e1), although he did explicitly object to the Athenian procedure of holding in one day trials that can result in execution (37a6-

b2, 38c1, see note on 37a8). It is also worth noting that apparently some of the jurors who voted "not guilty" voted for the death penalty (see note 38b9b). Socrates seems not to blame them, nor does he blame the guard, for carrying out what is, in his judgment, an unjust sentence (substantively, though perhaps not procedurally, unjust; see note on 50c2 above). This makes sense if he assumes the justice of legal "bifurcation," in this instance, separating the *liability* and the *penalty* phases of a trial. If Socrates accepts the justice of bifurcation, then he may think that although he is innocent of the crimes for which he was convicted, nevertheless the guard is acting justly in seeing that the penalty for violating those laws is duly applied.

54d3 ["Corybantes"]: in Greek myths, the Corybantes were divine beings who danced around the newborn Zeus, guarded the newborn Dionysus, and danced to the sound of flutes in the orgiastic celebrations of Dionysus. Sometimes the reference to a Corybantic dance suggests a state of frenzy (e.g. Aristophanes, *Wasps* 8), but it may also refer simply to the fact that the music is so loud that one cannot hear anything else (cf. *Euthydemus* 277d7, *Symposium* 215e1-2, *Ion* 533e8-534a1, *Laws* 7.790d4).

54d6 ["speak in vain"]: typically, Socratic discussions produce more discussions, not fewer; this is the only place where Socrates seems to say that further discussion is pointless. But this passage seems incoherent. On the one hand, he says that the arguments of the laws render him unable (*mē dunasthai*) to hear anything else, and that if Crito mounts any counter-arguments he will argue in vain (*matēn ereis*). But on the other hand, he clearly can hear things other than the arguments of the laws, since he hears Crito's response, and he qualifies his bold statement with "as it seems to me now." Recall that Socrates presented his arguments as a re-consideration of conclusions he had already reached (46b4-c6), so any further arguments Crito makes would count as a re-re-consideration. Given Crito's response at 54d8 (and his earlier responses at 51c5 and 52d7), perhaps Socrates' confidence that there was nothing further to say was based on his familiarity with Crito. In my opinion, what is significant here is that after all this, and given how clear it is that the argument is over, Socrates still encourages Crito to say anything he has in mind to say.

NOTES ON PROTAGORAS

309a2 ["the pack"]: *kunēgesion* literally refers to a pack of hunting dogs. Metaphorically it refers to the group of people who follow an attractive person. In ancient Greece, homosexual attraction was perfectly acceptable, but it is probably no accident that (1) the two individuals Plato clearly indicates Socrates felt some attration for were on the fast track to political power (Charmides at *Charmides* 155d3-e3; Alcibiades at *Alcibiades* 103a1-104c6, *Gorgias* 481d3, *Symposium* 216d2-219e5); and (2) we have no indication that Socrates ever had sex with a man (in fact, we have evidence that he never had sex with any man, *Symposium* 217a2-219e5). Socrates married late in life and had three children with his wife Xanthippe, with whom he appears to have had quite an affectionate relationship (*Phaedo* 60a1-8, 116a7-b5). On these matters, I am inclined to take Socrates at his word (*Symposium* 218d6-219a4, *Alcibiades* 104e4-6). I suspect that Socrates was very concerned about the next generation of political leaders, and he hoped that they would not suffer from the false pretentions to knowledge from which current and previous leaders suffer (cf. *Apology* 21b9-e2, *Meno* 92e3-95a1).

309a3 ["fine"]: *kalos*, see note on *Charmides* 154a3.

309a4-5 ["his beard really is filling in"]: youth set the standard of beauty for both men and women in ancient Greece (cf. *Alcibiades* 131c11-12).

309b1 ["his beard is just filling in?"]: at *Iliad* 24.348 and *Odyssey* 10.279 Hermes travels in disguise as a young man just beginning to grow facial hair, since this is when "the charm of youth is fairest." This is a disguise because Hermes has a full beard (although some artists like to depict him as a youth, since that was considered more beautiful).

309b6 ["support of my side"]: Alcibiades comes to Socrates' defense at 336b7-d5 and 348b2-8.

309c5 ["foreigner"]: *xenos*, see note on *Meno* 78d3.

309c8 ["Abdera"]: the port city of Abdera is in Thrace, west of the Hellespont. It was very wealthy because a great deal of maritime trade went through it, and also because of its substantial grain production. It owed the third largest tribute in the Delian League.

310c1 ["bed"]: here we learn that Socrates did not sleep on a *klinē* (the usual word for a bed or couch) but on a simple *skimpous* (a pallet). Apparently this was well known because Aristophanes made comic use of it in the *Clouds* (lines 254 and 709).

310c3 ["Oenoë"]: two demes had this name. One was northeast of Athens near Marathon, and other was northwest of Athens on the border with Boeotia. Both were probably only about 40 kilometers away from Athens.

310d7-8 ["he'll make you a wise man"]: if Socrates truly believes this, why hasn't he become Protagoras' student (cf. *Euthydemus* 304b6-c5)? On the other hand, if he believes that Protagoras is not wise, then he is lying to his friend. There is a third, intermediate possibility: Hippocrates is the one who just called Protagoras a wise man, and as usual (e.g. *Laches* 190c4-5) Socrates goes along with his partner's claim unless and until it is examined and refuted. Socrates does distinguish different degrees of belief (cf. *Charmides* 168a10-11, *Meno* 86b7, *Phaedo* 63c1-4, 114d1).

310e3 ["talk to him"]: *dialegomai* is used over two dozen times in the *Phaedo*. It's basic meaning is to converse with someone, but more pointedly it can refer to a discussion about a particular topic. It can also be used to refer to something much more specific, and is related to *dialektos*, the root of the English word "dialectic" (cf. *Republic* 5.454a4-9). The usual word for "debate" is simply *logos* (or *agōnizomai*, e.g. *Republic* 7.517d8; Demosthenes, *Erotic Essay* 61.43; Aristotle, *Rhetoric* 3.12; or *sumbouleuō*, e.g. Demosthenes, *Exordia* 10.1). I usually translate *dialegomai* as "discuss" (etc.).

310e5 ["first visited Athens"]: about a decade earlier. Pericles invited Protagoras to draw up the constitution for a new colony at Thurii in Italy. So Hippocrates is probably in his early 20's, and it would indeed be a bit forward of him to walk right up to Protagoras and introduce himself.

311b6 ["Hippocrates of Cos"]: we know virtually nothing for certain about this Hippocrates. He was a contemporary of Socrates, a serious medical expert, many medical treatises are alleged to have been written by him, and a school of medical science grew up around him, but beyond that we cannot be sure of exactly who he was or what he accomplished. Socrates refers to what we today would call his "holistic" approach to medicine at *Phaedrus* 270c1-7, cf. *Charmides* 156e3-6. The island of Cos (*Kōos*, in classical Greek) is off the southwestern coast of Asia Minor (modern day Turkey), in the southeast Aegean, northeast of Crete. It became famous in the 5th century BCE as a school for healers.

311b6 ["Asclepiad"]: myths about Asclepius the "blameless healer" go back at least to the *Iliad* (e.g. *Iliad* 4.194, 11.518). By the 5th century BCE a school of healers on the island of Cos (see note on 311b6) claiming to be biological descendants of this Homeric hero became famous. Their methods were quite varied and included divinatory "incubation" (sleeping in a sacred room so that one's dreams could be analyzed the next day for signs of a cure), herbal decoctions, as well as careful attention to diet and exercise. It is not too misleading to say that many engaged in empirical medical science. "Asclepiea" (local centers of Asclepiads) evolved into some of the earliest European hospitals and nursing homes.

311c3 ["Polycleitus the Argive"]: sculptor, active c.460-410. He worked in bronze and developed a detailed and precise set of mathematical ratios for portraying the human body, so that fingers, toes and each muscle would be proportionate. His most famous work was "The Spear-Bearer" (*Doruphoros*), and many copies of it exist today. He established an extremely influential school for sculptors. Ancient opinion seems to have been that he was second only to Phidias as a sculptor.

311c4 ["Phidias the Athenian"]: sculptor, active c.465-425. Phidias was responsible for the gigantic Athena Promachos on the Acropolis, which allegedly could be seen all the way from Sunium (modern day Cape Sounion, about 70 kilometers southeast of Athens). He was also responsible for the famous Zeus at Olympia. Both the Athena Promachos and the Zeus at Olympia were made of gold and ivory over a wooden core, and embellished with jewels, silver, copper, enamel, glass and paint. Pericles may have put him in charge of his entire building program for the Acropolis. Ancient opinion seems to have been that he was the greatest and most versatile of all sculptors. Pupils from his school dominated sculpture for quite a while. Unfortunately, it seems that Phidias was prosecuted (perhaps in 438) for embezzling ivory from the Athena Parthenos; he died in prison or fled to Olympia.

311c8 ["A sculptor, obviously"]: the answers to these questions are indeed obvious, and the questioning can seem tedious. Socrates does this often—in fact, it is a sort of trademark of Socratic reasoning: Aristotle claims that Socrates is responsible for introducing two things: universal definitions and inductive arguments, *Metaphysics* 13.4.1078b17-19. Socrates regularly induces his interlocutors to reason on the basis of known particular examples, not on hearsay or conjecture. See notes on 312a8 and 312d9.

311e4 ["Sophist"]: see note on *Laches* 186c3. Socrates is about to emphasize the relationship between the title "Sophist" (*sophistēs*), the adjective "wise" (*sophos*), and the abstract noun "wisdom" (*sophia*). By way of contrast, Pythagoras (c.570-c.495) did not call himself a *sophistēs*, but a *philosophos*: he did not claim to be wise, he claimed only to love wisdom.

312a7 ["if I have to say what I think"]: Socrates encourages his interlocutors to express their sincerely held beliefs (sometimes called "The Sincerity Requirement;" see 331b8-d1 below, and *Meno* 75d6, 83d2; *Laches* 193c7; *Crito* 49d1; *Gorgias* 495a5-b6, 500b; *Republic* 346a; *Theaetetus* 154c7-e6).

312a8 ["not like the other cases"]: the principle underlying inductive reasoning (see notes on 311c8 and 312d9) is that the future (or cases examined in the future) will resemble the past (or cases examined in the past; see note on 312d9). Socrates understands that inductive reasoning can be misleading, since cases examined in the future may only appear to be like cases examined in the past.

312b1 ["grammar teacher"]:in the *Republic* Plato distinguishes three branches of education: *grammata* (i.e. basic literacy, reading and writing; 3.402a7-b3), *gumnastikē* (physical, athletic and military training; 3.403c9-d5), and *mousikē* (music in our modern sense, but also including poetry, and hence theology, history and whatever poets write about; see notes on *Laches* 180d1 and *Phaedo* 60e6). Here Socrates distinguishes the *grammatistēs*, the *paidotribēs*, and the *kitharistēs*, but he probably has in mind the same threefold educational distinction.

312b4 ["every free person deserves to become"]: this is probably the first definition of a liberal education in the European tradition. See note on *Meno* 84d2.

312b8 ["soul"]: *psuchē*, see note on *Charmides* 154e1.

312c1 ["trained"]: *therapeuō* is the verb related to the noun *therapeia*, from which we derive the English word "therapy." See notes on *Euthyphro* 12e7 and *Laches* 185e4.

312c6 ["knowledgeable in wise matters"]: Hippocrates is correct that the name "sophist" (*sophistēs*) implies "wisdom" (*sophia*). The connection with "knowledge" (*epistēmē*) is certainly reasonable, since *sophia* can refer to skill (e.g. sculpting or poetic skill), which can be thought of as a body of knoweldge (e.g. knowing how to sculpt or write poetry); when Odysseus strung his bow "expertly," he strung is *epistamenos* (*Odyssey* 21.406). This makes Socrates' next point equally reasonable.

312d5 ["manage"]: *epistatēs* literally means to stand near or over, but it looks like it is related to the infinitive *epistasthai*, which is related to *epistēmē* (knowledge). This pun eases the way into the commercial analogy Socrates is about to use.

312d7 ["clever speaker"]: Socrates denies being a clever (*deinos*) speaker at *Apology* 17b1.

312d9 ["For example"]: more inductive argumentation (see notes on 311c8 and 312a8). Based on examples like this one here, we should probably say that Socratic induction often amounted to "illustrative parallels" (cf. Aristotle, *Rhetoric* 2.20.1393a30-b9). E.g. (i) athletes and steersmen ought not be selected by lot, so public officials ought not be selected by lot; or (ii) both Darius and Xerxes subdued Egypt prior to invading Greece, so if the present King of Persia subdues Egypt, then he will invade Greece. Obviously inductive arguments are not deductively valid, but they can have significant heuristic value, especially as ways to help us discern differences: as Socrates just pointed out (312a7-8), sometimes new situations are not like the ones already considered.

312e1 ["*kithara*"]: see note on *Laches* 192a3.

312e3 ["make you a clever speaker"]: some scholars accuse Socrates of the fallacy of equivocation. A "clever speaker" can be (a) a knowledgeable speaker on a particular topic, or (b) a skilled orator (i.e. someone with excellent diction, who can speak audibly to a large crowd in an open space, is adept at rousing various emotions in an audience, and so on). But Socrates is not equivocating, with Hippocrates he is insisting on (a), see *Apology* 22c5 and the note on that passage.

313a9 ["condition of your soul"]: this seems extreme. What about luck? What about the intervention of the gods? See 344c4-d5. A similar issue is raised at *Euthydemus* 279c7-280b6.

313d1 ["Grocers"]: Plato elaborates on this analogy of the sophist as a peddler of merchandise at *Sophist* 223c9-224e5.

313e2 ["doctor of the soul"]: it seems to me that Socrates is the originator of the notion of the scientific study of human psychology, i.e. psychological science.

314b8 ["become his students"]: Socrates does not explicitly say this, but I think it is implied by what he has said. Since you cannot unlearn what you have learned, he is not proposing that they go and become Protagoras' students just yet—he wants to give the man a fair hearing and then make their decision later.

314c2 ["wise men"]: here Socrates uses the adjective *sophos* instead of the noun *sophistēs*. He might intend to be distinguishing two very different kinds of people they are likely to encounter.

314c8 ["a eunuch"]: Greeks were disgusted at the eastern practice of castration (Herodotus 8.105; Xenophon, *Cyropaedia* 7.5.61). The English "eunuch" is a transliteration of the Greek *eunouchos*, which is derived from the phrase "*ho tēn eunēn echōn*," which means "the one who has the bed," i.e. the man who manages and protects the King's bedchamber or harem. In addition to managing the wives or daughters of powerful men, some cults of female deities employed eunuchs as priests, and—the practice that particularly disgusted Greeks—children were castrated to be used for sexual purposes. I suspect that Callias bought his doorman as a slave during a visit to Asia Minor. Eunuchs were not common in Athens, which is why Socrates makes note of it.

314e4 ["portico"]: ancient Greek houses were planned around a central courtyard, and in lavish houses the courtyard would be ringed by the portico (*prostōon*), a roofed walkway lined with columns. Protagoras is described as *peripatounta*, which is related to the English word "peripatetic," which is often associated with Aristotle.

315a4 ["on the other side"]: to make this passage readable, I've cut out some of the relational information Socrates includes. He mentions that Callias is the son of Hipponicus, that Paralus is Callias' half-brother and the son of Pericles, that Charmides is the son of Glaucon, that Xanthippus is Pericles' son, Philippides is the son of Philomelus, and that Antimoerus is from the town of Mende (on the peninsula of Chalcidice on the north of the Agean). This is a cosmopolitan group of people with money and power.

315a8 ["charming"]: *kēleō* (translated as "under a spell" at 315b1, and translated as "captivated" at 328d4-5; see note on 328d4-5). This word can refer to offering someone a gift, an inducement, or bribe (cf. *Laws* 10.885d4) Plato argues that "charming" people so that they control their bodily desires (especially sexual desire) is a good thing (*Laws* 8.840c2-3). Socrates mentions that cicadas can charm lazy people dozing in the midday sun (*Phaedrus* 259 a3), and that Protagoras was adept at arousing various feelings in a crowd by his spells—by which he seems to men artful speeches (*Phaedrus* 267d1). This is a familiar effect people often intend with words (*Lysis* 206b2). Alcibiades uses this word to describe Socrates, comparing him to the mythical Marsyas who bewitched people by playing the aulos (*Symposium* 215c1).

315b2 ["chorus line"]: *choros* literally refers to a dance, but it took on the reference to the chorus in a tragedy because the chorus danced while it sang or chanted its lines.

315b9 ["after him I recognized"]: *Odyssey* 11.601. Odysseus uses some such transition many times in Book 11 as he sees and talks with souls in Hades. This particular transition introduces "mighty Herakles."

315c3 ["Andron"]: again, I've simplified the text. Socrates mentions that Eryximachus is the son of Acumenus and that Phaedrus is from Myrrinus (a small town near Athens), and that Andron is the son of Androtion. Eryximachus and Phaedrus were friends and both appear in Plato's *Symposium*; Phaedrus plays a large role in Plato's *Phaedrus*. Both Eryximachus and Phaedrus were implicated with Alcibiades in some of the religious offenses of 415. Andron was a friend of Callicles (*Gorgias* 487c3), and was also a member of the oligarchic government of Athens that briefly held power in 411.

315c8 ["next I saw Tantalus"]: *Odyssey* 11.582.

315d5 ["sheepskins"]: perhaps the suggestion is that Prodicus has a cold. Perhaps this is accidental, but the three main intellectuals seem to be in declining positions of vigor: Protagoras is peripatetically holding forth in the courtyard; Hippias is pontificating while seated; Prodicus is bellowing from his bed.

315d7 ["Pausanias"]: Socrates mentions that he is from Cerames, another small town near Athens. Pausanias and Agathon are prominent in Plato's *Symposium*. Agathon became a prominent tragedian

315d8-e1 ["fine and good"]: see note on *Laches* 186c4.

315e5 ["Leucolophides"]: we know nothing of Adeimantus the son of Cepis, but the son of Leucolophides was implicated, with Alcibiades, Eryximachus and Phaedrus in the religious offenses of 415. He served in the military (sometimes with Alcibiades) but he was accused of treachery after Athens was defeated by Sparta. Adeimantus seems to have been a fairly common name, Plato had a brother with that name.

316a1 ["divine man"]: high praise indeed, and it seems sincere, cf. *Theaetetus* 151b5.

316a5 ["Critias"]: Socrates refers to him in the normal Greek fashion, i.e. with his patronymic: Critias the son of Callaeschrus. Critias' nephew Charmides has already been mentioned (315a1; see *Charmides* 154b1-2), and since Charmides is probably a teenager, it is only natural that he would have a guardian present (cf. *Charmides* 155a4-7). Critias was implicated in the religious offenses of 415, and both he and Charmides were involved in the government of the "Thirty Tyrants" (see note on *Charmides* 157e3).

316c5 ["circumspect"]: because Socrates is willing to pursue the conversation in private. As Protagoras is about to explain, if it becomes widely known that he is considering taking Hippocrates on as a student, some people might get upset. He's not wrong (see Anytus' reaction to sophists at *Meno* 91c1-5).

316d7 ["Simonides"]: Simonides of Ceos (where Prodicus was born) was an extremely successful poet in the late 6th and early 5th century (most sources point to about 556 for his birth, and he was traditionally thought to have lived for 90 years). It is traditional to cite Homer and Hesiod, plus Orpheus and Musaeus, in the way Protagoras does here (cf. *Apology* 41a6-7); but it is odd to stick Simonides in here. On Orpheus, Musaeus and "Orphism," see note on *Crito* 44b2.

316d9 ["Iccus of Tarentum"]: Tarentum was a Spartan colony in southern Italy. Iccus seems to have flourished in the 6th century as an athlete, athletic trainer and doctor. Plato seems to have admired his temperance (*Laws* 8.839e-840a4).

316e1 ["Herodicus of Selymbria"]: Selymbria was a little west of Byzantium, on the coast of the Propontis, in between the Hellespont and the Bosporus. Protagoras also mentions that he was originally from Megara, which is in between Athens and Corinth, but he does not say why Herodicus emigrated. Plato attributes to Herodicus the invention of what is today called "extraordinary life-sustaining treatment," i.e. medical procedures administered to terminally ill patients and designed to delay death (*Republic* 3.406a5-b8). He also recommended that Athenians should exercise by walking all the way to Megara and back (*Phaedrus* 227d2-5), about an 80 kilometer round trip (almost two marathons).

316e2 ["Agathocles as well as Pythocleides of Ceos"]: prominent music teachers. Agathocles is mentioned at *Laches* 180d1, Pythocleides is mentioned at *Alcibiades* 118c5.

317b4 ["educate"]: this is first use of the verb *paideuō* in the Protagoras (it also occurs at 319e4, 320a1, 320a7, 342d3, 342d6, 343a1, and 347d3). The related noun *paideutēs* is used only once, at 324b6. It is possible for *mathēteia*, *didaxis* and *paideia* and to be used interchangeably as "education," but it is also possible to distinguish them as "learning" (e.g. mathematical learning), "teaching" (e.g. grammatical instruction) and "education" (e.g. moral education). Of the three words, *paideia* can most easily bear a very robust meaning that includes reading, writing and arithmetic, physical and martial training, as well as the moral, social and political education younger men receive from mentors who help them make valuable business and political connections. If education includes shaping the hearts and minds of the youth (as we say today), and it influences their political inclinations, then community leaders may be wary of, or hostile to, foreigner educators.

317c2 ["lived for many more"]: he practiced his craft for 40 years, and lived for 70 (*Meno* 91e5-6).

317c7 ["lovers"]: *erastastēs* is the word normally used for a man who sexually desires another—usually younger—man, although it can also be used in a colorful way to refer to an admirer, or metaphorically to refer to a passion for something (cf. *Meno* 70b2-5, *Lysis* 221e7-222a7). Here it suggests that Socrates suspects a three-fold vanity in Protagoras, i.e. (1) Socrates and Hippocrates choose Protagoras as teacher over Prodicus and Hippias, (2) they admire him, and (3) they pursue him like a lover pursues a younger man (cf. the modern phrase, "I've still got it" when an older person feels as if they are not still too old to be attractive to younger people).

317e5 ["on the young man's behalf"]: I take this as evidence that Socrates' suspicions (see note on 317c7) were correct. Protagoras could have asked Socrates to raise the issue of how a well-born, able young man might best make a name for himself in the city, but instead he wants everyone to hear that for Hippocrates' improvement, they have come to Protagoras, and so, by implication, they did not come to Prodicus, Hippias, or even to Callias.

318b7-8 ["Zeuxippus of Heraclea"]: more often Zeuxis. Heraclea in Italy (modern day Policoro) is on the southern coast of Italy (between the "heel" and the "toe"); it was a colony of nearby Tarentum, which itself was a colony of Sparta. Zeuxippus became quite a famous painter—allegedly his grapes actually fooled birds. Arrogantly, he gave his paintings away on the grounds that no one could afford to pay what they were truly worth.

318c5 ["Orthagoras of Thebes"]: Thebes is north of Athens. The fourth century BCE philosopher, and student of Aristotle, Aristoxenus of Tarentum said that Orthagoras taught the famous Theban general Epaminondas to play the *aulos*.

318c8 ["playing the flute"]: one form of *aulos* was played horizontally, like the modern flute, and so "flute" is now the traditional translation. However, most *auloi* were reed instruments, and so unlike the modern flute. The double *aulos* (shaped like the letter "V") is often seen on vase paintings. Some *auloi* were double-reeded, and so were much more like the modern oboe than the modern flute. Other *auloi* had an air bag attached to allow for a continuous drone, and so were more like the modern bagpipe.

318d8-9 ["any other sophist"]: remember that Protagoras thinks that poets, musicians, and presumably painters too, are sophists (316d3-e5).

318e2-3 ["arithmetic, astronomy, geometry and music"]: this list is very close to the curriculum Plato recommends for rulers at *Republic* 7.525a9-531d4.

318e5 ["good deliberation"]: *euboulia*. Plato uses the related adjective *euboulos* to describe the city that is wisely governed (*Republic* 428b3-d10). Aristotle discusses the intellectual virtue of *euboulia* at *Nicomachean Ethics* 6.9.1142a31-1142b33. The idea that you can be a good manager without knowing anything about arithmetic, astronomy, geometry and music is similar to Critias' notion of temperance and political power in the *Charmides* (e.g., see *Charmides* 170a6-172a6).

319a1 ["as influential as possible"]: *dunatōtatos* is the superlative of *dunatos*, which can refer to strength, might or power. Protagoras could be insinuating that he can make young men politically powerful. Thucydides' description of Pericles at 1.139.4 is remarkably similar to what Protagoras promises here.

319a5 ["good citizens"]: Socrates' inference from teaching the political craft to teaching good citizenship is invalid in an indirect democracy, but valid in a direct democracy. In an indirect democracy, citizens are not judges—at most, they are jurors; in a direct democracy, citizens are judges (see note on *Apology* 40a2). In an indirect democracy, citizens are not legislators—at most, they vote for legislators; in a direct democracy, citizens are legislators (they are members of the *Ekklēsia*, see note on *Laches* 179d7). In an indirect democracy, citizens do not hold office—at most, they vote for people who hold office; in a direct democracy, offices (with few exceptions, e.g. military generals) are assigned on a basis of equality, e.g. by sortition. See also note on 326e1.

319a10 ["what I actually have in mind"]: scholars who think that Socrates is regularly ironic with his interlocutors might interpret this claim as ironic; scholars who think that we should be restrained in attributing irony to Socrates might take him at his word here. Whichever interpretation we accept, his claim here is worded carefully so as not to insult Protagoras, because what he's about to say implies that Protagoras does not in fact possess the skill he claims that he possesses.

319a10 ["teachable"]: see also *Meno* 90b4-96d4. In the *Republic*, Plato not only seems to think that the political craft is teachable, he appears to provide a fairly detailed sketch of how it is teachable. Perhaps Plato contradicts Socrates. However, Plato acknowledges that the conditions for the teachability of virtue are almost unattainable, though possible (e.g. *Republic* 5.473c2-e5). Unless Socrates' denial is intended in an unreasonably absolute sense (a sense not supported by his reasoning), then it is not incompatible with the view Plato defends in the *Republic*.

319b1 ["I have no basis for doubting it"]: "cognitive dissonance" is mental discomfort felt by someone who simultaneously holds what seem to be mutually exclusive beliefs. If Socrates is intolerant of such discomfort, then he must give up at least one of the beliefs that are apparently in conflict; so if we assume that Socrates is very intolerant of such discomfort, then we might assume that he is being ironic here. Alternatively, if he is fairly tolerant of such mental discomfort, then he may be perfectly sincere; after all, as he is about to show, he does have reason to think that virtue is not teachable (at least not under current or foreseeable circumstances, see note on 319a10), and it would be grossly presumptuous of him at this point in the dialogue to assume that Protagoras is lying or deluded about his own abilities.

319b4 ["I go along with that"]: is this agreement that the Athenians are wise compatible with what Socrates says at *Apology* 23b2-4?

319d1 ["speak"]: see note on *Laches* 178a4. Herodotus argues that freedom of speech is part of what made Athens great (5.78).

319e3 ["Pericles"]: see note on *Meno* 94b1.

319e3 ["two young men"]: Pericles' two sons by his first wife, Paralus and Xanthippus, died shortly before Pericles in the great plague of 429.

320a2 ["sacred cattle"]: cattle that belonged to a temple (for eventual sacrifice) were allowed to graze anywhere they liked. The comparison would, if anything, be considered a compliment, not an insult.

320c3 ["demonstration"]: on the *muthos/logos* contrast see notes on *Phaedo* 60c2 and 99e5.

320c7 ["tell you a story"]: Protagoras just distinguished between giving a *muthos* and giving a *logos*, and here he says that he will tell [*legein*] a story [*muthos*]. Perhaps this is a joke: Protagoras draws and then immediately blurs a verbal distinction. See also note on 324c4.

320d4-5 ["Prometheus and Epimetheus"]: the names of these brothers mean, respectively, forethought and afterthought. So the first joke in this story is that Prometheus is not the one to assign powers to the various creatures; the second joke is that the guy whose name means forethought doesn't do the final inspection until the very last minute (321c6-7). They are gods and the sons of the Titan Iapetos (the parents of the Titans were Ouranos and Gaia), so they are of the same generation as Zeus (whose father was the Titan Cronus). Hesiod tells their stories at *Theogony* 507-616, see also *Works and Days* 42-105.

320b1-2 ["skin without hair or blood"]: like the foot pads of dogs. In fact, these pads do have blood, but they are insulated with a thick layer of fat, so shallow abrasions do not make them bleed.

321c1 ["lack rationality"]: *alogos* could also mean without speech, but speech (*phonē*) is mentioned separately at 322a6, so "reason" is probably best here. It is common for people (a) to complain about human irrationality, and (b) to emphasize the intelligence of non-human species. However, Plato links the concept of *logos* as a distinctive human capacity with the adjective *logistikos* (e.g. *Republic* 4.439d5). So perhaps intead of human "rationality," we should think of *logos* as the human capacity for planning our lives logistically. Our technological and logistical superiority over all other known species does seem quite substantial, even if these do occasionally outstrip our wisdom, compassion and respectfulness.

321c1-2 ["human race was left unadorned"]: Protagoras appeals to the objective fact that humans lack claws or fangs (etc.), and not to the subjective fact that humans feel vulnerable. Similarly, at 322c3-4 Protagoras will appeal to the absolute fact that shame and justice are necessary for the existence of political communities, and not to the relative fact that (many or all) political communities value shame and justice as essential for the existence of the community. This objective and absolute basis for his view seems at odds with the subjectivism and relativism with which he is closely associated (cf. *Theaetetus* 167c4-5, 172a1-5).

321d1 ["Hephaestus and Athena"]: although today Athena is typically thought of as the goddess of war (focusing especially on wise tactics), in Athens she shared a temple and a festival with Hephaestus since both of them were patron deities of technology, e.g. weaving, tailoring, pottery, smithing, carpentry.

321d5 ["political wisdom"]: Protagoras seems to draw a close connection between (1) the individual staying alive and (2) the political community. Perhaps he thinks that the political community is only an instrumental means to each individual staying alive, so that if each individual could be assured of staying alive without having to resort to participation in a political community, it would be rational to avoid political associations. Hippias may see things differently (see 337d1 and the note on that line).

321d7 ["the guards"]: *Kratos* and *Bia*, i.e. Might and Force (Hesiod, *Theogony* 385-8). Their siblings are *Zēlos* and *Nikē* (Jealousy and Victory). Their mother is the river Styx (who is the daughter of Ocean). Might and Force are prominent at the beginning of Aeschylus' *Prometheus Bound*.

322a3 ["the divine allotment"]: or "the divine fate," since the noun *moira* is often translated as "fate." However, the word literally refers to a part, portion, share or allotment, e.g. when an inheritance is divided among brothers, each receives his own share. The human lot in life partakes of the divine because we have fire and technology, which was stolen from Zeus by Prometheus.

322a4 ["shares kinship with the gods"]: perhaps this kinship consists simply in the fact that we too now possess fire and technology. Alternatively, the suggestion may be that because human beings were fashioned in the earth (320d2), Gaia is their mother, just as Gaia is the mother of the Titans, and the grandmother of the Olympian gods (cf. Hesiod, *Works and Days* 108; Pindar, *Nemean* 6.1-3). Presumably, dogs, horses, deer and so on were not fashioned underground, but above the ground (*Menexenus* 237d4 is unclear on this point). At *Menexenus* 237b6, Socrates emphasizes the autochthony of Athenians—the fact that the first Athenians arose from Athenian soil.

322a4 ["acknowledge"]: see note on *Euthyphro* 3b3. Socrates mentions this exceptional trait of human beings at *Menexenus* 237d6-e1. This human exceptionalism may not have been universal in the ancient world: Psalm 104:21 interprets the lion's roar after a successful hunt as an acknowledgement of God.

322a6 ["names"]: *onoma* means name, but in an extended sense it can refer generically to words or phrases. If Protagoras really does mean "name" here, then his account is similar to the account in Genesis according to which Adam's first speech act was to name the animals (Genesis 2:19).

322b1 ["there were no cities"]: this may be a false opposition since it is possible for human beings to live in groups without living in cities (*homo sapiens* is a social species that evolved from social primates, so our ancestors lived in organized social groups for millions of years before there were cities). Protagoras seems to concur with the English philosopher Thomas Hobbes (1588-1679) in separating a pre-social period of human life from a eusocial period, and also in arguing that the in the pre-social period human beings were in danger of being killed off by wild animals and by each other (Hobbes does explicitly allow that presocial human beings lived in small families—very much like Homer's Cyclopes at *Odyssey* 9.112-15). As Hobbes so eloquently put it, in our pre-social period, human life was "solitary, poore, nasty, brutish, and short" (*Leviathan* 13.5; cf. *Laws* 1.626d7-9). Aristotle's view is closer to the truth because he believes that human beings are by nature social animals (*Nicomachean Ethics* 1.7.1097b11; *Politics* 1.2.1253a7; though Aristotle did not know that our sociality is an evolved trait of many primate species, including our own; the Sicilian philosopher Empedocles (c.492-432) seems to have been the only ancient Greek to believe that human beings were the result of a process of evolution—though his theory is by no means Darwinian). Protagoras and Hobbes seem to think that human sociality is merely instrumentally useful, and perhaps necessary for the long-term survival of our species; Aristotle argues that human relationships (both intra-familial and inter-familial) are essential components of the human good (e.g. *Politics* 1.2, 3.9).

322b5 ["political craft"]: *technē* is an art or a craft in a sense that includes carpentry, pottery, blacksmithing, weaving, building and so on. I often use "technology" (etc.) to translate it.

322b6 ["band together"]: perhaps an over-translation of *athroizō*, which simply refers to collecting together, gathering or mustering. A family would seem to be a band, or collection, of individuals, so is Protagoras saying that in our pre-social period we didn't even have families? Historically this is false since *homo sapiens* evolved from social primates. It is possible that the banding together is a banding together of separate families (e.g. into a "clan," though he does not say this), but why? There are at least three possibilities. (1) Human bands are purely instrumentally valuable, so that civil society, a large number of obedient slaves, or a large number of robots (to use a modern example) could all be equally effective solutions to the problem that must be solved. If slaves (or robots) could solve the problem, then civic virtues would not be absolutely necessary, simply necessary for one possible solution to the basic problem. (2) Human bands are intrinsically valuable in addition to being instrumentally valuable for protecting us from wild animals. But how is this intrinsic value to be explained? (2a) Non-rationally, human bonds can consist in strong feelings, e.g. affection, desire. But feelings can change, and so would seem to be an insufficient ground for relations of justice (you still owe basic duties of justice to people for whom your feelings have changed). This option also allows the possibility of solving the basic problem by means of slaves or robots, since some people can feel great affection for slaves or robots (especially if the robots are made to look like people). (2b) Rationally, human bonds can consist in mutually fulfilling relationships (e.g. friendship, co-workers, allies) based on mutual recognition that each of us deserves to be treated with a basic level of respect. This option can be a sufficient ground for relations of justice (since recognition that others deserve respect depends upon what they are, not upon how we feel about them), and does not allow the possibility of solving the basic problem by means of slaves or robots, since the correct sort of mutual recognition is not possible in either relationship (unless the robots were truly sentient and rational).

322c2 ["shame"]: *aidōs*, see notes on *Charmides* 158c6 and *Apology* 28b3. By affirming that we can be rational without having a sense of shame or justice, Protagoras seems to imply that shame and justice are non-rational feelings. This would make sense of Apollo's claim that *aidōs* is both a great benefit and a great harm for human beings (Homer, *Iliad* 24.44-45): it benefits us when we happen to feel it appropriately (or appropriately fail to feel it), but it harms us when we happen to feel it inappropriately (or inappropriately fail to feel it). Aristotle connects shame with rationality (*Nicomachean Ethics* 4.9) because he argues that we have perfectly good reason to respect others and to maintain friendly relations with them (e.g. in 9.8-9), and to judge ourselves harshly if we fail to treat them as they deserve to be treated. While Aristotle accepts that justice is a virtue, he denies that shame is a virtue (except, perhaps for young people), because mature adults should never do something to be ashamed of, although he allows that a sort of conditional shame might be a good trait, i.e. hypothetically if you did do something to be ashamed of, you would indeed feel ashamed of yourself.

322d4 ["unable"]: Zeus' answer to Hermes is unclear. If cities cannot exist when only a few have a share in shame and justice, then shame and justice has to be possessed by many, not few. If that is what Zeus intends, then why kill the moral defectives (who are not able to have any share in shame or justice)? People with especially low intelligence can lead productive lives with a guardian, and many morally insensitive people never commit capital offenses (not all sociopaths are criminals). Alternatively, Protagoras may mean that unless everyone living has a share in justice and shame then cities are impossible, it would be necessary to exterminate every moral defective before cities can exist. This gives a reason to kill the moral defectives, but it's not reasonable to think that the necessary condition for the existence of cities is so high. A third alternative would be to say that those who are unable to share in justice and shame are "incurable" (cf. *aniaton* at 325a8, and *Phaedo* 113e1-6) in the sense that although justice and shame are in them by nature, and despite repeated attempts at correction by parents, civil society, and the criminal justice system, they persist in criminal behavior, once it is clear that they are indeed incurable (e.g. by committing murder or some grave impiety, see note on *Phaedo* 113e3), they deserve to be executed, and they must be executed lest their example induce others to greater boldness in shameless and unjust behavior. See note on 322d5.

322d5 ["killed as a disease in the city"]: is this a deterrence theory of criminal justice? If so, then protecting the health of the city could justify killing people who do not deserve the death penalty, e.g. they are morally defective (see note on 322d4) but have not actually committed any capital offenses, or they are so defective that they lack self-control and so cannot be held responsible for their actions. This seems inconsistent with what Protagoras says at 323c7-324a4. Alternatively, the metaphor of disease and health might indicate that Protagoras has in mind only "incurable" people (again, see note on 322d4).

322d7 ["architectural virtue"]: this sounds odd in English, but the Greek *aretē* applies in non-moral cases, like architecture, animal husbandry and so on. See notes on *Charmides* 158a1 and *Apology* 20b6.

322a6 ["men"]: Prometheus switches from the gender-neutral *anthrōpos* to the gender-specific *anēr*. Does he mean to say that it is only men and not women who have a share of justice and shame (or temperance)? This raises a serious problem: Hermes' question about the distribution of shame and justice, and hence Zeus' answer, was posed using *anthrōpos*. If about half of the population lacks shame and justice, aren't cities impossible?

323a3 ["it belongs to everybody to have a share of this virtue"]: three translations are possible. He might be saying that (1) social life is impossible unless everybody is just (emphasizing *metechein*, to have a share in); or (2) social life is impossible unless everybody is required to be just (emphasizing *prosēkon*, to be fitting or proper); or (3) social life is impossible unless everybody is minimally just and temperate (taking *prosēkon* as belonging to, and *metechein* as having at least a minimal share in). Of these, (1) seems false because every society has criminals; (2) seems true but insufficient because society breaks down if a sufficient number of people refuse to do what they are required to do; (3) seems both true and consistent with Protagoras' claim to teach virtue: perhaps those who are not just or temperate at all can never be taught to be just or temperate, but those who are minimally just and temperate may well be taught to possess both virtues to an excellent degree.

323b1 ["reprimand"]: *noutheteō* literally means to put something in someone's mind, but in practice what one is putting in the other's mind are standards of behavior, i.e. reminding them of how they should behave and pointing out that they have violated those norms (it is used here and at 323d1, 323e3, 324a2, 325c6, 326a1, and 341a8). Hence "admonish," "rebuke," "warn" or even "advise" can be good translations. Part of Protagoras' point here is that this is the sort of thing we do with people who have minds. We hold people responsible for their actions in ways that we do not hold animals or inanimate objects responsible for the things they play some role in causing to happen. So "blame" is sometimes a good translation.

323d3 ["feel sorry for them"]: the verb *eleeō* is often translated as mercy or pity, and is the root of the English adjective eleemosynary (i.e. relating to charity). Protagoras' point here is very interesting and extremely important because he seems to be distinguishing what is voluntary from what is involuntary. This distinction is important for understanding the nature of agency, free will and moral responsibility.

323d7 ["habituation"]: *askēsis* is the noun related to the adjective *askētos*, see note on *Meno* 70a2.

324a6 ["corrects or punishes"]: *kolazō* refers to checking or chastising disfavored behavior or even conditions (it can refer to pruning trees). I usually translate it as "correct" in the sense in which the phrase "correctional facilities" (e.g. prisons) uses the term. Protagoras is about to use *timōreō* four times (324b1-2), and I think that he uses it to mean "retaliation" (in fact, "lashing out" might even be correct); but at 324c1 he seems to use *timōreō* in a generic sense, so I translate it as "punishment." According to Aristotle, *timōria* and *kolasis* differ in that *kolasis* is inflicted for the sake of the person being punished, but *timōria* is inflicted for the sake of the person doing the punishing, i.e. to satisfy his feelings (*Rhetoric* 1.10.1369b12).

324a7 ["they did the wrong thing"]: actually, Athenians did this. It seems that only with homicide did the Athenians consider the criminal's intent. Also, in cases where an unknown person, an animal, or even an inanimate object, was responsible for killing someone, a sort of trial was held at the Prytaneion, with the Basileus presiding. Such "trials" performed some of the functions of modern day coroners in determining the cause of someone's death. If an unknown person was determined to be responsible, they were punished with exile (a proclamation of exile was issued against "the person who killed" the deceased). If an animal was determined to be responsible, it was probably killed or driven beyond the border. If the culprit was an inanimate object (e.g. a tree or rock), it may well have been moved beyond the border ("exiled"). More generally, homicide seems to be the only kind of case in which Athenians took the intention of the alleged criminal into account (they distinguished intending to harm from not intending to harm, even if you intended only non-lethal harm but the victim died anyway, or your intention to harm was not premeditated but a sudden outburst of anger). See note on *Euthyphro* 4d4.

324b1 ["like a wild animal"]: Protagoras is wrong about this. First, some wild animals are social beings, and some of their retaliations against one another have to do with maintaining or enhancing their status in the social hierarchy—perhaps this qualifies as "thinking." Second, retaliation for being wronged may be revenge, which is done with the thought of protecting one's own dignity or regaining lost social status, and sometimes this can be grossly disproportionate to the original wrong (Achilles is the famous example, *Iliad* 9.307-429). Third, retaliation may follow the *lex talionis*, which is guided by the thought that the punishment should be proportionate to the crime. The "eye for an eye" principle is generally considered too literal a way to make the punishment fit the crime, but something like this seemed reasonable to many Greeks ("hateful word for hateful word" and "deadly blow for deadly blow," Aeschylus, *Libation Bearers* 309-313; cf. Pindar, *Nemean* 4.32). For a famous problem with the "eye for an eye" principle, see note on 324b3. Plato solves this problem with a myth involving reincarnation (*Laws* 9.872d7-873a3).

324b3 ["undo what has already been done"]: retributivist theories of justice are sometimes said to focus on the past because they hold that punishment is justified by the fact that it is right to inflict some evil upon someone who has done wrong, whether or not the punishment has any beneficial consequences. Normally retributivists also hold that a just punishment is proportionate to the crime, but a "proportionate" punishment does not need to be exact equality. For example, the German philosopher Georg Wilhelm Friedrich Hegel (1770-1831) pointed out that "an eye for an eye" will be grossly unequal if the original crime took one of two eyes, but the punishment takes the only eye the criminal has left: punishing an act of partial blinding is not equal to an act of total blinding (*Philosophy of Right* section 101, Note).

324b3 ["Instead"]: Protagoras does seem to pose retribution and deterrence as exclusive alternatives, i.e. we ought to implement the latter and not the former. Lysias proposes that just punishment should do both (Lysias, *Against the Corn Dealers* 22.20).

324b4 ["again"]: *authis* means again for at least a second time, as the Achaeans donned their armor yet again (*Iliad* 4.222). This word is important because without it Protagoras would be expressing a pure deterrence view of punishment (see note on 324b5), which, in theory, can allow that innocent people may be punished for crimes they did not commit because of the deterrence value of the punishment (e.g. police may be justified in framing an innocent person, and courts may be justified in punishing him, knowing that he is innocent).

324b5 ["will never do wrong"]: deterrence theories of justice are in danger of (1) supporting punishments that do not fit the crime, and of (2) not treating like cases alike. E.g., (1) it was said that Draco (7th century) reformulated Athenian law so that there was only one punishment for any offense: death. Even if this did deter crime, it seems unfair to people who commit minor offenses. E.g. (2) circumstances other than guilt (e.g. social status) can affect how much deterrence value there is in punishing someone, so two equally guilty people may not receive the same punishment on a deterrence theory. Deterrence theorists often reply to such objections by arguing that violations of the principle that "like cases should be treated alike," and the principle that "the punishment should fit the crime" can themselves produce bad results, and so those principles should not be violated.

324b6 ["dissuade"]: *apotropē* is literally a turning away or averting, e.g. diverting a water supply (*Laws* 8.845d7. So called "apotropaic magic" was designed to turn away harm and thus offer protection. Ritual offerings to the gods was supposed to have a similar effect, but only by gaining the favor of a particular god. Ancient ritual and magical beliefs might lend support to an apotropaic theory of criminal justice (e.g. see note on *Euthyphro* 4c1). See note on 354b7.

324c4 ["according to this account"]: here he claims to have given a *logos*, although earlier he said that he would give a *muthos* as opposed to a *logos* (though see the possible joke in the note on 320c7). In addition, he's about to say that he will no longer give a *muthos*, instead he will give a *logos* (324d6-7). While it may be possible to draw a distinction (sharp or not) between stories and accounts, the Greek words *muthos* and *logos* do not rigorously mark that distinction. Plato is explicitly uninterested in drawing a distinction between the two at *Laws* 9.872e1.

324e2 ["suppose there is"]: Protagoras' sentence is long and complex. I've broken it down into stages.

325c5 ["From the time when they are very small"]: I think that we should consider this to be a very early theory of developmental psychology.

325c7 ["nursemaid, mother, guardian"]: the *trophē* nursed (breast-fed) the child and did basic infant care. The *paidagōgos* was a sort of chaperone and private tutor for the adolescent; he would take the young man to and from a gymnasium for grammar school and physical education, and he would keep the boy out of trouble. The *paidagōgos* was typically a slave, and a highly trusted member of the household (cf.

Herodotus 8.75; the institution of slavery in the ancient world was very different from modern slavery). The paid help of both a *trophē* and a *paidagōgos* was not out of reach for what we would today call "middle class" families—they were quite typical (ancient economies allowed for the possibility of extreme wealth, but when they aggressively drained money away from the middle class to the upper class, the middle class occasionally rebelled; the economic reforms of Solon were aimed largely at stopping this destructive cycle).

326b1-2 ["harmonies"]: see notes on *Phaedo* 85e3 and 95a4.

326b3 ["tame and civilized"]: *hemeros* refers to animals that have been tamed, or trees that have been cultivated (e.g. olive trees for the production of oil). It does not seem a distortion to say that Protagoras' view is that from birth children are like wild animals that have to be systematically tamed by both praise and blame, rewards and corporal punishment. This kind of view is easily absorbed by Christian theology (e.g. St. Thomas Aquinas, *Summa Theologiae* IaIIae q.82 a.3 on "original sin"). This view is at the opposite end of a spectrum from something like the modern Montessori approach to the education of children.

326b3 ["disciplined and cooperative"]: *euruthmia* and *euarmostia* are related to *rhuthmos* (rhythm) and *harmonia* (harmony), which he just used at b1-2, so his Greek is far more elegant than my English. Literally, *euruthmia* refers to rhythmical order or movement, but a physical gracefulness or dignity of bearing is usually meant when referring to people. *Euharmostia* refers literally to something that is well fitted, a perfect match, but when describing people it often refers to an ability to get along well with others or to social or political concord.

326d5 ["traces outlines for living"]: I've expanded a bit on Protgoras' use of *hupographō*, which can be just a sketch. The question is: just what is being sketched? On a very minimal view, the point of law is to maximize individual liberty and protect the mutual alliance between citizens. This was the view of the sophist Lycophron (Aristotle, *Politics* 3.9.1280b10-12). A more robust view holds that the point of law is to provide guidelines directing citizens to living happy, virtuous and fulfilling lives (Aristotle, *Nicomachean Ethics* 5.1).

326e1 ["give an account"]: Protagoras uses the verb *euthunō* twice (once in the form of a participle). Literally it refers to guiding in a straight line, but in Athenian law it referred to the investigation of a public official's conduct that automatically took place after his year in office was over. The first part of the accounting was financial, but the second part took place in the central marketplace (*agora*) and anyone was allowed to lodge any allegations of misconduct (if the official deemed the allegation to have merit, then it was considered by the appropriate court, with, of course, a democratic jury). In a direct democracy, public officials are directly accountable to the people for the conduct (see also note on 319a5).

327d4 ["Pherecrates"]: comic poet, older than Aristophanes. He won his first competitions between 440 and 430, but according to Athenaeus (fl. c.200 CE) his play *Savages* was produced during the archonship of Arisitus, which was in 421/420, so he accuses Plato of anachronism for having Protagoras refer to this play (which is set probably at about 433). The play does not survive, but apparently a group of men leave civilization to live with savages who eat herbs and snails in good times, their own fingers in bad times.

327d4 ["Lenaea"]: a festival of Dionysus in Athens that took place during the winter (January/February, the Greek month of Gamelion). The word "Lenaea" is derived from the Greek *lēnē*, which refers to a maenad, i.e. a woman inspired to a ritual frenzy by Dionysus. The Lenaion (probably a sanctuary space for ritual celebrations of Dionysus combined with a theatre) was probably located in the Agora (the central market place). Also called the "Lesser Dionysia" (the "Greater Dionysia" took place in March, in the Athenian month of Elaphebolion). It was probably first organized around 440. In addition to comedies, two tragedians competed, each submitting only two tragedies.

327d6-7 ["Eurybatus and Phrynondas"]: these two were just as proverbial for dishonesty and vice as Benedict Arnold is in the USA for betrayal. We don't know about Phrynondas, but Eurybatus was said to have been a traitor to Croesus and a burglar. When his prison guards asked him to demonstrate how he was able to climb walls and get into people's homes, he asked for his shoes and a couple of sponges. With his spiked shoes he climbed the prison wall to the roof, and once there he put the sponges on his shoes so nobody could hear which way he went, and he escaped.

328b1 ["gladly welcome"]: *agapētos* is an adjective related to the noun *agapē*, which is famous among Christians as the love of God for sinful mortals (Romans 5:8), and brotherly love or charitable love (1 Corinthians 13:1). In ancient Greek it usually refers to affection, fondness (e.g. *Lysis* 215a1), or simply being content with someone or something (e.g. *Alcibiades* 104e7). It can also refer to familial love, e.g. the love of a father for his son (Homer, *Odyssey* 6.401). See note on *Euthydemus* 303d3.

328c2 ["donate that amount to the temple"]: Protagoras wrote a book entitled *Justice Concerning A Fee* (*Dikē huper misthou*). The question of how to measure a fee accurately is acute for someone who famously claims that "man is the measure of all things: of things that are that they are, and of things that are not that they are not" (*Theaetetus* 152a2-4). How the student measures the value of his lessons seems consistent with that principle. The point of swearing an oath in a temple is to ensure that neither Protagoras nor the student is trying to cheat the other: if the student swears that the lessons were worth less than Protagoras charged, then either (a) the student is telling the truth, in which case the wrath of the god will fall upon Protagoras; or (b) the student is not telling the truth, in which case the wrath of the god will fall upon the student. Similarly, it seems that a student named Eualthus made a special deal with Protagoras: he would not pay Protagoras until he won his first court case. After his lessons, Eualthus never went to court, and so never paid Protagoras. Hence, Protagoras threatened to sue him and ask the court to demand that he pay for his lessons. Protagoras reasoned as follows: "if I win this lawsuit, then Eualthus will have to obey the court and pay me my fee; but if Eualthus wins and the court does not order him to pay me, he has to pay me anyway because he will have won his first court case; either way, I get paid." But Eualthus reasoned as follows: "if I win this lawsuit, then the court's decision is that I do not have to pay Protagoras; but if I lose this lawsuit, then by the terms of my agreement with Protagoras I do not have to pay him; either way, I don't have to pay."

328d2 ["hope for them still"]: by unexpectedly mentioning Paralus and Xanthippus, but then almost immediately stopping his speech, Protagoras makes a very abrupt ending that is deliberately like a cliff-hanger, making us expect more, which is just how Socrates responds.

328d4-5 ["captivated"]: *kēleō* (also at 315a8 and 315b1). This is exactly the effect Socrates said that Protagoras has on people (315a8, b1), so "spellbound," "charmed" or "bewitched" are possible translations. Perhaps he is being ironic and he really means that he was bored out of his mind. However, this is not the only place where Plato portrays Socrates as being affected just like others without losing his self-control (e.g. *Menexenus* 235b1, *Charmides* 155c5-e3, and presumably *Symposium* 219e5-220c1 and 223c4-d12). Possibly the sort of bewitchment or charming he has in mind is when someone manages to focus all your attention so that you temporarily forget about other things (cf. *Phaedo* 81b3). This is a familiar effect people often intend with words (*Lysis* 206b2). See notes on 315a8 and 339c8.

328e4 ["impediment"]: it sounds as if Socrates is contradicting himself by saying that he is persuaded, but he is not persuaded. Perhaps he is being ironic and deliberately putting up a false front of being impressed with Protagoras in order to get Protagoras to let down his guard. Alternatively, Protagoras' speech had its desired emotional effect, and now Socrates is going to give him the sincere benefit of the doubt and see whether or not he can back up his claims. Since Protagoras himself mentioned the fairness of his fees (see note on 382c2), perhaps Socrates is taking Protagoras' speech as a sort if IOU, and now he wants to give Protagoras a fair opportunity to prove that he truly can pay it.

329a1 ["public speakers"]: *dēmēgoras* is the root of the English word "demagogue," although the related verb *dēmēgoreō* means to address the assembly (the legislative body). He's probably referring to the many people who put themselves forward as persuasive public speakers. Socrates uses this word referring to Protagoras' speeches at 336b.

329a3 ["books"]: at *Phaedrus* 275d4-e5 Socrates compares books to paintings in that both can appear lifelike (paintings can look visually like people, and books appear to express intelligent thoughts), but you cannot fruitfully engage them in question-and-answer. He makes the same objection about poets and poetry at *Protagoras* 347c-348a6, but he cites four distinct causes for this problem. First, his point about orators here is that they don't seem smart enough to ask or answer intelligent questions (like the vapid people at typical wine parties, 347c3-e3). Second, prose works can express intelligent claims, but they are inanimate objects and so cannot engage in dialogue. Third, poetry can express only amgiguous claims (and poets are no help in disambiguating their works, see *Apology* 22a8-c8). Fourth, many poets are dead and so cannot be questioned. Presumably it is the importance of engaging fruitfully in question-and-answer that explains why Plato wrote dialogues and not treatises: intelligent questions and answers are right there in the text. Of course, the text cannot give answers to questions that are not in the text, but at least it is modelling good dialectical behavior. Also, Plato worries that too much reliance on writing instead of memory will lead to people having poorer memories (*Phaedrus* 275a2-6). Presumably that is why Plato occasionally has characters in his dialogues model good mnemonic behavior (e.g. *Phaedo* 58d4-6, *Menexenus* 236a8-d3, *Euthydemus* 272d4-e1, *Symposium* 172a1-173c2 and, of course, *Protagoras* 310a1-7).

329b5 ["when you question someone else"]: see 335b7-8.

329c3-4 ["you repeated the claim"]: literally he claims that Protagoras said it "in many places" (*pollachou*). See 322e2-323a3, 323e3-324a1, and 324e2-325a2.

329d1 ["different names for one and the same thing?"]: as usual, Socrates is not focusing on the meanings of words (that's what Prodicus does, see notes on *Charmides* 163d4 and *Meno* 71b4). The Greek words for justice, temperance and piety obviously do not mean the same thing. Socrates is considering the possibility that they all refer to the same thing, e.g. to the same state of person who is virtuous. E.g. the final analysis of temperance considered in the *Charmides* is that it is the knowledge of good and bad (*Charmides* 174b11-c3), which is one and the same thing that is considered as the final analysis of courage in the *Laches* (*Laches* 199c3-d2). Perhaps the knowledge of good and bad is called courage when it is displayed on the battlefield, but it is called temperance when it is displayed in the barroom, and it is called justice when it is displayed in the courtroom, and so on. Some scholars refer to the claim that the names of the virtues all refer to one state as the "Unity Thesis." At 329e4 Socrates mentions a weaker thesis that is sometimes called the "Reciprocity Thesis," which claims only that the virtues are mutually entailing: if you have one virtue, then necessarily you have all the others. The theory Plato develops in Book 4 of the Republic seems to entail the Reciprocity Thesis but not the Unity Thesis.

330b4 ["knowledge"]: Socrates and Protagoras used *sophia* three times at 329e6-330a2, but here Socrates substitutes *epistēmē*.

330c1 ["real thing"]: the noun *pragma* is related to the verb *prassō* (to achieve, effect or accomplish) and the noun *praxis* (action, business, doing; see note on *Meno* 97b9). At *Cratylus* 391a8-b2 and 436a3-b3 Socrates contrasts *onoma* with *pragma*, i.e. the name of a thing and the thing that is named. Presumably, then, when he says that justice is a *pragma*, he is distinguishing justice itself from the word "justice" (*dikē* or *dikaiosunē* in Greek). This is a clear rejection of nominalism and affirmation of realism with respect to the universal justice (see note on *Euthyphro* 5d1). Also, Hippias will soon oppose *phusis* to *nomos* (337d1-3; cf. "nature" vs. "culture"). The use of *pragma* here probably implies that justice is a matter of *phusis* and cannot be dismissed as exclusively an artifact of *nomos*.

330c5 ["is it just or unjust?"]: on the "theory of forms" see notes on *Phaedo* 65d4-5, 74a11 and *Euthyphro* 5d3. On the "self-predication" of forms (i.e. the view that the form of F explains why all F things, including the F itself, are F) see notes on *Phaedo* 102d6 and *Euthydemus* 301b5.

331a8-9 ["justice is not the sort of thing to be pious"]: Socrates is constructing the following argument.

1. Justice is a real thing (330c1).
2. Justice is pious [something Socrates thinks Protagoras will admit].
3. So justice is a pious thing.
4. The form of piety explains why all pious things are pious (see note on 330c5).
5. So the form of piety explains why justice is pious.

Of course, the question then will be: how can piety explain why justice is pious unless piety and justice are one and the same thing? At the very least, this suggests that Socrates' view is closer to the truth than Protagoras' view.

331b1 ["piety is unjust?"]: if it is not unreasonable to infer that ears are blind and that eyes are deaf, then it is not unreasonable to infer that without some explicit qualification of what he's said so far, Protagoras is indeed committed to these worrisome conclusions. Some would not worry about the claim that courage is intemperate or that temperance is cowardly (though some would), it is more troubling to say that justice is impious because justice is closely associated with Zeus (e.g. 322c1-2).

331c5 ["if you want"]: Protagoras violates this request at 331e1 and 333c4.

331c6 ["put myself to the test"]: *elenchō* could refer to refuting (or disgracing) someone (cf. *Charmides* 166c3-e2), and I translate Protagoras' use of it this way below at 331e1. In a way, you might say that the Socratic *elenchos* is the dialectical equivalent of "trial by ordeal:" Socrates tries to refute you by reasonable means: if he fails, then you may well have shown yourself to be knowledgeable on the subject; but if he succeeds, then either your view is false, or at least you do not know that it is true—either way, you have more work to do.

332a6-7 ["correctly and beneficially"]: I think this is the crux of the argument (premise 4 below, and see also 333d9, where this premise would play a crucial role in Socrates' next argument, if he were allowed to finish it).

> 1. If the virtues are separate, then one virtue can cause us to violate another.
> 2. If one virtue can cause us to violate another, then one virtue can cause us to act incorrectly or harmfully.
> 3. So if the virtues are separate, then one virtue can cause us to act incorrectly or harmfully.
> 4. But no virtue can cause us to act incorrectly or harmfully.
> 5. So, the virtues are not separate.

Greek common sense does seem incoherent in just the way Socrates is pointing out: they could give up premise 4 above and coherently maintain the separability of the virtues, but it will be intolerable to many to deny that they want their sons to grow up to be courageous men; but if they maintain that courage is truly a fine and good quality their sons ought to develop, then they must give up the separability of the virtues.

332a7 ["temperately or intemperately?"]: on *sōphrosunē* see note on *Charmides* 157a6.

332c4 ["ugly"]: beautiful and ugly are one-dimensional translations of *kalon* and *aischron*; fine and shameful are a bit better.

332c8-9 ["just one opposite, not many"]: the adverb *enantion* literally refers to being on the opposite side, and so it is quite easy to have one thing stand *enantion* in relation to many things. E.g. at *Iliad* 1.534 all the gods reverently stand up to face Zeus as he enters Olympus, and so the one Zeus stands *enantion* many Olympian gods. E.g. enemies stand *enantion* one another (*Iliad* 3.433), and as the modern phrase goes, "the enemy of my enemy is my friend," but he doesn't have to be only me. Perhaps Socrates' "Principle of Unitary Opposition" is related to the discussion of opposites in the *Phaedo* (see notes on *Phaedo* 70e3 and 72d3), and so perhaps we should think of Socrates as trying to discover basic laws of human psychology. E.g. some modern psychologists contend that the emotion of hope is opposed not only to fear but also to anxiety, and on this basis they accept that fear and anxiety are one and the same thing, although the words "fear" and "anxiety" do not have exactly the same meaning—the two words refer to one and the same human emotion (even if that one emotion may come in a variety of intensities or qualities, as one species can be divided into multiple sub-species). Similarly, if justice is necessarily opposed not only to injustice but also to impiety (on the grounds that all unjust acts necessarily offend Zeus, or on the grounds that a just person treats others—whether mortal or immortal—as they deserve, cf. *Gorgias* 507a7-b4), then although the words "injustice" and "impiety" do not have the same meaning, the two words refer to one and the same human character state (even if that one character state comes in a variety of qualities depending upon the circumstances in which it is exhibited, e.g. in the courtroom as opposed to in the temple).

333b6 ["pretty well"]: this qualification blurs a distinction. In order to oppose Protagoras' view that the virtues are separable, Socrates needs to say only that the virtues are not separable, i.e. that it is impossible to have one without also having all the others (which some scholars call "The Reciprocity of the Virtues"). A stronger thesis would be that all the virtues are actually one and the same with all the others (which some scholars call "The Unity of the Virtues").

333c5 ["the many"]: *hoi polloi*, see notes on *Euthydemus* 303d1 and *Apology* 20c8.

333c6-7 ["whether you agree with them or not"]: this is peculiar for Socrates, who usually encourages his interlocutors to say only what they sincerely believe. See note on *Euthydemus* 275e1.

333c9 ["being examined as well"]: although it is peculiar for Socrates to invite someone to give answers that they do not personally believe, his focus on the truth of a claim and on examining the people involved in the discussion is quite familiar (see *Charmides* 161c3-6, 166c7-d6).

333d2 ["the discussion"]: Socrates says that Protagoras alleges that the *logos* is annoying. *Logos* could refer to the subject matter, the particular argument Socrates has been pursuing (i.e. that the parts of virtue are not like the parts of a face but like the parts of a lump of gold), the question-and-answer mode of discussion that Socrates has been employing, or more generally that he had grown weary of talking with Socrates. I hope that "discussion" is vague enough to allow for all of these interpretations.

333d5 ["sound mind"]: the point Socrates is making here is obviously reasonable in Greek. To act temperately is *sōphronein* and to act with a sound mind (to act sensibly) is *eu phronein*: the "*phronein*" is identical and in both cases is related to the noun "*phrēn*" (heart, mind, will) and to the verb "*phroneō*" (to understand, to be wise, to think, to know, to will). See note on *Charmides* 157a6. Compare the argument Socrates is making here with the argument he gives at *Gorgias* 507a5-c7.

333d7 ["turned out well"]: *eu prattousin*. It would be closer to the Greek if I could use the somewhat dated English phrase "fare well," because "faring well" in English often connotes "doing well" in the sense of being happy or living a good life, which is precisely the connection Greeks tend to make between *eu prattein* and *eudaimonein* (cf. *Euthydemus* 280b6).

333e3 ["belligerent in answering questions"]: as will soon be clear, Protagoras' previous answer brought up something irrelevant. Socrates asked whether being good and being beneficial were connected, and he is assuming that they are discussing this in relation to people, since they are discussing human virtue. Protagoras accepts the connection between being good and being beneficial and so he should simply have answered Socrates' question by saying, "Yes." Instead, he's about to bring in the irrelevant point that what is beneficial for some may not be beneficial for others. That's true, but the only relevant point would be that therefore what is good for some may not be good for others. Changing the topic in a discussion can be a way to shift from losing ground to winning ground, if you are more interested in victory than in truth (see *Phaedo* 89e4-90b7). Notice the response Protagoras gets from the crowd.

334a3 ["Certainly not"]: this admission paves the way for the following argument, which ruins Protagoras' attempt to defend the separability of the virtues.

1. Each of the five vices causes us to do things that are harmful.
2. Each of the five virtues cannot allow us to do anything that is harmful.
3. So, each of the five virtues is incompatible with all of the five vices
4. So, each of the five virtues requires each of the other five.

Courage, therefore, will not allow us intemperately to get drunk, since intemperate drunkenness is harmful to us, but courage is beneficial to us (cf. it sometimes takes courage to say 'no' to your friends when they are daring you to do something that you know to be harmful). Perhaps Protagoras sees that his admission has imperiled his view and so deliberately changes the subject.

334a2 ["those kinds of things are good"]: Socrates undermined the separability of (a) justice and piety at 330b6-331b8, and (b) temperance and wisdom at 332a4-333c3, and he has now begun to undermine the separability of (c) temperance and justice (333d4-334a2). Notice that this closes the loop: if all three of these arguments are successful, then piety, justice, temperance and wisdom are inseparable. Protagoras seems to concede this to Socrates at 349d2-8 (see note on 349d5), which is where Socrates begins his argument that courage is not separable from knowledge (which he seems to treat as one and the same as wisdom, see note on 330b4). He takes this to unite all the virtues at 361a5-b3. See note on 360d4-5.

334c8-9 ["apt to forget some things"]: Alcibiades will say that this is a joke (*paizō* at 336d3), but he he's clearly misunderstood Socrates' claim. Alcibiades takes Socrates to be referring to the fact that a long speech can function as a distraction that impairs our ability to recall what the question was (*hotou to erōtēma ēn*). No doubt this often happens to Alcibiades; but when Socrates asks a question, he doesn't forget it, nor does he forget relevant answers to it (see 359a2-c2). Socrates said that long speeches disrupt his ability to recall what the *logos* was about (*peri hou an ē ho logos*). Socrates is referring to logical disruption, not memory gaps, as when someone rambles on and on, changing the subject several times (see "keeping to the question that is asked" at 336a7): after a disjointed digression, it can be genuinely unclear whether the discussion has switched topic (or whether the discussion is actually over, cf. 335b-3-c7), especially if you recall all the different topics that have been broached (cf. *Hippias Minor* 373a2-3; see also the notes on Protagoras' speech from 320c8-328d2 and consider how difficult it would be to have a genuine philosophical discussion of all the interesting points he made). Notice that after Protagoras' protracted answer at 350c6-351b2 Socrates doesn't balk because everything Protagoras says stays on the topic at hand. Socrates thinks of recollection somewhat differently than most people, because he thinks that mathematical and logical reasoning is a form of recollection (*Meno* 82e12-13, cf. *Phaedo* 73c1-76a7). For Socrates, changing the topic in the middle of an argument is a disruption of memory. See note on 349a8.

335a4 ["debates"]: Socrates just used *dialegō* (discussion, dialogue, dialectic; 335a2) to characterize what they are doing. Protagoras characterizes it as *agōn logou*, i.e. a contest of words. The difference is important because the goal of a discussion is the truth, while the goal of debate is victory, and therefore it is appropriate to approach these differently (see *Meno* 75c8-e5).

335c6 ["somewhere I should go"]: see note on 362a2.

335e3 ["defeated the Persians"]: Crison of Himera was in his prime sometime in the 440's, when he won first place in the *stadion* (a foot race of over 200-yards) in three successive Olympiads. Socrates does not actually mention Pheidippides; he mentions (1) people who run the *dolichos* (about 12 times longer than the *stadion*) and (2) people who run all day. Pheidippides is the most famous example of the latter, and the run from Marathon to Athens after the battle was not his most remarkable accomplishment: when the Persians arrived at Marathon, he was sent to Sparta to request their help—a distance of about 150 miles, and apparently he ran the entire distance without stopping (he had a vision—or hallucination—of Hermes along the way; Herodotus 6.105-6).

336b7-8 ["Callias"]: Alcibiades puns on Callias' name because it is similar to the adjective *kalos* (beautiful): "You do not speak beautifully [*ou kalōs*] O Kallias [*ō Kallia*]." Plato often puns on proper names: 348b3-4, 361d3-4, 362a2-3; *Apology* 25c1-3; *Phaedo* 80d5-6; *Hippias Major* 281d9; *Gorgias* 481d5 (the son of Pyrilampes was named *Dēmos*); *Symposium* 174a6-b5, 185c1-5; *Republic* 10.614b2-3.

336c4 ["Socrates will be satisfied"]: on Socrates' attitude towards the love of victory as opposed to the love of wisdom see *Phaedo* 91a2-3. Alcibiades has noticed something important about Socrates, but as usual his insight turns superficial (Critias' critique at 336e1-2 seems on the nose). Socrates has an excellent track record in discussion by question and answer because (a) he understands better than anyone the ways in which Greek common sense is incoherent (cf. note on 332a6-7), and (b) Socrates has modified his beliefs so that they are more coherent. If, in addition, (c) Socrates relies on (mostly) true beliefs to drive the modification of his beliefs (cf. note on *Charmides* 336c4, and see Aristotle, *Nicomachean Ethics* 7.1.1145b2-7), then his novel beliefs may count as genuine discoveries, and his belief system may count as knowledge (see notes on *Meno* 98a3-4 and 98a5).

336c6 ["dodging"]: *ekkrouō* literally refers to knocking someone or something out. Less violently it means to repulse or drive back, and hence to put someone off or elude them. Alcibiades seems to be insinuating that sophistry is Protean (cf. *Euthyphro* 15d3 and the note on that passage).

336d2 ["Because"]: *epei* is clearly not temporal here, so it must be causal, but why? Perhaps he is citing Socrates' keen memory as explaining why Protagoras should stick to normal questions and answers: his attempts to elude Socrates' refutations will be no more successful than Proteus' metamorphoses were in eluding Menelaus (see note on *Euthyphro* 15d3, and see note on *Protagoras* 336c6).

337a3-4 ["fair but not equal"]: "fair and equal" or "fair and balanced" is perhaps as common a phrase today as *koinos kai isos* was in Socrates' day (Plato, *Letter 7* 337a5; Andocides, *Against Alcibiades* 4.7; Demosthenes, *Against Aphobus* 29.1; Aristotle, *Politics* 4.11.1296a30). In this context, *koinos* probably refers to impartiality, and *isos* probably refers to equality in the sense of being nondiscriminatory. Prodicus' point here is important and extremely influential. Aristotle is usually given credit for it because he devotes a chapter to it in the *Nicomachean Ethics* (i.e. 5.3 on distributive justice), but if Prodicus is not given credit for this distinction then either it should go to Hesiod (*Works and Days* 286-319), or to Isocrates (*To Nicocles* 2.14-16; *Nicocles or the Cyprians* 3.14-16; *Areopagiticus* 7.21), or to Plato (*Laws* 6.756e9-758a2). One way to exlain the distinction is to say that justice demands that each be given what they deserve, and so in that sense everybody will be treated equally, but since some deserve more than others, they won't all be treated equally in this other sense. Plato refers to "geometric equality" (*Gorgias* 508a4-8) and lambastes democracy for violating it (*Republic* 8.558c3-6). Aristotle develops the geometric vs. arithmetic analogy and points out that this helps to explain differences in governments. E.g. in a hereditary aristocracy people will think that if one person is more noble than another, then the more noble person should have more (e.g. honor, power, status, wealth) than the less noble person, and the difference in how much they have should be proportionate to the difference in their nobility (e.g. if I am twice as noble as you, then I should have twice as much authority as you).

337a8-b1 ["argue without fighting"]: *amphisbēteō* literally refers to parting ways or standing apart, while *erizō* is related to the noun *eris* which is strife. Both are often translated into English as "wrangle," and Socrates may treat the two as synonyms at 343d3-5 (and at *Lysis* 207c2-3), so it is possible that while Plato thinks Prodicus' first distinction is quite important (see note on 337a3-4), he may think that this is a distinction without a difference. It is worth comparing Prodicus' distinction here with Hesiod's distinction between two kinds of *eris* at *Works and Days* 11-26.

337b5 ["acclaim without praise"]: *eudokimeō* and *epaineō*. *Eudokimeō* is related to the adjective *eudokimos* which, when used of persons, is a term of approval, affirming that the person is trustworthy and genuinely valuable (e.g. they actually can accomplish the things they say they can). The related verb *dokimazō* refers to assaying something to ascertain its true value; it is an examination or putting someone to the test. Also the *dokimasia* was an examination of magistrates after having been elected to office, but prior to executing their duties, to make sure that actually did fulfill all the requirements of office. On the other hand, while *epaineō* can refer to approval, its primary use is to indicate praise as in "singing someone's praise." It can refer to any public compliment paid to someone, and it is associated with the songs of rhapsodes (see *Ion* 536d3, d6, 541e2). It seems to have been an "open secret" that praise is often undeserved (see *Menexenus* 234c4).

337c1-2 ["gladdened without being pleased"]: Plato is clearly having a bit of fun with Prodicus by having him draw four distinctions in a row—all using the explicit *men...de...* antithesis. Here he distinguishes the verbs *euphrainō* and *hēdomai*, which must have been quite deliberate on Plato's part because *hēdonē* (pleasure) will become quite important in the discussion (cf. 354b5-c5). This particular distinction accords with Greek idiom (Xenophon, *Hiero* 7.4), and Plato in particular seems to have thought it important (*Timaeus* 80b5-8).

337c8 ["family, friends and neighbors"]: *suggenēs*, *oikeios*, and *politēs* might more literally be translated as "relatives, members of a common household, and fellow citizens." We might think that *suggenēs* refers to a direct, biological connection, and so is a matter of *phusis* (nature, from *phuō* which refers to growth); while the people who happen to be citizens of the same city with you are connected to you only by accident because they happened to be born within the same political boundary line as you, and hence your relation to them is a matter of *nomos* (custom, convention or law) not *phusis*. The suggestion that it is natural to care about others to whom you are not biologically related seems to be in stark contrast to Protagoras' story, according to which political association is not part of our original design—it was added on later so that we wouldn't go extinct (see note on 321d5). Also, in Protagoras' account it isn't even clear whether direct biological connections matter. Hippias' view is more obviously compatible with Aristotle's (see note on 332b2).

337d1 ["nature, not by custom"]: this is the famous *phusis/nomos* distinction, which was prominent in Greek political theory in the 5th century. Actually, two different distinctions may be drawn.

(1) Absolute truths vs. relative truths, e.g. although Arabia and Egypt are geographically continuous with one another regardless of human laws or conventions, Arabia is said to end at the Arabian Gulf by human convention and by political boundaries (cf. Herodotus 4.39.1).

(2) Objective truths vs. subjective truths, e.g. although the gods really exist regardless of human laws or conventions, some hold that they do not really exist and that all the different social conventions and laws regarding them are nothing more than that—different conventions and laws maintained by different societies (cf. Plato, *Laws* 10.889e4).

Probably Hippias is saying that those gathered together share a real connection with one another that consists in more than simply the fact that they feel friendly towards one another (*phusis*-2, not *nomos*-2). The real connection between them is wisdom, which objectively unites them with each other, and objectively divides them from the unwise.

337d2-3 ["contrary to nature"]: "Man is born free; and everywhere he is in chains" is the first sentence of the first chapter of *The Social Contract*, written in 1762 by Genevan philosopher Jean-Jacques Rousseau (1712-78). If the view of Protagoras as expressed in his story about Epimetheus and Prometheus is similar to that of Thomas Hobbes (see note on 322b1), then Hippias' view may be similar to that of Rousseau.

338b2 ["agreeable to all"]: Socrates said "all" (*pantes*) but then indicates a lone hold out, i.e. himself; and that's just what he does at e2 below (*pasin*), where Protagoras is the lone hold out. Perhaps by "all" he doesn't mean literally everyone present, or perhaps by "all" he means all those who voiced an opinion, i.e. not counting those who abstained from voicing an opinion.

338b5 ["inferior"]: *cheirōn* can be an adjective or a substantive (here Socrates uses it as a noun). As an adjective it is used as the comparative of *kakos* (i.e. "bad"), and so means "worse." But *cheirōn* is derived from *chereiōn*, which means inferior in worth, rank or wealth. Which form of inferiority does Socrates have in mind here? 5th century Athens had a direct democracy, and they were very sensitive to issues of class and equality.

339a7 ["Simonides"]: see note on 316d7. What we get in this dialogue is our main source for the poem in question. Others quote parts of the poem, but those quotations only corroborate, they do not expand upon, what Plato gives us.

339b1 ["Indeed"]: when Protagoras quotes the poem, I translate it the way he interprets it; when Socrates quotes it, I translate it the way he interprets it. Here, the Greek word *men* can be used to express certainty, which is how Protagoras interprets it. Socrates, however, will interpret it in an alternative, but extremely common, way, i.e. as part of a *men...de...* antithesis indicating one of two contrasting correlatives, e.g. this *rather than* that. For example, Prodicus used the *men...de...* antithesis to draw his four distinctions at 337a1-c4. See note on 343d1.

339b9 ["contradicts himself?"]: Socrates agrees that self-contradiction is a poetic flaw, see *Meno* 95c9-96b4.

339c3 ["Pittacus"]: c.650-570; from the city of Mytilene, on the island of Lesbos, which is off the coast of Asia Minor (modern day Turkey). Similar to Solon in many ways—both were counted among the "seven sages" of ancient Greece—Pittacus overthrew the tyrant Melanchros, but when he did not help to perpetuate aristocratic rule he was himself accused of being a tyrant by his former ally Alcaeus. He is perhaps the earliest defender of the principle of the rule of law when he claimed that the greatest protector of the city is "painted wood" (laws were painted on wood). Apparently the occasion for his claim that it is difficult to be good was when he heard that a powerful man similar to himself in another city had indeed become a tyrant. Fearing that he might end up doing the same he asked to be allowed to step down before his term of office was over.

339c8 ["I was afraid"]: this is just the sort of comment that many scholars take to be ironic on Socrates' part. But he isn't saying this to Protagoras, nor is it an aside to anyone else in the room. This is spoken to his anonymous friend later that day after he's left Callias' home, and it is a parenthetical comment. Why would he be ironic in this way? Alternatively, he is sincerely reporting his feelings at the time, and Plato is showing that although Socrates feels all the same emotions that we feel, he doesn't allow his feelings to control him (see note on 328d4-5). On this view, Plato is presenting Socrates not as a paragon whose virtue is to be admired but not emulated; rather, Plato presents him as a role model, whose self-control is something we may attain ourselves. In fact, Plato may be giving us very practical advice on how to develop Socratic self-control at 339e1-5.

339d8-9 ["either the first claim or the second is incorrect"]: Socrates is about to indicate one way to resolve the apparent contradiction. Another is to say that Simonides is distinguishing between perfect goodness (i.e. "true" and "foursquare") and imperfect goodness, and so his two compatible claims are: (1) it is difficult for mortals (as opposed to gods) to become perfectly virtuous, but (2) Pittacus was wrong to say that it is difficult for mortals to become imperfectly virtuous (i.e. it is easy for mortals to be good in good times, but they turn bad easily in bad times).

340a4 ["the might of this man"]: an exact quotation of *Iliad* 21.308 (this line is enjambed, so Socrates quotes the verb, which is the first word on line 309). Scamandrius and Simois are rivers—they are "brothers" because of their confluence (*Iliad* 5.773-4).

340a8-b1 ["distinguish between wishing and wanting"]: Prodicus did not distinguish *boulomai* (wish) from *epithumeō* (want) at 337a1-c4, but at *Charmides* 167e1-6 Socrates appears to distinguish them by saying that we desire (*epithumeō*) pleasure and wish (*boulomai*) for good (see note on *Charmides* 167e1 ["desire"], and note on *Euthydemus* 278e3). Both may, depending upon the context, be translated as "want," which is why Socrates can substitute *boulomai* (*Meno* 78b3) for Meno's *epithumeō* (*Meno* 77b4) and Meno simply replies, "Yes, I did say that" (see note on *Meno* 78b4). In fact, *boulomai*, *epithumeō* and *ethelō* may all be lumped together as at least roughly equivalent, as Plato does at *Republic* 4.437b7-c10— see especially 439b1 where he brings in not only *boulomai* but also *oregō* (desire) and *hormaō* (impulse). Plato's pleonasm in *Republic* 4 is all the more striking because there he famously draws an important and influential threefold distinction among appetites or desires—a distinction that Aristotle follows, though Aristotle is verbally more fastidious than Plato. For Aristotle, the genus is desire (*orexis*, cf. *Nicomachean Ethics* 3.3.1113a9-12), and its two species are rational desires (*boulēsis*, cf. 3.2.1111b26-29) and non-rational desires, which come in two varieties: appetite (*epithumia*, cf. 3.1.1111a32-3) and spirit (*thumos*, cf. 3.2.1111b18-19). See note on 352b4.

340c6 ["which is not the same thing"]: at 345c1 Socrates will finally say explicitly that he interprets "*be good*" as meaning "be *continuously* good." No doubt this is a tendentious interpretation, but in Socrates' view, every interpretation of a poem is tendentious (see 347e3-7).

340d5 ["before it was difficult"]: *Works & Days* 289-92, the quotation is not exact. Socrates is correct to suggest that many people agree with this point, i.e. the path of vice is easy at first but it becomes much more difficult later, while it is the opposite with virtue, i.e. it is difficult at first, but once you are on it things get much easier (e.g. Jesus gives a version of it at Matthew 7:13-14). Prodicus indicates that he agrees with it, but Socrates does not (cf. 344c2).

340e7 ["as everybody agrees"]: Protagoras relies on the truth, and the alleged universal agreement, to interpret Simonides' poem. Not all literary theorists agree that this is a legitimate hermeneutic principle, since (1) poets may have false beliefs, and (2) poets may have unpopular beliefs. Socrates relies on this same principle (e.g. at 345d9-e6). See notes on 342a7 and 345e3-4.

341a1 ["divine and ancient"]: cf. Cratylus 425d1-426b3.

341a4 ["one of Prodicus' students"]: see Charmides 163d3-4, Meno 96d5-7, Cratylus 384b2-c1.

341a5 ["difficult"]: *chalepos*. Prodicus is simplistic to say that *chalepos* means *kakos* (bad), but we shouldn't say that he is wrong. *Chalepos* means difficult in the sense of being hard to bear or hard to deal with, and we may well think of a road that is difficult to traverse as being a bad road, or a person who is troublesome, harsh, or cruel as being a bad person. See also notes on 341c2 and 341b1-2. Protagoras is right to say that *chalepos* is the contradictory of *rhadios* (easy; 341d4-5).

341b1-2 ["saying that it is bad]: Prodicus also says that "difficult" is bad (see 341c2 and the note), so is he saying that "terrible" and "difficult" have the same meaning? Socrates will say that he is joking about "difficult" (*paizein* at 341d7), but perhaps the joke is only that he expresses his view in so laconic a manner that it sounds absurd. Probably he divides adjectives into ones that imply (or often suggest) a negative evaluation and others that imply (or often suggest) a positive evaluation (and perhaps others that are neutral), and he is simply indicating that both *chalepos* and *deinos* are in the first category.

341c2 ["bad"]: perhaps Prodicus answers with one word in order to demonstrate how adept he is at giving short answers, and perhaps even with some professional rivalry to show that he is better at this than Protagoras (cf. 334e4-335a1).

341c8 ["foreign language"]: the Greek inhabitants of Lesbos spoke Aeolic Greek (so the poets Alcaeus and Sappho wrote in Aeolic). Prodicus and Simonides spoke Ionic Greek because they were from Ceos (Homer and Hesiod both wrote in Ionic Greek). This is probably a chauvinistic insult, implying that Aeolic is a barbaric form of Greek.

341e3 ["God"]: the singular was not uncommon and did not signify monotheism—the Greeks were polytheists.

341e7 ["a fraud"]: literally, "in no way a Caen." The inhabitants of Ceos were renowned for eschewing indulgence, and saying something scandalous about the gods would be thought libertine.

341e8 ["ode"]: *asma* is related to the verb *aeidō*, which refers to singing or chanting, so an *asma* is a song or hymn. The more traditional word for many of Simonides' compositions was *melos* (melody), but since these songs were typically accompanied by a lyre in the Hellenistic period they were called *lurikos* (lyric). *Melos* (lyric poetry) was typically contrasted with *epos* (epic poetry), though *epos* could refer to poetry generally—which is the way that Protagoras has been using it. Probably because his teacher Prodicus is standing right next to him Socrates is being a bit picky about words.

342a7 ["what I think about this ode"]: in what follows it is not always clear if Socrates is expressing (1) what he believes to be true, or (2) what he thinks Simonides believes to be true. Socrates is well aware of this because at 345d9 he explicitly indicates something on which he does agree with Simonides.

342b4 ["Protagoras said earlier"]: at 316d3-317a2.

324b4-5 ["battle and courage"]: the similarity of Crete and Sparta was as commonplace as the belief in their emphasis on military superiority (*Laws* 1.626a5-c5; Herodotus 1.65.4-66.1; Aristotle, *Politics* 7.2.1324b7-9). Socrates knows that at the very least, his claim that this is mere pretense will be unexpected.

342b8 ["Spartan sympathizers"]: the *Protagoras* is set prior to the outbreak of the Peloponnesian War, and so the verb *Lakōnizō* probably should not be read with political overtones; it probably referred simply to those who imitated Spartans in the kinds of ways Socrates mentions. The English word "laconic," referring to the habit of speaking succinctly, is parallel to Socrates' *Lakōnizō*. But it is worth asking the extent to which Socrates himself would have been seen as a Spartan sympathizer (see note on *Apology* 37a8; Crito 52e5; see also Aristophanes, *Birds* 1281-3). Also, Socrates' response to Protagoras at 334c8-9 (see note) is remarkably reminiscent of a famous anecdote about the laconic Spartan way of speaking. The

Samians were in desperate need of help, so they sent a delegation to the Spartan authorities. The delegation made a long speech requesting aid, but Spartans said something like, "You talked for so long that we forgot what you said at the beginning, and so couldn't understand what you said after that." In frustration the Samians showed an empty barley sack and said something like "sack needs barley," to which the Spartans replied, "Still too long—'sack' is redundant" (Herodotus 3.46). The Spartans did help the Samians.

343a4 ["Seven Sages"]: Socrates does not use the exact phrase "Seven Sages," but he concludes the list by saying that Chilon "was said to be the seventh." This is the earliest explicit list of Seven Sages extant. We are uncertain of all their dates, but they all lived in the 6th century BCE. Four were from islands east of the Greek mainland (Thales, Pittacus, Bias, and Cleobulus), the others were from the mainland (unless Myson's village of Chen was on Crete and not near Sparta). Other versions of the list include Periander of Corinth instead of Myson of Chen, but because Periander was a brutal tyrant (whose crimes include not only murder but necrophilia, see Herodotus 5.92.η) he did not seem fit for the list. Herodotus is a good source for several on the list: Thales (1.74-5, 170), Bias or Pittacus (1.27), Solon (1.30-33), Chilon (1.59). Diogenes Laertius devotes a chapter to each of them (including Periander): Thales (1.22-44, e.g. when asked why he never had any children of his own he answered, "because I love children," 26; he also said, "know thyself," 40); Pittacus (1.74-81, e.g. when asked what is best he answered, "to do well whatever you are currently doing," 77); Bias (1.82-88, e.g. his most famous saying was, "most people are bad," 88); Solon (1.45-67, e.g. his most famous saying was, "nothing in excess," 63); Cleobulus (1.89-93, e.g. he once said, "one ought to benefit a friend to make him more a friend, and one ought to benefit an enemy to make him a friend"); Myson (1.106-108, e.g. he once said, "do not seek facts from arguments, but arguments from facts, because facts are not brought about for arguments, arguments are constructed for the facts," 108); Chilon (1.68-73, e.g. he once said, "do not desire what is impossible," 70).

343b5 ["laconic"]: *Lakōnikos* is indeed a pun; see note on 342b8. It is probably a further joke that Socrates uses a pleonasm here.

343d1 ["Rather"]: see note on 339b1. Socrates does not quote the line, but I've put it here the way Socrates is clearly understanding it. At 339b1 I translated it the way Protagoras is clearly understanding it. Either translation is grammatically possible. Since we do not possess the full poem, and since we have little reliable information about Simonides or his poetry, I think we do not have sufficient grounds for deciding who is right on this point (if, indeed, it is appropriate to talk about right and wrong in the interpretation of a poem).

343d2 ["Starting with this word"]: actually "the insertion of this one word" is more literal because the *men* is the third word in the line, not the first (as in my translation here and at 339b1). It adds one short syllable to the line and fits the metre, which was undoubtedly one of Simonides' considerations in using it.

343d4-5 ["argues against him saying"]: *amphisbētounta epein* is parallel to *erizonta legein* ("fighting against his view" on line 343d3). Socrates seems to treat *amphisbēteō* and *erizō* as if they are just as synonymous as *eipon* and *legō*. Prodicus explicitly distinguished *amphisbēteō* and *erizō* (see note on 337a8-b1). Here we have a clear example of just the sort of thing Prodicus scolds Socrates for (341a7-9), i.e. failing to observe a useful distinction. Perhaps Plato is doing this deliberately to indicate that he, the author, understands full well that the interpretation Socrates is giving is perverse. Alternatively, just because a distinction is useful it does not follow that we must always use it. The fact that what Socrates says here is perfectly understandable may indicate that occasionally Prodicus goes too far in being a stickler for distinctions.

343e3 ["hyperbaton"]: *hyperbaton* = *huper* (over) + *bainein* (to step, walk). E.g., in Act II, Scene I of Shakespeare's *Measure for Measure*, Escalus says, "Some rise by sin, and some by virtue fall." To put "some...fall" together as they belong, we need to "step over" the intervening phrase "by virtue." In my translation we need to "step over" the words "it is" to connect the phrase "truly...difficult." In the Greek, the word *alatheōs* ("truly") is separated by one word to its left from *agathon* ("good"), and by one word on its right by *chalepon* ("difficult"). It is an hyperbaton either way, but grammatically it can modify either.

Since Simonides is no longer around to say which way he intended the hyperbaton to go (if he had a clear intention, and if his intention decides the matter), and so either reading of the poem seems permissible (which may help to explain why Socrates isn't interested in the interpretation of poems; see 347e3-7).

343e4 ["separated from the word 'difficult'"]: Socrates thinks it does not make sense to say that some people are good, but not truly, and he thinks this is not something Simonides would say. Presumably, then, he thinks that it does make sense, and is something Simonides would say, to claim that some things are difficult, but not truly. Here's one way to make sense of the distinction: (1) to be good is to be virtuous, (2) the virtues are not like parts of a face (329d3-e6) because it is impossible to have one without having all the others, and so (3) to be good is to be completely virtuous, and so (4) to be good is to be truly good; however, (5) it is possible for something to be difficult in one way but not in another, and it is possible for difficulty to come in degrees, and so (6) there are two ways in which it is possible for something to be difficult without being truly difficult. Why doesn't Socrates bother to explain why "truly good" presents problems that "truly difficult" does not? Perhaps because that would give the interpretation of the poem more time than it deserves (see 347c3-348a6).

344c5 ["has knocked down"]: the idea that people are good only in good times was a matter of dispute among ancient Greeks. Odysseus' excellent hunting dog Argos lost his excellence when he lost his beloved master, and the faithful swineherd Eumaeus commented that Zeus takes away half a man's excellence (or virtue, *aretē*) on the day he becomes a slave (Homer, *Odyssey* 17.322-3). Theognis (6th century poet from Megara) held the opposite: good men show their good character in bad circumstances, and bad men show their bad character even in good circumstances (Theognis 319-22).

344c7 ["he's already down"]: my translation of the next two sentences aims at the sense rather than the literal content of what Socrates says. The Greek words I translate as "manage" and "unmanageable" are closely related to one another, and so the point comes across in Greek better than a more literal translation would in English.

344d5 ["unmanageable illness"]: here Socrates appears to accept that there are such things as unmanageable disasters that can prevent the successful completion of tasks like piloting a ship, growing crops or healing a sick person. Does that contradict his point at *Euthydemus* 281b2-3 (see note on *Euthydemus* 281b3)? Is this something Socrates believes, or is it something that Socrates thinks Simonides believes (see note on 342a7)?

344d5 ["become bad"]: there are two problems here. First, the word I translate as "honorable" (i.e. *esthlos*) can be (1) a synonym for "good" (*agathos*), (2) an adjective referring specifically to moral virtue (e.g. courageous), or (3) morally neutral excellence (e.g. good fortune, prosperity, well developed skill). Second, the word I translate with the phrase "it is allowed" literally refers to opening territory, and hence means to give room to or to allow. But this is ambiguous between (1) believing that something is possible, and (2) stating that something is possible.

344d8 ["sometimes honorable"]: we do not know who wrote this line. Xenophon quotes it and suggests that the author was someone other than Theognis (*Memorabilia* 1.2.20).

344e1 ["always necessarily bad"]: as a philosopher, this sentence vexes me. The medieval French philosopher Peter Abelard (1079-1142) distinguished two kinds of necessity: *de re* ("about the thing") and *de dicto* ("about what is said"). For example, the sentence "necessarily Héloïse sits" is false if we have in mind *de re* necessity because the property of sitting does not belong to Héloïse necessarily: she can get up and walk around if she so chooses. However, the sentence "necessarily Héloïse sits, if Héloïse sits" is true if we have in mind *de dicto* necessity because any sentence of the form "If F, then F" is necessarily true. So in this case, "a bad man is always necessarily bad" is false if it uses *de re* necessity, but it is true if it uses *de dicto* necessity (which Socrates seems clearly to intend).

345a2 ["successfully reads or writes"]: he asked two questions but gives only one answer (as in the next two sentences). In this entire section, Socrates' Greek is quite compressed and my translation is much more expansive so that it is easier to understand. Again (see note on 343e4), Socrates seems uninterested in giving a full defense of his interpretation of Simonides' poem. He's being perfunctory.

345b2 ["only a good man can become bad"]: he's not ruling out the possibility of someone who is neither good nor bad becoming bad; rather, he's summing up the point he's already made more explicitly with the ship's pilot and passengers, i.e. if your patients keep dying of the plague despite your best efforts to save them, then the unmanageable plague is ruining your medical practice; but if you aren't a doctor at all and hence don't have a medical practice, then we cannot say the same about you.

345d4 ["voluntarily"]: I set *hekōn* off with commas to indicate how Socrates construes the grammar. He thinks this is another hyperbaton so that instead of going with "who" (*hostis*) to which it is adjacent, it goes with the first person subject of the verbs *epainēmi* ("I praise") and *phileō* ("I love" or "I befriend").

345e3-4 ["involuntarily"]: this is quite a provocative statement because it seems obvious to many that we often give in to temptation and voluntarily do something that we know full well to be shameful (cf. Aristotle, *Nicomachean Ethics* 7.2.1145b27-28). This issue will be discussed at 352a1-357e8, and it appears to be an assumption of an argument he makes during his trial (*Apology* 25d8-26a7). His claim that no wise man disagrees with him follows from his use of the adjective *apeideutos* ("uneducated") at 345d7: Socrates thinks that an accurate understanding of voluntariness shows that no one does wrong voluntarily, and so anyone who believes that people often do wrong voluntarily demonstrates *ipso facto* that they are uneducated with respect to voluntariness, and hence cannot be wise. Hence, either you accept Socrates' interpretation of Simonides, or you must reject the claim that he was a wise man. Today we do not think that such interpretive arguments are persuasive, but it does seem to have been acceptable in Socrates' circumstances (cf. Hippias' assessment at 347a6-7, and see note on 340e7). Perhaps the acceptability of such arguments partially explains Socrates' dim view of the interpretation of poetry (see 347c3-348a6).

345e7 ["under compulsion"]: *hekōn* is typically contrasted with force, necessity and compulsion, just like our modern contrast between volunteer service and compulsory service (e.g. volunteering for the military as opposed to being conscripted). Aristotle's notion is somewhat different, and he would disagree with Socrates' characterization of the upcoming example as being involuntary: even in a case where a tyrant threatens to kill your children unless you do something shameful, if you choose to do the shameful thing rather than allow your children to be killed, Aristotle thinks there is still a sense in which your action is *hekousios* (probably a synonym for *hekōn*; see *Nicomachean Ethics* 3.1.1110a4-b17).

346c4 ["sound mind"]: actually he says "healthy man" (*hugiēs anēr*) but the line makes no sense if he is referring simply to physical health. The use of *hugiēs* to refer to moral soundness is not uncommon in the 5th or 4th century (e.g. Euripides, *Bacchae* 948; Plato, *Phaedo* 89d6).

346e2 ["Mytilenean dialect"]: Pittacus was from Mytilene, the most important city on the island of Lesbos where Aeolic Greek was spoken. In the poem, where Simonides says "I praise and am a friend to all," he used the Aeloic form of "praise" (which is *epainēmi*, as opposed to the Attic *epaineō*).

347b1 ["I too have a good account of it"]: if Plato was having a bit of fun with Prodicus at 337a1-c4 by comically exaggerating his proclivity for drawing distinctions (see note on 337c1-2), here is is probably having a bit of fun with Hippias (cf. *Hippias Minor* 363c7-d4, *Hippias Major* 286a5-6).

347c4 ["drinking parties"]: in fact much lyric poetry, including many poems by Simonides, were deliberately written to be sung at symposia.

347d7-e1 ["even if they drink quite a lot"]: cf. *Symposium* 223c4-5.

347e22 ["most of us"]: Socrates and Hippocrates do not claim to be wise.

347e4 ["impossible to question poets about what they say"]: cf. note on 329a3, *Apology* 22a6-c8, *Hippias Minor* 365c8-d1.

347e7 ["impossible to prove either way"]: presumably, then, Socrates believes that he failed to prove that his interpretation of Simonides' poem is correct, and he also believes that Protagoras or Hippias could give at least as convincing a case for incompatible interpretations.

348a8 ["in the middle of discussing something"]: Protagoras derailed their discussion at 333e2-334c6.

348d1 ["when we go together"]: *Iliad* 10.224, and his next quotation is the second half of line 225. Together, lines 224-226 read: "When two go together, one perceives before the other how gain may be had, but if one alone perceives, his attention is shorter and his resources fewer." Diomedes says this to Nestor after volunteering for the mission to spy on the Trojans. He chooses Odysseus to accompany him, so perhaps Socrates = Diomedes and Protagoras = Odysseus? It is interesting that after saying that they should leave poets out of the discussion, Socrates quotes Homer.

348d5 ["they can confirm it"]: *bebaioō* can refer to official confirmation or validation by someone specially qualified to determine validity (cf. Isocrates, *Dicaeogenes* 5.23; Demosthenes, *Against Pantaenetus* 37.12). But in the middle voice (as we have here), it can refer to making one's grasp on something secure (cf. Thucydides 6.10.5, 6.78.1). This is how Plato uses this word elsewhere in the context of argumentation (cf. *Gorgias* 489a5). Securing an argument may consist in corroboration (e.g. *Crito* 53b8-9, *Laches* 194c6). Here it looks like corroboration is what he means.

348d7 ["best person"]: this is the sort of claim many scholars call "Socratic irony." But in this case, as he makes clear in what immediately follows, he is clearly taking Protagoras at his word since he has not yet had the opportunity to put his extravagant claims fully to the test. It would be presuming that he knew something that he did not know if he simply assumed that Protagoras' boasts are all false.

349a8 ["remind me of"]: Socrates clearly remembers the question he asked (compare 349b1-6 with 329c6-d8). He is also able to remember accurately when Protagoras gives different answers to the question that he wants answered (see 359a2-c2). His earlier claim about a poor memory was not about simple recall, but rather about his ability to keep to one line of reasoning when his interlocutor confuses the issue by changing the subject (see note on 334c8-9). Also, given the disputes about authors' intentions in poetry, Socrates' request that Protagoras remind him of what he said is also an invitation to clarify (or modify) his earlier comments in case Socrates misinterpreted anything he said (or he's changed his mind).

349d5 ["different from all the others"]: this is not the view Protagoras stated at 329d3-330b6. Socrates undermined the separability of (a) justice and piety at 330b6-331b8, and (b) temperance and wisdom at 332a4-333c3, and he began to undermine the separability of (c) temperance and justice at 333d4-334a2 when the conversation broke down. Notice that if all three of those arguments are successful, then Protagoras cannot separate piety, justice, temperance and wisdom: all four are inseparable. Notice further that courage is the only one of the five left out, which is precisely the one Protagoras picks on here as separable from the rest. Perhaps this is the closest he will come to admitting that he has no good responses to Socrates' earlier arguments, and so he concedes the inseparability of all but courage to Socrates.

349e2 ["Do you say that courageous people are daring people"]: in Greek, the locution "I say x to be y" can be predicative (e.g. *Charmides* 159b8), i.e. it is to say that x has the property of being y, as in "I say Achilles to be angry". But this locution can also be used to state an identity (e.g. *Euthyphro* 6e10-7a1), i.e. it is to say that what it is to be x is to be y (x and y are one and the same thing, or x and y are two names for one thing, cf. 349b1-3), as in "I say Achilles to be the son of Peleus". Socrates may be assuming that he is asking the identiy question, but Protagoras clearly interprets it here as a predicative question (350c7-9).

350a2 ["they know how to"]: the name of the virtue is *sophia* (349b1), but here he uses the verb *epistamai* (related to the noun *epistēmē*), and he switches to *sophos* (the adjective related to the noun *sophia*) at 350c2. Protagoras uses *epistamai* at 350d3, then switches to *sophia* at d5, then to *epistēmē* at 351a2. Similar switching occurs in the *Euthydemus* (see note on 292b1). See note on 352c7.

350c1-2 ["are daring, but they won't be courageous"]: this part of Socrates' argument works exactly like his standard refutations in the *Charmides* and *Laches* (see note on *Charmides* 159c1).

Step 1: courage and daring are one and the same thing.

Step 2: courage is fine.

Step 3: daring is fine.

Step 4: daring is not fine (as illustrated by examples of excessive daring).

Protagoras avoids the refutation by denying Step 1: he was not giving an analysis of courage. If this were a definitional dialogue like the *Charmides*, *Laches* or *Euthyphro*, then Socrates would, presumably, indicate to Protagoras that he failed to answer the question Socrates asked, since he would have asked a question whose proper answer would have been in the form: "courage and x are one and the same thing" (cf. *Charmides* 158e6-159a10, *Laches* 190d7-192b8, *Euthyphro* 5c8-6e6). But this is not a definitional dialogue, and this section is aimed not at defining courage but at considering the unity of the virtues (see note on *Protagoras* 350c4-5).

350c4-5 ["won't wisdom be courage?"]: if by "wisdom" (*sophia*) Socrates means here what he means by "knowledge (*epistēmē*) of good and bad" in the *Charmides* and *Laches* (cf. *Charmides* 174a10-e2, *Laches* 199d4-e1), then he is only hinting at quite a complex argument, i.e. separate analyses of the five virtues show that "virtue and the knowledge of good and bad are one and the same thing" is the only irrefutable analysis of virtue, hence it is the only reasonable account of virtue.

350e3 ["Yes"]: I've put this as a dialogue to help make it clear. Also, here is where Protagoras ends his ersatz dialogue—he vaguely waves his hand at the next inferences, which I spell out for him.

351a1 ["not the same thing"]: "capability" translates *dunamis* (from which we get "dynamite"), and "strength" translates *ischus*. Because it is often our strength that makes us capable of doing some things, *dunamis* and *ischus* can be difficult to distinguish. Homer is probably using *dunamis* to refer to physical strength at *Iliad* 13.786-7, 22.20, 23.891. Homer never uses *ischus*, but Hesiod uses it to describe (a) the Cyclopes, (b) the hundred-handed giants Kottos, Briareos, Gyges, and (c) the monster Typhoeus (*Theogony* 146, 153, 823 respectively). In all three cases, *ischus* seems to refer to bodily strength. For Aristotle, the two are distinct: a master builder has the capacity for building, and this crucially involves his physical strength, but people who have equal or greater physical strength do not necessarily have the same or greater capacity for building (see *Metaphysics* 9.1-7). This seems close to the distinction Protagoras is drawing.

351b2 ["courage is like strength"]: some people find these kinds of arguments easier to follow using set theory, Venn diagrams and so on. Protagoras is suggesting, in effect, that the set of strong people is a proper subset of the capable people (so that all strong people are capable, but not all capable people are strong since their capacity can derive from something other than strength, e.g. training). Similarly, the set of courageous people is a proper subset of the daring people (so that all courageous people are daring, but not all daring people are courageous since their daring can derive from something other than courage, e.g. madness).

351b4 ["some men live well and some badly"]: some scholars see this as an abrupt change of topic, and speculate that it has resulted from Plato splicing an earlier version of the *Protagoras* into a later version. On the contrary, I think the idea of living well or badly would occur quite naturally to Socrates and this coterie in a discussion of courage, daring, wisdom and fine actions. E.g., when Socrates wants to encourage Clinias to love wisdom and virtue he naturally begins by asking him about doing well (*Euthydemus* 278e3); when Socrates describes his dream in which temperance rules us, he naturally concludes the dream with everyone living well and being happy (*Charmides* 173a7-d5).

351d7-e1 ["produce pleasure or are pleasant in themselves?"]: see 353c4-d2. For example, eating will produce the pleasure of satiety, but if the food is tasty then the act of eating is pleasant in itself.

352b4 ["it doesn't rule us"]: "I know that I should stand and fight, but I'm too afraid, so I drop my shield and run" is an example of *akrasia*, i.e. "weakness of will" or "incontinence," i.e. lack of control over one's own non-rational desires. Aristotle discusses incontinence at *Nicomachean Ethics* 7.1-10; he argues that something like the view Socrates defends here (352a1-357e8) is correct (*Nicomachean Ethics* 7.3.1147b13-17. What does Socrates mean when he says that knowledge rules us? At least, he means that non-rational inclinations do not necessarily deprive us of the voluntary control of our actions (they don't necessarily overpower us, or drive us literally insane—a sub-theme of the *Protagoras*, see 323b2, 349e6, 350b6, 350c2, 360b4-5). Aristotle certainly would agree with this (cf. *Nicomachean Ethics* 7.5 on bestiality and disease). At most, Socrates means that non-rational inclinations cannot disrupt the connection between

(a) what we know to be a better course of action, and (b) what course of action we take. Aristotle's account of incontinence seems to allow for just such disruption (cf. *Nicomachean Ethics* 7.3 on incontinence and ignorance). Plato's division of the *psuchē* into three parts also allows for just such disruption (*Republic* 4).

352c4 ["if someone knows"]: so far he's been using *epistēmē*, but here he switches to *gignōskō*. Perhaps he's using the two as synonyms (see note on 352c7).

352c7 ["intelligence"]: now he switches to *phronēsis* (see note on 352c4). All five main epistemic terms (*sophia, epistēmē, phronēsis, oida, gignōskō*) appear not to be sharply distinguished by Socrates (see notes on *Charmides* 154a4, 162b5, 170b12; *Laches* 192c8, 194e8; *Meno* 88b4, 97a6; *Phaedo* 73c7). Perhaps we should assume that prior to a detailed analysis of knowledge, Socrates simply uses these terms to indicate an elevated cognitive condition.

352e1 ["overcome"]: *hēssaomai* to be less than, to be weaker than or to be inferior to. It can refer to being overpowered and defeated by someone stronger, or it can refer to giving way or yielding to someone. Hence, in this context, it is ambiguous in an important way (see note on 352b4).

353b3 ["you still think"] see 351e10-11.

353c1 ["THE MANY"]: Plato writes much of what follows in indirect speech, which makes it indirect speech nested within indirect speech. I've converted this to direct speech because I think it's easier to follow that way. As a result, I've trimmed some of Socrates' narration (e.g. "Protagoras agreed" at 353e5). Also, "the many" translates *hoi polloi*, see notes on *Euthydemus* 303d1 and *Apology* 20c8. Both Socrates and Protagoras have used this label several times so far (I usually translate it as "most people").

353c6 ["eating, drinking, or having sex"]: Aristotle argues that this narrowly constrained cluster of pleasures constitutes the focus of the virtue temperance (*Nicomachean Ethics* 3.10). Plato also accepts this cluster as a suitable way to identify the focus of the appetitive part of the *psuchē* (though he adds a phrase that opens the door to including other related but unspecified pleasures; *Republic* 4.439d6-8). Here Socrates introduces this list with the demonstrative pronoun *hode* (dative plural *toisde* at 353c5), and not the demonstrative pronoun of quality *toiosde*, and so it is possible that he intends this list as exhaustive. If so, this could be evidence that (a) he truly is treating *hoi polloi* with disdain (see the delightfully disdainful description at *Republic* 9.586a1-b4, which is all the more notable because Plato has quite an inclusive notion of *hēdonē*, see note on 353c7), and (b) he himself does not believe the form of hedonism he attributes to *hoi polloi* (and which Protagoras appears to affirm at 354c3).

353c7 ["pleasure"]: *hēdonē*, from which we derive the English word "hedonism" (see note on 354c1-2). According to Aristotle, Prodicus distinguished three kinds of *hēdonē*: *chara* (joy, delight), *terpsis* (enjoyment, delight), and *euphrosunē* (mirth, merriment, festivity, gladness, good cheer; Aristotle, *Topics* 2.6.112b22-23). Notice that at 337c1-4 Plato has Prodicus distinguish between *euphrainō* and *hēdomai* (see note on 337c1-2). Plato has quite an inclusive notion of *hēdonē* at *Republic* 9.580d7-583a11 (cf. Aristotle, *Nicomachean Ethics* 3.10.1117b28-1118a1).

353c7 ["wrong"]: *ponēros* is typically opposed to *chrēstos*, and so can mean "harmful" or "base" as opposed to "beneficial" or "noble," but this pair of opposites is often associated with (a) the *agathos/kakos* opposition, and so *ponēros* often means "bad" (cf. the switch from *ponēros* to *kakos* at 353d5, and using *agathos* as the opposite of *ponēros* at 354a3), or (b) the *dikaios/adikos* opposition, and so *ponēros* often means "wrong." Here it is clearly referring to the rejection of a possible course of action. It is used at 313a4, 313a8, 313d2, 313d8, 313e3, 334a8, 346a3, 353c7, 353c9.

353d1-2 ["produces pleasure and is pleasant in itself?"]: see note on 351d7-e1.

353e6 ["as Protagoras and I maintain"]: this is ambiguous between (a) Protagoras and Socrates maintain that the action is bad for no other reason than that it causes pain, etc., and (b) Protagoras and Socrates maintain the most people think that the action is bad for no other reason than that it causes pain, etc. Protagoras seems to agree with most people at 354c3, but aside from this ambiguous phrase, we have no indisputable evidence that Socrates also agrees with what most people say about pleasure/pain, and good/bad.

354a2 ["opposite"]: actually, Socrates addresses this to Protagoras (see note on 353c1). The opposites Socrates has in mind are (1) a course of action is thought to be pleasant but wrong (*ponēros*), and (2) a course of action is thought to be painful but good (*agathos*). Normally we'd expect the opposite of *ponēros* to be *chrēstos*, but see note on 353c7.

354b7 ["prevent"] *apotropē* means to turn away (see note on 324b6 above). The idea of turning away or warding off pain or harm made sense to ancient Greeks in both ritual and magical practices. Ritual offerings to the gods could win their favor, and hence both protection from disaster and possibly the showering of blessings (see note on *Euthyphro* 12e7). Amulets worn around the neck were thought to form a sort of protective zone around the wearer. Such amulets often contained a lamella (often a small, thin, rolled sheet of metal, usually iron, occasionally gold) on which protective verses were inscribed; e.g. one lamella contained these three verses from Homer's *Iliad* (10.564, 521 and 572, in that order):

So saying, over the trench he drove the single-hooved horses

And the men gasping in painful bloodshed

But for themselves, much sweat they washed off in the sea

Papyri Graecae Magicae IV.2219-26, edited by K. Preisendanz (1926) and updated by A. Henrichs (1973-4), Stuttgart.

354c1-2 ["good other than pleasure and pain?"]: "evaluative hedonism" is the view that only pleasure is good and only pain is bad (aka "normative hedonism"); "psychological hedonism" is the view that only pleasure and pain motivate people (aka "motivational hedonism"); "rational hedonism" is the view that only pleasure and pain give us reasons for action; "ethical hedonism" is the view that right and wrong are determined exclusively by pleasure and pain (e.g. it is wrong to choose a more painful course of action when a more pleasant course of action is available). The response of *hoi polloi* to Socrates' question commits them to evaluative hedonism (and Protagoras' comment at 354c3 commits him to evaluative hedonism). Every form of hedonism is less plausible if the relevant notion of pleasure is limited in the way that Socrates seems to limit it at 353c6. Plato rejects rational hedomism (even with a very inclusive notion of pleasure, cf. note on 353c7 ["pleasure"]) because he thinks that independently of the reason we have to pursue pleasure, we also have reason to pursue both (a) freedom (*Republic* 9.577c1-580c8), and (b) a life suitable for human beings (*Republic* 9.588b1-592b6). So, regarding (a) freedom: if two courses of action are equally pleasant, but the first also gives us freedom denied us by the second, then we have reason to choose the first. At the end of *Republic* 9 Plato gives a fantastical summary regarding (b) a life suitable for human beings, but Aristotle agrees and argues that if two courses of action are equally pleasant, but in the first we develop into mature adults while in the second our development is stunted and we remain immature children, then we have reason to choose the first (*Nicomachean Ethics* 10.3.1174a1-4).

354c6 ["enjoyment"] *to chairein* is related to *chara* (see note on 353c7 ["pleasure"]).

354d8 ["goal"]: *telos* refers to an objective, an aim, a target, goal or end. So it is easily used as a standard for judging degrees of success or failure. This sentence in Greek is extremely similar to the final sentence of the previous paragraph, so instead of repeating the same language, I took the opportunity to elaborate on the Greek notion of a *telos*.

355a4-5 ["whatever results in pleasure or pain"]: if in some sense good = pleasure and bad = pain (see note on 355c5), then this statement could go either way. Socrates could equally say "good is what results in pleasure" and "pleasure is what results in good." He never does this. He speaks as if the promotion of pleasure explains why something is good and not the other way around. Some have called this "epistemological hedonism," i.e. judgments about goodness are known or justified on the basis of claims about pleasure and not *vice versa*.

355a6 ["ridiculous"]: some scholars think that what is ridiculous is the hedonism just expressed at 355a2-3. For an alternative, see note on 355d3.

355c2 ["he does it anyway"]: after this point, Socrates narrates a dialogue. Technically it is a dialogue (between someone taking the side of The Many and someone constructing the *reduction ad absurdum*)

within a dialogue (between The Many and Socrates/Protagoras), which is itself within a dialogue (between Socrates and Protagoras) that is within another dialogue (between Socrates and his friend). I simplify the situation by simply continuing the discussion between The Many and Socrates/Protagoras.

355c5 ["substitute"]: Socrates is clearly not saying that the words "pleasure" (*hēdonē*) and "good" (*agathos*) have the same meaning; he's only saying that they have the same reference.

355d3 ["overcome by something good"]: it certainly does seem ridiculous to say that I choose what I know to be the worse option because I know that it is the better option. For a different view of what is supposed to be ridiculous, see note on 355a6.

356a6 ["some later time"]: the notion of measuring pleasure/pain on a time scale was already a part of the conversation at 355a3 when he asked about living out a "whole life." One set of choices might be appropriate if we are seeking to maximize the pleasure of one whole day; an incompatible set of choices might be appropriate if we are seeking to maximize the pleasure of one whole life. As Aristotle says, "one swallow does not make a spring" (*Nicomachean Ethics* 1.7.1098a18-19; cf. the pain of torture now can lead a slave to say something for which he will suffer a far more painful death later, Antiphon, *On the Choreutes* 6.25). Presumably, the proper standard to use when consider pleasure for a human being is a whole life because a human being is by nature a temporally extended thing. So if we can discern other natural features of human beings, they might also affect our calculation of which pleasures are appropriate for them (see note on 354c1-2).

356d4 ["science of measurement"]: perhaps *technē* should be translated as "craft," "skill" or "expertise," but the connection with precise measurement and with knowledge (*epistēmē* at 357a1 and seven more times from 357b4-e1) is a good match for what people today think of as science.

357c5 ["knowledge"]: here Socrates switches from *epistēmē* to *oida* (see note on *Charmides*162b5).

358b7 ["knows or believes"]: by expanding his point to cover both knowledge and belief, Socrates seems to be giving an explanation of all human behavior that is not literally insane, i.e. all sane people always do what they believe at the time to be the best option open to them. Ignorant people are at the mercy of appearances which can (1) lead them to choose the worse option because it falsely appears at the time to be better, and (2) lead them to change their minds often because appearances are highly variable. This sort of view has been extremely influential in the history of European philosophy because it is related to what many scholars refer to as "intellectualism," i.e. the view that the will is determind by the greater good as presented by reason. See note on *Euthyphro* 10d6.

358d1 ["isn't in human nature"]: on Socrates' account of human nature (especially the *psuchē*), *akrasia* (see note on 352b4) is either rational (e.g. you changed your mind about what you ought to do) or irrational (e.g. you know/believe that you ought not do what you are doing, and you simultaneously know/believe that you ought not do what you are doing). (On "know/believe" cf. "knows or believes" at 358b7). There seems to be no recognition of the possibility of non-rational (as opposed to irrational) inclinations. Aristotle does allow that by nature, the human *psuchē* does include non-rational inclinations, and this allows him to develop an intermediate third alternative: *akrasia* can be compared to sleepwalking, acting when we are drunk, and it reduces knowledge to something like an actor on a stage speaking lines that are disconnected from reality (*Nicomachean Ethics* 7.3.1147a10-14, 18-24). In my opinion, we can use the modern diagnosis of dissociative psychogenic amnesia in the *Diagnostic and Statistical Manual of Mental Disorders, Fifth Edition*, to understand Aristotle's intermediate position. I think that Aristotle was the first to identify what we may call "dissociative psychogenic akrasia" (DPA), i.e. sudden, retrograde, loss of behavioral norms not due to structural brain damage or brain lesion. DPA is sudden because it is a response to stimuli (e.g. a tempting pleasure); it is retrograde because it impairs our ability to implement behavioral norms that have shaped our behavior in the past (i.e. it does not prevent us from developing new norms in the future); it is psychogenic and not induced by trauma (which would be a different kind of problem), and so its roots and appropriate therapy lie within our character, and hence should be dealt with in the education we receive as children, or, failing that, in taking responsibility for our feelings, choices and actions as adults.

359a7 ["a unique capacity"]: see 329d3-330b6.

359b1 ["different from all the others"]: see 349d2-8.

359e6 ["what is fine is also good?"]: see 358b5-6.

359a3 ["we did agree to that"]: see 358a5-6.

360b3 ["if they are not shameful, then aren't they fine?"]: at *Symposium* 201e8-202b5 Diotima instructs Socrates that the inference from "x is not fine" to "x is shameful" is invalid because it is possible for something to be intermediate between fine and shameful. But here he is not drawing an invalid inference because he is talking specifically about courage: as long as you are not doing anything shameful in (a) carrying out your military orders and facing the enemy boldly, or (b) in making a strategic retreat from a lost battle, then you are indeed acting finely.

360d2 ["opposite of ignorance"]: in English, the antonym of "wisdom" is "folly," and the antonym of "ignorance" is "knowledge." In Greek, *sophia* and *amathia* are antonyms (see note on *Charmides* 155d4).

360d4-5 ["courage is wisdom"]: notice that this closes the final gap, thus making all five virtues inseparable (see note on 334a2).

360e1 ["at first"]: see 349d6-8.

360e3 ["eager to win"]: on Socrates' attitude towards the love of victory as opposed to the love of wisdom see *Phaedo* 91a2-3.

361d2 ["to the various creatures"]: see 320c8-322a2.

361d5 ["as I said at the beginning"]: see 347b9-c2 (cf. 328d3-329d2).

361e1 ["I'm not bad at it myself"]: literally he says that he thinks he's not a "bad person" (*kakos einai anthrōpos*), but I think that by "bad" he means "inferior," and that his next comment about envy shows that his ego is wounded by the fact that Socrates got the better of him in argument. He's trying to put on a show of magnanimity after behaving like a petulant child at 360c6-e5.

362a2 ["I mentioned earlier"]: see 335c3-7. Apparently Socrates was supposed to meet his friend to whom he recounts the entire conversation (309b5-7). Presumably, Socrates had promised to meet him. No doubt his friend wouldn't be surprised at Socrates being very late, having been delayed by some prolonged conversation. Three other dialogues have similar endings: *Euthyphro* 15e3-4, *Meno* 100b7, *Apology* 42a2.

362a4 ["we left"]: the plural is probably referring to Socrates and Hippocrates. If that is what he means, then it seems that Hippocrates was not as eager to become Protagoras' student as he was earlier that day.

NOTES ON MENO

70a2 ["virtue"]: *aretē*, see notes on *Charmides* 158a1 and *Apology* 20b6.

70a2 ["habituation"]: *askētos* refers to practice. The question of whether virtue is a matter of instruction (*mathēton*) or habituation is also raised at *Cleitophon* 407b1-8. The speech Socrates gives in the *Menexenus* clearly distinguishes *askētos* from virtue, saying that the former without the latter is shameful and bad (*Menexenus* 246d8-e2). In the *Republic*, *askētos* refers to training or regimen (3.404a1, a7, c7; cf. *Protagoras* 342b6). Aristotle asks a question that is very close to the question with which the *Meno* begins, but Aristotle's question is about happiness (*eudaimonia*) and not virtue (*Nicomachean Ethics* 1.9.1099b10). For Aristotle, *askētos* is probably a synonym for *ethismos*, which Aristotle takes to be helpful but not sufficient for virtue (see *Nicomachean Ethics* 2.2).

70b1 ["wisdom"]: see note on *Charmides* 155d4.

70b2 ["Larissa"]: Thessaly is about halfway between Attica (where Athens is) and Macedonia, and Larissa is in the north of Thessaly.

70b2 ["Aristippus"]: clearly not Aristippus of Cyrene (see notes on *Phaedo* 59c3 and 60a7); this is Aristippus the Aleuad (see note on 70b4). In 404, Lycophron the tyrant of Pherae (an important city in the southeast of Thessaly) attacked and defeated Larissa, led by Aristippus. In the wake of this loss, some prominent Larissans fled to Athens. Xenophon says that Aristippus was attracted to Meno because of his youthful good looks (*Anabasis* 2.6.28; note that Xenophon has a very poor opinion of Meno, e.g. he calls Meno a liar at 2.6.26).

70b3 ["passion"]: *erastēs*. Socrates is making a pun, since he uses *erastēs* at b5 in the sense of a homosexual lover, but here he uses it in a non-sexual sense.

70b3 ["Gorgias"]: Gorgias of Leontini (c.485-c.380). Leontini was a colony in Sicily established by the Greeks of the island of Naxos. Gorgias was a student of Empedocles, and in 427 he served as ambassador to Athens where his rhetorical methods became extremely influential.

70b4 ["Aleuad clan"]: the leading families of Larissa for generations. They were scandalous because in 485 they actually invited Xerxes to invade Greece, promising him their loyalty and help (Herodotus 7.6.2).

71a6-7 ["I don't know what virtue happens to be"]: Anytus might appear to be a counter-example to Socrates' claim that this is what any Athenian would answer (cf. 92e3-6). But Socrates seems perfectly well aware that many Athenians falsely claim to know much about virtue (cf. *Apology* 23a5-b4). Perhaps he means that if people spoke the truth upon examination—as opposed to what they falsely believe to be the truth—this is what they would say (see *Apology* 20e8-23c1).

71b4 ["how could I know what qualities it has?"]: the implied answer seems to be "I could not." It is worth considering whether the ends of the *Charmides*, *Laches*, *Euthyphro* and *Lysis* support such an answer to this question. E.g., if Euthyphro cannot say what piety is, then how can he be so sure that prosecuting his own father is pious? Some scholars speak of Socrates as affirming a principle of the priority of definition (something like, "if you do not know what a thing is, then you do not know any of that thing's qualities"). Austrian philosopher Ludwig Josef Johann Wittgenstein (1889-1951) took Socrates to task in his *Blue Book* (1933-34) for insisting on such a principle of priority. But rather than a priority of *definition*, *Meno* 71b4 and *Lysis* 223b4-8 suggest that Socrates' principle is rather a priority of the *universal*: if you admit to being confused about the universal, then you look ridiculous when you confidently claim to identify particulars that fall under it. Euthyphro looks ridiculous when he runs away from Socrates (*Euthyphro* 15e3-4), and Socrates is about to make Meno look ridiculous (*Meno* 79e7-80b7). Of course, Socrates does not apply the priority of the universal to every universal; if he accepts such a principle, he applies it only to virtue and the virtues. Wittgenstein seems more concerned with the legitimate use of words, something Socrates associates with Prodicus (cf. 75e3 and the note on *Charmides* 163d4); Socrates seems concerned with real universals (see "the same," at 72c7 and 75a5). Identifying a real universal is more like identifying a real person than it is like establishing the correct use of words.

71b5 ["doesn't know at all"]: whatever claim Socrates is making here (see note on 71b4), it's content and reasonability depend crucially upon what he means by "know," but he switches from *oida* at b4 to *gignōskō* at b5 then back to *oida* at b6 (see note on *Charmides* 162b5). If he has in mind the facile affectation of cognitive superiority alluded to at 70b6-c1 above, then his principle is quite reasonable: if you lecture others on x as if you are an expert on the subject, but upon questioning you turn out not to know what x is, then nobody is going to take anything you say on the subject seriously. Also, it may be legitimate to compare not knowing what virtue is with not knowing who Meno is only if we assume a black and white contrast between knowledge and ignorance: not knowing at all who Meno is seems to entail total ignorance, and so if this is comparable to not knowing what virtue is, then Socrates seems to be assuming that ignorance of what virtue is entails total ignorance of virtue. We don't normally assume this, but again, perhaps Socrates has in mind the facile affectation at 70b6-c1: if you try to lecture me on virtue as if you are the expert and I am the ignorant pupil, but then I manage to show that you don't actually know what virtue is, then I may well conclude that you don't know anything at all about virtue—you're just "full of hot air" as the saying goes.

71c8 ["My memory isn't excellent"]: perhaps Socrates is actually saying that his memory is quite poor, which may be contradicted by dialogues like the *Protagoras* and *Euthydemus*, in which Socrates recounts in great detail very long dialogues he had earlier. At *Protagoras* 334c8-9 he says that he loses track of the point if someone makes a long speech (cf. *Hippias Minor* 373a2-3), and that may be what he is saying here, since Gorgias probably made many long speeches when he was in Athens (in 427, which is probably 24 years prior to the date when this discussion with Meno is set). If upon examination Gorgias had impressed him as someone who knew what virtue is, he would probably remember it. Blaming his memory, therefore, is a polite way to avoid directly contradicting someone for whom Meno has great admiration, and it obeys Socrates' principle that we should be ready to blame our own poor mental abilities if someone seems to us to fail to prove their claim (*Phaedo* 89d9-91a3).

71e3 ["managing the city's affairs"]: "help your friends and harm your enemies" is what I call the Pagan Golden Rule. Different versions of it are expressed by the poets Archilochus (7th century) and Theognis (6th century), as well as Solon (c.638-c.558), Isocrates (*To Demonicus* 1.26) and Xenophon (*Memorabilia* 2.3.14, 2.6.35). Polemarchus mentions this in Plato's *Republic* at 1.332d5-8. What is surprising about Meno's list is not that he includes the Pagan Golden Rule, but that he incorporates it into the alleged virtue of competently managing affairs of state. Sophistry typically emphasized public speaking as a way to succeed in both law and politics (cf. *Protagoras* 318e5-319a2, *Gorgias* 452d5-e8). In other words, Meno's account of virtue for a man implies that sophists are godsends, and that any man should be happy to pay whatever fee the sophist asks.

72c7 ["form"]: *eidos*. See notes on *Euthyphro* 5d4 and 6d11. Socrates uses *eidos* here, at 72d8 and at 72e5. Meno uses it at 80a5.

72e2 ["health is the same"]: men don't get pregnant, so in that sense, health for a man is different from health for a woman. What Socrates and Meno seem to have in mind is something like what Socrates says at *Phaedo* 104a3-b1, e.g. it doesn't matter whether you have three olives, three apples or three oranges, if there are three then the number of items is odd, not even. Similarly, it doesn't matter whether you are a man or a woman, if you are healthy then you are neither ill nor injured (although men and women have some distinctive illnesses and injuries). This is the sort of response Socrates would likely give to Aristotle's criticisms in *Politics* 1.13.

72e5 ["a strong woman"]: at *Politics* 3.4.1277b20-23 Aristotle says that a man would be thought a coward if he were no braver than a brave woman, so he might also argue that a man would not be considered strong if he were no stronger than a strong woman. But Socrates clearly intends his point here to be the same that he just made with health, so probably a good example of what he has in mind is that the strength to lift 100 lbs doesn't differ whether it is in a man or a woman. Compare the way that Plato deals with the differences between men and women at *Republic* 5.452e4-457c2: if someone is capable of doing a particular job, then they should be allowed to do it—their gender is irrelevant.

73b1 ["temperately and justly"]: in theory, Meno could claim that temperance and justice for women are different than they are for men, but there would be two problems with such a response. First, it seems false. The Greek cultural stereotype that women are morally weaker than men when it comes to resisting temptations of food, drink and sex does not seem to entail that women's temperance is different from men, rather it seems to entail that women are less temperate than men. Also, if justice is rendering to each their due (*Republic* 1.331e3-4), or helping one's friends and harming one's enemies (*Republic* 1.332d5-8), then it holds equally with men and women. Second, this response on Meno's part might be *ad hoc*, or question-begging: it's not clear that he could give any reason for such a claim other than that he has to say it in order to defend his view that virtue is different for women and men.

74a5 ["magnificence"]: *megaloprepeia*. Aristotle distinguishes *megaloprepeia* (*Nicomachean Ethics* 4.2) from *megalopsuchia* ("magnanimity," 4.3): magnificence has to do with great sums of money, magnanimity has to do with large honors.

75a5 ["the same in all these cases?"]: here and at 75a7 Socrates uses the pronoun *autos* (the same) and not the adjective *homoios* (similar). The latter is compatible with nominalism with respect to universals, the former is not (if Socrates intends it literally). See note on *Euthyphro* 5d1.

75c2 ["foolish"]: *euēthēs*. This is the word Socrates uses to describe his own claim that "nothing other than beauty itself makes something beautiful" (*Phaedo* 100d4-5): the claim seems uninformative, and to someone who does not understand "beauty itself" it is unhelpful. This may be an example of *ignotum per ignotius*, i.e. an explanation of something unknown (or unfamiliar) by citing something even less known (or even more unfamiliar). Here Meno may have in mind the related *ignotum per aeque ignotum*, i.e. an explanation of something unknown (or unfamiliar) by citing something equally unknown (or equally unfamiliar). Explaining shape in terms of color won't help anyone who is equally ignorant of both shape and color. These need not be fallacies—especially if you go on eventually to clarify these unknowns by reference to things known—because reality is often stranger than fiction, and there are cases where the true explanation of something known is incomplete until we figure out something currently unknown to us.

75c5 ["didn't understand what color is"]: if the question, "what is the same in all shapes" puzzles you, then you will probably be equally puzzled by "what is the same in all colors." Both are indeed puzzling questions, because ordinarily we content ourselves with a simple grasp of particular shapes and particular colors, rarely pausing to ask about the universal.

75c9 ["eristic"]: see *Euthydemus* 272b10. Euthydemus and Dionysodorus are clear examples of eristics. "Debaters" translates *agōnistikos*, which means fit for contest or combat. Both eristics and debaters seem to be the sort of people Socrates does not want to become, i.e. those who love victory more than they love wisdom (*Phaedo* 91a2-3).

75d4 ["more suited to dialectic than to eristic"]: perhaps all Socrates says here is that he would answer in a more conversational tone. But I do think the is contrasting dialectic with eristic. To see what the difference is, contrast the way Euthydemus and Dionysodorus carry on an argument in the *Euthydemus* with the way that Socrates carries on an argument here in the *Meno* (cf. *Charmides, Laches, Euthyphro*). Two important differences between dialectic and eristic are about to be mentioned. See note on 75d6.

75d6 ["the person being asked questions says that he knows"]: this is Socrates' regular "Sincerity Requirement." See 83d2 below, as well as *Laches* 193c7; *Crito* 49d1; *Protagoras* 331b8-d1; *Gorgias* 495a5-b6, 500b; *Republic* 346a; and *Theaetetus* 154c7-e6. Neither Euthydemus nor Dionysodorus express a sincerity requirement. Socrates does not want his interlocutors to be willing to contradict themselves if they say what they sincerely believe the truth to be; he does not want them to say things they don't believe simply in order to avoid contradicting something they've already admitted. Socratic dialectic, therefore, is more concerned with truth than with victory, whereas eristic and agonistic is more concerned with victory than with truth.

75e3 ["Prodicus"]: see *Charmides* 163d4 (and the note). See also *Laches* 197d3.

76b5 ["good-looking"]: *kalos*. On the difference between *kalos* and *kallos* see note on *Charmides* 154a3. Perhaps "handsome" is a better translation here, but since he uses *kalos* in a more general way at 76c2, the same translation is probably best in both places.

76c7 ["emanations or effluences"]: *aporroē*. Literally this means a flowing off, an outflow or a stream, e.g. streams of blood (Euripides, *Helen* 1587). Socrates immediately brings up Empedocles because Gorgias studied with him.

76d3 ["comprehend my meaning"]: we no longer have the original poem by Pindar, so we do not know the original context of this phrase. Phaedrus quotes this line to Socrates at *Phaedrus* 236d2 when he is begging Socrates to give a speech. At *Birds* 945 Aristophanes has a poet utter this line when he's indirectly asking for a handout. So this phrase can be an ancient equivalent of "catch my drift," when you are begging something from someone but don't want to come right out and ask for it. Tone is not always easy to discern: some scholars think that this quotation adds to an air of mock-profundity. Alternatively, by including the likes of Gorgias, Empedocles and Pindar, Socrates is keeping the conversation on grounds that are quite familiar to Meno. I cannot imagine Socrates uttering the next sentence to Charmides, Laches or to Euthyphro.

76e3 ["distinguished"]: *tragikos* is an adjective derived from *tragos*, which refers to a male goat, so literally it means male-goat-like. But since the Greek "tragedies" derived ultimately from primitive "goat songs" (probably sung at the ritual sacrifice of a goat), the adjective *tragikos* came to refer to the majestic or stately style of Greek tragedies. But tone is difficult to discern; this word can be used to imply that something is pompous or overblown.

76e4 ["shape is the limit of a solid"]: Socrates does not explicitly repeat this account here, so he could be referring to his earlier claim that shape is the only thing that always accompanies color (75b10-11).

76e6-7 ["it is not the better of the two"]: Socrates doesn't say why. Empedocles' theory raises at least three concerns. (1) The emanations strike inanimate objects, which seems to entail that inanimate objects have perceptions. (2) Empedocles also believes that emanations fitting pores explains magnetism and the fact that leaves drop from trees in the fall, so the emanation-pore theory doesn't seem to be a theory of perception as much as a basic theory of physics. (3) This emanation-pore theory seems to give only an account of the material causes perception, not of what it is to perceive something (cf. *Phaedo* 96a10 and the note on that passage).

76e9 ["the mysteries"]: the Eleusinian mysteries were founded on the myth of Persephone's abduction by Hades and her return to her mother Demeter. Socrates compares initiation into philosophy with initiation into mysteries in several places: *Gorgias* 497c3-4, *Symposium* 209e5-210a2, *Phaedrus* 250b8-c6, *Theaetetus* 155e3-6. Quite the opposite of making philosophy seem exotic, this rather compares philosophy to something with which Greeks are quite familiar.

77a6 ["as a whole"]: *kata holou*. Probably this phrase is closely related to *kata pantōn* ("applies to everyone") at 73d1 and *kata...pantos* ("every") at 76a5. Compare *kata holon* at *Republic* 3.392d9, and *kath holon* at *Timaeus* 40a7 and 55e7. Socrates' use of *kata holou* here is probably the ultimate source of Aristotle's noun *to katholou*, which he contrasts with *to kath hekaston* ("according to each") at *Metaphysics* 5.1023b29, and with *to kata meros* ("according to part") at *Rhetoric* 1.2.1357b1. This is the distinction between universals and particulars. Aristotle defines a universal as that which is naturally predicated of more than one thing (*De Interpretatione* 7.17a39-40). So universals are properties (e.g. beauty) and relations (e.g. equality). These should be taken broadly so that they include species and types. Universals may also be called "explanatory properties" because they play necessary roles in laws of nature (e.g. Newton's First Law of motion refers to the properties rest and motion, and to the relation force). Modern scientists often claim to be "nominalists" about universals, and so describe laws of nature as mere generalizations or statements based on observations, but both Plato and Aristotle (and probably Socrates) were realists about universals (see note on *Euthyphro* 5d1).

77b3 ["to rejoice in what is fine"]: this exact line does not occur in any extant Greek poem, but the sentiment seems related to Pindar, *Olympian* 1.103-5 and *Pythian* 11.50-1.

77e3 ["things that they think are good"]: we should say that American philosopher W.V.O. Quine (1908-2000) wrote an influential footnote to this passage when he distinguished between *de re* ("of a thing") and *de dicto* ("of a statement") belief-attribution. Consider the famous ancient case of giving someone a love potion to drink, but instead of making them fall in love, it poisons and kills them (Aristotle, *Magna Moralia* 1.16.1188b29-38). I believe (*de dicto*) that "this love potion will make Melitta fall in love with me," and so I want her to drink it. But if it is actually poison that will kill her, I do not believe (*de re*) that this poison will make Melitta fall in love with me, and I do not want her to drink it. This is related to the distinction between *referential transparency* (like *de re*) and *referential opacity* (like *de dicto*). If the sentence "Melitta drank the love potion" is true, and if the love potion is in fact lethal poison, then "Melitta drank the lethal poison" is also true. Hence, "Melitta drank the love potion" is *referentially transparent*: other terms referring to the same thing as "the love potion" can be substituted for that phrase without changing the truth-value of the sentence. However, if the sentence "I want Melitta to drink the love potion" is true, and if the love potion is actually lethal poison, it is nevertheless false to say that "I want Melitta to drink the lethal poison." Hence, "I want Melitta to drink the love potion" is *referentially opaque*: I want her to drink the love potion only under the description "love potion."

78a2 ["are struggling"]: the adjective *athlios* is obviously related to the English word "athletic," and it refers primarily to winning first place in an athletic competition. However, metaphorically its emphasis is on the striving or struggling of competition, and it was used to refer to people who were going through hard times, e.g. suffering through financial or health-related difficulties. Often it means unhappy, wretched, miserable, pitiful.

78a3 ["unhappy?"]: *kakodaimōn* is the opposite of *eudaimōn*, see note on *Charmides* 172a3.

78d3 ["guest-friend"]: *xenos*. *Xenia* was an ancient and extremely important ritualized form of friendship between aristocratic families in different cities. Travel outside your home city left you vulnerable not only to bandits, but to ill treatment by citizens of the city in which you travelled, since you had rights only in your home city. Hence, aristocrats formed bonds of *xenia* with aristocrats in other cities. Your *xenos* would serve as your sponsor and protector when you visited them, and you were expected to do the same for them when they visited you. The relationship involved the exchange of gifts. Part of what made Paris' abduction of Helen so terrible was that it was a profound violation of *xenia*. The relationship between Meno's family and the King of Persia was probably forged when Xerxes invaded Greece (see note on 70b4 above).

78e7 ["refusal or failure"]: *aporia* refers to being without a *poros*, i.e. a means of passage, a ferry or a ford to get over a river. In general it means to be at a loss or to be in a difficulty. The difficulty Socrates has in mind is the desire to acquire gold or silver, but seeing no way to do so justly. He does not clearly indicate a firm moral stand ("refusal") or simply dithering and losing out ("failure").

80a1 ["puzzled"]: *aporeō* (verb related to the noun *aporia*, see note on 78e7); also used at 75c6, 80a2, 80a4, 80c8, 80c9, 80d1, 84a7, 84b1, 84b6. *Aporeō* can refer to doubt, but Socrates has not called Meno's knowledge, or the justification of his beliefs, into question. Alternatively, Meno might be claiming to be "stumped" because he can't seem to find a satisfactory answer to Socrates' question. However, he seems to be implying something more than the obvious. Perhaps he is referring to confusion, but in this case there is an important ambiguity: (a) was Meno perfectly clear prior to talking with Socrates, and Socrates has managed to confuse him, or (b) has Socrates revealed that there is an important issue on which Meno has always been confused without realizing it? In short, is Socrates creating or revealing confusion?

80a6 ["bewitching"]: *goēs*. Orators sometimes use this word in a string of insults where it seems to be the equivalent of swindler, cheater or fraud (e.g. Demosthenes, *On the Crown* 18.276, *On the False*

Embassy 19.109; Aeschines, *On the Embassy* 2.153, *Against Ctesiphon* 3.137). Plato's proposed harsh law against sorcery is against swindlers (*Laws* 10.909b5-6, cf. *Republic* 10.598d3, 602d2) and poisoners (*Laws* 11.933a5). It is unlikely that any Greek city at the time had laws against sorcery or any form of magic because these practices could be used for good purposes (e.g. protection against harm, healing illness, drawing material benefits) as well as for bad (e.g. inflicting harm, causing illness or death, drawing misfortune upon someone). In these latter kinds of cases, the legal action would be for the harm inflicted, not for the use of sorcery or magic in itself. Perhaps some cases against sorcerers could be lodged on the grounds of impiety. That would make sense of Meno's claim here, and it would make this comment a foreshadowing of Anytus' more ominous warning to Socrates later (94e3-95a4).

80c8 ["not because I have all the answers"]: see *Apology* 22e6-23b4.

80c9 ["I am more puzzled than anyone"]: if *aporeō* refers to confusion (see notes on 78e7 and 80a1), then Socrates is probably being ironic. He certainly does not seem to be confused. But if he means that he is more puzzled than anyone, then he may be sincere: he probably is familiar with far more puzzles related to understanding virtue than anyone, and since he regularly claims not to know what virtue is, he cannot claim to know any of the answers to the puzzles he's noticed. See note on 84a4.

80d6 ["you do not know at all what it is?"]: Meno is almost directly quoting Socrates from 71b5-6. But in that earlier passage, Socrates' point was about knowledge, not inquiry.

81a10 ["priests and priestesses"]: possibly Orphics or Pythagoreans. We do not have the poem by Pindar to which Socrates refers.

81b8 ["For when Persephone"]: the meter is dactylo-epitrite, which is often used by Pindar (as well as Bacchylides, and is often found in tragic choral odes). I have alternated iambic and trochaic octameter.

81d1 ["all of nature constitutes one large family"]: obviously Socrates isn't even trying to give more than just a vague sketch of a theory, but the key seems to be the view that the cosmos is not a random collection of unrelated individuals. Why? If the soul has been everywhere and seen everything, then it could contain all information, even if all information consisted in isolated and unrelated facts. The relatedness of things suggests that Socrates isn't thinking of mere recall, but something more like reminding (see *Phaedo* 72e3-76e7; I take it that if seeing x makes me recall seeing y, then earlier I saw y; however, if seeing x puts me in mind of y, it does not necessarily follow that I saw y earlier, though it might imply that in some sense y was in my mind implicitly all along). E.g., if I know that Al is a bachelor, then in some sense I know that he can be married without violating any laws against bigamy, even if it has never occurred to me to think explicitly about Al violating bigamy laws.

82b4 ["Is he Greek?"]: Solon outlawed debt slavery among Athenians, and in general there was a growing sense that it was not right for Greeks to enslave other Greeks (this correlated with a growing sense that it was right for Greeks to enslave non-Greeks). But slavery came in many gradations. Many slaves earned their own livings, made profits and eventually bought their own freedom. Slaves functioned in many capacities, including serving as a sort of police force for the city, clerks for judges, teachers and nannies, as well as the more obvious forms of domestic and agricultural labor. Meno's slave is called "Boy," but that is a sign of lower status, not necessarily a young age. The fact that he was born in Meno's house probably means that his mother (and possibly father) was one of Meno's slaves.

82e12 ["in connecting things together"]: *ephexēs*. This word indicates order, succession or connection. Probably he has in mind the same thing he meant when he said that all of nature is one large family (see note on 81d1). Again, by "recollection" Socrates does not simply mean remembering.

83d2 ["always answer according to your sincere beliefs"]: this is Socrates' "Sincerity Requirement." See 75d6 above, and also note on *Euthydemus* 275e1.

84a1 ["point to where"]: in effect, Socrates is asking the slave what the square root of 8 is. But the square root of 8 is an irrational number (approximately 2.8284). Obviously there is no way that the slave can guess that number accurately. At this point, all he can be sure of is that the number he's looking for is larger than 2 but smaller than 3. Allowing the slave to point to some place on the diagram between 2 and 3 feet makes an impossible arithmetic task manageable—at least as an approximation.

84a4 ["did not realize that he was in fact puzzled"]: Socrates claims that the slave was not in fact clear about the matter—he was puzzled about it all along, in the sense that his thinking about squares and square feet was muddled, but he didn't realize that his thinking was muddled. This suggests that in the earlier conversation with Meno, Socrates believes that he did not confuse Meno, rather, he helped Meno to realize that his own thinking about virtue was in fact muddled (see note on 80c9.

84b10 ["asserted many times to many people"] compare Meno's earlier claim at 80b2-3 that he has "delivered countless grand speeches on virtue to many people." Socrates is clearly drawing parallels between Meno's experience with Socrates' questions and the slave's experience.

84d2 ["gave him any answers"] *diexeimi* refers to going out or through. In a general sense Socrates has already been taking the slave through the issues by drawing diagrams, describing them carefully and in detail, and asking very cleverly designed questions to get him to focus on specific features of the figures involved. None of this is what teachers typically did. Teaching was typically done by giving students step-by-step instructions, and expecting them to repeat these steps accurately many times in a row. In effect, Socrates is insisting on the difference between a liberal and an illiberal education: an illiberal education simply requires teaching students how reliably to accomplish a task; a liberal education focuses on getting the students to understand why the correct solution is correct, regardless of whether that understanding is necessary for reliably accomplishing the task. See note on Protagoras 312b4.

85c4 ["these opinions were inside him"]: Socrates never suggests that the slave had ever before been asked these questions, so it is not clear what he means by saying that these opinions were "inside him." Socrates' most famous opponent on this issue is English philosopher John Locke (1632-1704) who argued that at birth the human mind is a *tabula rasa* ("blank slate"), and that we acquire opinions only by sense perception. In reply, Socrates might point to three features of his conversation with the slave. First, although Socrates did draw figures in the sand, surely they were quite imprecise, which means that the slave did not immediately perceive with any precision the relative sizes of the squares they were comparing (in fact, probably none of the figures drawn were, technically, squares, since their sides could not have been perfectly straight, and their angles could not have been precisely 90-degrees). Second, when the demonstration is over, the slave has learned something about all squares, not just about the ones he saw Socrates draw. If we cannot know things we have not yet perceived, then the slave should be unable to derive knowledge of squares he has not yet seen from squares that he has seen. Third, Socrates asks the slave about what is necessarily true (e.g. at 83d4). Even if we can know by perception that something is actually true, it is not clear how we could know by perception that something is necessarily true. Socrates might argue that after the demonstration the slave clearly knows things that he did not come to know by perception, and that therefore his mind must not have been a *tabula rasa*.

86a7 ["awakened in him to become knowledge"]: Socrates will later emphasize the distinction between true opinion and knowledge (99a1-5). If he is relying on that distinction here, then perhaps he rejects the assumption that knowledge must be based on knowledge (if you know that x is true, and you base your knowledge of x upon y, then you must know that y is true). Socrates' most famous opponent on this issue is French philosopher René Descartes (1596-1650) who seems to insist not only that knowledge is based on knowledge, but that it must be based ultimately on absolutely indubitable knowledge (*Mediations on First Philosophy* 1). If Socrates does reject the assumption that knowledge must be based on knowledge, then he is emphasizing the importance of the truth: as long as (some of?) your beliefs are true, then by the process referred to at 85c9-d1, you will be able to generate genuine knowledge.

86a8 ["for all time?"]: Socrates' argument is valid, but relies on an unproven premise. If the slave has true opinions inside of him for the entire period when he exists in either human or non-human form, and if that period of time is always, then the slave has true opinions inside of him always. What he has not proven is that the slave exists always. The connection between recollection and the immortality of the soul is explored more fully at *Phaedo* 72e3-78b3 (possibly because Plato was himself unsatisfied with this argument here, cf. "I cannot draw all these conclusions definitively" at 86b7).

86d7 ["because you are a free man"]: slaves were not allowed to testify in courts, but their testimony could be considered if it had been acquired by torture. Presumably slaves were expected to say whatever their owners wanted them to say, and that torture was the only way to get the truth from them (perhaps this shielded them from being beaten by their owners if they said something their owners hadn't wanted them to say). Meno, by contrast, is a free man, so he cannot be compelled to do anything against his own will. But this suggests a paradox: insofar as it is a form of control, self-control seems incompatible with freedom; but insofar as it is a form of self-governance, self-control (as opposed to control by someone else) seems to be the very essence of freedom.

86e6 ["whether a given area"]: there have been at least half a dozen proposals as to what the geometrical problem here is supposed to be.

87b7 ["knowledge?"]: *epistēmē*. See note on *Charmides* 154a4, and note on *Meno* 88b4 below.

87d6-7 ["nothing is good that is not encompassed by knowledge"]: *periechō* means encompass, surround or embrace, and so it introduces a crucial ambiguity. Is a knife good or bad? If it is used knowledgeably, then you can do lots of good with it, but if you use it stupidly, you might hurt yourself with it: we might say that a knife is *conditionally good*. So if "encompassed by knowledge" applies to the knowledgeable use of things, then Socrates is saying only that knowledge is necessary for virtue (e.g. if endurance is separated from knowledge, then it is not courage; but if it is encompassed by knowledge, then it is courage). Alternatively, if "encompassed by knowledge" means "is comprised of knowledge" (i.e. it consists of knowledge, cf. 88b1-3), then he is saying that knowledge is sufficient for virtue (e.g. we do not need any additional endurance to make us courageous if we possess knowledge), and he is implying that things like knives (and money, good looks, noble birth and so on) are in fact not goods at all, any goodness they are associated with applies only to the knowledgeable use of such assets. This latter, more extreme view, seems to be what Socrates claims at *Euthydemus* 281e3-5; the former, more moderate view, seems compatible with what Socrates says at *Euthydemus* 281d6-e1. See note on *Euthydemus* 281d4-5.

87d7 ["has something to do with knowledge"]: the manuscripts differ. (1) if Plato wrote *tin' auto*, then he's inferring that virtue is a kind of knowledge, which is highly controversial (many believe that it is possible to know the right thing to do, but fail to have the willpower to do it, so that either virtue is not knowledge or it includes something in addition to knowledge, e.g. willpower). However, (2) if Plato wrote *ti autou*, then he's only inferring the weaker claim in my translation. I've chosen *ti autou* because it is vaguer and is not incompatible with the stronger claim. See note on 89a3.

87e7 ["we say"]: here he uses *legomen*, but just after mentioning health he added *phamen* ("we say," omitted in my translation). Perhaps he means that they definitively, unequivocally, and indefeasibly affirm that they are in fact good. Alternatively, he may mean only that this is what we ordinarily say, but upon reflection (e.g. the considerations Socrates is about to introduce) we will have to change our minds.

88a3 ["what is leading us"]: *hēgeomai* can mean to rule a country. If Socrates has this strong sense in mind, then he is looking for some controlling factor. Alternatively, *hēgeomai* can mean simpy to lead or to guide. This seems a weaker sense, emphasizing the possibility of disobedience.

88a4-5 ["correct use"]: compare *Euthydemus* 280e3.

88a8 ["discernment"]: *eumathia* refers to someone who learns readily (*Charmides* 159e1-7).

88b4 ["intelligence"]: *phronēsis*, see note on *Laches* 192c8, and the note on *Meno* 87b7. Socrates is assuming that *epistēmē* and *phronēsis* are one and the same, or at least that the difference is not significant for his purposes here. Perhaps we should heed his caution at 75e2-5.

88b8 ["Learning and training with sense"]: see *Laws* 8.808d1-809a6 where Plato compares school boys with wild animals. Presumably "training" (*katartuō*) is what temperance amounts to if it is not a form of knowledge or intelligence (*katartuō* occurs at *Laws* 8.808d6). Socrates appears to treat courage and temperance differently. At 88b3-5 he seems to say that courage without intelligence is recklessness, which never benefits us: thoughtful and intelligent action—without recklessness—benefits us. This fits the more extreme view mentioned in the note on 87d6-7. But at 88b6-8 he seems to say that temperance without intelligence is training, which benefits us—and hence is good—on the condition that it is encompassed by sense. This fits the more moderate view mentioned in the note on 87d6-7.

88c6 ["themselves by themselves"]: *auta...kath hauta* (this phrase is used in a similar context at *Euthydemus* 281d4-5, and d8-e1). If he means to say that these things are neither beneficial nor harmful, then he is denying that they are good or bad: goodness and badness attach only to the knowledgeable or ignorant use of them. If he is consistent, then when he says below that wealth is "good sometimes" (see note on 88d5), he's saying only that it can be used to benefit us, and hence that the goodness is in the correct or incorrect use. See note on 87d6-7, and also note on *Euthydemus* 281d4-5).

88d5 ["good sometimes"]: if he is saying that under some conditions things like wealth can be good, then he is affirming that they can be conditionally good (or conditionally bad), and his view here sounds as if it is at odds with the view he expresses in the *Euthydemus* (see note on *Meno* 87d6-7, and also note on *Euthydemus* 281d4-5). If he is asserting here that wealth can be conditionally good, then at 88c6 (see note above) he was not denying that they could be conditionally good, he was only denying that they are unconditionally good (or unconditionally bad).

89a3 ["Intelligence, then, is virtue"]: or "Virtue, then, is intelligence." The difference is significant. If intelligence is the subject, then Socrates is allowing for the possibility that intelligence is only one part of virtue, which is compatible with recognizing other parts of virtue, e.g. endurance. This, in turn has serious implications for Meno's main question: if virtue is part intelligence and part endurance, then it is part teachable and part non-teachable, and the non-teachable part is acquired either by birth or by training. On the other hand, if virtue is the subject, then he is ruling this possibility out: virtue is nothing but intelligence (or one species of intelligence), which would entail that it is entirely teachable (as are all forms of intelligence). See note on 87d7 above.

89b4 ["Acropolis"]: a large hill inside Athens that had been fortified in the 13th century BCE with a massive wall. The most important temples were on the Acropolis, and the treasury was kept in them. Literally, Socrates adds that they would set the city seal upon these blessed children, indicating that they are precious possessions of the city (the door to the public treasury had the seal of Athens on it).

90a4-5 ["the Theban Ismenias"]: in 404 BCE Thebes radically changed its position on the Peloponnesian War from advocating the destruction of Athens to providing refuge for exiled Athenian democrats. This change was probably the result of a group of wealthy democratic Athenians bribing the Theban politician Ismenias (cf. *Republic* 1.336a6 on Ismenias' venality). Maybe an Athenian named Polycrates was one of those who contributed to this bribe. Maybe it was Polycrates the sophist who lived c.440-370 BCE (he was about 11 years older than Plato and he who wrote a work called *The Accusations Against Socrates* which may have been what provoked both Plato and Xenophon to write their works on the same topic). Maybe. But my money is on Polycrates the son of Aiakes. In about 535 BCE he made himself tyrant of Samos (on the island of Samos, off the coast of Asia Minor, due east of Athens), and he was notoriously greedy (Herodotus 3.122-125). His greed led him to a death so disgusting that Herodotus couldn't bring himself to describe it (Herorotus 3.125.3). I suspect that "Polycrates' money" was proverbial for money that you pursues to your own ruin.

90b1 ["raised and educated"]: *trephō* and *paideuō* can both refer to rearing children, but *trephō* tends to refer more to physical growth and maturation, while *paideuō* tends to refer more to training the character, and can refer to correction or discipline. The usual verb for "teach" in the Meno is *didaskō*, which refers to pointing something out, and so is much closer to what we today think of as a teacher.

90b2-3 ["since they select Anytus for the highest offices"]: what is the connection between high political office and raising your son well? Probably it is the same attitude that underlies St. Paul's command that a bishop must "manage his own household well, keeping his children in good order with respect, for if a man does not know how to manage his own household, how will he take care of God's assembly?" (1 Timothy 3:4-5).

90d4 ["anyone who wishes to learn"]: see note on *Charmides* 155b2. Then, as now, not everybody who claims to be a doctor is entirely on the up and up.

91a2 ["he was telling me"]: Meno never explicitly told Socrates of this desire in this dialogue. Either Socates is lying; or we are to understand that Meno expressed this desire to him before the beginning of this dialogue (e.g. during a speech that Meno delivered just prior to engaging with Socrates); or Socrates is assuming that during their conversatition, Meno implicitly expressed this desire.

91b6 ["Who are you referring to"]: Anytus is surprised. He blandly accepted Socrates' premise regarding doctors, shoemakers, flute players and so on, but Socrates' previous question clearly describes sophists like Protagoras, Gorgias and Prodicus, to whom Anytus seems to have an antipathy. In other words, Socrates' question was deliberately provocative.

91c1 ["Herakles!"]: invoking Herakles is not as common as the exclamation "by god" or "by Zeus," which is rather bland (like "by heavens!" today); and sometimes it expresses more emotion. Here Anytus is clearly agitated by the Sophists. Keep in mind that (1) Athens had recently lost the Peloponnesian War (with a tremendous number of casualties), (2) the democracy has been forcibly replaced by an oligarchy of anti-democratic Athenians (3) who purged as many pro-democracy advocates as they could, but (4) the democratic faction re-took the city in a bloody battle, and (5) many people in the restored democracy wanted revenge against the supporters of the oligarchy who had done them wrong (e.g. murdered a family member). It was a time of closing ranks, and knowing who your friends were and who your enemies were. The amnesty of 403 (imposed by Sparta) prevented Athenians from "remembering wrongs" committed by anyone except for a few named oligarchs, and so much desire for legal revenge was thwarted. Clearly the sophists played no direct role in Athens' recent calamities, but were they "us" or "them"?

91d2 ["enough evidence to trust you"]: *pisteuō* refers primarily to placing trust or faith in, or relying upon, a person, thing or statement. Typically, a basis for trust is assumed or implied, and Socrates has already laid out evidence in support of the sophists, so here he challenges Anytus to provide evidence against them. Some think Socrates is ironically supporting the sophists here. Alternatively, he is inducing Meno and Anytus to base their judgment of the sophists on a fair consideration of all the relevant evidence.

91d4 ["Phidias"]: see note on *Protagoras* 311c4.

92b2 ["the cities that allow these people in"]: cf. *Laches* 197d6-8 where Laches takes a similar but less radical position against the sophists. Notice also the opposition drawn by Laches as well as here (*Meno* 90b2-3) between sophists and elected political leaders. The latter fear the former as rivals.

92b4 ["or citizens"]: among other things, this is a reference to the trial and execution of Socrates.

92c6 ["seer"]: see notes on *Laches* 195e1, 199a2 and *Euthyphro* 3e3.

92d5 ["I was just describing"]: at 91a2-6.

92d7 ["I supposed"]: *oiomai* covers a spectrum of attitudes from definite belief to indefinite suspicion or foreboding. Since Socrates' case in favor of the sophists was purely superficial and obvious (e.g. they claim to teach it) he's probably not asserting here that he definitely belives that they do teach virtue.

92e4 ["fine and good"]: *kaloi kagathoi* is an old phrase that used to refer to the upper class, and so in a superficial sense it implied that they were well adorned and wealthy. In a political sense it implied that they they acted in the state's best interest and were powerful. In a moral sense it implied that they were magnanimous and courageous. But it is deliberately vague, implying a range of admirable attributes. In democratic Athens its implicit reference is not to the upper class, but to the *dēmos* generally, and it applies to people who are respectable, law-abiding and hard working. Anytus would not apply this phrase to rich people with aristocratic lineages and who sought to undermine or overthrow the democracy.

93a5-6 ["there are many good statesmen here"]: Socrates denies that there are good statesmen in Athens at *Gorgias* 517a1-2. The touchstone he uses in both places is quite similar because both here and in the *Gorgias* Socrates looks to the effect that statesmen have on those around them—here he focuses on their children, in the *Gorgias* he focuses on the people more generally. It is important to note that Socrates' claim at *Gorgias* 517a1-2 happens after a substantial argument about numerous individual statesmen, whereas this statement here occurs prior to any consideration of cases. Also, the denial in the *Gorgias* is strong ("we know none," *oudena hēmeis ismen*) but the affirmation here is weak ("they seem to me to be," *Emoige...einai dokousin*).

93b7 ["Themistocles"]: c.524-459 BCE. Themistocles' most famous success was in leading the Athenian fleet against the Persians at Salamis in 480. Sometime before 460 he was ostracized from Athens, and later he was condemned to death. After 465 the Persian King Artaxerxes I made him governor of Magnesia, where he eventually died. Thucydides admired him (see *The Peloponnesian War* 1.138.2-3).

93d4 ["accurately throw a javelin while riding"]: humans probably began riding horses around 4000 BCE. The earliest saddles known are from Assyria around 700 BCE, but they were elaborate and expensive and so probably only to display the wealth of the owner. The earliest known saddles for non-ceremonial use are from northern Iran in the 5th century BCE. Stirrups seem to have been invented in India in the 2nd century BCE. Neither saddles nor stirrups were used in Greece in Plato's lifetime, and so accurately throwing a javelin from horseback was indeed a significant accomplishment.

93d5 ["taught"]: here Socrates uses *paideuō*, but then he switches immediately to *didaskalos* for "teachers" on the next line. See note on 90b1. At 94a5 he uses *didaskalos* and then switches immediately to *paideuō* (and again at 94b4-6).

93e5 ["certainly not"]: Socrates points out the failure of putatively virtuous fathers to pass on their virtue to their sons at *Alcibiades* 188d10-e8, *Laches* 179b7-180c4, and *Protagoras* 319d7-320b3. Together, Socrates and Anytus consider several possible explanations: (1) virtuous fathers are unable to teach their virtue (rejected at 92e3-93a4), (2) virtuous fathers are unwilling to teach their virtue (rejected at 93c5-d7), (3) the children are morally ineducable (rejected in the case of Cleophantus at 93d9-e1). If this phenomenon cannot be explained, then more radical possibilities should be considered, e.g. (4) virtue cannot be taught (cf. 93e8, 94e2), or (5) allegedly virtuous fathers are not in fact virtuous (cf. 93e10-11; such morally complacent people might well be in need of a divinely sent gadfly to sting them out of their self-satisfied slumber, cf. *Apology* 30e1-31a7).

94a1 ["Aristides"]: a contemporary of Themistocles; but whereas Themistocles was associated with democracy and the common citizen, Aristides was associated with aristocracy and the upper class. Famously called "Aristides the Just," one story has it that during an ostracism vote he helped a man write a name on his *ostrakon* (pottery shard). He asked the illiterate man what name he wanted written, and the man said "Aristides the Just." When Aristides asked why the man replied, "Because I'm sick and tired of hearing everyone call him 'the Just'." Aristides wrote his own name on the *ostrakon*, which was indeed the just thing to do. In the *Gorgias*, Socrates admires him for not being corrupted by power (526b2), though he would fail the test for being a good statesman that he sets for Pericles, Cimon, Miltiades and Themistocles (cf. 515b6-517a6).

94a1 ["Lysimachus"]: Aristides' father and first born son were both named Lysimachus. It was common for Athenians to name their first born son after their father (*Laches* 179a3-4), so having a grandfather with your same name was common. Pericles' father and first born son were both named Xanthippus (94b2). Lysimachus, the son of Aristides, tells the sad story of how his father neglected him at *Laches* 179b7-180c4.

94b1 ["Pericles"]: c.495-429 BCE. The most famous statesman of Classical Athens. Culturally, religiously, militarily and politically he was very involved and influential in the city's affairs. He and his two sons died from the plague. Socrates (or Plato) seems to have thought that he was not a good statesman (*Gorgias* 515b6-516d4).

94b6 ["everything else that takes skill"]: *technē* applies to quite a lot, and I'm fairly certain that Pericles did not teach his sons stonecutting, sculpting, painting, carpentry, tanning and every other craft. Probably he has in mind something like the generic distinction drawn in the *Republic* between three branches of education: *grammata* (i.e. basic literacy, reading and writing; 3.402a7-b3), *gumnastikē* (physical, athletic and military training; 3.403c9-d5), and *mousikē* (music in our modern sense, but also including poetry, and hence theology, history and whatever poets write about; see notes on *Laches* 180d1 and *Phaedo* 60e6); cf. *Protagoras* 312b1-2 where Socrates distinguishes the *grammatistēs*, the *kitharistēs*, and the *paidotribēs*.

94b9 ["careless"]: the superlative of *phaulos*, which can mean inferior, either socially or morally. If this is what Socrates is saying, then he is insulting people whom Anytus admires, and we might expect some immediate reaction from Anytus, even to the point of interrupting Socrates. But *phaulos* can be a compliment when it refers to someone who is simple, direct and honest, without artificiality or insincerity. This does not fit the context because whatever *phaulos* is doing here, it is not a compliment—it is explaining the failure to make one's own sons virtuous. A third sense of *phaulos* is related to the second: a simple and direct person can act without a lot of complicated scheming, and so can do things in an off-hand, comparatively thoughtless, indifferent or careless manner. I think this is what Socrates is saying: perhaps these great statesmen were so busy with running the city that they neglected the moral education of their own sons (cf. *Laches* 180b1-7).

94c1 ["Thucydides"]: born around 500 BCE, ostracized in 443, probably returned in 433 and died sometime later in old age. This is the son of Melesias, not the son of Olorus (the historian, though both were probably related). Thucydides was Pericles' main rival after the death of Cimon. He was said to have opposed Pericles' extravagant building plan.

94d4 ["common man"]: *phaulos*. Again (see note on 94b9), this word can be taken as an insult, though here it is explicitly opposed to the notion of being influential with a lot of people and having a substantial social network.

94d5 ["or her allies?"]: in this context Abdera (birth place of Protagoras) and Leontini (birth place of Gorgias) will likely come to mind. This tacit implication, together with the implicit but obvious contrast with the failure of luminaries like Themistocles, Aristides and Thucydides to educate their own sons in virtue, clearly explain Anytus' upcoming outburst (compare what prompted his earlier outburst at 91c1).

94e3 ["speak ill"]: how has Socrates spoken ill of Athenian statesmen? Some have suggested that Anytus is upset on the grounds that Socrates is implying that Themistocles and the others were not truly virtuous. However, Socrates' explicit argument so far has not been "if they were truly virtuous, then they would have taught their sons to be virtuous," but "if virtue were teachable, then they would have taught their sons to be virtuous" (see note on 93e5). Alternatively, because Anytus has accepted that everything Socrates said about Athenian statesmen was common knowledge, perhaps he is upset that Socrates would explicitly mention these embarrassing facts—especially in front of his guest-friend Meno. Also, the mere use of the word *phaulos* (see notes on 94b9 and 94d4) may have rubbed Anytus the wrong way (although, see note on 96d5).

94e6 ["easy to do ill"]: the manuscripts have the adjective *rhadion* (easy), but some have speculated that Plato actually wrote the comparative adjective *rhaon* (easier). If he wrote *rhaon*, then he has Anytus say that in other cities it is easier to do someone harm than to do them good, and in Athens it is even easier. While this may be true (see note on 95a1), it hardly puts Athens in a good light, and Anytus seems eager to defend Athens. In either case, Socrates is not worried because he thinks that the ability of the populace to do someone great harm or benefit is greatly over estimated (see *Crito* 44d6-10, see also notes on *Crito* 44d7 and 44d9).

95a1 ["in Athens it is much easier"]: I do not doubt that Plato intended the reader to recall that Anytus did join the prosecution against Socrates (cf. *Apology* 30b8). However, the explicit reference is probably to Athenian slander laws (Athens had no laws against libel, i.e. defamation in writing). In the 6th century BCE Solon made it illegal to speak ill of the dead, and illegal to speak ill of the living while in a temple, a legal trial, a festival contest or while carrying out official public duties. We don't know how long Solon's laws against speaking ill of the living remained in effect, but his law against speaking ill of the dead was still in force during the 4th century BCE. Sometime prior to 384 a law was passed that forbade several specific slanders, e.g. falsely claiming that someone was a murderer, a father-beater, a mother-beater, had thrown his shield away (Lysias, *Against Theomnestos* 10.6-9), or that someone's mother had worked as a common laboror in the marketplace (Demosthenes, *Against Eubulides* 57.30). Other specific allegations may have been forbidden the law. There were also laws against the verbal abuse of magistrates. Prior to 414 (but not after), public comedies (e.g. the plays of Aristophanes) were exempt from libel laws (except for a brief period from 440-436).

95a5 ["to slander someone"]: some scholars speculate that this is a foreboding prophecy that Plato placed here, knowing that indeed Anytus later did fall victim to slander. Alternatively, Plato is employing dramatic irony since we know that in the end it is Socrates who will fall victim to Anytus' slander (cf. *Apology* 23d7-24a4), and not the other way around.

95c4 ["clever speakers"]: this is exactly the sort of speaker Socrates claims not to be (*Apology* 17b1).

95d1 ["Theognis"]: 6th (or 7th) century poet from Megara (between Athens and Corinth). He composed elegiac verse (i.e. poems consisting of couplets in which the first line is dactylic hexameter and the second is dactylic pentameter). "Elegy" derives from *elegos*, which is a sung lament, so probably the elegiac metre was stereotypical of such songs, though poets (including Theognis) used it for a wide variety of purposes (including bawdy drinking songs for banquets). We have a collection of 1,400 verses that are attributed to Theognis, but probably they were not all written by him.

95d3 ["In the elegiac lines"]: my translations are very literal, not elegiac. Apparantly these four lines were quite popular, since we see them quoted or referred to by several people (e.g. Xenophon, *Memorabilia* 1.2.20, *Symposium* 2.4; Aristotle, *Nicomachean Ethics* 9.9.1170a11-13, 9.12.1172a12-14). Socrates' quotation here does not exactly match the manuscripts we have of Theognis (see note on 95d6). There are other places where Socrates' quotations do not seem exact (e.g. see notes on *Apology* 28c6 and 28d2), but there are places where our manuscripts of Theognis are clearly errant (e.g. some manuscripts have the fourth line of this poem begin with *summigēs*, which is metrically unacceptable).

95d6 ["you will learn"]: Socrates uses *didaxeai*, which is related to *didaskalos* (see notes on 90b1 and 93d5). This word makes these lines obviously relevant to what Meno, Anytus and Socrates have been discussing, and in that context it does not seem unreasonable to interpret Theognis as affirming that virtue is teachable. Our manuscripts of Theognis do not have *didaxeai* but *mathēseai*, from *manthanō*, which means to learn (it is the root of the English word "math"). Some have argued that this was a deliberate verbal trick on Socrates' part to distort Theognis' poem for his own purposes. However, *mathēseai* provides just as reasonable a basis for interpreting Theognis as affirming that virtue is teachable, especially if you agree with Meno and Socrates that without *didaskaloi*, there can be no *mathētai* (96c1). A more important issue with this line is that Aristotle clearly thinks that the form of education Theognis has in mind is *askēsis*, i.e. practice, exercise or cultivation (*Nicomachean Ethics* 9.9.1170a11, cf. 1.9.1099b9-20). For Aristotle, the difference is important: virtue requires training so that we feel pleasure and pain properly. E.g. a continent person will stand fast in battle, but he'll suffer from great fear, a virtuous person will stand fast in battle and will not suffer from such fear (2.3.1104b5-9). It is not clear that Socrates agrees with Aristotle on this point.

95e4 ["says something like this"]: I've put the next five quoted lines together and eliminated Socrates' comments breaking them and indicating that he is not entirely certain that he's quoting them exactly right.

96a1 ["by teaching"]: *didaskōn*. There is no dispute about this word in these lines, and so if *didaxeai* is correct at 95d6 (see note on 95d6), then Socrates does have sufficient textual warrant for interpreting these lines as being on the same topic as the lines he quoted earlier. Furthermore, if the distinction between the good and the bad is between people who are and people who are not virtuous, then the former lines imply the answer "yes" while the current lines imply the answer "no" to the question, "Is it possible to get people who are not virtuous to be virtuous by teaching them?"

96a3 ["exactly the opposite"]: Socrates has sufficient textual warrant to draw this conclusion (see note on 96a1). But, of course, alternative interpretations of the quoted lines may be equally warranted. E.g. if

Theognis would allow that it is possible to lack virtue without being bad, then in these lines he may be saying that it is not possible to teach bad people to be virtuous, while in the lines quoted earlier he is implying that it is possible to teach non-virtuous people to be virtuous as long as they are not bad. Or in the earlier lines Theognis may be implying that naturally good people can be benefitted by associating with cultivated people, while in these lines he is implying the compatible claim that people who are naturally bad can never be made good.

96a6 ["this seems to be, Meno"]: this sentence is not in the text, but what Socrates says in Greek is long and complex, so I've make the syntax simpler and added bits to make it clearer.

96c3 ["didn't we agree"]: see 89d6-e5.

96d6 ["negligent"]: *phaulos*. This remark expresses self-deprecating humility, not shameful self-insult. This suggests that Socrates' use of this word in reference to the allegedly fine and good statesmen of Athens was not intended as an insult (see notes on 94b9 and 94d4). Some scholars see irony in Socrates' reference to Prodicus: he *says* that he is Prodicus' student and hasn't learned enough, but he *means* that what Prodicus does is worthless. Alternatively, he means just what he has said, and that either they have more to learn from Gorgias and Prodicus respectively, or they've learned as much as they can about virtue from their respective teachers and must begin to look elsewhere.

97a1 ["Were we right to agree"]: at 87e1-2.

97a6 ["knowledge"]: literally, "if they were not *phronimos*." Normally I would translate this adjective as "intelligent" (*phronimos* is related to *phronēsis*, see note on *Laches* l92c8). But given what Socrates goes on to say, it seems that he is not distinguishing *phronēsis*, *oida* (97a9) or *epistēmē* (97b2). Socrates associates the careful distinction of word meanings with Prodicus (see *Charmides* 163d4 with its note, and also *Laches* 197d3).

97a9 ["Larissa"]: chief city in Thessaly. It was named after a nymph who was the legendary mother of several local heroes. Larissa was the seat of power for the Aleuad clan (see 70b2-5 and notes on 70b2 and 70b4).

97b1 ["true belief"]: *orthōs…doxazōn*, or "correct opinion."

97b9 ["action"]: *praxis* is used here and at 98b8, 98c2, 99b2 (and earlier it was used at 72a3, 79b9, 79c5). Both *praxis* and *poiēsis* can refer loosely to doing something, but Aristotle sometimes restricts *praxis* to actions that are done (a) intentionally, or (b) both intentionally and because of a reasoned decision, or most strictly of all, to actions that are done (c) intentionally, because of a reasoned decision, and partly for its own sake, not exclusively for some goal, aim or end beyond the action itself. When Aristotle contrasts *praxis* and *poiēsis*, he has (c) in mind, so that *poiēsis* refers to productive activity that aims at producing something separate from the activity itself (*Nicomachean Ethics* 1.1, 6.4-5). A professional potter making a pot for commercial purposes may be an example of *poiēsis* ("production"); an amateur potter making a pot simply for the joy of making pots may be an example of *praxis* ("action" in the strictest sense). If we rely on this Aristotelian distinction, then Socrates' point would be more clearly put if he used *poiēsis* as opposed to *praxis*: he is concerned exclusively with the outcome of the activity, not whether the activity is done knowledgeably.

97c11 ["I wonder"]: at *Theaetetus* 155d2-4 Socrates says that philosophy begins with wonder.

97d6 ["Daedalus"]: see note on *Euthyphro* 11c1. Two theories are supported by ancient evidence. One is that an ancient sculptor created statues that actually moved, either by the judicious use of mercury (Aristotle, *De Anima* 1.3.406b18-18) or by some mechanical contrivance (Callistratus, *Ekphrasis* 8). Alternatively, several revolutions in Greek sculpture were in the direction of remarkably more lifelike productions (e.g. eyes open, one leg stepping forward), leading new audiences to marvel at how the statues seem as if they could get up and walk away (Diodorus Siculus, *Library of History* 4.76.2-3).

98a3-4 ["figuring out what is responsible"]: *aitias logismō*. My intention in this translation is to be quite literal, and hence to be neutral with respect to the many different views that scholars have taken of this phrase. One prominent view is that Socrates is here giving what has been the dominant view in European philosophy, i.e. knowledge is justified true belief. Of course, this analysis is little help without an explanation of what justification consists in. Alternatively, it has been argued that Socrates is saying that knowledge is true believe with an explanatory account of what we believe to be true. Of course this is little help without an explanation of the difference between explanation and justification. This passage also bears on two other important issues. First, metaphysically Socrates seems to assume that we can have knowledge and true belief of the very same things (since we first have a true belief about it, and then when we figure out what is responsible for it's being true we have knowledge of it). Some scholars have argued that in the *Republic*, Plato denies that we can have knowledge and true belief of the very same things (roughly, and allegedly, knowledge is of forms and not sensible particulars, belief is of sensible particulars and not forms). Second, epistemologically Socrates seems to assume that we can gain knowledge by relying on mere true beliefs. In other words, knowledge does not have to be based upon knowledge. If this is what he is implying here, then his view is probably incompatible with what has come to be called "epistemological foundationalism," which assumes that in order to know a proposition P, we must prove that it is true by relying upon premises that are already known to be true.

98a5 ["as we agreed earlier"]: this is the first mention of an *aitias logismos*, so perhaps Socrates is simply connecting this point with their earlier claim that recollection is the way that we turn true beliefs into knowledge (i.e. 85b8-86b4).

98b5 ["one thing I know"]: perhaps the fact that he uses *oida* and not *epistēmē* is significant, but perhaps not (cf. note on 97a6). In any case, this is a remarkable admission for Socrates to make.

99b8 ["it isn't because of knowledge"]: a thoughtful Greek reader who is familiar with Plato's Socratic dialogues will perceive a duality here. On the one hand, the mention of *tuchē* ("chance") at 99a3 above will suggest divine intervention; but on the other hand, the denial of knowledge and wisdom will suggest ignorance and folly. If we think that Socrates is implying the former, but means the latter, then we will think that he is being ironic. On the other hand, if he is honestly and openly following a line of reasoning, then we will think that he is allowing for the possibility of the former without explicitly ruling out the latter.

99b11 ["good judgement"]: *eudoxia* usually refers to the good opinion that people have of you. This suggests another duality (see note on 99b8): (1) people like Themistocles lead the people because of the true beliefs they have about which policies are best, or (2) they lead the people only because people have a good opinion of them (e.g. people naively assume that they know what they are doing).

99c3 ["prophets or seers"]: see *Apology* 22c2 where Socrates uses both *chrēsmōdos* (prophet) and *theomantis* (seer). The "-*ōdos*" part of *chrēsmōdos* is related to the English word "ode," and refers to a chant, song or poem. If an oracle did not deliver a simple "yes" or "no" answer, then it might convey the will of the gods in verse (which, of course, must be interpreted carefully). On *mantis* see notes on *Charmides* 169b4;, *Laches* 195e1, 199e2; and *Euthyphro* 3e3.

99c5 ["what they are saying is true"]: a more extreme translation is possible, e.g. "they are in a state of religious ecstasy and are not in their right minds, so they do not comprehend what they are doing." My translation is modest because most of us are familiar with enthusiastic (*enthousiazō*, 99c3-4) people who get caught up in the moment and succeed in doing something wonderful, despite the fact that they didn't actually know that they were doing the right thing, or that they would succeed. In terms that have been explored in the *Meno* we might say that they are recollecting some truths from within their souls, but they have not worked out in detail what is actually responsible for the truth of their true beliefs.

100a2 ["impart his expertise to others"]: here Socrates envisions a form of virtue that could be taught, given that the form of virtue they've been assuming so far seems clearly incapable of being taught.

100a5 ["flitting shadows"]: Homer, *Odyssey* 10.495. Socrates also quotes this line at *Republic* 3.386d7. Compare (a) political leaders who set the country's economic policy without consulting the science of economics with (b) hypothetical political leaders who are scientific experts in both macroeconomics and microeconomics, and whose policies rest on conclusions that are just as surely known as the firmest results in mathematics, geometry, physics, chemistry and biology. The opinions of the former may shift with every change in the political breeze, though they may occasionally be correct, and may occasionally recommend policies that turn out to be more beneficial than detrimental, but this will be accidental.

100b2-3 ["divine allotment"]: *theia moira* could also be translated "by divine fate." *Moira* refers to a part as opposed to a whole, and so can refer to a portion of land, or one's share of an inheritance. The notion of one's allotted portion (e.g. "my lot in life") can be blamed on the gods as one's "destiny," "fate" or "doom." But the notion of fatalism (i.e. some events are matters of inescapable necessity, so that if we are fated to do something, it will occur no matter what we choose or do) has not arisen in the discussion so far. They have not ruled out, e.g., the possibility that we can influence the gods' decision to give us virtue.

100b5 ["in what way people become virtuous"]: see 71a1-b8, 86d3-e1.

100b6 ["itself by itself"]: *auto kath hauto*. Sometimes Socrates uses this phrase to indicate separation (i.e. independent existence; cf. *Phaedo* 64c6 and the note on that passage). Here there is no indication that virtue could exist in separation from a person who is virtuous, so he is probably thinking of the virtue of the virtuous person in isolation from other properties the person may have.

NOTES ON PHAEDO

57a1 ["You yourself"]: *autos* ("self") is the first word of the *Phaedo* (it is also the first word of Phaedo's reply). Self examination is a hallmark of Socratic philosophy (cf. *Apology* 38a5-6).

57a2 ["hemlock mixture"]: Echecrates does not explicitly mention hemlock (*kōneion* never occurs in the *Phaedo*, but we know from other sources that this was the plant used to make the poison, cf. Lysias, *Against Eratosthenes* 12.17). He uses the word *pharmakon*. This is a dangerous word for translators since it can mean either "cure" or "poison," and it can refer to a natural herbal "decoction" or to a supernatural magical "potion." It is the root of the English word "pharmaceutical." Since a major concern of this dialogue is whether death is to be feared or welcomed, I suspect that Plato wanted to plant these ambiguities in the mind of the reader at the outset.

58a4 ["so long after"]: normally the penalty was imposed immediately after the jury determined it.

58a6 ["Coincidence"]: *tuchē* is a tricky word. On the grand side it can refer to unalterable fate, divine providence or the direct intervention of a god. It is sometimes personified as a savior (Pindar, *Olympian* 12.2; Aeschylus, *Agamemnon* 664). I mention this because Plato is about to use the verb for salvation three times (*sōzō* at 58b1-2). Literally *tuchē* is related to the verb *tunchanō*, which simply means "to happen," so "happenstance" might be a good translation. Sometimes "fortune," "luck" or "chance" are appropriate translations, but today those English words are often associated with games or with the notion that some events can be truly random, and probably those associations are not what Plato intends here.

58a10-11 ["the very ship that Theseus sailed"]: this ship was, and continues to be, the focus of a paradox (sometimes called "The Paradox of Theseus' Ship," or just "Theseus' Paradox"). It's earliest written statement is by Plutarch (*Theseus* 23.1). The ship had been preserved from the mythical time of Theseus down to the reign of Demetrius Phalereus (c.350-c.280 BCE), replacing rotting wood as necessary. But if the material components were not the very same ones that had composed the ship when Theseus sailed it, can the ship itself truly be one and the same as the ship that Theseus sailed? Plutarch poses this as a question of "growth" (*auxanō*), which makes the problem urgent: through eating, drinking and elimination we continually lose and replace the material components that make up our bodies—if the ship that existed in the time of Demetrius Phalereus was not one and the same as the ship that Theseus sailed, then the adult you is not one and the same as the infant you. Or, to couch the same paradox in Heraclitean terms: if you cannot step into the same river twice, then you cannot meet the same person twice. This exacerbates a main problem of the *Phaedo*: if we cannot account for our survival from one moment to the next, then how can we possibly account for our post-mortem survival?

58a11 ["the Minotaur"]: Plato does not explicitly mention the Minotaur, he mentions only the "Twice Seven," i.e. the tribute of seven boys and seven girls brought every nine years to Crete. Of course there were many different versions of the story, but the outline is that Androgeos, the son of King Minos and Queen Pasiphaë, travelled from Crete to Attica and was murdered in Athens. In retaliation, Minos repeatedly attacked Athens. As if that wasn't enough, Athenian rivers dried up and pestilence was upon the land. To atone for its crime, Athens was required to make the sacrifice of the "Twice Seven" every nine years. Some say that the half-man, half-bull Minotaur ate the sacrifices in the inescapable labyrinth beneath the palace. Others say that the fourteen youths were simply enslaved (Plutarch, *Theseus* 16). Before his voyage to save the youths, Theseus dedicated an olive branch decorated with pure white wool to Apollo.

58c9 ["without his friends"]: see note on *Apology* 40c5.

58d2 ["tell us"]: it is clear that there are more people in addition to Phaedo and Echecrates assembled, but there is no indication of how many or who they are (cf. 102a8).

58d8 ["as accurately as you can"]: at *Symposium* 173b1-6 Apollodorus says that after hearing an account of the speeches he later repeats, he checked on some of the details with Socrates who confirmed them. Even so, scholars find it difficult to believe that the *Symposium* is anything other than a Platonic fiction—though perhaps it was based on a real event. Such a skeptical view seems even more justified in this case: both in philosophical method and doctrine the Socrates we have in this dialogue seems quite distinct from the Socrates of the *Charmides*, *Laches*, *Euthyphro*, *Euthydemus*, *Apology*, *Crito*, and *Protagoras* (though there is some similarity with Socrates at *Meno* 81b3-e2). One crucial question is how we interpret the "I think" at 59b10 where Phaedo says, "But Plato, I think, was sick."

58e5 ["Hades"]: the pagan Hades is not to be confused with the Christian Hell. See note on *Apology* 41a1.

59b6 ["Apollodorus"]: of the people mentioned here, Plato also says that Apollodorus, Critobulus, Crito, Epigenes, Aeschines (and Plato himself) were also present at Socrates' trial (*Apology* 33d8-34a2). Ctesippus of Paeania is in Plato's *Euthydemus* and *Lysis*. Menexenus was a good friend of Lysis' (*Lysis* 212a1), and sought Socrates' political advice in the *Menexenus* (at 234b3-7). Simmias and Cebes brought money to help Socrates escape from prison and presumably to take him back with them to Thebes (*Crito* 45b4-5). Aeschines would later achieve some notoriety for his Socratic dialogues and as a legal speech writer. Antisthenes would later become a very influential "Cynic" philosopher. Euclides, perhaps with the help of Terpsion, founded a philosophical school in Megara, where Plato took refuge after the death of Socrates. Of the people here named as present, it is inconceivable that only Simmias and Cebes took a prominent role in the discussion during Socrates' final day—again (see note on 58d8), this dialogue is clearly fictionalized to some extent.

59c3 ["Aristippus and Cleombrotus"]: clearly many people were not present (e.g. Evenus of Paros, 60d3 and *Apology* 20a2-c1); why mention just these two? Perhaps some accident detained them and Plato wanted to do them the honor of mentioning their names as people who would have been there if they could have. "Some honor" might be the reply: why pick them out as *not* being there? According to Diogenes Laertius, Aristippus charged a fee for teaching, and on one occasion sent 20 minae to Socrates, but Socrates' divine sign would not allow him to keep it, and Socrates said that the offer had bothered him (*Lives of the Philosophers* 2.65). In the 3rd century BCE a poem by Callimachus mentions that someone named Cleombrotus committed suicide by jumping off a cliff into the ocean after reading about the immortality of the soul in Plato's *Phaedo* (*Epigram* 23). Perhaps Plato wanted explicitly to separate these two from Socrates. See note on 60a7 below.

59e6 ["the Eleven"]: see notes on *Apology* 37c2 and *Crito* 44a4.

60a2 ["Xanthippe"]: Xenophon composed a dialogue between Socrates and his eldest son Lamprocles in which the latter complains about his mother's temper (*Memorabilia* 2.2.7). The context brings out the obvious point that short-sighted children often fail to appreciate the correction they receive from their parents (see 2.2.1-10)—indeed, *Memorabilia* 2.2.10 is an encomium of Xanthippe. Diogenes Laertius tells stories of Xanthippe scolding Socrates, drenching him with water, and even ripping his cloak off of him in the *agora* (*Lives of the Philosophers* 2.36-37). But Diogenes is not the most reliable of sources: he often records scandalous stories regardless of their provenance, and he wrote more than six centuries after Socrates' death. Plato's only portrait of her is here and, presumably, at 116b2.

60a9 ["beating her breast"]: two misunderstandings lead modern scholars astray here. First, Xanthippe's lament about the last time Socrates and his friends will talk is not superficial sentimentality, it clearly lays Socrates' own heart bare (see note on *Apology* 40c5). This is deliberate on Plato's part, so that in what is to follow we do not misinterpret Socrates as placid due to apathy, but as admirably maintaining an equanimity despite being profoundly saddened by precisely the fact that Xanthippe mentions. Second, Xanthippe's emotional display would be considered excessive in a Puritanical community, but in her culture it does honor to her husband and to the entire household. Presumably, Socrates' body would be brought to his home, where the funeral procession proper would begin, and so Xanthippe will probably spend the day preparing the house for the arrival of the body. Although she is not named, she no doubt returns with all the household women and children at 116b2.

60b7 ["pursues one of them"]: Socrates "pursued" his shackles in the sense that he could have escaped from prison with Crito, Simmias and Cebes (*Crito* 45b4-5), but he chose to remain in jail. The pleasure of having the shackles removed is unexpected, but welcome, and it suggests not only that relief from pain is pleasant, but also that the loss of pleasure can be painful. Clearly Socrates is not making the false claim that "pleasure always follows pain, and *vice versa*." First, he undercuts the certainty of the connection (*schedon* at b7); but second, and more importantly, he limits his claim to pleasures and pains that we pursue (*diōkē* also at b7). The sick man pursues painful medicine in the hope of pleasant recovery; the courageous man pursues painful battle in the hope of pleasant victory; the intemperate man pursues pleasant alcohol forgetting the painful hangover the next morning. To employ a simplistic metric, the extent to which a pursued pleasure of $^+3$ tends to be followed by a pain of $^-3$, or *vice versa*, is the extent to which we will be disillusioned with the "science of measurement" mentioned at *Protagoras* 356d4, and with the similar calculus Socrates criticizes below at 68d2-69c3. Aristippus seems to have learned this lesson but to have drawn the wrong conclusion; he seems to have thought that we should give up on long range calculation and content ourselves with trying to beat the odds on a daily basis, hoping that a great enough pleasure will not be entirely cancelled out by an equal but opposite pain (Diogenes Laertius 2.87, 68). I am not surprised that Plato says Aristippus was absent this day (see note on 59c3 above).

60c2 ["story"]: *muthos* occurs here and also at 61b4, 61b6, 94d8, 110b1, 110b4, 114d7. The related adjective *muthologikos* occurs at 61b5. Because a *muthos* is a word or a speech, "*muthos*" has a wide range of uses, e.g. simple statement of fact, a pubic speech, a piece of advice, a threat, an unspoken intention, a rumor. It also has a special use referring to a narrative, story or tale—whether true or false—though in some contexts it clearly refers to fiction as opposed to historical fact (e.g. *Timaeus* 26e4-5, Pindar, *Olympian* 1.28-29). But *muthos* and *logos* can be used interchangeably to mean "story;" Pindar does this at *Nemean* 7.21-23, and Plato does this here, having Socrates refer to the "*muthon*" of Aesop at 60c2, and having Cebes refer to the "*logous*" of Aesop at 60d1. See note on *Protagoras* 320c3, and the notes on *Phaedo* 61b4, 70c6, and 99e5.

60c8 ["jumped in"]: *hupolambanō* literally refers to taking something up by getting under it (see also note on 86b6). Often it means to sieze something, or to come upon it suddenly. There is no indication that Cebes is rudely interrupting Socrates—there is no harm to Socrates' grammar. Clearly the mention of Aesop suddenly reminded Cebes of what Socrates has been doing, and he impetuously—though politely—asks Socrates about it.

60d2 ["hymn"]: a *prooimion* is an introduction, preamble or prelude, but because the *Homeric Hymns* were preludes to longer songs, "*prooimion*" could refer to a short hymn that introduced a longer one (cf. Thucydides 3.104.4). I assume that both of these were meant to be sung to the *kithara*, which Socrates had been learning to play (*Euthydemus* 272c3). Apollo was named at 58c2—surely Socrates' choice of deity was not random.

60d5 ["Evenus"]: see note on *Apology* 20c1.

60e2 ["fault"]: *aphosioō* is related to *hosia*, a divine law, which is examined in the *Euthyphro*. Violations of divine law include immoral actions like murder, but they also include actions that are not immoral but incur only what we might call "ritual impurity" (see note on *Euthyphro* 4c1). Failure to heed a divine command may incur just such an impurity, from which one needs to be cleansed or purified. Apollo is especially associated with purification rituals.

60e4 ["The same dream"]: if the appearance varies from dream to dream, why does Socrates call it "the same dream"? Because it always gives the same message. This parallels the identity conditions for propositions, e.g. "*Emoige dokei*" and "It seems so to me" express the same proposition, though they are different sentences because they are in two different languages. Aesop's fables ask us to apply a similar principle if the fable and the moral attached to the fable are to be taken as expressing the same truth. Socrates' versification of a fable by Aesop is another example of the propositional identity of two non-identical expressions. How far does Socrates take this principle? E.g. does he think "All mortals are stationed on guard duty" (62b4) expresses a truth that could be expressed in more scientific language? Is this how we are to understand his belief in the concluding myth (108e4)?

60e6 ["heed the Muses!"]: the English word "music" is semantically far narrower than the Greek word "*mousikē*," which included anything over which the Muses presided. Poets like Homer and Hesiod range over many subjects (e.g. history, cosmology, ethics, politics), and so "music" could legitimately be thought by Socrates to include philosophizing.

61a7 ["violate the command"]: in both law and cult, *mens rea* is usually irrelevant for Greeks. Pagan versions of "Pascal's Wager" could be strongly motivating.

61b3 ["it occurred to me"]: this is perfectly natural since it is common for Homeric Hymns to end with something like, "Hail, children of Zeus, and honor my song! But now I will remember you and also another song" (*Hymn to the Muses and to Apollo* 25.6-7). Many hymns are short preludes and were probably sung before singing a much longer passage from Homer. It simply will not do to write a prelude without then going on to write the thing it is a prelude to.

61b4 ["tell stories and not come up with arguments"]: this is the famous distinction between *muthos* and *logos*, unfortunately it is not clear what Socrates means by it. In the *Protagoras* the distinction seems a superficial one, as if the exact same point may be made either way (320c3, 324d6, 328c3). Aesop's fables fit this perfectly, since the story and the moral attached to it allegedly convey exactly the same meaning in two different ways. See notes on 60c2 and 99e5.

61b5 ["I'm no storyteller"]: some scholars make heavy weather of this comment since Socrates tells a whopper of a story at 107d5-114c8. But obviously Socrates is not saying he is incapable of telling stories—he is currently explaining why and how he told a story. A philosopher can say that he's "no storyteller" just as a storyteller can say he's "no philosopher" despite the fact that a philosopher can tell stories and a storyteller can philosophize.

61b6 ["Aesop"]: it is not certain that a collection of Aesop's fables existed before the 3rd century BCE. Diogenes quotes one line of a hymn to Apollo that some say (and some deny) was the hymn produced by Socrates; and he quotes two lines from what he claims was the fable of Aesop that he turned into a poem (*Lives of the Philosophers* 2.42). Personally, I like to think that Socrates versified "The Miller, His Son and Their Ass," since it colorfully makes a point that is quite important to Socrates (see *Crito* 44c6-9).

61b8 ["follow me quickly"]: if Evenus were facing the growing shame of a debilitating old age, the suggestion that he end his own life soon may not have sounded bad or wrong (Socrates may have in mind only that he refuse medical treatments to extend his life, not that he actively kill himself, cf. 61c9 and also 84b2 and the note on that line, and the note on *Apology* 41d4). Greeks were highly motivated by shame, and "death before dishonor" was taken quite seriously, though precipitation (hurling oneself off of a great height, e.g. into the sea to drown, see note on 59c3) and hanging were thought to be shameful ways for men to die (though acceptable for women and slaves). Plato records what sounds like a calloused attitude towards the care of the deathly ill (*Republic* 3.407c7-e2). Keep in mind that Socrates dies by his own hand at the end of this dialogue, and though sad, there is no indication that Plato or his friends thought his suicide was shameful or wrong. In his condemnation of suicide at *Laws* 9.873c2-d8 Plato admits three exceptions for (1) disastrous calamity, (2) intolerable disgrace, and (3) a command of the state. See note on *Apology* 19a4.

61c6 ["a philosopher?"]: Evenus would probably have called himself a *sophistēs*, though he probably would not object to being described as a *philosophos*. I suspect that Plato deliberately brought this word in so early because of the Pythagorean context (see note on 61c10). The word "*philosophos*" was invented by Pythagoras (c.570-c.495) as a term of humility—only god is wise, the most a human should claim is to be a *lover* of wisdom. Pythagoras was famous for his eponymous geometrical theorem, but was probably more famous for his discovery of the *tetractus*, i.e. ten dots in the shape of an equilateral triangle in which the top three dots are arranged like this ∴ so that the rows have 1, 2, 3 and 4 dots respectively. This configuration has a great many applications, but chief among them is the comparative lengths of strings on a lyre, thus producing the octave (ratio 2:1), the fifth (ratio 3:2) and the fourth (ratio 4:3). It is no accident that Pythagorean astronomy recognizes exactly ten heavenly spheres: the central (invisible) Divine Fire (1); the paired Earth and (invisible) Counter-Earth (2); the trio of Sun, Moon and Mercury (3); and finally Mars, Venus, Jupiter and Saturn (4). Hence, Pythagoras unified mathematics, harmonics and cosmology. Pythagoras himself was said to be the only person able to hear the octave, fifth and fourth made by the revolution of the spheres around the Divine Fire (the "harmony of the spheres").

61c10 ["not permitted"]: on *ou...themiton* see notes on *Apology* 21b6 and 30c9. The implication is that suicide incurs ritual impurity since it violates a sacred law, which means that the real question here is who "they" are, since ordinary Greeks did not think that suicide violated any divine ordinance. Perhaps the reference to Philolaus at 61d7 suggests that we are to assume a Pythagorean context (see note on *Crito* 45b4).

61d8 ["Not clearly"]: two strains of Pythagoreanism can be detected. The mathematici followed the written mathematical proofs, and the acusmatici followed the oral traditions. It is not clear how these strains were related to one another, and even if they were mutually consistent. The acusmatici believed that Pythagoras had a golden thigh, the ability to hear the harmonics of the celestial bodies, the ability to recall his previous incarnations, and the ability to bilocate (he was said to have given one lecture at one time in two discrete locations: one in Italy, the other in Greece). If Cebes and Simmias had learned about the philosopher's attitude towards death from the acusmatici, they might well say that the account they received was not clear.

61d10 ["what I've heard"]: the proper contrast is with *Charmides* 161b3-162e6. It is surprising that Socrates is willing to explain another's view.

62a2 ["surprising to you"]: often Plato is a beautiful writer. Not here. The Greek text of 62a2-7 can be taken a number of ways. To make a long story short, I think that Socrates is doing little more than summing up what he's already been said.

62a7 ["do the deed himself"]: impartiality may suggest that (1) the respect we give to ourselves is owed equally to others, and that (2) the abuse we give to ourselves is permitted equally to others (see note on *Crito* 50e5). We might then infer that if another may kill us under certain circumstances, then we may kill ourselves under those same circumstances.

62a8 ["By Zeus"]: "By god" would be a legitimate translation. However, tradition has it that the two simplest plane figures—the triangle and the tetragon—were sacred to Pythagoras. It will take four equilateral triangles or three squares inscribed within a circle to make twelve contact points with the circle—one contact point for each sign of the zodiac (introduced to Greece from Mesopotamia by Cleostratus of Tenedos in the 6th century BCE). Connect the twelve contact points with straight lines and you have a dodecagon. There were twelve Olympian gods, Zeus was their leader, and so Zeus was associated with the dodecagon, and as such was sacred to Pythagoreans. I think Cebes and Simmias exclaimed "by Zeus!"

62b4 ["guard duty"]: a *phroura* is a look-out, or someone on guard duty, so by extension it can refer to a guardhouse, and at *Gorgias* 525a7 it seems to refer to a stockade or prison. At *Gorgias* 493a2-3 Socrates mentions hearing some wise person say that the body (*sōma*) is a tomb (*sēma*); and at *Cratylus* 400b11-c9 he attributes a similar view to the "Orphics" (an ill defined collection of people with esoteric rituals and doctrines allegedly derived from the Orpheus who, according to myth, descended to Hades while alive, and emerged still alive).

62b5 ["Profound as it may be"]: Diogenes Laertius relates the story that Euripides once gave Socrates a copy of Heraclitus' book and asked what he thought of it. Socrates told him that what he understood was excellent, but what he did not understand would take a Delian pearl diver to get to the bottom of (*Lives of the Philosophers* 2.22). Of course what is striking here is that Socates actually *does* go on to explain the unfamiliar doctrine (see note on 61d10).

62b7 ["gods who take care of us"]: in the *Statesman* Plato's Stranger puts the era of divine care in the distant past (*Statesman* 271d4) so that the hallmark of the current era is that we take responsibility for ourselves (274a3-e1).

62c7 ["it is impermissible to kill oneself"]: Socrates' strategy is valid if we assume that by "impermissible" (here expressed by the negative command *mē* plus the infinitive) he means *ou themiton* (from 61c10, see note above). If we accept the premise that the gods care whether we live or die (a controversial assumption for a pagan), and we assume that the will of the gods can be violated by ignorant or impious humans (a non-controversial assumption for a pagan), then the only question remaining is how to discern the will of the gods with respect to our deaths (usually settled by divination for a pagan). But notice that this will not settle the issue of the morality of suicide without the addition of premises connecting the will of the gods to morality (premises that will be controversial for pagans, and will be scrutinized by Socrates, see *Euthyphro* 10a1-11b1).

63a6 ["wise men"]: *andres sophoi* are wise men—as opposed to wise women, or wise people. At 60b4 and b6, when Socrates was making his point about the association of pain and pleasure, he did use *anthropos* to indicate the ubiquity of the phenomenon. So the use of *anēr* (adult human male) as opposed to *anthropos* (human being) is often sexist. I keep the sexism in my translation.

63b8 ["better than the men here"]: is it rude of Socrates to say that he will be among better men than the ones he is currently with? Or should we read this paragraph through the eyes of the author who still misses his mentor and must believe that he has not turned to dust but received a blessed welcome on the other side? If so, then a seriously anachronistic portrayal need not be the "heartless mystification" Burnet rightly rejected (*Plato's Phaedo*, Oxford 1911, xii).

63e9 ["it seems to me suitable"]: a far cry from absolute certainty (underscored by the potential optative at 64a2, "might be"). *Eikotōs* is an adverb that derives from *eikos* which, in turn, derives from the verb *eoika*, which means to be like or to look like. All three are used when something seems likely, fitting, suitable, appropriate, probable or plausible. For example, according to Aristotle, the Pythagoreans posit the existence of an additional heavenly body named *antichthōn* (anti-earth) not on the basis of observational evidence (*antichthōn* cannot be seen directly from the earth because it orbits the central Fire opposite the Earth at exactly the same rate of speed), but because ten is a perfect number (see note on 86b6 below) and without *antichthōn* there would only be nine heavenly bodies in motion (*Metaphysics* 1.986a8-12). The existene of *antichthōn* seems perfectly fitting, appropriate and plausible to Pythagoreans, although this argument fails to impress Aristotle. Socrates' use of *eikotōs* here should make us wonder whether Socrates is committed to giving sound arguments for his conclusions, or whether he will be content simply to make his conclusions seem appropriate to Pythagoreans like Simmias (or Echecrates).

63e10 ["really spent his life in philosophy"]: *tō onti* indicates the reality as opposed to the mere appearance. This qualification may be relevant to Evenus (see note on 61c6), though it also paves the way for the "no true Scotsman" fallacy.

64b2 ["most people"]: *hoi polloi*, see notes on *Euthydemus* 303d1 and *Apology* 20c8.

64c1 ["leave others out of it"]: this is much more than a simple acknowledgement of who happens to be in the room. If you try to convince *hoi polloi* of something, then you will have to rely on premises that *hoi polloi* can be expected to accept. If *hoi polloi* are very ignorant, then arguments for exotic claims can be laborious: starting from what they believe, you need to convince them of a first set of conclusions which may then be used as premises to derive a second set of conclusions, and this procedure will have to be repeated until they've agreed to the premises that entail one's main conclusion. If Socrates is talking to a group of philosophically sophisticated Pythagoreans, his arguments can be much more efficient.

64c4 ["the soul"] *psuchē*, see note on *Charmides* 154e1.

64c6 ["itself by itself"]: *auto kath hauto* (and *autēn kath hautēn* on lines 7-8) here clearly refer to separation, i.e. the body existing without the soul, and the soul existing without the body. To grant this point seems already to grant the post-mortem persistence of the soul, which seems to entail that Socrates is arguing in a circle—assuming here what he will later "prove." However, when he later proves the immortality of the soul, he initially allows two possibilities: (1) at death the soul withdraws from the dead body, or (2) at death the soul is destroyed (102d9-e2). Also, to define death as separation of soul and body does not in itself entail the post-morem persistence of either partner: pop an air balloon and you separate the air from the balloon, but the air immediately dissipates leaving only a piece of rubber, not a balloon (cf. 70a5 and the note on that line). Immolate a balloon filled with hydrogen gas and not even the rubber will survive the separation of partners. Perhaps we should not think of Socrates as giving any arguments here at all, but as elucidating a common thought about death.

65b3 ["the poets"]: perhaps this was a popular trope in the 5th (or early 4th) century, but we lack evidence for it (except, possibly, Epicharmus fr. 249, "the mind sees, the mind hears, the others are deaf and blind"). Alternatively, Plato may have in mind Homer's repeated trope of gods concealing things from human perception, e.g. *Iliad* 3.381, 5.127-30, 20.321.

65b5 ["neither accurate nore clear"]: this point seems contrary to much Socratic practice. E.g. at *Laches* 192a9-b3 Socrates defines the swift as that which accomplishes much in little time, including running and speaking. He seems to treat ordinary sense perception—watching the runners or hearing the speakers—as adequate to the task of determining accurately and clearly who is swifter than whom. But of course some important issues are not so easily settled, and sense perception does not seem up to the task of settling them (cf. *Euthyphro* 7b6-8a8). Perhaps in the *Phaedo* we are to assume that the discussion is at a more advanced level than we have in dialogues like the *Laches* and *Euthyphro*, and that some of these elementary epistemological, ethical and metaphysical points may be taken for granted. But just how much can we take for granted? This question is made more problematic at c3 ("anything real") and d4-5 ("just itself").

65d4-5 ["justice itself"]: *dikaion auto* is an odd expression, and it is odd that Simmias responds as if it is perfectly normal. Probably some "theory of forms" (see note on 65d12) is being taken for granted (see note on 65b5). At a minimum, justice itself is not the same as, e.g., a just law or a just verdict in a trial. Even if our eyes can discern—accurately and clearly—a guilty verdict (assuming that our eyes can count votes and hence distinguish between two votes seen at one time and one vote seen at two times), how could they discern the *justice* of the verdict (see note on 74e3)? After all, it's not as if all just verdicts come in a particular shade of blue. Justice itself is not the same as the culturally relative meanings of the various words for justice (e.g. *dikē* in Greek), nor is it the same as the personally subjective notions that we may have of justice. Justice Itself is an objective and absolute reality (which is why Socrates asks if it is "something or nothing," and part of why he emphasizes "reality" at d13 below), and hence its significance is universal: just as the Pythagorean Theorem is objectively and absolutely true of all right triangles at any place and at any time, so also facts of justice apply anywhere and any time there is something just. Hence, we can say that Platonic Forms have the power of bilocation (see note on 61d8): justice itself can simultaneously be in an ancient Athenian law that no longer exists and in a modern English law that exists now but did not exist back then. Platonic Forms do not have the spatial or temporal limitations that material beings have.

65d7 ["Beauty Itself"]: usually I translate *kalos* as "fine" (see note on *Charmides* 154a3). Socrates has used adjectives for the three forms he's mentioned, so "just itself," "beautiful itself" and "good itself" would be more literal translations, but I think the adjectival versions make the Forms harder to grasp: adjectives modify nouns, and so we are inclined to think that an absolute adjective that modifies nothing is utter nonsense. Platonic Forms are metaphysically interesting, and perhaps they cannot exist, but they are not nonesense. For example, if beauty is in the eye of the beholder, then we may reject the existence of an absolute and objective form of beauty itself as a patent falsehood, but not as a patent absurdity.

65d12 ["forms"]: no word for "forms" occurs in the text right here, but Plato will soon use both *eidos* (102b1, 103e3, 104c7, 106d6) and *idea* (104b9, 104d2, 104d6, 104d9, 104e1, 105d13). On these words see notes on *Euthyphro* 5d4 and 6d11.

65e2 ["truest"]: Plato assumes that truth comes in degrees. E.g. "Al is healthy" and "Betty is healthy" may both be true, though the latter may be truer than the former (Betty may be healthier than Al). I may draw two circles in the dirt, and one of them may be a truer circle than the other (i.e. closer to being truly circular), but the truest circle would be circle itself, i.e. what it is to be a circle, i.e. the form of the circle. Notice that truth and reality (or "being") go hand-in-hand: if there are degrees of truth, then there are degrees of being (e.g. degrees of being a circle).

66c8 ["Every war"]: Plato gives the same theory of war at *Republic* 2.373d7-e7. Perhaps I won't be going too far to speculate that it was when he wrote this passage in the *Phaedo* contrasting war with philosophy that Plato first conceived of the Kallipolis he describes in the *Republic*. "What would it be like," Plato must have thought to himself, "to have a society that simultaneously minimizes the risks of war, and maximizes the security that promotes philosophy?" The key to his answer: the abolition of the private possession of wealth (cf. *Republic* 5.462a9-c5).

66d2 ["no time"]: *ascholia* is the opposite of *scholē* (i.e. leisure, time for study), from which we derive the English word "scholar." Literally, a "scholar" is someone who has enough time away from gainful employment to study. Such free time is even more difficult to come by if the study is not directed to subjects that will evidently produce a profit in the near term.

66e3 ["we love: wisdom"]: Socrates just condemned *epithumia* and *erōs* (66c2), but here they are both validated. Similarly, possession (*ktēsis*) of wealth is condemned at 66c8, but possession (*ktaomai*) of knowledge is validated at 66e6. The difference, obviously, derives from wisdom (here, as often in what is to follow, *phronēsis* must clearly be translated as "wisdom") and from truth: it is one thing to choose x over y simply because one feels more strongly inclined to choose x than to choose y; it is quite another to feel more strongly inclined to choose y than to choose x, but to choose x instead after a wise consideration of all relevant facts and determining that in truth, x is better than y. (This process may indeed change one's initial pre-reflection inclinations so that in the end one does what is in accord with one's post-reflection inclinations—the difference, obviously, derives from wisdom).

66e5 ["pure knowledge"]: *katharōs gnōnai* seems to mean the same as *katharōs ti eiseisthai* on line d8 above. Here and perhaps elsewhere Plato treats *oida* and *gignōskō* as interchangeable.

67c8 ["collecting its thoughts and regaining"]: *sunageirō* and *athroizō* are perfectly normal words for gathering, collecting, and assembling, e.g. mustering an army. This combination could be used by a materialist philosopher who assumed that the *psuchē* was literally a fluid (e.g. associated with blood) or a gas (e.g. associated with breath). Alternatively, they could be used metaphorically, e.g. my consciousness of my painful gouty toes might be thought of as being in my toes, so that when I re-direct my consciousness to justice itself I may be said to be gathering my soul from my toes and withdrawing it into itself.

67d12 ["at the beginning"] i.e. 61c8-d2 or 63c4-7.

68a3 ["a lover, a wife or a child"]: *paidika* was used interchangeably with *erōmenos*, which referred to a younger man who was sexually desired by an older man—in Greek culture younger people (both male and female) were generally considered more sexually attractive than older people. Orpheus is exactly the sort of person who is not being considered here, because it was precisely his unwillingness to go to Hades in the proper way (i.e. by dying) in order to be with his beloved Eurydice that condemned him to failure (*Symposium* 179d2-e1). Alcestis died not to be with her husband but in place of her husband (*Symposium* 179b4-d2). Evadne hurls herself on her husband's funeral pyre (Euripides, *Suppliants* 980-89), though this could be in the thought that it is better for her to die at this point and escape the sort of life to which she would be condemned if she lived on. Jocasta kills herself when her children die (Euripides, *Phoenissae* 1454-59), but again, this could simply be that life beyond this point would be too terrible to contemplate. The only clear example of just the sort of thing Socrates mentions here is Achilles dying to be with Patroclus, but this is not Homeric—this particular detail seems invented by Plato (*Symposium* 180a1). In Homer, Achilles dies to avenge Patroclus, not to be with him.

68a7 ["wisdom"]: when *phronēsis* is what the *philosophos* loves, (e.g. here, at 168b4 and 169a10) I think that we can no longer avoid translating it as "wisdom."

68c1 ["wisdom-lover"]: parallel to *philosophos* Socrates uses *philochrēmatos*, *philotimos*, and *philosōmatos* (this is the only use of this word by Plato, who probably invented it). In the *Republic*, Plato uses *philochrēmatos* about a dozen times, and he associates it with the part of the soul he calls the *Epithumētikon* (e.g. 9.580d10-581a7). He uses *philotimos* a bit more often, and obviously he associates it with the part of the soul he calls the *Thumos* (e.g. 9.581b2-3). At *Republic* 9.582d7-9 Plato distinguishes all three: *philokerdēs* (= *philochrēmatos*, cf. 581a6-7), *philotimos* and *philosophos*. Perhaps while he was writing the *Phaedo* Plato was already developing the theories he would elaborate in the *Republic*. See also note on 82a4.

68d8 ["Fear of a greater evil"]: Socrates will appear to be arguing unsoundly here if we attribute to him the false assumption that choosing the lesser of two evils entails acting out of fear. But there is no reason to attribute this false assumption to him. First, Socrates is probably assuming an understanding of his cultural context in which successful prosecution for cowardice (see note on *Apology* 28d8) could have serious consequences, which an ordinary Athenian could safely be assumed to fear. Second, Socrates clearly understands the difference between acting *despite fear* and acting *because of fear* (83b2-c3): philosophers can fear x more than y but still choose x despite their fear because they love wisdom, and hence truth, and it may be true that x is better than (or not as bad as) y. If non-philosophers do not love wisdom or truth as do philosophers, then this option for escaping the determination of their actions by their philosophically unanalyzed fears is not open to them. Third, we do Socrates a serious injustice if we fail to attribute to him the gadfly's critique of cultural hypocrisy: Athenians claim to value wisdom and strength, but upon analysis their actual behavior fails to achieve their lofty goals (*Apology* 29d7-e3, cf. 30e5). With respect to courage, Athenians claim to prefer death to dishonor (cf. *Apology* 28b5-29b1), and so it is an embarrassing revelation (not a sophistic fallacy) when Socrates points out that in fact Athenians choose death not out of a commitment to doing the right thing (as do philosophers, e.g. 32a9-33a5), but only because they happen to feel a greater philosophically unanalyzed fear of the outcome if they are prosecuted for cowardice.

68d12 ["fear and cowardice?"]: Socrates will appear to be arguing unsoundly here if we attribute to him a fallacious verbal equivocation between *deidō* (fear, on d11) and *deilia* (cowardice, on d12). But there is no reason to attribute this equivocation to him. Socrates is providing a gadfly's critique of cultural hypocrisy (see note on 68d8 above): Athenians claim to prefer death to dishonor, but upon a more honest analysis it appears that they overcome their fear of death not because of a stronger commitment to honor, but only because they feel a greater philosophically unanalyzed fear of the outcome if they are prosecuted for cowardice. The charge of cowardice (*deilia*) follows not simply from the fact that their actions are determined by their philosophically unanalyzed fears (*deidō*), but because of the combination of the facts that (i) their actions are so determined and (ii) their actions are (hypocritically) not determined by considerations of honor.

68e3 ["temperate because of intemperance?"]: on *sōphrosunē* see note on *Charmides* 157a6. *Akolasia* is the opposite of *sōphrosunē*; literally *akolasia* is to be lacking in correction or chastisement (it also refers to the pruning of trees). The opposition between *akolasia* and *sōphrosunē* naturally suggests the hotly disputed claim in the *Gorgias* that punishment for wrongdoing is in one's own best interest (491d7-492a3, 505b1-12, 507c8-e3, 525b1-c1; cf. proper pruning is good for trees and shrubs).

68e7 ["the lure of those other pleasures is too powerful"]: Socrates' argument may appear to entail that the drunkard is intemperate because of temperance when he is successful at *overcoming the pleasures* of health and financial security to pursue a ruinous course of drink. But this ignores what Socrates has repeated, i.e. it is the philosopher's concern for wisdom and truth that is the basis for the proper sort of "overcoming" (see note on 66e3 above).

69a9 ["correct coin"]: the coin metaphor is confusing. If the "correct coin" is legal tender, then the other "coins" are counterfeit. In this case, we might think that *phronēsis* has value, while pleasures, pains and fears (etc.) lack value. We might expect to hear something like this from a Cynic or Stoic philosopher. Alternatively, if the "correct coin" is a coin of special value, then pleasures, pains and fears (etc.) have value, they simply lack the special value that is possessed by *phronēsis*—and Socrates owes us an account of this special value. Book 2 of the *Republic* begins with Glaucon asking Socrates to defend the view that justice has special value. Most confusing of all is the claim at b1-2 that in addition to trading other coins for the coin of *phronēsis*, the exchanging should be done with *phronēsis*, i.e. intelligently. Scholars have been much exercised by the text here, and I think the blame is Plato's: in mid-sentence he drops the metaphor of *phronēsis* being a coin and instead uses *phronēsis* literally as the intellectual virtue we ought to employ when we decide which pleasures, pains and fears to avoid and which to seek.

69a10 ["exchange all these others for it"]: we exchange pleasure for pleasure when we, e.g., give up a second dessert after dinner for the pleasures associated with health. We exchange pleasure for *phronēsis* when we, e.g., have a simple, small meal that does not require a lot of planning and does not leave us bloated and unable to concentrate on our studies.

69b3 ["justice"]: justice easily fits the model he has just given for courage and temperance. A vendor avoids charging an unjustly high price for wares in order to earn the trust of customers and hence maximize his profits in the long run. So he is just because of his greed.

69b7 ["fit only for a slave"]: it will turn out later that this form of virtue is not entirely worthless; see note on 82a11-b1.

69c1 ["purification"]: even today we speak of "pure motives." E.g., the vendor mentioned in the note on 69b3 has an "impure motive" for being just, since he is motivated both by virtue and by money. In theory, if the circumstances change, his policy of maximizing his expected profits in the long run could motivate him to be unjust. Someone who is motivated purely by virtue and not by money won't "sell out" for any price. But this raises the question mentioned in the note on 69a9 of whether pleasure and pain (etc.) have any value at all, or simply have such little value that no amount of them could ever make it worth someone's while to "sell out." E.g. "the light of a lamp is eclipsed by the brilliance of the sun" (Marcus Porcius Cato as quoted by Cicero, *De Finibus* 3.45).

69c6 ["stuck into the mud"]: at *Republic* 2.363d5-7 Adimantus mentions the story that the unholy and unjust are stuck into the mud when they reach Hades, and they are compelled to fetch water with a sieve. The context suggests that Plato has Orphism in mind (cf. 364e3-4).

69c8 ["celebrants are many, worshippers are few"]: more literally, "Narthex-bearers are many, but Bacchants are few." The narthex is a giant fennel plant whose stalk was decorated and used as a wand (a thyrsus) in the frenzied rites of Dionysus. Perhaps it is not too misleading to compare this quoted line to Jesus' "many are called, but few are chosen" (Matthew 22.14).

69d7 ["my defense"]: see 63b2.

69d8 ["my masters"]: see 62e1, 63a6, and 63c2.

70a5 ["puff of smoke"]: on Greek views of the *psuchē* see note on *Charmides* 154e1. The *psuchē* of Patroclus visits Achilles to beg for a funeral pyre so that he may cease his vain wanderings through the house of Hades, and when Achilles promises to provide it he tries to embrace Patroclus but his *psuchē* vanishes like a puff of smoke (*Iliad* 23.100). Similarly, when Odysseus summons the dead he tries to embrace the *psuchē* of his mother Anticleia, but it flies away like a shadow or a dream (*Odyssey* 11.207-8, cf. 222). But of course in both of these cases, not only does the *psuchē* still exist, it is treated as numerically identical to the living person, not merely a remnant of the person—though after entering the gates of Hades thoughts are no longer in them unless they drink sacrificial blood (see *Iliad* 23.104 with *Odyssey* 11.152-154, and see Cebes' challenge at 70b3-4). Plato quotes Homer's lines about the smoke (*Iliad* 23.100-101) at *Republic* 3.387a2-3 and argues that they should be bowdlerized on the grounds that they are not suitable for the ears of those who should fear slavery more than death (3.387b1-6).

70a7 ["you mentioned"]: at 66b3-d7.

70b6 ["conversation"]: *diamuthologeō* is a peculiar word since it combines *muthos* and *logos*, which are sometimes contrasted (e.g. *Protagoras* 320c3, see notes on *Phaedo* 60c2, 61b4, 70c6, and 99e5). In Plato it occurs only three times: here, *Apology* 39e5, and *Laws* 1.632e4-5. Probably it means simply talking together, conversing, or even chatting.

70c1 ["comic poet"]: "babbling" translates *adolescheō*, which Aristophanes has Strepsiades use to describe the conversations at Socrates' silly school (*Clouds* 1485). See also *Apology* 19c2, and the note on *Apology* 18d2.

70c6 ["ancient account"]: again Socrates disrupts the tendency to keep *muthos* and *logos* separate—here he uses *logos* where we might expect *muthos* (i.e. "story"). See *Protagoras* 320c3, and the notes on *Phaedo* 60c2 and 61b4 above. Herodotus records an Egyptian view of reincarnation that involves a cycle of birth, death and re-birth: the soul cycles through every kind of living being and it takes 3,000 years to complete the cycle and be re-born as a human being (1.123.2-3). He also mentions that some Greeks have adopted this view, and he may have the Pythagoreans or Orphics (or both) in mind. Plato has Socrates give a version of such a view at *Meno* 81a10-d5, quoting Pindar at b8-c4.

70c9 ["wouldn't it necessarily follow that"]: perhaps a bit of an over-translation on my part because this isn't much of an argument. But we should not criticize it as circular: it is a hypothetical argument from authority, i.e. if this ancient authority is correct, that would indeed answer the question. The one missing premise is the assumption that the souls of the dead are in Hades (and not, e.g., among the stars).

70d8 ["the easy way"]: *rhadios* is an adjective that describes something as easy as opposed to difficult (*chalepos*), and when it describes a person it can refer to someone who is easy-going and adaptable or to someone who makes light of serious matters, and so is reckless or unscrupulous. Simmias used the adverb *rhadiōs* twice to describe Socrates as taking his death too lightly (63a7 and a8). Perhaps (a) this argument is *rhadios* because it reaches the conclusion directly from assumptions his audience already accepts, or (b) Socrates doesn't take this argument seriously.

70d9 ["becomes"]: *genesis* is obviously where we get the English word "genesis," and it refers to the origin, source, beginning or birth of something. It is related to *genesthai*, which is contrasted with *einai*: "to become" as opposed to "to be." But "to become" and "to be" share a threefold ambiguity: existential ("to be" in the sense of "to exist;" "to become" in the sense of "to come to exist"); predicative ("to be" in the sense of "to be qualified in some way," e.g. to be large; "to become" in the sense of "to become qualified in some way," e.g. to become large); veridical ("to be" in the sense of "to be true," e.g. I know it to be true that an elephant is a large animal; "to become" in the sense of "to become true," e.g. it is not true now that this baby elephant is large, but as it grows it will become true). Plato often fails to distinguish these senses.

70e3 ["the noble is the opposite of the shameful"]: or "the beautiful is the opposite of the ugly." This argument is difficult to evaluate because Socrates does not explicitly distinguish contradictories (e.g. black and not-black) from contraries (e.g. black and white) or from contrasting comparatives (e.g. darker and lighter). At least since Anaximander in the 6th century BCE a consensus grew among intellectuals that the fundamental laws governing change involve opposites (e.g. moist and dry, cool and warm). The Pythagoreans endorsed this sort of view with a table of ten pairs of opposites (Aristotle, *Parts of Animals* 3.7.670b21; *Nicomachean Ethics* 1.6.1096b6; *Metaphysics* 1.5.986a23, 14.6.1093b12). Aristotle notes this consensus, with which he concurs, and he argues that because the laws of change are not random the termini should not be contradictories (e.g. musical from not-musical, since chairs are not-musical but they do not learn music) but contraries (e.g. musical from unmusical, since only people capable of learning music learn music) or intermediaries (e.g. musical from rhythmic, since unmusical people might learn rhythm as an intermediate to fully learning music); see *Physics* 1.5.188a19-b8. It is important to note this context or we will be tempted to attribute silly views to Socrates, e.g. that we cannot change from being single to being married, we can only change from being divorced to being married; or that we cannot change from feeding the chickens to feeding the goats since goats are not the contraries of chickens. See note on 71c12.

71a9 ["we've made this point sufficiently"]: if this indicates a conclusion then the argument is inductively weak (it rests an a mere four examples), or deductively invalid (his examples relied on comparatives but his initial statement of the view appealed to contraries). Perhaps he is resting content with weak arguments that are impressive to a particular audience (see note on 63e9).

71c12 ["come to be asleep from being awake"]: this example makes more sense of the universal principle that coming to be requires contraries (or intermediaries, as Aristotle points out, see note on 70e3). We do not say that we come to be asleep from being fishing, building or writing, although it is possible to fall asleep while fishing, building or writing. Those all fit the model of becoming between contradictories because fishing, building and writing are all forms of not-sleeping. But there is no law-like connection between any of them and becoming asleep. Nevertheless, despite Cebes' credulity, there is something deeply unsatisfactory in Socrates' account of becoming; Aristotle supplements a theory of change requiring contraries with a theory of potentialities (*Metaphysics* 8): the persisting potentiality for sense perception (*On Sleep* 1.453b25-454a11) explains why sleep and waking are termini of a law-like change (our senses go from active to inactive) as opposed to, e.g. sleep and fishing (although it is possible for our senses to go from inactive to fishing).

71e2 ["our souls are in Hades?"]: at least two cultural assumptions are required to make this inference reasonable. First, obviously, is the assumption that Hades is, by definition, the realm of the dead, so that if our dead souls are anywhere they are in Hades. Second, is the rejection of material reductionism—just as it is impious to say that the moon is dirt (cf. *Apology* 26d5) and not a goddess, so also it is one of those silly egg-head theories ridiculed by Aristophanes in the *Clouds* to say that the human soul comes into being from, or passes away into, a dead gas or fluid. Even if we accept Aristotle's more sophisticated version of the "change involves opposites" theory it is hard to see how to avoid the persistence of the soul: we can explain the change from sleeping to waking as the actualization of the persistent potentiality for sense perception, but what persistent potentiality could possibly explain the change from dead to living? The persistent potentialities of non-living combinations of earth, water, air and fire do not seem complex enough to be actualized in, e.g., singing, farming, or legislating. Perhaps Socrates himself suggests this point later (cf. 96b4 and his discussion that follows).

72b1 ["pendulum"]: Socrates refers to a circle and a straight line to appeal to Cebes' intuitions. I added the images of the pendulum and the rock because I think they make a similar appeal to modern intuitions.

72c1 ["Endymion"]: the point of the story depends upon the version. Perhaps in dread of old age Endymion asked to be preverved forever in youthful beauty, but permanent sleep was the price of the gift. Alternatively, Zeus may have inflicted the state on him out of jealousy, fearing that Hera may fall in love with him. Alternatively, Selene, the goddess of the moon, fell in love with him and preferred gently kissing him to feeling his ardent passion.

72c4 ["Anaxagoras"]: see *Apology* 26d6 and the note on that passage. We know little of his philosophy aside from what Socrates refers to here, what he calls the *homoiomerē*: the opposites were separated out from an initial state in which there was a portion of everything in everything. It seems that on this view, the initial state of the cosmos was a sort of chaos in which everything was simultaneously moist and dry, warm and cool, and so on for every opposition. In theory, this would be exactly the opposite of "prime matter" which would be matter without any properties whatsoever (neither moist nor dry, neither warm nor cool, and so on). My translation in this entire paragraph is a bit loose; I think the argument is clear enough, but Plato's expression is terse.

72d3 ["everything ends up dead"]: in my opinion, Socrates' arguments from 69e6-72e2 have been unfairly maligned for two main reasons. First, commentators fail to place this discussion in its proper philosophical context, i.e. the philosophical interest in discovering the basic laws that govern change (especially generation and corruption) in the cosmos (see note on 70e3). Because law-like patterns of change are not random, they require termini that are not mere contradictories (e.g. egg to not-egg) but are contraries in the sense of being opposite ends of a real process (e.g. egg to chicken for one type of egg, but egg to hawk for a different type of egg). Of course this raises an ultimate question: by what natural law is death connected to life? Intellectuals have rarely been satisfied with Hesiod's claim that simply by combining earth and water Hephaestus could create a living, breathing woman (*Works and Days* 61, *Theogony* 571; as if the task were no more difficult than making tripods that move themselves, *Iliad* 18.368-79). Protagoras' alternative recipe is no better (*Protagoras* 320d2-3). We've always had some understanding of the natural process by which living tissue can become dead, but the discovery of natural processes that can turn non-living material into living beings has been far more elusive. In other words, until very recently, Socrates' theory in this section was among the leading rational contendors as an answer to the ultimate question about the origin of life.

72e5 ["recollection"]: see *Meno* 81a10-86c2, *Phaedrus* 248e3-253c6. The reference at 73b1 to diagrams may be a reference to the *Meno*, which is evidence that the *Phaedo* was written after the *Meno*. Why are these three dialogues the only ones in which Plato explicitly uses the theory of recollection?

73c7 ["coming to know only it"]: here Socrates uses *gignōskō*, but in "knowledge of the second thing" he switches to *epistēmē*. Presumably this is because *gignōskō* is more closely associated with perception. It is clear that his concern in this argument is not with the mere association of ideas but with knowledge. The first time I saw a koala it was sitting upright on a tree branch asleep and I immediately thought that it should be sleeping lying down in a burrow. Since I had no *knowledge* of koalas, this does not count as a case of recollection (see note on 74e3 below).

74a10 ["equality?"]: again (see note on 65d7) I translate Plato's adjective with an abstract noun. Plato seems to do this himself at 74c1 where he shifts from "the equals themselves" (*auta ta isa*) to "equality" (*hē isotēs*). But shifting from adjectives to abstract nouns is even more controversial here than elsewhere since "the equal" is even more obviously troubling than "the beautiful" or "the just." Even if we can accept an absolute adjective that modifies no noun, how can we accept an absolute *comparative* adjective with nothing to which to compare it (what is "the equal" equal *to*?). Using "equality" rather than "the equal" does not avoid the many philosophical and interpretive problems of the argument Socrates is about to give, and it has the benefit of yielding a less forbidding translation for those who are coming to this dialogue for the first time.

74a11 ["beyond all these things"]: one important question about Plato's "theory of forms" is whether he "separated" them, i.e. whether he believed that the form could exist independently of the things that instantiate it, e.g. whether the form of beauty could exist if nothing were actually beautiful, or justice could exist if nothing were actually just. The phrase "beyond all these things" could express "separation," but it could also simply express difference, i.e. the form of equality is not the same thing as the the many particular things that are equal to one another.

74b3 ["Certainly"]: this answer is surprising if we are familiar with dialogues like the *Charmides*, *Laches* and *Euthyphro*, which seek forms of the virtues but fail to discover them. Consider also the requirement of knowledge at 76b4-c3.

74b8 ["equal to one"]: to one *person* or to one *thing*? The text can mean either. If Socrates means "to one *person*," then he's saying that sometimes two people will be assuming different contexts when they consider whether this stick is equal: a 3-foot long stick is equal to the 3-foot long stick that I have in mind, but it is unequal to the 2-foot long stick that you have in mind. His point is that this never happens with the form of equality: if one person is "looking at" a form and in the context he's considering the form looks unequal, then whatever form he's looking at, he's not looking at the form of equality. Alternatively, if he means "to one *thing*," then he's ignoring the people who are considering the sticks and simply focusing on the fact that any stick will be equal in length to some things, but unequal in length to other things. On this view, his point would be that the form of equal is equal, but not equal to anything, so it can never be unequal to anything else.

74c1 ["the equals themselves"]: "the equals themselves," "equality" and "the equal" all seem to refer to the form of equality, so perhaps we should ignore the differences. One alternative is that he thinks the form of the equal is a pair of perfectly equal particular objects. A second alternative is that he is distinguishing equality itself (the form of equality) from the equality that is in these two equally long sticks. However we interpret "the equals themselves," the basic strategy of this argument is clear: equal sticks possess a property that equality lacks, and so equality cannot be identical to the equal sticks (just as the butcher and the baker must be two people and not one if the butcher has the property of being married but the baker does not have that property). The property the equal sticks have, and which equality lacks, is the property of suffering from "the compresence of opposites," i.e. the equal sticks "appear equal to one but appear not equal to another," but this is not true of equality (see note on 74b8). This is a different approach to the one Socrates uses in dialogues like the *Charmides* and *Laches*, in which he emphasizes the ability of forms to be in more than one place at one time (see note 65d4-5).

74e3 ["knew beforehand"]: if forms are standards we use to judge particulars we see, does it follow that we knew the forms before seeing the particulars? David Hume (1711-76) would deny the inference and argue that the standards are derived from perceptions of particulars: "Five notes played on a flute give us the impression and idea of time" (*A Treatise of Human Nature* 2.3 paragraph 10). For Hume, it is because we are able to perceive the sequence of notes that we are able to judge whether things take too much or not enough time. But this example rather proves the opposite: noticing a *temporal* sequence of notes presupposes that our experience is already ordered temporally (see note on 65d4-5). Also, I presume that Socrates does not have in mind foolishly judgmental people (see note on 73c7 above). For example, the very first time I see a koala I might judge that it is ill because it fell asleep in a tree instead of in a burrow. This judgment does not require that I recollect burrow-sleeping koalas I've seen in the past, it requires only that I be foolishly judgmental. I presume that Socrates has in mind justified judgments, e.g. if I am justified in claiming that these two sticks are only approximately but not exactly equal, then I must already be justified in believing that equality and inequality are real phenomena, which requires already having some justified beliefs about equality.

75b10 ["using our senses from birth"]: if the first of the two alternatives Socrates mentions at 76a4-7 is true, then it will follow that in our initial use of our senses we recognize sensible equals (e.g. equal size sticks). If the second alternative is true, then it may be a while before our senses actually stimulate recollection of equality. This second alternative does not ruin the argument for pre-natal knowledge since the period of time between first opening our eyes and first recognizing sensible equals does not include any substantive change in our eyes.

75c7-8 ["had it when we were born"]: this seems to contradict 76c1-3, especially if we emphasize *apollumi* (destroy) at 75d10, 75e2-3 and 76d1. Presumably Socrates intends 76c1-3 as a correction that allows him to have it both ways: newly born babies are incapable of actually recognizing equal sticks or stones (i.e. because they have forgotten equality), and yet they are capable of precisely that (i.e. because the knowledge of equality is still within their souls).

76b5 ["give an account"]: because *logos* can mean so many things, it is not clear what it means to give one. "Definition," "explanation" and "proof" are all possibilities, but since each of those clearly stand in need of further clarification, I think that the "account," which is perhaps as semantically pliable as *logos*, is probably the best translation.

76c6 ["our souls"]: if our *psuchai* are the very things that give us a psychology, then our souls are us. So why doesn't Socrates just say "us"? Perhaps this curious phrase was set up by Simmias' curious comment about "tomorrow at this time" (76b11). Perhaps Socrates and his *psuchē* can be compared to a character and the actor who plays that character. However, if you care more for the character than the actor, then you won't be comforted by the knowledge that the latter will outlive the former.

76e1 ["recovering our own knowledge"]: Socrates is tersely encapsulating many points he's already made, and I'm attempting to make his economical prose more perspicuous. In particular, it is easy to miss the connection between his *hēmeteran* here and his *oikeian* at 75e5.

76e5 ["complete waste of time"]: the pre-existence of the soul and the theory of forms are connected, but how? Perhaps their link derives from the link Socrates describes between the theory of opposites and the theory of recollection. This linkage is reasonable. Prior to the triumph of evolutionary biology in the 20ᵗʰ century, it was unreasonable to think that any combination of non-living materials could actualize living processes, e.g. farming, legislating (see note on 72d3). Similarly, prior to the triumph of ethology and developmental psychology in the 20ᵗʰ century, it was not unreasonable to think that human cognition was different in kind, not simply degree, from mammalian cognition generally. An understanding of the evolutionary basis of human biology and cognition simultaneously undermines Socrats' arguments for his theory of opposites and his theory of recollection.

77b3 ["Cebes' concern"]: see 70a5.

77c7 ["put this argument together with"]: what is the relationship between the argument from opposites and the argument from recollection? At 72d9-e1 the argument from opposites is wrapped up with the claim that "dead souls continue to exist." Then at 72e3 Cebes said that the recollection argument could be added to the argument from opposites as additional confirmation. But, of course, the recollection argument is strictly about a pre-natal career of a soul, so when it concludes, Simmias and Cebes point out that the recollection argument fails to prove the post-mortem existence of the soul (77b3-c5). Simmias mentions the ordinary fear that the soul will be dispersed at death (77b4-5). Socrates quickly reminds them that the post-mortem existence of the soul was already proven by the argument from opposites (77c6-d5, cf. 72d9-e1 again). The clue to what is going on here is exactly what Socrates emphasizes, i.e. the childish fear (77d7) that the soul will be dispersed at death. Childish fear can make people forget something they just proved rationally a few minutes earlier.

78a1 ["good at charms"]: see note on *Charmides* 155e5.

78a8 ["amongst yourselves"]: some are tempted to see in this comment an attempt by Plato to claim Socrates' mantle for himself. But I suspect that this comes from readers who are too familiar with Matthew 26:20-25 and too unfamiliar with *Phaedo* 59b10. Clearly Socrates is humbly pointing out that there are many philosophers worth associating with, and most importantly that each person should take responsibility for "charming" his own inner child.

78c2 ["suffer dispersion"]: the specific childish fear Socrates is confronting is the one that likens the soul to breath or smoke, both of which can be dispersed upon the winds (77d7, cf. note on 70a5). Dispersibility does indeed presuppose a composite nature, but dispersion is not the only way, in theory, for something to cease to exist.

78e3 ["never remain the same"]: this claim seems clearly false. I have a beautiful shirt that has remained beautiful for quite some time. Does this refute Socrates? Perhaps not, for at least five reasons: (1) not everybody thinks that the shirt is beautiful (see 74b8 and the note on that line), (2) the shirt does not look beautiful if I wear it with the wrong pants or wrong jacket, (3) look at the shirt inside out and it is not beautiful, (4) I've worn it next to someone who was wearing a much more beautiful shirt and by contrast my shirt did not look beautiful, and (5) the shirt is getting old and soon will be worn out and no longer beautiful. Socrates seems to count these as five ways of being inconstantly beautiful. This is one of the crucial passages scholars point to as an indication of Plato's Heracliteanism. Heraclitus of Ephesus (died after 480 BCE) claimed, among other things, that "all things are in motion, nothing is still" (*Cratylus* 401d5). See also note on *Euthydemus* 294b2.

79b12 ["invisible?"]: *aoratos* is the negation of *horatos*. Simmias also uses *aoratos* at 85e5. These are the only two uses of the word in the dialogue. Usually Socrates contrasts *horatos* with *aidēs*, which means unseen or secret, and which is related to *Haidēs/Hadēs*, i.e. Hades. Socrates makes this pun at 80d6. At *Cratylus* 404b1-4 Socrates notices the close similarity of *Haidēs* and *aidēs*, but claims that the former was actually derived from *eidenai* (from *oida*) because of Hades' knowledge of all fine things. Since *Phaedo* 80d6 is not alleging a derivation, it does not contradict *Cratylus* 404b1-4.

79b16 ["more like"]: the comparative seems to serve the double function of associating souls with forms, but also distinguishing them—the soul is only *like* the forms (it is not visible), the soul is not itself a form (the soul is a particular, not a universal). God, soul and the form of life play special roles in Socrates' view (see 106d5-e3, see note on 106e7).

79c2 ["a while ago"]: at 65a9-67b5.

80b10 ["or very nearly so?"]: perhaps Plato adds this qualification because in fact he believes that the soul is divisible (see *Republic* 4.436a8-c1 and following). It is worth considering whether Plato's theory of the soul in the *Republic* is compatible with the theory presented in the *Phaedo*.

80c2 ["although it is fitting"]: Socrates is either contradicting or qualifying what he just said (i.e. "quickly dissolved").

80d7 ["the good and wise god"]: when Socrates made this point at 63b6-7 he used *sophos* instead of *phronimos*, and he used the plural *theoi* instead of the singular *theos*. He reverts back to the plural *theoi* at 81a9. Clearly he is simply varying his language, not drawing distinctions.

81a9 ["initiates"]: *mueō* means to initiate someone into mysteries. It derives from *muō*, to have one's eyes shut. So initiation is an opening of the eyes. At *Phaedrus* 249a3 Plato seems to say that the philosophical life must be lived three times before the soul is released (this matches Pindar's count at *Olympian* 2.68). Perhaps this passage contradicts the *Phaedrus*, although perhaps Plato thinks that the purity he refers to here will not be achieved until the third time one lives a philosophical life.

81b1 ["polluted"]: see note on *Euthyphro* 4c1.

81d3: ["apparition"]: an *eidōlon* is a ghost, but the word derives from *eidos*—one of Plato's words for a "form" (e.g. the form of goodness). This irony was probably not lost on Plato (cf. note on 83c7). Some scholars worry about the coherence of Plato's thought here: if he thinks he has established the immateriality of the soul, then how can he countenance them showing up visibly? In my view, the problem is not with Plato, but with modern scholars who cannot completely free their thinking from modern materialist assumptions. Plato believes that he refuted materialism with his argument from opposites (see especially note on 72d3), and so he thinks he's refuted the view that the soul is any kind of attenuated, rarefied or sublimed fluid or gas (see note on 71e2). If the truth is closer to the opposite of materialism, then soul is not any kind of emanation from the body, perhaps the body is a sort of radiation or emanation from the soul—in which case quasi-physical appearances of the soul are less problematic.

82a4 ["hawks, buzzards or wolves"]: probably these two sets of animals map onto the *Epithumētikon* and *Thumos* from *Republic* 4.439c2-441c2 (see also note on 68c1).

82a11-b1 ["personal and social virtues"]: it is not clear what Socrates means by describing virtue as *dēmotikos* or *politikos*; in a democracy the two can be quite close. What is clear is that he has in mind the sort of virtue that he earlier said was "fit only for a slave" (69b7). In comparison with philosophical virtue, these demotic and politic virtues are quite poor, but they are not entirely worthless. This view seems similar to Plato's notion in Books 8 and 9 of the *Republic* that virtue comes in gradations.

82b10 ["a philosophical life"]: Socrates believes that he has lived a philosophical life (67b7-d2, 69d3) and that the best outcome awaits him (63b7). He argues, "philosophers deserve the best outcome, and I am a philosopher, so I deserve the best outcome;" but we may suspect him of arguing: "I deserve the best outcome, and I am a philosopher, so philosopher's deserve the best outcome." Upon reflection (see *Republic* 9.580d3-583a11), Plato may think that something like the latter argument can be rationally convincing—after all, whose judgement is more likely to be fact-based, someone who loves learning (*Phaedo* 82c1) or someone who loves drinking (81e5)?

82c1 ["love learning"]: it is important to remember that Socrates' notion of a philosopher is not nearly as restricted as ours today.

82c2 ["for the sake of joining the gods"]: the plural *toutōn* could refer to several reasons, but I think its clear that it refers to the plural *theōn* at the beginning of the previous sentence. Is this attitude just as mercenary as the attitude he is about to condemn: do philosophers love wisdom only to gain a post-mortem reward and to avoid reincarnation in an animal? This suspicion overlooks the fact (as I see it) that *toutōn* refers to *theōn*: what he says is the philosophers act "for the sake of the gods," not "for the sake of *joining* the gods." It seems to me that Augustine added a footnote to this passage when he wrote, "if there is something more excellent than the truth, then that is God; if not, the truth itself is God" (*De Libero Arbitrio* 2.15): in loving wisdom, philosophers love the truth, and they love (the) god(s).

83b2 ["different in something different"]: *Laches* 190e4-191b7 is a perfect example of this. Use your eyes to examine courage and it will appear one way if you are looking at hoplite soldiers, but then turn your gaze to the Scythian cavalry and courage will look quite different.

83c3 ["incalculably"]: Socrates appears to contradict himself because he begins this thought by saying that the philosophical soul has calculated (*logizomai*) what follows, but he ends by saying that it has not calculated (*logizomai*) the final consequence. My translation goes beyond what Socrates literally says, but I think it expresses his meaning.

83c7 ["manifestly clear"]: at 77a3 Socrates associates being *enargēs* with the form of the good and so on. The ultimate fraud is the ultimate betrayal (83a4, 5): the philosopher's highest aim is the form of the good, and intense feelings prop an impostor on the throne. This is incalculably bad in the way that a compromised immune system is incalculably bad for our health: the damage caused by a particular illness is calculable, but the potential havoc resulting from a weakened immune system is not. Perahps this resolves the apparrant contradiction between 83c2-8 and 89d2-3: the latter says that nothing is worse than misology, and the former says that worst thing is being compelled to believe that whatever causes intense pleasure or pain is the truest and most manifestly clear being there is. Though not identical, perhaps each condition entails the other.

83d7 ["whatever the body believes"]: *homodoxeō* does seem to imply that the body has beliefs. I suppose this is no more (or less) problematic than the ability of the body to tell the soul what is true.

84a6 ["Penelope"]: according to the suitor Antinous, for three years Penelope put off her suitors on the pretense that before divorcing Odysseus and marrying another, she had to finish weaving the burial shroud for Odysseus' father. However, at night she would unweave what she had woven during the day. In the fourth year of this pretense, one of Penelope's servants revealed the deception and she was forced to complete her work (*Odyssey* 2.93-110). Usually this incident redounds to Penelope's moral and intellectual credit: it shows that she is faithful to her husband and her husband's house, and it also shows remarkable prudence. Socrates' narrow focus on unweaving what was just woven makes the act appear irrational.

84b2 ["as long as there is life within him"]: here Socrates seems to affirm that a philosopher will not commit suicide. It is worth considering whether this comment is compatible with the advice Socrates gave to Evenus at 61b7-8.

85b9 ["the Eleven"]: see notes on *Apology* 37c2 and *Crito* 44a4.

85c3 ["certainty"]: *saphes eidenai* is to know something clearly, for the truth of something to be manifest. *Saphes* is used of prophets whose prophesies are unerring, a sure thing, certain to come to pass (Sophocles, *Oedipus Tyrannus* 390, 1011). On the one hand, the fact that our knowledge may never be *saphes* means that we must perpetually be open-minded to alternative viewpoints; but on the other hand this fact ensures that we have not fallen into sophistry and that we remain committed to objective knowledge of absolute facts, where the truth transcends (is not reducible to) any possible evidence we can have for it.

85d3 ["divine doctrine"]: if Alfred North Whitehead (English philosopher, 1861-1947) was correct to say that "the safest general characterization of the European philosophical tradition is that it consists of a series of footnotes to Plato" (*Process and Reality: An Essay in Cosmology* 2.1.1), then much of the philosophy of Søren Kierkegaard (Danish philosopher, 1813-1855) is a footnote to this passage. But Simmias' *modus ponens* (i.e. "if we cannot sail on the ship of divine doctrine, then we must float on the raft of unending proof") is Kierkegaard's *modus tollens* (i.e. "since we must not float on the raft of unending proof, we must sail on the ship of divine doctrine"). See note on 86e2-3.

85e3 ["tuning"]: *harmonia* is the root of "harmony," but it derives from the verb *harmozō*, which refers to the act of joining things together, or fitting things to one another. With musical instruments the verb *harmozō* refers to the act of tuning, so the noun *harmonia* refers to the state resulting from the act, so "tuning" or "attunement" are more accurate translations than "harmony." E.g. a four-stringed lyre may be tuned to the notes A-D-E-A so that it has a fourth, a fifth and an octave; this is called a *pipa* tuning because it is how the Chinese lute of that name is traditionally tuned. We might also call this a Pythagorean tuning (see note on 61c6).

85e3-4 ["the tuning of a lyre"]: some modern scholars would say that the tuning "supervenes" on the strings, and so the tuning is a "supervenient property." A more traditional account would be to say that the tuning is "ontologically dependent" on the strings insofar as what it is for the tuning to be is for the strings to be and for the strings to be modified in that particular way. Lewis Carroll famously played with this concept in the Cheshire cat's grin, which survives the vanishing of the Cheshire cat's lips (1865, *Alice's Adventures in Wonderland*, Chapter 6). Closer to home, Aristotle's response to the argument of Antiphon's Bed champions the "formal cause:" if the rotting of the wooden bedpost, and the subsequent sprouting of a tree, proves the need to recognize a "material cause," then the fact that man comes from man proves the need to recognize a "formal cause" (*Physics* 2.1). If it is a material law that earth, air, fire and water comes to be from earth, air, fire and water, then it is a formal law that dogs give birth to puppies and not to kittens, while cats give birth to kittens and not to puppies. It is not the material constitution of cats and dogs that accounts for this formal law, it is the different forms that the material takes that determines the forms of the progeny.

86b6-7 ["we think"]: perhaps Simmias is referring to Pythagoreans, but this idea could in fact be nothing more than a popular view at the time. The latter possibility underscores the point Socrates just made: no matter how well verified a theory happens to be, any new hypothesis that arises demands that the established theory be supported anew.

86d3 ["soul is the first thing to perish?"]: Simmias' objection is brilliant. Even if Socrates' earlier argument dealing with the opposites proves that we must reject pre-Socratic materialism (i.e. the theory that a complete account of reality can be given relying on nothing more than the basic material elements), all he has shown is that some form of dualism is needed (see notes on 70e3 and 71c12). One obvious candidate is "substance dualism," i.e. there are two basic kinds of substances, material and non-material. We might also call this "transcendent dualism" because it allows non-material substances to have a non-material (disembodied) existence (and in that sense they "transcend" matter). The trouble is that "transcendent dualism" raises the question of how the two kinds of substances can interact with one another (see note on 81d3). Simmias' objection raises the alternative possibility of "property dualism," i.e. there are two basic kinds of properties, material and non-material. Aristotle's recognition of formal and final causes is the most famous and influential version of property dualism. Property dualism (1) does not raise any interactionist worries, (2) solves the problems with pre-Socratic materialism as well as substance dualism does, but (3) supports only "immanent dualism," i.e. it does not allow non-material properties a disembodied existence.

86e2-3 ["agree with them"]: here Socrates is agreeing with the point of Simmias' raft analogy at 85b10-d10—given that absolute certainty on such matters is denied us, we must perpetually be on the defensive, and if a new view overturns the view upon which we have based our whole journey in life, we must be prepared to abandon it after due consideration. Such an attitude seems unacceptable to some (see note on 85d3). What grounds this willingness to abandon even a view upon which one's entire life has been based is the love of learning (cf. 82d9), and hence love the truth (66b7).

86e7 ["a while ago"]: at 77e7 where Cebes challenged Socrates to prove to them that the should not be afraid of death.

87b8 ["one he'd made himself"]: this detail prepares us for Cebes' idea that the soul makes the body (87e1), i.e. a material body is like Theseus' ship (see note on 58a10-11), and like a Heraclitean river—you cannot step into the same river twice, and you cannot meet the same body twice. The material components (e.g. "cells," as we would say today) are constantly passing away so that without constant replenishment our bodies would simply die.

87d7-8 ["soul wears out many bodies"]: Cebes' objection is clever. He grants that Socrates has so far proven what came to be called "vitalism" in the 19th century, i.e. that materialism cannot account for living processes (see notes on 70e3 and 71c12), and he is willing to admit that the soul has no physical parts and so is by nature more durable than any composite material object (as Socrates argued at 78b4-81a2). So unlike Simmias, Cebes is willing to admit that the death of the body (the unstringing of the lyre) does not automatically destroy the soul. And he is also willing to admit that what destroys the body cannot destroy the soul. But from this it does not follow that nothing can destroy the soul. To complete the argument we need to be able to say, "what destroys the body cannot destroy the soul, *and nothing else can destroy the soul*."

88a9 ["final death"]: like the proverbial cat with nine lives nearing the end of its ninth.

88b4 ["we are fools"]: this is precisely why Simmias demurred at 84d6-7. Both of their objections give reason to think that Socrates is being a fool for facing his own demise with such equanimity. It seems downright cruel to deprive someone facing imminent death of their confidence.

88b5-6 ["deathless and indestructible"]: Socrates argues for deathlessness at 102b-105e and indestructibility at 106a-e.

88c1 ["uncomfortable"]: *aēdēs* derives not from *hēdonē* (pleasure, enjoyment, satisfaction) but from *ēdos* (delight, but also it refers to vinegar used as a flavoring for food). So *aēdēs* is not simply "unpleasant," but rather "distasteful" or even "nauseous." I think there are two aspects to this nausea, and both are connected to Simmias' liferaft analogy (85d1). First, Cebes ended his objection by almost calling Socrates a fool for facing his imminent death calmly (thus, apparently trying to rip Socrates' liferaft away from him at death, when he needs it most, see note on 88b4); second, the two objections seem to have in fact ripped away everybody else's liferafts. At this point it may appear that sustained rational scrutiny of reality reveals that it is reticent to moral order, beauty and meaning—in which case, the novel *La Nausée* (by French Philosopher Jean-Paul Sartre, 1905-1980) and the essay *Le Mythe de Sisyphe* (by French Philosopher Albert Camus, 1913-1960) are footnotes to this passage.

88d7 ["start over from the beginning"]: this seems to be an exaggeration driven by his current emotion. He won't be starting over from the beginning since the discussion so far has laid bare a number of the important issues that will have to be dealt with by whatever turns out to be the true theory. Proceeding from an awareness of some of the main issues and problems is quite different from starting out from the beginning without any understanding of the issues or problems.

89b4 ["tease me"]: Phaedo was a bit too old to be wearing his hair long, and so probably it was a bit of vanity that induced him to keep it long. Socrates probably teased him for caring so much about the beauty of his body when the beauty of his soul was much more important.

89b5 ["cut your beautiful hair"]: in mourning; he would also wear black clothing (see Isaeus, *Nicostratus* 4.7; cf. *Iliad* 23.135-7, 141-53; *Odyssey* 4.197-8, 24.45-6; Aeschylus, *Libation Bearers* 6-7).

89c2 ["the town of Thyrea"]: Socrates mentions only the oath of the Argives because the oath was so famous. I've filled in some details. Herodotus' account is thrilling (*Histories* 1.82).

89c3 ["win back our account"]: this attitude towards an argument sounds more like that of the sophists Euthydemus and Dionysodorus (see *Euthydemus* 272b1). Is Socrates contradicting everything he's said so far about loving wisdom and seeking the truth (e.g. *Phaedo* 66b2, b7, d7, 67b4)? Perhaps not: he proposes only that the cost of defeat is cutting off their hair not their heads (and Socrates seems to think that Phaedo ought to cut his hair for independent reasons, see note on 89b4). So Kierkegaard's *modus tollens* would be Socrates' *modus ponens* (see note on 85d3). Probably we should see this comment as Phaedo's third point at 89a5-7: he is not encouraging them to think that victory is everything, he is merely rallying them so that they don't give up so easily—their view has substantial rational support and so it is worth fighting for, not simply abandoning as false at the first sign of trouble. When Alexis Bouvard (French astronomer, 1767-

1843) discovered that the orbit of Uranus seemed to contradict Newton's laws of motion, he did not give up on Newton's laws: he predicted the existence of an unseen planet, which was discovered three years after his death (Neptune was discovered in 1846 by Johann Gottfried Galle, German astronomer, 1812-1910).

89c5 ["not even Herakles"]: see *Euthydemus* 297b9-d2 and note on 297c1.

89c8 ["daylight"]: Socrates was not allowed to live out the day, so he was required to drink the hemlock no later than dusk.

89d1 ["misologists"]: Immanuel Kant (German philosopher, 1724-1804) argued that misology arises when when someone with a cultivated reason strives for happiness, since reason is ill suited to this purpose (*Groundwork for the Metaphysics of Morals*, Section 1). But Kant here conceives of "happiness" as satisfaction. In the *Phaedo*, therefore, Socrates would probably agree with Kant's point, because he would agree that reason's highest function is not to serve the satisfaction of the body (63b4-69e5). In the *Gorgias*, however, Socrates would probably disagree with Kant, because he would point out the adaptive function of reason: if we have 4 desires and satisfy only 3 of them, then we enjoy only 75% satisfaction; if reason is unable to satisfy the fourth desire, then it may eliminate it, because satisfying 3 of 3 desires yields 100% satisfaction (cf. *Gorgias* 492d1-494a5; a related view seems entailed by the view in the *Republic* that the *logistikon* ought to rule both the *thumos* and the *epithumētikon*, cf. *Republic* 4.435c4-445b4).

89d6 ["sound"]: *hugiēs* literally means "healthy." More generally it refers to being in good condition (e.g. "safe and sound"), or being wholesome. He is about to apply this adjective to *logoi* (arguments, accounts or theories), and it is not clear what he means by it. Today logicians define a "sound" argument as one with true premises, and whose premises necessarily entail the conclusion (and so a sound argument succeeds in proving that the conclusion is true). Probably he would allow that an argument can be *hugiēs* even if it is not "sound" in this sense, e.g. inductive arguments are not "sound" in this sense, but they can provide sufficient warrant for believing the conclusion, and the conclusion may in fact be true.

90b8 ["sometimes the conclusion is true"]: perhaps he is referring to something like Laches' claim that courage is standing fast (*Laches* 190e4-6); sometimes this is true (e.g. for hoplite soldiers), but sometimes it is false (e.g. for Scythian cavalrymen).

90c1 ["contradicting arguments"]: *antilogikos* is also used at 101e2. See also *Sophist* 225b10, *Phaedrus* 261d10. Perhaps Socrates has contrarians in mind—people who make a habit of contradicting any view put forward. There are other possibilities, e.g. litigious or polemical reasoning, dialectical argumentation, Zeno's strategy of deriving contradictory conclusions from someone's thesis, or the exercise that teachers of rhetoric sometimes gave their students of requiring them to write persuasive arguments both for and against any given position (a practice well illustrated by Thucydides' practice of pairing political speeches on two sides of a disputed proposal). Around 400 BCE a collection called *Dissoi Logoi* ("doubled arguments" or "contrasting arguments") was written, and it paired arguments on opposed sides of various issues. It is not clear what the purpose of this work was: Socrates might find it worthwhile since it helps readers to consider alternative argumetns; however, he might also fear that it could induce misology in some (for every argument there is an equally strong but opposed argument, so we can never place our trust in any argument)

90c5 ["strait of Euripus"]: a narrow channel of water between the Greek mainland and the Aegean island of Euboea. Today its narrowest point is only 125 feet and the water changes direction four times each day. In ancient times it was said to change direction seven times each day. Euripides set his tragedy *Iphigeneia at Aulis* by this strait, and the inconstant water served as a metaphor for the repeatedly shifting views of the main characters.

90d3 ["instead of laying the blame on himself"]: Socratic wisdom involves self-scrutiny (e.g. *Apology* 23a3-c1). Perhaps, then, Martin Heidegger (German Philosopher, 1889-1976) underestimated the extent to which traditional philosophers make the inquirer a prominent subject of inquiry (*Being and Time*, Introduction, Section 2). Hence, Socrates might admonish Antoine Roquentin (the protagonist of Sartre's *La Nausée*, see note on 88c1) to consider the possibility that his inability to discern rational order, beauty and meaning in reality is a problem with him, not reality, and that he ought to make the inquirer a more prominent focus of his inquiry.

92d5 ["in geometry"]: at *Theatetus* 162e4-7 Socrates says that Theodorus would be a worthless geometer if he argued from premises that were merely likely. In the *Euthydemus* he says that arguing from such premises is appropriate for the kinds of orators who aren't exactly philosophers, but aren't exactly politicians (305e1). At *Meno* 82e3, when Socrates is proving that learning is recollection, the slave boy first makes a guess which seems likely (though it is not explicitly said to be so) but it leads to the wrong answer.

92d9 ["itself by itself"]: see 75d2, 76d7-e7, and 78d1.

93a11 ["return to this point later"]: not in the text. I've added this because Socrates employs an odd structure in this section.

> Premises for argument A: 92e4-93a10
> Premises for argument B: 93a11-c10
> Argument B: 93d1-94b3
> Argument A: 94b4-95a3

93a12 ["insofar as it is tuned"]: this point is obvious in Greek (see note on 85e3). Although he uses this principle immediately in argument B (see premise (2) in note on 93a14), it is not necessary (premise (3) is independently just as reasonable as premise (2) and so does not need to be inferred from it). But this principle is more important in argument A.

93a14 ["tunes one lyre more fully"]: argument B (see note on 93a11) has been translated and interpreted in many different ways. In my view (see notes below), it works as follows.

> Hypothesis: the soul is an attunement (94b1).
> (1) Attunements follow tunings (93a11-12).
> (2) Tunings do not come in degrees (93d6-7).
> (3) So attunements do not come in degrees (93d9-10).
> (4) If a soul can be bad, then attunements come in degrees (93e7-9).
> (5) A soul cannot be bad (94a1-6).
> (6) So, all souls are good (94a8-10).
> Conclusion: the Hypothesis entails a false claim (6), so it is false (94a12-b3).

If one four-stringed lyre is tuned to A-D-E-A and another to C-F-G-C, the second is not a wrong, bad or lesser tuning. The normative language appropriate to souls (cf. *Crito* 47d3-48a1, *Republic* 4.444d13-e2) is not appropriate to tunings, and so souls are not tunings.

93b2 ["fuller or more complete"]: I've added the musician and the lyre because Socrates' statement is extremely abstract. Only two points are clear in the text: (1) Socrates is applying the principle he just stated (see 93a12 and the note on that line), and (2) he is using comparative words that indicate matters of degree. So his point is that if the original act of tuning is a matter of degree, then the resulting attunements will be matters of degree. Not all comparative degrees are normative (e.g. the tree is farther to the right than the bush), but some are (e.g. the second patient is sicker than the first). Socrates makes it clear that in this argument he is not concerned with comparative degrees as such, but only in normative degrees (93b9-c1).

93c7 ["have only one attunement"]: it is possible to understand the Greek as saying that the bad soul has zero attunements, not one, but this does not fit well with what he has said so far. More importantly, the clear focus of Socrates' question is the *allos* on lines c5, c7 and c8 i.e. the *additional* attunement. So the question about the bad soul is not whether it has any attunement at all, but whether it has an additional attunement, i.e. given the fact that it already has the attunement of being a soul—this is the hypothesis upon which the entire argument rests.

93d3 ["this is the agreement"]: here my translation is very literal. The relationship between the two agreements is not clear; obviously they are not word-for-word identical. What would make sense would be to say that the two agreements are equally reasonable in themselves, and each is equally a reason to believe the other—though the former probably helps to illuminate the latter, which explains the order in which he places them in this paragraph. Possessing a soul seems to be an all-or-nothing matter: either you have one or you don't; the same seems to go for possessing an attunement. We might prefer hearing a lyre with the A-D-E-A tuning to hearing the one with the A-D-E#-A tuning (depending upon how they are played), but both count equally as tunings. So here is where Socrates is pointing out that they've rejected the "supposing that is possible" allowance from 93b1.

93d7 ["no more or less tuned"]: applying the abstract principle briefly stated at 93a11-12. We might say that the musician did a better or more complete job of tuning the first lyre as opposed to the second (e.g. she brought the E# down to an E on the first but not the second lyre), but this is a normative judgment of the musician (e.g. she failed fully to accomplish her goal for the second lyre), not the tuning (cf. note on 93d3). Although we can rank tunings according to our preferences, this does not entail that the tunings we don't like are wrong or bad, and they don't entail that the one's we don't like aren't tunings at all (or aren't tunings to some degree—if that even means anything). Alternatively, lyres may be bad if they are incapable of holding the same tuning for very long, but the badness of the lyre does not entail that the various attunements through which it goes as it goes increasingly out of tune are in themselves bad or wrong, even if we like them less and less.

94b8 ["does it resist them?"]: cf. *Republic* 4.436b8-441c2.

94b10 ["despite being hungry?"]: argument A (see note on 93a11) might be reduced thus: if the soul is an attunement, then dieting is impossible; but dieting is not impossible; so the soul is not an attunement. We might be skeptical of the first premise since it may be possible for one body to contain two attunements, and when played, one may cancel out the other. But this would seem to be a case of one bodily appetite overcoming another, which was already rejected as a true form of virtue (at 68d2-69d6).

94c3 ["didn't we agree just now"]: at 93a6-9.

94c6 ["the soul follows the strings"]: I've added the implicit reference to the strings, which is implied by the explicit reference to tightness and looseness. I think Socrates' point is about explanatory priority: the fact that a lyre is attuned to A-D-E-A does not explain why the four strings are as tightly strung as they are, rather, the fact that the strings are as tightly strung as they are explains why the lyre is attuned to A-D-E-A (though, of course, the fact that the musician intended the lyre to be attuned to A-D-E-A explains why the four strings are as tightly strung as they are).

94e1 ["worse you've endured"]: an exact quote of *Odyssey* 20.17-18 (Plato also quotes line 17 at *Republic* 4.441b6). I've added a bit more of the context than Socrates actually gives since his audience was probably more familiar with the *Odyssey* than a modern audience.

95a4 ["Harmony"]: *Harmonia* is the goddess of joining or bringing together (see note on 85e3). Naturally, her parents were Aphrodite (goddess of love) and Ares (god of war). Her name is the word I've been translating as "tuning" and "attunement." *Harmonia* was married to the mortal Cadmus, the legendary founder of the city of Thebes—hometown of both Simmias and Cebes.

96a6 ["When I was young"]: scholars disagree on much of the following account was intended by Plato to be an autobiography of Socrates, or how much of it was in fact true of Socrates.

96a8 ["natural science"]: literally he says *peri phuseōs historia*, i.e. "natural history," or "inquiry into nature." But today "natural history" tends to be limited to the study of plants and animals in their environments. What Socrates goes on to describe includes issues of metabolism and astronomy, so probably "natural science" is closer. But even that may be too narrow: "natural philosophy" or "the philosophy of reality" might be more accurate.

96a9 ["what is responsible"]: *aitia* can refer to a cause, a reason or an explanation, but it can do so because it refers primarily to responsibility. I hope that my use of "why" in the rest of the sentence preserves the ambiguity.

96a9 ["why each thing comes to be"]: *gignomai* is ambiguous. First, it can be use existentially (or in an unqualified or complete way) to refer to something coming into existence (e.g. being born or created). Second, it can be used predicatively (or in a qualified or incomplete way) to refer to something acquiring a property (e.g. coming to be blue by being painted blue). Socrates does not distinguish these senses: sometimes what he says makes more sense on one meaning than on another.

96a10 ["why each thing exists"]: if you know why something came to be and why it has not yet perished, don't you *ipso facto* know why it exists? Socrates goes on to mention what Aristotle will later call "material causes" (e.g. food causes us to grow) and "efficient causes" (e.g. eating causes us to grow), but not until he mentions Anaxagoras (97c1) will he consider a "final cause" (e.g. we grow in order to reach maturity), and, of course, Socrates is most concerned about what Aristotle will call the "formal cause" (e.g. we grow because we are essentially human beings).

96b3 ["those people"]: Socrates briefly sketches the theory of Archelaus, who was probably Athenian. Archelaus was a student of Anaxagoras, and a teacher of Socrates (Diogenes Laertius 2.16). I've supplemented what Socrates actually says with Diogenes' account of Archelaus' view. Perhaps 97b8 is actually a reference to Archelaus.

96b4 ["by which we think"]: in the 5th century, Empedocles defended the blood theory, Diogenes of Apollonia defended the air theory, and the Heracliteans defended the fire theory. From a modern perspective, these theories seem so simplistic as to be silly non-starters, but we must remind ourselves that they are inventing an entirely new way of understanding reality. Instead of explaining natural phenomena by appealing to multiple, incommensurable, external divine beings, whose intentions can be discerned only through divination, these early thinkers seek to explain natural phenomena by appealing to as few as possible, commensurable, internal material compositions, whose causal powers can be discerned by the very same capacity that allows us to plan logistically. Perhaps no more profound a revolution in thought ever has or will happen in the history of our species.

96b5 ["the brain"]: Alcmaeon of Croton and Hippocrates (both 5th century) defended the view that the brain is the seat of consciousness.

96b9 ["everything in the heavens?"]: *ouranos* refers to the sky, which was thought of as a sort of dome, arch or roof over the earth (hence a vaulted roof and the roof of the mouth could metaphorically be called an *ouranos*). At *Apology* 19d3-5 Socrates denies ever discussing "even a little bit" such matters (see note on *Apology* 19d5). Given the comparative lengths of these four questions, it seems that his most avid pursuit was more Hippocratic than anything else—which is irrelevant to his concerns in the *Apology*. For all he says in the *Phaedo*, Socrates' astronomical research amounted to no more than reading Anaxagoras' book—which is perfectly compatible with his denial at *Apology* 19d3-5.

96e7 ["I do not know"]: the text makes it seem that Socrates is denying that he knows what makes one man taller or one number greater, but it will soon be clear that in his view the forms give the correct answers to these questions (see 101b9-c5). My guess is that here he is expressing confusion about the answers that used to seem perfectly clear and reasonable to him. The text is highly abstract and admits of different interpretations; this is one of those passages that makes me think that Plato sometimes neglected to edit or re-write passages he could have done a better job with. But I don't want my translation to be unnecessarily difficult or confusing, so I've taken the liberty of making the passage more concrete: I've added the reference to the olives, a widely cultivated fruit in Greece.

97c6 ["best for it"]: perhaps Socrates thinks that if things are arranged by mind, they are arranged intentionally to achieve particular goals—*teloi* in Greek—and hence are arranged teleologically. E.g. if it is my goal to hit the bullseye of a target, and my first arrow lands ten inches from the bullsey but the second lands only five inches away, then my second shot was *better* than my first shot. *Teloi* are norms, but not all norms are intentional. Health is a norm. Similarly, you fail to understand a cheetah if you fail to understand why its tail is as long and as heavy as it is: it would be a worse tail for a cheetah if it were substantially longer or shorter, heavier or lighter, i.e. you must understand how its actual tail is *best* for it. This teleological conception of reality would dominate European thought into the early modern period—when it was seriously challenged by a mechanistic conception.

97d8 ["flat or round"]: the views of the Ionians and the Pythagoreans respectively.

97e3 ["the earth is in the center of the cosmos"]: probably the view of both Anaxagoras and Archelaus. The Pythagorean philosopher Philolaus (see 61d7 and note on *Crito* 45b4) argued that the earth is a planet circling an unseen central fire (not the sun).

98e5 ["By the dog"]: see note on *Charmides* 172e4 and *Apology* 22a1.

99b6 ["whirlpool"]: Empedocles' view (Aristotle, *On the Heavens* 2.13.295a6-20).

99b8 ["column of air"]: the view of Anaximines, Anaxagoras and Democritus (Aristotle, *On the Heavens* 2.13.14-23).

99c8 ["deprived"]: because Anaxagoras turned out to be a fraud (see 98b8).

99c9 ["second sailing"]: although this could refer to a second attempt at a voyage after being turned back by the weather, it probably means using the oars when the wind died, because in practice the phrase seems to imply an inferior second-best method (cf. *Statesman* 300c2, *Philebus* 19c2-3; Aristotle, *Politics* 3.13.1284b19, *Nicomachean Ethics* 2.9.1109a35). The "first sailing" was to learn from Anaxagoras how mind controls the entire cosmos; Plato would later attempt this in the *Timaeus*.

99e5 ["argumentation"]: *logos* could be word, statement, theory, argument, computation, accounting, consideration and so on. I prefer argument here because so far they have relied quite a lot on arguments, and also because a focus on arguments is probably quite inclusive, e.g. it can include the examination of statements and theories, but it can also include the collection and examination of evidence. Some scholars assume that the praise of *logos* here entails a condemnation of *muthos*, which would be hypocritical of Socrates since he himself gives a *muthos* at 110b5-114c8. But even if *logoi* are the only way to gain knowledge of the truth, it doesn't follow that *muthoi* can play no positive role at all. Elsewhere Plato condemns many traditional *muthoi*, but just because *muthoi* can be badly constructed it doesn't follow that they cannot be well constructed to make a good impact on listeners.

99e6-100a1 ["my analogy isn't exact"]: a reflection of the sun is a *less* accurate image of the sun than a direct perception of it, but a *logos* of the truth can provide a *more* accurate image, so the analogy isn't exactly parallel.

100a3 ["hypothesis"]: cf. *Meno* 86e3. We might call this, Socrates' "hypothetical method." It is worth asking how this method relates both to the "Socratic method" of refutation in dialogues like *Charmides*, and *Laches*, and how it relates to what is today called the "scientific method." In the *Meno*, Socrates compares it to a method of proof used by geometers. It would be difficult to overstate the significance of Socrates' critique of pre-Socratic philosophy and his development of a new method of inquiry. In the history of European philosophy, it can be compared to Francis Bacon's *Novum Organum* (1620) and René Descartes' *Discourse on Method* (1637).

100a4 ["account"]: a *logos* could be an hypothesis, e.g. a proposition, theory, explanation.

100a4 ["sound"]: *errōmenos* refers to sound health, so "robust" might be a better translation. Why doesn't Socrates explain what he means? If a robust hypothesis is one that survives the sort of Socratic questioning we see in the *Charmides*, *Laches* and *Euthyphro*, then perhaps he thinks this part of his hypothetical method is so obvious that it goes without saying.

100a5 ["agreement"]: Socrates does not use *sumbainein* but *sumphōnein* (also at 101d5), so he probably has something broader in mind that just logically necessary entailments of the hypothesis. Also, Socrates assumes that he will consider a plurality of *logoi*, not just one. Again (see note on 100a4b), this fits with the sort of Socratic questioning we see in the *Charmides*, *Laches* and *Euthyphro*—hence the necessity of selecting a robust hypothesis: the hypotheses put forward by, e.g., Charmides entail false claims.

100b6-7 ["and all the others"]: at *Republic* 10.596a6-7 Socrates says that they (plural) posit a form when many things have a single name. This is often called the "one over many" assumption, but surely it needs to be narrowed: is there a form of the dirty, the bald and a form of everybody named "Frank"? See notes on *Laches* 191e10 and *Phaedo* 102b2.

100c5 ["participates"]: *metechō* (like *metalambanō*, see note on 102b2) means to partake of or to share in. For example, to spend time focusing on how you are dressed is to partake of (64e1, cf. 65a5) that sort of thing; a ghost that can be seen partakes of (81d4) the visible, to partake in land is to possess or to control a portion of it (Herodotus 1.204.1). Can a beautiful sculpture possess a portion of the beautiful itself? Can a large person possess a portion of the large itself, and if so, how large a portion will that be? Plato worries about such questions at *Parmenides* 130e5-131d3. See also 100d6 below.

100d3-4 ["openly, simply and perhaps foolishly"]: perhaps Socrates is ironically asserting that his theory is far wiser than that of the so-called wise men. Alternatively, to say flat out that beauty is what makes beautiful things beautiful does seem truly to speak openly, simply and perhaps foolishly—especially when (1) the forms are a hypothesis, and not a proven fact, (2) you fail to say what beauty is, and (3) you stumble for a way to explain the relationship between a beautiful thing and the form of beauty. Nevertheless, perhaps no assertion—other than "the element and principle of all things is water" by Thales—was more momentous in the history of European science than this: in addition to studying the intrinsic material properties of things, science cannot advance without concerted study of configurational, structural or formal properties.

100e9 ["by a head"]: a textbook case of the "Dative of Measure of Difference." Taken out of context, this would be confusing because Socrates is not challenging our ability to measure differences in length. What he is objecting to is answering the question, "What is responsible (*aitia*) for the fact that this man is taller than that man?" with "he's a head taller," and leaving it at that. Perhaps Socrates should not have shied away from geometrical examples. Suppose you answer the question, "What is responsible for the fact that this wooden triangle has three sides?" with "that carpenter nailed a third side onto the other two." If you are satisfied with that answer, then perhaps you think that the only reason the carpenter didn't create a four-sided triangle is that she knocked off for lunch. For the significance of Socrates' point, see note on 100d3-4.

101a8 ["by something small"]: again (see note on 100e9) it is not easy to see Socrates' point with this example. If one man is taller than another, but just barely, then the measure of the difference in their height is very small, and there's nothing ridiculous about that. The ridiculousness (or monstrosity, *teras* at 101b1) is more evident in my case of the wooden triangle: it would be monstrous to say that the addition of one board is what is responsible for the fact that this object is a triangle—again, as if the addition of one more board was all that was needed to create a four-sided triangle. Scholars are correct to worry about the multiple distinct senses that *aitia* can have (see note on 96a9a), but I think the more important problem with Socrates' account is that it appears to entail that a form is in itself a sufficient cause (thereby failing "to distinguish the cause of an action from the necessary conditions for the cause to be effective," 99b3-4). If we accept that the form of the large itself is alone responsible for the largeness of this large man, then it appears as if we do not need to appeal also to his bone mass (which Aristotle would count as a "material cause" of his largeness), or to the parents who created him (which Aristotle would count among the "efficient causes" of his largeness). Aristotle explicitly criticizes this oversight in the *Phaedo* at *Generation and Corruption* 2.9.335b7-29. The way Socrates speaks here will make it appear as if forms transcend matter, and hence can exist uninstantiated (this is often called Plato's doctrine of "separation," and it was criticized by Aristotle, e.g. *Metaphysics* 13.9.1086b6-7). Socrates supplements the view he defends here at 105b5-c7.

101d3 ["focuses"]: I just translated a form of *echō* as "stick with," and many scholars are uncomfortable giving it a different translation a mere two lines below. Perhaps Plato should have re-written this passage, though I think the idioms involved would not have confused native speakers. So far Socrates has been emphasizing the part of his "hypothetical method" in which you give answers to questions that would be true if your hypothesis is true. Now he considers people who ask about substantiating the hypothesis independently of the consideration of its consequences—he thinks that this approach simply confuses things (*kukaō*, 101e5).

101e1 ["something adequate"]: Socrates does not say what would be adequate (sufficient, befitting, satisfactory; *hikanos*). In particular, he gives no indication that adequacy consists in something substantially different from the consideration of coherence he just mentioned (*sumphōnei ē diaphōnei*, 101d5). If this is correct, then Plato resolves a deep worry about the Socratic method by a sort of coherentism (see notes on *Charmides* 163c2, *Laches* 195c12). In the *Republic*, the third stage of "The Line" employs hypotheses that are not adequate until the form of the good is employed in a synoptic view of things (7.537c6-7). However, he makes this point in the context of philosophical research; perhaps a less robust form of adequacy will suffice with non-philosophers.

101e2 ["the hypothesis and its consequences simultaneously"]: if we assume that knowledge is based on knowledge (KBK), then this approach would be reasonable. Perhaps René Descartes accepted this assumption if he thinks that claims such as 'I think' and 'I exist" are known and are based on themselves (they are self-justifying). Socrates appears to reject KBK in the *Meno* e.g. 85b8-86c2, 97c11-98a8. Socrates quickly uses a hypothetical method at Meno 87b5-c10, and then immediately challenges the hypothesis on which he just relied. True to form, he continues by positing a "higher" hypothesis, i.e. one that would justify their acceptance of the first hypothesis. Notice that the "higher" hypothesis will likely have broader significance than the one hypothesis currently being challenged, which would explain why a plurality of propositions will inevitably be considered (see note on 100a5).

102b2 ["called by the name"]: literally he says they are "eponymous" (*epōnumia*). This suggests that he really is attracted to the "one over many" argument for the existence of a form (see notes on *Laches* 191e10 and *Phaedo* 100b6-7). Here, instead of *metechō* he uses *metalambanō* for "participate" (see notes on *Euthydemus* 301a4 and *Phaedo* 100c5).

102b6 ["largeness and smallness"]: Socrates consistently focuses on forms of the qualities and relations possessed by beings, not forms of the beings themselves, e.g. the form of largeness or equality rather than the form (genus and species) of human beings that can be large or equal in size to one another. It is not clear why. However, one thing that is made clear by this focus is that in some cases (if not all), forms are related to one another. Perhaps we should not expect to get a complete account of any one form in isolation from others.

102c2 ["the magnitude that he happens to have"]: Socrates implicitly relies on one of the most important distinctions in philosophy, i.e. the distinction between an *essential* and an *accidental* property. Most philosophers define this distinction by saying that an essential property of an object is a property that the object must have (to gain the property is to come into existence, and to lose the property is to go out of existence), but an accidental property of an object is a property that it happens to have, but it could lack (to gain or to lose the property is simply to change, not to come into or go out of existence). A triangle that gained an extra side would stop being a triangle and start being a quadrangle (the triangle ceased to exist and was replaced with a quadrangle): having exactly three sides is an essential property of all triangles. A triangle that got painted blue would simply undergo an alteration; it could become green, then red and so on—the color it happens to have is an accidental property of a triangle.

102c7 ["in relation to"]: most scholars are side-tracked by this passage because largeness is a *relational property*, but the more important point is that Socrates recognizes that largeness and smallness are *essentially contextual* (cf. the difference between a large mouse and a small elephant). This is part of the significance of some of the claims he is about to make, which might otherwise appear to us to go without saying, e.g. the number ten cannot possibly be an odd number (105a7). There are systematic relations between forms such that we cannot fully understand any one without seeing its relations to others. Whether or not an action participates in the form of the good may depend upon whether it participates in the form of the just, which may depend upon whether it violated any law of the city in which it was done. We should not think of "participation" in a form on an analogy with cookies stamped out by cookie-cutters (see notes on *Euthydemus* 301a4 and *Phaedo* 100c5).

102d6 ["largeness itself will never be simultaneously large and small"]: the form of the large is itself large (see also *Euthyphro* 6e3-6, *Hippias Major* 291d1-3, *Protagoras* 330c4-e2, *Parmenides* 132a6). The claim that the form of the large is itself large, or, in general, that the form of F is itself F, is called "Self-

Predication." But this label may be misleading: large is predicated of an elephant because it is a property that elephants gain as they grow. Surely the form of the large did not acquire the property of being large by growing. Perhaps "Self-Explanation" would be more accurate: the form of the large *explains* why all large things are large, and since the form of the large is precisely what explains the largeness of things, it is self-explanatory, hence it is large.

102d7 ["the largeness in us"]: what is the largeness in us? Hopefully it is just that, i.e. the form of the large itself, which currently is in us. That forms can be in us seems to be implied by his claim at 100d5-6 that beauty itself is "present with" (*parousia*) or "associates with" (*koinōnia*) the beautiful thing (see notes on 100c5, 102b2, and *Euthydemus* 301a4). If the form of largeness in us is something in addition to the form of the large (perhaps Socrates is distinguishing an *idea* from an *eidos*), then Socrates is multiplying explanatory entities beyond necessity (he's violating Ockham's Razor). Some scholars refer to the largeness in us as an "immanent character." See note on 103e5.

102d8 ["it won't agree"]: Socrates' verbs personify the largeness in us. Presumably this is simply colorful language and not to be taken literally. But if this is not to be taken literally, what else in this passage is not to be taken literally?

102d9 ["departs"]: *hupechrōeō* is used here and at 103d8, 104c1 and 106e7. Literally it means to give place to something. Clearly Socrates is not using this word literally, but (1) it's not clear what it's non-literal meaning is, and (2) Socrates applies it in very special cases (see 106d5-7 and note on 106e7).

102e2 ["the largeness in us has been destroyed"]: if you think that the form of largeness cannot be destroyed, then you might infer that the largeness in us is not the same thing as the form of largeness itself (see note on 102d7). But Plato never says that the largeness in us, or any of the forms in us, can be destroyed—destruction is simply one of two alternatives. E.g. it is true that when this bachelor gets married there are only two options: either he ceases to be a bachelor, or he continues to be a bachelor despite being married. The fact that the second option is the only alternative to the first does not entail that sometimes the second option happens. Also, if you think that the form of largeness cannot flee or move around, then you might infer that the largeness in us is not the same thing as the form of largeness itself. But obviously not all of Socrates' colorful language is to be taken literally (see note on 102d8); the form of the large can "flee" simply in the sense that a material object can stop being large (the form is no longer in it). See note on 103e5.

103a4 ["someone else"]: it is difficult to believe that on Socrates' final day, the conversation was almost exclusively between Socrates, Simmias and Cebes. This seems artificial, and so perhaps Plato included this detail to make the dialogue seem less unrealistic.

103a6 ["what we agreed earlier?"]: at 69e6-72e2.

103b3 ["one contrary thing"]: Socrates is explicitly distinguishing between a thing and its properties. This may be the first place where this happens in European philosophy.

103b4 ["for example"]: here and at c1 below I've added the example; see 70e6-8.

103d2 ["the hot"]: if you think that Socrates distinguishes between the form of the hot itself and the hot in us, then it is not clear to which he is referring here. This is one of the many unnecessary complications that arise if Socreates is violating Occham's Razor (see notes on 102d7 and 102e2).

103d6 ["That phrase we used a little while ago"]: at 103a1.

103e5 ["character"]: here and at 104d10 Socrates uses *morphē*, which means shape, form, appearance, and, by extension, kind, sort or type (*Republic* 3.397c5; Euripides, *Ion* 382). If Socrates distinguishes *eidos* and *idea* (a transcendent form and an immanent form; see note on 104b9), then it would stand to reason that a *morphē* is a third kind of form, which seems profligate (see notes on 102d7 and 102e2). It could be that Socrates has no interest in standardizing a philosophical vocabulary, and so he casually uses *eidos*, *idea* and *morphē* all to suggest what he has in mind by the forms.

104a4 ["The number three"]: is Socrates referring to (a) the form of threeness itself, (b) the immanent character of threeness that is in, e.g., a group of three olives, or (c) three things, e.g. three olives? In my view, we can ignore (b), see notes on 102d7 and 102e2.

104b8 ["they are always opposed"]: more literally, Socrates says that while they are not opposites, they have opposites. But that sounds contradictory, and he is simply repeating what he's already said, e.g. there is no such thing as the opposite of a snowball, but a snowball is always opposed to heat in the sense that heat melts snowballs—there's no such thing as a hot snowball, there's only a warm puddle where a snowball used to be.

104b9 ["character"]: this is the first occurrence of *idea* in the *Phaedo* (see note on 65d12). It could refer to what some philosophers call "immanent characters," e.g. the large that is in us as opposed to the form of the large itself (see notes on 102d7, 102e2, and 103e5). If that is it's function in the *Phaedo*, then perhaps that was its function in the *Euthyphro* (see note on *Euthyphro* 5d4). But, of course, it could also refer to the form itself.

104c5 ["three and even"]: the only thing Socrates actually says here is, "two is not the opposite of three." Scholars speculate on why. My suggestion here is conservative, i.e. he is simply spelling out what he just said at 104b9-10, i.e. there is no such thing as the opposite of the number three. Europeans did not embrace negative numbers (-3 might be thought of as the opposite of 3) until the 17th century (Chinese mathematicians were the first to recognize them, and our earliest evidence of this is from the Han Dynasty (206 BCE–220 CE).

104d1 ["when it takes hold of something"]: this passage is grammatically uncertain, which complicates its philosophical uncertainty, especially given how abstract it is. As usual, my translation is conservative, fitting the example he just gave, and also the examples he's going to give at 104e7-105b3. When the number three takes hold of some olives (i.e. there are three olives), the number three compels the olives to take on the distinctive character of three (e.g. take one away and you'll be left with only two), but it also compels the olives to take on one of a pair of opposites (i.e. when the number of olives is three, the number of olives is necessarily odd, which is the opposite of being an even number of olives). Similarly, when typhoid fever (not just the bacterium *Salmonella typhi*, see note on 105c4) takes hold of a body, it compels that body to take on the distinctive character of typhoid fever (e.g. malaise and a rise in body temperature), but it also compels the body to take on one of a pair of opposites (i.e. illness, which is opposed to health). In both cases, when the second of the pair of opposites takes hold of the bodies, the first is destroyed, it doesn't withdraw: the oddness of the three olives doesn't automatically migrate to another set of olives when someone eats one of them, and this person's typhoid fever doesn't automatically transfer to another person when the doctor cures her.

104d9 ["as long as"]: I've added this; Socrates cannot mean that once something becomes three, it can never become four (once I was three feet tall, but I grew; once the measurement of my height was odd, but later it was even).

104e7 ["Earlier"]: at 104c11.

105b7 ["Earlier"]: at 100c3-102a1.

105c4 ["fever"]: *puretos* is the name of an illness, and not—as we think of it today—a symptom of an underlying infection (cf. Hippocrates, *On airs, waters and places* 10). Hence, by fever coming into your body, you are ill. Notice a difference: (a) it is not true in every case that by the bacterium *Salmonella typhi* coming into your body you come down with typhoid fever (Mary Mallon, aka "Typhoid Mary," never suffered from typhoid fever), but (b) since typhoid fever is an illness, by it coming into your body you do become ill, and if your doctor brings health to your body, then either your typhoid fever withdraws from you or it is simply destroyed (you cannot be completely healthy and suffering from typhoid fever simultaneously, though you can be completely healthy and have *Salmonella typhi* in your gall bladder). Illness is a generic contextual property of a living body; typhoid fever is one species of that generic contextual property. I assume that Socrates is not claiming that *puretos* is the only illness—this is just an example.

105c6 ["one"]: 7 is odd because it is not evenly divisible by 2; when you divide it by 2, 1 is left over; 7 is 3+3+1 so the additional 1 is what makes 7 odd.

105c9 ["that body will be alive?"]: a detailed answer to this question will be a full analysis, definition or account of what it is to be alive. As in the case of illness (see note on 105c4), you misunderstand Socrates' question if you answer, "it is because of Typhoid Mary that I am ill," you make a parallel mistake in this case if you try to cite some "vital spark," "vital force," "élan vital" or "quickening agent" in answer to his question. In Aristotelian language, Socrates is seeking a formal cause, not an efficient or material cause (see note on 96a10).

105c11 ["Soul"]: there is no definite article with *psuchē* here. The manuscripts do not agree on whether Plato used the definite article with *psuchē* at d3, d10, e4 and e6. *Psuchē* can refer to a particular person, a particular soul, a soul-stuff (as if soul is a quasi-material substance), the form of the soul itself, or an individual immanent soul. Nevertheless, what he says here (and especially what Socrates says at d3-4) is consistent with the earlier view that no combination of non-living materials could actualize living processes (see notes on 72d3 and 76e5), and so there must be some non-material principle of life, and this principle may be called *psuchē*.

106d3 ["eternal"]: *aidios* is rare in Plato. It occurs here and at *Republic* 10.611b5, *Philebus* 66a8 (though the manuscripts disagree), and at *Timaeus* 29a3, 29a5, 37c6, 37d1, 37e5, 40b5.

106e7 ["withdraws from death"]: here Socrates uses the principle enunciated at 102d9-e2. Presumably this applies to "god, the form of life itself, and anything else that is immortal" (106d5-7), which now includes soul (105e6). It seems to be a restricted conservation principle. Empedocles famously endorsed a principle of the conservation of matter, claiming that it is neither created nor destroyed, it simply scatters and re-forms. In a parallel way, Socrates seems to affirm a "conservation of life" principle, according to which life is neither created nor destroyed, it simply moves from place to place. This is unlike, e.g. my 3-foot tallness: when I grew taller than 3-feet, my 3-foot tallness didn't somehow pop up somewhere else, my 3-foot tallness was simply gone—destroyed. Empedocles also famously endorsed an "effluence" or "emanation" (*aporroē*) theory of perception (*Meno* 76c7): we see objects when their effluences come into contact with our sensory apparatus. In this way, one and the same object can create multiple appearances in multiple perceivers simultaneously; and just because I stop perceiving something does not mean that it no longer exists. Rather than this theory of material effluences, Socrates here seems to suggest what we could call a theory of ideal effluences: non-living material comes to life when an effluence of life itself comes into contact with it. In this way, one and the same ideal form (i.e. life itself) can create multiple living entities simultaneously, and just because this heap of matter dies does not mean that the living effluence that used to animate it ceases to exist. Compare Socrates' effluence theory of beauty at *Phaedrus* 251b2.

107a1 ["Our souls shall indeed be in Hades."]: the full argument works thus.
1. Soul brings to the body life, which is opposed to death.
2. If A brings to x F, which is opposed to G, then A is opposed to G.
3. So, soul is opposed to death.
4. If soul is opposed to death, then soul is immortal.
5. If soul is immortal, then soul cannot be destroyed.
6. So, Soul cannot be destroyed
7. Either soul can be destroyed, or soul withdraws when death approaches.
8. So, Soul withdraws when death approaches.
9. Hades is where soul goes if it withdraws when death approaches.
10. So, soul goes to Hades after death.

The premises that raise the most questions are 1, 2 and 7. On 1 see note on 105c9. On 2 see note on 104d1. On 7 see note on 106e7.

107c6 ["a godsend to bad people"]: notice that the "godsend" is simply that bad people do not have to continue with bad souls; the problem with immortality is that if you are bad, you continue after death with a bad soul. It is not that the good are rewarded and the bad punished; in a sense, goodness is "its own reward" and badness is "its own punishment."

107d6 ["guardian spirit"]: on *daimōn* see notes on *Apology* 24c1, 27c1, 31d1 and *Euthydemus* 272e4. The notion of a guardian spirit for each person seems to have been common at the time, perhaps dating back to Hesiod's reference to what became of the golden race of men after they all died (they are called "blessed ones" at *Works and Days* 141). The guardian spirit and the guide mentioned at 107e1 seem to be two different individuals.

107d7 ["takes him by the hand"]: perhaps I'm taking *epicheireō* too literally, but this expresses the kindness of the *daimōn* and it reflects the fact that Socrates often talks as if the dead have bodies.

107d8 ["judgment"]: compare *Gorgias* 523e1 and *Republic* 10.614c3. Post-mortem judgment is mentioned by Pindar at *Olympian* 2.58, and Aeschylus says that Hades himself holds us to account after death, apparently in much the same way that government officials in Athens were called to account after their year in office to see whether they had acted corruptly (*euthunos* at *Eumenides* 273; Zeus seems to play a similar role at *Persians* 828).

107e2 ["received their due"]: Socrates is vague, so my translation is vague. He could have some kind of necessity in mind, but is it moral or metaphysical necessity? He's simply sketching a typical story, so probably he is deliberately leaving the details vague.

107e4 ["cycles"]: *periodos* is marching around or going around, e.g. making a circuit, going in a circle. This word is used to refer to the cycle of games (e.g. Olympian, Isthmian) which recur regularly. Perhaps this simply means "a long time" (e.g. many summers come and go before they return to this life), but it could refer to the cycle of life-Hades-life, and it could be saying that this cycle happens many times.

107e5 ["Telephus"]: we know only the title of this tragedy. As usual, there were different versions of this myth, and Aeschylus probably did something original with it. Perhaps the main focus of the Telephus stories is that he was wounded by Achilles, and his wound could be healed only by Achilles—which he did in exchange for Telephus guiding the Achaeans to Troy.

108a4 ["triple forks"]: Hecate was the goddess of roads, and offerings to her were laid at crossroads. Triple masks were left for her where three roads met. Hecate is associated with the moon, witchcraft, and Persephone's journey to and from Hades. It is not unreasonable to interpret the roadside offerings to Hecate as being related to anxiety at the thought of getting lost, and hence trapped, after death—never reaching Hades.

108a7 ["not disoriented"]: since the soul is separated from the body, the soul no longer has eyes to see, ears to hear, hands to feel, and so on, so unless you are used to navigating by pure thought alone, death can be very disorienting.

108a8 ["as I was saying before"]: at 81c10.

108c6 ["Earth"]: *gē* is the prose version of *gaia*. Socrates is not changing the subject entirely because Hades is an invisible realm only because it is hidden deep inside the earth. Hades was not thought of as "another dimension," but as being underground, and possibly accessible through certain caves.

108d4 ["craft of Glaucus"]: several ancient authorities explained this reference in several different ways, but if this is the same Glaucus to whom Plato refers at *Republic* 10.611d1, then the craft is *manteia*, i.e. divinatory power that enables the possessor to see many things hidden from mortals (cf. Euripides, *Orestes* 360-67).

108e5 ["round like a ball"]: *peripherēs* means "carried around" and it can refer to revolving or to being surrounded. It can mean round like a flat, circular wafer, but Socrates explicitly uses *sphaira* (sphere) at 110b7, so probably here he is referring to the same shape.

109a4 ["equilibrium"]: this is the theory of Anaximander (c.610-c.547/6). Aristotle rejects it by claiming that if a fire were in equilibrium with itself and were placed at the center of a homogeneous space it would still move up, it wouldn't stay at the center (*De caelo* 2.13.295b10-296a23).

109b1 ["Pillars of Herakles"]: the Pillars of Herakles are the promontories that flank the entrance to the Strait of Gibraltar, where the Mediterranian Sea joins the Atlantic ocean. The Phasis river is today called the Rioni, and it is at the east coast of the Black Sea in Georgia. The Greeks knew of India, which lies far to the east of the Phasis river (the Kallatians mentioned by Herodotus at 3.38.4 are from India). The Greeks thought of the Phasis as where Europe ends and Asia begins. The Greeks also knew Herodotus' story of the circumnavigation of Africa—which they called Libya (ordered by the Egyptian king Nechos II sometime between 610 and 595; 4.42). The main reason historians take this account seriously is that Herodotus records a report that he doesn't believe, i.e. that when the Phoenicians were sailing west around what we now call the Cape of Good Hope, the sun was on their right. In the Northern Hemisphere when you face west the sun is on your left; on the equator the sun is directly above you; in the Southern Hemisphere the sun is on your right. The journey took two years.

109b8 ["aither"]: Zeus dwells in the *aithēr* (Homer, *Iliad* 2.412). Probably Greeks developed the notion of *aithēr* from experiencing how thin the air can get at the tops of mountains, and how thick the air is in low areas with lots of fog. The English word "ether" derives from *aithēr*.

109d7 ["sea of air"]: Socrates does not use this phrase, but it is clearly implied by his account. The idea that we live at the bottom of a sea of air which constantly exerts pressure on us ("atmospheric pressure") was verified by the ingenius Puy-de-Dôme experiment in 1648 by Florin Périer, brother-in-law of Blaise Pascal (1623-1662). The experiment refuted the notion that suction pumps work by creating a vacuum: it is not that "nature abhors a vacuum" (so that everything around it tries to fill it), rather suction pumps create an area of low pressure, so the surrounding high pressure pushes the surrounding medium towards it.

110b1 ["story"]: *muthos*, see notes on 60c2 and 90e5.

111a6 ["islands surrounded by air"]: probably a kenning for clouds. I suspect that part of Plato's design in having Socrates defamiliarize the familiar is to provoke a sense of wonder at the natural world, since wonder is the beginning of the love of wisdom (*Theaetetus* 155d2-4). I suspect that he is trying to create stories that do not merely delight young listeners, but provoke in them a sense of curiosity, e.g. "there couldn't possibly be such things, could there?" In this case, he is using a sort of ratio: systematically comparing and contrasting the realm of the sea with that of the land and that of the air. Intellectual puzzles can be useful (cf. *Theaetetus* 155b4-d7).

111e1 ["like in Sicily"]: Mt. Etna is in Sicily, and is the tallest active volcano in Europe.

111e6 ["chasms"]: *chasma* refers to a wide opening, like a yawning mouth or a huge hole in the earth. It may be that a "chasm" is simply a large "pit" (*koilos*, I translate *chasma* as pit at 111c8).

112a1 ["opening"]: *tetrainō*. Perhaps it is only an accident that Hippocrates mentions the size of the urinary opening (*tetrainō*) in his discussion of passing kidney stones (*De aere aquis et locis* 9.50). I suspect that Plato designed his description of the earth to pique medical curiosity about the functioning of the human body, as well as scientific curiosity about the physics of fluid dynamics. Some myths (see 110b1, 114d7 and note on 60c2) prompt flights of unrealistic fantasy, but some can spark intellectual curiosity (see note on 99e5). No doubt Plato prefers the latter, especially for young minds just beginning to mature.

112a3 ["Very far off"]: *Iliad* 8.14. Zeus threatens the other gods with throwing them into Tartarus if any of them helps either the Greeks or the Trojans. One remarkable thing, certainly from Plato's point of view, is that Zeus describes Tartarus as being as far below Hades as the heavens are above the earth—in other words, Zeus uses a mathematical ratio. Compare Hesiod's measurements at *Theogony* 720. At *Meteorology* 2.2.355b32-356a31 Aristotle criticizes the theory that Socrates is about to give.

112a7 ["tastes and colors"]: Socrates does not explicitly mention tastes and colors; I follow Aristotle's interpretation of what he means (*Meteorology* 2.2.355b32-356a31).

112e3 ["flowing uphill"]: here I follow Aristotle's interpretation in *Meteorology* 2.2.355b32-356a31. Plato is making the point that on a sphere, "down" is relative, so if you get to the center, then any direction you go—even if you keep going the direction you were going, you will be going "up." Since water never flows uphill, the water would all get stuck at the center of the earth if it weren't for the tremendous gale force winds that blow constantly (112b8).

112e7 ["in a circle"]: in 1961, Dutch graphic artist Maurits Cornelis Escher (1898-1972) created a lithograph called *Waterfall* in which water flowed in a perpetual circuit.

113b7 ["Cocytus"]: I've ruined Socrates' dramatic delay in naming this river (he saves it for the very last word of this paragraph at 113c8). The word *kōkutos* means "shrieking" or "wailing" and its mere mention could send shivers down the spine (*Republic* 3.387b8-c5, cf. *Odyssey* 10.514). I suspect that this reveals a main point of the entire story up to here: the speculative geography is not especially thrilling, so it saps the terror away from the underworld, replacing it with a geometrical interest in mapping symmetry, and a scientific interest in studying fluid dynamics.

113c3 ["terrible powers"]: Socrates doesn't say what these powers are, but given Aristotle's interpretation of 112a7 it could mean that the water is not potable, either it tastes and smells bad or perhaps it is outright toxic.

113d7 ["purified"]: *kathairō* refers primarily to cleaning, i.e. washing away dirt. Normally we would assume that the purification refers only to the penalties for injustice, but grammatically it seems to include the rewards for good deeds. Perhaps the notion is that the slate is wiped clean: the immortality of the soul Socrates envisions does not seem to be a personal immortality in the sense that you carry your personal baggage with you forever. At the end of each life, your slate is wiped clean and you begin a new life fresh, to make of it what you will, unhampered and unhelped by whatever you did in your previous life.

113e2 ["faults"]: *hamartēma*, see notes on *Charmides* 157b5, 171d6, 171e7.

113e3 ["sacrilegious"]: usually "sacrilege" refers to robbing a temple, but Plato also counts murdering a parent as sacrilege (*Laws* 9.869b3-4), and he may include other crimes as well (cf. *Laws* 10.884a1-885b9).

113e6 ["depart"]: *ekbainō* means to step out of, to disembark or to leave. It does not mean to escape (which would be *pheugō* or *diakrouō*, cf. *ekpheugō* at 115c5). If Tartarus is truly their fair share or fitting lot (*hē prosēkousa moira*), then perhaps they themselves judge that there is no more appropriate place for them than with their own kind, the incurable i.e. those who never become better people (recall 107c5-8). Perhaps also they would prefer to stay in Tartarus than to endure what the curably bad people must endure (i.e. 114a8-b1). The moral of this story for the living seems to be that one shouldn't play with vice since it is possible to make oneself incurably vicious.

114a2 ["in such a state"]: see notes on *Euthyphro* 4d4 and 4d9.

114a3 ["must fall into Tartarus"]: *anankē* is necessity, e.g. compulsion, so perhaps they "fall" because they are forcibly pushed into Tartarus against their will. But *anankē* can also refer to anguish (Sophocles, *Philoctetes* 206, 215) or distress (Euripides, *Bacchae* 89). Perhaps they fall of their own free will into Tartarus as part of their deliberate penitence for the wrongs they committeed in life. The moral of this story for the living seems to be that one shouldn't play with vice since it is possible to make oneself incurably vicious.

115a2 ["journey to Hades"]: I think Burnet is right to bracket the additional phrase "whenever destiny (*heimarmenē*) summons him." This is the sort of sentiment Socrates is about to mock, and it would be easy for a copyist to allow his eye to slip down to the *heimarmenē* at 115a6 and accidentally add the appropriate phrase in at 115a3.

115d8 ["I would remain"]: this is all Socrates says in the text. I've added what scholars reasonably presume he's referring to.

116b6 ["a lot of time inside"]: probably he spoke with his wife and children for quite a while.

116b8 ["the Eleven"]: see notes on *Apology* 37c2 and *Crito* 44a4.

117b5 ["right in the eye"]: Socrates' usual expression was mentioned at 86d5, but here it is said to be "like a bull" (*taurēdon*). It's not clear if Plato intends any special significance to this description.

118a4 ["when it reached his heart"]: *Conium maculatum*, the poison hemlock, works like curare; both inhibit muscle contraction causing ascending paralysis. Death is caused when the effect reaches the lungs, resulting in asphyxiation. If the affected person is kept alive by artificial respiration for 2-3 days the effect will wear off, though kidney damage may also result.

118a7 ["we owe Asclepius a rooster"]: perhaps this means nothing and indicates that Socrates was delusional. Alternatively, at his trial Socrates claimed that he was poor (*Apology* 23c1), so perhaps he had a neighbor named Asclepius who once gave him a chicken to eat and Socrates wanted to pay him back. Alternatively, Apollo's son named Asclepius was a doctor, so perhaps the rooster is an offering to the god in exchange for healing Socrates—which entails that Socrates thinks of human life as an illness. I suspect that Socrates does not think of human life as an illness but as a state in which the soul is in a body, and hence is impure. So the sacrifice to Asclepius would be not for curing him of an illness, but for purifying his soul by separating it from his body. My guess is that the man who mixed the hemlock was in fact a member of an Asclepius cult (the closest thing to a licensed doctor at the time).

118a17 ["most just"]: *dikaiotatos* is the final word of the *Phaedo*.

SELECT BIBLIOGRAPHY:

I have benefitted from so many translations, commentaries, books and articles that I cannot list them all. Here I will simply list the works that I've used most frequently (I list the translator in place of the author, since Plato is the author of all the dialogues).

Allen, R.E. 1984. *The Dialogues of Plato, Vol. 1: Euthyphro, Apology, Crito, Meno, Gorgias, Menexenus.* New Haven, CT: Yale University Press.

Bluck, R.S. 1961. *Plato's Meno.* Cambridge: Cambridge University Press.

Brann, Eva, Peter Kalkavage and Eric Salem. 1998. *Plato's Phaedo.* Newburyport, MA: Focus Publishing/R Pullins Company

Cooper, John M. *Plato: Complete Works.* Indianapolis, IN: Hackett Publishing.

 G.M.A. Grube, *Euthyphro, Apology, Crito, Phaedo, Meno*

 R.K. Sprague, *Charmides, Laches, Euthydemus*

 S. Lombardo and K. Bell, *Protagoras*

Denyer, Nicholas. 2008. *Plato Protagoras.* Cambridge: Cambridge University Press.

Gallop, David. 1988. *Plato Phaedo.* Oxford: Clarendon Press.

Hackforth, R. 1955. *Plato's Phaedo.* Cambridge: Cambridge University Press.

Hamilton, Edith and Huntington Cairns (eds.). 1980. Princeton: Princeton University Press.

 Hugh Tredennick, *Apology, Crito, Phaedo*

 Benjamin Jowett, *Charmides, Laches*

 Lane Cooper, *Euthyphro*

 W.K.C. Guthrie, *Protagoras, Meno*

 W.H.D. Rouse, *Euthydemus*

Hornblower, Simon, Antony Spawforth and Esther Eidinow (eds.). 2012. *The Oxford Classical Dictionary.* Oxford: Oxford University Press.

Lombardo, Stanley, and Karen Bell. 1992. *Plato Protagoras.* Indianapolis, IN: Hackett Publishing.

Ostwald, Martin. 1956. *Protagoras.* New York: Liberal Arts Press.

Sprague, Rosamund Kent. 1973. *Plato: Laches and Charmides.* Indianapolis, IN: Bobbs-Merrill Educational Publishin.

Tatham, M.T. 1896. *The Laches of Plato.* New York, NY: MacMillan and Co.

Taylor, C.C.W. 1976. *Plato Protagoras.* Oxford: Clarendon Press.